The Stonehenge Environs Project

English Heritage

Archaeological Report no 16

The Stonehenge Environs Project

Julian Richards

with contributions by
Mike Allen, Alister Bartlett, Martin Bell, Wendy Carruthers, Rosamund Cleal, Anne Ellison, Roy Entwistle, Rowena Gale, Philip Harding, Janet Henderson, Julie Jones, Helen Keeley, Mark Maltby, Joshua Pollard, Frances Raymond, Hazel Riley, Fiona Roe, and Olwen Williams-Thorpe

Historic Buildings & Monuments Commission for England

1990

First published 1990 by
Historic Buildings and Monuments Commission for England, Fortress House, 23 Savile Row, London, W1X 1AB

Printed by Hobbs the Printers of Southampton

British Library Cataloguing in Publication Data

Richards, Julian, C.
The Stonehenge environs project.
1. Wiltshire. Stonehenge region. Prehistoric antiquities
I. Title II. Allen, Mike
936.2319

ISBN 1-85074-269-3

Contents

Appendices

List of illustrations

List of tables

Microfiche contents

Microfiche 1

Microfiche 2

Acknowledgements

The appearance of this volume owes much to the efforts of Anne Ellison and John Coles. Anne Ellison was responsible for the concept and initiation of the Stonehenge Environs Project and, as the Director of the Wessex Archaeological Unit, guided it through its formative years. The structure of this volume owes a great deal to John Coles, who has guided a major revision of the original format and the subsequent editing. In between these stages, a lot of people have been involved in the many and varying aspects of fieldwork and post-excavation analysis that have gone into the production of this volume.

The project was commissioned and funded by English Heritage. Of the many inspectors from this organisation who have shown considerable interest in the project, I would particularly like to thank Geoff Wainwright for the perceptive criticism that was a feature of his site visits.

The project would not have been possible without the cooperation and kindness of the landowners and tenants in the Stonehenge area, many of whom not only allowed surface collection and excavation to take place on their land but also acted as hosts to the excavation campsites.

The assistance of the Wessex Regional Office of the National Trust, both in practical and financial terms, is most gratefully acknowledged, as is the financial assistance provided for excavation by the Society of Antiquaries of London, the British Academy, and the Prehistoric Society. The assistance of Roy Canham of the Wiltshire Library and Museums Service is also most gratefully acknowledged. In addition, I would like to thank Dr Rupert Housley of the Oxford University Radiocarbon Accelerator Unit for the provision of dating facilities.

Many of those involved in specialist studies are acknowledged by their written contribution, but I would like to add to this my personal thanks. Roy Entwistle in particular has been a lively contributor to both fieldwork and subsequent reflection. Of my colleagues in the Trust for Wessex Archaeology, all of whom have been supportive and all of whom will be greatly relieved that this project is complete, I would like specifically to acknowledge the current Director, Andrew Lawson, for his valued comments on both drafts of the report and for his support, and Rob Read, Illustrations and Records Officer, who has supervised the long-term and much-revised drawing programme.

A special debt is also owed to Jo Mills, Frances Raymond, Hazel Riley, and Ros Cleal for their help at varying times from 1981 onwards in structuring the project report and archive.

Final thanks must go to those, particularly Richard Bradley and Isobel Smith, whose interest in the project has been of considerable assistance in both the development of methodology and the interpretation of the results.

Organisation of the report

The illustrations and tables run in sequence throughout text and microfiche. Those which appear in the microfiche are identified in the contents list by the use of italics. In the main report, references to the microfiche are given as, eg, MF1 B3.

Within the text of the report all dates quoted are calibrated according to the method recommended by Pearson *et al* (1986), and in most cases are used generally, for example 'early third millennium BC'. Where a specific date is referred to, then the one sigma calibrated range is quoted and the laboratory identification is appended, enabling reference to be made to Table 137 and Figure 156. In both cases the prefix 'cal' has been omitted throughout.

The project archive is deposited in Salisbury and South Wiltshire Museum together with a comprehensive indexed guide. A brief introduction to the archive is contained in appendix 1.

1 The study area

1.1 Introduction to the study area

The term 'Stonehenge Environs' was originally employed by Sir Richard Colt Hoare in the early nineteenth century to delineate the rich archaeological landscape surrounding Stonehenge itself. Situated on the undulating chalk of Salisbury Plain approximately eight miles (13km) north of Salisbury (Fig 1), his 'Environs' (Hoare 1810, map facing p 170) extend from the town of Amesbury and the henge monument of Durrington Walls in the east, as far west as the valley of the River Till, and from the Wilsford barrow group in the south northwards to beyond the Lesser Cursus (Fig 2). The concept of the area, if not its exact boundaries, was employed by the Royal Commission on the Historical Monuments of England in their review of the field monuments it contains (RCHME 1979), a review providing the basis for the work which this volume describes. For the purposes of the Stonehenge Environs Project the southerly and easterly limits of the area defined by the Royal Commission were accepted, and while that on the west was slightly extended, in practice no fieldwork was carried out west of the SU 10 grid line. This line coincides broadly with a modern boundary, the A360 Salisbury to Devizes road. The study area was extended to the north to include Robin Hood's Ball causewayed enclosure, considered, with associated long barrows, to be a focal element of the early monumental landscape. At the time that the study area was defined, this additional area was thought to have little potential for fieldwork, particularly surface collection, as it lay within the Salisbury Plain Military Training Area.

The best known archaeological monument in the area is, of course, Stonehenge itself, and the concentration of archaeological sites within its immediate surroundings is remarkable in both composition and density (RCHME 1979). The monuments within the study area (Fig 3), tabulated below in broad functional groups (Table 1), demonstrate an intensity of prehistoric activity within the Wessex chalklands paralleled only in the Avebury area (R W Smith 1984) and on the south-east Dorset Ridgeway (RCHME 1970, iii; Woodward forthcoming). In contrast to the areas noted above, however, the Stonehenge area exhibits an unparalleled diversity of monuments which clearly demonstrate that Stonehenge was constructed in a landscape already of some ceremonial and funerary significance.

Robin Hood's Ball causewayed enclosure (N Thomas 1964), the long barrows and long mortuary enclosure (F de M Vatcher 1961), together with the Lesser Cursus can all be suggested as predating the earliest phase of construction at Stonehenge (Atkinson and Evans 1978). Later Neolithic monuments include the three more traditional henges, in terms of both morphology and association, at Durrington Walls (Wainwright and Longworth 1971), Woodhenge (Cunnington 1929), and Coneybury (King 1970).

Contemporary with the major phases of construction at Stonehenge (Atkinson 1979) the surrounding landscape develops extensive and diverse cemeteries of round barrows around which a less coherent pattern of settlements, fields, and boundaries, assumed to have contemporaneous origins, can be identified. Evidence for the development of a more formalised agricultural landscape is distributed primarily on the western side of the study area, contrasting with the sparse evidence for subsequent prehistoric activity. The apparently real absence of Iron Age activity over much of the study area provides as great a contrast with surrounding areas, as do the spectacular concentrations of sites from the earlier prehistoric periods.

1.2 The objectives of the project

In 1979 the review of the monuments in the Stonehenge area by the Royal Commission on the Historical Monuments of England presented a graphic illustration not only of the extent and complexity of the archaeological remains in such a restricted area but also of the extent

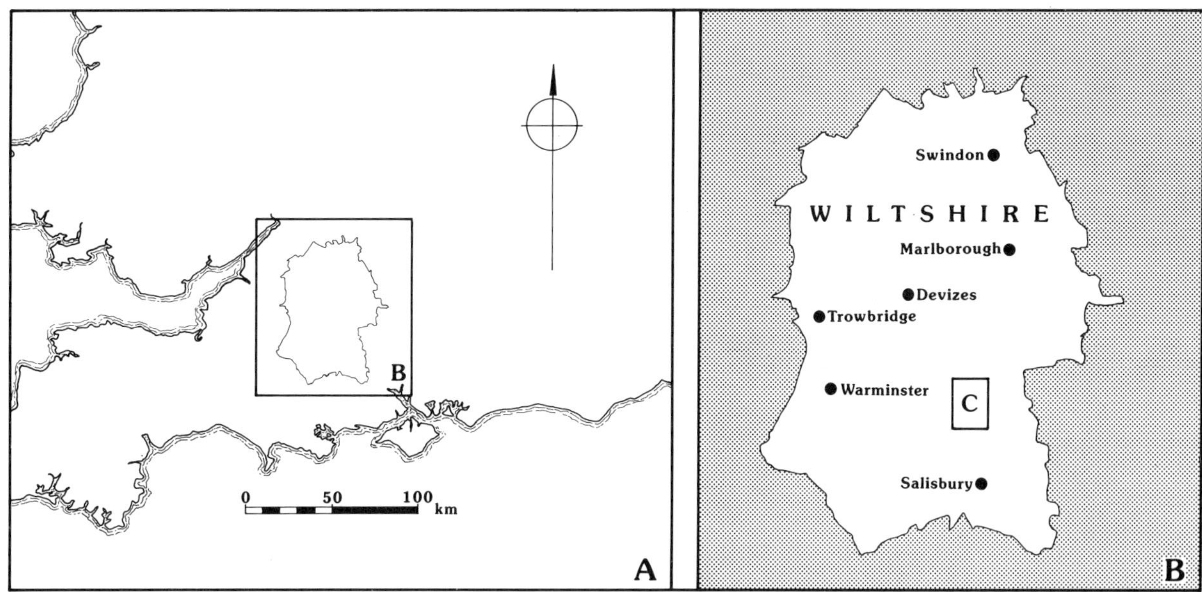

Fig 1 Location map

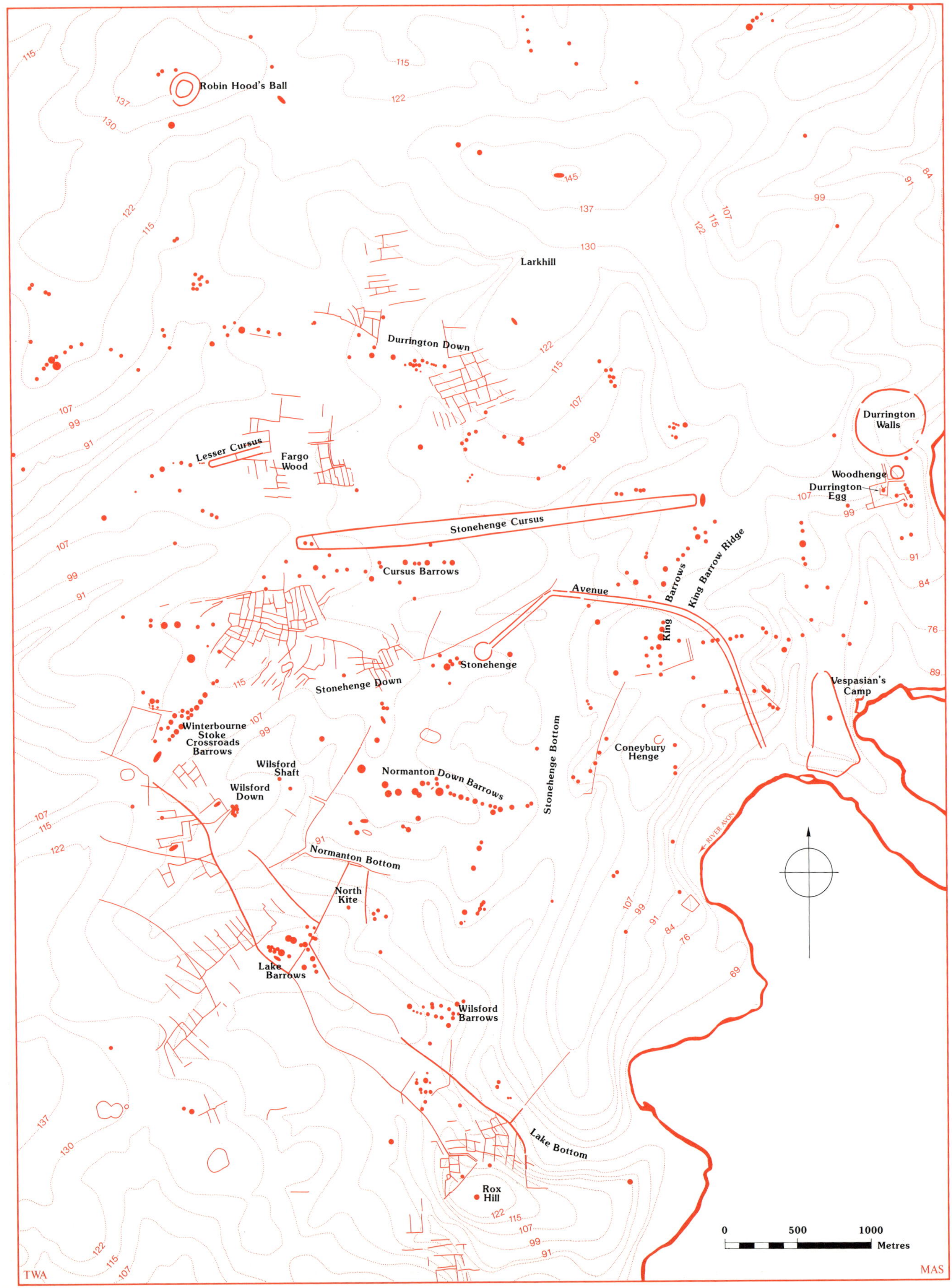

Fig 2 The topography and major monuments of the study area

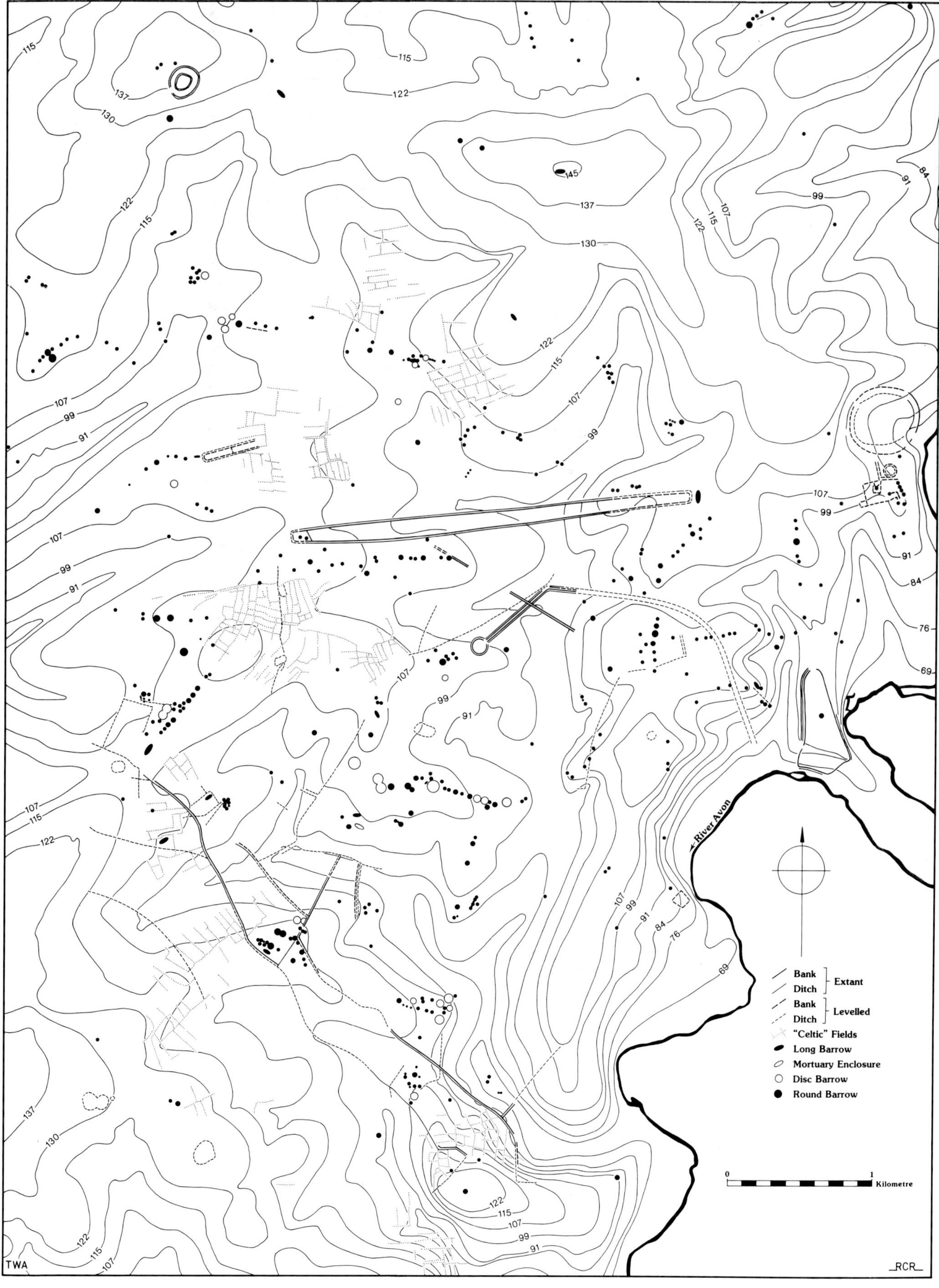

Fig 3 All archaeological monuments within the study area

Table 1 Monuments within the study area

Ceremonial and communal	
Cursus monuments	2
Henges and associated monuments	5
Long barrows	
Long barrows	10
Long mortuary enclosures	1
Round barrows	
Bowl	256
Bell	32
Disc	29
Saucer	10
Pond	17
Unspecified	31
Ring ditches	99
Total	474
Settlement and land use	
Hillforts	1
Enclosures	5
Field systems	462ha
Linear earthworks	22.35km

of damage, both ancient and modern. The land use map (RCHME 1979, map 3) provided the historic context for much of the erosion, concentrated within a broad band of former open fields to the west of the River Avon.

In addition to its comprehensive inventory, the RCHME publication made reference to the need for further investigation, both general and specific, and also emphasised the necessity for proper management of the monuments. In these aspects, the RCHME survey provided both academic and practical stimuli for the Stonehenge Environs Project, initiated in 1980 by the then Wessex Archaeological Committee.

'A policy for archaeological investigation in Wessex' (Ellison 1980) summarised outstanding priorities relating to archaeological activity and presented them in the framework of a series of projects. The individual projects were related to a series of general themes and period-based priorities and, in many cases, identified potential study areas. Project 2, 'Neolithic and Bronze Age settlements and their associated landscapes', was to investigate major themes of subsistence, population, and social organisation by means of locating and excavating earlier prehistoric occupation and activity sites. The area around Stonehenge was suggested as a possible study area and a draft project design for what was to be known as the Stonehenge Environs Project was circulated in April 1980. After wide consultation and approval by the Department of the Environment Inspectorate of Ancient Monuments, the project commenced with the implementation of a specific RCHME recommendation, namely the geophysical survey and evaluation excavation of the ploughed henge monument on Coneybury Hill (RCHME 1979, xv (e); 13). This was followed by the first short season of surface collection work (Table 2).

In 1981/2 it was intended to concentrate research on the environmental potential of the Neolithic monuments within the study area, and also to examine an exterior sample of the Coneybury henge, where the 1980 excavation had indicated an area of possible Beaker settlement. These proposals were not accepted, however, and work in 1981/2 was restricted to the completion of the excavation of a large Early Neolithic pit located adjacent to the Coneybury Henge monument and to a further short season of surface collection work.

In October 1981 the Inspectorate of Ancient Monuments defined the objective of the project as being to 'identify the prehistoric settlements in the Stonehenge region, and to establish their state of preservation with a view to the Department developing a management strategy for them'. This was the main brief of the developed project.

Initially the project was wholly funded from the Inspectorate's rescue budget and, subsequent to 1981, was geared primarily to the location and evaluation of surface scatters. Further seasons of fieldwalking and excavation were carried out in 1982/3 and 1983/4. As this side of the project progressed, however, several potential areas of ancillary research became apparent and, in order to pursue these, external research funding was sought. The Society of Antiquaries of London and the British Academy originally supported a programme designed to define and examine colluvial deposits within the study area. When the initial phase of this project failed to locate significant colluvial deposits, funding was transferred to a monument-based research programme, examining environmental themes falling outside the DoE-funded project brief. This eventually led to the development of a more specific programme of sample excavation designed to examine aspects of the earlier Neolithic landscape in the vicinity of Robin Hood's Ball causewayed enclosure. This project will be the subject of a separate report (Richards in prep a).

Additional research funds were made available by the Prehistoric Society in 1983 for sample excavation of what appeared to be anomalously early linear earthworks in the Wilsford Down area (RCHME 1979, xv (f)).

As part of the preparations for the production of a management plan for the area, the final 1983/4 season of fieldwork incorporated the field assessment of all 'monuments' (in the broadest sense) within the study area. Data were used in the production of an internal management document (Richards 1984a) which identified both general and specific problems in the management of the archaeology within the project area.

During phases of project fieldwork and subsequent post-excavation, papers have been produced examining aspects of both methodology and interpretation. The former (Richards 1982; 1985a) are primarily concerned with surface collection. The latter (Richards 1984b; Entwistle and Richards 1987) deal respectively with broad aspects of Neolithic and earlier Bronze Age landscape change and the specific comparative interpretation of the geophysical and geochemical attributes of two project excavations.

Table 2 Stonehenge Environs Project fieldwork

Year	*Excavation*	*Funding*	*Extensive survey*	*Intensive survey*
1980	W2 Coneybury Henge	DoE	87.5ha	none
1981	W2(81) Coneybury 'Anomaly' Early Neolithic pit	DoE	182.875ha	W31 prelim W32 prelim
	W17–22 dry valleys	SA and BA		
1982	W31 Wilsford Down flint scatter	DoE	199.625ha	W58 prelim W59 prelim
	W32 Fargo Wood I flint scatter	DoE		
	W34 Fargo Wood II pottery scatter	DoE		
1983	W51 Wilsford Down linear earthwork	PS	302.5ha	W53 total collection
	W52 North Kite linear earthwork	PS		
	W55 Lesser Cursus	DoE		
	W56 Stonehenge Cursus	SA and BA		
	W57 Durrington Down round barrow	DoE		
	W58 Amesbury 42 long barrow	SA and BA		
	W59 King Barrow Ridge flint scatter	DoE		
1984/86	W83 Robin Hood's Ball flint scatter	SA and BA	ongoing research project	
	W84 Robin Hood's Ball pottery scatter	SA and BA		
	W85 Netheravon Bake long barrow	SA and BA		
			Total 752.5ha	

SA Society of Antiquaries BA British Academy PS Prehistoric Society DoE Department of the Environment

Fig 4 Normanton Down, with Stonehenge in the distance, viewed from Wilsford Down

The post-excavation stage of the project has also involved the production, with commercial sponsorship, of a new interpretative guide book to the Stonehenge area (Richards 1985b).

1.3 The topography and geology of the study area

The study area consists of *c* 33km^2 of Middle Chalk, lying between the valleys of the Till to the west and the Avon to the east, ranging in height from between *c* 130m OD to a little over 60m OD in the Avon Valley (Fig 2). This area of largely uncapped chalk is bisected by the major Stonehenge Bottom/Spring Bottom dry valley system, the occasionally steep sides of which form the only effective constraint to present-day arable cultivation. With the exception of these and similar slopes at the river valley margins, the gently undulating topography of the Stonehenge Environs is unremarkable in the context of Salisbury Plain as a whole. Figures 4 and 5 illustrate the general topography of the area.

On the chalk, drift geology, in the form of superficial deposits of chalky drift, loess, and clay-with-flints, is more important as a soil parent material than the solid geology. Chalky drift deposits are the products of periglacial erosion of the chalk and make a major contribution of minerals in soil genesis. Loess is an ubiquitous component of the chalk soils throughout southern England; erosion of this fine deposit, intensified in the early Holocene and the later Bronze Age, has resulted in only *c* 0.1–0.4m of loess over chalk and other superficial deposits in many places (Catt 1978). Clay-with-flints occurs mainly in isolated patches in the study area, although more extensive deposits occur to the south, near the village of Wilsford-cum-Lake and on Rox Hill. The only deposits occurring close to sites excavated during the project are those on the low plateau by Fargo Wood (W32 and W34), and slightly to the north on Durrington Down (W57). This patchy distribution may be all that remains of more widespread deposits which have been much reduced by erosion.

These drift deposits give rise to three main soil types in the study area. Depending on variables such as topography and cultivation history these soil types are mapped as rendzinas, brown calcareous earths, and argillic brown earths.

Rendzinas are the characteristic soils of the chalklands. They form over solid chalk or chalky drift and are mapped as the Icknield, Andover, and Upton series in the study area. The humic rendzinas of the Icknield series are mostly soils which have been in cultivation for a number of years, with some consequent loss of humic material. In some cases this is sufficient for soils

Fig 5 Wilsford Down viewed from Normanton Down

to be transitional with the Andover series. Uncultivated Icknield soils remain only on the steeper slopes and in areas of long-standing pasture around some of the major monuments. Outside the study area, towards the interior of the Plain where there has been none of the intensive tillage common near the major settlements, Icknield soils have a more widespread distribution. Brown rendzinas are mainly represented by soils of the Andover series. They are mostly deeper than the Icknield soils and contain greater amounts of drift material. Some of the Andover soils may have developed from the Icknield series where tillage has been sustained over many years. On the more sloping valley sides, prolonged cultivation has given rise to grey rendzinas of the Upton series. These are chalky grey soils which characteristically contain much less organic matter than either the Icknield or Andover series soils.

Brown calcareous earths may form wherever solifluxion debris and associated colluvium from the chalk scarp and valley sides have accumulated to sufficient depth. The shallower of these soils, less than 0.5m deep, have been mapped as the Coombe series. This includes soils of a silty clay loam texture, highly calcareous throughout, and sometimes containing large quantities of flint. Where decalcification has taken place, the non-calcareous Charity series soils are mapped.

Argillic brown earths form over superficial deposits over the chalk and contain material derived from clay-with-flints and loess. Soils of this type are not common in the study area, although examples are to be found over clay-with-flints near Fargo Wood and on Durrington Down.

1.4 Land use and preservation

The first observations of the landscape surrounding Stonehenge, those of William Stukeley in the 1720s, record a traditional downland landscape, although even he was able to note and lament the rapid encroachment of the plough. In the eighteenth and nineteenth centuries arable was largely concentrated on the eastern side of the study area, in the former open fields of Amesbury and the Avon Valley villages. This pattern, confirmed by the distribution of tile and recent pottery from project surface collection, is also reflected in the preservation of monuments. To the east of the King Barrow Ridge a high proportion of round barrows exist solely as ring ditches and the true morphology of both Woodhenge and Coneybury henge was only revealed by aerial photography. The course of the Avenue, initially recorded by Stukeley as far as the King Barrow Ridge, was subsequently extended, again by the use of aerial photographs, as far as the River Avon at West Amesbury, again emphasising the contrast in land use and monument preservation.

Subsequent observers have also noted increased destruction, largely through clearance and arable cultivation, but also through military construction, roads, and services. Areas of Wilsford Down and Winterbourne Stoke Down are known to have been converted from grassland within the last 40 years, the conversion often accompanied by means of highly destructive soil-busting methods.

In 1979 the RCHME survey presented a view of the land use in 1971 (map 3), subsequent to which small-scale but destructive changes have taken place (documented in Richards 1984a, overlay 2). Present land use, and in consequence the state of preservation of many of the monuments within the study area, can be considered under four major categories.

1 Old grassland represents a mere 4% of the study area and, with the exception of isolated pockets on and around individual monuments and small groups of monuments, is located in only three areas. Two of these, the Stonehenge Triangle, within which the monument lies, and the slopes of Rox Hill, are small and isolated. The third area, to the north of the Packway Road in the north of the study area, is effectively part of the more extensive Salisbury Plain Training Area given over to military training. It is unfortunate that of all the major monuments and monument groups within the study area, only the barrow cemetery at Winterbourne Stoke lies largely within land used in this way.
2 Reintroduced grassland forms *c* 7% of the study area and, with the exception of Durrington Walls henge monument, is restricted to the National Trust estate where a block of approximately 190ha was removed from cultivation during the 1970s. This move represents a stabilisation of a considerable area within which the previously evident problems of ploughing margins have been eradicated. This has had particularly beneficial effects for the Stonehenge Cursus, the Cursus barrow cemetery, and for the surviving earthwork section of the Avenue.
3 Woodland forms *c* 3% of the study area. Much of it is plantation belt, ranging in date from Fargo (*c* 1840) to the recent conifer belts which screen Larkhill army camp. Areas of older, deciduous woodland include those on the King Barrow Ridge, which cover the Old and New King Barrows, that within which Vespasian's Camp hillfort lies, and woods to the south which include the Wilsford and Lake barrow cemeteries. In preventing cultivation, woodland can be regarded as a beneficial form of land use, although the unmanaged state of many of the areas of older woodland outside the National Trust's estate is now causing damage to standing monuments.
4 Cultivated land forms between 70 and 75% of the study area, some areas having been under cultivation for several centuries, others for a matter of decades. In both cases specific monuments which have not been deliberately levelled for cultivation survive as 'island' sites, devoid of both immediate context and, in many cases, less obvious elements such as associated ditches. The original morphology of the individual monument has, in many cases, determined its vulnerability to the effects of ploughing. In consequence the mounds at least of bowl and bell barrows have survived more consistently than have entire disc or saucer barrows. Within the arable areas the state of preservation of monuments for which there is some indication of original morphology can rapidly be assessed. The state of preservation of less definable sites or areas of activity is less easy to determine although the occurrence,

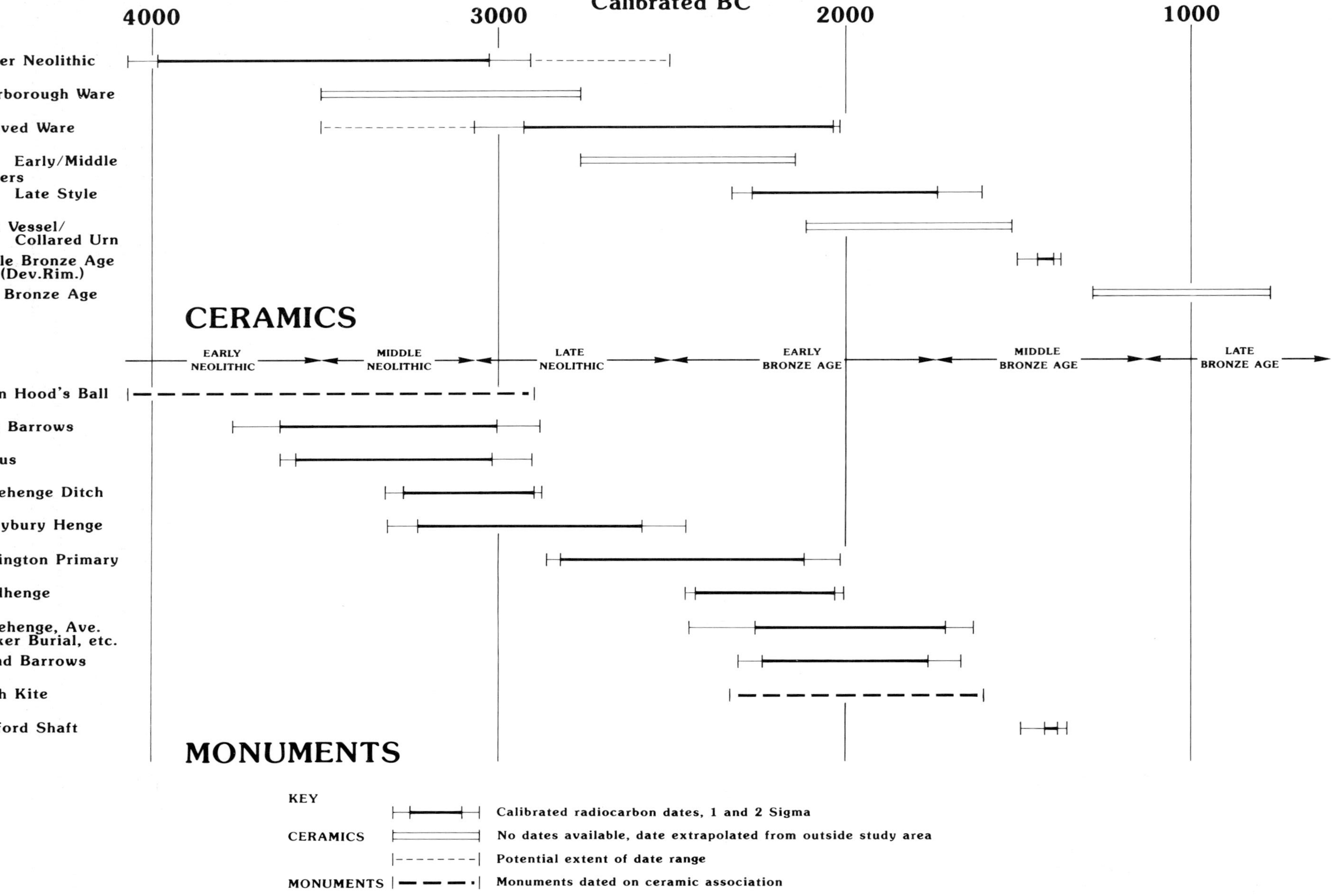

Fig 6 The chronology of monuments and ceramic styles

size, and state of abrasion of prehistoric pottery recovered from surface collection provides some measure of rapid assessment.

Continued cultivation can be regarded as the major threat to the surviving archaeology of the study area and is certainly the cause of erosion of monuments characterised by the construction of ditches, banks, or mounds. However, on sites that have already been levelled, or on those perhaps never characterised by upstanding earthworks, the cultivation of an established ploughsoil may not cause continuing serious erosion. The stability of cultivation over such an area may not be erosive beyond the continuing effect on ploughsoil artefacts and their spatial patterning, but any change in method involving deeper cultivation may disrupt this state of apparent equilibrium.

1.5 Introduction to the archaeology of the project area

The Stonehenge Environs represent a unique parcel of prehistoric Wessex, a physically undistinguished area of chalkland within which lies the densest and most varied complex of Neolithic and Bronze Age monuments in southern England, and perhaps in western Europe. Certain elements are unique – Stonehenge, the Wilsford Shaft, and the North Kite – and as such they are isolated but significant aspects in any wider scheme of classification and analysis in prehistoric Britain. Other elements of the landscape, however, have a more central position in the construction of wider chronological and evolutionary schemes, and these elements form the focus of this report.

Without doubt a rich landscape in the Neolithic and perhaps more spectacularly in the Bronze Age, the wealth of the Stonehenge Environs has often been subjected to analysis in terms of social, economic, political, and religious power, but this is all based on the ritual and funerary aspects of the visible monuments. Such monuments make up the ceremonial and funerary landscapes and need no further enhancement here. They provide the Stonehenge Environs with their unusual if not unique character. This study tries to move beyond the traditional view, and will show that the area is also unique in terms of its prehistoric settlement record, demonstrating a range and density of human activities hitherto unstudied and essentially unknown. These activities are to be seen against a background of a complex and shifting human impact on the landscape, within which the demonstrable organisation of land for well-established and successful arable cultivation is of far-reaching consequence.

The Stonehenge Environs, either as the setting for struggles of economic and ideological power, or as a microcosm of changing prehistoric subsistence strategies, can be seen as playing a crucial role in the evolution of human societies in the fourth, third, and second millennia BC.

In order to provide a clear indication of the types of monument and associated ceramics to be found within the study area, Figure 6 sets out a chronologically ordered scheme to which the reader can refer throughout both descriptive text and discussion. In suggesting some broad chronology for the ceramic styles which are discussed extensively in chapter 6, radiocarbon dates from both within and beyond the project area are employed. The solid heavy lines indicate good stratigraphic associations between clearly identified pottery and dating material. The dotted lines indicate some uncertainty, either between the pottery and the dating material (in the case of the earlier Neolithic material from beneath the Durrington Walls bank), or in the identification of the ceramic tradition (in the case of the possible Grooved Ware from the King Barrow Ridge). The majority of the monument classes, and specific episodes of construction, are dated by radiocarbon, although some monuments must rely on less precise ceramic association.

Period divisions are also indicated on Figure 6. Although they should be used with some caution, they do provide a positive reinforcement of some apparently well-established associations between monuments and ceramics.

1.6 A history of previous enquiries

Within the study area, and prior to the attentions of Sir Richard Colt Hoare (1810), antiquarians had tended to focus their interest on Stonehenge itself (Chippindale 1983). The major exception to this rule was William Stukeley who in the early part of the eighteenth century recorded many of the field monuments in the area (Stukeley 1740) and also excavated a number of round barrows. This particular field of investigation was continued into the nineteenth century, in the first two decades of which Colt Hoare and Cunnington examined over 200 round barrows within the study area. This understandable concentration of effort in an area so rich in a wide variety of barrows was part of a national emphasis on the examination of such sites which developed throughout the nineteenth century. Similarly extensive campaigns of excavation were carried out not only within Wessex but also in the Peak District and in Yorkshire (Mortimer 1905).

During this century research has again concentrated on monuments, with particular attention focused on both barrows and henges (Table 3). Many of the former were excavated by contract archaeologists working for the then Ministry of Public Buildings and Works during the 1950s and 1960s. Little thematic coherence can be identified within the work carried out during these decades, with sites apparently selected on an *ad hoc* basis determined largely by the immediacy of the perceived threat. Inevitably this meant a further emphasis on previously defined, and in many cases scheduled, sites, with ploughed examples of both long and round barrows most commonly examined.

Stonehenge saw specific and rapidly published investigation in the early years of this century (Gowland 1902) followed by the more extensive work of Colonel Hawley during the 1920s and Professor Atkinson more recently (Atkinson 1979). Colonel Hawley's work in particular, although inconclusive in the case of Stonehenge, can be seen as a continuation of the broad research themes being promoted at Avebury (Gray 1935) and Maumbury Rings (Bradley 1976).

Table 3 Recorded excavations in the study area, with principal references

Site	Reference
Eighteenth- and nineteenth-century excavations	
5 round barrows	Stukeley 1740 Atkinson 1984
1 round barrow	Thurnam 1868
12 round barrows	Duke unpubl
208 round barrows	Hoare 1810
Twentieth-century excavations	
Ceremonial and communal monuments	
Stonehenge	Gowland 1902 Hawley 1921; 1922; 1923; 1924; 1925; 1926; 1928 Atkinson *et al* 1952 Atkinson and Evans 1978 Atkinson 1979 G Smith 1979–80 Pitts 1982 Bond 1983 Evans 1984
The Avenue	Clay 1927 Vatcher and Vatcher 1968 G Smith 1973
Durrington Walls	Wainwright and Longworth 1971
Woodhenge	Cunnington 1929
Stonehenge Cursus	Farrer 1917 Stone 1947 Christie 1963
Normanton Down long mortuary enclosure	F de M Vatcher 1961
Round barrows	
Amesbury 26	Pitts 1979–80
Amesbury 39	Ashbee 1979–80
Amesbury 51	Ashbee 1975–6
Amesbury 98	Crawford 1928
Amesbury 101	Passmore 1940
Amesbury 103	Pitts 1979–80
Amesbury 132 and 133	F de M Vatcher 1960
Durrington 65b	Booth 1951
Durrington 67, 68, 69, 70	Cunnington 1929
Durrington 74	Stone *et al* 1952
Wilsford cum Lake 1, 33	Field 1961
Wilsford cum Lake, Lake Group: 36f, 36g 37, 38, 38a, 38b, 39	Grimes 1964
Wilsford cum Lake 51, 52, 53, 54	Greenfield 1959
Wilsford cum Lake 83	Haslam 1960
Winterbourne Stoke 30	Christie 1963
Winterbourne Stoke 31 and 32	H L Vatcher 1962
Winterbourne Stoke 45	Christie 1970
Winterbourne Stoke 38, 39, 46, 47, 49, 50	F de M Vatcher 1962
Inhumations	
Durrington	Ruddle 1901
Durrington	Farrer 1918
Fargo	Stevens 1919
Durrington	Anon 1920
Amesbury	Cunnington 1935
Fargo	Stone 1938
Larkhill	Shortt 1946
Larkhill	Moore 1966
Stonehenge	Atkinson and Evans 1978

Table 3 continued

Site	Reference
Settlement	
Wilsford Shaft	Ashbee 1963 Osborne 1969
Settlement at Longbarrow Crossroads	Vatcher and Vatcher 1968
Settlements near Durrington Walls	Cunnington 1929 Stone *et al* 1952 Wainwright and Longworth 1971 Wainwright *et al* 1971
The Durrington 'Egg'	Cunnington 1929
Packway enclosure	Wainwright and Longworth 1971
Pits/postholes	
Woodhenge	Stone and Young 1948
King Barrow Ridge	Vatcher and Vatcher 1969
Stonehenge Bottom	F de M Vatcher 1969
Stonehenge	Vatcher and Vatcher 1973
Boundary systems	
Linear earthwork near Stonehenge	Vatcher and Vatcher 1968
North Kite linear earthwork	Greenfield 1959

Woodhenge was excavated shortly after its discovery in 1925 (Cunnington 1929) as, perhaps more surprisingly, was the nearby Durrington 'Egg' (ibid). The sample excavation of Durrington Walls during road construction between 1966 and 1968 (Wainwright and Longworth 1971) formed part of a broader programme of investigation of large Wessex henges which also included those at Mount Pleasant (Wainwright 1979) and Marden (Wainwright 1971).

The themes of past investigation noted above, many of which were pursued on a national basis, have inevitably resulted in an emphasis on the excavation of a restricted repertoire of monuments. This has resulted in the enhancement of the funerary and ceremonial aspects of the landscape whilst, with a few notable exceptions, investigators have ignored some of the more fundamental elements of prehistoric society and economy. Some pioneering surface collection work was carried out in the 1930s (Laidler and Young 1938), resulting in the definition of surface flint industries, but no subsequent emphasis was placed on the necessity for enhancing and extending this potential. The location and investigation of settlement traces remained a chance phenomenon, until changing emphases in prehistoric research priorities during the 1970s provided the stimulus for investigations such as the Stonehenge Environs Project.

2 Methodology

2.1 The general strategy

The main objective of the project, to record the nature of the existing archaeological record for the area and the predominant land use, dictated the main emphasis of fieldwork, a concentration on surface collection ('fieldwalking'). The strategy considered most conducive to the achievement of the objective within the duration of the project was to involve stages of identification, further surface definition, and finally evaluation by means of sample excavation. In addition to this multi-stage approach to what at the initiation of the project was merely an abstract concept, the 'surface scatter' as yet unlocated and undefined, more defined monuments were also to be evaluated by sample excavation.

The project area provided the overall sample frame within which areas, either whole or part modern field units, were selected for extensive surface collection. This selection was governed initially by the availability of suitably weathered fields and, later, by the intention of broadly sampling a number of areas of varying terrain and within contrasting monumental zones. The selection of areas for subsequent, more detailed surface examination, with the implication that such work could be the prelude to excavation, inevitably resulted in a concentration on areas or 'sites' with immediate definition. After surface evaluation of varying degree, three such areas were sampled by excavation in 1982 (W31, W31, and W34) and in 1983 an additional area (W59) was sampled after a exhaustive programme of surface evaluation.

2.2 Extensive surface survey

The considerable increase in surveys employing some form of surface collection has been matched by an increase in methodological discussion (Hazelgrove *et al* 1985). The surface collection techniques employed by the Stonehenge Environs Project have previously been discussed in some detail (Richards 1985a) and can here be summarised as extensive and intensive, the former employed as a broad sampling technique, the latter

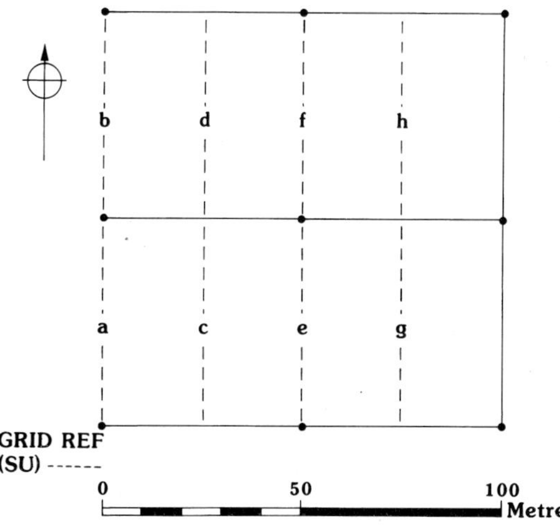

Fig 7 Extensive surface collection hectare sampling strategy

primarily as part of a suite of pre-excavation surface surveys.

Extensive surface collection methods involved the systematic collection of a *c* 10% sample of surface artefacts within extensive sample areas. In all cases, collection was carried out employing hectare squares based on the national grid as the sampling unit. Within each hectare eight transects, each 50m long and spaced at 25m intervals, were walked in a north–south direction (Fig 7). Field conditions and observations, soil variation, microtopography, weather, lighting, and personnel were all recorded on standardised field forms and annotated 1:2500 scale map extracts. Potential areas of soil accumulation were tested by augering on an *ad hoc* basis.

In practice, the finds recovered consisted primarily of worked (struck) flint with smaller quantities of pottery and worked stone. Burnt flint was not collected, although in retrospect this would have provided valuable data, but concentrations were noted in the field. All foreign (non-local) stone was, in theory, collected, although some selectivity was practised in areas of previous military activity. Sarsen of the hard, 'rooty' type occurs naturally in small boulders and its occurrence was therefore recorded without collection.

Table 4 Stonehenge Environs Project extensive surface collection 1980–84

Year	*No*	*Field name*	*Ha walked*	*Total ha/year*
1980	50	Winterbourne Stoke Crossroads	17.625	
	51	Coneybury Hill	27.25	
	52	North of the Cursus	42.625	87.5
1981	54	Stonehenge Triangle	33.5	
	55	South of Stonehenge	31.125	
	56	Normanton Down	26.75	
	57	King Barrow Ridge	34.125	
	59	The Diamond	20.75	
	60	Woodhenge	16.625	162.875
1982	61	Normanton Gorse	10.5	
	62	Cursus West End	62.25	
	63	Fargo Road	34.125	
	64	Horse Hospital	21	
	65	Durrington Down	26.375	
	66	Sewage Works	8.625	
	67	Normanton Bottom	12.125	
	68	West Field	24.625	199.625
1983	69	King Barrow Ridge (East)	19.875	
	70	Nile Clump	15	
	71	Railway	19.5	
	72	Home Fields	20.75	
	73	Whittles	6.75	
	74	Pig Field	6.5	
	75	Bunnies Playground	8	
	76	Destructor	9	
	77	The Ditches	6.125	
	78	Spring Bottom	23.625	
	79	Aerodrome	16.375	
	80	Ammo Dump	13.875	
	81	King Barrow Ridge (addit)	4	
	82	Rox Hill	27.25	
	83	Well House	4.875	
	84	Luxenborough	13.875	
	85	South of the Cursus	12.75	
	86	Rox Hill (unsown)	11.375	
	87	New King	20.75	
	88	Normanton East	29.5	
	89	Lake Bottom	2	
	90	Wood End	10.75	302.5
			Total	752.5

By this method a total of 752.5ha were examined over the winters of 1980–1 to 1983–4. The 39 individual collection areas, each designated by a traditional or assigned name (Table 4), are located on Figure 8. In discussion of the results of surface collection reference to specific collection areas will be by means of the area name followed by the number shown in Table 4, eg Stonehenge Triangle (54). Names employed for more general description, for example the area north of the Cursus, will be distinguished by the absence of a number suffix.

This first, locational, stage of surface collection is capable of suggesting broad spatial variation, the limitations on its refinement being primarily those imposed by the spacing of the individual collection units.

2.3 Intensive (pre-excavation) surface survey

2.3 a *Intensive collection*

This involved the collection of a 'total' surface assemblage, in this case including both burnt flint and sarsen, within a more rigidly defined and, of necessity, more restricted grid. A 5m or 10m grid was generally employed, within which all surface artefacts were collected. Defined types of artefacts – pottery, worked stone, and identified flint tools – were individually recorded in the field and their position accurately plotted.

This approach, providing a great deal more spatial refinement, was employed initially as a pre-excavation technique on specific monuments. It was subsequently used in the same way on areas initially defined by extensive surface collection. The accurate, surveyed grids constructed for this stage of surface collection were, in the fully developed methodology, also employed for surface analyses of the type described below, and were subsequently utilised as the excavation grid.

2.3 b *Geophysical survey*

(incorporating conclusions by A D H Bartlett)

The magnetometer survey carried out by the Ancient Monuments Laboratory at the first project excavation, Coneybury Henge (W2), demonstrated the advantages of pre-excavation geophysical survey, in this case providing an accurate ditch plan and facilitating the application of a precise sample design. Similar surveys, in each case carried out by the Ancient Monuments Laboratory using a fluxgate magnetometer, were employed on subsequent excavation sites wherever possible. Apart from the benefits for sample application already noted, the survey prior to excavation of sites located only by surface scatters of artefacts was used to suggest the location of subsoil features, crucial as 'traps' for associated environmental and economic data.

Topsoil excavation at Coneybury Henge was also preceded by field measurement of soil magnetic susceptibility, in this case integrated with less extensive soil sampling for laboratory susceptibility measurement. Both stages of analysis were carried out by the Ancient Monuments Laboratory. Subsequent magnetic susceptibility surveys were carried out using field coils loaned by the Ancient Monuments Laboratory and by Reading University, the data processing in each case being carried out by the Ancient Monuments Laboratory.

The Stonehenge Environs Project provided an opportunity to test geophysical techniques across a series of sites of varied archaeological character, but in reasonably uniform and favourable geological conditions. Subsequent excavations showed that the magnetometer could detect both natural and anthropogenic features, primarily substantial and earth-filled, but that employed alone, it could produce only a very incomplete picture of the archaeological character of a site.

The project has demonstrated that, by deploying a full range of fieldwork techniques (magnetometer, magnetic susceptibility, and phosphate – see below), significant information can be recovered even from sites where much of the archaeological evidence is confined within the ploughsoil. It has also shown the potential value of magnetic susceptibility measurements in studies of this kind. The susceptibility results showed that, although non-archaeological influences such as cultivation or terrain could not necessarily be excluded from the total response, a pattern of activity which related well to the other archaeological evidence could still be observed. It appears not only that information about the broad disposition of an area of activity can be obtained, but also that there is the possibility of identifying distinct small-scale anomalies if the site is surveyed in sufficient detail.

Summaries of individual Ancient Monuments Laboratory reports can be found in chapter 4, with full reports in microfiche (Bartlett, this vol, MF1 B2-5).

2.3 c *Geochemical survey*

The laboratory measurement of soil phosphates has been employed as part of other extensive Trust for Wessex Archaeology survey projects (the Kennett Valley Survey, Lobb and Rose in prep; the Isle of Purbeck Survey, Cox and Hawkes forthcoming). The methodology, developed during the 1982 Stonehenge Environs Project excavation season by Roy Entwistle (1984), was applied to all subsequent surface scatter excavations.

The methodology employed was essentially that used at Grimes Graves and at Fengate, and is described in detail in the respective publications (Sieveking *et al* 1973, 192–9; Craddock 1980). Spot samples were taken by the Ancient Monuments Laboratory from W2 Coneybury Henge and W2 (1981) Coneybury 'Anomaly' in order to compare the ditch deposits and the pit fill. Subsequently systematic samples were taken along sample transects at W31 Wilsford Down and at W32 and W34, Fargo Wood I and II. The buried soil at W52, the North Kite, was sampled on a 1m grid, as was the topsoil within a suggested urnfield (area A) at W57 Durrington Down barrow. The flint scatter at W59 King Barrow Ridge was sampled at 1m intervals for phosphate analysis, as part of a systematic strategy incorporating intensive surface collection, geophysical and

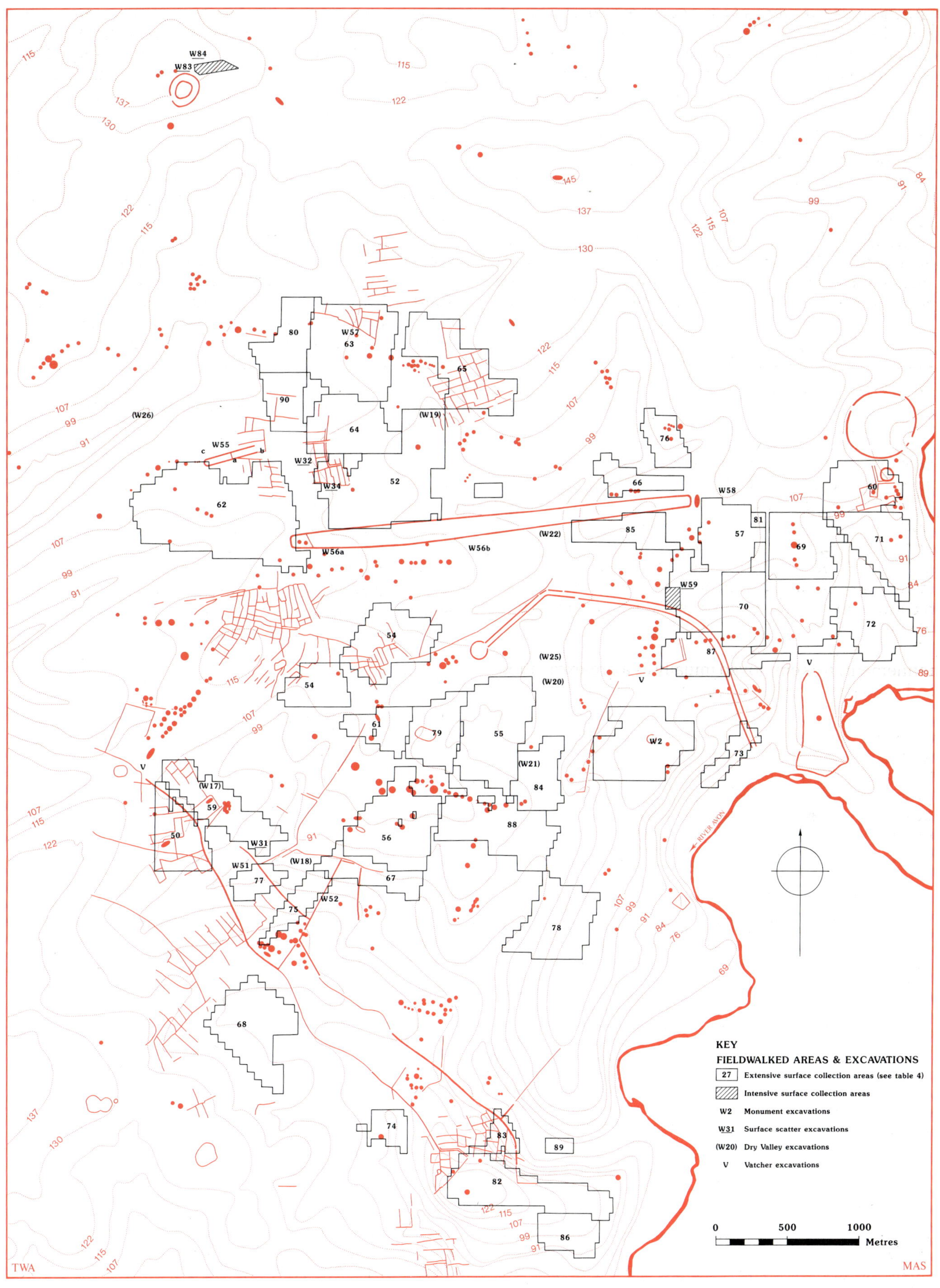

Fig 8 Location of extensive and intensive surface collection areas and project excavations

geochemical survey, and excavation. Spot samples from features were also taken.

The methodology of both magnetic susceptibility and phosphate survey work within the project has recently been discussed in a paper which makes specific reference to the comparative characteristics of two project excavations, W31 and W59 (Entwistle and Richards 1987). At W31 Wilsford Down a correlation was noted between enhanced phosphate values and higher magnetic susceptibility reading, corresponding with a general area of *in situ* domestic activity (Entwistle and Richards 1987, fig 3.3). The systematic survey of W59 King Barrow Ridge showed a general correlation between enhanced phosphate readings, higher magnetic susceptibility readings, concentrations of lithic material, burnt flint, and, where examined, archaeological features (Entwistle and Richards 1987, figs 3.4, 3.5). However, comparative data from W32 and W34 at Fargo Wood suggest a correlation between enhanced phosphate values and soils which had formed on a substrate of clay-with-flints rather than chalky drift. This emphasises a pedological boundary which had already been noted and introduces a cautionary note in seeking an entirely anthropogenic origin for observable patterns within soil phosphate data (Entwistle 1984; Entwistle and Richards 1987, fig 3.6).

2.4 Excavation

The combination of artefact collection from the surface of the topsoil, and an increasing awareness of the geophysical and geochemical properties of such deposits, necessitated a careful and consistent approach to their excavation. The methodological reasoning behind the project's approach to the topsoil has been previously published (Richards 1985a) and emphasises the value of the combined physical, chemical, and magnetic records, particularly in the comprehension of prehistoric domestic activity (Entwistle and Richards 1987).

On all project excavations, topsoil has, with one exception (W55 the Lesser Cursus), been excavated by hand on a 1m grid. Extensive topsoil sieving has also been carried out in order to retrieve a representative artefact sample, of particular importance for recovery of the lithic assemblages. Topsoil sieving was carried out using 4mm mesh box sieves; in the majority of cases the friable chalk-derived soils enabled soil to be passed dry through a sieve suspended from a shaker frame. More cohesive soils were wet-sieved (W32 and W34, Fargo Wood I and II), or, alternatively, dry-sieved residues too dirty for artefact recognition were subsequently wet-sieved, effectively washing the residues.

The sample fraction for topsoil excavation was determined after the first project excavation, Coneybury Henge (W2), where a nested sampling strategy was devised for the topsoil sieving (Fig 94), 50% eventually being achieved. This exercise provided a series of data sets which, combined with a new-found awareness of the time taken to sieve and sort topsoil residues, enabled a minimum sample fraction of 20% to be selected. This was applied to all project excavations from W31 Wilsford Down onwards (1982), with the exception noted above. All sieve residues from both topsoil and stratified deposits were sorted on site by core personnel with proven ability in the recognition of artefacts. Beyond this overall approach to the sampling of topsoil, the sampling strategies were site specific and as such will be described in the introductory sections for each report.

The sieving approach to stratified deposits varied according to their nature and extent. Ditch deposits were generally excavated in such a way that remaining central baulks, or a 1m central column through the baulk, could be sieved through a 4mm sieve after refinement of the stratigraphic sequence determined by initial excavation. The fills of features such as pits were totally sieved to 4mm with, as in the case of ditch deposits, sub-samples taken for 1mm wet-sieving/flotation.

All excavated ditch deposits were sampled for possible molluscan analysis, although in reality it was unlikely that all samples would be analysed. Key ditch sections exhibiting dated horizons were either fully analysed or sub-sampled, while others, for which there is at present no dating evidence, were reduced to sieve fractions and deposited within the archive.

For the purposes of artefact studies all 'bulk' finds (primarily worked flint and burnt flint) are recorded by context, although identified activities involving such artefacts, for example flint knapping clusters, were recorded in more detail (see for example W58). On all project excavations, specified artefacts (pottery, metal objects, worked stone, flint tools, and bone) from non-topsoil contexts were precisely located. It was hoped that such an approach could refine the record within accumulative deposits and suggest the nature of deposition in more restricted areas.

2.5 Comments on the methodology

The project involved four seasons of fieldwork, during which the methodology for surface survey and excavation was devised and tested. Ideally the project would have commenced with the application of a fully developed suite of methodological approaches which could have been refined as appropriate. More practically, the timetable of project fieldwork meant that the fully developed methodology was only applied to one specific surface scatter site (W59 King Barrow Ridge) during the final (1983) season of excavation.

Data recovered by the range of techniques outlined above vary considerably in their interpretative capacity. The integration of such varying data levels may be easiest, and indeed most informative, where all levels can be demonstrated as applying, with increasing refinement, to a specific focus (the 'site'). Here the processes of identification, definition, and further surface assessment, when followed by characterisation of the ploughzone and the recovery of dated economic and environmental data, represent achievement of the methodological aims of the project.

3 Surface collections

3.1 Extensive surface collection evidence – the material

This section outlines the nature of the data recovered by extensive surface collection. The range of material recovered from surface collection and also from the excavation of ploughsoils is restricted to durable materials, primarily flint and stone. Such material is susceptible to spatial analysis appropriate to the method of recovery, and only a limited number of individual pieces embody either chronological or functional attributes. In the case of more detailed collection or ploughsoil excavation, associated geophysical or geochemical data can, however, enhance the interpretative capacity of such data.

3.1 a Lithics

The programme of extensive surface collection recovered a total of 102,175 pieces of worked flint. The recovery, processing, and cataloguing of this bulk of material (approximately 12 cubic metres of storage space), in order to enable basic functional and chronological assessment to take place, formed a major part of the project fieldwork.

3.1 b Ceramics

The pottery recovered from extensive surface collection ranged in date from Early Neolithic to post-medieval, the former represented by a single sherd, the latter, more durable, by considerable quantities, often associated with ceramic roof tile. It is clear from the discussion below of the distribution of pottery of various periods that past land use has had a considerable effect on the survival potential of certain types of prehistoric pottery. Nevertheless the survival, recovery, and analysis of such material, embodying not only chronological but in many cases ideological attributes, has proved an important aspect of the surface collections.

3.1 c Other material

Foreign (non-local) stone, including querns and fragments of stone axes, form the only additional class of artefacts recovered in significant quantities by extensive surface collection.

3.2 Surface collection analysis

The main aims of the programme of extensive surface collection were to locate and define areas of prehistoric activity. From the start of the project there was an awareness of the potential range of activities represented by the surface artefact record, and this work was not seen simply as an exercise in finding 'sites'. However, within the context of the broader brief, to evaluate further such located areas, there was an inevitable emphasis placed on areas with definition and preferably of manageable extent. The diminishing sample fraction that is the inevitable consequence of a more intensive approach, culminating in excavation, has previously been noted (Richards 1985a). The problems inherent in the excavation of samples which could be considered unacceptably small (see for example W31) are considerable and may be compounded by the initial selection of an over ambitious sample frame.

3.3 Lithics

Within the Stonehenge Environs Project study area it was obvious that the main tool for both location and definition would be worked flint, the most durable element of the majority of prehistoric artefact assemblages. Other types of surface finds, such as pottery, were likely only to be useful in an adjunctive capacity as their survival, affected considerably by land use history, could not be guaranteed.

3.3 a Sorting

The first stage – sorting of all lithic material by recorded context (hectare and transect) into the categories shown in Table 5 – provided the basic data for broad spatial analysis. This involved the construction of objective plots of defined categories of lithic material.

3.3 b Basic spatial analysis

In the absence of computer facilities, the definition of categories for plotting was carried out by constructing a histogram (Fig 9) showing occurrences of values of all worked flint per 50m run (transect). The divisions on the Poisson distribution thus generated were taken at the point of inflection of the curve and where the curve started to break up (Hodder and Orton 1976). This produced categories of: 0–10, 11–39, 40–89, and 90+ pieces of worked flint per 50m run, categories which, with the exception of 0–10 (omitted for clarity), were then plotted as a distribution map (Fig 10). This basic distribution of all worked flint makes possible the identification at a positive scale both of broad zones of activity and of some measure of extent and intensity. At this level note must be taken not only of the more positive and defined aspects of the distribution patterns thus generated but also of less intensive yet often widespread associated patterns. These cannot simply be regarded as indications of similar but less intensive activity; the potential for a complementary suite of activities should not be ignored.

The initial spatial analysis should go some way to explaining where specific and recognisable activities were taking place but, if the data are capable of supporting further inference, attempts must be made to answer questions relating to both function and chronology.

3.3 c Functional analysis

Functional assessment depends on an understanding of the processes by which worked flint enters the ar-

Table 5 Worked flint sorting categories

Category	*Criteria*
Core	Piece showing traces of flake removal by percussion
Core fragment	Fragment of above, generally showing signs of flake removal by percussion, but broken, for example, along incipient fracture line
Flake	Complete piece removed by percussion and exhibiting full length from bulb to distal end
Broken flake	Incomplete example of above
Burnt worked flint	Any worked piece subsequently burnt
Retouched flake	Flake showing traces of consistent secondary flake removal/modification by percussion
Scraper	See Figure 15 for type series
Other tool	Other recurrent consistently modified piece with apparent functional potential

chaeological record. These can be summarised as: procurement, manufacture, use, and discard.

Procurement of flint can be by means of mining, surface grubbing, or collection. In manufacture the reduction sequence can encompass a range of processes, from raw material testing and discard of unsuitable flint, through various stages of production, to resource exhaustion. The first stages of reduction may often be associated with the procurement site, together constituting the 'industrial' side of the process. Such an association, particularly if a specific flint resource is consistently utilised, will render industrial activity largely static and thus potentially more archaeologically visible.

Subsequent stages, involving more portable elements of the reduction sequence, such as prepared cores or selected flake blanks, may take place on, or near, habitation areas. The degree of mobility in what must be regarded as a wide range of activities is less easy to assess, as is their potential archaeological visibility .

In the absence of microwear potential, the result of mechanical damage and of surface patination ('cortication'), use can only be characterised by the occurrence of retouch and 'tools', recurrent modified forms falling within broad, often well-established, functional categories. Discard, the means by which an object enters the archaeological record, encompasses a range of processes including chance loss, deliberate deposition in a range of circumstances, or incorporated dispersal within, for example, manuring debris.

Although both use and discard can take place both on or off 'site', relatively high proportions of both tools and retouched material, particularly where clustered, can, in very general terms, be suggested as indicating 'domestic' activity, if not necessarily settled habitation.

3.3 d Chronological assessment

With regard to problems of chronology, the lithic assemblages can all be suggested as dating in conventional chronological terms to the Neolithic and Bronze Age. Evidence for Mesolithic activity is extremely slight, although the sampling strategy for the extensive collection may be unsuitable for the recovery of diagnostic Mesolithic artefacts. Equally, there is little evi-

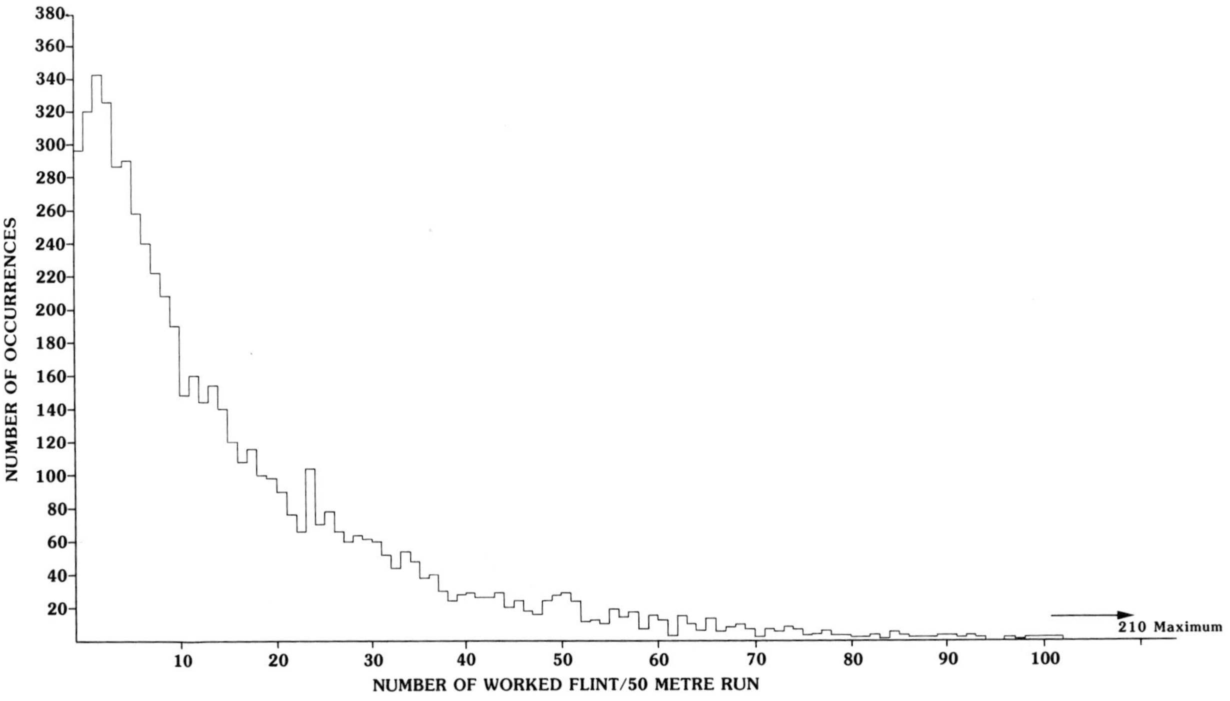

Fig 9 Recovery of total number of worked flints per 50m collection unit

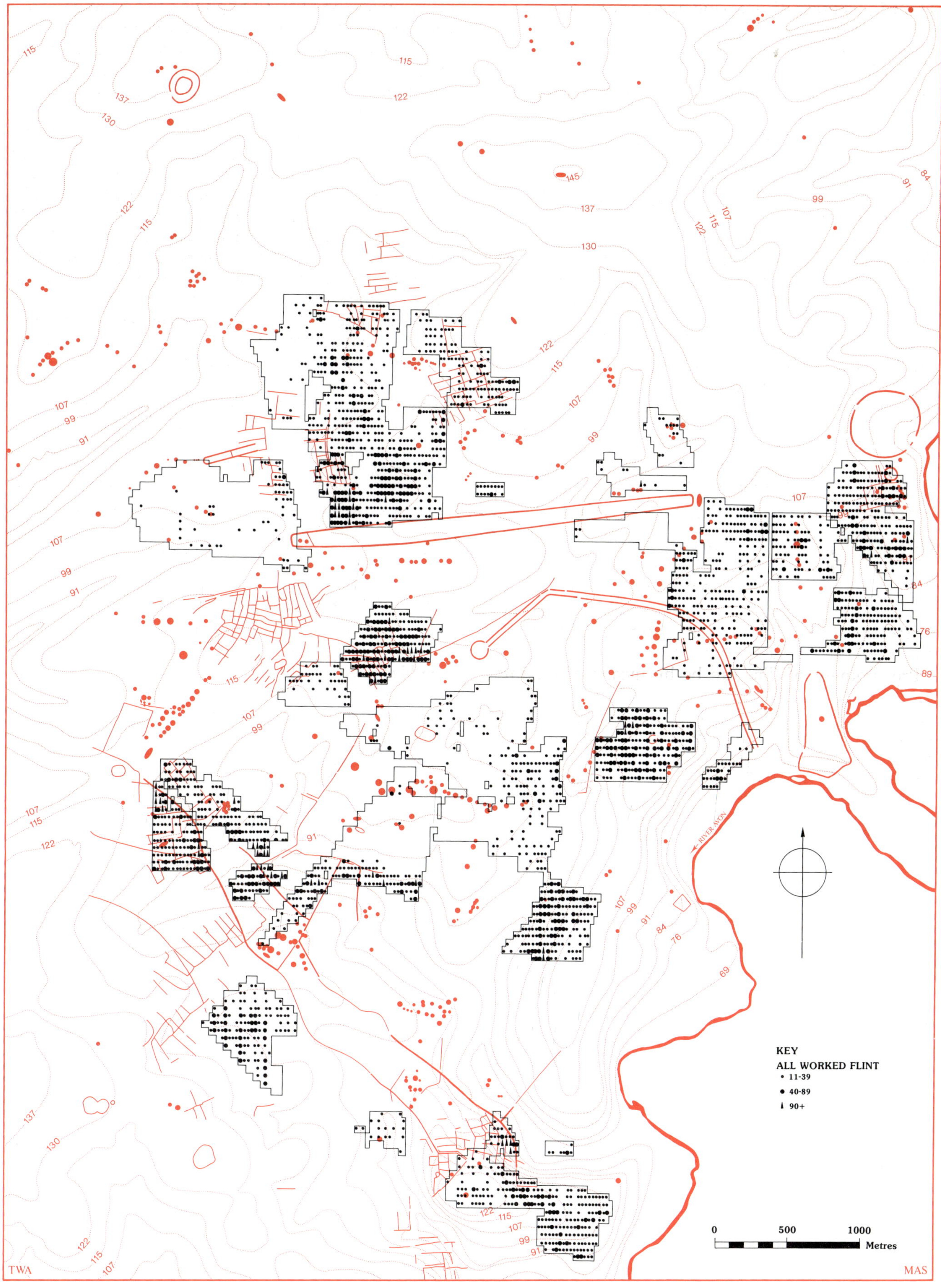

Fig 10 The distribution of all worked flint from extensive surface collection

dence for activity of any form during the first millennium bc, although the extensive use of lithic resources is generally suggested as having ended in the later Bronze Age (Ford *et al* 1984). Attempts at chronological refinement within what are basically the third and second millennia bc must rely on a series of attributes, some related to specific tool types and therefore individually applicable, others generated by, and therefore only applicable to, assemblages.

It was hoped that the analysis of a range of stratified lithic assemblages would result in the identification of a suite of technical attributes with additional chronological value. Such attributes, if identified, could be sought on a sampling basis from within the material recovered by surface collection. However, the degree of technical variation observed within groups of both Early and later Neolithic date appeared insufficient to warrant this approach as a part of the initial analysis. Rather, a broad range of chronological attributes was used in the overall assessment of the lithic assemblage obtained from extensive surface collection. Table 6 shows these, and Figure 11 illustrates a sample of the less specific tool types referred to in the table.

The broad assessment of the material from surface collection and the identification of both functional and chronological attributes enable a series of models to be constructed. These models are used as an aid to the interpretation of the distribution plots and relate to defined stages in the movement of lithic resources within the landscape.

Three stages can be suggested:

i Procurement/reduction (industrial)
Spatial attributes: possibly extensive with nucleated elements, but strongly topographically based (related to the availability of lithic resources).
Assemblage composition: hammerstones (particularly heavy ones), 'tested' nodules, flawed cores, high proportions of primary flakes.
Chronologically diagnostic attributes: potentially few.

ii Reduction (manufacture)

Table 6 Chronological attributes used in overall worked flint assessment

Tool type	*Early Neo*	*Later Neo*	*Beaker*	*Later Bronze Age*
Arrowheads	leaf	transverse	barbed and tang →→	
Scrapers	double end		thumbnail	expedient
	long end			
	D-shaped →→			
Axes	ground flint	ground stone		
	chipped flint →→			
Other tools	microdenticulate	fabricator	plano/convex	tool kit
		Y-shaped	knife	
	backed blade	discoid	borer →→	
	truncation element	rod		

→→ continuation into next period
See Figure 15 and Table 125 for scraper type series
See Figure 7 for illustrated examples of tool types

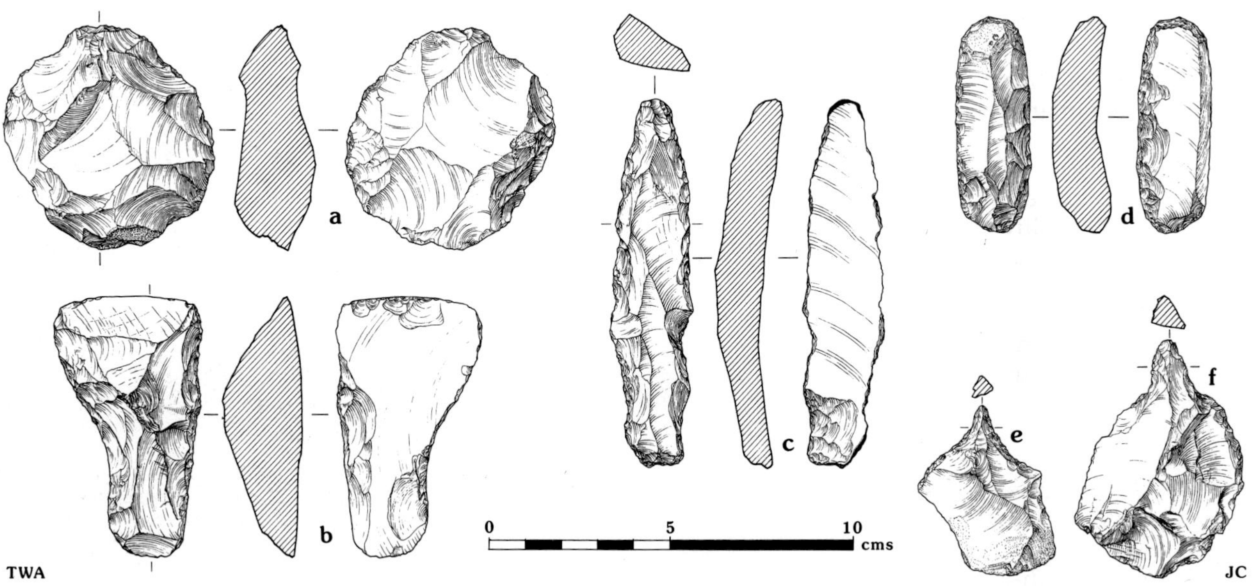

Fig 11 Flint tools with chronological attributes

Spatial attributes: more likely to be nucleated, even within broad areas of activity.

Assemblage composition: hammerstones, cores (particularly exhausted or failed examples), high proportions of both broken and apparently unutilised flakes.

Chronologically diagnostic attributes: platform technique and consequent reasons for core abandonment, specific 'blank' production.

iii Use/discard (domestic)

Spatial attributes: will depend on the nature of the overall economic base, the range of potential activities, and consequently on the discard patterns generated.

Assemblage composition: high proportions of utilised (retouched) pieces, tools, burnt worked material, tool variability.

Chronologically diagnostic attributes: wide range of individual items, and recurrent retouched forms (tools) (see Table 6 for examples).

3.4 Distribution patterns

Having set out the theoretical basis on which the evidence is judged, the basic data from extensive surface collection can now be reviewed. Figure 10 shows the distribution of all worked flint from the project's sample areas. Perhaps the most striking aspects of the distribution pattern are the areas producing little or no evidence of prehistoric activity in the form of high densities of worked flint (for the location of collection areas see Fig 8 and Table 4). Areas such as Ammo Dump (80), Wood End (90), Cursus West End (62), Sewage Works (66), and Destructor (76) may be regarded as peripheral to the major zone of activity represented by monument clusters. This is not the case for the area represented by the southern part of Stonehenge Triangle (54), Normanton Gorse (61), Aerodrome (79), South of Stonehenge (55), Normanton Down (56), and part of Normanton East (88). The latter encompasses a wide range of monument types and is surrounded by areas producing positive evidence for the range of activities discussed below. Despite this, there is little or no evidence in the form of high densities of worked flints from surface collection. The topography and soils of this apparently blank zone cannot be regarded as explanatory factors.

Surface finds in South of the Cursus (85) were collected under unsuitable field conditions and the results obtained cannot be regarded as a valid sample.

Turning to the positive side of the distribution, several broad zones of activity can be suggested. The extent of these zones does, to a certain extent, seem to be defined by the Avon Valley and the dry valleys of Stonehenge Bottom and Spring Bottom. The Avon Valley forms an obvious physical and topographical boundary whereas the dry valley systems, while not presenting physical boundaries, nevertheless appear to have influenced the nature and extent of prehistoric activity. Project fieldwork also demonstrated them to be devoid of colluvial deposits which may have masked activity areas.

The area to the south-west of Stonehenge Bottom and Spring Bottom (Lake Down and Rox Hill) shows consistent values of between 11 and 89 pieces of worked flint per 50m collection unit, with no apparent nucleation of activity.

A markedly different pattern of activity can be identified within the dry valley running from Winterbourne Stoke Crossroads (50), The Diamond (59), through The Ditches (77), Bunnies Playground (75), and Normanton Bottom (67). Here, the dry valley itself forms the focus for consistent values of worked flint in excess of 90 pieces per 50m collection unit. The contrast is strongest between the activity represented by Normanton Bottom (67) and the almost total absence of worked flint from Normanton Down (56) immediately to the north. Around the head of the dry valley, strongly nucleated activity at Winterbourne Stoke Crossroads (50), The Diamond (59), and The Ditches (77) lies within a more extensive area of activity. Well House (83) lies within the same dry valley, closer to the point at which it joins the valley of the River Avon, and produced an area of strongly nucleated activity, within which the highest levels of surface worked flint from the study area were recorded.

To the north of the blank zone already noted, two extensive areas of consistently higher density can be identified. North of the Cursus (52) and the northern part of Stonehenge Triangle (54) show consistent values of between 40 and 89 pieces of worked flint per 50m collection unit and also broad areas of intensive activity (in excess of 90 pieces of worked flint per 50m collection unit). These two areas may be part of the same broad zone of activity which continues in a more fragmentary manner to the north, for example, through Horse Hospital (64) and Fargo Road (63). The Stonehenge Triangle (54) element of this zone appears to mark its southernmost limit, demarcated topographically by the summit of Stonehenge Down.

Coneybury Hill (51) and Spring Bottom (78) lie on the ridge top between Stonehenge Bottom to the west and the Avon Valley to the east. Both demonstrate a broad distribution of similar values: 11 to 89 pieces of worked flint per 50m collection unit, with occasional higher values. This pattern begins to break up west of Coneybury Hill, but may continue into the eastern half of Luxenborough (84).

The remainder of the 'Durrington Zone' is perhaps not as coherent as has been suggested (Richards 1984b, 183). Much of the King Barrow Ridge shows a fragmentary pattern of values below 39 pieces of worked flint per 50m collection unit. To the east, within Woodhenge (69), Railway (71), Home Fields (72), and New King (87), the distribution becomes more regular and values above 40 pieces of worked flint per 50m collection unit become more common. The higher values within this area suggest a linear distribution, reflecting the influence of the river valley to the east and perhaps partly masked in the south-east corner by alluvial soils.

The distribution patterns shown in Figure 10 and discussed above appear to suggest broad zone preferences. An element of topographic determinism can be suggested, perhaps associated more with soil variability and the availability of lithic resources, discussed below and by Harding (this vol, 5.2). Alternatively, the distribution of a proportion of the surface material may be affected by ideological considerations, represented by ceremonial and funerary monuments. There is little

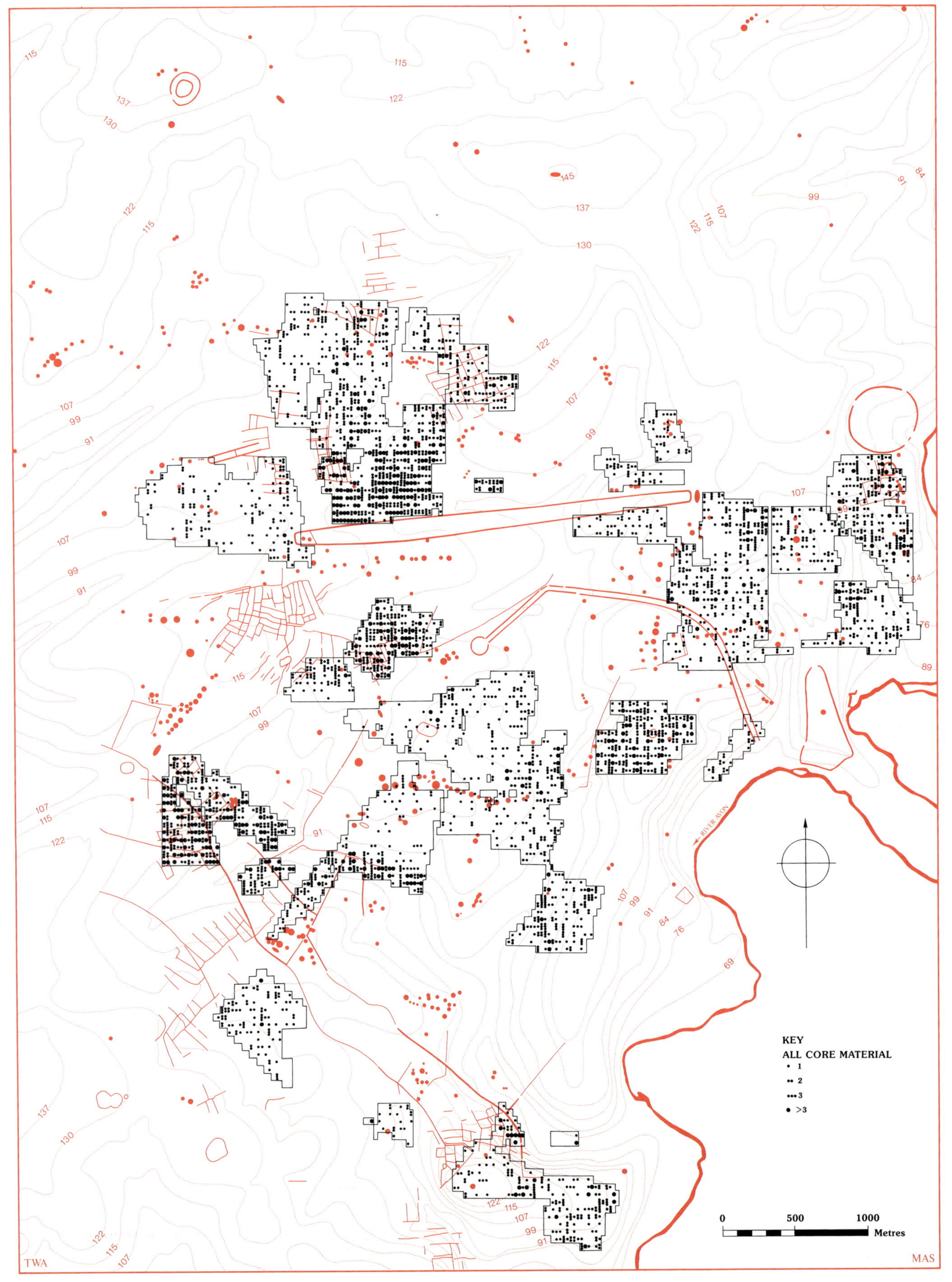

Fig 12 The distribution of all flint cores from extensive surface collection

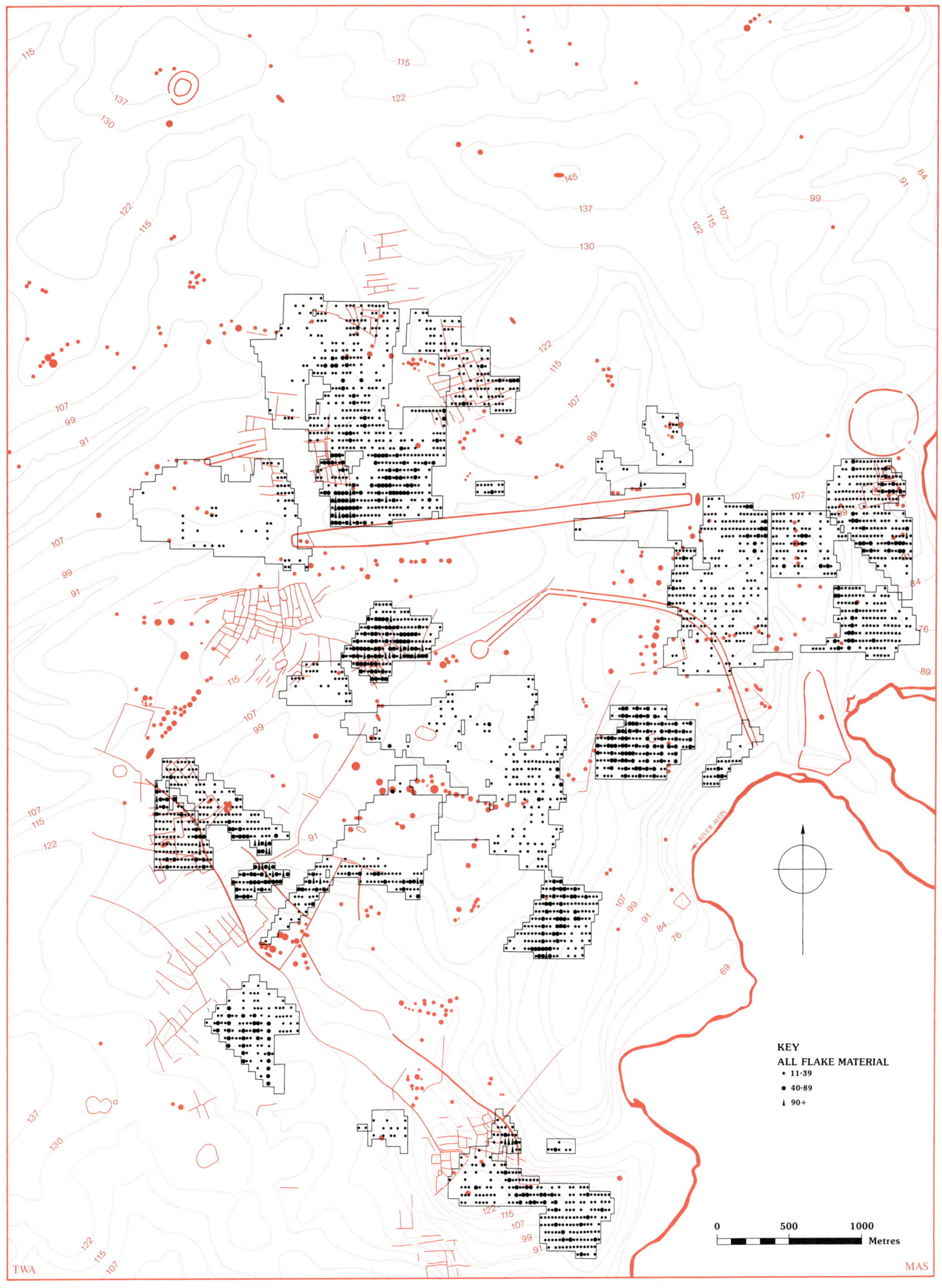

Fig 13 The distribution of all flint flakes from extensive surface collection

Table 7 Extensive surface collection: flint core and flake analysis

Sample area	*Sample size ha*	*No of cores in sample*	*Mean core weight*	*No of flakes in sample*	*Primary %*	*Secondary %*	*Tertiary %*
Well House (83)	0.075	55	366.13	696	8.33	57.47	34.20
Normanton Bottom I (67)	0.1125	59	150.63	296	4.05	72.64	23.31
Normanton Bottom II (67)	0.125	48	134.63	538	4.46	66.91	28.62
The Diamond (59)	0.05	10	132.60	264	3.79	63.26	32.95
The Ditches (77)	0.075	28	128.46	415	9.88	66.75	23.37
North of the Cursus (52)	2.5	124	94.51	1315	10.34	58.02	26.99
King Barrow Ridge (57)	0.5375	89	93.61	973	6.47	65.36	28.06

else to explain the apparent avoidance of Normanton Down discussed above.

Within this study a distinction has been made between 'lithic' (flint) and non-local stone. The following discussion is concerned with the former.

3.5 Interpretation of lithic material from extensive surface collection

3.5 a Functional assessment

The models suggested above for stages of procurement and manufacture involve greater numbers of both cores/hammerstones (means of production) and flakes (product), shown plotted in Figures 12 and 13. The first of these clearly suggests two lithic resource zones: one in the area north of the Stonehenge Cursus, where surface nodules from relict clay-with-flint deposits appear to have been exploited, and a major zone along the sides and base of the dry valley running from The Diamond (59) through Normanton Bottom (67). The occurrence of grassland further south-west along this dry valley prevents clarification of the extent of this activity, but the major industrial area at Well House (83) may be a continuation of this extensive zone rather than an isolated phenomenon. A more detailed consideration of the lithic resources exploited within the project area is contained within the flint report (Harding, this vol, 5.2).

As has been suggested above, the potential for chronological refinement within industrial assemblages recovered from surface contexts relies primarily on the identification of specific products. Figure 12 suggests a number of both extensive and nucleated core clusters, the cores from which were rapidly assessed and a number of attributes recorded. These were: weight; raw material; potential product; whether the core had been rejuvenated; and whether the core had been utilised as a hammerstone. No attempt was made to classify cores by an established typology such as that devised by J G D Clark (1960, 216).

Stratified assemblages recovered from W31 Wilsford Down, a site with a considerable industrial emphasis located immediately adjacent to this flint source, have, however, been examined in some detail (Harding, this vol, 4.10 b). Here analysis suggests that small, possibly surface nodules were the most commonly used raw material, although evidence from refitting material suggests that core tools (axes) were a part of the product of this site and may have required an alternative raw material source. Other flint tools, specifically transverse arrowheads and associated pottery, suggest that at this particular site major exploitation was taking place in the later Neolithic.

The suggested exploitation of two lithic resources, each potentially with raw material of varying productive capability, makes the modelling of lithic movement across the landscape more difficult. Modelling is further complicated by the suggestion made by Harding (this vol, 5.2) that the majority of the raw material needs of the sites examined in detail could have been met by selected locally available surface nodules. If the movement of lithic resources is restricted to those necessary for the production of more specialised, and usually larger, tools, then the position is further complicated.

If, however, resource areas can be identified and were being extensively utilised, then the basic models introduced above would suggest that the weight of cores should fall off with distance from source, as should both overall flake numbers and the percentage of primary (cortical) flakes. The mean weights of cores from the sample areas examined are shown in Table 7, which emphasises the 'heavy' industrial nature of the assemblage from Well House (83) and the consistency of the core size within the remainder of this, the Normanton Bottom industrial zone.

The mean weight of the cores from a broader but still consistent zone, North of the Cursus (52), suggests the exploitation of a flint source with smaller nodules. In comparison to the results from the two zones examined above, the core weights from both surface collection and the excavated sample on the King Barrow Ridge are consistently lower. This may suggest a greater curation of raw material, reflected in the reasons for core abandonment or, as suggested by the assemblage from Amesbury 42 long barrow (W58), may involve the utilisation of small, locally derived nodules (Harding, this vol, 4.7 b).

The distribution of all flake material provides a complementary distribution to that of cores, emphasising that the procurement of raw material may be expected to be accompanied by some form of production. The initial stages of reduction, involving the removal of cortex and the preparation of potentially productive platforms, should be represented by primary (wholly cortical) and secondary (partially cortical) flakes. Table 7, showing the relative proportions of primary, secondary, and tertiary (non-cortical) flakes associated with the examined core samples, fails to demonstrate this

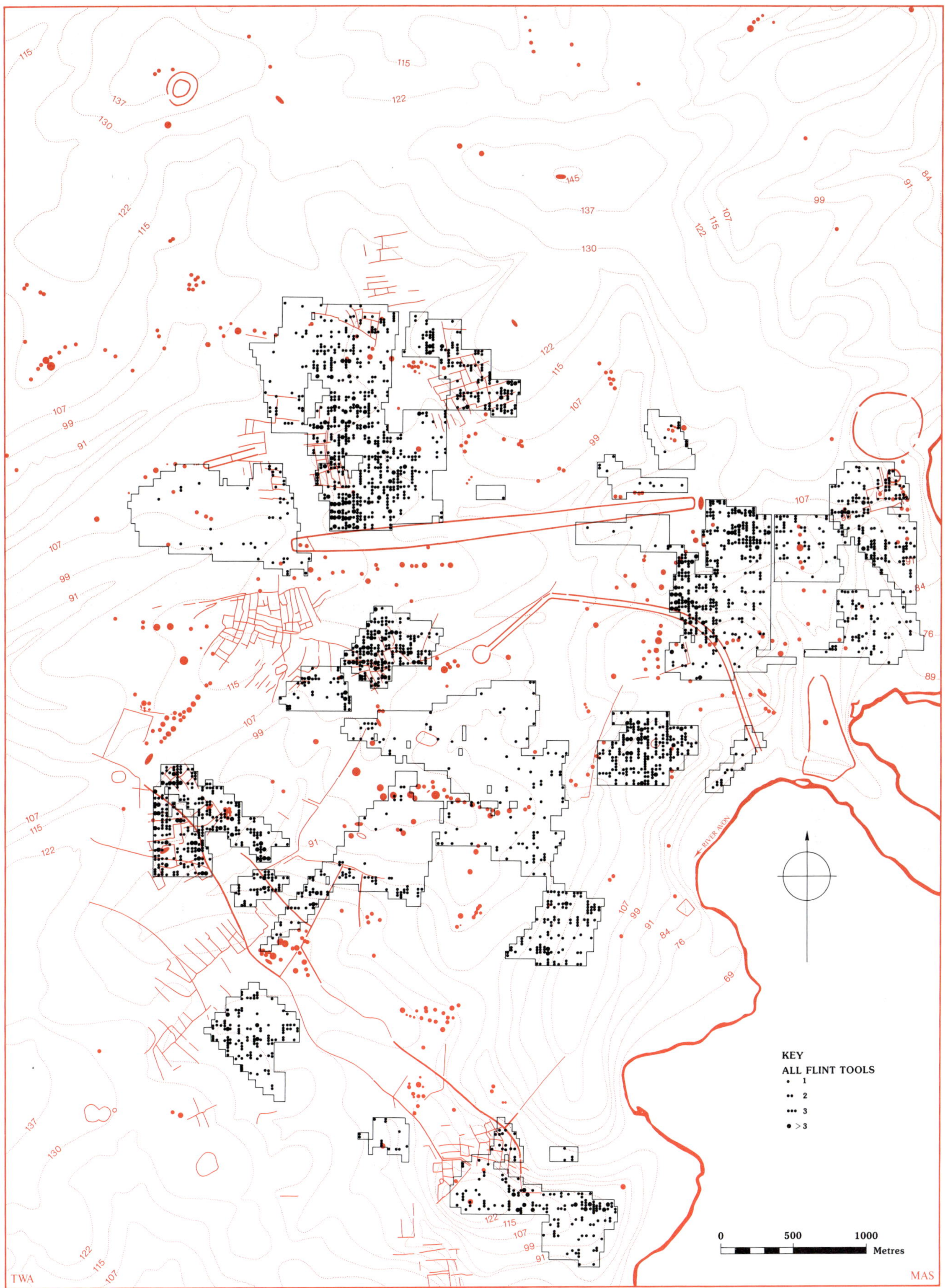

Fig 14 The distribution of all flint tools from extensive surface collection

suggested trend. As it seems unlikely that such flakes were the intended product and have been removed, it can be suggested that the under-representation of such flakes from surface collection may be due to their having one surface (the dorsal) entirely natural, and consequently unrecognisable.

Figure 14 shows the distribution of all flint tools – all recurrent retouched or modified forms identified during sorting. This plot intentionally has no chronological refinement, and contains forms that can be demonstrated to date from the Early Neolithic to the Middle Bronze Age or later. No attempt at functional refinement has been made, as the range of tools relates to both sedentary and mobile activities and is likely to have entered the archaeological record via a wide range of processes. This distribution provides an indication of zones which can be suggested as demonstrating a consistently domestic emphasis. These zones may not appear as significant in the overall lithic distribution, discussed in detail above.

Certain areas can be shown to combine elements of both industrial and domestic activities. In the case of North of the Cursus (52) and the northern part of the Stonehenge Triangle (54), the correlation appears to be direct, whereas at Winterbourne Stoke Crossroads (50), The Diamond (59), and The Ditches (77) the domestic activity appears to be peripheral to the main industrial areas. In contrast, the concentrations of tools from the King Barrow Ridge (57 and 81) were not associated with high densities of lithic debris. This suggests activities involving the use and careful curation of flint presumably arriving as either prepared cores or flake blanks.

3.5 b Chronological assessment

A number of tool types have been assigned to period, either on the basis of observed or published association (Table 6). A number of specific types are illustrated in Figure 11. Scrapers formed the greatest proportion of all tools recovered (over 2500 examples or *c* 78% of all flake tools) and, as might be expected from such an ubiquitous tool type, these are generally difficult to assign to period. Some examples from the earlier Neolithic are made on flakes of blade proportions, but the examination of substantial groups of stratified scrapers from both Early and Middle Neolithic contexts – Coneybury 'Anomaly' (W2 (1981)), Robin Hood's Ball (W83), and King Barrow Ridge (W59) – suggested groups effectively indistinguishable, certainly so in rapid assessment. The small, 'thumbnail' type does appear to be a Beaker association, confirming earlier suggestions (Gibson 1982). Expedient types appear to have a later association, but may equally relate to functionally specific activities in earlier periods. Based on the observation of stratified groups, published data, and examination of mixed groups, a classification scheme of ten scraper types was devised, designed to separate types with a broad chronological significance (Riley, this vol, 5.3). This type series is shown in Figure 15.

3.6 Discussion

The lithic assemblage recovered by the extensive surface collection programme reflects considerable human activity within the area sampled. The assessment outlined above attempts to identify aspects of the distribution relating to consistent factors such as topography, and then to provide both generalised functional and chronological schemes. It is not intended to provide a justification for site identification, the emphasis of the more positive and consequently explicable elements of a distribution to the exclusion of all else. Some chronologically ordered concept of wider, more contextual

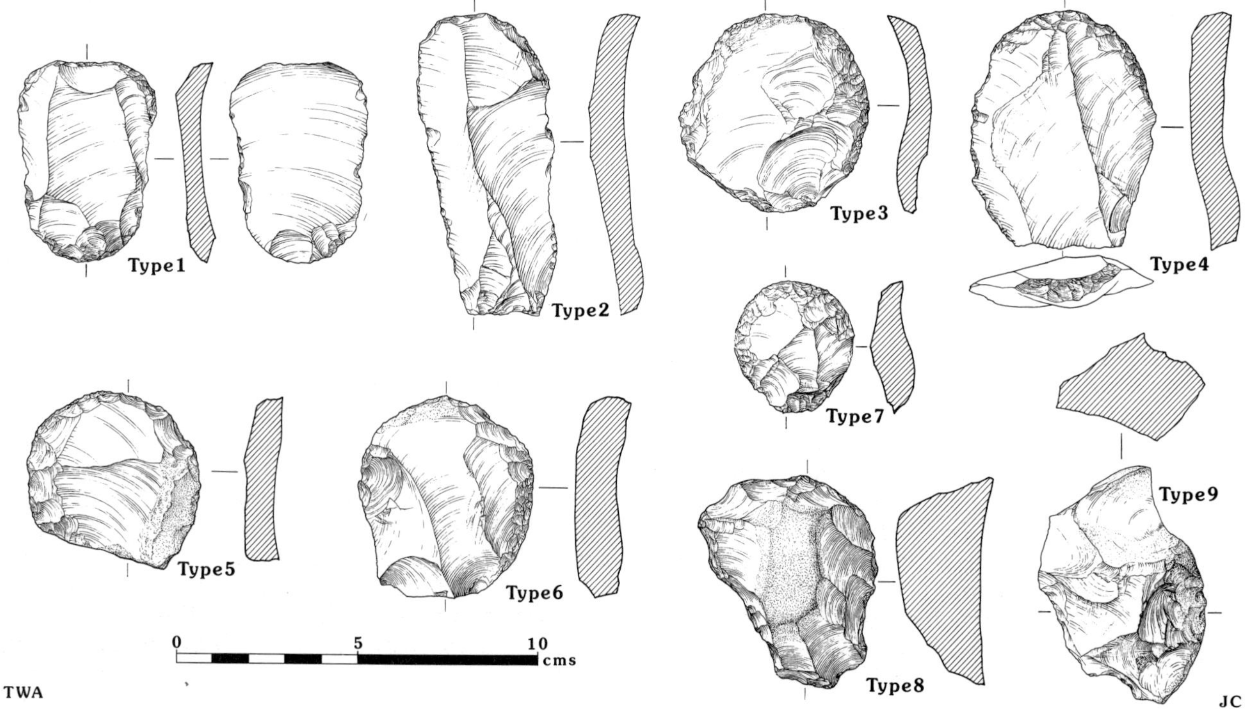

Fig 15 Flint scraper type series

patterns can also be suggested, discussion of which will be introduced within chapter 9. However, in the consideration of the overall development of the prehistoric landscape emphasis will inevitably be placed on the more defined aspects of the surface collection work.

The approach adopted here is neither site, nor non-site, nor off-site (Foley 1981) in conscious preference. Caution in interpretation could be recommended given the nature of the main surface artefact group and an awareness of the range and potential mobility of activities during the periods under consideration. The interpretation offered within chapter 9 does include 'site' identification, considered to be an appropriate term of reference for an identified and apparently spatially defined area of activity. For the purposes of excavation, the term 'site' can conveniently be used in reference to the overall unit to which the excavation sample is to be applied.

There are inevitably limitations to the approach outlined above, some related to the nature of surface sampling, others to the constraints imposed by the sheer size of the artefact assemblage. The use of a restricted range of tool types as domestic indicators may only identify specific types of activity, the emphasis lying with sedentary activities, employing a consistent, and possibly restricted, repertoire of tool types. A considerable range of potential activities may be recoverable from a more detailed analysis of, for example, unspecified retouch, coupled with a more sophisticated spatial approach. It is also certain that the further examination, on a sampling basis, of elements of the surface collection lithic assemblage would produce a considerably refined concept of resource movement, use, and discard.

Areas or zones selected on the basis of preliminary analysis of extensive collections were sampled on a more intensive basis. The methodology has been described above and, as this work was generally a preliminary stage to excavation (W32, W58, W59), the strategy and interpretation are described within the individual site reports in chapter 4.

3.7 The distribution of non-local stones

Of the three identifiable classes of non-local stone discussed above, both the small numbers of stone axe fragments and the 'bluestones' have a wide distribution within the Stonehenge area. The former category are shown on Figure 157, following Bradley's suggestion (1984, 53) that the fully developed stone axe trade is a later Neolithic phenomenon. Bluestone fragments occur more frequently and some patterns can be identified. Finds from the western half of the Stonehenge Cursus may provide some confirmation of the 'bluestone scatter' recorded by Stone (1947, 17) the specific location of which, now within an area of reintroduced pasture, cannot be checked.

Certainty as to the precise location of whole saddle querns should be tempered by an awareness of their portability and nuisance value to the farmer, a combination which may explain the occurrence of some examples towards the edges and corners of fields. Their distribution and that of recognisable fragments (plotted on Fig 160) do, however, show a strong association with areas of later Bronze Age activity, themselves integrated with areas of 'Celtic' fields. A notable concentration occurs within the fields to the north of the Stonehenge Cursus, close to the Fargo Wood I Bronze Age settlement (W34, this vol, 4.14), the sample excavation of which produced over 60% of all quern fragments recovered from excavations.

Three fragments of rotary querns were recovered, of which the distribution, and that of rock fragments potentially representing undiagnostic quern fragments, correspond well with that of Roman pottery (Fig 17). The emphasis consequently lies within Rox Hill (82), Winterbourne Stoke Crossroads (50), and Woodhenge (60).

3.8 Ceramics

The prehistoric pottery recovered from extensive surface collection has been analysed as part of the overall assemblage from the project. The methodology employed is discussed in chapter 6. An explanation of the coding system for the description of the prehistoric pottery fabrics is given in appendix 3. Figure 16 shows the distribution of all prehistoric pottery by weight per 50m collection unit, a distribution which shows a distinct concentration to the west of the study area. This is particularly marked in the area north of the Stonehenge Cursus, at Stonehenge Triangle (54), and The Diamond (59).

The overall distribution of prehistoric pottery (Fig 16) shows a negative correlation with all later ceramic material recovered from extensive surface collection. The distribution of Roman pottery (Fig 17) shows three clear foci. At Winterbourne Stoke Crossroads (50) an extensive scatter of pottery is associated with a 'Celtic' field system. Within the Woodhenge collection area (60) a scatter of pottery was recovered lying to the south and south-east of the settlement examined in 1970 (Wainwright *et al* 1971). In the Rox Hill area (82 and 86) a nucleated scatter lying on the hill top is associated with considerably abraded earthworks of fields within which potential settlement areas can be identified.

The distribution of both medieval and post-medieval pottery (Fig 18), and also that of ceramic tile (Fig 19), are heavily biased towards the eastern side of the study area. This combined distribution shows a strong correlation with areas of eighteenth- and nineteenth-century arable cultivation (RCHME 1979, map 3) and probably represents debris from the manuring of the open fields of the Avon Valley villages.

The distributions outlined above suggest that the emphasis exhibited by prehistoric pottery does not reflect a genuine distribution, but rather the inconsistent survival of a fragile class of artefact. The potential survival of this type of artefact in areas not subject to ploughing was demonstrated adjacent to Robin Hood's Ball where intensive collection of an area of *c* 2ha ploughed apparently for the first time in the historic period produced over 2000 sherds of pottery ranging in date from Early Neolithic to Late Bronze Age (Richards in prep a). The effects of historic ploughing, reflected in the almost total absence of prehistoric pottery within

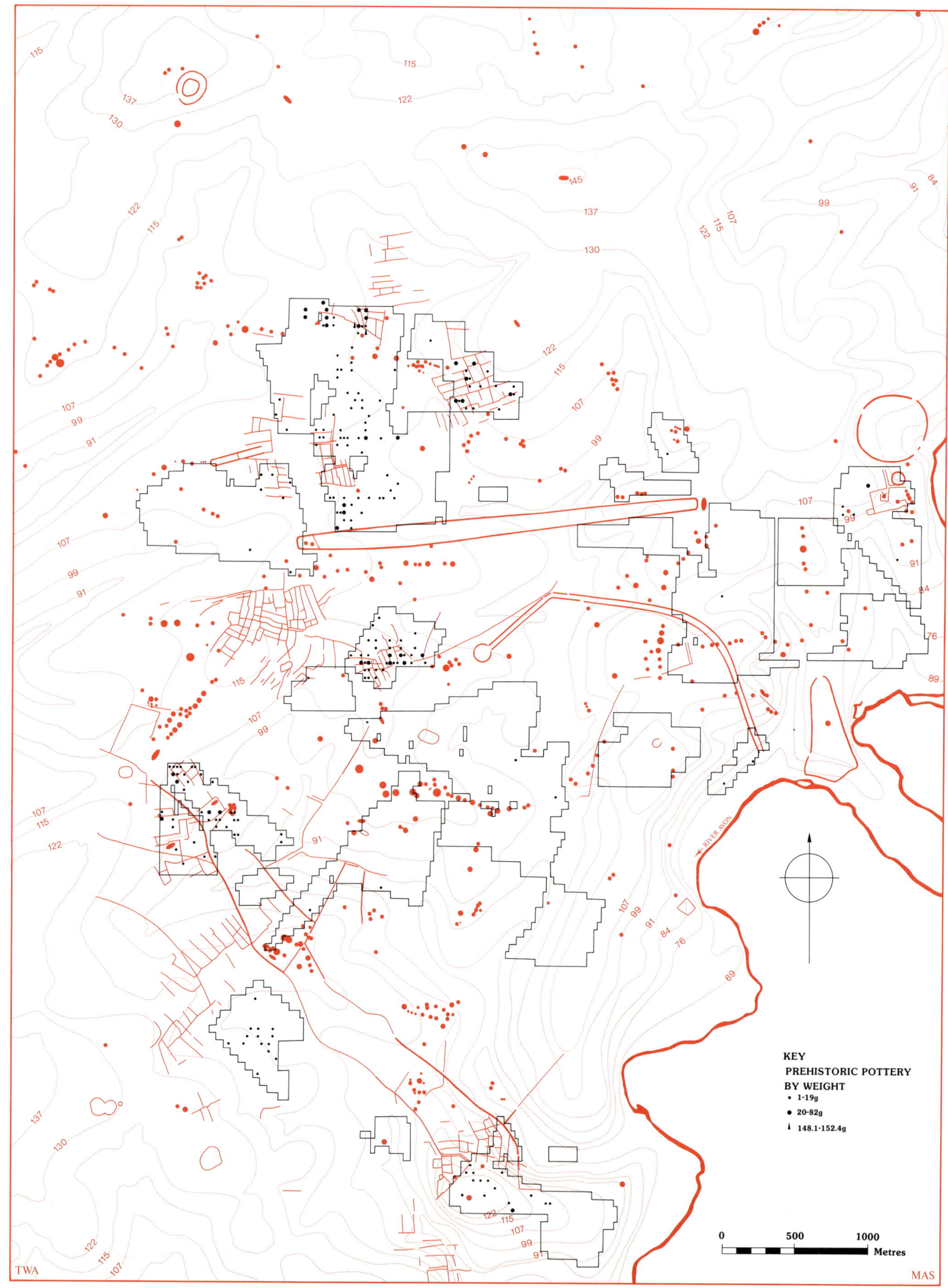

Fig 16 The distribution by weight of prehistoric pottery from extensive surface collection

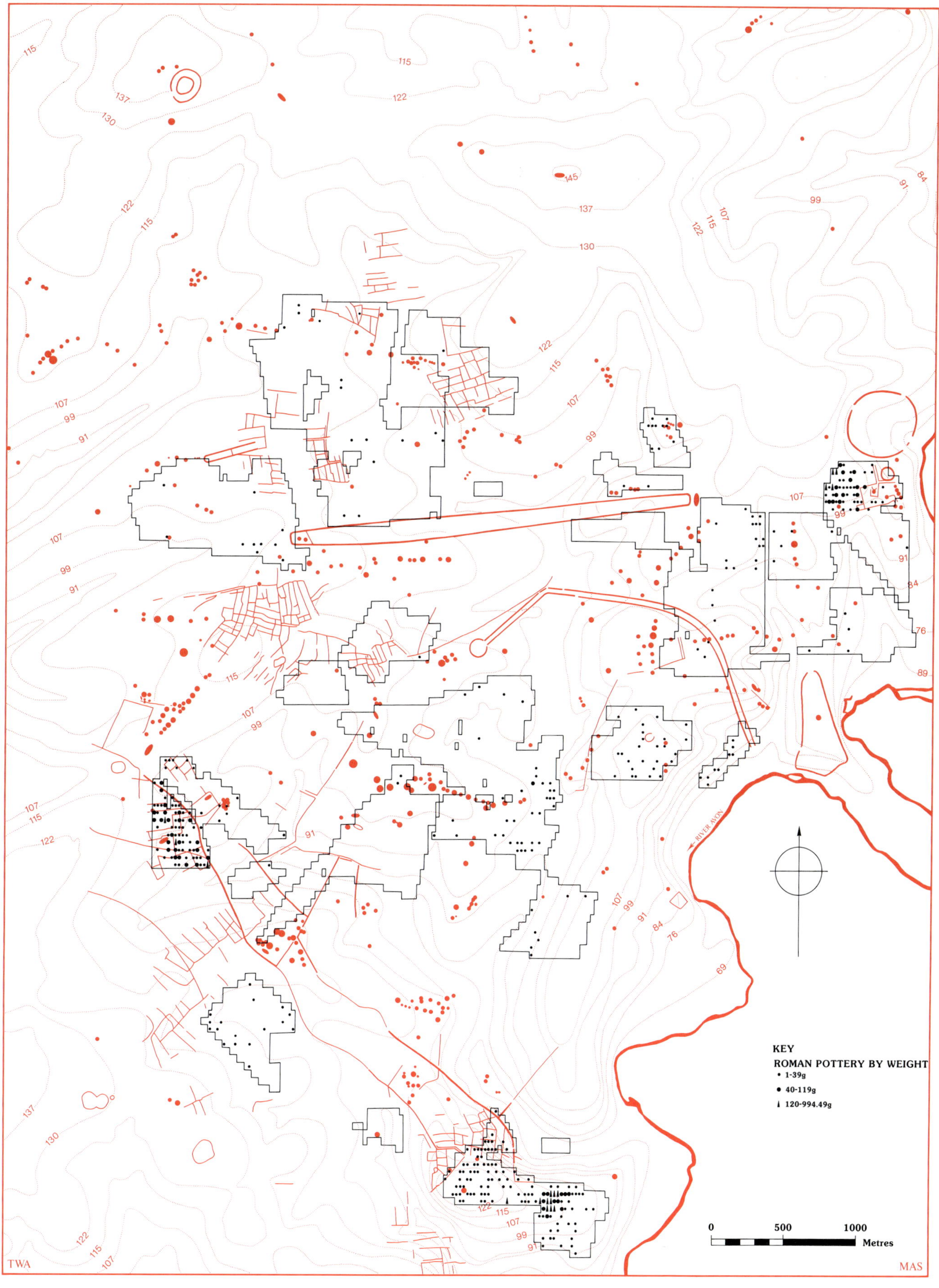

Fig 17 The distribution by weight of Roman pottery from extensive surface collection

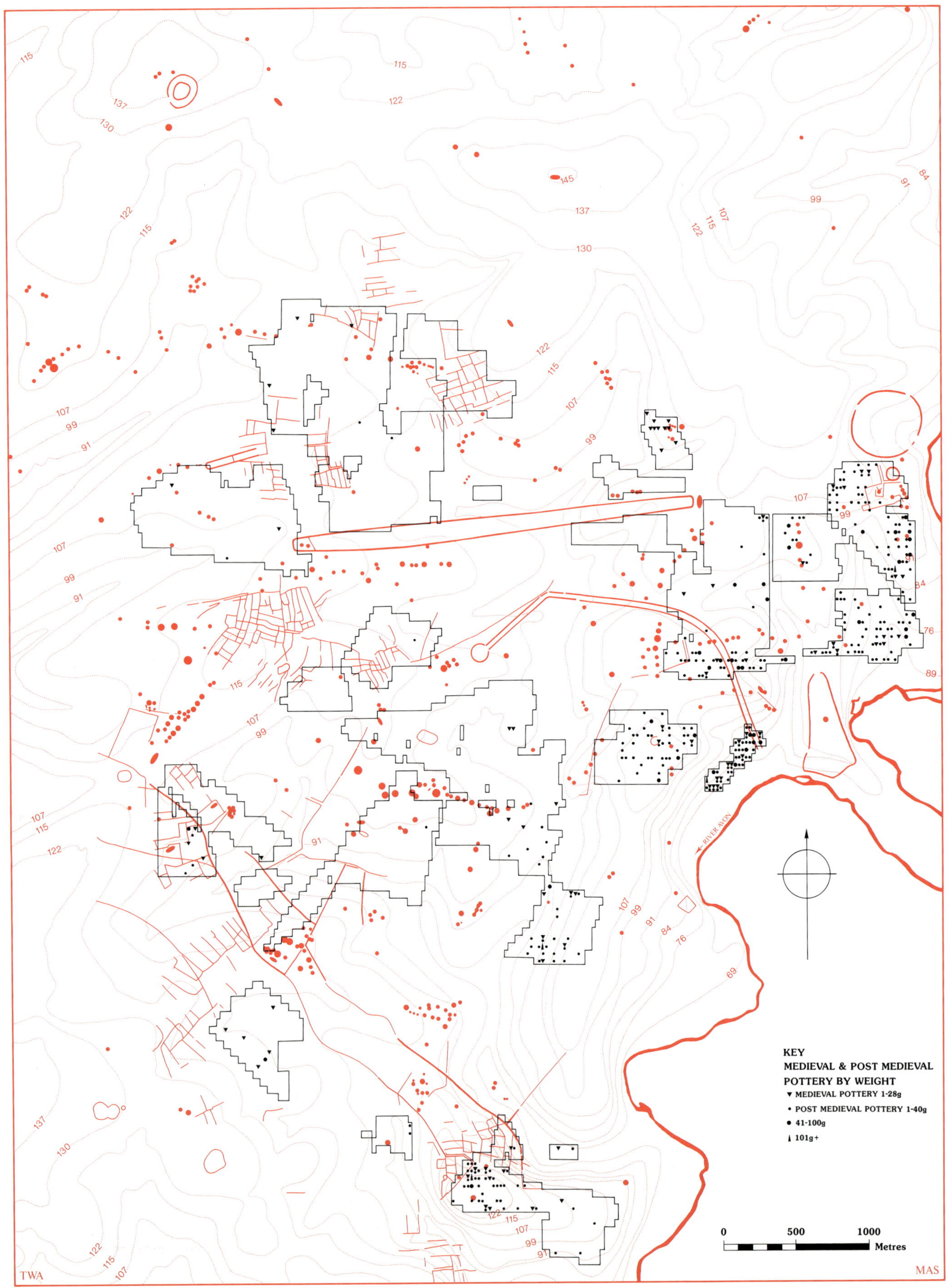

Fig 18 The distribution by weight of medieval and post-medieval pottery from extensive surface collection

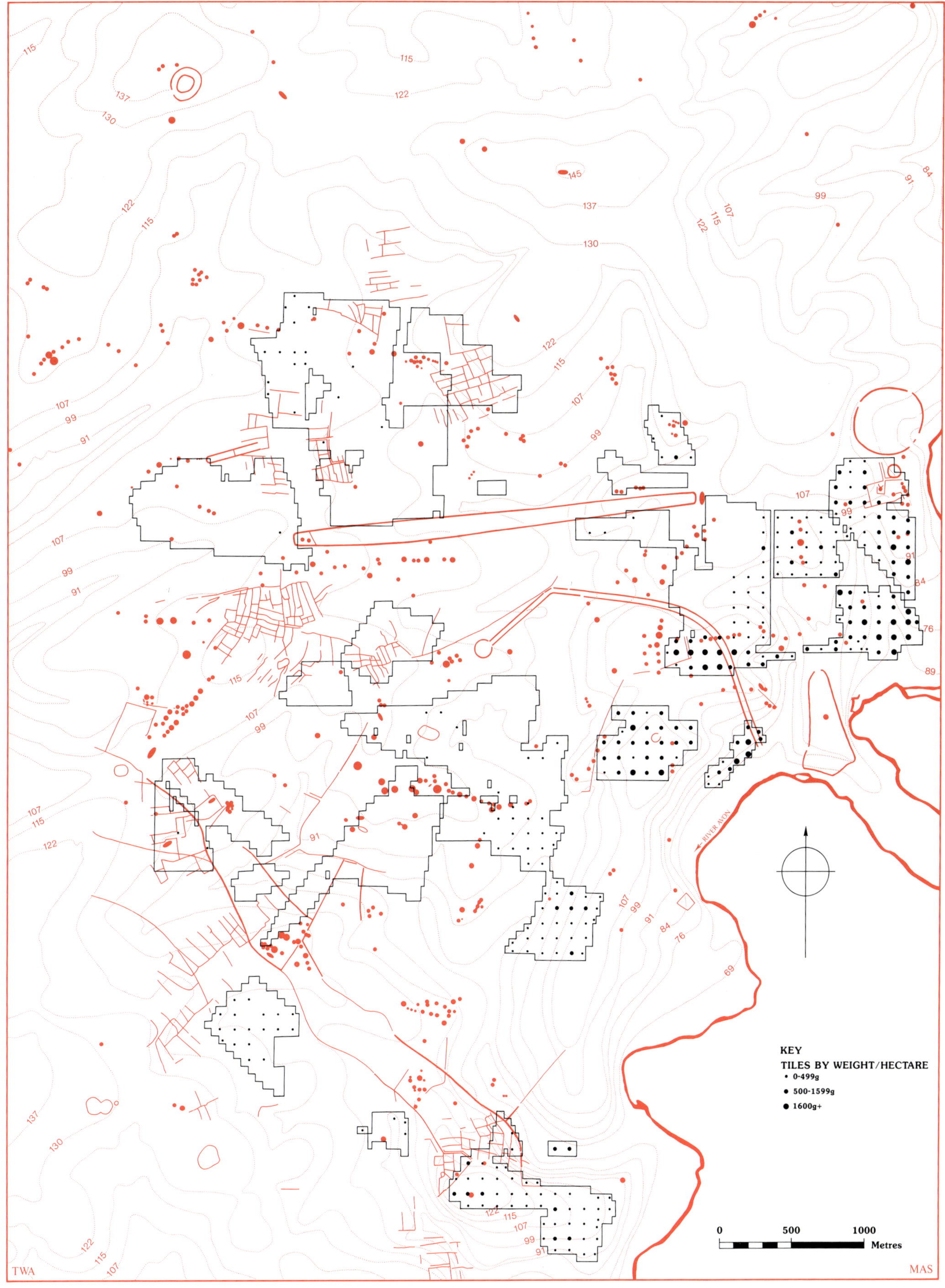

Fig 19 The distribution by weight of ceramic tile from extensive surface collection

the eastern half of the study area, has been confirmed by ploughsoil excavation (W59, this vol, 4.8). Such effects can also be seen in the abraded state of associated surface flint assemblages.

3.9 Prehistoric ceramics from surface collection

by Rosamund Cleal, with illustrated pottery descriptions by Frances Raymond

A total of 581 sherds, weighing 2.332kg, were recovered from surface collection. Details by collection area and ceramic fabric area are shown in Table 8, the data from which have been used to compile the summaries by field group (see below) shown in Figure 20. The majority of featured sherds are illustrated; only small or extremely weathered sherds have been excluded from Figures 21–23. For the purposes of illustration and discussion the material is divided into four groups:

i Fields north and west of the Stonehenge Cursus
ii Stonehenge Down (Stonehenge Triangle) and south as far as the Normanton barrows
iii Wilsford Down/Winterbourne Stoke Crossroads and south down to Rox Hill
iv The entire King Barrow Ridge and east as far as the River Avon

The distribution of prehistoric pottery by period is shown in Figure 154.

3.9 a *Group i: Fields north and west of the Stonehenge Cursus (Fig 20a, illustrated sherds Fig 21)*

Earlier Neolithic

A single sherd may belong to this period, but the identification is on fabric alone, and should be regarded as tentative.

Peterborough Ware

This is a fairly common ceramic in this area, mainly occurring in a broad north–south band in Fargo Road (63), Horse Hospital (64), and North of the Cursus (52). All but one of the sherds are likely to come from Mortlake or Ebbsfleet Ware bowls, but the rim sherd P273 is not from such a vessel. Although superficially P273 appears to belong to a Fengate Ware form, the angle of the rest of the rim is clearly almost horizontal, and the internal bevel shows this strongly by its marked curvature. Away from the rim, at the sherd's extremity, there is a slight change in angle, suggesting that the form may be deeper than the saucer-like profile it at first appears to represent. However, although it is impossible to establish the form of P273 with certainty, its affinities are clearly with the Fengate substyle of the Peterborough tradition. This is suggested by the strongly bevelled rim form, the herringbone on the rim bevel, and the fabric, which is shelly and laminated,

Table 8 Extensive surface collection: prehistoric pottery by collection area and fabric
Figures in table represent number/weight in grammes.

Fabric code	*Field no*							
	F50	*F52*	*F54*	*F55*	*F57*	*F59*	*F60*	*F61*
FS:Neo/3				1/13.3				
F:Pet/2						4/1.8		
F:Pet/3						1/3.4		
Ffe:Pet/1		3/16.1						
Ffe:Pet/3			2/12.0					
FS:Pet/7			19/62.7					
CFGS:LN/EBA/1						4/25.6		
feGS?:LN/EBA/1	1/3.4							
GM:LN/EBA/1						5/23.2		
Cfe:Bkr/1		1/2.4						
CG:Bkr/1			11/27.3					
CGS:Bkr/1						3/3.9		
FfeS:Bkr/1		1/3.4						
fe:Bkr/1		1/9.7						
feG:Bkr/1		4/9.2						
feG:Bkr/3						3/4.5		
feG:Bkr/4		1/6.4						
feGS:Bkr/1		2/36.6						
feGS:Bkr/3			2/4					
feGS:Bkr/8						9/28.5		
Indet Bkr		4/1.6	2/2.5			1/0.6		
CfeG:CU/1	1/3.8					9/71.2		
G:CU/1					1/6.6			
GS:CU/3		4/30.6						
Ffe:DR/1	4/19.7					6/43.0		
Ffe:DR/12	1/5.7							
FfeM:DR/1		4/18.4						
FfeS:DR/3			25/131.3					
FG:DR/1								1/8.7
FGS:DR/2						10/60.4		
FS:DR/5						5/41.6		
Fsh:DR/1			2/11.4					
sh:DR/1						3/36.4		
CFG:LBA/1		1/3.9						
F:LBA/3		2/37.5						
FfeG:LBA/1			3/40.4					
FfeGM:LBA/1								
FfeS:LBA/1		1/16.5						
FfeS:LBA/3		3/6.0						
FfeS:LBA/5								
FfeS:LBA/7							2/13.8	
FfeSV:LBA/5							2/11.2	
FG:LBA/1			18/41.7					
FG:LBA/2						9/58.1		
FGV:LBA/1						5/54.9		
FM:LBA/1			7/30.0					
FS:LBA/12	4/40.1					5/5.1		
FV:LBA/2		2/26.7						
CFfe:Indet/1						18/27.5		
FfeMS:Indet/1						2/17.6		
FS:Indet/3						5/18.2		
FS:Indet/4						1/3.6		
Fsh:Indet/1						2/5.0		
sh:Indet/1							1/4.3	
Indet		5/2.7	11/8.1			10/9.5		
Total no	11	39	102	1	1	120	5	1
Total wt (g)	72.7	227.4	371.4	13.3	6.6	543.6	29.3	8.7

Table 8 continued

	F62	*F63*	*F64*	*F65*	*F67*	*F68*	*F71*	*F73*
FS:Neo/2		1/10.2						
Ffe:Pet/4						5/11.4		
FfeS:Pet/4		1/14.4						
FM:Pet/1		1/2.4	4/26.9					
FS:Pet/8			2/12.9					
FV:Pet/2		1/5.3						
GV:Pet/1			2/34.1					
FfeS:Bkr/1	1/5.7							
FG:Bkr/1		1/6.2						
FGS:Bkr/1				1/4.5				
fe:Bkr/1		5/45.7	1/1.5	2/6.4				
feG:Bkr/1		2/13.8	1/1.3					
feGM:Bkr/2		2/2.9	2/3.0					
feGS:Bkr/2			4/33.9					
feGS:Bkr/3				2/2.2				
G:Bkr/3		2/22.5	1/7.6	3/39.1				
GS:Bkr/1						1/1.9		
Indet Bkr			1/0.5					
GS:CU/3				3/29.4				
Ffe:DR/1		17/93.4						
FfeG:DR/1		2/37.8		1/16.6				
FfeM:DR/1	1/6.7			1/3.2				
FfeMV:DR/1		2/8.7						
FfeS:DR/1		20/167.3						
FfeS:DR/2		9/29.0						
FfeS:DR/4				2/29.0				
FfeV:DR/1		1/4.2	1/4.0					
FM:DR/1		1/6.1						
FS:DR/1		1/1.9						
FS:DR/3								2/6.1
FS:DR/6		5/39.0	3/12.2					
FS:DR/7				2/9.8				
FSV:DR/1		23/97.8						
FSV:DR/2			7/108.6	10/123.1				
F:LBA/3	2/10.3			3/65.5				
F:LBA/4						3/14.2		
FfeGM:LBA/1	2/16.1							
FfeS:LBA/5	1/2.6							
FfeS:LBA/6						2/22.5		
FfeSV:LBA/5							1/3.9	
FS:LBA/12						4/9.7		
FS:LBA/13				1/12.5				
FS:LBA/15						5/13.0		
FV:LBA/2				1/5.4				
FV:LBA/3						1/3.4		
feSsh:LBA/1			1/2.5					
fesh:LBA/1		1/4.1						
S:IA/1		1/14.3						
FfeM:Indet/3		1/6.7						
feM:Indet/1		1/5.8	2/8.3					
feMsh:Indet/1						1/5.0		
feSV:Indet/1			1/3.2					
Msh:Indet/1				16/19.2				
Indet		1/1.0	3/3.6	13/1.9	1/2.4	1/1.4		
Total no	7	102	36	61	1	23	1	2
Total wt (g)	41.4	640.5	264.1	367.8	2.4	83.5	3.9	6.1

Table 8 continued

	F75	*F76*	*F80*	*F82*	*F84*	*F90*	*KBR tot coll*
FS:Neo/3					1/13.8		
FfeS:Pet/1							2/14.4
FS:Pet/9							1/2.7
GV:Pet/1						1/13.5	
S:LN/EBA/1							1/2.7
feGM:Bkr/2						2/6.2	
Ffe:DR/1			12/32.8				
FfeS:DR/1			5/37.6				
FfeS:DR/2			1/9.9				
FS:DR/1			3/2.9				
FS:DR/7				1/6.2			
feMsh:DR/1				1/6.9			
Ssh:DR/1			2/5.1				
F:LBA/5			1/2.0				
FGS:LBA/1				4/36.4			
FS:LBA/2			2/3.0				
FS:LBA/5			1/5.2				
FS:LBA/12				1/1.2			
FS:LBA/14				4/20.6			
FSV:LBA/5			5/40.3				
feSsh:LBA/1			1/2.1				
Cfe:Indet/1				2/4.0			
F:Indet/1				1/5.4			
Ffe:Indet/2				1/4.9			
FfeGM:Indet/1	1/9.2						
FfeM:Indet/3			2/7.9				
FfeS:Indet/1							1/2.5
feGS:Indet/2				2/8.0			
feSV:Indet/?							1/4.0
GS:Indet/1		1/3.9					
LMSV:Indet/1				1/6.5			
S:Indet/2				2/18.4			
Indet							1/0.7
Total no	1	1	35	20	1	3	7
Total wt (g)	9.2	3.9	148.8	118.5	13.8	19.7	27

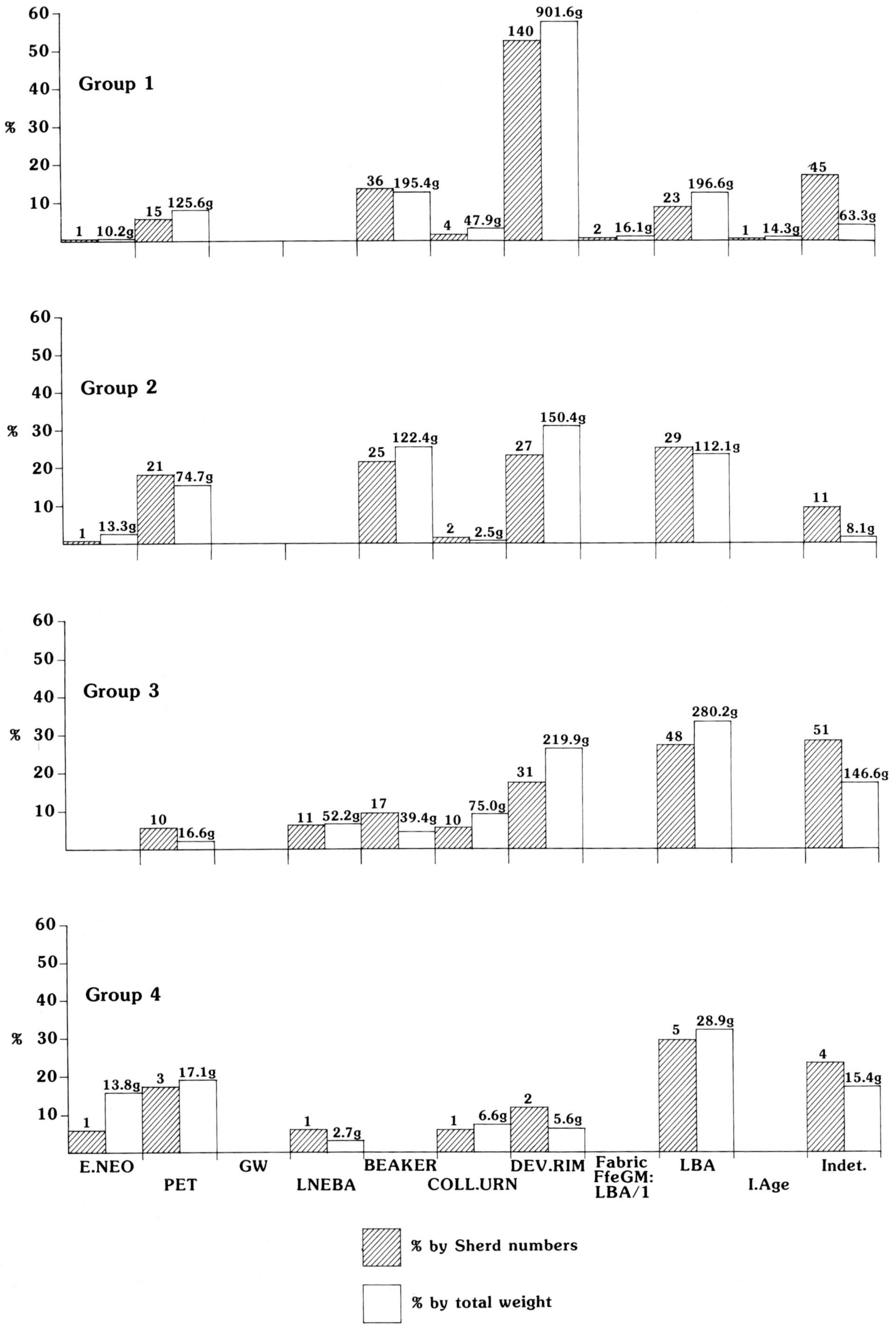

Fig 20 Prehistoric pottery from extensive surface collection: sherd number and weight by ceramic style (field groups 1–4)

unlike the majority of Peterborough Ware of other substyles within the area.

Beaker

The Beaker sherds are all small and unclassifiable. However, P287 may belong to a Middle Style Beaker of Clarke's W/MR group (Clarke 1970) as it is fine and has a distinctive red surface colour. It is possible that all the sherds belong to the Middle Style, as there are no certainly Late Style features: lattice filled bands (P277) are common in the Middle Style, as are pendant triangles above the base (P275).

With the exception of a minor concentration immediately north of the Stonehenge Cursus, Beaker material is widely scattered across all the collection areas within this group.

Early Bronze Age

Apart from a small scatter of plain grog-tempered sherds from North of the Cursus (52), the Collared Urn, Food Vessel, and indeterminate Early Bronze Age sherds all come from the vicinity of the barrows on Durrington Down. In particular, P285 and P286 were recovered from the immediate vicinity of, respectively, round barrows Durrington 72 and 23 and seem almost certain to be derived from disturbed burials.

Deverel-Rimbury

Three major concentrations of pottery can be identified, two of which lie within areas of field systems. In Fargo Road (63) sherds P292–P297 were found, with unillustrated sherds, within an area of poorly preserved 'Celtic' fields. This material is very similar in form and fabric to the assemblage from W57 (this vol, 4.11 c): all the fabrics represented among the illustrated pottery from surface collection are well represented in that assemblage, and P293 and P294 in particular closely resemble P248 and P249, and P251 at W57. This is not surprising as the cluster of surface finds occurs within a 200m radius of the excavated barrow. It is suggested that the pottery from W57 exhibits traits which place it at the transition between Deverel-Rimbury ceramics and the post-Deverel-Rimbury complex, and this must also apply to the assemblage from surface collection. The sherds from further to the east on Durrington Down, P299–P301 and plain sherds of both Deverel-Rimbury and Late Bronze Age date, may relate to the field system centred around SU 121440. The third concentration lies to the north of the Stonehenge Cursus and east of Fargo Wood, and is probably related to the settlement and fields sampled by excavation (W32 and W34, this vol, 4.4 and 4.14). The field system shown by the RCHME as lying on either side of the northern part of Fargo Wood (1979, map 1) actually extends to the south, covering part of the Stonehenge Cursus (W56A, this vol, 4.6), and the area in which the pottery occurs. Although the relationship between the surface material and the excavated pottery is not as clear here as in the case of Fargo Road (63) and W57, fabric FfeM:DR/1, which occurs among the surface pottery, is one of the more common fabrics at W32 (20% by weight).

Late Bronze Age

The distribution of this material is similar to that of the Deverel-Rimbury sherds. The two illustrated sherds, P302 and P303 are probably related to, respectively, the Fargo Wood field system and the system immediately to the north. Unillustrated sherds in Late Bronze Age fabrics also occur in all the areas in which Deverel-Rimbury pottery occurs.

Illustrated pottery

Group i (Fig 21)

P269 Fargo Road (63) 111443/D
FV:Pet/2. Peterborough Ware. Rim sherd. Too eroded to classify as to shape. Twisted cord impressions arranged in three parallel rows set on a diagonal axis.

P270 Horse Hospital (64) 112436/D
FM:Pet/1. Peterborough Ware. Rim sherd. Pointed with external bevel. Parallel twisted cord impressions arranged on a diagonal axis across the top of the rim and on the interior of the vessel. Two or three lines of cord impressions run more or less horizontally across the exterior.

P271 Fargo Road (63) 113440/B
FM:Pet/1. Peterborough Ware. Very fragmentary rim sherd, with only a small length of original rim top surface surviving. The exterior has flaked away entirely. Twisted cord impressions on the interior.

P272 Horse Hospital (64) 115436/B
GV:Pet/1. Peterborough Ware. Body sherd. Twisted cord impressions.

P273 Horse Hospital (64) 116436/C–D
GV:Pet/1. Peterborough Ware. Rim sherd. Flattened top with internal expansion. Fingernail impressions arranged in a herringbone pattern along the top of the rim. Plastic finger-pinched motif arranged in parallel lines on a vertical axis on the exterior of the vessel. Fengate Ware. The rim curvature suggests that the vessel is a bowl, rather than the more usual type of Fengate Ware vessel.

P274 Wood End (90) 107439/H
feGM:Bkr/2. Beaker. Body sherd. Impressed motif arranged in five parallel lines at right angles to a sixth impression.

P275 Cursus West End (62) 108427/G
FfeS:Bkr/1. Beaker. Base sherd. Comb-impressed (square-toothed comb) motif arranged in a zig-zag pattern.

P276 Wood End (90) 108438/B
feGM:Bkr/2. Beaker. Body sherd. Impressed motif.

P277 Fargo Road (63) 111443/H
feG:Bkr/1. Beaker. Comb-impressed motif arranged in two narrow bands defining an area infilled with cross-hatching.

P278 Fargo Road (63) 111443/H
feG:Bkr/1. Beaker. Body sherd. Comb impressions arranged in two narrow bands.

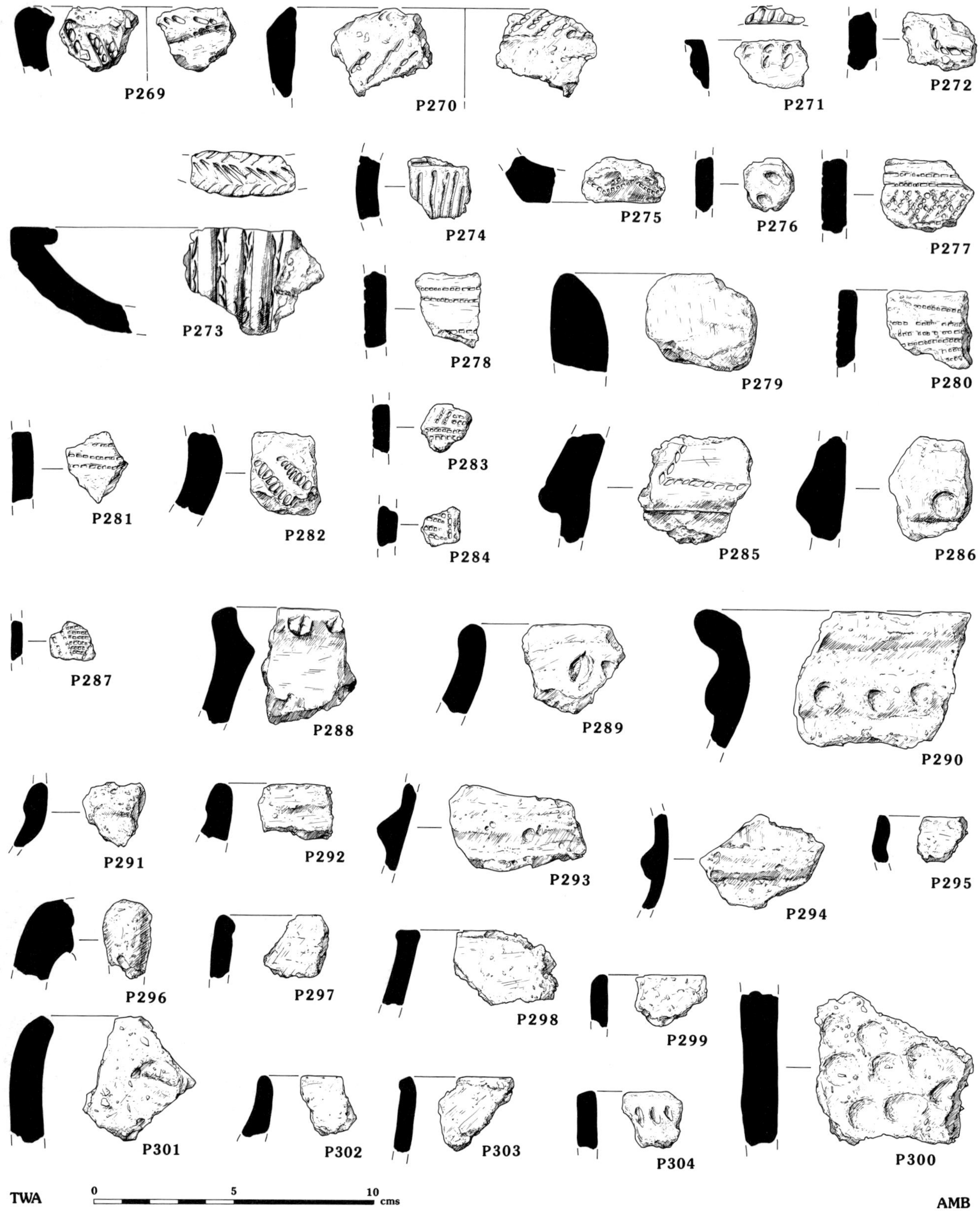

Fig 21 Surface collection prehistoric pottery (P269–P304)

P279 North of the Cursus (52) 112431/E
feGS:Bkr/1. Indeterminate. Rim sherd. Pointed.

P280 Fargo Road (63) 112440/A
FG:Bkr/1. Beaker. Rim sherd. Rounded. Comb-impressed motif arranged in parallel lines on a horizontal axis.

P281 North of the Cursus (52) 113430/B
feGS:Bkr/1. Beaker. Body sherd. Narrow band consisting of three parallel comb impressions.

P282 Horse Hospital (64) 113436/E
feGS: Bkr/2. Beaker. Body sherd. Two parallel whipped cord impressions arranged on a diagonal axis.

P283 Horse Hospital (64) 113438/D
feGM:Bkr/2. Beaker. Body sherd. Comb-impressed motif, possibly representing an infilled pendant.

P284 Horse Hospital (64) 113438/D
feGM:Bkr/2. Beaker. Comb-impressed motif, possibly representing an infilled pendant.

P285 Fargo Road (63) 11364414
fe:Bkr/1. Collared Urn. Twisted cord impression.

P286 Durrington Down (65) 120441/C
G:Bkr/3. Indeterminate, possibly EBA. Body sherd with cordon. Sub-spherical impressed motif.

P287 Durrington Down (65) 121440/C
feGS:Bkr/3. Beaker. Body sherd. Two parallel comb impressions defining an infilled pendant.

P288 Durrington Down (65) 118442/F
GS:CU/3. Food Vessel. Rim sherd. Flattened top with concave internal bevel. Fingertip motif.

P289 Durrington Down (65) 120441/C
GS:CU/3. LN/EBA, possibly Beaker. Rim sherd, rounded. Fingertip impressed motif.

P290 Horse Hospital (64) 110436/Area
FSV:DR/2. Deverel-Rimbury. Rim sherd with cordon. Rounded and everted with internal bevel. Fingertip motif along cordon.

P291 North of the Cursus (52) 113431/B
FfeM:DR/1. Deverel-Rimbury. Rim sherd. Rounded with convex external surface.

P293 Fargo Road (63) 114443/A
FSV:DR/1. Deverel-Rimbury. Cordoned body sherd. Barrel Urn associated vessel.

P294 Fargo Road (63) 114443/A
FSV:DR/1. Deverel-Rimbury. Cordoned body sherd. Barrel Urn associated vessel.

P295 Fargo Road (63) 114443/A
FS:DR/1. Deverel-Rimbury. Rim sherd. Rounded with convex internal surface. Barrel Urn associated vessel.

P296 Fargo Road (63) 114444/A
FSV:DR/1. Deverel-Rimbury. Round-sectioned handle.

P297 Fargo Road (63) 114444/D
FfeS:DR/2. Deverel-Rimbury. Rim sherd. Rounded with internal bevel. Barrel Urn associated vessel.

P298 North of the Cursus (52) 115432/H
FfeM:DR/1. Deverel-Rimbury. Rim sherd. Upright with flattened top and convex exterior surface. Barrel Urn associated vessel.

P299 Durrington Down (65) 121440/A
FfeM:DR/1. Deverel-Rimbury. Rim sherd. Flattened top. Barrel Urn associated vessel.

P300 Durrington Down (55) 123439/B
FSV:DR/2. Deverel-Rimbury. Body sherd. Fingertip-impressed motif. Barrel Urn.

P301 Durrington Down (65) 124439/B
FfeG:DR/1. Deverel-Rimbury. Rim sherd. Rounded with internal bevel and an inward curve. Impressed motif, probably fingertip impression.

P302 Cursus West End (62) 108432/C
FfeS:LBA/5. Late Bronze Age. Rim sherd. Rounded.

P303 Fargo Road (63) 114443/A
fesh:LBA/1. Late Bronze Age. Rim sherd. Rounded and everted.

P304 Horse Hospital (64) 112435/B
feM:indet/1. Indeterminate. Rim sherd. Rounded with external bevel.

3.9 b Group ii: Stonehenge Down (Stonehenge Triangle) and south (Fig 20b, illustrated sherds Fig 22)

Earlier Neolithic

Only one sherd, from South of Stonehenge (55), is of this date. This sherd, P305, is a horizontally perforated oval lug from a South-Western style bowl. In fabric and form this sherd can be matched by P55 in the small group from the King Barrow Ridge pit (this vol, 4.3) 1km to the north-east, and in fabric by the assemblage from the Coneybury 'Anomaly' (W2 (1981), this vol, 4.1), 1km to the east.

Peterborough Ware

The 21 decorated and undecorated sherds of Peterborough Ware from the Stonehenge Triangle (54) form a small concentration of this type of pottery, at a similar distance to the south of the Stonehenge Cursus as the concentration in Horse Hospital (64) is to the north. The sherds are not assignable to substyle.

Beaker

Although a scatter of Beaker sherds occurs across the whole of the collection area, almost all are featureless body sherds in Beaker-type fabrics. The two illustrated sherds, P309 and P310, are of indeterminate type.

Later Neolithic/Early Bronze Age

One rim sherd, P311, although in a fabric which also occurs in Beaker sherds, is of an unusual form. The rim is inturned, with a slight internal bevel, and the decoration is executed in comb impression. Not only would the rim form be extremely unusual on a Beaker, but the comb impressions are quite unlike those typical of Beaker pottery: the comb appears to have been slightly curved, to have possessed only three irregular teeth, and to have been very short (*c* 5mm long). The rim form could be accommodated within Grooved Ware, as might the fabric, but the decoration would be extremely unusual, although not completely unparalleled, in that tradition: at Durrington Walls several Grooved Ware vessels carry comb-impressed decoration (Wainwright and Longworth 1971, P392–P400).

Deverel-Rimbury

Sherds of this tradition occur as a concentration in Stonehenge Triangle (54) and as a single find, P312, in Normanton Gorse (61). Unlike much of the material from the Fargo Road (63) concentration and that to the east of Fargo Wood, which is difficult to classify, the sherds from Stonehenge Triangle, and in particular P314, appear to belong to typical Bucket or Barrel Urns. This may be related to the occurrence in round barrow Amesbury 3, 400m from P314, of a true Barrel Urn (Annable and Simpson 1964, fig 576). Both this pottery and that of Late Bronze Age type occur within an area of 'Celtic' fields.

Late Bronze Age

This is represented only by plain body sherds in fabrics which elsewhere in the area occur in vessels of Late Bronze Age form. The sherds are concentrated in Stonehenge Triangle (54), in the same area as the Deverel-Rimbury pottery.

Illustrated pottery

Group ii (Fig 22)

P305 South of Stonehenge (55) 124414/F
FS:Neo/3. Earlier Neolithic. Vertically pierced lug.

P306 Stonehenge Triangle (54) 115421/G
FS:Pet/7. Peterborough Ware. Rim sherd. Not clear which is interior and which exterior. Twisted cord impressions on the rim top, running close to and parallel with one edge, and also on one surface of the vessel, on a diagonal axis.

P307 Stonehenge Triangle (54) 115424/A
Ffe:Pet/3. Peterborough Ware. Body sherd. Sub-spherical impressed motif.

P308 Stonehenge Triangle (54) 116421/H
FS:Pet/7. Peterborough Ware. Rim sherd. Rounded. Incised linear motif.

P309 Stonehenge Triangle (54) 115422/G
feGS:Bkr/3. Beaker. Body sherd. Narrow band consisting of three parallel comb impressions.

P310 Stonehenge Triangle (54) 115422/H
CG:Bkr/1. Beaker. Body sherd. Sub-spherical impressed motif.

P311 Stonehenge Triangle (54) 115424/A
CG:Bkr/1. LN/EBA. Rim sherd. Pointed with internal bevel. The impressions have been made with a slightly curved comb, possessing only three irregular teeth, and only 5mm in width (unstraightened).

P312 Normanton Gorse (61) 114417/C
FG:DR/1. Deverel-Rimbury. Body sherd. Linear impression. Globular Urn.

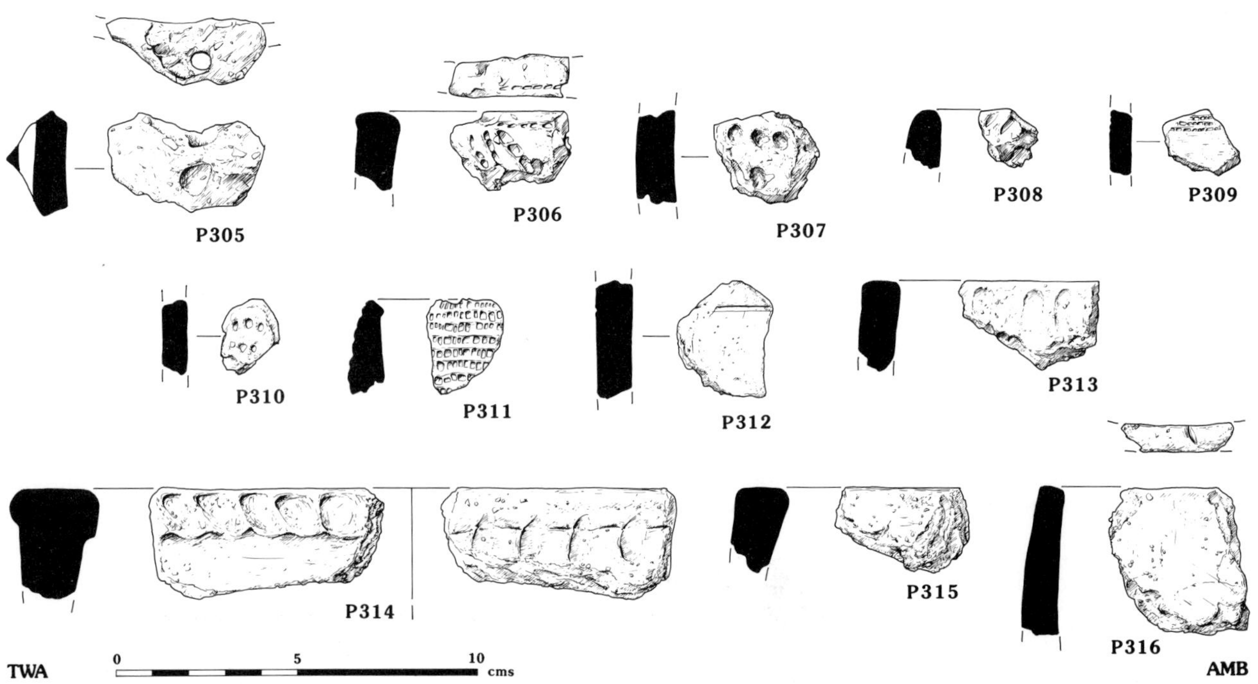

Fig 22 Surface collection prehistoric pottery (P305–P316)

P313 Stonehenge Triangle (54) 115422/H
FfeS:DR/3. Deverel-Rimbury. Rim sherd. Upright with flattened top. Fingertip-impressed motif. Barrel Urn.

P314 Stonehenge Triangle (54) 116421/G
FfeS:DR/3. Deverel-Rimbury. Rim sherd. Flattened top, expanded internally and externally. Fingertip-impressed motif along the top of the rim and on the exterior of the vessel. Barrel Urn.

P315 Stonehenge Triangle (54) 116422/E
Fsh:DR/1. Deverel-Rimbury. Flattened top with convex interior surface. Barrel Urn.

P316 Stonehenge Triangle (54) 118421/B
FfeS:DR/3. Deverel-Rimbury. Upright with flattened top and slight internal bevel.

3.9 c Group iii: Wilsford Down/Winterbourne Stoke Crossroads and south (Fig 20c, illustrated sherds Fig 23)

Peterborough Ware

Only one sherd, P317, is certainly of this tradition, and belongs to the neck of a Mortlake Ware or Ebbsfleet Ware bowl. It is located approximately 300m from W31 (this vol, 4.10), where sherds of several Peterborough Ware vessels were found during excavation, and this find suggests that the area of activity associated with Peterborough Ware on Wilsford Down continues to the west of W31.

Later Neolithic/Early Bronze Age

In the case of several sherds, P318–P321, it is impossible, on the basis of form, fabric, and decoration, to assign them with any confidence to a particular style group. Two of these sherds, P318 and P319, occur in a concentration of finds to the south-east of Winterbourne Stoke Crossroads which include material from the Beaker period to the Late Bronze Age, while the others are widely spaced across The Diamond (59).

Beaker

Beaker sherds occur as a scatter throughout The Diamond (59), with a concentration at the north-west end. One sherd of AOC Beaker, P328, was recovered from the surface close to W31, where excavation also produced AOC Beaker (this vol, 4.10 c). The remaining sherds could be Middle or Late Style although there are some indications that they are Late. P323 appears to belong to a Beaker with a slight collar; this feature is rare, but occurs several times on Beakers of Clarke's S2

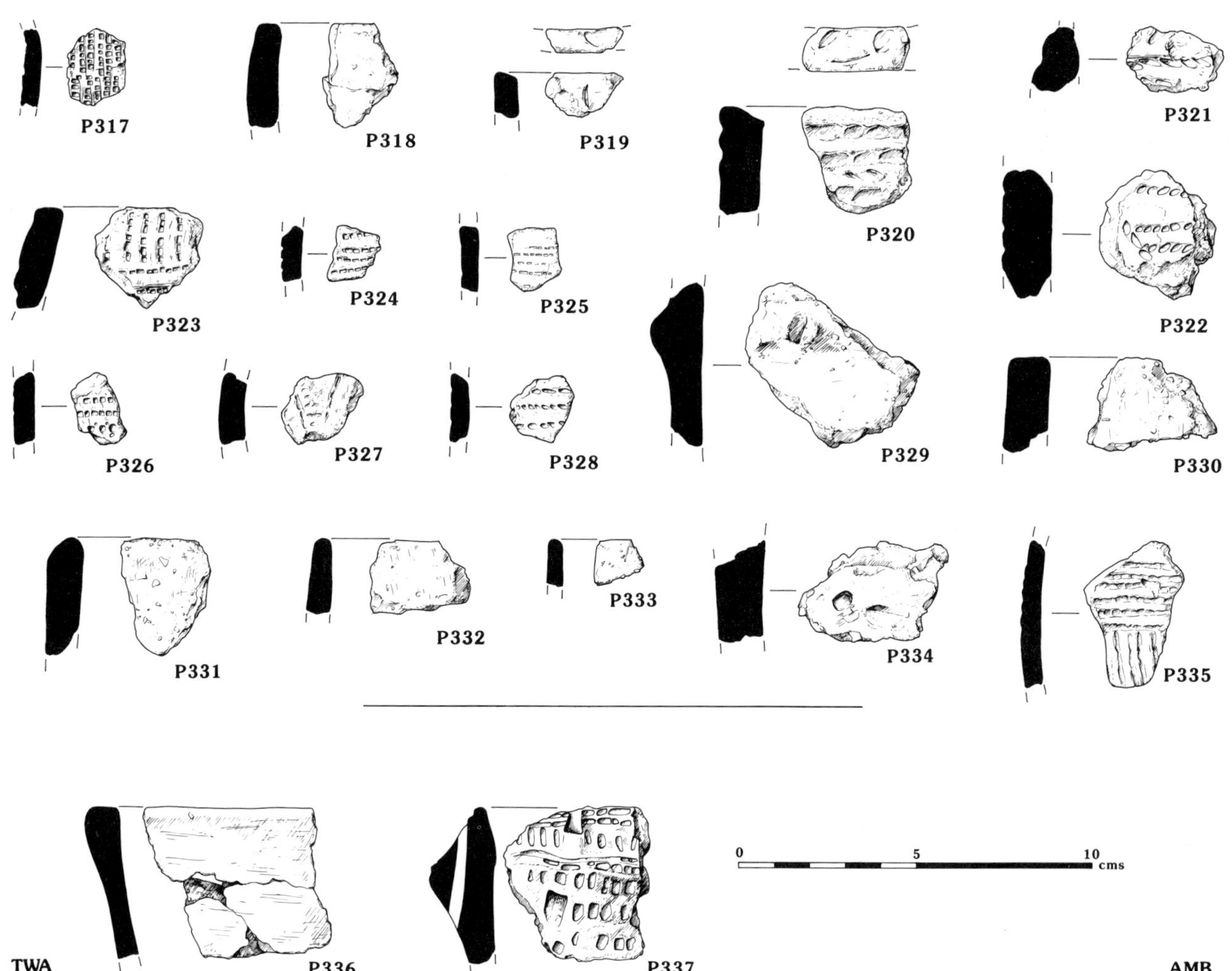

Fig 23 Surface collection prehistoric pottery (P317–P335), Winterbourne Stoke Crossroads (P336) and Durrington Walls (P337)

group (Clarke 1970, figs 876–879). The small sherd P327 is decorated with a filled triangle but there are also traces of another line of comb impressions running along the edge of the sherd. If this is the case then the decorative motif represented is almost certainly a reserved bar chevron, a diagnostic feature of Clarke's Southern tradition and therefore of Late Style. A single featureless body sherd in a Beaker type fabric was recovered from West Field (68).

Early Bronze Age

In addition to the single illustrated sherd from a collared urn (P322), several plain sherds in similar fabrics were recovered from The Diamond (59) and from Winterbourne Stoke Crossroads (50), in both cases from the parts of the collection areas closest to the Winterbourne Stoke Crossroads barrow cemetery. Although the cemetery does not extend into either of the collection areas it is difficult to avoid the conclusion that the concentration of Early Bronze Age pottery is related to the location of the barrows.

Deverel-Rimbury

Two of the illustrated sherds (P329 and P330) and a considerable number of plain sherds in similar fabrics were found at the Winterbourne Stoke Crossroads end of The Diamond (59), and in Winterbourne Stoke Crossroads (50). This concentration must form part of the settlement excavated by the Vatchers prior to the construction of the Winterbourne Stoke roundabout (RCHME 1979, 22; this vol, 4.15), which would appear to be of the same date, and the distribution of surface finds suggests that the settlement extended to the south-west of the area excavated. A large area to the south-west of Winterbourne Stoke Crossroads is covered by 'Celtic' fields, also presumably related to this settlement. To the south two Deverel-Rimbury sherds occur on Rox Hill (82).

Late Bronze Age

Sherds in Late Bronze Age fabrics occur in the concentration at the Winterbourne Stoke Crossroads end of The Diamond (59), on Rox Hill (82), and in West Field (68). The Winterbourne Stoke Crossroads concentration includes the two illustrated sherds P332 and P333.

Illustrated pottery

Group iii (Fig 23)

P317 The Diamond (59) 105410/E
F:Pet/2. Peterborough Ware. Body sherd with whipped cord impressions. The sherd appears to be from the neck of a bowl, with the decoration on the interior.

P318 The Diamond (59) 102414/A
GM:LNEBA/1. LN/EBA or later. Rim sherd. Upright with flattened top and convex exterior surface.

P319 The Diamond (59) 102414/A
GM:LNEBA/1. LN/EBA or later. Rim sherd. Flattened top sloping towards the interior of the vessel. Fingertip-impressed motif on the top of the rim and exterior surface.

P320 The Diamond (59) 103411/C
CFGS:LNEBA/1. LN/EBA or later. Rim sherd. Flattened top with internal bevel. The decoration consists of rows of plastic fingernail impressions beneath the rim, with non-plastic fingernail impressions below.

P321 The Diamond (59) 105409/Area
GM:LNEBA. LN/EBA. Body sherd. Twisted cord impressions arranged in at least two parallel lines.

P322 The Diamond (59) 101413/A
CfeG:CU/1. Probably Collared Urn. Body sherd. Twisted cord motif.

P323 The Diamond (59) 101413/A
feGS:Bkr/8. Beaker. Rim sherd. Flattened top. Comb-impressed motif arranged in parallel lines on a vertical axis directly below the rim and above two horizontal impressions.

P324 The Diamond (59) 10141/C
feGS:Bkr/8. Beaker. Body sherd. Comb-impressed motif arranged in four roughly parallel lines.

P325 The Diamond (59) 101414/Area
feG:Bkr/3. Beaker. Body sherd. Comb-impressed motif arranged in parallel lines.

P326 The Diamond (59) 102413/H
feGS:Bkr/5. Beaker. Body sherd. Comb-impressed motif arranged in two parallel lines associated with sub-spherical stabbed impressions.

P327 The Diamond (59) 103411/C
feGS:Bkr/8. Beaker. Body sherd. Infilled pendant.

P328 The Diamond (59) 108409/D
feGS:Bkr/8. Beaker. Body sherd. Twisted cord impressions (z-twist impressions) arranged in three parallel lines.

P329 The Diamond (59) 101414/Area
FS:DR/5. Deverel-Rimbury. Cordoned body sherd. Fingertip-impressed motif along the cordon. Possibly Barrel Urn.

P330 The Diamond (59) 101414/Area
FGS:DR/2. Rim sherd. Flattened top. Possibly Barrel Urn.

P331 Rox Hill (82) 121386/H
feMsh:DR/1. Rim sherd. Rounded. Barrel Urn associated vessel.

P332 The Diamond (59) 101413/F
FGV:LBA/1. Late Bronze Age. Rim sherd. Rounded with slight internal bevel.

P333 The Diamond (59) 101414/Area
FS:LBA/12. Late Bronze Age. Rim sherd. Rounded.

P334 The Diamond (59) 105410/Area
CFfe:Indet/1. Indeterminate. Body sherd with non-plastic fingernail impressions.

P335 Rox Hill (82) 122386/H
feGS:Indet/2. Indeterminate. Body sherd. Impressed motif.

Pottery not recovered by the project

P336 Winterbourne Stoke Crossroads settlement (excavated 1967). Context noted as 'co-ordinates N 4'E., –3' to 5' from natural chalk'. In posthole filling, in post replacement. Thickened rim of a slightly splayed but straight-walled vessel.

P337 Durrington Walls henge monument. Post-hole 44 (Southern Circle Phase 2). Published as P24 in Wainwright and Longworth 1971. Redrawn. Rim sherd with a slight internal bevel. On the exterior a large oval lug with two vertical perforations is attached just below the rim; the sherd has broken along the line of one of the perforations, which shows only in section. It is clear from the form of the applied piece that it is a lug rather than a cordon, as although it is not complete it shows a more marked curvature than the vessel wall. The section shows evidence of ring- or coil-building. The exterior surface, including the lug, is rusticated, with rows of impressions, some slightly plastic. Lines of joining impressions occur below the rim, and along the upper surface of the lug. The sherd was originally considered as probable Mortlake Ware (Wainwright and Longworth 1971, 55); at that time the perforations were presumably obscured by soil and chalk, as they only became apparent with cleaning. Perforated lugs are only a rare feature on Grooved Ware (eg Wainwright and Longworth 1971, P219 and P220), but are unknown on Mortlake Ware. The sherd would therefore seem more likely to be Grooved Ware than Mortlake Ware.
Fabric: not paralleled within the Project fabric series. Hard fabric with a hackly fracture, containing sparse calcareous inclusions (irregular, sub-angular, >2mm, possibly limestone), sparse grog (rounded, >2mm), rare flint (>3mm) and sparse fine sand). (Salisbury Museum catalogue of finds from Durrington Walls No. 884)

3.9 d Group iv: King Barrow Ridge and east (Fig 20d)

Very few featured sherds were recovered from this area.

Earlier Neolithic

One plain body sherd was recovered from Luxenborough (84). Earlier Neolithic activity is also attested in this part of the study area by the assemblage from the Coneybury 'Anomaly' (W2 (1981), this vol, 4.1) and by residual sherds from Coneybury Henge (W2, this vol, 4.9, P1–P52, P57).

Peterborough Ware

Three sherds (including one small decorated sherd not illustrated) were found in the King Barrow Ridge total collection area (W59, this vol, 4.8).

Early Bronze Age

One plain sherd, in a fabric similar to Collared Urn fabrics, was recovered from King Barrow Ridge (57).

Deverel-Rimbury

Two sherds, both plain, were recovered from Whittles (73).

Late Bronze Age

A scatter of sherds in Late Bronze Age fabrics occurred in Woodhenge (60), and are presumably associated with the Bronze Age activity recorded by Cunnington and others (Cunnington 1929; RCHME 1979, 23–4) in the vicinity of the Durrington 'Egg'.

4 Excavations

A wide range of sites was examined both in the course of project fieldwork and as integrated elements of backlog post-excavation analysis. The results of intensive surface collection, together with those from geophysical and geochemical survey, form part of the evidence discussed here within the individual site reports.

Summary reports for these sites are arranged by chronology (prehistoric), in the order in which they appear in Table 9. Where excavated sites span more than one period then the major emphasis of the site will dictate its position within the overall sequence. Data from specialist reports are, where appropriate, presented in text, with the remainder of the specialist reports contained within the fiche.

Table 9 Summary of sites examined

Site	*Type*	*Stratified deposits*	*Pottery*	*Flint*	*Animal bone*	*Molluscs*
W2 (1981)	pit	yes	**	**	**	
W83 (int.)	pits	yes	*	**	**	
Vatcher	pits	yes	**	*	*	
W32	flint scatter	no	*	*	*	
W55	cursus	yes	*	*	*	**
W56	cursus	yes	*	*	*	**
W58	long barrow	yes	*	**	*	**
W59	flint scatter	yes	**	**	**	
W2	henge	yes	**	**	**	**
W31	flint scatter	yes	*	**	*	
W57	round barrow	yes	**	*	*	
W52	enclosure	yes	**	*	*	*
W51	linear ditch	yes		*		*
W34	pottery scatter	no	**	*	**	
Vatcher	settlement	yes	*		*	
W17–22	dry valleys	no	*	*		

** major group
* minor group

4.1 W2: the excavation of the Coneybury 'Anomaly', an Early Neolithic pit on Coneybury Hill, 1980–1

A magnetometer survey carried out by the Ancient Monuments Laboratory prior to the excavation at Coneybury Henge (W2) in 1980, in addition to locating the henge ditch and internal features, also produced a strong and discrete response immediately to the northwest of the assumed area of the former henge bank (Bartlett, this vol, MF1 F6–12; see Fig 89, MF1 F14 for location). Although an extensive exterior sample was not part of the initial excavation design, it was decided to sample a small and specific area in order to examine the potential relationship of this assumed feature to the adjacent henge. The sample excavation of what became known colloquially as 'the Anomaly' commenced during the 1980 excavation season and was completed during 1981.

4.1 a Excavation

The excavation commenced with the clearance of topsoil from an area 4m by 4m (area K). This revealed what appeared from the surface to be a very substantial circular subsoil feature, cut 2104. A further smaller feature (cut 2115, Fig 97) lay partly within the cleared area and proved on excavation to be of Early Bronze Age date. This pit is considered within the report of the excavation of the henge (W2, this vol, 4.9).

In 1980 three quadrants of the pit were excavated to a depth of *c* 1.05m, at which point the nature of the fill changed radically from a localised colluvial soil to a dark, fine soil containing considerable numbers of artefacts, specifically animal bone and large sherds of pottery. A small sample of artefacts was planned and lifted before the deposit was covered and the pit backfilled. The excavation was completed during August 1981 when area K was re-excavated. After the removal of the remaining quadrant of upper fill, the artefact-rich deposit, which was then found to be primary, was completely excavated, with all finds of pottery, bone, and flint tools individually recorded and planned. This precision of finds recording within a single feature was carried out in order to investigate the possibility, suggested by the density of artefacts, that the pit contained one or a series of 'placed' deposits, reminiscent of those recovered from the ditches of causewayed enclosures (Mercer 1980; Pryor 1987).

The pit was 1.25m deep from the present chalk surface and must originally have been *c* 1.9m in diameter (Fig 24). The base of the pit was flat and the sides below the weathering slope almost vertical. No traces of tool marks were noted.

The upper fills

The uppermost fills consisted of *c* 0.20m of brown silty clay loam (context 2105), containing later Neolithic and Beaker pottery (Cleal, this vol, 4.1 c). Below this was the upper colluvial fill (context 2231), *c* 0.40m of reddish brown silty clay, containing chalk and flint. The lower colluvial fill (context 2256) was similar to this, but contained a higher proportion of chalk.

The primary deposits

The primary deposit consisted of a dark grey to black fine soil (overall context 2538) interleaved with and in part overlying lenses of cemented chalk wash (context 2539). The dark soil contained charcoal, both in small lumps and more finely divided, the latter retrieved from wet sieving down to 600 microns. Oak and hazel can be positively identified, with *Rosaceae* sp (cherry/blackthorn and hawthorn/rowan/whitebeam) also represented (Gale, this vol, 8.2). Samples from the primary deposits of the pit show very high levels of soil phosphate, five samples producing an average value of 280 parts per million, compared to a single value of 30 parts per million from a sample of the upper colluvial filling. Such high phosphate values may be suggested as resulting from the decay of an organic rich deposit which, to judge from its charcoal content, may also have been burnt. It can be suggested that this primary deposit, no more than 0.20m deep when excavated,

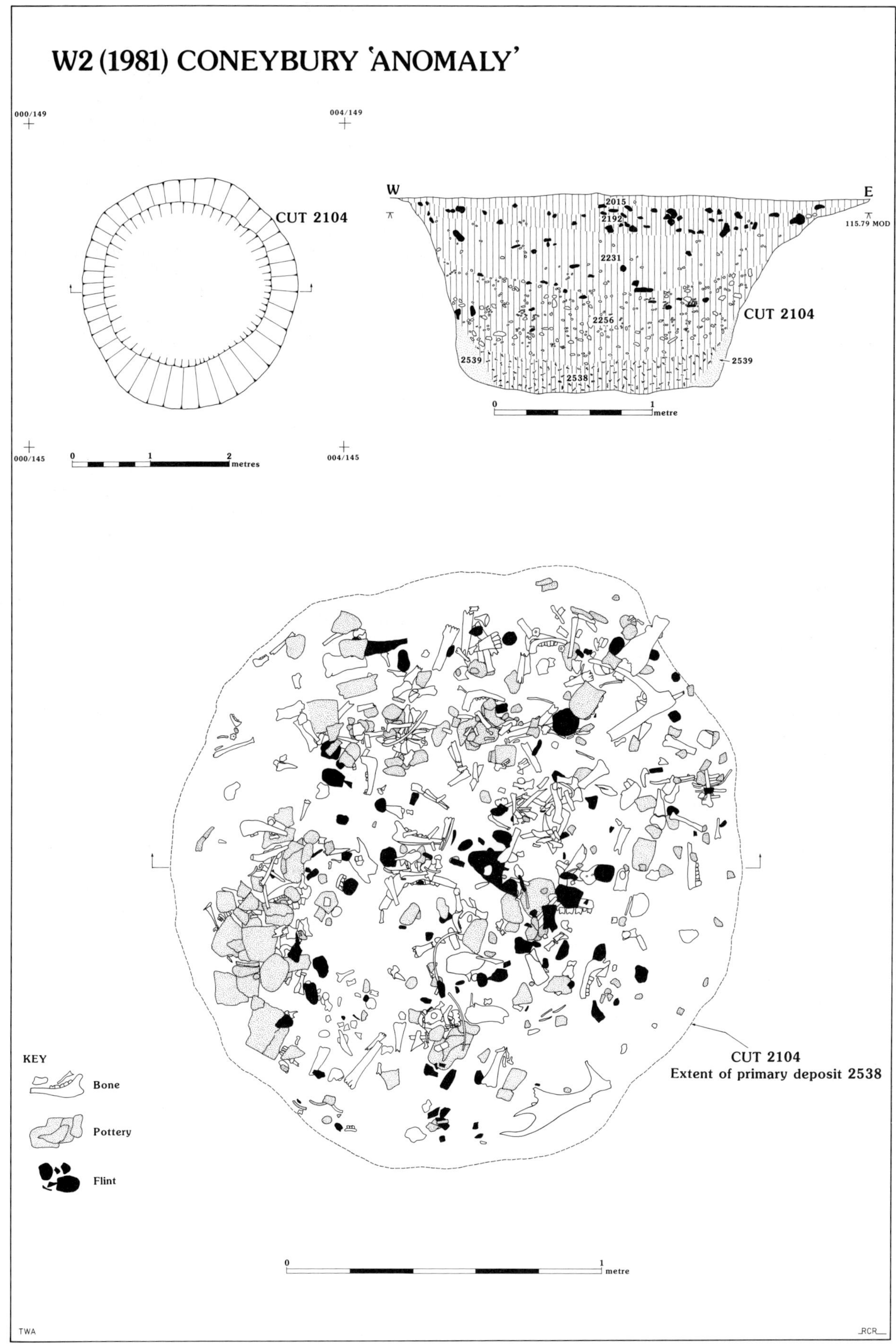

Fig 24 W2 (1981) Coneybury 'Anomaly': plan, section, and distribution of finds in primary deposit

may originally have been considerably deeper. The artefacts recorded from this reduced deposit are thus likely to have little spatial integrity, at least in a vertical plane.

The density of artefacts within the primary deposit, hinted at in the 1980 sample, was confirmed by the subsequent stage of the excavation (Figs 25, 26). Major assemblages of pottery, animal bone, and worked flint were recovered. Animal bone from the primary deposit produced a radiocarbon date of 3980–3708 BC (OxA 1402).

Artefacts from the primary deposits

The assemblage of pottery from the pit, including the upper colluvial fills, consisted of 1744 sherds, weighing over 16kg. However, nearly 92% of the assemblage by weight (1375 sherds, weighing 14.695kg), was recovered from the primary deposit. During excavation it was suggested that some primary material, specifically pottery, but including elements of the bone assemblage, had been deliberately 'placed', rather than dumped at the base of the pit. While this suggestion cannot be confirmed for all the material within the primary deposit, particularly as the pit fill is now realised to be much compressed, the position of some sherds with 'nested' curved surfaces may indicate that this idea should not be entirely dismissed.

Analysis of the pottery assemblage from the primary pit fill (Cleal, this vol, 4.1 c) suggests that it represents a minimum number of 41 vessels, belonging within the South-Western style of earlier Neolithic pottery (Figs 28–31). A number of vessel forms from cups to a range of bowls can be identified, one of the largest bowls (P1) also being one of only two to be certainly carinated. Cleal suggests that the condition of the majority of the sherds, although fresh, indicates that they may have been incorporated within a midden deposit for a short time prior to burial. The general absence of sooting from the assemblage is also noted by Cleal, who suggests that this may be a feature of post-depositional processes. As the faunal assemblage discussed by Maltby (this vol, 4.1 d) appears to involve large scale meat consumption, it is also possible that the vessels represented were used for cooking.

The faunal remains from the primary fills of the pit are 'unparalleled in Britain' (Maltby, this vol, 4.1 d). A total of 2110 animal bone fragments were recorded,

Fig 25 W2 (1981) Coneybury 'Anomaly': detail of the primary deposit (scale 25cm)

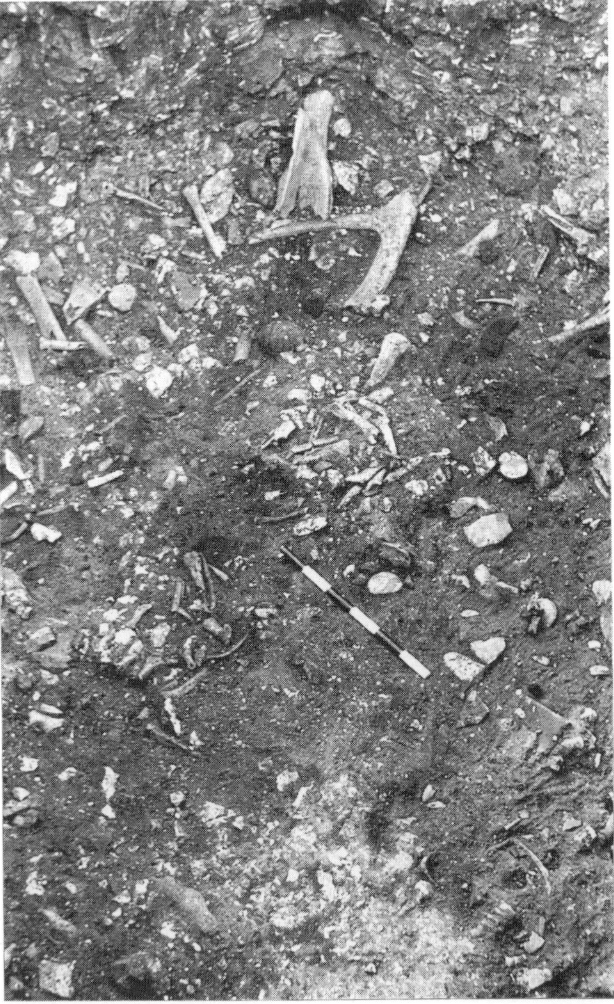

Fig 26 W2 (1981) Coneybury 'Anomaly': detail of the primary deposit (scale 25cm)

with the assemblage dominated by cattle and roe deer. Smaller numbers of pig, red deer, and beaver, together with one fish, were also represented. The assemblage appears to represent a major episode of butchery in which at least ten cattle, several roe deer, one pig, and two red deer were processed. Maltby suggests that the roe deer bones represent the remains of meat consumed immediately after butchery. In contrast, those of cattle and red deer suggest the removal of carcases either for consumption elsewhere or for preservation for later consumption.

Although domestic cattle would have provided the majority of the meat represented by the bones from the pit, wild animals form a significant part of the assemblage.

In contrast to the large-scale consumption of meat shown by the animal bones, samples taken from the primary deposits produced only a small quantity of poorly preserved cereals. Identifiable cereals were all glume wheats, probably emmer, which had been subject to intense heat (Carruthers, this vol, 8.1).

The flint from the primary deposits (Harding, this vol, 4.1 b) gives the overall appearance of a curated assemblage, with little potential for refitting and a high proportion of retouched material. Apart from tools identified by retouch, it can be suggested that elements of this assemblage, particularly blades/bladelets, may be regarded as unretouched flake tools. Some confirmation of this is provided by limited microwear analysis. Of the groups analysed, this assemblage contains the highest proportion (24%) of blades/bladelets and provides a strong contrast to the broadly contemporary material from W83. The occurrence of burnt scrapers suggests a strong association of tool use and discard with the activity suggested by the other artefact groups.

Discussion

Although the occurrence of other Early Neolithic pits within the general area of Coneybury Henge (see, for example, Vatcher King Barrow Ridge pit, this vol, 4.3) suggests an area of extensive, if sporadic, activity, there is little direct evidence for the immediate context of the 'Anomaly'. That recovered by extensive surface collection on Coneybury Hill (51) is restricted largely to scraper types potentially of earlier Neolithic date (Riley, this vol, 5.3), with an absence of more distinctly diagnostic flint tools. The pit and its contents must therefore be considered in isolation, a consideration which will inevitably be more concerned with the contents and the circumstances of their deposition. The reasons for the original digging of the pit, whether the disposal of rubbish was a primary or secondary function, cannot be ascertained.

In considering the contents the faunal remains, and specifically the contrast in the exploitation of wild and domestic animals, provide the strongest indications of the type of activity that may be represented. As noted above, it appears that the meat from culled cattle and from red deer was either taken away for consumption elsewhere or was preserved, whereas the meat from the roe deer, and potentially from the other wild animals represented, was possibly consumed immediately after butchery. This would appear to indicate either a single major feast, or possibly a period of feasting, suggested by Maltby on the basis of immature animals, having taken place during the summer months. If a period of feasting is envisaged, it can be suggested that the debris may have accumulated in a temporary midden. This may help to explain the occurrence of carnivore gnawing marks on 24 cattle fragments, as well as the incomplete representation of the large number of pottery vessels.

The pottery assemblage is unusual in quantity, if not in terms of vessel type and fabric. The absence of gabbroic ware, the fine component within the South-Western regional style, is noted by Cleal, who comments that the form of P1, the large ('serving') vessel, is identical to a shape occurring in gabbroic wares. Gabbroic pottery occurs at both the causewayed enclosure at Robin Hood's Ball (Thomas 1964) and within W83, the recently excavated pit group outside the enclosure (Cleal pers comm).

The evidence from the pottery may therefore be taken to suggest that the group of people responsible for the butchery/feasting episode represented within the 'Anomaly' were outside the exchange network within which gabbroic pottery circulated. This network, within which enclosures played a particularly significant role, can be suggested as being based on the more sedentary aspects of the earlier Neolithic. Many aspects of the 'Anomaly' suggest a more mobile emphasis, particularly the significant proportions of wild animals within the bone assemblage. Specific if minor elements such as beaver and brown trout also suggest a continuity of emphasis on the adjacent river valley, and on an at least partly 'Mesolithic' economy. This is reflected again within the lithic assemblage which utilises a small proportion of river gravel flint and includes 24% blades/bladelets. The latter can be regarded not only as the maintenance of a technological tradition but as evidence of the continuity of an essentially mobile economy. This is supported by the early fourth millennium BC radiocarbon date.

The deep upper colluvial fills of the pit contain material of Early Neolithic to Bronze Age date, including transverse arrowheads. This, together with the weathered nature of the upper edges of the pit, suggest that at the time of the henge construction the pit was still visible as a substantial depression, approximately 2m in diameter and potentially up to 0.70m deep.

4.1 b Lithics

by Philip Harding

i Recovery and condition

This analysis relates to lithic material from the primary deposits described above. Within the feature flint finds were recorded by context, with all tools and cores from the primary deposits recorded in three dimensions. The nature of the primary deposits and the method of excavation enabled small pieces to be recovered, although chips may be under-represented as the entire deposit was not wet-sieved.

Flint from primary and secondary contexts was in mint condition but had developed a mottled, dark/light blue patina, making it generally unsuitable for microwear analysis. Some surfaces were covered by calcium carbonate concretion. Flint from the upper pit fills was patinated light blue to white.

ii Raw material

The assemblage contains flint from several sources, most of them probably local. Narrow vertical bands of tabular flint appear on the surface of the Upper Chalk of Coneybury Hill. It is of poor quality with limited usable material between the chalky cortex. Cores of this material show that it was worked bifacially and for the production of bladelets and was also used for hammerstones. Domestic requirements including scrapers were also served by irregular shaped surface nodules, generally between 300 and 400g in weight, together with occasional pebbles of river gravel flint. These were of variable quality and were prone to thermal fractures.

The presence of axe thinning flakes (Newcomer 1971) and large flakes of lighter grey flint suggest the possible exploitation of better quality flint from industrial sites in the area. It is not certain in what form this flint would have arrived at the site.

iii The flint industry

This includes material from the production of flake tools, blades/bladelets and core tools. There are few cores, and core tools are represented by ten probable thinning flakes. Refitting, which demonstrates nearby knapping, appears to have limited potential within this assemblage, suggesting that only a proportion of the potential total waste component is represented. The assemblage is probably derived from small-scale production with a basically domestic content rather than specialised industrial activity. Most of the flakes can be considered as waste although some, particularly the blades, could include unretouched flake tools, their association with the scrapers representing some form of tool dump. All stages of blade production from core preparation are likely although complete sequences cannot be demonstrated. Retouch phases are proved by refitting.

Although the flint is of a uniform type the distinctive raw materials and refitting pieces are generally contained within single or adjacent contexts near the base of the pit. There has, therefore, been little mixing of material since deposition. Initial infilling probably occurred as an individual event although compression of the pit fills has undoubtedly taken place. Refitting of material from primary and upper fills suggests the later incorporation of associated horizontal deposits in colluvial fills. This observation is borne out by the study of pottery from the upper fills (Cleal, this vol, 4.1 c).

Cores

The 13 cores from the primary contexts provide very little reliable technological evidence as most are failed examples and as such are probably atypical of those producing blanks with use potential. Five cores may have produced flakes found in the pit, although none refit. A refitted broken core shows that core fragments were reused to produce small blanks if the flint appeared sound. Many striking platforms were fractured thermal surfaces which had been used unprepared, while other platforms were prepared by the removal of a flake. One core has a crude bifacial crested edge which has not been removed totally by the following blade blow. It is uncertain whether this represents deliberate cresting, as no crested blades (*lame à crête*) were found among the waste. Although some nodules were worked at right angles to their longest axis, the exploitation of ridges combined with narrow butts, made possible by platform abrasion, was used to produce bladelets and long flakes. Faceting to modify the flaking angle is rare although platform rejuvenation flakes do exist. There is one exhausted multi-platform flake core but the ratio of blade production to flakes is uncertain. Some tabular flint blocks which have crude alternate flaking may represent failed or rudimentary core tools.

It is possible that, with nodules of relatively small size and of unreliable quality, successful core preparation was not achieved easily. It is also possible that the number of productive cores were few in relation to failed examples.

Flakes

All complete flakes from the pit were measured, although results are only shown from the primary deposit from which the majority of the flint was recovered. Table 116 shows the total number of flakes, broken flakes, and burnt flakes from analysed groups. The majority probably result from core trimming and represent the initial stages of flake or blade production. As such they were probably not primarily manufactured as tool blanks and can be considered as waste. Distinctive flakes, such as core rejuvenation flakes and core tool thinning flakes, are also present; details are contained within the archive.

The presence of blades demonstrates that some control and predetermination of blank form was possible, although the absence of distinctive blade by-products and techniques, including *lame à crête*, suggests that production was not specialised.

The recognition by microscopic analysis of unretouched flake tools amongst the blades is significant (E Moss pers comm). The total of such pieces is unknown but the use of non-specialised blanks ('waste flakes') indicates a flexible selection of pieces for use. Their association with retouched tools and a high proportion of burnt flakes (22%) reinforces the argument that the contents of this feature represent a deposit of selected pieces with a strongly domestic component.

Figure 149 shows the combined results of the analysis of the flint flakes and confirms the presence of a blade/bladelet element (2.5:5=25%). The flake class histogram (Fig 149) substantiates the effects of flake ridges on breadth/length and confirms the importance of conserving ridges at the front of the core for guiding flake length. Most flakes show that they have been struck from cores worked in a single direction.

Although flake platforms were not normally prepared, the removal of overhang by abrasion is present, and it is possible that this technique was employed in the production of deliberate blanks. Plain butts predominate throughout; however, a few show the remnants of identifiable negative flake scars which may result from alternate flaking. Percussion angles were consistently high and were sufficiently well maintained to allow some continuous production. Some blades have patches of cortex on the distal end which indicates that in some cases it was possible to maintain the length of the pieces produced.

The number of accidents of debitage from this assemblage – Siret fractured, hinged, and plunged pieces – were not recorded accurately but in relationship to the other examined assemblages appear comparatively low.

Scrapers

The 47 scrapers, in common with the majority of Neolithic flint assemblages, form the largest retouched tool category (56.4%). The primary fills contained 25 examples of which 3 were burnt and only 19 suitable for analysis. The results (Figs 150, 151) demonstrate recurring features of blank selection. All scrapers are on flakes of nodular flint. Blanks consistently exceed 40mm in both length and breadth, and average 4.6–5.5:5 breadth/length. These factors, together with cortical cover and flake class, show that large trimming flakes, preparation flakes, or large non-cortical flake blanks were normally selected.

Flake scars on the dorsal surfaces of the scrapers show that blanks were removed during core preparation phases or from flake cores but were not part of the blade core technology. The ventral surfaces indicate that some soft hammers were used to remove blanks, although the presence of 'softened' (less accentuated) hard hammer characteristics suggests that these might be flint hammers with cortical surfaces.

Blanks were generally modified by direct retouch at the dipping distal part of the flake (end scrapers) and there are only two side scrapers. Most retouch is semi-abrupt (10 examples between 50° and 59°), regular, and continuous, forming a convex scraping edge. Only 4 scrapers have retouched edges which do not remove cortex, compared with 11 which are totally retouched through cortex. The scrapers as a group can be considered to be well made.

Scraper manufacture/resharpening is also represented within the assemblage from the pit. Three scrapers made on cortical flakes of a distinctive flint were found in close proximity. At least two were broken during or after manufacture while the third was made on a flake with a hinged distal end. It is possible that these represent the failed pieces of tools made in bulk. There are also flakes, including retouch chips (Newcomer and Karlin 1987), which are apparently from the same nodule. Specific evidence for manufacture/sharpening is present in the form of a retouch chip which refits to its scraper (Fig 27), although whether the activity represented here is manufacture or sharpening is impossible to define in the absence of visible scraper edge wear. It does, however, indicate the expendability and possible life span of retouched flake tools including well-made pieces which show no obvious reason for rejection. The retouch chips show similarities in hammer mode with the blanks.

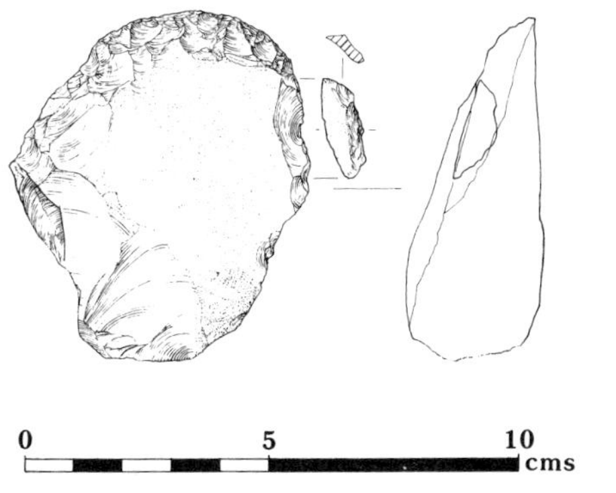

Fig 27 W2 (1981) Coneybury 'Anomaly': flint scraper with refitting resharpening chip

Other tools

The primary deposits also contained two leaf-shaped arrowheads and a broken ground flint axe (not illustrated).

4.1 c The prehistoric pottery

by Rosamund Cleal

A total of 1744 prehistoric sherds, weighing 16,182g, were recovered from the fill of this feature, the majority contained within the primary fill. Only a small amount of the pottery, exclusively from the upper fill, is datable to the later Neolithic or Bronze Age, and the majority of the assemblage is earlier Neolithic in date. A summary of sherd counts and weights, by context, is given in Table 10.

Methodology

Fifteen fabrics were identified by examining the material at ×10 magnification with a hand lens; a small number of sherds were also examined under a microscope at ×30 magnification. These fabrics are listed and described in Table 11 (and in more detail in Table 12, MF1 A4–5).

Estimates of the number of vessels represented by the sherds were calculated by two methods:

i By visual examination of all the rims. Joining rims were counted as belonging to a single vessel, but in addition rim sherds judged likely to belong to a single vessel on the grounds of form, finish, and to some extent colour were also counted as such for the purposes of the vessel count. Very small rim sherds were excluded from this, as were body sherds not joined to rims, unless they were in fabrics not otherwise represented.

ii By a count of all rims, with joining rims counted as single units.

No certainty can be attached to either method, and they are both used in the subsequent discussions of vessel numbers. The illustrated vessels (Figs 28–31) are designated by a 'P' prefix, and those with an asterisk indicate sherds which have been counted as separate vessels in the estimate of vessel numbers. The illustrated pottery is described in the catalogue below (P1–P52).

Table 10 W2 (1981) Coneybury 'Anomaly': pottery sherd count and weight by context

Fabric	*Unstratified*		*Ploughsoil in area K*		*Recent deposits*		*Upper colluvial*		*Lower colluvial*		*Primary deposits*		*Totals*	
S:Neo/1	–		–		6	14g	2	4g	47 (5)	130g	187 (11)	740g	242	888g
FS:Neo/1	3 (1)	10g	–		34	157g	13 (2)	69g	171 (7)	727g	1174 (85)	13927g	1395	14890g
CFS:Neo/1	2	6g	–		–		–		6	5g	14 (1)	28g	22	39g
S:Bkr/1	–		–		1	2g	1	2g	–		–		2	4g
FeM:Bkr/1	–		–		1	5g	–		–		–		1	5g
GS:Bkr/1	–		–		–		1	5g	–		–		1	5g
FGS:Bkr/1	–		–		2	3g	–		–		–		2	3g
Ffe:DR/4	–		–		1	9g	–		–		–		1	9g
FfeS:DR/1	–		–		1 (1)	1g	–		–		–		1	1g
G:LBA/1	–		1	4g	1	2g	–		–		–		2	6g
FV:LBA/1	–		–		1	3g	–		–		–		1	3g
FS:Indet/1	–		–		–		–		1	1g	60	297g	61	298g
GS:Indet/1	–		–		–		1 (1)	7g	–		–		1	7g
SV:Indet/1	–		–		1	1g	–		–		–		1	1g
SSh:Indet/1	–		–		–		–		–		6	18g	6	18g
FS:–	–		–		5	5g	–		–		–		5	5g
Totals	5	16g	1	4g	54	202g	18	87g	225	863g	1441	15010g	1744	16182g
Romano-British sherds			1		1									
?medieval			1											

Figures in parenthesis represent rim count; rim count is also included in sherd count

Table 11 W2 (1981) Coneybury 'Anomaly': summary prehistoric pottery fabric descriptions (see also Table 12 (MF1 A4–5) for more detailed descriptions)

Descriptive terms

Abundance of inclusions recorded using the following terms, in order of increasing density – rare, sparse, moderate, common, very common, abundant

Size: terms used as follows – <2mm small; 3–5mm medium; >6mm large

Fabric descriptions are arranged in chronological order, where possible (ie Neolithic, Beaker, Indeterminate), and within each chronological group by alphabetical order.

Fabric code	*Description*
CFS:Neo/1	Soft fabric with sparse small to large CHALK (max diam 6mm), sparse large FLINT (max length 10mm), and moderate fine SAND
FS:Neo/1	Hard fabric with sparse to common FLINT of varying size (max length 10mm), and moderate to abundant SAND (fine to coarse). This fabric is very variable, even within single vessels, and the inclusions are patchily distributed.
S:Neo/1	Hard, sandy fabric with moderate to very common fine SAND and rare flint
FGS:Bkr/1	Hard fabric with sparse small FLINT, sparse small GROG, and sparse fine SAND
GS:Bkr/1	Soft fabric with sparse small GROG and moderate fine SAND
S:Bkr/1	Soft, sandy fabric with very common fine SAND
FS:Indet/1	Hard fabric with common to very common small to medium FLINT (max length 4mm) and common fine SAND
GS:Indet/1	Hard fabric withh sparse small to medium GROG, moderate coarse SAND, and rare flint
SSh:Indet/1	Soft laminated fabric with moderate fine SAND and common small to large fragments (max length 6mm) of SHELL
SV:Indet/1	Soft fabric with moderate fine SAND, and common, small to medium, rounded VOIDS

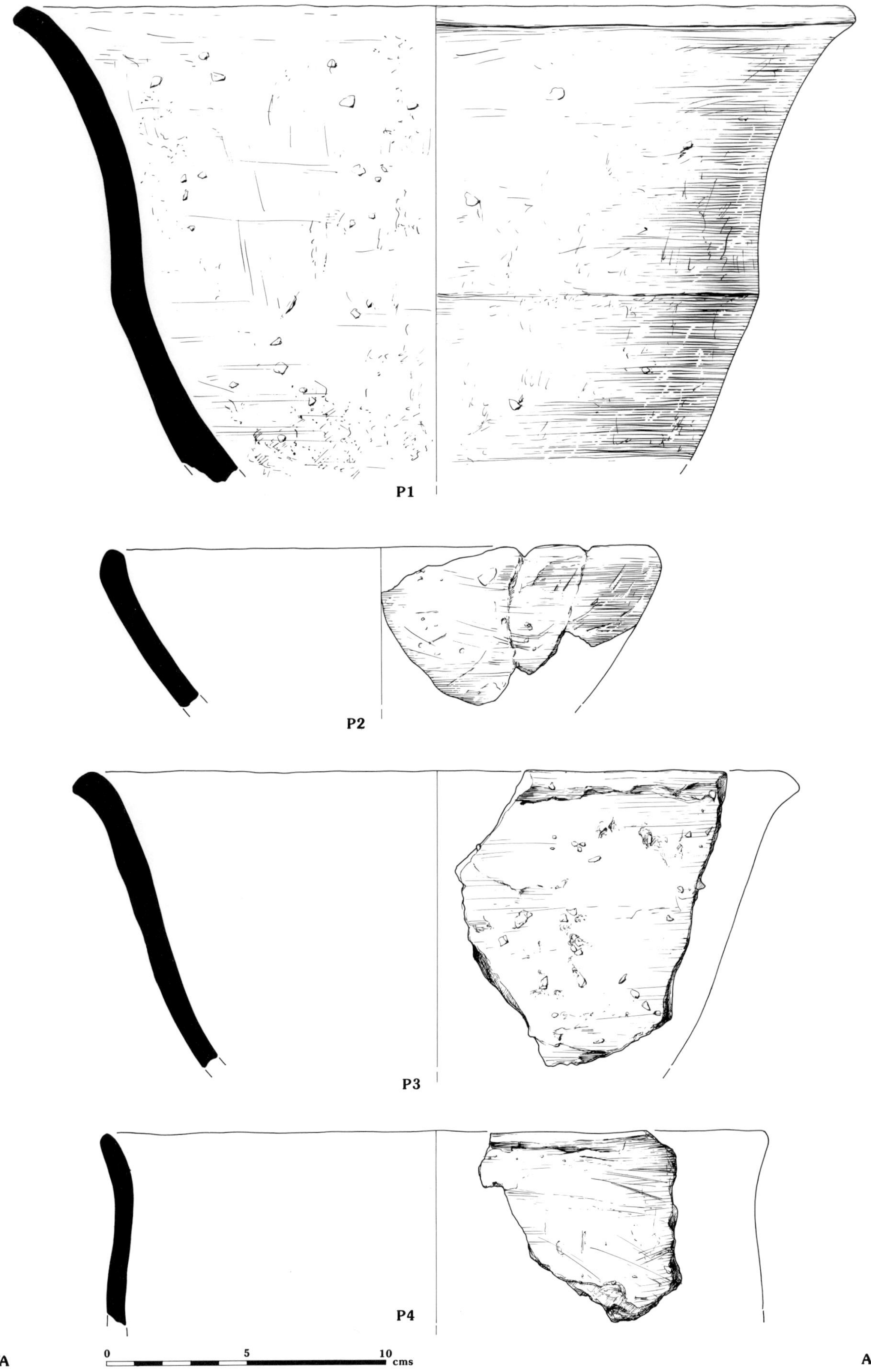

Fig 28 W2 (1981) Coneybury 'Anomaly': prehistoric pottery (P1–P4)

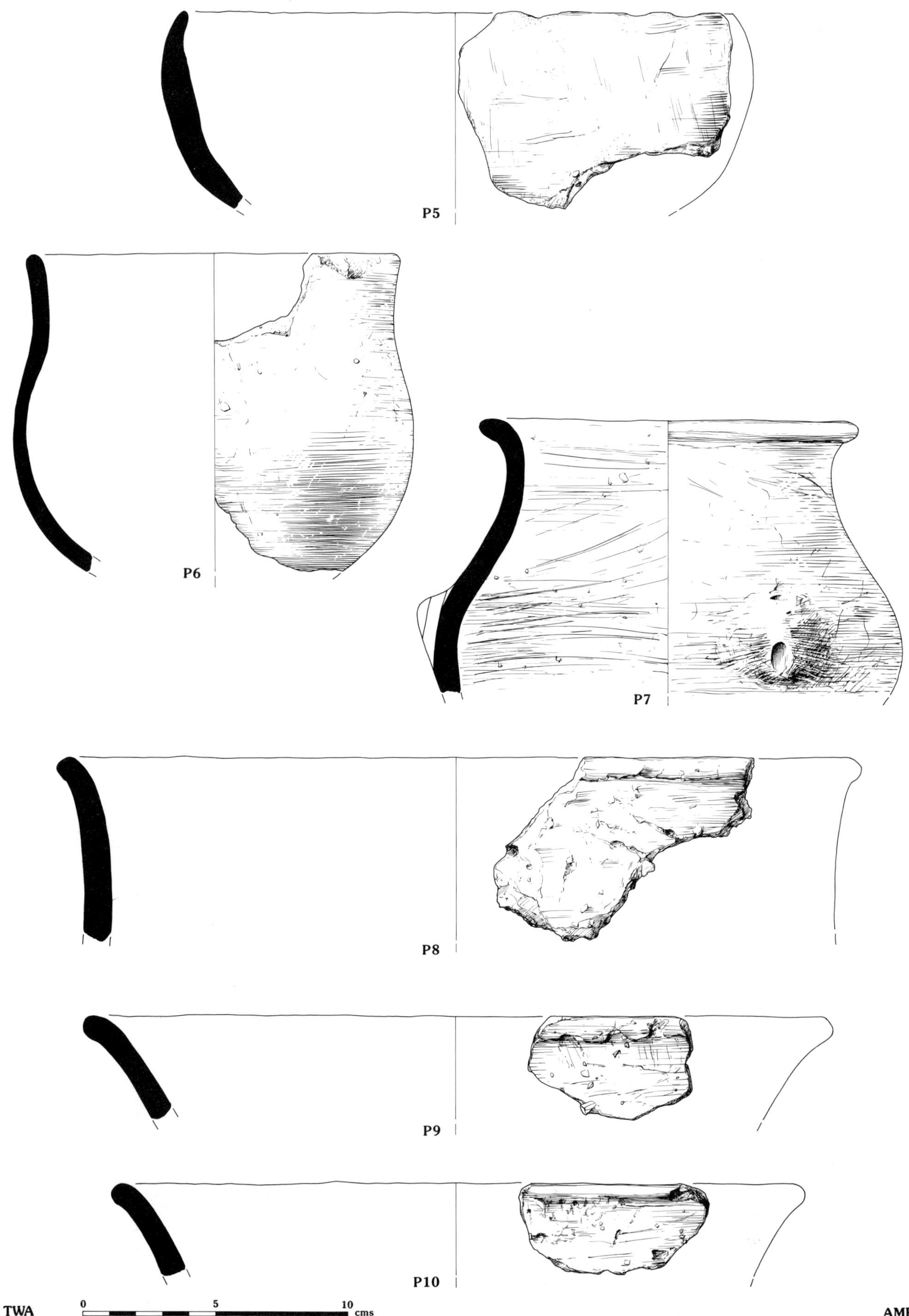

Fig 29 W2 (1981) Coneybury 'Anomaly': prehistoric pottery (P5–P10)

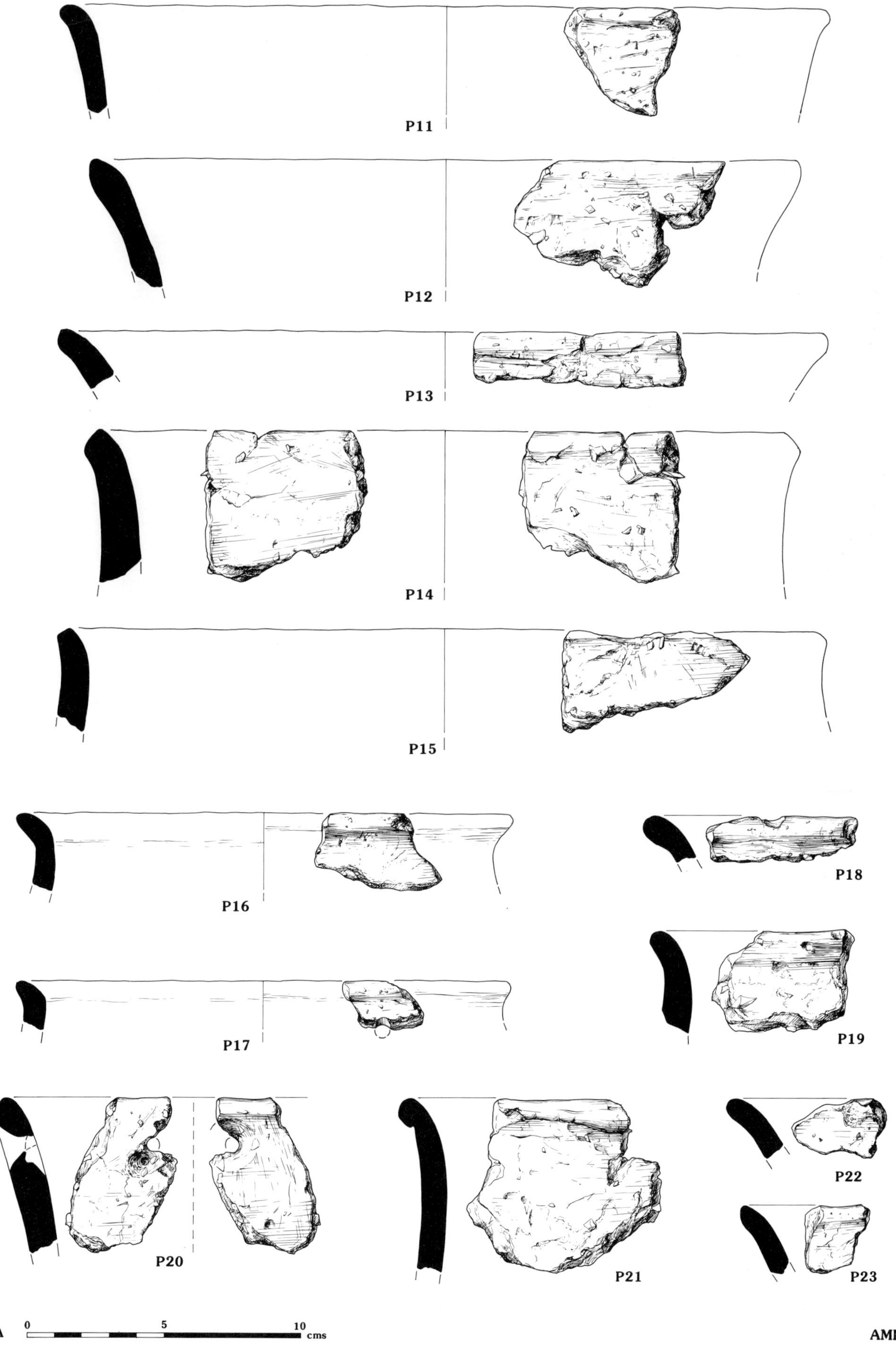

Fig 30 W2 (1981) Coneybury 'Anomaly': prehistoric pottery (P11– P23)

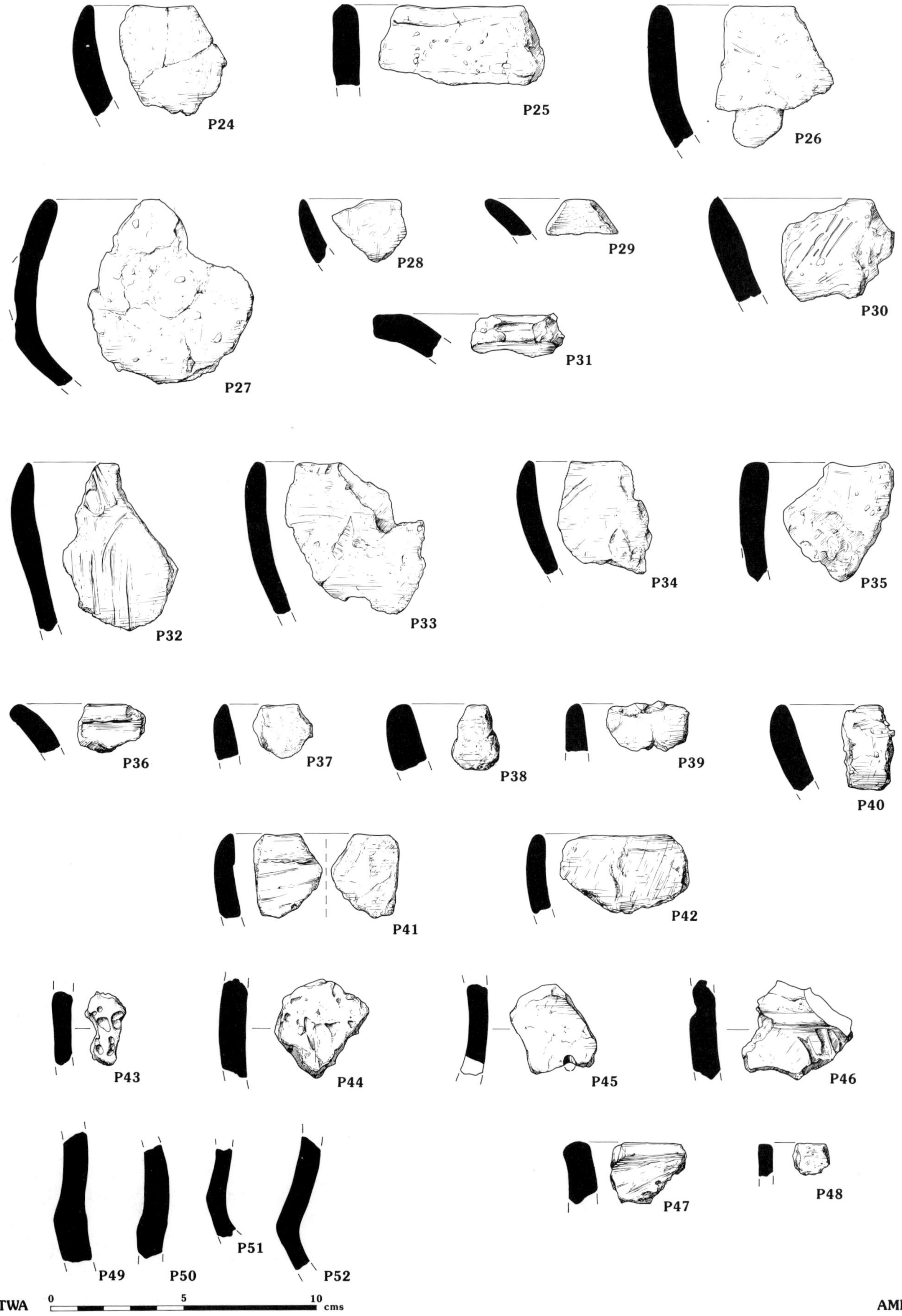

Fig 31 W2 (1981) Coneybury 'Anomaly': prehistoric pottery (P24-P52)

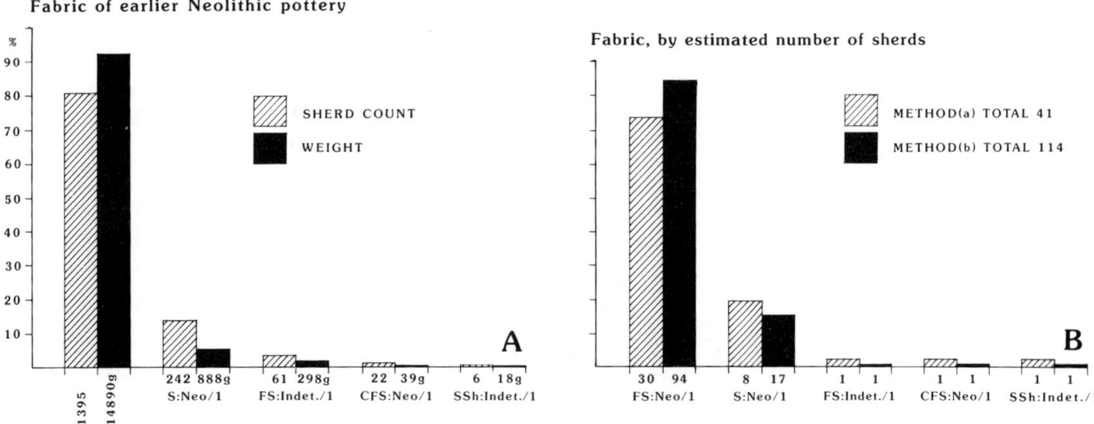

Fig 32 W2 (1981) Coneybury 'Anomaly': prehistoric pottery fabric histograms

Earlier Neolithic

Fabric

Three certainly earlier Neolithic fabrics were identified (FS:Neo/1, S:Neo/1, and CFS:Neo/1), and two more (FS:Indet/1 and SSh:Indet/1) are likely to be of this date, although represented only by plain body sherds (see Table 11 and Table 12, MF1 A4–5, for descriptions). Two fabrics, however, account for the majority of the sherds: FS:Neo/1 and S:Neo/1. The former is a coarse fabric with flint and sand inclusions, and the latter a sandy fabric. The flint is almost certainly an added ingredient, but the sand may or may not have been introduced by the potter. Fabric CFS:Neo/1 may only be represented by a single vessel.

There is some variation in the degree of sandiness within fabric S:Neo/1, but not enough to warrant subdivision, and Fabric FS:Neo/1 also varies considerably in sandiness, in the distribution of flint temper, and in the quality of finish. Subdivision of this fabric was initially attempted during sorting but was found to be unwarranted as joining sherds sometimes presented quite differing frequencies of inclusions.

The absolute dominance of Fabric FS:Neo/1 is clearly demonstrated by Figure 32A, which gives the total number of sherds and total sherd weight for each fabric, and illustrates that other than fabric FS:Neo/1 only Fabric S:Neo/1 is present in any appreciable amount. However, although sherds of fabric S:Neo/1 make up nearly 14% of the total sherd assemblage, it only constitutes 5% of the total weight. The average weight per sherd in fabric S:Neo/1 is only 3.7g, whereas for fabric FS:Neo/1 the comparable figure is 10.7g; this reflects the fact that vessels in fabric FS:Neo/1 tend to be larger and have thicker body walls than those in fabric S:Neo/1. Figure 32B gives the total number of vessels in each fabric, using the estimates of vessel number arrived at by both methods described above. In both cases the sandy fabric S:Neo/1 is clearly in the minority, and at most it constitutes only 20% of the total.

Table 13 W2 (1981) Coneybury 'Anomaly': earlier Neolithic pottery rim classification

This includes all classifiable rims (ie all those where the rim angle is determinable, except that joining rim sherds count as one. A more detailed breakdown of rim types, including those for which the rim angle is not determinable, is given in Table 14, MF1 A6–8. The classification is based on the same criteria, and is in the same form, as that used by I F Smith in the report on the assemblage from Carn Brea (I F Smith 1981).

Rim form	*Rim count and %, by fabric*					
	FS:Neo/1		*S:Neo/1*		*CFS:Neo/1*	
Simple						
Pointed	5	5.3%	4	4.3%	0	–
Rounded	14	14.9%	8	8.5%	1	1.1%
Squared	1	1.1%	0	–	0	–
Indeterminate			1	1.1%		
Sub-total	20	21.3%	13	13.9%	1	1.1%
Everted						
Rolled-over	11	11.7%	0	–	0	–
Pointed	8	8.5%	1	1.1%	0	–
Featureless	37	39.4%	0	–	0	–
Squared	2	2.1%	0	–	0	–
Indeterminate	1	1.1%	0	–	0	–
Sub-total	59	62.8%	1	1.1%	0	–
Totals	79	84.1%	14	15.0%	1	1.1%

Morphology

Rim form

Table 13 lists the rim forms exhibited by the earlier Neolithic pottery, using Isobel Smith's classification. A slightly more detailed breakdown of rim form is given in Table 14 (MF1 A6–8). Smith has used this system for several years, and has applied it to the large assemblage at Windmill Hill, Wiltshire (I F Smith 1965), and, apparently with some modification, to that from Carn Brea, Cornwall (I F Smith 1981), as it is suitable both for the plain rims of South-Western style assemblages and for assemblages with a high proportion of thickened rims. The rims from W2 (1981) have been classified in the same way as the Carn Brea assemblage, and are presented in the same manner, as both assemblages belong within the South-Western regional style. In this scheme 'simple' denotes basically unmodified rim forms, approximately upright, and 'everted' are similar forms, set at an outward-leaning angle to the main vertical axis of the pot. Most of the subdivisions are self-explanatory. 'Featureless', as used in the Carn Brea

Table 15 W2 (1981) Coneybury 'Anomaly': earlier Neolithic pottery rim classification by estimated number of vessels

Rim form	*FS:Neo/1*	*S:Neo/1*	*CFS:Neo/1*
Simple			
Pointed	2	3	0
Rounded	6	3	1
Squared	1	0	0
Sub-total	9	6	1
Everted			
Rolled-over	6	0	0
Pointed	3	1	0
Featureless	10	0	0
Squared	1	0	0
Sub-total	20	1	0

Total number of vessels is 37 (ie estimated number of vessels arrived at by method (a), minus 2 vessels represented only by body sherds, and 2 with uncertain rim angles)

report, appears to denote completely unmodified, usually rounded, rims.

The assemblage from the pit is clearly a limited one in terms of the number of rim types exhibited, as is to be expected from an assemblage of the South-Western style. No heavy, thickened rims are present, and most of the rims are everted or upright, with a small number showing a slightly inturned attitude, though not qualifying as inturned in the sense used by Smith (ie form F, I F Smith 1965, 48, and fig 11). Of the 15% of rims which are in the sandy fabric S:Neo/1 at least 6% are of this slightly inturned form (Table 14, MF1 A6–8).

In terms of Smith's classification the most common type of rim is the everted, featureless type (eg P1, P4), all of which are in fabric FS:Neo/1; everted rims overall account for more than half of all classifiable rims (63.9%). All except one of these rims is in fabric FS:Neo/1 (Table 13).

The overwhelming dominance of everted rims must surely be a reflection of the importance of open-mouthed bowls in the assemblage, though this cannot be supported by reconstructions of the vessels, as the profiles of most are not reconstructable.

If the estimate of vessel numbers as calculated by method i is used, excluding those which do not have rims, the percentages are similar to those obtained from the 94 rims used in Table 13. Ten of the 37 possible vessels have everted featureless rims (*c* 27%), all in fabric FS:Neo/1, and everted rims overall account for more than half the total number of vessels (57%) (Table 15).

Vessel form

Only one vessel, P1, is even partially reconstructable, the others being represented mainly by rim sherds, as it was generally not possible to assign body sherds to particular vessels. In only 14 cases out of the minimum number of 41 vessels established by method i were rim diameters determinable, and these are presented in Figure 33A. However, in 15 other cases it was possible to define a size range within which the vessel rim diameter must have fallen, and these are presented in Figure 33B, in which the vessels with measurable diameters are also included. The size ranges in Figure 33B are: cups (<120mm), small bowls (130–200mm), medium bowls (210–300mm), and large bowls (310mm and larger). The use of 120mm diameter as the dividing line between cups and bowls is a widely used one (eg Whittle 1977, 77), but the other divisions are arbitrary.

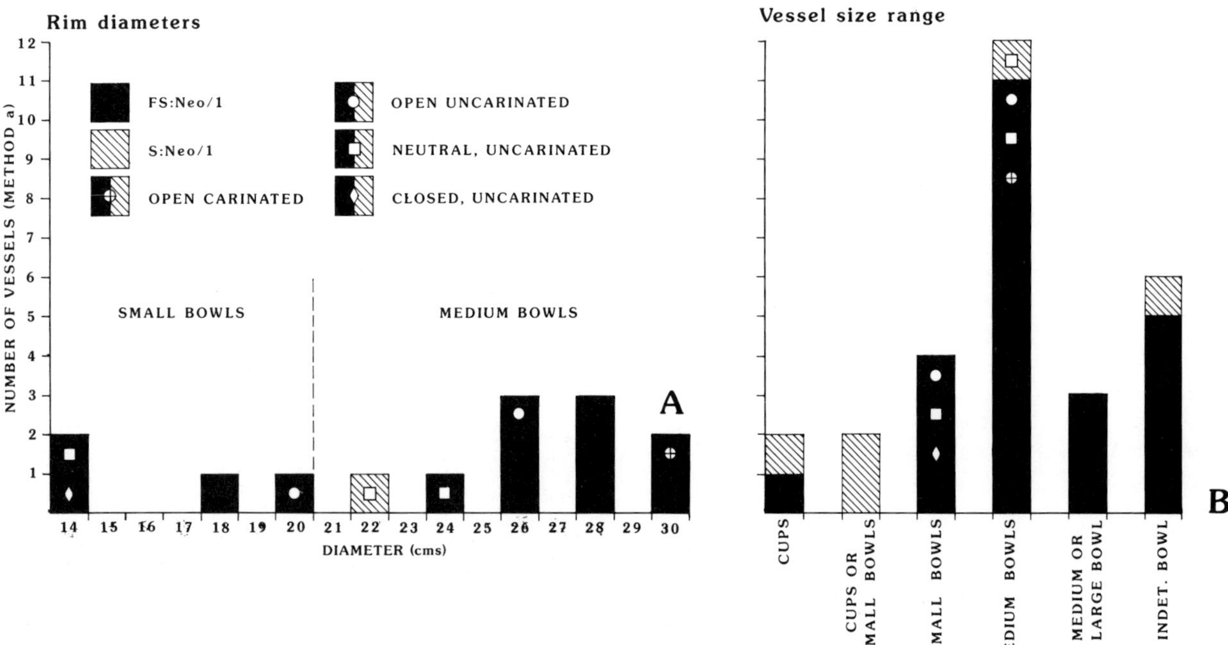

Fig 33 W2 (1981) Coneybury 'Anomaly': prehistoric pottery form histograms

P1 is one of the largest vessels from the pit, and is one of only two of the 41 identified vessels to be certainly carinated, although the shoulder is an extremely weak one. However, there are 11 carinated body sherds in the assemblage which may not belong to vessel P1 (some of which are illustrated as P49–P52); fewer than 11 vessels are likely to be represented by these sherds, but they do demonstrate, with P1, that there is a minor carinated component to the assemblage.

It is unfortunate that so few vessel profiles are reconstructable, but the presence of open forms, particularly P1, and simple, unthickened rims clearly indicate that the assemblage belongs within the South-Western (or Hembury) style. As such it is comparable with the assemblages from Maiden Castle, Dorset (Wheeler 1943), Carn Brea, Cornwall (I F Smith 1981), and Hembury, Devon (Liddell 1930; 1931; 1932; 1935) to the south-west, and to the South-Western component of the Windmill Hill, Wiltshire (Smith 1965), assemblage to the north.

The presence of a vessel with a lug (P7)in the Coneybury 'Anomaly' also suggests that the assemblage belongs to the South-Western style. The lug on P7 is oval, set horizontally, and is vertically perforated; this type of lug is not common, but occurs in such large South-Western style assemblages as Maiden Castle (Cleal forthcoming a) and Windmill Hill (I F Smith 1965, fig 22: P119, fig 23: P132).

Decoration

Several of the earlier Neolithic sherds from the Coneybury 'Anomaly' exhibit surface features but few, if any, of these are likely to represent deliberate decoration. Only two of the illustrated vessels have decoration: P32, a cup or bowl, has grooves and shallow irregular impressions, and P33 and P34, which are likely to be part of the same vessel, have impressions and faint, possibly accidental, fingernail(?) impressions. The other vessel, P30, a cup or small bowl, has a set of multiple scored lines.

Eight other body sherds have surface features. Three sherds, including one of the carinated sherds (P46), have grooves, four have impressions (P43, P44), one a pair of fingernail impressions, and one (P45) a perforation made before firing. P45 may belong to the vessel represented by rims P16 and P17, as the latter also has a pre-firing perforation. The grooves in each case appear to be deliberate, but the fingernail impressions are faint and may be accidental. Decoration is rare in assemblages of the South-Western style, but when it occurs it does include grooving and shallow impression (Field *et al* 1964, fig 3: P10 and P19; I F Smith 1981). Pre-firing perforations are rare, but single examples do occur at Carn Brea (I F Smith 1981, fig 74: P146) and Maiden Castle (from the recent excavations; Cleal forthcoming a).

Context

The majority of the sherds were recovered from the primary fill, within which the distribution of conjoining sherds was plotted in an attempt to establish whether parts of the same vessel were located close together. This did not appear to be the case as several of the groups of pottery noticed during excavation were found to include sherds of several vessels, and sherds apparently belonging to single pots, in particular P1, were found in more than one group.

Function

Vessel function is a difficult area of analysis, and one especially difficult when, as in this case, the material is fragmentary and few vessels are reconstructable. Few attempts at analysis of function have been made on earlier Neolithic assemblages, the most pertinent in this connection being Hilary Howard's treatment (1981) of the earlier Neolithic assemblage from the causewayed enclosure at Windmill Hill. Howard divided the fabrics into two classes: cookwares and non-cookwares, based on their likely resistance to thermal shock, and identified several classes of vessel for which she offered functional interpretations. This type of approach, although interesting, is difficult to apply to the Coneybury 'Anomaly' assemblage because the number of vessels is small, few rim diameters can be established with any certainty, and even fewer profiles can be reconstructed. In addition, there is also less variation in fabric than at Windmill Hill: both FS:Neo/1 and S:Neo/1 would be classed as cookwares in Howard's terms, as both have high densities of inclusions. However, the presence of large inclusions in FS:Neo/1 would probably render it more resistant to thermal shock than S:Neo/1.

It is clear that the 'Anomaly' assemblage shows less variety than that from Windmill Hill, but this could largely be due to its smaller size and to the more restricted repertoire of the regional style to which it belongs. In spite of this, a few tentative points may usefully be made regarding the way in which the assemblage may have functioned.

Firstly, it does seem likely that the assemblage was made and used within a fairly short period of time. The fabrics of the assemblage are fairly homogeneous, and apart from the few small sherds with shell inclusions, all could have been made using materials available within a few kilometres. Although the vessels were fragmentary, few showed excessive wear; however, it seems unlikely that the vessels were deposited immediately after breakage, as more fully reconstructable vessels would be expected if that were the case. A few sherds showed complete or partial loss of surfaces and, although this might be due to conditions after burial, it might also result from exposure in a midden. It must be stressed that the condition of the sherds does not suggest that they were exposed on a used surface for any length of time, as the large size of some of the sherds and their general condition are not consistent with the material having been trampled in a living area. The presence of a repair hole on P20 suggests that at least some of the vessels had been used for some time before discard, unless the break or crack was a result of firing.

It was extremely difficult to estimate the number of vessels, and it is quite possible that the true figure is considerably more or less than the estimate. However, the following elements are certainly present:

at least one very large carinated vessel in fabric FS:Neo/1 (P1)

several open or neutral bowls, mainly, if not all, uncarinated, and of moderate size, mainly in fabric FS:Neo/1, but at least one in S:Neo/1 (eg P2, P3, P4, P5)

small shallow bowls or cups, mainly in fabric S:Neo/1 (eg P24, P32–P34, P41, P42)

one small neutral bowl with an ill-defined neck, in fabric FS:Neo/1 (P6)

one small closed bowl or jar with a perforated lug, in fabric FS:Neo/1 (P7)

In addition, the approximate volumes of six vessels can be calculated. Volumes were calculated by projecting the existing line of the vessel wall to a round base in those vessels in which it seemed unlikely that there would have been a sharp change in angle in the lower body (ie the angle was already present (P1) or sufficient of the wall survived to be fairly certain that there was no change in angle), and the vessel was then divided into a series of truncated cones, for which volumes were calculated and then summed to give the total for the whole vessel.

P1 6895cm^3
P2 1374cm^3
P3 3718cm^3
P5 2095cm^3
P6 1422cm^3
P7 1926cm^3

P7 has been treated as a bowl rather than a jar, and its volume may therefore be a considerable underestimate.

This suggests one vessel of around 7ltr capacity, one of around 3.5ltr, two around 2ltr, and two around 1.5ltr. Vessel P2, a shallow open bowl in fabric S:Neo/1, and with a capacity of about 1.4ltr, seems likely, on the basis of form and capacity, to be an individual eating or drinking vessel. P6, however, with a similar capacity, although possibly an eating or drinking vessel, is of a form unusual in the assemblage, and might be more readily suited, because of its necked form, to cooking rather than eating. P5 resembles P2 in form and is also in fabric S:Neo/1, but its capacity is larger at about 2ltr, which would seem rather large for an individual eating bowl: an alternative might be a cooking or food preparation vessel. P3, at 3.7ltr, might also have been intended for these purposes. The closed bowl or jar P7 is more difficult to explain: although in fabric FS:Neo/1 it is relatively well finished in comparison with most of the assemblage, and its very restricted form would seem to preclude its use as a cookpot. However, the restricted form and the presence of the rolled-over rim and the lug, which could both be used to attach a hide cover, would all be consistent with use as a storage vessel. The lugs may also have been used for suspending the vessel during transportation. Although the capacity is small (approximately 1.9ltr), this could be a considerable underestimate if the body was actually a deep jar form, and large storage vessels would have been impractical if transportation was necessary. Finally, the large open vessel P1, with a likely capacity of nearly 7ltr, is clearly either a food preparation vessel, a cookpot, or a serving vessel, or indeed all three combined. Its large size and lack of handling aids (eg lugs/handles, rolled over or thickened rim) would render it unwieldy to handle when full, when it would be extremely heavy, which might perhaps be taken as an indication that it was not used for cooking. It does not show any signs of sooting, but sooting is generally absent from the assemblage, a feature which is possibly the result of post-depositional processes.

It is clearly impossible to establish with any certainty how the assemblage was used or how many people used it. Although the very restricted nature of the assemblage does not suggest the presence of a large group, if the group were mobile the lack of much of a storage element in the assemblage might be the result of unbroken storage vessels being removed and/or the use of non-ceramic storage containers.

The question of precisely what sort of consumption is represented is even more problematic, and obviously the pottery cannot be considered alone in this connection. Whether the assemblage is particularly special or unusual is difficult to ascertain; in terms of vessel type and fabric it is certainly not unusual, but the quantity of pottery is much greater than is usual in similar deposits. Small pits containing parts of several vessels are not uncommon in the earlier Neolithic, such as at Rowden (Woodward forthcoming) or Pamphill (Field *et al* 1964), both in Dorset. The rarity of lugs in an assemblage the size of that contained within the Coneybury 'Anomaly', however, is slightly unusual, as is the form of the only lugged vessel (P7). This may suggest that this group represents a variant within the South-Western style (I F Smith pers comm). The South-Western regional style generally lacks decoration, but the fine component of such assemblages is usually taken to be represented by gabbroic ware, which is conspicuous by its exceptionally fine black finish. No gabbroic ware is present at Coneybury 'Anomaly', but it is perhaps of interest that the very large bowl P1 is identical in form to a shape common in gabbroic ware vessels (ie carinated bowl with an open flaring mouth). This is also true of the very fragmentary carinated vessel represented by P16, P17, P45, and P52, which also has a very fine surface finish and is well fired. It must be stressed, however, that there is no other resemblance between P1 (or P16, P17, P45, and P52) and gabbroic ware, as the colour and finish are quite different. The Coneybury 'Anomaly' assemblage, then, shows little internal variation, and lacks the fine component of the South-Western regional style which is known to have been circulating at this period. The homogeneity of the fabrics and the appearance of the vessels suggests manufacture during a fairly restricted period, and this fact, in combination with the unusually large size of the group, rather than any qualities of the material itself, render the assemblage unusual.

Catalogue of illustrated earlier Neolithic pottery (Figs 28–31)

The asterisks denote the 39 illustrated vessels considered likely to be separate vessels. Descriptions of rim form (and codes) are Cleal rather than Smith types. For conversion to Smith types see Table 14 (MF1 A6–8).

P1* 24 sherds of an open bowl with a slight shoulder carination and a simple, everted, rounded rim (A1a)
Fabric: FS:Neo/1. Colour: exterior pale grey; exterior margin orange; core dark grey, black; interior pale grey

P2* Nine sherds of an open uncarinated bowl with a simple, inturned, rounded to pointed rim (A3a/b)
Fabric: FS:Neo/1. Colour: exterior varied – dark grey-brown, orange-brown, dark grey; core dark grey, orange, black; interior dark grey, orange-brown

P3* One large rim sherd of an open uncarinated bowl with a rolled-over, everted, rounded rim (B2b)
Fabric: FS:Neo/1. Colour: exterior absent; core dark grey; interior pale grey

P4* Three conjoining rim sherds of a neutral uncarinated bowl with a simple, everted, pointed rim (A1b)
Fabric: FS:Neo/1. Colour: exterior dark grey; exterior margin dark brown; core black; interior dark grey

P5* Ten sherds of an open uncarinated bowl with a simple, inturned, rounded rim (A3a)
Fabric: S:Neo/1. Colour: exterior pale orange; core dark grey; interior: pale orange

P6* One rim and one body sherd (conjoining) of a neutral uncarinated bowl with a weakly defined neck and a simple, upright, rounded rim (A2c)
Fabric: FS:Neo/1. Colour: exterior obscured; core dark grey; interior: grey

P7* Two rim sherds and two body sherds (conjoining) of a closed, uncarinated bowl with a rolled-over, upright, rounded rim (B1a) and a vertically perforated oval lug
Fabric: FS:Neo/1. Colour: exterior grey-brown, grey; exterior margin orange; core dark grey; interior grey

P8* Two rim sherds of a bowl with a simple, upright, rounded rim (A1a)
Fabric: FS:Neo/1. Colour: exterior grey-brown, grey; exterior margin orange; core dark grey; interior grey

P9* One rim sherd of a bowl with a simple everted rounded rim (A1a)
Fabric: FS:Neo/1. Colour: orange throughout

P10* Seven rim sherds (two conjoining) of a bowl with a simple, everted, rounded rim (A1a)
Fabric FS:Neo/1. Colour: exterior pale orange, grey, brown; core black, dark grey; interior pale orange, pale grey

P11* Four rim sherds of a bowl with a simple, everted, rounded rim (A1a)
Fabric: FS:Neo/1. Colour: orange throughout

P12* Two conjoining rim sherds of a bowl with a simple, everted, rounded rim (A1a)
Fabric: FS:Neo/1. Colour: exterior brown, grey-brown; core dark grey; interior black

P13* Two conjoining rim sherds of a vessel with a simple, everted, pointed rim (A1b). Both sherds have broken along the junction of two coils which were insufficiently joined by the potter; this shows as a concave smooth surface along the broken edge
Fabric: FS:Neo/1. Colour: exterior dark grey, grey-brown; core dark grey; interior brown, pale brown

P14* Three conjoining rim sherds of a vessel with a simple, everted, squared rim (A1c)
Fabric: FS:Neo/1. Colour: exterior pale grey; core grey; interior pale grey

P15* Single rim sherd of a bowl with a simple, upright, squared rim (A2c)
Fabric: FS:Neo/1. Colour: exterior grey; core black; interior grey

P16*,P17 Seven rim sherds, three conjoining, of a bowl with a rolled-over, everted, rounded to pointed rim (B1a/b). P17 has a hole made before firing, approximately 4mm in diameter. The concave neck sherd illustrated as P45 may also be part of this vessel
Fabric: FS:Neo/1. Colour: exterior orange throughout

P18* Two rim sherds of a cup or small bowl with a rolled-over, everted, rounded rim (B1a)
Fabric: FS:Neo/1. Colour: exterior grey; core dark grey; interior dark grey

P19* Single rim sherd of a bowl with a simple, everted, rounded rim (A1a)
Fabric: FS:Neo/1. Colour: exterior worn; core dark grey; interior dark grey, pale brown on the rim interior

P20* Single rim of a bowl with a simple, everted, rounded rim (A1a). The hole was drilled after firing, from the exterior, although a previous attempt was made from the interior, a few millimetres away, but abandoned apparently because a particularly large flint inclusion barred the way
Fabric: FS:Neo/1. Colour: exterior brown, grey-brown; core dark grey; interior dark grey

P21* Single rim of a bowl with a simple, everted, rounded rim (A1a)
Fabric: FS:Neo/1. Colour: exterior pale brown; core dark grey; interior dark grey

P22* Two rim sherds of a cup or small bowl with a simple, everted, rounded to pointed rim (A1a/b)
Fabric: FS:Neo/1. Colour: exterior grey-brown; core black; interior grey-brown

P23* Three rim sherds of a cup or small bowl with a simple, everted, pointed rim (A1b)
Fabric: FS:Neo/1. Colour: orange throughout

P24* One rim sherd and four plain body sherds of a cup or small bowl. The angle of the rim is uncertain
Fabric: S:Neo/1. Colour: orange throughout, except for a patch of black immediately below the rim on the interior

P25* One rim sherd of a bowl with a simple, upright, rounded rim (A2a)
Fabric: FS:Neo/1. Colour: exterior buff; core black; interior grey

P26* Single rim sherd of a cup or small bowl. The angle of the rim is uncertain
Fabric: FS:Neo/1. Colour: exterior grey, patchy orange; core black; interior grey

P27* Single sherd, showing the profile of what appears to be a small neutral or closed bowl or cup. The rim angle is uncertain, but that illustrated seems to be the most likely angle. The rim diameter is uncertain, but the diameter around the body seems to be approximately 120mm

Fabric: FS:Neo/1. Colour: exterior grey-brown; interior surface abraded

P28* Single rim sherd of a cup or bowl. The angle of the rim is uncertain
Fabric: S:Neo/1. Colour: grey throughout

P29* Single rim sherd of a cup or small bowl with a simple, everted, pointed rim (A1b)
Fabric: S:1. Colour: exterior orange; core grey; interior orange

P30* Single rim sherd of a cup or bowl. The angle of the rim is uncertain. A group of scored lines on the exterior appear to be a deliberate feature
Fabric: FS:Neo/1. Colour: grey throughout

P31* Single rim sherd of a vessel with a rolled-over rim of unusual form
Fabric: FS:Neo/1. Colour: grey throughout

P32*,P33,P34 Four rim sherds and seven body sherds of one vessel (two conjoining) with a simple, inturned, rounded to pointed rim (A3a/b). Some of the sherds appear to be decorated, although P34 in a random fashion. The decoration includes wide shallow grooves (P32), shallow impressions (P32, P33), and what appear to be fingernail impressions (P34), although these are indistinct
Fabric: S:Neo/1. Colour: exterior dark grey; core dark grey; interior grey-brown

P35* Single rim sherd of a bowl with a simple, upright, rounded (A2a) rim
Fabric: FS:Neo/1. Colour: exterior grey (immediately below the rim), orange; core black; interior grey

P36* Single rim sherd of a cup or small bowl with a rolled-over, everted, rounded rim
Fabric: FS:Neo/1. Colour: exterior pale brown; core dark grey; interior dark grey

P37* Two rim sherds of a cup or small bowl with a simple, upright, pointed rim (A2b)
Fabric: FS:1. Colour: exterior brown, grey-brown; core black, grey; interior grey, dark grey

P38* Single rim sherd of cup or bowl. The angle of the rim is uncertain
Fabric: S:Neo/1. Colour: exterior orange; core black; interior orange

P39* One rim sherd and six plain body sherds of a cup or bowl with a simple, upright, rounded rim (A2a)
Fabric: CFS:Neo/1. Colour: orange throughout

P40* Single rim sherd of a cup or bowl. The angle of the rim is uncertain
Fabric: FS:Neo/1. Colour: exterior grey; core black; interior grey

P41* Two rim sherds and three plain body sherds of a cup or bowl. The rim angle is uncertain. The rim interior has a flattened, bevel-like appearance which may be an accidental feature
Fabric: S:Neo/1. Colour: exterior orange, but with a black band running below, and parallel to, the rim

P42* Two conjoining rim sherds of a cup or small bowl with a simple, inturned, rounded rim (A3a)
Fabric: S:Neo/1. Colour: exterior orange-brown; core obscured; interior grey

P43 One small body sherd with rounded impressions
Fabric: S:Neo/1. Colour: dark grey throughout

P44 One body sherd with elongated impressions
Fabric: FS:Neo/1. Colour: exterior red-brown; core and interior dark grey

P45 One sherd from the concave neck of vessel, probably that represented by P16 and P17. Approximately half of a pre-firing perforation survives
Fabric: FS:Neo/1. Colour: exterior pale orange; core and interior pale grey

P46 Carinated sherd with cuneiform impressions
Fabric: FS:Neo/1. Colour: exterior and core dark grey; interior obscured

P49 Carinated sherd
Fabric: FS:Neo/1. Colour: pale orange throughout

P50 Carinated sherd
Fabric: FS:Neo/1. Colour: dark grey throughout

P51 Carinated sherd
Fabric: FS:Neo/1. Colour: dark grey throughout

P52 Sherd, with a well-defined carination; almost certainly part of the same vessel as P16, P17, and P45
Fabric: FS:Neo/1, but at the fine end of the range. Colour: exterior orange; core grey; interior pale orange. All the sherds of this vessel (ie P16, P17, and P45) show well-oxidised and evenly-oxidised surfaces.

Other pottery

Only a very few sherds, none of which were from the primary fill, were not of earlier Neolithic date. Two sherds are illustrated:

P47 Context 2231. Plain rim sherd, probably from a Beaker
Fabric: GS:Indet/1 Colour: exterior orange-red; core black; interior orange-red

P48 Context 2105. Plain, flat-topped rim sherd, probably of the Deverel-Rimbury tradition
Fabric: FfeS:DR/1. Colour: exterior pale brown; core black; interior pale brown

In addition, four Beaker sherds (none illustrated) were recovered from the upper fills of the pit:

Sherd from just above the junction of base and body wall of a Beaker; decorated with one row of rectangular-toothed comb impressions
Fabric: GS:Bkr/1. Colour: exterior and interior orange; core obscured

Body sherd of a Beaker with very worn parallel lines of comb impression
Fabric: S:Bkr/1. Colour: exterior orange; core dark grey; interior: pale orange

Two small body sherds with very worn comb impressions
Fabric: FGS:Bkr/1. Colour: exterior pale brown; core black; interior pale brown

Other plain body sherds in non-Neolithic fabrics are included by count only in Table 10.

The Beaker sherds are not datable, except that they are unlikely to be very early in the Beaker series as they are comb-impressed rather than cord-impressed. Their presence in the upper fill of the Coneybury 'Anomaly' may be connected with the Beaker associated activity represented in the immediately adjacent pit 2115 and in the nearby terminal of the henge ditch (this vol, 4.9 c).

4.1 d *Animal bones*

by Mark Maltby

A total of 2110 animal bone fragments were recorded from this feature. The species represented by the 2107 fragments positively located to context are shown in Tables 16 and 17.

Table 16 W2 (1981) Coneybury 'Anomaly': animal species represented in primary deposits

Species	*Context* 2235	2247	2248	2516	2517	2518
Cattle	10	20	3	24	29	4
Pig	–	2	–	–	–	–
Red deer	–	2	–	–	2	–
Roe deer	5	35	–	5	32	2
Beaver	–	1	–	–	1	–
Unidentified large mammal	7	16	12	10	24	3
Sheep-sized mammal	8	16	1	45	31	2
Unidentified mammal	13	59	2	75	32	2
Fish (brown trout)	–	–	–	11	–	–
Total	43	151	18	170	151	14

Species	2519	2520	2536	2538	2539	*Total*
Cattle	4	1	4	336	15	450
Pig	–	–	–	17	–	19
Red deer	–	–	–	17	–	21
Roe deer	8	1	5	194	17	304
Beaver	–	–	–	–	–	22
Fish (brown trout)	–	–	–	–	–	11
Unidentified large mammal	2	–	1	149	10	234
Sheep-sized mammal	3	–	1	128	15	251
Unidentified mammal	5	3	4	192	16	403
Total	22	5	16	1052	73	1715

The majority of the faunal assemblage (1715 fragments) was recovered from the primary deposit where a dense accumulation of extremely well-preserved bones was located. Only 60 of the 1715 fragments were slightly eroded. There was evidence of canid gnawing on 32 fragments and 125 fragments displayed various degrees of burning.

Cattle and roe deer bones dominated the assemblage, with pig, red deer, and beaver represented in small numbers. At least one fish was also represented. Sheep-sized and large mammal fragments were roughly equally represented amongst the unidentified fragments. The vast majority of these probably also belonged to roe deer and cattle respectively.

Table 17 W2 (1981) Coneybury 'Anomaly': animal species represented in upper fills

Species	*Total*
Cattle	94
Sheep/goat	2
Pig	7
Red deer	6
Roe deer	18
Beaver	3
Unidentified large mammal	123
Sheep-sized mammal	53
Unidentified mammal	87
Total	393

The excavation of the primary deposit was carried out extremely carefully and involved three-dimensional recording of all identified finds. Most of the remainder of the bones were recovered by dry-sieving through a 4mm mesh and in addition sub-samples of approximately 10 litres were wet-sieved through a 1mm mesh. These, from contexts 2247, 2516, and 2538, produced 253 fragments of bone, of which 142 were small unidentified mammal fragments, many of them burnt. A further 57 sheep-sized mammal and 17 large mammal fragments were not identifiable to species. Those which were identifiable belonged to cattle (20 fragments), roe deer (4 fragments), beaver (2 fragments), and fish (11 fragments). The sieving programme can therefore be demonstrated as having increased the number of recorded species, since these were the only fish bones represented in the deposits. However, in general, the results from the wet-sieving did not add greatly to the information obtained from the 4mm dry-sieving.

Cattle

Cattle fragments were the most commonly identified in the primary deposits. The bones represented in the cattle assemblage are listed in Table 18 and consist almost entirely of bones from the head and neck or from the limb extremities. The sample was dominated by skull fragments, mandibles, cervical vertebrae, metapodia, and phalanges. The upper limb bones, ribs, and other vertebrae were rarely encountered. Carpals and some of the tarsals were slightly more common.

This assemblage is a classic example of the disposal of cattle primary butchery waste. Bones with little meat value were dumped, whereas the major meat-bearing bones were taken away for further processing and consumption. The impression gained during the excavation was that the primary fills were formed over a short period of time. It is possible, therefore, that these cattle bones were dumped in one butchery episode. It is thus important to estimate how many animals were butchered in this manner to form some impression of the scale of the processing activity.

Table 19 gives the minimum number of cattle represented by each bone in the primary deposits. The calculations were made by taking the side of the body,

Table 18 W2 (1981) Coneybury 'Anomaly': fragments of cattle represented

	Context			
Cattle	*2538*	*Other primary*	*Upper fills*	*Total*
Skull fragments	75(19)	34	14	123
Mandible	31	5	10	46
Hyoid	6	–	–	6
Loose teeth	23(2)	16	25(2)	64
Scapula	2(1)	4	2	8
Humerus	–	1	5	6
Radius	–	1	–	1
Ulna	–	1	–	1
Os Coxae	3	2	1	6
Femur	3	1	3	7
Tibia	5	–	1	6
Carpals	5	–	2	7
Calcaneus	1	–	1	2
Astragalus	1	–	3	4
Centroquartal	2	1	1	4
Other tarsals	4	1	–	5
Metacarpal	24	2	6	32
Metatarsal	28(1)	3	4	35
Metapodial	7	6	3	16
1st Phalanx	30(1)	6	1	37
2nd Phalanx	25(1)	5	1	31
3rd Phalanx	22(2)	6	1	29
Sesamoids	8	4(1)	–	12
Ribs	1	3	–	4
Cervical vertebrae	25(1)	9	8	42
Thoracic vertebrae	5	2(1)	2	9
Lumbar vertebrae	–	1	–	1
Total	363(18)	114(2)	94(2)	544

( ) number from 1mm wet-sieved samples

Table 19 W2 (1981) Coneybury 'Anomaly': minimum number of cattle elements in primary deposits

	Neonatal	*Immature*	*Adult*	*Immature adult*	*Total*
Skull fragments	3	3	1	–	7
Mandible	3	5	1	–	9
Hyoid	1	–	–	2	3
Scapula	1	1	–	1	3
Humerus	1	–	–	–	1
Radius	–	–	–	1	1
Ulna	1	–	–	–	1
Os Coxae	1	1	–	1	3
Femur	1	–	–	1	2
Tibia	1	–	1	1	3
Carpals	1	–	–	1	2
Calcaneus	–	–	1	–	1
Astragalus	–	–	–	1	1
Centroquartal	1	–	–	1	2
Other tarsals	1	–	–	1	2
Metacarpal	2	4	–	3	9
Metatarsal	3	2	–	2	7
Metapodial	1	1	–	–	2
1st Phalanx	2	1	–	2	5
2nd Phalanx	2	1	–	3	6
3rd Phalanx	2	–	–	3	5
Sesamoids	1	–	–	1	2
Ribs	1	1	–	–	2
Cervical vertebrae	1	2	–	1	4
Thoracic vertebrae	1	1	1	–	3
Lumbar vertebrae	–	–	1	–	1
Total	3	5	1	3	10

age, and the size of the bone into consideration. The various calculations showed that at least ten cattle were represented. Three of these were young calves (neonatal), five or six were immature, and one or two were adults. Although only a minimum of nine animals were represented by any individual bone, at least seven immature or adult cattle were represented by the metacarpus and, in addition, at least three neonatal animals were represented by some of the other bones. Consequently, at least ten cattle of various ages had been butchered.

It was possible to plot 232 of the cattle fragments on to the horizontal distribution plan of recorded finds. There was no clear distinction between the distribution of bones from the head and neck and those from the feet, nor between bones of calves and older cattle. In several instances, however, there were several groups of bones located in close proximity which probably belonged to the same animal. Several of the skull fragments and phalanges were probably still attached to each other when originally deposited in the pit. The recovery of a large number of unfused epiphyses together with their diaphyses also suggests that these may still have been joined together by gristle when dumped.

Ageing data were obtained from the study of mandibular toothwear and epiphyseal fusion data. In addition, bones of young calves could be recognised by their porosity and these were duly recorded. Table 20 (MF1 A9) shows the epiphysial fusion and the porosity data for the limb bones. The results confirm that at least three young calves were represented by the very porous bones. Many of the phalanges, however, belonged to older animals, since their proximal epiphyses, which fuse between 15 and 24 months (Grigson 1982a), were fusing or had fused. The distal metapodia were, unusually, still unfused. These are generally thought to fuse between 24 and 36 months, although the age varies owing to a variety of factors. At least three animals, however, had reached this stage of development, since the distal epiphyses of their metacarpi had fused.

There was evidence of tooth eruption wear on 13 mandibles (Table 21, MF1 A10). Six or possibly eight of these mandibles could be paired with each other and may have belonged to the same animals. Four mandibles from at least two cattle had none of the deciduous premolars fully erupted whilst the first molar was unerupted. These belonged to calves that were probably less than a month old (Higham 1967). Two other mandibles had the first molar only in an early stage of wear and belonged to animals perhaps about a year old. Six other mandibles belonged to older, although still immature, cattle. These still had their deciduous premolars in wear. In one specimen, the second molar was in an early stage of wear but the third molar was unerupted. These may have belonged to animals under 16 months of age (Higham 1967). Only one specimen had a fully developed toothrow and this belonged to quite an old animal, judging by the wear patterns on the teeth. The dominance of immature animals supports the epiphyseal fusion evidence.

A total of 22 of the cattle bones bore evidence of butchery in the form of fine cuts made with a sharp blade (Table 22, MF1 A11). Most examples were found near the proximal articulation of the first phalanx.

These were produced during the disarticulation of the phalanges from the distal metapodia. The presence of cuts on the medial surfaces of three of these phalanges indicates that the toes were carefully separated from the metapodia. At the other end of the metapodia, cuts on three tarsals and near the proximal articulation of a metacarpus and a metatarsus indicate how these bones were detached from the upper limbs.

Cuts on the skull fragments may be indicative of filleting, although skinning marks cannot be ruled out. A calf's mandible bore cuts on the lateral aspect of the ramus. An os coxae had cuts inflicted during the detachment of the femur from the pelvis. A radius had knife cuts on its posterior aspect near the proximal articulation. These were probably associated with the separation of bones at the radio-cubitus joint. A rib and a thoracic vertebra bore cuts near their attachments, indicating how the ribcage was separated from the vertebrae.

Further evidence for the treatment of cattle carcases can be gleaned from the study of the fragmentation pattern of the metapodia (Table 23, MF1 A12). Only two (belonging to young calves) were complete. Most of the rest appear to have been deliberately broken. The metatarsi tended to be more fragmented than the metacarpi. The breakage pattern, however, appears to have been quite consistent. One side of the shaft appears to have been struck by, or hit against, a sharp edge to crack open the bone, which was then twisted apart. This would have enabled the marrow to be removed. This process may have been done in association with fire. Seven of the metacarpi and two of the metatarsi fragments bore evidence of burning. Bones processed for marrow are often heated to facilitate the operation (Binford 1981, 148). The high fragmentation of the skulls would also suggest that these had been broken open to remove the brain for food.

Some of the fragmentation of the limb bones can be explained by carnivore scavenging. Twenty-four cattle fragments (mostly metapodia and phalanges) bore gnawing marks and a few bones may have been totally destroyed by such activity.

Measurements were taken where possible, although the high frequency of immature animals limited the scope for metrical analysis (Table 24, MF1 A13). All the bones belonged to animals of domestic cattle of a similarly large size to those represented on other Early Neolithic sites in southern England.

Roe deer

The 304 fragments identified to this species are shown in Table 25. A much more balanced representation of the different skeletal elements was encountered. The minimum number of animals represented by each element is given in Table 26. At least seven animals were represented by the radii and tibiae, six by the mandibles, and four by the humeri. Most of the other bones belonged to at least two or three animals. Context 2247 produced two sets of lumbar and some thoracic vertebrae and ribs, which formed two articulated groups. In addition to these, several sets of phalanges and tarsals seem to have been dumped in articulation, as were some of the major limb bones.

Table 25 W2 (1981) Coneybury 'Anomaly' : fragments of roe deer represented

Roe deer	*2538*	*Other primary*	*Upper fills*	*Total*
Skull fragments	15	7	1	32
Mandible	6	5	1	12
Hyoid	5	–	–	5
Loose teeth	14(1)	3	4	21
Scapula	3	3	1	7
Humerus	3	2	1	6
Radius	11	4	1	16
Ulna	8(1)	2	–	10
Os Coxae	3	2	3	8
Femur	4	3	–	7
Patella	2	–	–	2
Tibia	9	1	–	10
Carpals	9	4	–	13
Calcaneus	2	1	–	3
Astragalus	2	–	–	2
Centroquartal	4	1	–	5
Other tarsals	2	1	–	3
Metacarpal	9	1	–	10
Metatarsal	10(1)	5	4	19
Lateral Metapodial	2	1	–	3
Metapodial	4	–	–	4
1st Phalanx	11(1)	5	2	18
2nd Phalanx	9	4	1	14
3rd Phalanx	5	4	–	9
Ribs	27	13	–	40
Cervical vertebrae	11	3	–	14
Thoracic vertebrae	4	17	–	21
Lumbar vertebrae	–	15	–	15
Sacrum	–	1	–	1
Total	194(4)	110	19	323

( ) number of fragments found in 1mm wet-sieved samples

Table 26 W2 (1981) Coneybury 'Anomaly' : minimum number of elements of other species in primary deposits

	Pig	*Red deer*	*Roe deer*	*Beaver*
Skull fragments	1	1	3	1
Antler	–	1	–	–
Mandible	1	1	6	–
Hyoid	–	–	2	–
Scapula	–	–	2	1
Humerus	–	–	4	1
Radius	–	–	7	2
Ulna	–	–	5	1
Os Coxae	–	–	2	–
Femur	–	–	2	2
Patella	–	–	1	–
Tibia	2	–	7	2
Fibula	1	–	–	–
Carpals	–	–	2	–
Calcaneus	–	–	3	1
Astragalus	–	–	2	–
Centroquartal	–	–	3	–
Other tarsals	–	–	2	–
Metacarpal	1	1	2	–
Metatarsal	–	–	3	–
Lateral Metapodial	–	–	1	–
Metapodial	–	1	1	–
1st Phalanx	–	2	2	1
2nd Phalanx	–	2	2	–
3rd Phalanx	–	–	2	–
Ribs	–	–	3	1
Cervical vertebrae	1	–	2	1
Thoracic vertebrae	–	–	2	–
Lumbar vertebrae	1	–	3	–
Sacrum	–	–	1	–
Total	2	2	7	2

Most of the roe deer bones represented belonged to skeletally mature animals. Table 27 (MF1 A14) shows the epiphysial fusion data with nearly all the surviving articular surfaces of limb bones and phalanges fused. In addition, at least four very young roe deer were represented by porous bones. However, only the radii and tibiae produced more than one porous specimen.

The mandibular tooth eruption data (Table 28, MF1 B1) revealed that at least one roe deer had a fully erupted toothrow. Two other mandibles which had their permanent premolars erupted but not in wear may have belonged to animals aged between 12 and 15 months. Two others had the deciduous premolars in an early stage of wear and at least one of these specimens had an unerupted first molar. These belonged to animals under six months old.

Twenty roe deer bones bore cut marks (Table 22, MF1 A11). Cuts on the anterior surfaces of the carpals, metacarpus, and centroquartals were made during the disarticulation of the feet from the upper limb bones. Marks on the distal humeri and proximal ulna and radii were associated with the disarticulation of the radio-cubitus joint. Cuts on the distal scapula revealed how this was disarticulated from the proximal humerus. Two mandibles bore cuts on the lateral aspect of the ramus, probably associated with the disarticulation of these bones from the skull. A thoracic vertebra had cuts on its articulating surface with the rib made during the separation of these two bones. The butchery evidence indicated that the skeletons had been disarticulated in a systematic manner and, although no evidence for the filleting of meat from the bones was found, such procedures need not have left any trace. Most of the limb bones, however, appear to have been broken open for marrow. Few bones bore canid gnawing marks.

Other species

Red deer (*Cervus elaphus*) was represented by 21 fragments in the primary deposits. These belonged to at least two animals (Table 26). A very young calf was represented by two unworn deciduous premolars, three porous phalanges, and a mandible, in which the deciduous premolars were erupted but not in wear. An older animal (or animals) was represented by two fragments of metacarpus, five phalanges, and four skull fragments, three of which definitely belonged to the same skull. In addition, there were two substantial fragments of antler, which may have been associated with the digging of the pit. The red deer assemblage therefore resembled that of the cattle, since only head and feet bones were represented.

At least two immature beavers (*Castor fiber*) were represented by 22 fragments in the primary deposits (Table 26). Wet-sieving (1mm) produced the calcined remains of a third phalanx. Two animals were represented by the radius, femur, and tibia. No evidence of butchery marks was found on any of the bones, most of which were found in a relatively complete state.

Only 19 pig fragments were recovered, representing a minimum of two animals. One newborn (or possibly foetal) pig was represented by a tibia while the other bones could have belonged to a single, older, but still immature animal. These consisted of three skull fragments, two mandible fragments, five loose teeth, two cervical and one lumbar vertebrae, two fragments of the same tibia, two fibulae fragments, and part of a metacarpal. One of the mandible fragments articulated with a maxilla. These still possessed their deciduous molars and had only the first of the molars in wear. The second molars were unerupted. These bones belonged to an animal probably under a year old (Bull and Payne 1982).

A fish vertebra recovered from 1mm wet-sieving was a good match for a brown trout (*Salmo trutta*) of about 0.3m length. The other fragments of fish could have belonged to the same species and, indeed, the same fish.

The unidentifiable bones included a large number of small skull fragments of large mammal, probably belonging to cattle.

The upper pit fills

The species represented by the 393 fragments recorded in these levels are shown in Table 17. The sample was much less well preserved, with a high proportion of eroded fragments (178). The sample was dominated by cattle fragments (Table 18) of which 27% consisted of loose teeth, an indication of the poorer state of preservation of the assemblage. There was still a bias towards bones of the head, neck, and feet, but the fills also included bones from other parts of the skeleton. Two humeri fragments, a first phalanx, an astragalus, and a fragment of pelvis belonged to animals the size of aurochs (*Bos primigenius*). The remainder of the bones were of a similar size to those of the domestic cattle found in the primary deposits. One humerus in 2254 was charred in a similar manner to the specimens of humeri and radii found in the terminal ditch of the henge (Maltby, this vol, 4.9 d).

Only 18 fragments of roe deer (Table 17) were identified in the upper fills. Pig was represented by seven fragments (three loose teeth, two humeri, a scapula, and an ulna), red deer by six fragments (a mandible, an antler tine, a scapula, two first phalanges, and a third phalanx), beaver by two teeth and a first phalanx, and sheep by fragments of a radius and a metacarpus. These were the only identifications of sheep in this feature.

Discussion

The faunal remains from the primary fills of this deposit are unparalleled in Britain. They appear to represent a major butchery episode, in which at least ten cattle and several roe deer of varying ages were butchered. At least one pig and two red deer carcases were processed at about the same time.

The cattle were from domestic stock and the cull included at least three calves and two or three other immature animals. It is clear that their carcases were heavily exploited, with the metapodia showing clear evidence of systematic marrow extraction. The major meat-bearing bones must have been taken for consumption elsewhere. Although chronologically distinct, the bones from the upper layers of the ditch terminal at the adjacent Coneybury Henge (Maltby, this vol, 4.9 d) represent evidence for the same process which resulted in the spatial separation of different parts of cattle carcases.

The deer appear to have been butchered at the same time as the cattle. Unless the animals were killed nearby, people must have been prepared to carry their carcases to this site for processing. The beavers and the trout may have been caught in the nearby River Avon.

The roe deer assemblage did differ from those of cattle and red deer in that more of the major meat-bearing bones were represented. It is possible that these bones represent the remains of meat consumed immediately after butchery, whereas the dressed cattle and red deer carcases were either taken away for consumption elsewhere or were preserved (possibly by smoking) for later consumption.

If most of the meat was destined for immediate consumption, it implies that it was supposed to cater for a large gathering and could be evidence for the preparation of a major feast nearby. The presence of relatively large numbers of cattle major meat-bearing bones in the later henge ditch suggests that the site may have been the focus for such feasts and gatherings over a considerable period of time. The presence of the young calves of cattle, red deer, and roe deer would suggest that the butchery episode may have taken place during the summer months, assuming these animals were born in the spring.

The most remarkable aspect of the species represented in this feature is that, although domestic cattle would have provided the bulk of the meat, wild animals form a significant proportion of the assemblage. Sheep were not represented at all in the primary deposits and were probably not kept in the area at that time. Only one young pig was represented and it is not clear whether this was a wild or domestic animal. Beaver and trout were the other wild species exploited, although the former may have been processed for their skins only.

The colluvial fills probably contained some material that was associated with this major butchery event but was not immediately buried. This would explain the continued bias amongst the cattle assemblage towards bones of the head, neck, and the limb extremities, and the presence of most of the roe deer, red deer, and beaver bones. However, these upper fills also included bones that were incorporated into the deposits over a considerable period of time. These include bones of aurochs and sheep which were not present in the primary fills, and also some of the other pig and cattle bones.

4.2 W83: interim report on the excavation of an Early Neolithic flint scatter at Robin Hood's Ball

4.2 a Site description

Intensive surface collection within an area of formerly unploughed downland adjacent to the causewayed enclosure of Robin Hood's Ball (located on Fig 34) produced considerable quantities of both worked flint and prehistoric pottery. The preliminary analysis of the surface artefact collections demonstrated clear patterning, one of the strongest elements of which was a cluster of flint scrapers only 30m beyond the ditch of the causewayed enclosure. Excavation in 1984 of the 10m by 10m sample square within which the main scraper concentration had been recorded, and in 1986 of an adjacent area of undisturbed grassland, revealed a roughly circular cluster of shallow pits (W83). Within the area enclosed by the pits were over 200 flint scrapers, associated with leaf-shaped arrowheads and considerable quantities of worked flint.

The pits contained small quantities of pottery belonging to the South-Western style, and at least one decorated rim, probably of the Abingdon sub-style of the Windmill Hill tradition. Animal bone samples from two pits produced radiocarbon dates of 3640–3370 BC (OxA 1400) and 3361–3039 BC (OxA 1401).

The worked flint and animal bone from the five pits excavated during the first season have been examined in order to provide comparative samples for the material recovered from W2 (1981), the Coneybury 'Anomaly' (this vol, 4.1).

Discussion

The preliminary assessment of material from W83 suggests that the activity recovered was of a sedentary nature, both artefacts and associated geochemical data suggesting a consistent focus defined by the cluster of small pits. The emphasis on domestic animals and the proportionally low blade component within the analysed flint industry offer further confirmation of the stable nature of the recovered activity.

4.2 b Lithics

by Philip Harding

This report details the analysis of the worked flint from the pits excavated in 1984, material examined in order to provide a comparative sample to that from W2 (1981). Subsequent excavation at W83 has provided additional stratified pit groups together with associated horizontal deposits which will be analysed and published in a subsequent report (Richards in prep a).

The quantity of material from the five stratified pits is shown in Table 116. The analysis of the pit contents has included material from the upper fills which, in pits 108 and 114, forms the largest population by weight of material. There is no reason to believe that the upper pit fills are seriously contaminated by later material.

Refitting within this assemblage has been of limited success, but has confirmed that knapping took place on site and has shown some relationship between individual deposits within the filling sequence of pit 102. The limited quantity of material and the absence of distinctive raw materials makes recognition of individual deposits within features difficult.

i Recovery and condition

The features were excavated manually. Flints were recorded by context except for recognised tools which were recorded in three dimensions. All stratified deposits were dry-sieved through 4mm mesh and smaller (12–15 litre) samples were wet-sieved through 1mm mesh.

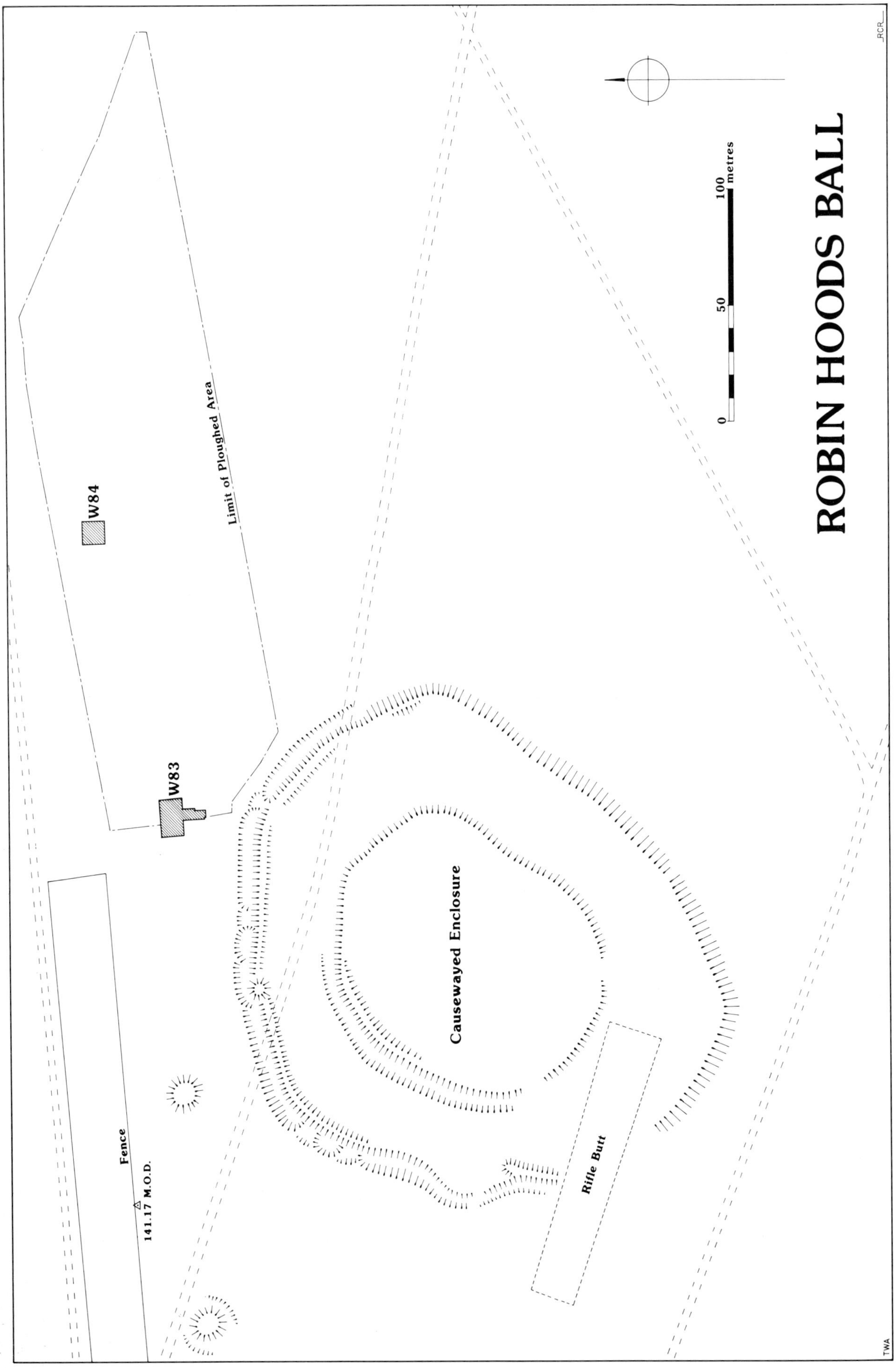

Fig 34 Robin Hood's Ball causewayed enclosure: location of areas of recent survey and excavation (W83, W84)

Flint from primary pit contexts was in mint condition with a light blue/grey patina. Material from the upper pit fills was in mint/sharp condition with a white patina. Patches of calcium carbonate concretion from groundwater precipitation were deposited on flint from all contexts, particularly those from primary positions.

ii Raw material

Nodules of flint from the local chalk appear to have been used as raw material. They are irregular, rounded, or subangular in shape, weigh generally between 200 and 400g, and contain thermal fractures. The flint is dark grey to black in colour with irregular grey cherty inclusions. The hard chalky cortex which can be up to 12mm thick is often weathered following erosion from the chalk. The flint served the majority of domestic needs although the production of large core tools would not have been possible from this raw material. Ground tools, of which fragments were found at this site, were undoubtedly the product of sites with larger raw material.

Flaking was probably by direct percussion using locally available flint hammerstones. There is no evidence for imported or organic hammers.

iii The flint industry

The material is the product of a flake industry, but includes a low (12%) proportion of blades. Differences between the 'waste' and scraper blanks suggest different forms of blank production; small blanks for composite tools and large blanks for scrapers rather than the 'waste' being a by-product of a single phase of scraper blank production.

There is no evidence of core tool production or modification on site, although ground tool fragments occur in all features with the exception of pit 106. The low quantities of material present and the lack of refitting pieces suggests that the sample examined does not represent larger scale 'industrial' knapping.

Variation within the pits examined suggests some selectivity in the disposal of elements of the overall assemblage. Pit 102 has a high proportion of cores, flakes, and refitting pieces and few tools suggesting that the fill contains knapping debris, while pit 108 includes ten scrapers together with probable retouch chips near the base, but with very little knapping waste. This may represent the manufacture, use, and discard of tools, associated with a surface concentration of scrapers around this particular pit.

Cores

Twenty-six cores representing a variety of types were recovered. All, with the possible exception of one which may have produced blades, were flake cores. Most have one or two platforms including Clark's flat-faced Aii cores (J G D Clark 1960, 2, fig 10), but semi-discoidal, biconical, and multi-platform examples are also present. Refitting indicates that at least some of the flakes recovered were removed from cores found within the pits. The cores include failed pieces and those from which control has been lost as well as exhausted productive examples. The expectations of thermal flaws within the surface flint industry probably meant that raw material selection was on a relatively haphazard basis. All cores were made on thermally fractured cortical nodules except one which was made on a flake. Complete knapping sequences were not present although the indications are that systematic core preparation/shaping was limited. Suitable striking platforms were used unmodified (19%), but a higher proportion (65%) were prepared by the removal of a flake or by alternate flaking until the striking platform angle was suitable for flake production. The absence of specialised end products is accompanied by a lack of specialised core preparation techniques (*lame à crête*) or shaping. No great care was taken to orientate the direction of percussion parallel to the longest axis of the nodule, although ridges were utilised to maintain flake length for the production of smaller blanks. This was of less importance in scraper production. Striking platforms were not modified extensively although faceting chips are present as are core rejuvenation flakes. The number of cores with two (32%) or more platforms suggests that the preferred rejuvenation technique involved rotating the core and recommencing flake production from a new flaking surface or by using alternate flaking. Crested rejuvenation flakes are, however, absent.

The largest recorded flake scars on each core show that 45% lie between 40 and 49mm in length, a range within which 54% of the scrapers lie. Flint from the site was certainly large enough to provide blanks for the scrapers.

Some cores have sinuous edges indicating where percussion has been set back from the edge of the striking platform. Flakes with broad butts, similar to those found on most scrapers, are produced in this way.

The single largest contribution to core rejection is an increase in flaking angle (37%). However, only 6% also show recession of the striking platform edge, caused by continuous percussion. This suggests that there was an appreciation of the point at which the core became unworkable. Similarly the number of exhausted cores/striking platforms (8%) also suggests a fairly high standard of ability.

Flakes

Table 116 shows the total number of measured flakes, broken flakes, burnt flakes, and chips from each pit. All complete flakes were measured and were divided into broad types according to their presumed position of origin on the core (Harding forthcoming a). The majority probably result from core trimming and were produced as by-products of flake and blade production or during core preparation.

Unretouched tools may be present within the flake assemblage, although their presence and proportions cannot be quantified. Much of the flake assemblage is unsuitable for scraper blanks, as shown in Figures 149 and 150.

Overall results of the analysis are shown in Figure 149, where they are compared with those from W2 (1981). More detailed results are contained within archive. The results show a greater proportion of blades at W2 (1981) which indicates a higher standard of technology (for a discussion of other potential aspects of blade/flake variation see overall lithic discussion, Richards, this vol, 5.4). The rarity of blades, including broken pieces, reinforces the argument that they were not part of the production at W83, and that presumably flakes were used instead. This is in contrast to W2 (1981) where flakes supplemented blade production.

The flake classes, compatible with other earlier Neolithic assemblages, confirm the importance of conserving ridges at the front of the core for guiding flake length. This has a corresponding effect on breadth/length ratios. Most flakes were struck from cores worked in a single direction, with scars from right angles to the direction of percussion being present from two-platform or multi-platform cores.

Plain butts predominate (67%) while 'others' are mostly those too small to determine, the effect of percussion near the core edge. Narrow butts are consistent with other Neolithic industries and are accompanied by platform abrasion which removes overhang and strengthens the edge of the striking platform. Platform abrasion is most common in miscellaneous trimming flakes/blades at both W2 (1981) and W83, which implies its use to remove blanks once the cores were prepared. The effects of abrasion on butt width can be shown by the variation between W83 (10% abraded) and W2 (1981) (30% abraded), where butts are generally thinner. Percussion angles, which can also effect flake length, are also lower at W83 than at W2 (1981) but are broadly consistent with the Neolithic industries from the Stonehenge area. Of the measured flakes, 10.36% have plunged and 3.64% hinged distal ends. Hinged flakes are most common amongst preparation flakes, accounting for 18% within this class; 11% of broken flakes have Siret fractures (accidental breakages, Bordes 1979, fig 4.2).

Chips

With an average ratio of two chips per flake, chips appear to be under-represented. This may be an effect of sieving strategies, but may in some cases suggest that the material has been incorporated within pits as secondary rubbish. Those recovered appear to substantiate the technological conclusions already suggested. Faceting chips (Newcomer and Karlin 1987) are virtually absent, although abrasion chips, of which about 10% have abraded butts, are undoubtedly present. Retouch chips are less easy to identify but chips from pit 108 may be of this type, related to an associated deposit of scrapers.

Scrapers

The scraper population is high (average ratio of 21 flakes per scraper) compared to W2 (1981) where the primary deposit contained a ratio of 58:1. Unretouched tools, suggested at the latter site on the basis of blades and traces of microwear, are much more difficult to suggest at W83.

A total of 151 well-made scrapers were found from all contexts excavated in 1984. The 46 from the pits, of which 11 are from upper fills, form 69% of the stratified retouched component and as such maintain the dominance of scrapers in Neolithic assemblages. Scrapers are made on flakes with a slightly dipping profile, although plunged flakes are generally avoided. Three are made on fragments, ten on flakes with no butt, and one is burnt. Results of analysis of blank form from 116 scrapers are shown in Figure 150 and indicate a well-defined selection of blanks. Sixty-nine per cent are between 40 and 59mm long, 72% are between 40 and 59mm broad, and 92% are over 10mm thick, a selection of broad thick blanks. Thickness appears to be particularly important towards the distal end. The blanks have less well ridged dorsal surfaces which can be produced by maintaining a flatter flaking surface to the core and placing the point of percussion well on to the striking platform (see butt width, Fig 149). Flakes with abraded butts are therefore rare. Suitable flakes are scarce amongst the waste flakes, with only 19% of waste flakes lying within one standard deviation of the mean for two or more measured attributes of scraper length, breadth, and thickness. This compares with 81% of scrapers with zero or one failed attribute.

Core preparation flakes (24%) and side trimming flakes (40%) are shown to be more suited for scraper selection than miscellaneous trimming flakes (22%). However, squat, thick, 'miscellaneous trimming' and 'miscellaneous trimming blanks' (31%) were also produced with broad butts for scrapers. They share few characteristics with the shorter, thinner, elongated, miscellaneous trimming waste flakes which argues for an independent scraper blank production. Although surface material has not been examined in sufficient detail to determine the presence of such blanks, their absence from the pits may suggest their production off site.

Retouch

The highest proportion (93%) of blanks were modified by direct retouch. Figure 151 shows the distribution of retouch on 106 examples of end scrapers. This shows that the majority occur around the distal end, but that retouch extends more frequently on to the right edge of the flake than the left. This may be related to the scraper being drawn towards a right-handed user. Additional retouch is rare and is generally limited to simple modification of the butt. Figure 151 also shows the relationship of scraper blade length to scraper blade angle. The scraper blades normally range from 30–55mm in length and are retouched at a relatively low angle (65–75 degrees) into a regular convex edge. This minimises the occurrence of scrapers with undercut edges. Cortical scraping edges are present. Scrapers replicated in experiments show that similar retouch can be achieved by low angle direct percussion using a flint hammerstone.

No refitting retouch chips were found; however, chips found with scrapers in the primary fill of pit 108 seem likely to represent retouching/resharpening activities. No scrapers with worn scraping edges were observed.

Details of the remaining 28 retouched pieces which include two leaf arrowheads, one fabricator, and four ground flint tool fragments are contained within the archive. This material will be discussed within the final report (Richards in prep a).

Table 29 W83 Robin Hood's Ball: animal species represented by context

Species	*Topsoil*	*Pit 102*	*Pit 104*	*Pit 106*	*Pit 108*	*Pit 114*	*Other*	*Total*
Cattle	3	2	2	1	3	11	1	23
Sheep/goat	–	–	–	–	2	1	–	3
Pig	–	7	1	–	–	–	–	8
Unidentified large mammal	1	3	–	–	2	6	1	13
Sheep-sized mammal	–	1	–	–	–	–	–	1
Unidentified mammal	1	14	–	–	6	3	1	25
Total	5	27	3	1	13	21	3	73

4.2 c Animal bones

by Mark Maltby

A total of 73 animal bone fragments were recovered from the 1984 excavation, from both the topsoil and five pits (Table 29). These totals include 22 fragments recovered from 1mm sieved samples. Twelve of those could only be assigned to the unidentifiable mammal category and four belonged to unidentified large mammal. The sieving programme produced three identifiable fragments of pig, two of sheep/goat, and one of cattle.

Cattle fragments were found in small numbers in all of the pits. The cattle sample consisted of 12 loose teeth fragments, a radius, two metacarpi, two metatarsi, a first and third phalanx, a proximal sesamoid, and a lumbar and two cervical vertebrae fragments. Pit 114 produced all but two of the postcranial fragments. The sparse ageing evidence indicated that immature cattle were represented. The distal articulations of one of the metacarpi and one of the metatarsi were both unfused and thus belonged to animals probably under three years of age (Silver 1969). The third phalanx was porous and belonged to a young calf, as did a deciduous fourth premolar which was only just coming into wear. On the other hand, older cattle were represented by the fused lumbar vertebrae, some of the teeth, and a metacarpus with a fused distal epiphysis.

Measurements were possible on three cattle bones. The radius had a maximum proximal breadth of 76.6mm, a metacarpus had a maximum distal breadth of 62.8mm, and the first phalanx had a maximum length of 59.2mm. These all fell within the range of measurements obtained for large domestic cattle found in other Neolithic assemblages in southern England.

Sheep/goat was represented in two of the pits. Two fragments of loose teeth were recovered in a sieved sample from pit 108 and pit 114 included a shaft fragment of a metacarpus, the slenderness of which indicated that the bone probably belonged to sheep rather than goat. All but one of the pig fragments were found in pit 102 and included at least four bones from the same animal. The proximal portions of a third and a fourth metatarsal were found in association. A sieved sample from the same context produced two of the tarsals that articulated with the metatarsals. Context 176 produced the distal half of the fourth metatarsal. This articulation was unfused and the bones belonged to an immature animal. The rest of the pig assemblage consisted of teeth fragments. A lower third molar in an early stage of wear had a length of 36.5mm. This was within the size range usually attributed to domestic pig rather than to wild boar.

The assemblage as a whole was poorly preserved. A total of 32 fragments consisted of loose teeth fragments, several not identifiable to species, and all but one of the other fragments had surface erosion which was moderate or severe in most instances. The cattle first phalanx bore evidence of gnawing, possibly by a dog. Four small fragments (three from sieved samples) had been burnt.

4.3 Neolithic pits on the King Barrow Ridge and Vespasian's Ridge

4.3 a An Early Neolithic pit on the King Barrow Ridge

The material from the pit under consideration was recovered by F de M Vatcher in the course of a watching brief carried out on the route of the A303 improvement in 1967.

The finds were contained within one box and there was no associated written or photographic archive. The position of the pit was recorded on the finds bags and labels and is consistently referred to as 'South of the A303, cut by road ditch, located approximately 100x west of the New King Barrow Wood'. If the distance is 100 yards then the position of the pit can be located with some precision at SU 13324198. No dimensions are given although the maximum depth recorded on individual finds labels is 0.90m. From this information it appears that the pottery was consistently at a lower level than the small number of flints that were recorded. There is no information for the location within the pit of the associated bone.

The finds

Five pieces of worked flint were recovered. The fact that two of these are scrapers suggests that some selectivity may have taken place. One end scraper is made on a thick cortical flake showing signs of bulb removal. The other is a side/end scraper made on a partly cortical flake.

The prehistoric pottery

by Rosamund Cleal

A minimum of five vessels are represented, all but one of which are certainly or probably of earlier Neolithic date (Fig 35).

Vessel 1: represented by the two body sherds of fabric FFeS: Indet/1 and possibly by one additional sherd which, although it seems to lack iron oxides, has a distinctive colouring which is very similar to the other sherds. Probably earlier Neolithic.

Vessel 2: represented by a sherd with a lug (P55). Although the sherd is in the common fabric FS:Neo/1, the vessel is of much finer quality than the rest of the sherds in that fabric. Certainly earlier Neolithic.

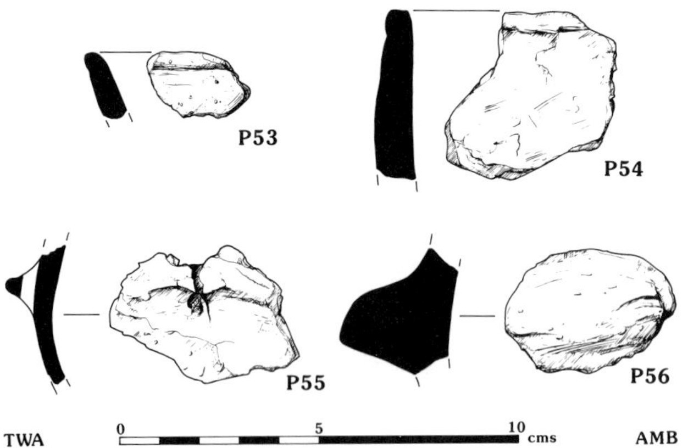

Fig 35 King Barrow Ridge earlier Neolithic pit: prehistoric pottery (P53–P56)

Vessel 3: represented by three body sherds in fabric S:Indet/1. The small plain rim (P53) probably also belongs to this vessel. Probably earlier Neolithic.

Vessel 4: represented by the plain rim (P54) in fabric FS:Neo/1 and probably also by two body sherds, one of which is large. Probably earlier Neolithic.

Vessel 5: represented by one plain body sherd in fabric S:Indet/1.

The lug (P56) could possibly belong to vessel 4.

The assemblage is small and fragmentary, but can be placed within the South-Western regional style on the basis of lack of decoration, lack of heavy rims (and presence of simple, unthickened rims), and the occurrence of the two lugs. Solid oval lugs such as P56 are a common feature of the large South-Western assemblage from Maiden Castle, Dorset (Wheeler 1943). Although vertically perforated lugs are not common in that assemblage, a broadly similar lug to that of vessel 2 (P55) does occur at W2 (1981) the Coneybury 'Anomaly', a clearly South-Western style site only 400m to the south-east (Cleal, this vol, 4.1 c). The fabrics of the pottery from the King Barrow Ridge pit also resemble those from the Coneybury 'Anomaly' assemblage, although FS:Neo/1 does vary considerably in frequency of inclusions, even within single vessels. Even fabric FFeS:Indet /1 here might be encompassed within fabric FS:Neo/1, as at Coneybury 'Anomaly'; iron oxides do occur in that fabric, although infrequently. Fabric S:Indet/1, however, is clearly different from the fabrics represented in the Coneybury 'Anomaly' assemblage.

Illustrated pottery (Fig 35)

P53 S:Indet/1. Small plain rim; simple, everted, rounded

P54 FS:Neo/1. Plain rim; simple, upright, rounded

P55 FS:Neo/1. Horizontally applied oval lug with a vertical perforation. The lug has broken across the perforation in antiquity. Exterior orange-brown, dark grey (over lug surface); interior pale grey-brown

P56 FS:Neo/1. Large horizontally applied oval lug, unperforated. Orange surfaces, grey core

Fabrics

FFeS:Indet/1. Soft fabric with moderate flint (mm), sparse iron oxides (small rounded grains mm), and common to abundant coarse sand

FS:Neo/1. As in W2 (1981) type series

S:Indet/1. Hard but brittle fabric with abundant coarse sand

Animal bones
by Mark Maltby

The bone included one almost complete domestic cattle femur represented by four fragments. Several fine cuts were recorded, made during dismemberment and filleting of meat from the bone. The breakage of the bone may have been the result of marrow processing, although the evidence is not conclusive. The only other bone was a fragment of cattle thoracic vertebra.

4.3 b A Neolithic pit on Vespasian's Ridge

The material from the 'Vespasian's Ridge (?) Neolithic pit' was recovered by F de M Vatcher in the course of a watching brief carried out on the route of the A303 improvement in 1967. The material was contained within one box and there was no accompanying written or photographic archive.

The exact location of the pit is unknown, but it can be assumed to be around SU 145421, the point at which the ridge running northwards from the Iron Age hillfort of Vespasian's Camp was cut by the road. There are no records of the dimensions of the pit.

The finds

The dating evidence for the pit is provided by a broken ground flint axe (not illustrated). The axe, which is in mint condition but very patinated, is of pale flint with some cherty inclusions. Length 104mm, maximum width 52mm, maximum thickness 25mm. The edge of the axe is regularly ground and exhibits only occasional chips which may be use damage.

The pit contained nine fragments of bone, only one of which can be positively identified. This is a large cattle calcaneus in a heavily eroded state, as were the other fragments, all of which appear to be large mammal (bone identified by Mark Maltby).

4.4 W32: the sample excavation of Fargo Wood I flint scatter

4.4 a Excavation location and pre-excavation definition

Extensive surface collection north of the Stonehenge Cursus in the winter of 1980/81 (52) located a dense and well-defined linear flint scatter at grid reference SU 111433. The scatter, which initially appeared to be approximately 50m long (north–south) and 10m wide, lay on a patch of heavier clay soil. The worked flints recovered from this soil exhibited a light patina and a relatively fresh appearance. Preliminary analysis of material recovered from the first stage of surface collection, a sample of 160 pieces of worked flint from one 50m transect, identified a blade component suggesting a date in the earlier Neolithic. The possibility that Mesolithic activity might be represented was not ignored, as it was felt that extensive surface collection could not be relied upon to recover such diagnostically Mesolithic artefacts as microliths. At this preliminary stage the scatter was interpreted as an area of Early Neolithic activity, with a tool component suggesting at least a partly domestic function. The nucleated nature of the area recorded provided a strong contrast to the extensive areas of activity, assumed to be of later Neolithic date, which the project had identified during the first season of surface collection.

The scatter described above, providing a considerable contrast to that located on Wilsford Down (W31, this vol, 4.10), was selected for further evaluation as part of the first (1982) season of surface scatter excavation. Prior to excavation a detailed surface collection was carried out in spring 1982. An area of 65m by 20m (see Fig 36 for location) was subdivided into 5m squares within which all surface artefacts were collected. All flint tools identified in the field and all sherds of pottery were precisely plotted. This collection, details of which are contained within the archive, confirmed the spatial integrity of the scatter, and served to define its edges more closely, but also introduced a confusing element. Sherds of Beaker pottery and flint tools of post-Neolithic date were recovered, their distribution entirely coincident with the limits of the flint scatter. A magnetometer survey carried out by the Ancient Monuments Laboratory prior to excavation suggested only one anomaly, a possible pit (Bartlett, this vol, MF1 B6; Figs 37 and 38, MF1 B7 and B8).

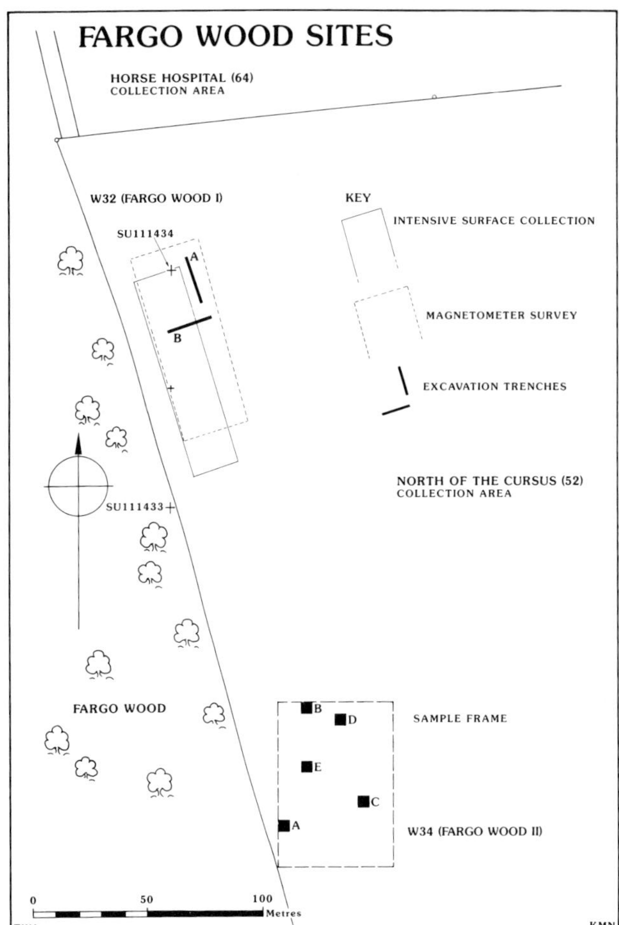

Fig 36 Fargo Wood sites: location of W32 and W34

Excavation

The initial sample transect, area B, was laid out across the long axis of the scatter and was also positioned in order to examine the one recorded magnetic anomaly. The trench, 20m by 2m, was hand excavated, the topsoil removed on a 1m grid with a 20% sample of the squares dry-sieved through 4mm mesh. The heavier nature of some of the soils encountered on this site rendered it necessary to wet-sieve some 'dirty' dry-sieved residues in order to recognise artefacts.

Some concept of the true nature of the scatter was achieved very rapidly, during the digging of the site cess pit. This was naturally dug in an area devoid of surface artefacts, in this case approximately 30m beyond the western end of area B at the edge of Fargo Wood. The sequence revealed in the pit section showed a stone-free clayey soil approximately 0.40m deep, overlying a sorted horizon (context 44 within the pit) which produced considerable quantities of worked and burnt flint together with a small quantity of prehistoric pottery. This sequence was repeated in the area excavated beyond the apparent western edge of the scatter, whereas to the east the distribution of worked flint appeared to correspond very accurately with the edge of the deeper clay soils. The linear nature of the scatter had been produced by differential plough penetration, deepest at the soil junction. The effects of this differential disturbance, recovered from the excavation of both the ploughsoil and, where located, the underlying sorted horizon, are shown graphically in Figure 39. In order to present the data as comparative histograms this figure laterally compresses data from adjacent 1m squares within the 2m wide transect.

Within area B the assemblage of artefacts included pottery of earlier Neolithic to later Bronze Age date together with considerable quantities of worked flint. This area produced over 73% of the combined flint tool total for both excavated areas, together with considerably higher levels of burnt flint.

A further trench, area A, was excavated running at right angles to that described above. This trench, again 20m by 2m, was excavated in order to examine a slight surviving element of an adjacent 'Celtic' field system (RCHME 1979, map 1). No trace of the field 'bank' apparent on the surface had survived within ploughsoil or subsoil and in contrast to the adjacent trench the soil profile was markedly more calcareous. A broadly similar range of artefacts was recovered from this trench, although a contrast is provided by the generally lower levels of worked and burnt flint and by the greater proportion of Neolithic pottery from this area.

Discussion

Prior to excavation, both initial surface collection and subsequent, more intensive work suggested that the activity under consideration had spatial, if not chrono-

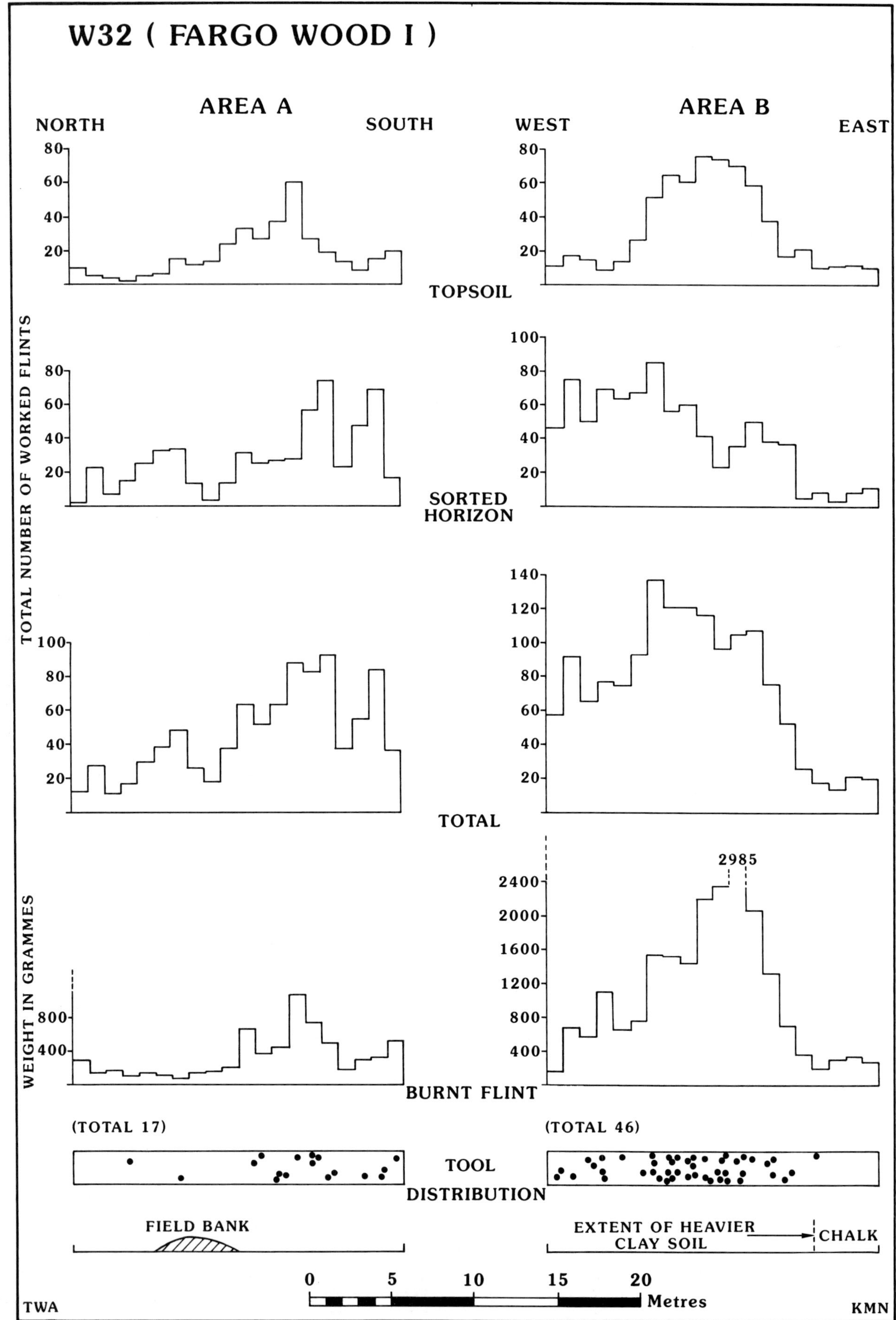

Fig 39 W32 Fargo Wood I: comparative artefact transects

logical integrity. The results of the excavation clearly demonstrate that the apparently nucleated activity is, to a certain extent, the product of differential disturbance, resulting in selective visibility of surface artefacts. However, the localised distribution of worked flints, even within a very restricted sample area, suggests that there is a positive correlation between activity and soil type. In area B the junction of the heavier clay soils and the lighter chalk soils is marked both by an identifiable physical change and by the apparent edge of a dense scatter of worked flint. The contrast is reinforced by the results from Area A, lying entirely on the lighter soils, where levels of worked flint are consistently lower than those from area B.

It is tempting to suggest that the overall nature of the activities represented by these two areas can be identified. Area A, on light soil and associated with an element of a field system, can be suggested as having a direct link with the later Bronze Age settlement immediately to the south (W34, this vol, 4.14 and Fig 37, MF1 B7). Area B, in contrast may be considered to demonstrate earlier Neolithic activity on a soil type possibly exploited as a source of flint. This suggestion is not reinforced by the ceramic evidence (Figs 40, 41, and 42). There is, however, a direct link between pottery fabrics identified from both the Fargo Wood sites (Tables 31, 32, MF1 B9–12, C1–14, and Table 103, MF2 E7–F8), perhaps adding weight to the suggestion that some of the W32 pottery may represent manuring from the settlement focus represented by W34.

It is perhaps unwise to speculate further on the nature of the activity recovered by this sample excavation. The overall sampling approach appears valid and the results, if inconclusive in the strict sense, did provide an immediate awareness of the potential variability of both preservation and consequent archaeological visibility. This awareness was of considerable value in subsequent seasons of excavation and fieldwork, and in the formulation of wider management recommendations.

4.4 b Lithics

Surface collection and excavation produced a total of 3874 pieces of worked flint. These can be considered within four broad groups: the surface collection flints, those from the two sample trenches (areas A and B), and the small group recovered from the excavation of the site cess pit. The composition of these groups is shown in Table 30.

Although, as discussed within the site report, there was some vertical separation of artefact groups within the two sample trenches, the groups of worked flint can all be considered as unstratified. Equally, although there is some variation in the composition of the two larger excavated groups, the relationship of which to recovered soil boundaries is also discussed within the site report, the proximity of the two trenches makes the examination of overall trends the most appropriate approach. Although the two trenches were closely spaced, the variation in soil type between them resulted in their respective flint groups exhibiting widely differing patination. All of the material is in mint to sharp condition but that from area A, located on a calcareous soil, is patinated pale blue to white, while that from the clay soil of area B is a dark to mid blue-grey in colour.

A stage 1 catalogue has been prepared for all the recovered material, data from which have been employed in the construction of the flint distribution profiles shown in Figure 39.

The preparation of this catalogue suggested a potentially wide date range for the material under examination. Specific tools include arrowheads of leaf type (two), petit tranchet derivative type (four), and barbed and tanged type (one). The scrapers from the whole assemblage again reflect the suggested chronological range (Riley, this vol, 5.3), with a small number of early types, the ubiquitous dominance of type 4, and a notable peak in the Beaker-associated type 7. In addition, four borers/awls, which may also be suggested as having a broadly Bronze Age association, were recovered. Despite the mixed nature of the overall assemblage, certain earlier Neolithic elements, apart from the more obvious arrowheads, can be identified from the results of the rapid assessment. The sample of 1737 complete flakes from areas A and B includes 7.8% of blade proportion (breadth:length 2.5:5), within which, and within the broken flakes, an actual (deliberately produced) blade component can be identified. However, despite the occurrence of a small number of systematic single platform cores, no specific blade cores were identified.

The raw material employed appears to be mainly chalk flint, although some larger nodules, represented by a range of unsystematic cores, may well derive from the clay soils to the south and west of the area examined. Two flakes of gravel flint were identified.

This flint assemblage, and most specifically that part of it recovered from area B, represents a potentially very small sample of what may be an extensive area of activity. This, and its demonstrably mixed nature, render inappropriate any immediate further stages of analysis.

Table 30 W32 Fargo Wood I: composition of the flint assemblage

	Cores		*Flakes*				*Scrapers*	*Other tools*	*Total*
	complete	*fragments*	*complete*	*broken*	*burnt*	*retouched*			
Surface collection	79	42	607	180	36	86	7	7	1044
Area A	24	29	786	266	37	25	17	6	1190
Area B	67	41	951	373	55	48	33	13	1581
Cess pit	5	5	33	14	1	1	–	–	59
Totals	175	117	2377	833	129	160	57	26	3874

4.4 c *The prehistoric pottery (Fig 40)*

by Frances Raymond

A total of 271 sherds, representing a minimum of 21 vessels, were recovered (Table 31, MF1 B9–12). These cover a broad time span within the prehistoric period, from the earlier Neolithic to the later Bronze Age (although the possibly earlier Neolithic material is extremely fragmentary and consists only of small body sherds of doubtful attribution) (Fig 41). While the same chronological range is present at both areas excavated within the site, the distribution of ceramics in area B is weighted towards the later Bronze Age (Fig 42). In ceramic terms this would appear to be the only significant distinction between the two areas excavated.

The average sherd weight of 2.0g remained constant between areas A and B and between ceramics of the various chronological phases. This apparent mixing, found also at W31 (this vol, 4.10), reflects the derived nature of the archaeological contexts. Identical fabrics occur in both locations, but unfortunately the small numbers of featured sherds made it impossible to identify different vessels within the same fabric group.

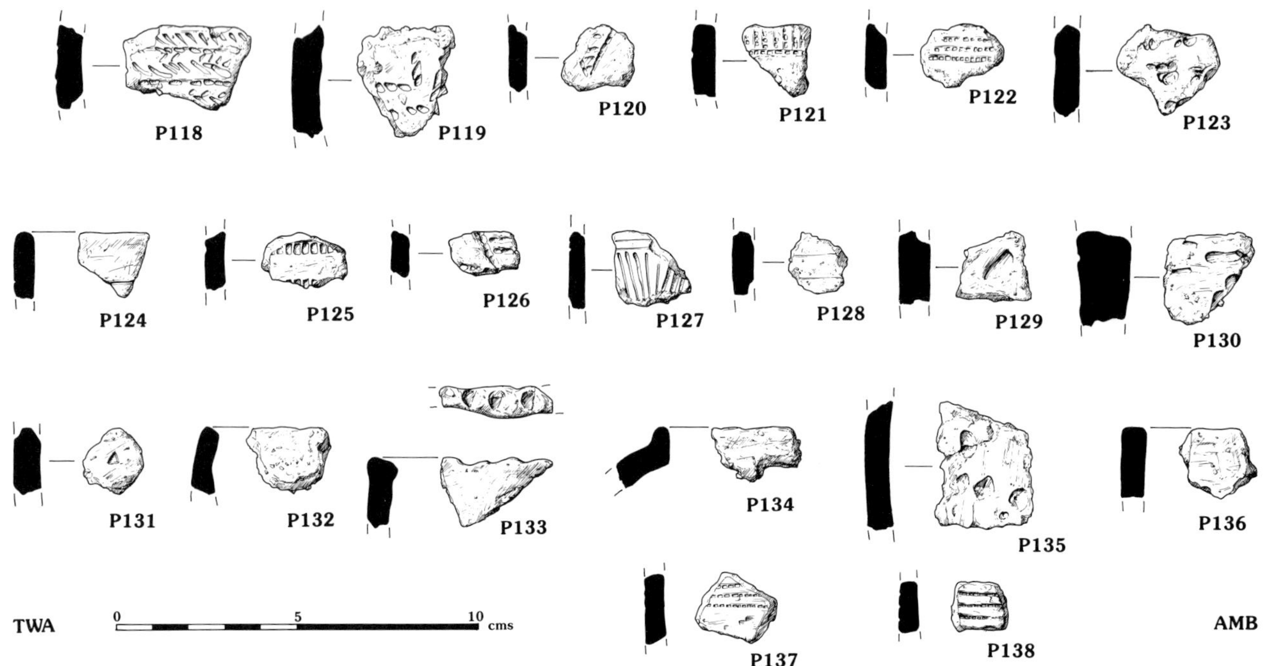

Fig 40 W32 Fargo Wood I: prehistoric pottery (P118–P138)

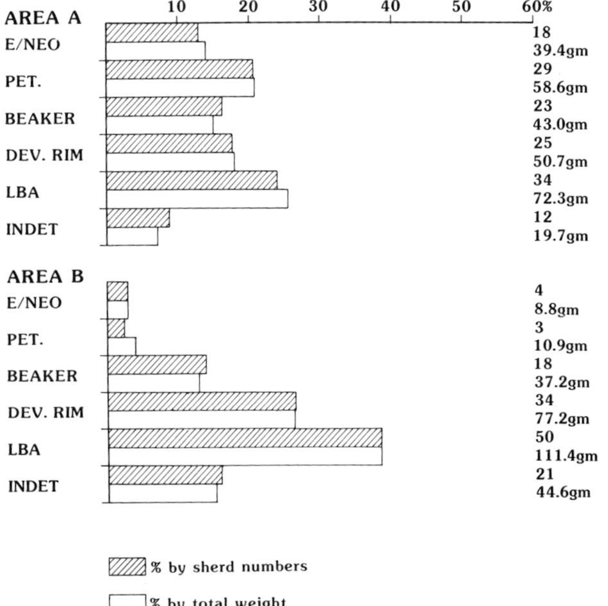

Fig 41 W32 Fargo Wood I: prehistoric pottery fabric histogram

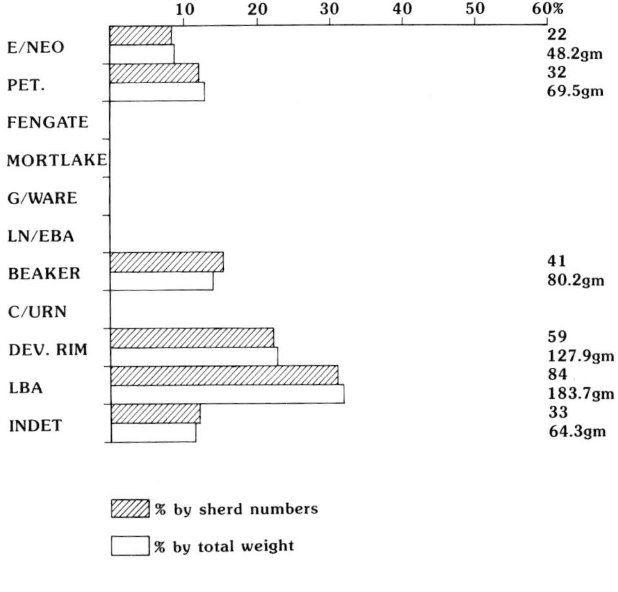

Fig 42 W32 Fargo Wood I: prehistoric pottery comparative fabric histograms

Details of the number of sherds assigned to each of these groups are given in Figure 41.

Earlier Neolithic

The sherds at W32 are small and do not provide enough evidence for a discussion of form or numbers of vessels. However, the fabric of one vessel (FS:Neo/2) was also noted in preliminary examination of the pottery from W83, the Robin Hood's Ball settlement site (Table 32, MF1 C1–14), and also occurs within material from W53, the associated intensive surface collection (Richards in prep a). In both locations it is used to produce plain Neolithic bowls.

Peterborough Ware

A minimum of three vessels are represented. Only two sherds, one in each area, survive from one of the vessels. One is a carinated body sherd (not illustrated), which includes seed impressions on the exterior surface (FV:Pet/1). The second vessel, represented by a single sherd (P118), is also unusual in the common inclusion of mica as an intrusive element within the clay paste (FM:Pet/1, see W31, the Peterborough Ware (this vol, 4.10 c), for discussion).

The final vessel is represented by the greatest number of sherds, only one of which is decorated (P119). At W32 it is not possible to assign this to a particular style group within the Peterborough series, although the same fabric (Ffe:Pet/1) occurs at W31 in Mortlake form.

Beaker

A minimum of 11 vessels are represented. Each of the nine Beaker fabrics recorded at W32, with the exception of G:Bkr/1, occurs elsewhere within the Stonehenge area (Table 33).

Eleven of the 41 Beaker sherds are decorated and five separate motifs are represented. The infilled pendant used in two vessels (P120 and P126) belongs to Clarke's Southern Motif Group 4 (1970, 427–8).

Deverel-Rimbury

A minimum of four vessels are represented, two Barrel and two Globular Urns. Fabric FS:DR/8 has been identified in Type 1 Globular Urns (Calkin 1962) in preliminary examination of the pottery from W85, Netheravon Bake long barrow (Richards in prep a). Of the Deverel-Rimbury sherds, 90% belong to the Barrel Urn fabric FfeM:DR/1, which occurs in the form of a small tub-shaped vessel North of the Cursus (52). At W32 the decoration takes the form of fingernail impressions with a single example of a triangular motif.

Table 33 W32 Fargo Wood I: associated findspots for Beaker ceramic fabrics

Fabric group	*Location*	
	Excavation	*Surface collection area*
FfeS:Bkr/1	W32 W34 W52 W55 (W53)	(52) (62)
feG:Bkr/1	W31 W32 W34 (W53)	(52) (63) (64)
feGM:Bkr/1	W32 W52	
feGM:Bkr/2	W31 W32 W34 W55 (W53)	(62) (63) (64)
feGS:Bkr/1	W31 W32	(52)
feGS:Bkr/2	W32	(64)
feGS:Bkr/3	W32 W34	(54) (65)
feS:Bkr/1	W32 W52 (W53)	

W53 preliminary analysis of pottery from surface collection adjacent to Robin Hood's Ball causewayed enclosure

Later Bronze Age

A minimum of nine vessels, identified on fabric differences alone, are represented. The distribution of fabrics represented at W32 is confined mainly to the area of the field system around Fargo Wood (ie to W32, W34, W55, and to the surface collection areas North of the Cursus (52) and Cursus West End (62), although three of the fabric groups (FfeS:LBA/1, FS:LBA/1, and FS:LBA/3) are also found at W53 (Richards in prep a). Although only two rim forms, one of which has simple fingertip decoration, are represented at W32 (P133 and P134), identical later Bronze Age fabrics occur at other sites within the area, where they are used to produce jars characteristic of Barrett's post-Deverel-Rimbury complex (Barrett 1980).

Illustrated pottery (Fig 40)

Peterborough

P118 Area A, context 89
FM:Pet/1. Body sherd. Three parallel twisted cord impressions. The areas these define are infilled with diagonal incisions arranged in a herringbone pattern.

P119 Area A, context 143
Ffe:Pet/1. Body sherd. Three twisted cord impressions, two of which form a right angle.

Beaker

P120 Area A, context 29
feGM:Bkr/2. Body sherd. Impressed comb motif used to form a pendant infilled with horizontal lines.

P121 Area A, context 133
FfeS:Bkr/1. Body sherd. Rectangular-toothed comb motif used to define an area infilled with seven parallel lines set at right angles to the first.

P122 Area A, context 153
feGM:Bkr/2. Body sherd. Three parallel lines of square-toothed comb impressions arranged in a narrow band.

P123 Area A, context 161
feS:Bkr/1. Body sherd. Five indistinct impressions, probably fingernail.

P124 Area A, context 164
feGM:Bkr/1. Rim sherd. Rounded. Horizontal linear impression.

P125 Area A, context 167
G:Bkr/1. Body sherd. Two parallel comb impressions.

P126 Area A, context 167
feS:Bkr/1. Body sherd. Impressed motif used to form a pendant infilled with horizontal lines.

P127 Area B, context 103
feGM:Bkr/1. Body sherd. Two linear incisions defining an area infilled with parallel lines radiating inwards.

Deverel-Rimbury

P128 Area A, context 130
FM:DR/1. Body sherd. Two parallel linear incisions. Type I Globular Urn.

P129 Area A, context 149
FfeM:DR/1. Body sherd. Fingernail impression. Tub-shaped Barrel Urn.

P130 Area B, context 55
FfeM:DR/1. Body sherd. Three fingernail impressions. Tub-shaped Barrel Urn.

P131 Area B, context 87
FfeM:DR/1. Body sherd. Impressed triangular motif. Tub-shaped Barrel Urn.

P132 Area B, context 118
FfeM:DR/1. Rim sherd. Asymmetrically rounded. Tub-shaped Barrel Urn.

Later Bronze Age

P133 Area A, context 161
FS:LBA/3. Rim sherd. Flattened top sloping towards the interior of the vessel. Fingertip impressions along top of rim.

P134 Area B, context 90
CFG:LBA/1. Rim sherd. Rounded.

Indeterminate

P135 Area A, context 159
feSV:Indet/1. Body sherd. Impressed motif.

P136 Area B, context 110
FS:LBA/2. Rim sherd.

Beaker

P137 Surface collection, context 231
(Sherd mislaid after illustration, so no fabric description). Body sherd with rectangular-toothed comb impressions.

P138 Surface collection, context 235
(Sherd mislaid after illustration, so no fabric description). Body sherd with grooves or worn comb impressions.

4.5 W55: the evaluation excavation of the Lesser Cursus

4.5 a Site description

The Lesser Cursus lies along the summit of a remarkably flat ridge top *c* 600m to the north-west of the western end of the Stonehenge Cursus. Running approximately WSW–ENE between SU 10354345 and 10734352, the monument is *c* 400m long and 60m wide. Aerial photographs show that it was levelled by ploughing between 1934 and 1954, but that it originally consisted of a ditch with an internal bank. The western end comprises a closed terminal with a slightly eccentric profile, while the eastern end is open, the two parallel ditches apparently terminating approximately 75m short of Fargo Wood. The monument is effectively divided in half by a slightly oblique cross ditch, the alignment of which appears to reflect that of the terminal ditch. The cross ditch appears to show traces of a bank on its eastern (exterior) side.

Certain aspects of the monument were suggested for investigation by the RCHME, specifically 'the E end of the Lesser Cursus and also the cross-bank within it and its relationship to the monument as a whole' (RCHME 1979, xv, (c)). The sample excavations carried out in 1983 were designed to investigate these points and also to sample the ditch deposits at the western end.

Previous excavations at the Stonehenge Cursus had demonstrated that the terminal ditch was much larger than those of the long sides and that its original form probably incorporated a substantial earthwork terminal bank (Stone 1947; Christie 1963; W56 and W58, this vol, 4.7). It was intended to investigate the possibility of a similar relationship at the Lesser Cursus.

Prior to the excavation, the most obvious sequence of construction that could be suggested for the monument was that it had been built in two stages: the first a short cursus extending as far east as the cross bank, the second a possibly unfinished stage doubling the original length. The only problem with this suggested sequence lay in the position of the ditch on the west (interior) side of the cross bank.

A combination of a magnetometer survey carried out by the Ancient Monuments Laboratory (Bartlett, this vol, MF1 D1; Fig 44, MF1 D2) and drought conditions during the excavation, which showed up the ditch as a clear parchmark in grass, meant that a complete ground plan of the monument could be obtained (Fig 43). On the basis of this plan three areas were examined:

Area A The intersection of the cross ditch with the southern flanking ditch

Area B The southern ditch terminal at the eastern open end

Area C A cutting through the western terminal ditch. The location of the trench at this point was in order to examine a magnetometer anomaly lying immediately within the terminal ditch. Considerable interference in this area made the identification of other anomalies impossible.

Within each area the topsoil was removed by hand, but not on a gridded basis and no sieving was carried out. The low numbers of artefacts recovered from both topsoil and stratified contexts may partly vindicate this approach, which was occasioned by constraints of time and personnel.

Area A (Figs 45–48)

After the removal of the topsoil from the area, it was observed that the chalk surface was very disturbed by weathering and deep ploughing. A series of amorphous soil marks were recorded pre-excavation, which seemed to indicate a possible irregular ditch or series of quarry scoops. Subsequent vigorous cleaning and the removal of some of the shattered natural chalk surface clarified the ditch edges. At this stage of the

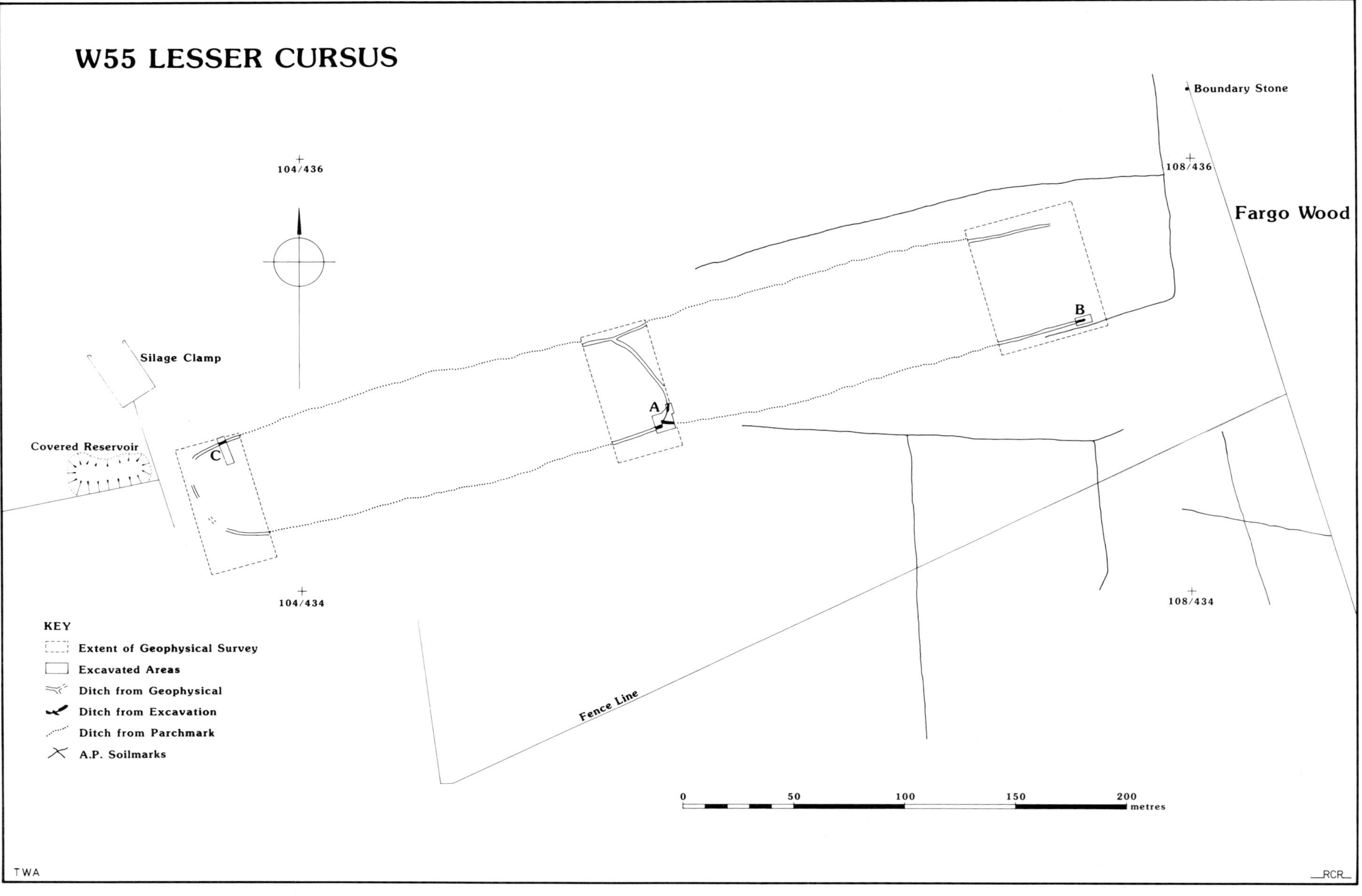

Fig 43 W55 Lesser Cursus: overall plan and location of excavated areas

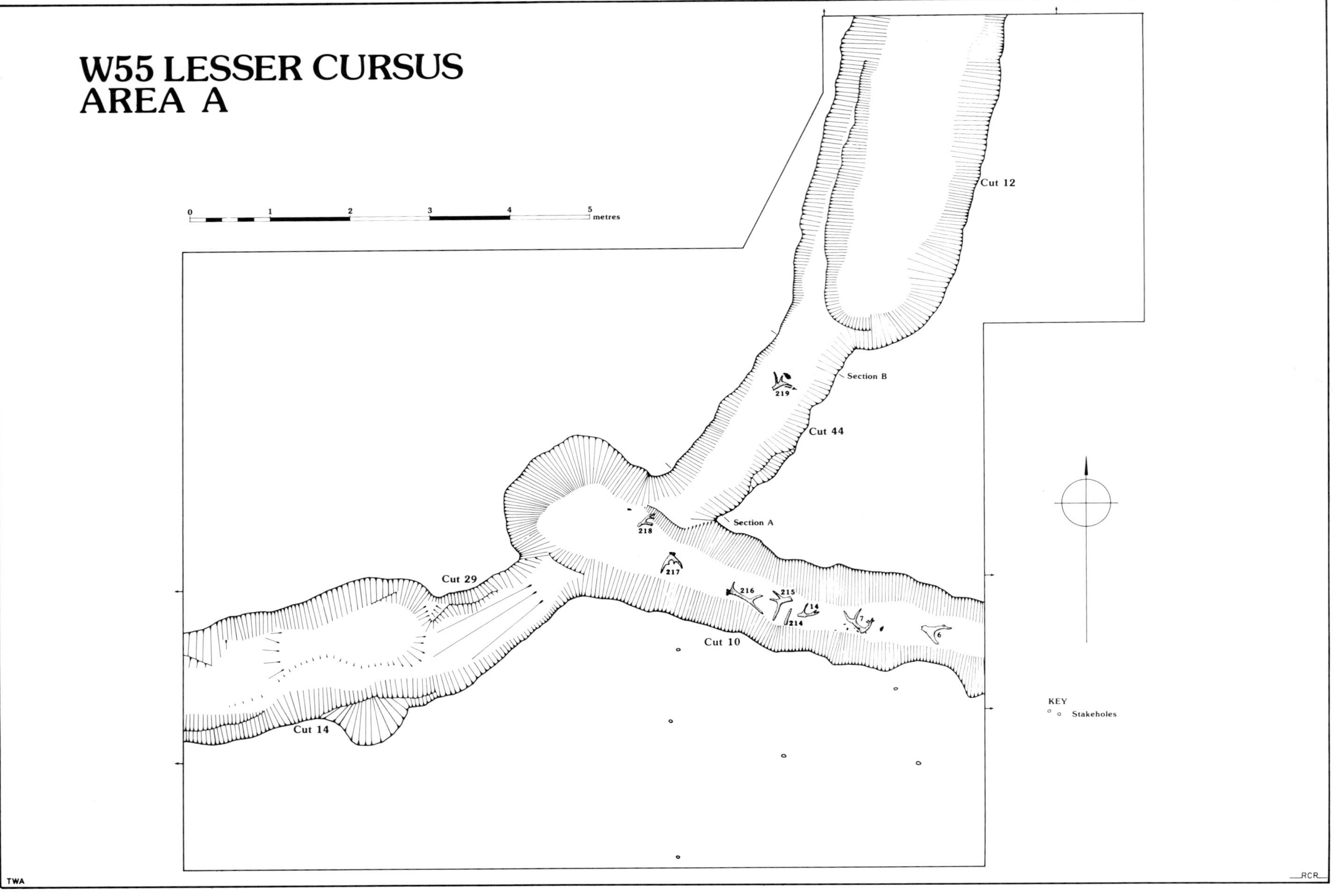

Fig 45 W55 Lesser Cursus: area A plan

Fig 46 W55 Lesser Cursus: area A fully excavated from the south-west (scale 2m)

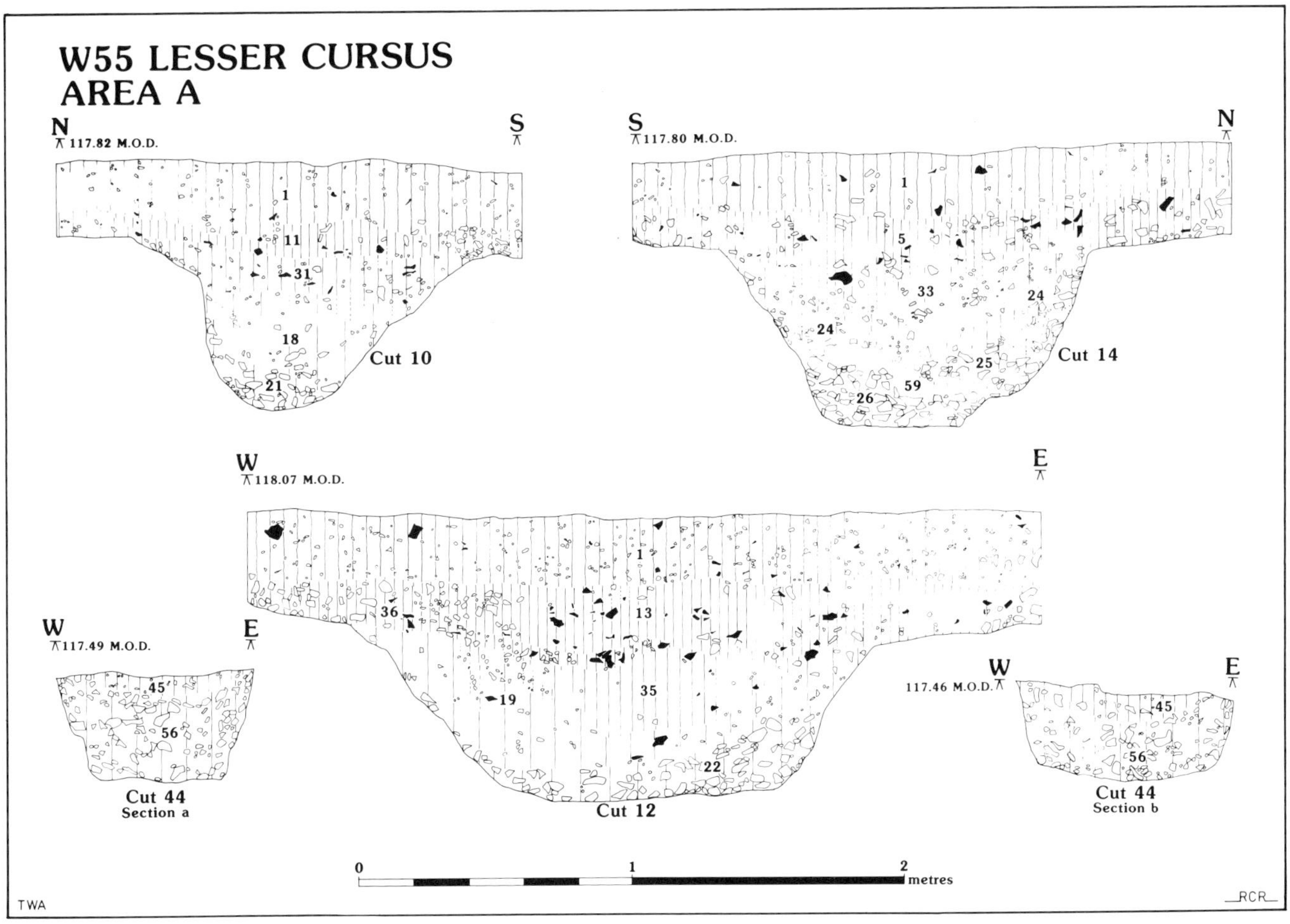

W55 LESSER CURSUS
AREA A

N S
117.82 M.O.D.
1
11
31
18
21
Cut 10

S N
117.80 M.O.D.
1
5
33
24
24
25
59
26
Cut 14

W E
118.07 M.O.D.
1
36
13
19
35
22
Cut 12

W E
117.49 M.O.D.
45
56
Cut 44
Section a

W E
117.46 M.O.D.
45
56
Cut 44
Section b

0 1 2 metres

TWA RCR

Fig 47 W55 Lesser Cursus: area A ditch sections

Fig 48 W55 Lesser Cursus: area A antler deposit on base of phase 2 ditch (scale 25cm)

excavation, three lengths of ditch were recognised. The terminal of the cross ditch to the north was allocated cut no 12, but the relationship of the remaining ditches could not be ascertained in surface plan. Consequently they were excavated as a series of quadrants, and were eventually defined as cuts 10 and 14 respectively.

As excavation of these ditches progressed, it became clear that they cut an earlier ditch, the outline of which was uncovered as more shattered chalk was removed and the surface plan clarified. The relationship of the ditches provides evidence for at least two phases of construction (Fig 46):

Phase 1 Two short lengths of ditch, cuts 42 and 44

Phase 2 Three ditch terminals: the cross ditch to the north, cut 12, the flanking ditch to the west, cut 14, and the flanking ditch to the east, cut 10.

The phase 1 ditch

The south-west length of cut 42, the first-phase ditch, was 2m long, 0.8–1.2m wide, and 0.6–0.8m deep, with a shallow U-shaped profile. It was filled with an angular chalk rubble primary fill, above which was a brown, soft, calcareous fill, probably the equivalent of the final phase of secondary silting of the phase 2 ditches. The only find from this length of ditch was a flint core from the primary fill.

To the north-east cut 44, the equivalent ditch, survived for a length of 3.3m. The profile and dimensions were similar to cut 42, as was the fill, with the addition of a further layer of primary chalk rubble, context 51. Again, this section of ditch contained few artefacts, but a heavily eroded fragment of red deer antler (SF219) was recovered from the primary chalk rubble. This appeared to be *in situ* and produced a radiocarbon date of 3496–3042 BC (OxA 1404).

The nature of the primary fills of the first-phase ditch, compact chalk rubble and wash, with little humic material, and the lack of artefacts, combined with the *in situ* deposit of antler, suggest deliberate backfilling.

The phase 2 ditches

The first-phase ditch was cut by three individual ditch terminals, cuts 10, 12, and 14. None of these have any recoverable relationship to each other, but are regarded as all belonging to the same phase of enlargement and modification.

The terminal of the second-phase cross ditch, cut 12, cuts the northern end of the first-phase ditch, cut 44. This was the largest of the three ditches, with a shallow U-shaped profile, 2m wide and a maximum of 1m deep at the northern edge of the trench.

The tertiary fill was a dark brown calcareous loam (context 13), which contained few artefacts but a quantity of bone, including a cattle fragment which compared in size to a large bull or aurochs. Below this was a rather disturbed relict soil (context 36), overlying a layer of loose humic sediment, both almost devoid of artefacts.

The upper secondary fill was a pale calcareous silt loam, below which, in the southern section, was a lens of very strongly cemented chalk wash, devoid of artefacts. This may have derived from erosion of the internal southern bank or it may represent deliberate backfill, using bank material. The lower secondary fill was also devoid of finds and consisted of soft, weathered chalk rubble with some humic material. Similarly, the primary chalk rubble filling the bottom of the ditch contained some humic lenses but no artefacts. The filling of this ditch appears to be accumulative, and as such provides a strong contrast to the apparently deliberate filling of the remaining examined ditches at the Lesser Cursus.

The second-phase eastern terminal flanking ditch, cut 10, again cuts the first-phase ditch and runs north-west/south-east for 7 metres to the edge of the excavated area. The ditch had a fairly uniform, U-shaped profile with a maximum width of 1.2m and a maximum depth of 0.9m. The tertiary fills consisted of a relict soil above its associated sorted horizon. This contained a quantity of worked flint and burnt flint and a few fragments of unidentifiable bone. The upper secondary fill, chalk wash and loose chalk rubble, contained far less worked flint and three fragments of unidentifiable bone. Below this was a lens of cemented chalk rubble, devoid of finds, which may be derived from the internal bank. The remainder of the secondary fills, which consisted of loose chalky rubble with a humic component, also contained no artefacts. The chalk rubble in the secondary fills suggests deliberate backfill rather than natural silting of the ditch.

The primary fills consisted of loose chalk rubble with humic and silty lenses. Lying on the floor of the ditch were eight substantial fragments of red deer antlers (Fig 48), including picks (Figs 56 and 57) which may have been used in the original excavation of the ditch. Although all of the antlers, in contrast to those from the first-phase ditch, were fresh in appearance, one, SF7, appears to have been worked using a groove and splinter technique (Fig 55). Although this might be taken to suggest that the antlers together constituted no more than a primary rubbish deposit, their apparently formal arrangement on the base of the ditch may suggest a more ceremonial deposit. A sample from one antler produced a radiocarbon date of 3606–3200 BC (OxA 1405).

The second-phase western flanking ditch terminal, cut 14, a 3m length of which was examined, cut the southern end of the first-phase ditch. It was of similar

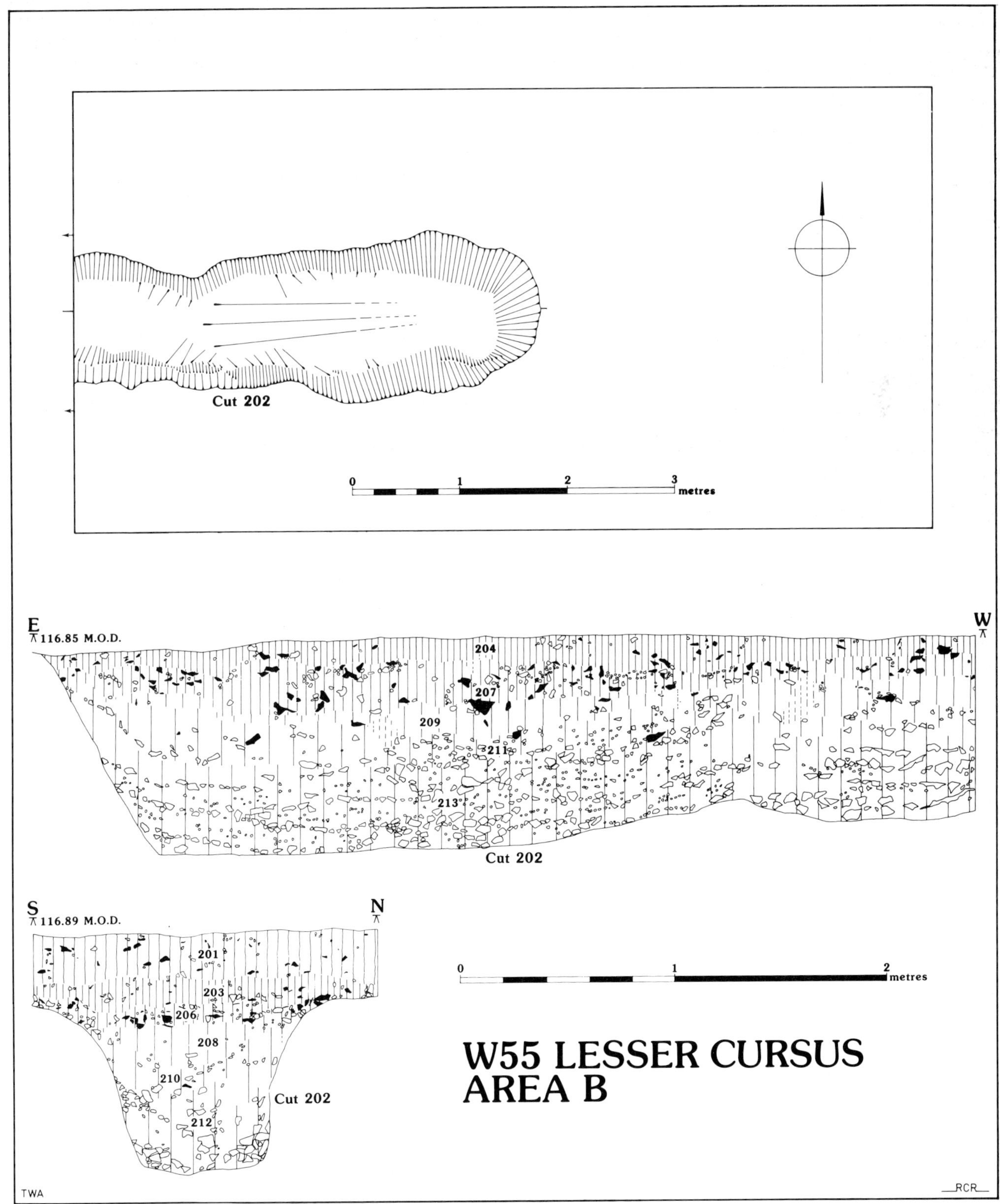

Fig 49 W55 Lesser Cursus: area B plan and ditch sections

Fig 50 W55 Lesser Cursus: area B fully excavated from the east (horizontal scale 2m)

dimensions to the eastern ditch described above: 1.4m wide and 1m deep, again with a U-shaped profile. The tertiary fill contained nine bone fragments, including cow and sheep/goat, a large quantity of worked flint, including two tools and two sherds of prehistoric pottery (Beaker and Late Bronze Age). The secondary fills, chalk rubble and humic sediments, contained only one flint flake. The chalky nature of these fills again suggests deliberate backfilling of the ditch. The primary chalk rubble contained no artefacts.

Columns of samples for molluscan analysis were taken from ditches cuts 10 and 12 (Entwistle, this vol, 4.5 e).

Area B (Figs 49, 50)

The exact position of the eastern terminal of the southern ditch was determined by a combination of magnetometer survey and parchmark recording. An area 8m by 4m was hand excavated and the upper fill of a 4.3m length of the ditch was revealed. The area stripped was intended to examine the possibility of either a marking-out ditch or postholes extending the line of the ditch beyond its apparent end, but no evidence for such features was recovered. At this point there was also no evidence for the former existence of a bank.

The ditch, a maximum of 1.1m deep and 1.5m wide at the surface, had a uniform U-shaped profile. The tertiary fills consisted of a fairly stone-free colluvial layer overlying a sorted horizon. This suggested stabilisation phase contained a quantity of burnt flint and a flint assemblage which, as well as flakes, contained 4 cores, 8 scrapers and a piercer. A total of 32 sherds of prehistoric pottery were recovered from the tertiary fills: 13 Beaker, 2 Deverel-Rimbury, and 17 Late Bronze Age (Raymond, this vol, 4.5 c; see Fig 53 for illustrated examples). Of the 36 pieces of bone, cow, pig, and red deer were recognised. The lower component of the colluvial soil, partly derived from the secondary silts, was disturbed by animals. It contained some worked flint, including 4 scrapers, 16 sherds of prehistoric pottery (one Late Neolithic/Early Bronze Age, 7 Beaker, 8 Late Bronze Age), and 56 pieces of animal bone. The bone was fragmentary and badly eroded, but pig, cow, and sheep/goat were identified (Maltby, this vol, 4.5 d).

There were no finds in the secondary and primary fills. The secondary silts consisted of a chalk wash with some chalk rubble. This may be frost-shattered chalk from the ditch sides, eroded bank material, or deliberate backfill using bank material. The primary fill was mainly vacuous chalk rubble with inclusions of cemented material and some humic material.

This sequence was also sampled for molluscan analysis (Entwistle, this vol, 4.5 e).

Area C (Figs 51, 52)

An area 12m by 4m was selected in order to sample a section of the north terminal ditch together with a possible feature suggested by the magnetometer survey as lying immediately within the interior of the Cursus. On excavation, this feature was found to be of natural origin, with an irregular profile and with a fill devoid of artefacts. Within area C the removal of the ploughsoil revealed the only direct evidence from the

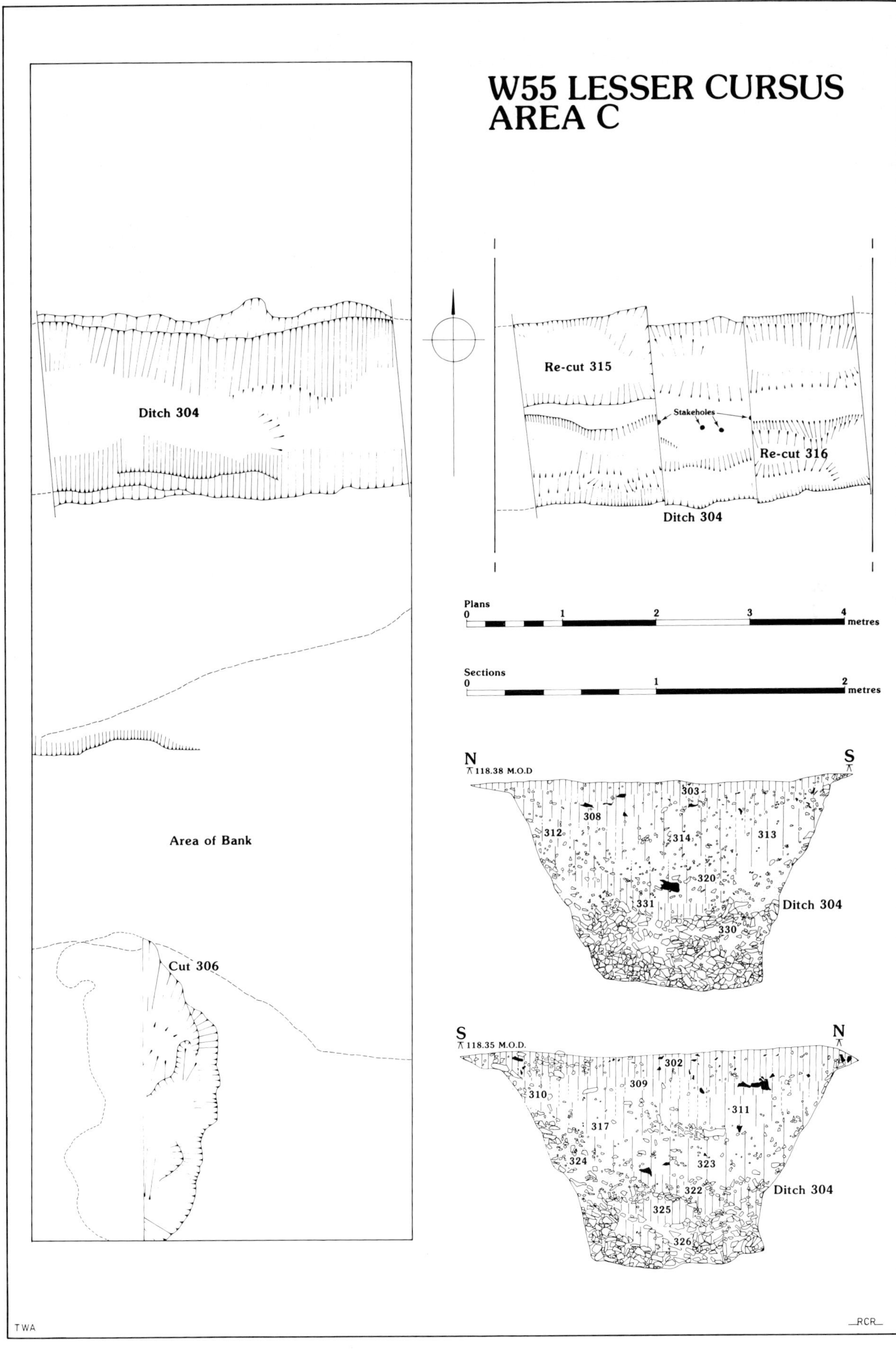

Fig 51 *W55 Lesser Cursus: area C plan and ditch sections*

Fig 52 W55 Lesser Cursus: area C ditch section central baulk from west (scales 1m)

entire monument for the former position of the internal bank. Here a band of 'protected' chalk between 2.2m and 4.6m wide ran parallel to and *c* 2m from the inner edge of the ditch. The size of the area of protected chalk, while suggesting the former position of the bank, cannot be used to determine its precise dimensions.

The ditch itself, some 1.8m wide and 1.1m deep, is considerably larger than any of those sampled in areas A or B, and also demonstrates a comparably more complex sequence of deposits. The 3m wide section was initially excavated leaving a 1m central baulk, providing four potential sections for recording/interpretation and for molluscan sampling. The removal of the baulk provided a sequence of samples for bulk sieving. Owing to the complexity of the sequence and considerable burrowing disturbance, certain contexts were only recognised in section and consequently only stratigraphically excavated within this baulk.

The tertiary fills represent the remains of a developed soil in the top part of the ditch, the clean, stone-free layer with an underlying sorted horizon indicating an undisturbed grassland soil. The tertiary fills contained a quantity of worked flint, a fragment of unidentifiable bone and one sherd of Deverel-Rimbury pottery. The secondary ditch silts, context 317, when first recorded, appeared to form a peak in the centre of the ditch. Although difficult to define and present in a drawn section, this is interpreted as being associated with two small recuts on the inner and outer ditch edges. The northern recut, cut 315, was 0.5m wide and 0.15m deep; that on the southern side, cut 316, was of a similar size (0.35m wide and 0.2m deep).

The secondary fills consisted of a layer of cemented chalk rubble, overlying vacuous chalk rubble within which a number of small lenses of silt were recorded. The combined chalk rubble deposits, which may represent bank material, deliberately dumped into the partly silted ditch, contained fragments of antler, one of which provided a radiocarbon date of 2860–2398 BC (OxA 1406).

The antlers recovered from the chalk contexts described above were in a more fragmentary condition than those from area A and included a further example (SF211) of groove and splinter (Fig 58).

The secondary fills contained only six pieces of worked flint and the primary chalk rubble contained no finds.

This section was also sampled for molluscan analysis (Entwistle, this vol, 4.5 e).

Discussion

The sample excavations have served to clarify a number of specific aspects of both sequence and chronology, suggesting two phases of construction, indistinguishable on the basis of the radiocarbon dates obtained.

Phase 1

The evidence for phase 1 of the Lesser Cursus is provided primarily by the two short lengths of ditch recorded within area A. Any attempts to reconstruct the original morphology of this phase of the monument are based on the assumption that the course of the phase 1 ditch was, in general, followed and totally removed by the subsequent, and much enlarged, ditch. If this is accepted, then the original monument appears to be a 200m by 60m enclosure of slightly trapezoidal form, defined by an small ditch and interior bank. The short lengths of surviving phase 1 ditch in area A could alternatively be suggested as representing a 'marker' ditch, but appear defined enough to have formed an independent if insubstantial monument.

Phase 2

The morphology of phase 2 appears clearer. The phase 1 monument is substantially enlarged, for the majority of its circuit was totally removed in the process. Within the circuit of the phase 1 cursus the position of the internal bank is maintained and presumably enhanced, with the exception of the newly enlarged cross ditch, the bank of which is now on the eastern side. The monument is also extended eastwards by means of roughly parallel ditches which, although no firm evidence was provided by the excavation of area B, can be suggested on the basis of aerial photographs as having internal banks. As far as can be ascertained from the location of excavated ditches and from magnetometer survey, the lengths of the phase 1 monument and the extension are exactly comparable, suggesting an element of conscious planning. The eastern end appears to have been deliberately left open, the neatly excavated ditch terminal mirrored by its northern counterpart located by magnetometer survey. These two terminals stop at a remarkably precise point relative to the layout of the enlarged monument.

Within area A, the termination of the enlarged cross ditch short of the southern flanking ditch appears to be suggested by the geophysical survey of the comparable, but more northerly, junction. This gap, and the suggestion of deliberate backfilling of the phase 1 ditch, may indicate the position of a formal access way into the otherwise totally enclosed western end of the monument. Alternatively it may merely indicate the position of the phase 2 internal bank, and suggest a width of approximately 2m, less than that suggested in area C, but in area A associated with a slighter ditch.

Despite some comprehension of the construction sequence and even the construction date of the Lesser Cursus, the potential for the reconstruction of associated activity seems slight. With the exception of the deliberately placed, and presumedly ceremonial, deposit of antlers within ditch cut 10 in area A, the primary fills of all the ditches were virtually devoid of artefacts. This appears not to be uncommon at other monuments of this type even where ditches have been extensively examined (F Pryor pers comm), and may suggest a deliberate attempt at maintaining a 'clean' monument (see also the primary fills from W56 A and B and W58, this vol, 4.6 and 4.7). It also appears likely that, with the exception of cut 12, the phase 2 cross ditch, all of the phase 2 ditches were deliberately backfilled. In some cases this appears to have taken place almost immediately after their original excavation, as the replaced chalk is totally clean and the condition of incorporated antlers is fresh. In contrast, the backfilling in area C, part of a complex sequence of events represented within the ditch deposits, may have occurred after a period of natural accumulation. The majority of the recoverable activity relates to the upper ditch fills, where molluscan analysis suggests major cultivation episodes associated with Beaker and later Bronze Age pottery.

4.5 b Lithics

A total of 750 pieces of worked flint were recovered from the excavation of the three sample areas (Table 34). Of these, 529 (71.23%) were from the ploughsoil or from the uppermost colluvial fills of the ditches, and are therefore essentially unstratified.

Despite the absence of stratified material, the spatial attributes of this limited assemblage can be employed to suggest a focus for later activity. The proportion of retouched material and tools, expressed as a percentage of the overall flake count, is similar within areas A and C (3.12% and 3.08% respectively). In area B, however, far greater tool numbers raise the level to 10.48%, with correspondingly greater numbers of burnt

Table 34 W55 Lesser Cursus: composition of the flint assemblage

Area	*Cores* complete	*Cores* fragments	*Flakes* complete	*Flakes* broken	*Flakes* burnt	*Flakes* retouched	*Scrapers*	*Other tools*	*Total*
A unstratified	7	–	75	5	2	–	–	5	94
cut 29	–	–	–	–	–	–	–	–	–
cut 44	1	–	5	2	–	–	–	–	8
cut 10	1	–	95	10	–	2	–	–	108
cut 12	1	–	25	2	–	1	–	–	29
cut 14	4	–	96	7	1	1	1	1	111
A (total)	14	–	296	26	3	4	1	6	350
B	16	4	181	23	10	9	15	3	261
C	9	2	105	19	1	3	–	–	139
Totals	39	6	582	68	14	16	16	9	750

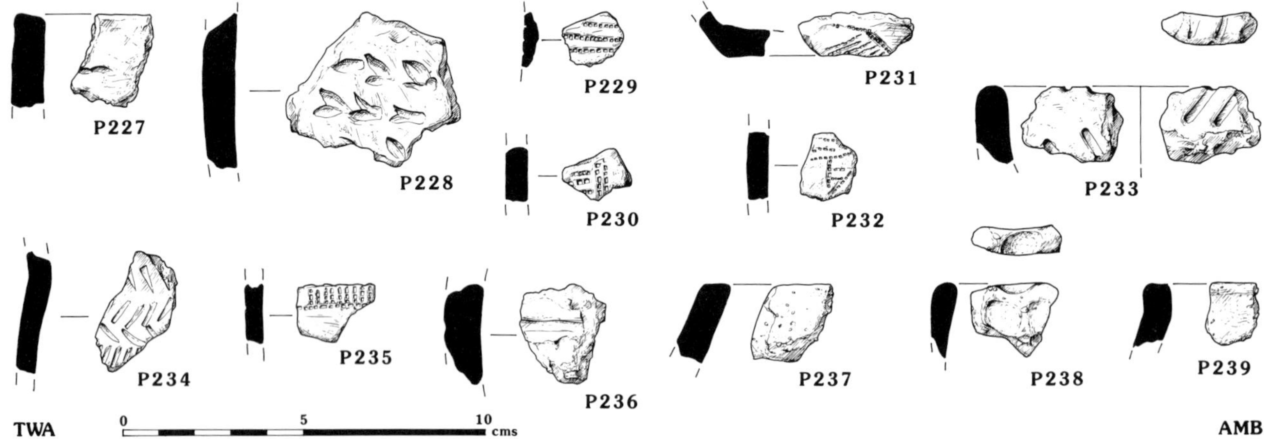

Fig 53 W55 Lesser Cursus: prehistoric pottery (P227–P239)

worked pieces, and also cores. This independently suggests that the Fargo Wood area, immediately beyond the eastern end of the Lesser Cursus (area B), was a focus for Bronze Age activity.

4.5 c *The prehistoric pottery (Fig 53)*

by Frances Raymond

A total of 63 sherds representing a minimum of 23 vessels was recovered (Table 35, MF1 D3–4). A major proportion (94%) of this assemblage comes from the secondary silts of the eastern ditch terminal (area B). Of the identifiable pottery 42% is of Beaker or Late Neolithic/Early Bronze Age date, while the remaining 58% can be attributed to the later Bronze Age period (see Fig 54). The vertical distribution of the two ceramic groups within ditch deposits is mixed.

Later Neolithic/Early Bronze Age

Three sherds, probably representing only a single vessel, were recovered from area B. The fabric used to produce this pottery also occurs at W31 and is unusual

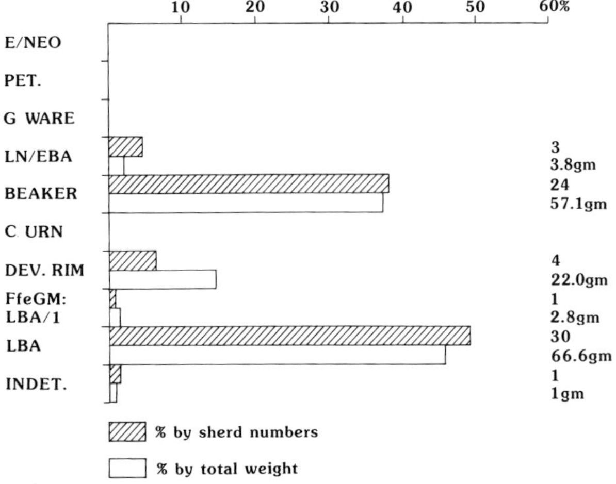

Fig 54 W55 Lesser Cursus: prehistoric pottery fabric histogram

in the inclusion of crushed bluestone within the clay paste. Although it is not possible to assign this to a specific ceramic group it has a greater affinity with Beakers than with Peterborough Ware.

In addition, P233, although in a fabric more typical of Beakers than of any other tradition, carries a decorative scheme which precludes its accommodation within that ceramic style, although it seems likely to be of later Neolithic or Early Bronze Age date.

Beaker

A minimum of seven vessels are represented, one from area A and the remainder from area B. The assemblage includes an element certainly identifiable as Late Style (Case 1977). P231 is notable in that although reserved triangles which spring directly from the base of a vessel are common, filled triangles in the same position are slightly less frequent: most of the examples illustrated by Clarke (1970, eg fig 965, from Cherhill, Wiltshire, or fig 795, from Undley, Suffolk) are from Southern tradition Beakers, although it is an occasional feature of other groups (eg Clarke 1970, fig 656, from Acherole, Caithness). Filled triangles are also a component part of complex designs around reserved bar chevrons, but this cannot be the case with P231 as a horizontal line is just visible directly above the apex of the triangle. P232 is also likely to belong to a Southern tradition Beaker: from the curvature of the sherd and the asymmetry of the motif itself, the triangular motif would seem to lie at an oblique angle, and is likely therefore to belong to a decorative scheme similar to those on Beakers from Deepdale, Staffordshire, and Seahouses, Northumberland (Clarke 1970, figs 862 and 866), both of which are S2(E) Beakers.

The fabric of P231 and P232, FfeGM:Bkr/1, which also occurs at W52, and fabric feGM:Bkr/2, which is found at W31, W32, and W34, and from surface collection North of the Cursus (52), seem to occur frequently in Late Style vessels.

The greatest number of sherds are representative of two vessels (Fabric feG:Bkr/4) with square rims, one of which (P227), located within area A in the upper fill of the southern Cursus ditch, is undecorated; the second (P228) exhibits plastic finger-pinching. Rustication, particularly of the 'crow's foot' type seen in P228, is a feature more commonly associated with Late Southern

Beakers (Bamford 1982). The two remaining pots survive in relatively small quantities and have been identified on fabric differences alone. Although the fabric FfeS:Bkr/1 is found in several locations within the study area, none of the sherds includes motifs exclusive to a particular style of Beaker, while at W52 fabric feGS:Bkr/4 occurs on AOC Beakers.

Deverel-Rimbury

A minimum number of three vessels, distinguished on fabric differences, are represented, two from area B and one from area C. All three are Globular Urns and the fabric in which one occurs, FS:DR/8, has been identified in preliminary examination of the pottery from W85, the Netheravon Bake long barrow (Richards in prep a), as belonging to vessels of the Type I series.

Later Bronze Age

The small number of diagnostic sherds within the assemblage belonging to this period have restricted calculations of minimum vessel numbers to fabric distinctions. Eight of the 12 fabrics identified also occur in the excavations in the Fargo Wood area, 7 at W34 and 1 at W32. Direct matching of clay pastes used to produce Late Bronze Age ceramics within the study area is very unusual and in this case can be used to argue for contemporaneity between the settlement adjacent to Fargo Wood at W34 and the field system extending to incorporate the Lesser Cursus. At W34 the same fabrics are used to produce the pottery of the post-Deverel-Rimbury complex (Barrett 1980). Fabrics unique to the Lesser Cursus (F:LBA/2, FSV:LBA/2 and Ssh:LBA/1) are consistent with this assemblage in terms of treatment and finish.

Illustrated pottery (Fig 53)

(see Table 32 for fabric descriptions)

Beaker

P227 Area A, context 5
feG:Bkr/4. Rim sherd. Upright with flattened top.

P228 Area B, context 204
feG:Bkr/4. Body sherd. Plastic finger-pinched motif arranged in parallel rows; orientation of the sherd is not certain as there is very little curvature in any direction.

P229 Area B, context 206
FfeS:Bkr/1. Body sherd. Three parallel comb impressions.

P230 Area B, context 207
feGM:Bkr/2. Body sherd. Infilled pendant defined by two parallel comb impressions.

P231 Area B, context 214
FfeGM:Bkr/1. Base sherd. Parallel comb impressions forming a triangle springing from the base angle and filled with oblique lines of comb impression.

P232 Area B, context 215
feGM:Bkr/2. Body sherd. Infilled asymmetrical pendant abutting three parallel comb impressions.

Later Neolithic/Early Bronze Age

P233 Area B, context 215
feG:Bkr/2. Rim sherd. Rounded. Deeply impressed diagonal lines along the top of the rim and on the interior and exterior of the vessel.

Beaker

P234 Area B, context 219
FfeGM:Bkr/1. Body sherd. Parallel linear impressions arranged in a herringbone pattern.

P235 Area B, context 219
FfeGM:Bkr/1. Body sherd. Parallel comb impressions set at right angles to a single row.

Later Bronze Age

P236 Area B, context 201
G:LBA/1. Body sherd. Slight linear impression or groove.

P237 Area B, context 206
feSsh:LBA/1. Rim sherd. Flattened top.

P238 Area B, context 207
FS:LBA/3. Rim sherd. Rounded with external bevel. Fingertip impression on the top of the rim.

P239 Area B, context 219
CFG:LBA/1. Rim sherd. Flattened top.

4.5 d Animal bones and worked bone

by Mark Maltby and Julian Richards

A total of 178 fragments of animal bone were recovered. The species represented are shown in Table 36. The assemblage was generally poorly preserved, with nearly all the bones displaying a considerable amount of surface erosion. This, together with the friable nature of many of the bones, explains the high proportion of unidentified fragments.

With the exception of the red deer antlers from area A, very few bones were recovered from the bottom of the ditches. Most of the antlers, which included both shed and unshed examples, were substantial pieces and all had presumably been used as picks during the digging of the ditch. At least two bore evidence of working (see below), as did an example from area C. The other red deer bone was a small fragment of a metacarpus from the terminal ditch.

A cattle metacarpus from area A cut 12, the phase 2 cross ditch, belonged to a large animal, either a large bull or possibly an aurochs (*Bos primigenius*). The other cattle bones from area A consisted of a fragment of a calcaneus, a metatarsus, and a loose tooth. The cattle bones from the upper fills of the eastern terminal (area

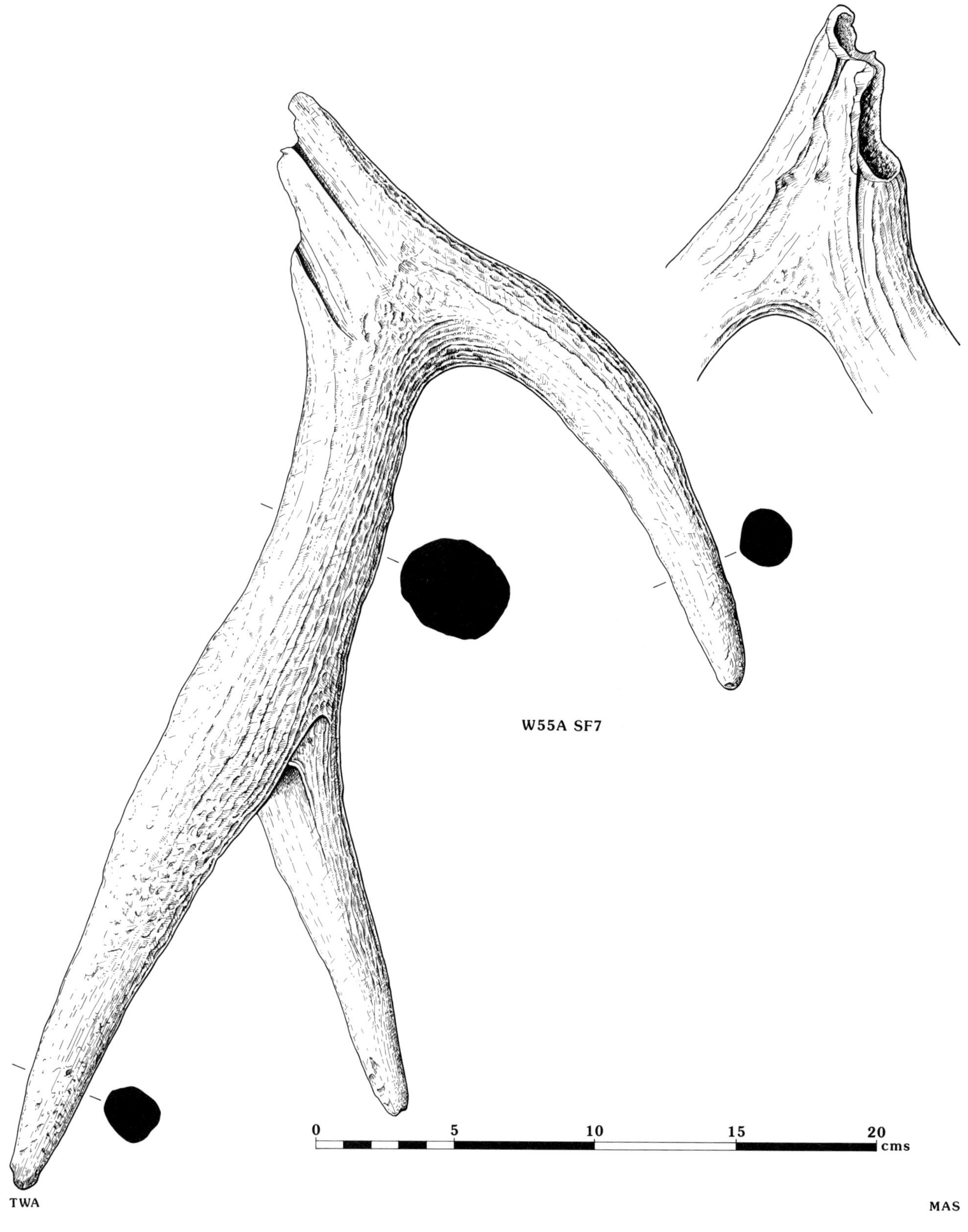

Fig 55 W55 Lesser Cursus: area A antler rake with groove and splinter SF7

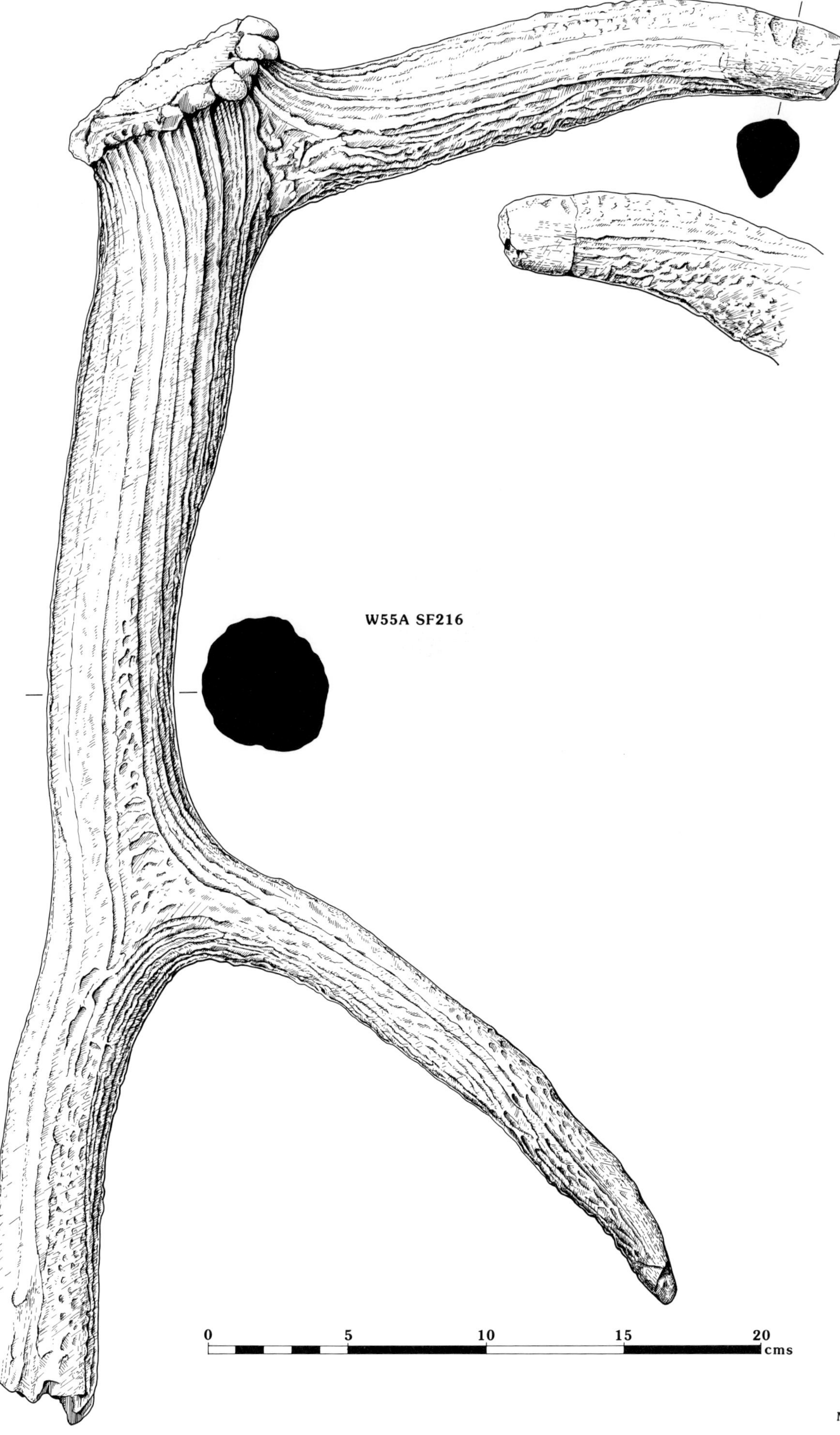

Fig 56 W55 Lesser Cursus: area A antler pick SF216

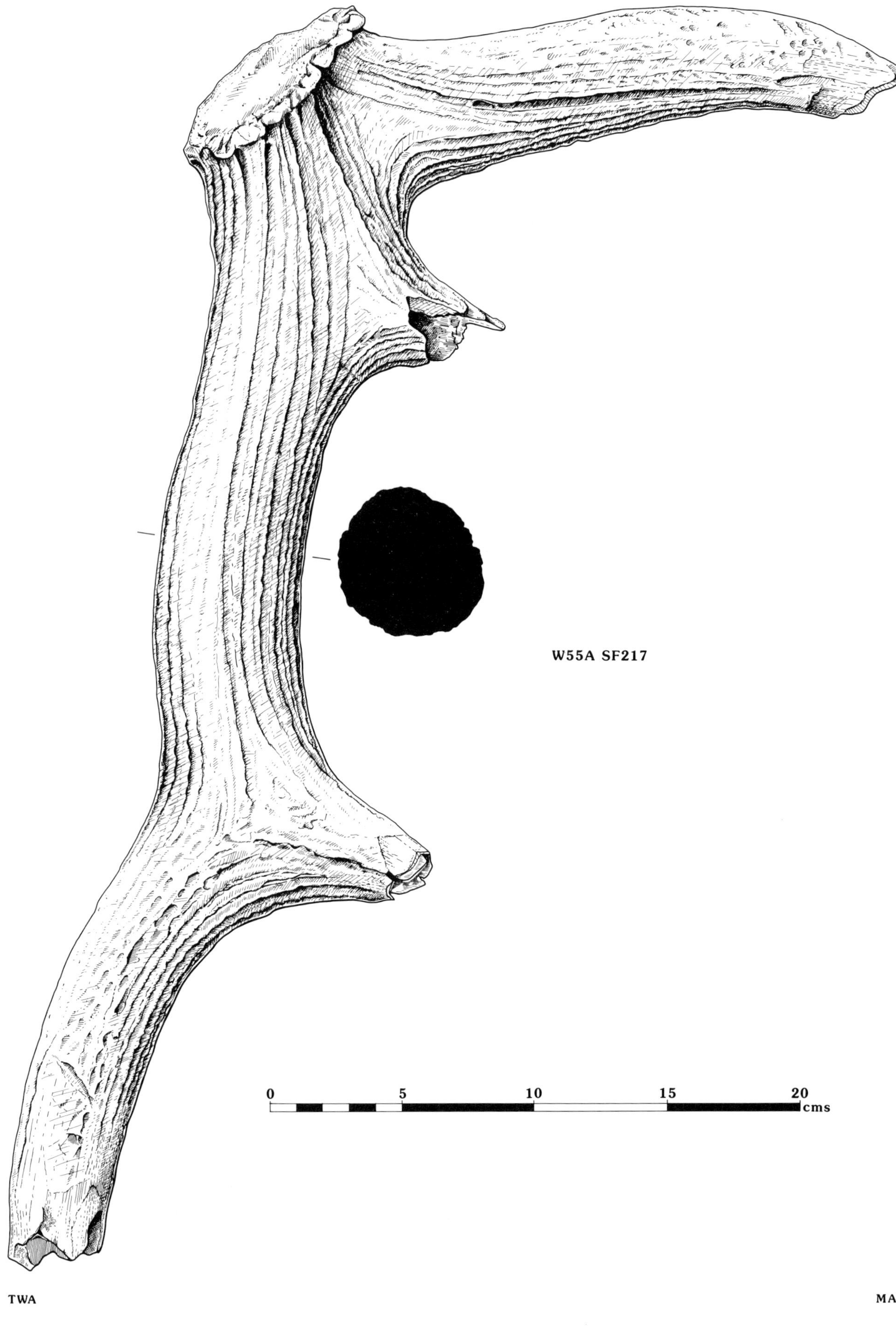

Fig 57 W55 Lesser Cursus: area A antler pick SF217

Table 36 W55 Lesser Cursus: animal species represented in areas A, B, and C

Species	*Area A Southern and Cross Ditch*	*Area B Terminal Ditch*	*Area C North Ditch*	*Total*
Cattle	4	11	–	15
Sheep/goat	2	4	–	6
Pig	–	4	–	4
Red deer	11	1	7	19
Unidentified large mammal	13	18	7	38
Sheep-sized mammal	2	26	1	29
Unidentified mammal	6	45	16	67
Total	38	109	31	178

B) consisted of two skull fragments, three loose teeth, two fragments of the same tibia, and fragments of a calcaneus, an astragalus, and a metatarsus. Five of the fragments from area B were charred, as were nearly all the fragments from area C.

Sheep/goat was represented only by tooth fragments and pig by three loose teeth and a radius. The sample was too small to merit further analysis.

Objects of antler

Area A context 21 SF7 (Fig 55)

This object, of a form conventionally referred to as a 'rake', lay on the base of cut 10, the phase 2 eastern extension ditch (Figs 45, 48). The evidence here for the use of the main antler beam for the production of splinters suggests that this example may be regarded as waste, although it may subsequently have been used as a rake.

The ends of four V-shaped grooves, each of markedly differing profile, demonstrate the removal of two blanks employing the groove and splinter technique (Semenov 1964, 152). Two of the grooves exhibit a clear association as they are linked by a straight cut across the antler. This would have produced a splinter with a maximum width of 25mm, the length of which, based on surviving grooves, must have been at least 45mm.

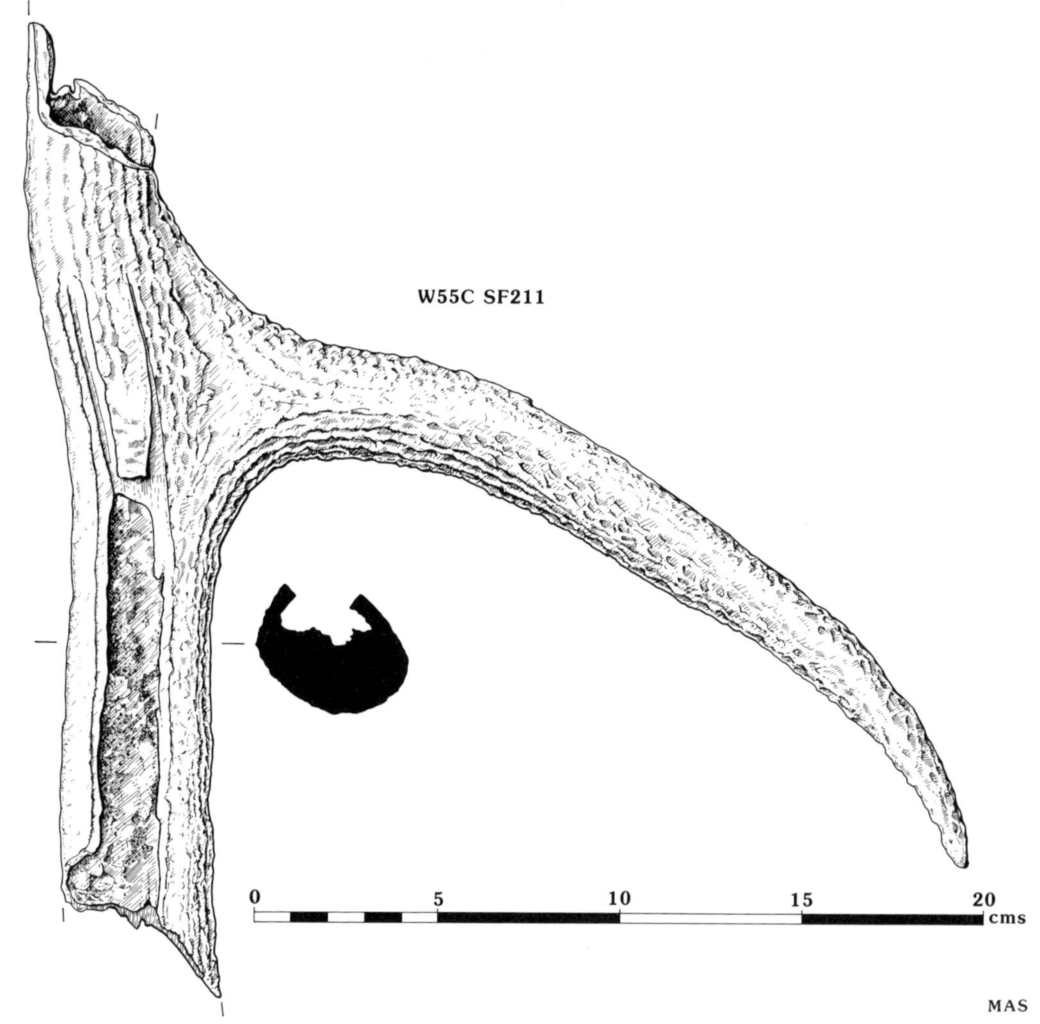

Fig 58 W55 Lesser Cursus: area C antler with groove and splinter SF211

Area A context 38 SF216 (Fig 56)

Pick of shed red deer antler from the base of cut 10, the phase 2 eastern extension ditch. The brow tine shows considerable wear and impact damage although the crown shows no signs of damage. The bez tine is left in place and shows some wear to the tip. The regularity of part of the truncated end suggests that it was partly sawn.

Area A context 38 SF217 (Fig 57)

Pick of shed red deer antler from the base of cut 10, the phase 2 eastern extension ditch. Both the brow tine and the crown show considerable wear and impact damage. The bez and trez tines are both broken off and the truncated end also appears to have been partly sawn.

Area C context 337 SF211 (Fig 58)

This heavily eroded section of antler, from the western terminal ditch cutting, shows evidence for the removal of a single splinter employing the groove and splinter technique (Semenov 1964, 152). Parallel V-shaped grooves, 140mm and 155mm long respectively, have outer edges on average 20mm apart. The remaining end of the removal shows no signs of a cross cut and must therefore have been snapped off. The removed splinter would have been *c* 10mm wide and a minimum of 125mm long.

4.5 e Land mollusca

by Roy Entwistle

Methodology

The methodology employed for the analysis of molluscan samples from this site, W55, is also applicable to those from W56, W58, and W52 (this vol, 4.6 g, 4.7 e and 4.12 e).

The extraction and analytical techniques were based on those outlined by Evans (1972). The results are presented in tabular form and as percentage frequency histograms for those samples containing sufficient

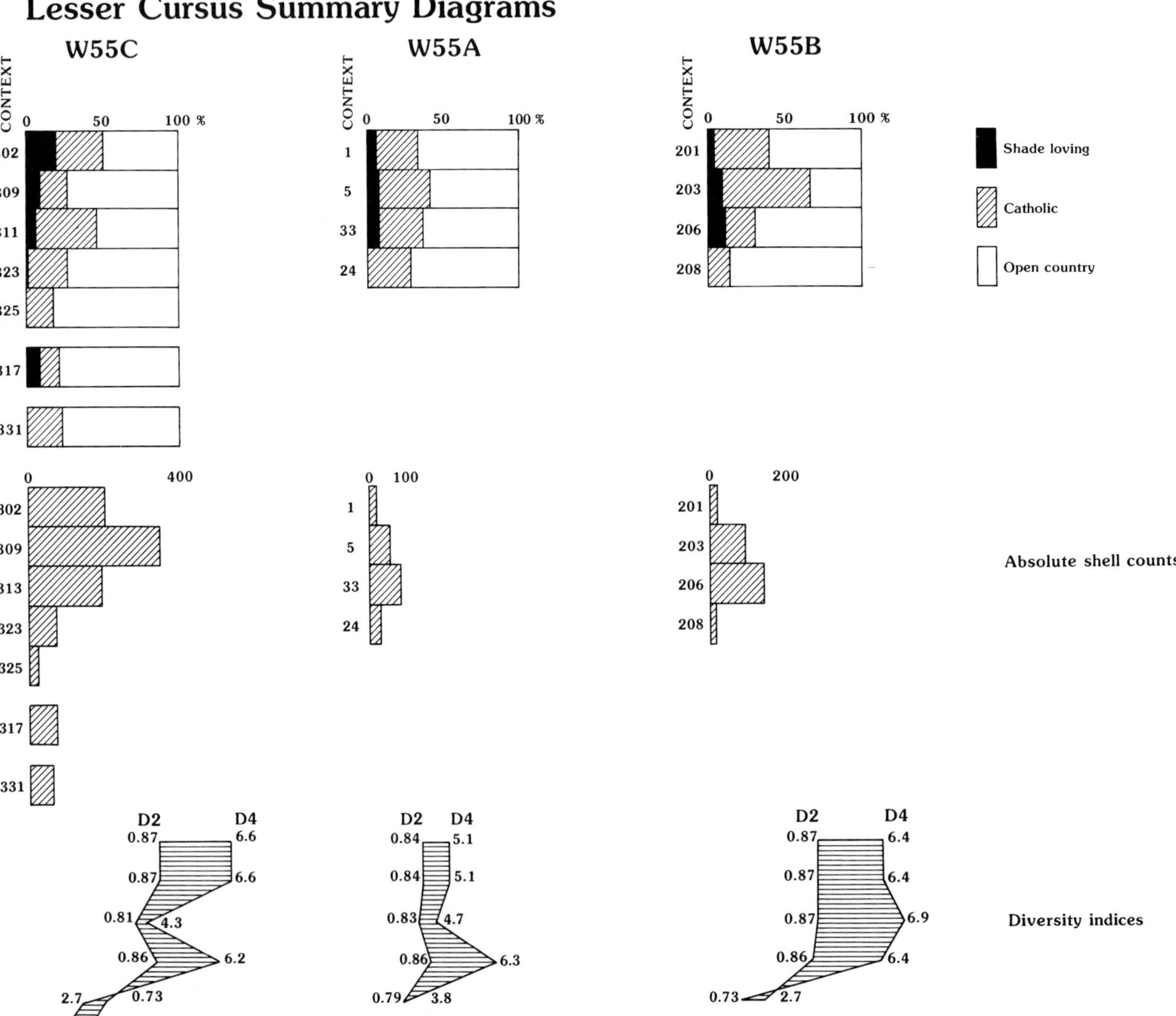

Fig 59 W55 Lesser Cursus: summary mollusc diagrams

numbers of shells (Tables 37–42, MF D5–10; Figs 60, 61). There are both ecological and mathematical objections to this method of analysing data trends (Thomas 1985, 131–56). However, since the main objective was to model fluctuations through time in the overall environmental sequence these objections are considered less significant. The use of percentage frequencies facilitated comparisons between data sets including those from previously excavated sites. Summary diagrams showing relative change between ecological groups, and diversity curves have also been included in order to enhance inter-site comparison (Fig 59; Tables 42, 43, MF1 D10, D11).

In the main mollusc diagrams some species are grouped and plotted together as single histograms since, individually, these species do not provide any additional information. These groupings, and those in the summary diagrams, follow the scheme used by Evans (1984, 7–30), with only minor additions. They are as follows:

Zonitidae: *Vitrea contracta*, *Vitrea cristallina*, *Aegopinella pura*, *Aegopinella nitidula*, *Oxychilus alliarus*, and *Oxychilus cellarius*

Carychium tridentatum: plotted separately in main diagram but otherwise included with shade-loving species

Discus rotundatus: plotted separately in main diagrams but otherwise included with shade-loving species

Other woodland: Clausiliidae, *Ena obscura*, and *Nesovitrea hammonis*

Catholic (or intermediate): *Cochlicopa* spp, *Punctum pygmaeum*, *Cepaea* spp, Trichia (*Trichia hispida*, *Trichia striolata*, *Vitrina pellucida* and *Vertigo pygmaeum*)

Pomatias elegans: plotted separately in main diagrams, but in all other respects is included with catholic species

Open country: Helicellids (*Helicella itala*, *Candidula gigaxii*, and *Cernuella virgata*), *Vallonia costata*, *Vallonia excentrica*, *Pupilla muscorum*, and *Vertigo pygmaeum*.

W55, sampling and analysis (Tables 37–43, MF D5–11)

Two columns, one from the southern ditch section (cut 14), and one from the cross ditch section (cut 12), were analysed from area A (numbered as columns 4, 5, 6, and 7); a single column was analysed from area B (cut 202, column 13); and from area C one column and two individual samples were analysed (cut 304, numbered as columns 8, 9, 10, 11, 12) (Figs 60, 61).

Much of the upper ploughwash sequence, especially in area A, had been disturbed by deep ploughing, suggesting that the biostratigraphy of the uppermost layers is unlikely to retain any chronological integrity.

A similar succession takes place in the top layers of area B.

Area A

In the sequence from the cross ditch (cut 12) a sorted horizon, context 36, had survived the effects of deep ploughing. Below this context 35, a ploughwash overlying the secondary silts, was one of the few contexts to produce shells in sufficient numbers to allow interpretation. Open country species make up most of the faunal assemblage from context 35 (sample 0.56–0.72m); *Vallonia excentrica* is more abundant than *Vallonia costata*, perhaps reflecting the ability of the former to tolerate slightly more moist and shaded conditions. A small but significant shade element is also present, composed mainly of members of the family Zonitidae. The presence of characteristically open country species, such as *Helicella itala* and *Pupilla muscorum*, along with shade-loving species, suggests an autochthonous fauna, specifically reflecting the microenvironmental conditions in the ditch, combined with derived elements. The latter are open country species, which reflect the broader environmental setting of the ditch. The colluvial origin of context 35 indicates that these open conditions were maintained by cultivation close to the monument. Although *Helicella itala* is not common in arable settings today, this is most probably the result of competition from more recently introduced Helicellids, such as *Cernuella virgata* and *Candidula gigaxii*. In the past, *Helicella itala* seems to have been more common in arable environments, occurring abundantly in hill wash deposits and lynchets (Evans 1972, 180–2). Similarly, *Pupilla muscorum* is rare today on arable land, but its abundance in colluvial deposits shows it to have been tolerant of mechanical disturbance in the past (Evans 1972, 147–50).

By 0.48–0.56m in context 36, the Zonitidae are completely absent but 'other woodland species' increase, whilst *Carychium tridentatum* and *Discus rotandatus* appear for the first time. This trend is accompanied by a decline in the numbers of open country species and an increase in species diversity. Both indices rise slightly: D2 from 0.8 to 0.83 and D4 from 3.94 to 4.99, but at the same time absolute shell numbers decline (Fig 60 and Table 42, MF1 D10). The increased stoniness in this context confirms this as a stabilisation horizon. The decrease in absolute shell numbers, mainly due to a sharp decline in the absolute numbers of open country species, is a function of reduced sedimentation. The marked increase in the numbers of *Pomatias elegans* is a further indication of more stable conditions, as sedimentation slows. This species has a preference for loose soils into which it can burrow; such conditions would have been present in the ditch at this stage. Increasing faunal diversity, the appearance of *Discus rotundatus*, and an increase in the numbers of Clausiliidae, strongly suggest shaded conditions. These were probably created by localised colonisation of the ditches by scrubby vegetation. The persistence of *Helicella itala* and reduced but significant numbers of *Vallonia*

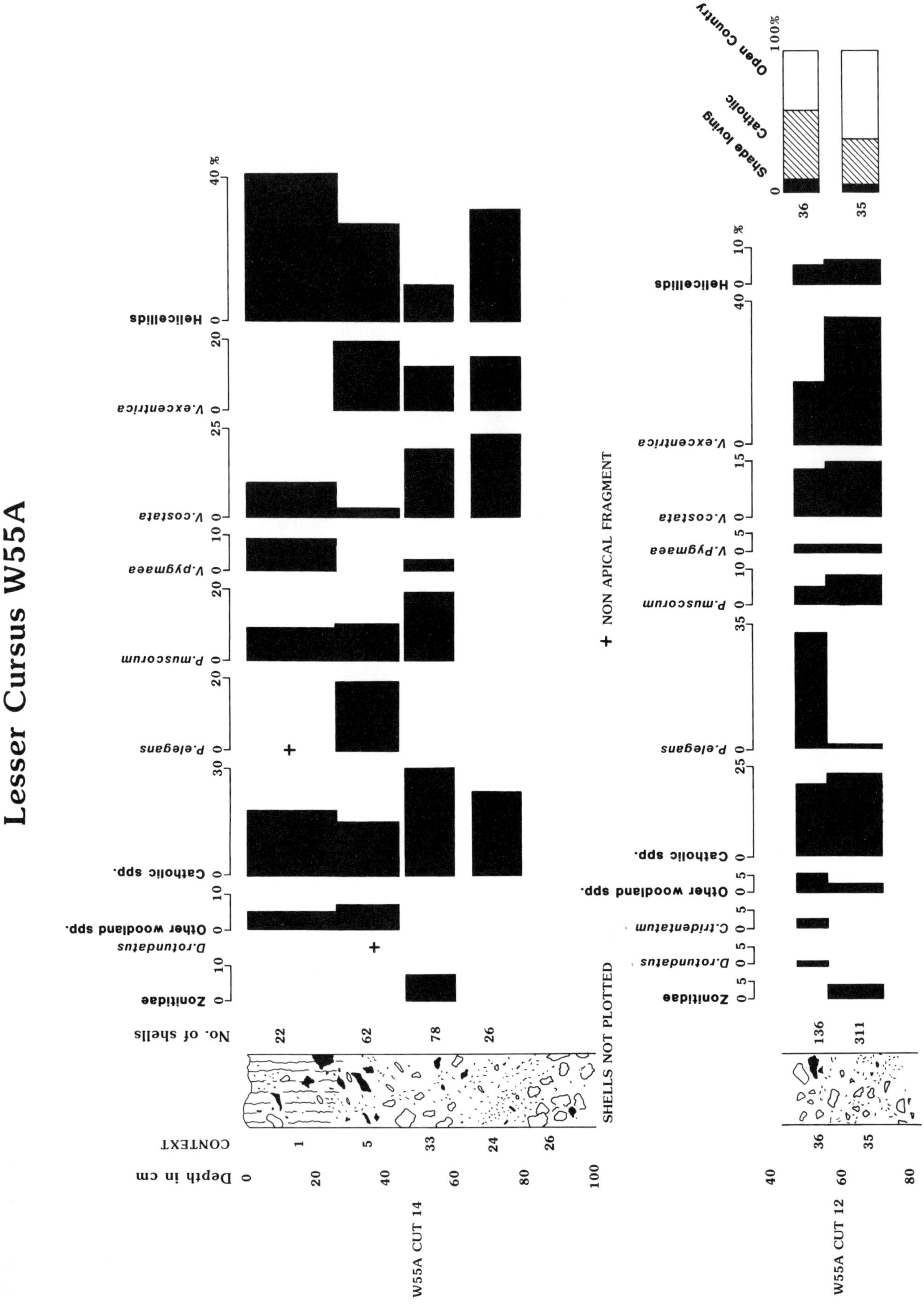

Fig 60 W55 Lesser Cursus: area A mollusc diagrams

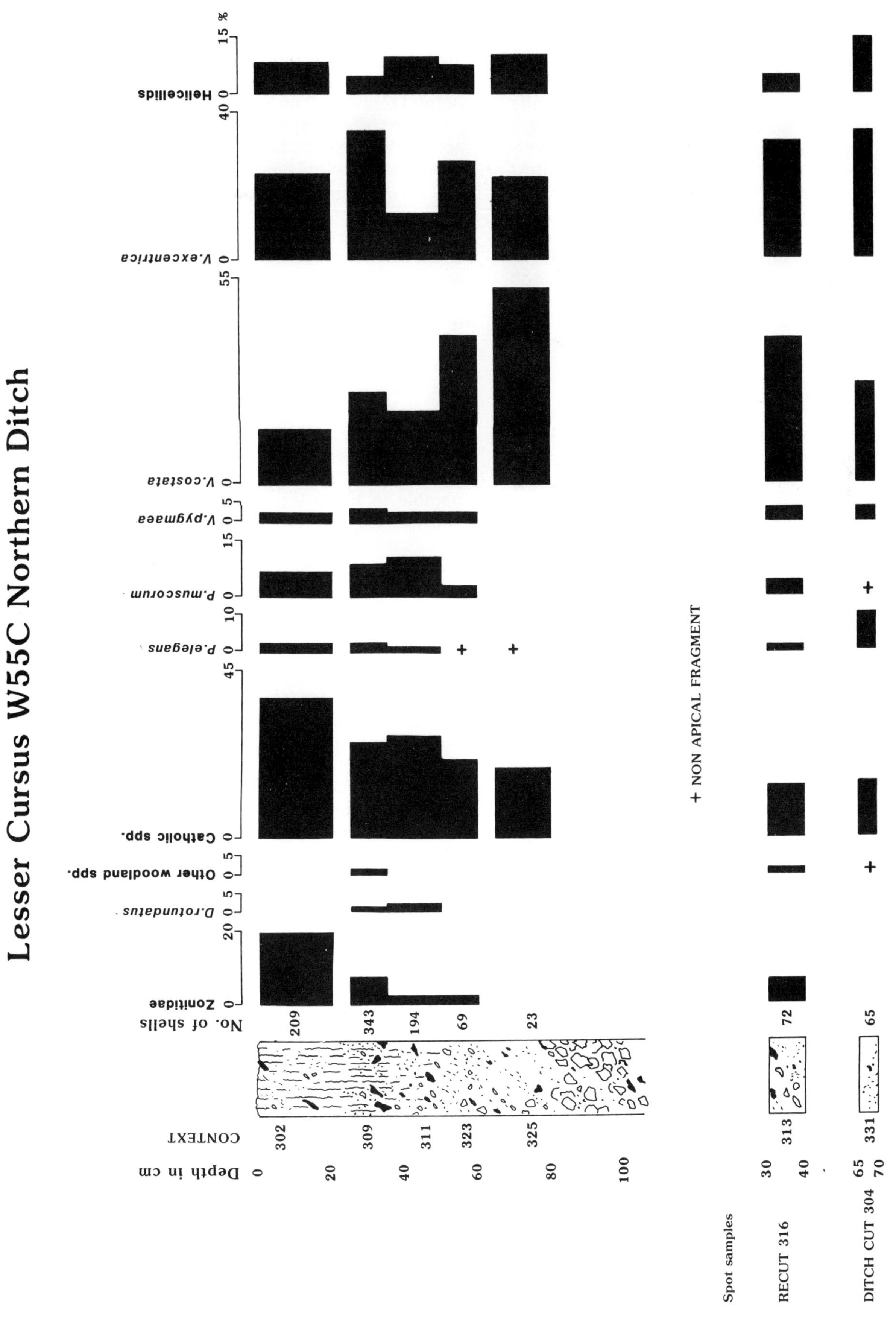

Fig 61 W55 Lesser Cursus: area C mollusc diagrams

costata and *Vallonia excentrica*, point to the existence of predominantly open conditions close by.

Within cut 14, the southern flanking ditch, context 5 (0.26–0.44m), despite disruption by deep ploughing, retained sufficient evidence of sorting to indicate a break in sedimentation. The fauna is dominated by *Helicella itala*, *Pupilla muscorum*, and *Vallonia excentrica*, but, unlike the earlier stabilisation horizon, the Zonitidae and Carychium tridentatum are absent and *Discus rotandatus* is represented by a single non-apical fragment. By the stage at which ploughing was actually passing over the completely silted ditch, it no longer presented a separate range of habitats. Species diversity had declined from a value of 0.86 for D2 in context 33 (this layer appears to be an equivalent of context 35 in the cross ditch, cut 12) to 0.83, and D4 from 6.28 to 4.7. Above this level, in sample 0–0.25m, shell numbers fall sharply but the open aspect is maintained, *Helicella itala* disappears and is replaced by *Cernuella virgata* and *Candidula gigaxii*, both apparently post-Roman introductions.

Area B

A similar sequence can be recognised in area B, where independent evidence for cultivation is provided by the alignment on the Cursus of elements of a field system (Fig 43). Within this sequence a stabilisation horizon, context 206, can be recognised, the species composition of which resembles that from context 36 in area A. The molluscs are predominantly of open country aspect but with a significant range of shade-loving species (Table 39, MF1 D7), including *Discus rotandatus*, *Aegopinella nitidula*, and the Clausiliidae family, all of which prefer woodland or scrub. A complex ecosystem is suggested by the high diversity indices, D2:0.86 and D4:6.39, which included a sufficiently open aspect to favour such species as *Helicella itala* and *Pupilla muscorum* (Fig 59). The recurrence of ploughwash recorded in context 203 is marked by a very slight change in faunal diversity; D4 increases from 6.89 to 6.39 and at the same time the number of shells has fallen by over half. This may be a function of renewed cultivation causing shell fragmentation, although at this level fragmentation does not appear to increase greatly. There is a limited rise from 25% in context 206 to just under 30% in context 203 (percentage fragmentation calculated as a proportion by weight of whole shells). By comparison with the modern ploughsoil, which has a fragmentation approaching 50%, this seems slight, therefore renewed cultivation at area B may have had less ecological impact than at area A.

Area C

Sampling in area C was made difficult by the complex stratigraphy which included evidence of deliberate backfilling and recutting. The lowest sample, 0.85–1.13m, from context 326 of the primary fill, produced only eight shells, all of open country species (Fig 61). Above this sample, 0.65–0.8m is from context 325, which appears in section as a lens of sediments at the base of the secondary silts. It clearly interrupts the tip line of the primary rubble eroding from the southern ditch side, suggesting incorporation as an intact object, possibly a large turf (Limbrey 1975, 291, fig 33). The mollusc assemblage is small, 23 shells in all, and composed predominantly of open country species, mostly *Vallonia costata* and *Vallonia excentrica*, which supports the interpretation of this as fallen turf. The absence of any shade-loving species in these lower strata suggests that the mollusca are derived from the margins of the ditch; presumably at this stage conditions in the ditch are too unstable to allow an autochthonous community to develop. The low diversity indices reinforce this point: D2 is only 0.66 and D4 is 1.91 (Fig 59).

Context 323, sample 0.5–0.6m, represents the slowly accumulating secondary silts. Conditions were still unconducive to colonisation and, as in the previous layer, low diversity indices suggest a derived fauna of exclusively open country species, D2:0.73 and D4:2.68. Overlying the secondary silts is a strongly cemented chalk rubble, context 317; this is almost certainly the result of backfilling, possibly with material derived from the cursus bank. The faunal diversity in this context is greater than in earlier layers. Although still dominated by open country species, there is a minor shade element represented by *Aegopinella pura*, *Vitrea crystallina*, and Clausiliidae.

Contexts 310 and 311 fill the inner and outer recuts which appear to have silted up naturally with poorly sorted colluvial silts. Context 311, sample 0.35–0.5m, produced a high-diversity fauna with values comparable to those for colluvial silts at the other two subsites, D2:0.86. The xerophyllic species *Helicella itala* and *Pupilla muscorum* are both present, as are other open country species such as *Vallonia costata*, *Vallonia excentrica*, and *Vertigo pygmaea*. The shade-loving species *Discus rotandatus* and *Vitrea contracta* are present in small numbers, suggesting conditions similar to those at the other areas. However, in the uppermost levels of the ditch the trend at area C begins to diverge.

There is an initial fall in diversity in context 309, a fall which occurs at area A in response to the re-introduction of cultivation. It is difficult to account for this abrupt change at area C, since in other respects it seems to be less affected by the ecological changes associated with cultivation. However, the more complicated stratigraphy in area C means that equivalent phases are difficult to identify. Above this in the uppermost layer faunal diversity increases to 0.87 for D2 and 6.57 for D4, and compared to the other areas the number of shells remains high. Shade-loving and catholic species increase proportionally from context 309 through to context 302, the top fill of the ditch. Both *Vallonia costata* and *Vallonia excentrica* numbers fall dramatically, but surprisingly those of *Helicella itala* and *Candidula gigaxii* hardly change. *Discus rotandatus*, *Aegopinella nitidula*, *Acanthinula aculeata*, and the Clausiliidae suggest a scrub vegetation over the ditch. The surface of context 317 was penetrated by a series of stakeholes, perhaps left by fence posts driven in through contexts 302 and 309. A hedgerow along the line of the fence, formed by scrub vegetation with the occasional tree, would adequately account for the more shaded conditions at this end of the cursus. The higher shell numbers in the tertiary silts suggest a slower rate of accumulation with less fragmentation than at the two other subsites. Moreover, there is no sign of the heavy ploughing responsible for truncating the ditches in area A.

Discussion

Despite the limitations placed on interpretation by a rather variable data set, the later environmental sequence for the Lesser Cursus can be reconstructed in some detail. Unfortunately, the evidence for the Neolithic environment is too sparse for detailed comment. There is no reason, however, to suppose that the open conditions revealed by other sequences in the area were not present during the construction of the monument. During later prehistory, temporal variation can be seen in the major cultivation episodes, with phases of intensification and contraction producing concomitant ecological change. Over the length of the monument these major episodes show spatial variations which are reflected in the ceramic assemblage and in the pedology of the ditch stratigraphy, as well as in the comparative environmental successions.

4.6 W56, sample excavation of the Stonehenge Cursus

4.6 a Site description

In September 1983 two small cuttings were excavated through the southern ditch and bank area of the Stonehenge Cursus, Scheduled Ancient Monument Wiltshire AM328. The first of these, W56 A, a cutting within the former area of Fargo Wood, was carried out for research purposes; the second, W56 B, was a cutting alongside the Stonehenge to Larkhill track, excavated in advance of the insertion of a sewage pipeline.

Reported separately in this vol, W58, the excavation of Amesbury 42 long barrow, must be considered as an integral part of the research into the Stonehenge Cursus and its associated monuments.

The Stonehenge Cursus, also referred to as the Amesbury Cursus, was first recorded by William Stukeley in 1723. His published engravings (Stukeley 1740) and, more informatively, his manuscript drawings (Bodleian Library Gough Maps 122, 125), show the full length of the Cursus as an earthwork, with Amesbury 42 long barrow lying beyond the eastern end, and the western terminal inexplicably shown as rounded. A combination of agricultural erosion and more deliberate destruction have now effectively levelled approximately 40% of the length of the Cursus, specifically the section both within and east of Stonehenge Bottom.

During this century a number of excavations have been carried out, in many cases linked to specific destructive episodes. These are located on Figure 62, to which reference can be made for all aspects of this report, and can be summarised as follows:

Farrer 1917. Unpublished observations and recording of a cutting made by the Army. Notes and finds in Devizes Museum.

Stone 1947. Excavations on the southern ditch. Ditch sectioned, no trace of bank. Causeway in ditch and antler from ditch bottom. Material in Salisbury Museum. Published Stone 1947.

Christie 1959. Excavations on and within the western terminal some time after the levelling for agriculture of the terminal bank. Several cuttings were made including one involving the total excavation of round barrow Winterbourne Stoke 30. Material in Salisbury Museum. Published Christie 1963; flint assemblage reappraised in Saville 1980.

W56 A, Fargo Wood

Area A was a 2m wide cutting in the southern flanking ditch, located at grid reference SU 11204288, approximately 100m west of Stone's cutting (Stone 1947). The trench was intended to examine the ditch, here visible as a slight depression, the apparent area of the bank, and also a small area beyond the tail of the bank.

The ditch, cut 21 (Figs 62, 63), was approximately 2.0m wide and 0.8m deep with a flat bottom approximately 1.3m wide. The sequence of ditch fills was markedly decalcified, only a small amount of calcareous primary fill (context 17) surviving. Above this, context 16 and subsequent deposits appeared clean, brown, and devoid of chalk content with the exception of small rounded particles. The decalcified nature of the ditch fill resulted in samples taken for molluscan analysis being almost devoid of shells (Table 45, MF1 D14). The upper secondary ditch fills produced very small quantities of later Bronze Age pottery (Raymond, this vol, 4.6 c, none illustrated), together with a small copper alloy ring from context 13.

The outer (southern) edge of the ditch showed a stepped profile, caused by two shallow scoops, cuts 22 and 23, neither of which contained any datable finds. The scoops were co-linear with the main ditch, although no stratigraphic relationship between any of the individual elements could be ascertained with certainty. It would seem unlikely that they formed a part of a counterscarp structure, no suggestions of which have previously been made for the overall structure of the flanking earthworks of the Cursus. Such an arrangement, however, appears to have formed a part of the western terminal (Christie 1963, fig 1).

No trace of the structure of the bank was recovered, although its former position was clearly indicated by a rise in the surface of the natural chalk. This corresponded with a 'protected' chalk surface, the 'compo' referred to by both Stone (1947, 15) and later by Christie (1963, 380). In contrast to the relationship recorded by Stone (1947), the ditch and bank did not appear to have been separated by a berm of any great width. This may be an indication of a somewhat irregular construction method for the flanking earthworks, possibly involving a series of individual dumps. The irregular appearance of these flanking earthworks, where they survive relatively intact, may therefore partly reflect their original morphology, although the effects of recent damage cannot be discounted. The sporadically segmental appearance of the ditch would also seem to be an indication of its original form as Stone located a causeway within the length of ditch he examined (Stone 1947, 12, fig 3). The two terminals here were of markedly differing shape, again suggesting an irregular, possibly gang-dug ditch.

The rear (north) of the apparent bank area within cutting A appears to correspond with a slight negative lynchet, the deposits associated with which again contained occasional sherds of later Bronze Age pottery. The lynchet may possibly be of relatively recent origin, but may also be associated with the incorporation of the

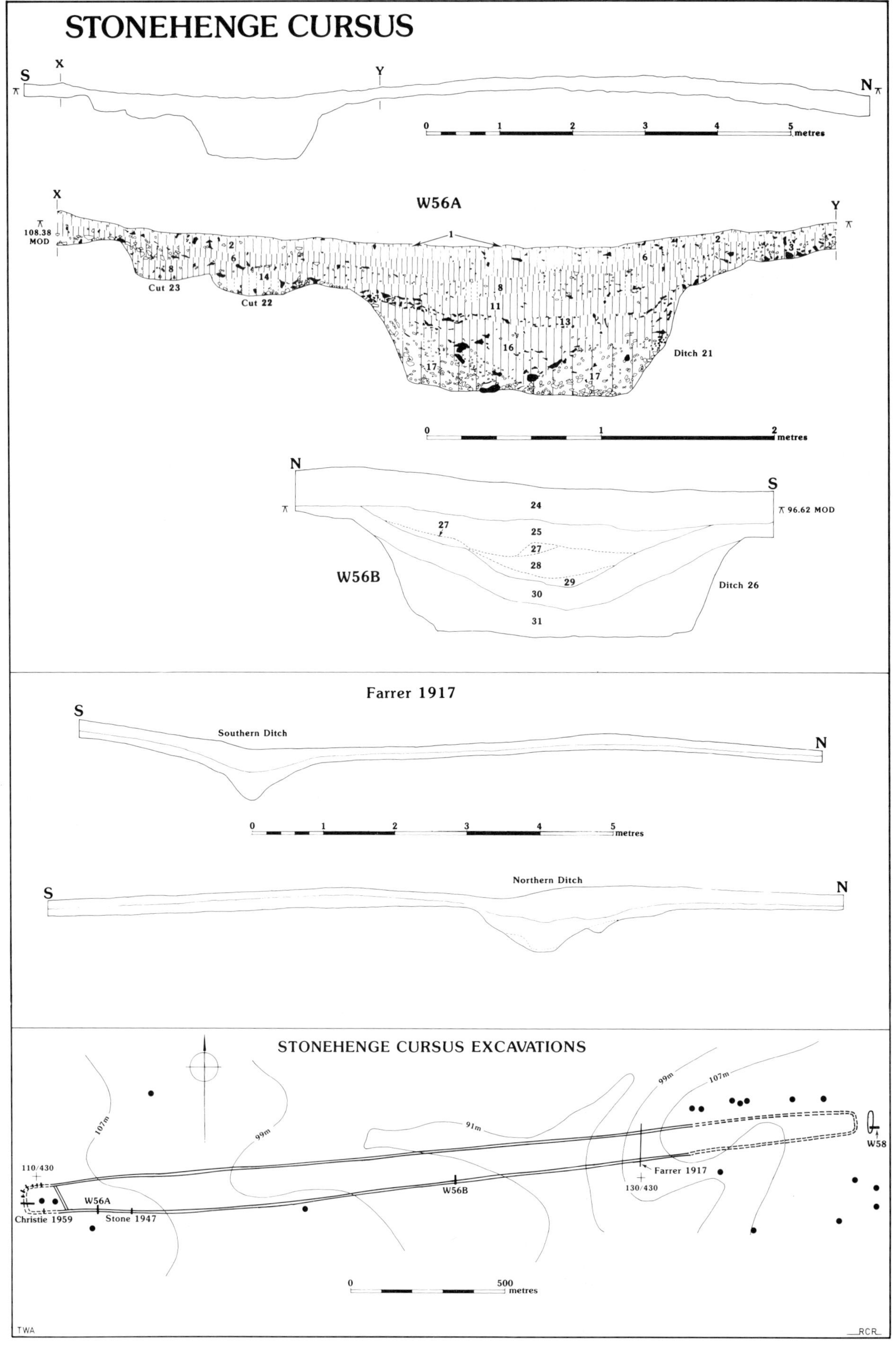

Fig 62 The Stonehenge Cursus: location of all previous excavations, W56 A and B ditch sections

Fig 63 W56 Stonehenge Cursus: area A, view from south-east over excavated ditch and former position of bank (scale 2m)

Cursus into the extensive and coherent 'Celtic' field system to the north and north-west (W34, this vol, 4.14).

W56 B, the Larkhill Track

Area B was immediately to the east of the Stonehenge to Larkhill track at SU 12384299, and also examined the southern ditch. The proximity of the metalled track and its verge meant that at this point no trace of the bank could be seen on the ground, partly the reason for the location of the crossing of the Cursus by the pipeline. This minimally destructive location was consequently unable to provide any further opportunity for the examination of the bank area of the Cursus.

The ditch, here sampled by means of a 1m wide hand-dug trench, was of similar dimensions to the section recorded at W56A. Approximately 2.2m wide at the surface and a maximum of 0.8m deep from tarmac level, the ditch had a flat bottom 1.45m wide. This sequence was also sampled for molluscan analysis. Although the filling here was markedly less decalcified than that from W56A, and consequently produced more shells, the totals are still too small for any detailed environmental interpretation. The results are therefore discussed less specifically in 8.3. Details of the molluscs are recorded in Table 46, MF1 E1. For the most part all that can be said is that open country species are dominant throughout the sequence. In the only two viable samples, 0.35–0.45m and 0.45–0.55m, a minor shade element and the catholic species presumably reflect the more moist and shaded conditions within the ditch.

No pottery was recovered from this section, whereas the flint assemblage, although too small for analysis, was considerably larger than that recovered from W56 A (Table 115).

As part of the watching brief a 1m wide strip running north–south across the interior of the Cursus was stripped of topsoil and track makeup and was thoroughly cleaned. In practice only the southern half of the monument was revealed in this way, as part of it was sealed by a considerable build up of soil and rubble forming a causeway on which the track ran. It was ascertained that the depth to which the pipe was to be laid would cause no damage to the northern ditch and bank and consequently this area was not examined. No features or finds were recorded within the somewhat restricted area thus observed.

Data from the two cuttings described above, together with Stone's published accounts and the observations made by Farrer, suggest a coherent pattern of filling for the southern ditch of the Cursus. The origin of the unusual decalcified ditch fill which, from Farrer's observations appears to be confined to the southern ditch, is still ill-understood. It does appear from the exposures discussed above that the sequence becomes progressively less decalcified from west to east along the southern ditch. The most marked contrast is provided, however, by the two extremities of the Cursus, where the sequences from both the western terminal (Christie 1963, re-examined in 1987, Richards in prep b) and from Amesbury 42 long barrow (W58, this vol, 4.7) are devoid of any decalcified deposits.

Summary and dating

The absence of datable and appropriately stratified artefacts from restricted cuttings of the type described above is not surprising, particularly when the general paucity of finds from Cursus excavations is considered. Stone's excavations, more extensive in a deliberate search for dating material, did, however, produce one stratified antler from the base of the ditch (Stone 1947, 14; fig 3D). A sample of this antler produced a radiocarbon date of 2878–2502 BC (OxA 1403). This date is considerably later than was estimated and cannot be accepted as dating the construction of the Cursus. It can be suggested that the 'recess' in the ditch edge, within which the antler lay (Stone 1947, 14; fig 3D), may have been a later intrusive feature, unrecognised in excavation. Further indication that the construction of the Stonehenge Cursus should date to the same phase as that of the Lesser Cursus (W55, this vol, 4.5) was provided by the *in situ* flint knapping cluster recovered from the base of the western terminal ditch of the former monument in 1987. This appears to have been a blade industry, suggesting, by analogy with industries recovered during the course of project fieldwork (Harding, this vol, 5.2), a date within the first half of the fourth millennium BC.

The sample excavations, which did not examine the interior of the enclosure and which together represent a minute sample of the ditch and bank area, were never intended to attempt to shed light on the potential function of the Cursus. This inevitably remains ill-understood.

4.6 b Lithics

The two cuttings produced a total of 294 pieces of worked flint, 131 from area A, and 163 from the smaller cutting in area B. The composition of these groups is shown in Table 115. In both cases the secondary ditch deposits (Fig 62, area A, context 16, area B, context 29) produced small groups of fresh flakes which may have limited refitting potential. No further analysis of these small groups has been undertaken.

4.6 c The prehistoric pottery

by Frances Raymond

A total of 12 sherds (Table 44, MF1 D13; none illustrated), representing a minimum number of five vessels, were recovered from the ditch silts and from essentially unstratified layers north of the bank area. All identifiable sherds are of later Bronze Age date and are probably associated with the field system extending south from W34 and encroaching on the Cursus. The estimate of number of vessels present is based on fabric differences alone. The clay pastes used to produce three of the vessels (FfeS:LBA/4, FS:LBA/4, and FS:LBA/5) occur commonly in the form of largely undecorated post-Deverel-Rimbury vessels.

4.6 d Copper alloy

Context 13, SF10 (not illustrated as in fragmentary condition).

Ring with one intact terminal, tapering towards the incomplete end. Made of circular section wire, maximum diameter 20mm.

4.6 e Animal bones

by Mark Maltby

A small number of animal bones were recorded from area A, including those of hare, pig, sheep-sized mammal, and unidentified large mammal. All these bones could be relatively recent intrusions into the deposits, and were consequently not computer-recorded.

4.7 W58, Amesbury 42 long barrow

4.7 a Site description

Amesbury 42 long barrow (Scheduled Ancient Monument Wiltshire AM328) lies at SU 13754318, approximately 30m beyond the apparent eastern end of the Stonehenge Cursus (Fig 62). Orientated broadly north–south, it is positioned almost on the crest of a very low ridge from which point it would have been visible from the western terminal of the Cursus. Stukeley's engraving of 1723 (Stukeley 1740) shows the barrow mound lying beyond the then extant eastern terminal of the Cursus, but also shows what may be smaller ditches connecting the two earthworks. The engraved and printed version varies, however, from the original drawing (Bodleian Library Gough Maps 229, 125), which shows the two elements unconnected. Hoare (1810, 158) considered the barrow to be the end of the Cursus while Thurnam obviously considered it to be a conventional long barrow, excavating it as such in the mid-nineteenth century and recovering inhumations, most probably not primary, and an ox skull (Thurnam 1868).

During this century the monument has been considerably damaged, and at present is barely recognisable as a long barrow. The main reason for its ill-defined state is the variety of land use to which elements of the barrow are subject. These are shown on Figure 64. Past cultivation has obviously reduced the mound considerably and has blurred the profile of the mound and ditch. Present cultivation continues to erode the eastern flank of the mound, along the main axis of which a metalled track now runs. The western flank is perhaps the most stable area of the monument, lying within a plantation belt where it has recently been cleared of trees and scrub.

Pre-excavation survey

Prior to excavation, an intensive surface collection employing a 5m by 5m grid was carried out within the area of arable cultivation. The collection area, 80m by 20m, included the eastern flank of the barrow and the eastern flanking ditch, here visible as a slight depression and corresponding soil mark. The collection, details of which are contained within the archive, together with close observation of elements of the barrow revealed by ploughing, suggested that the mound within the culti-

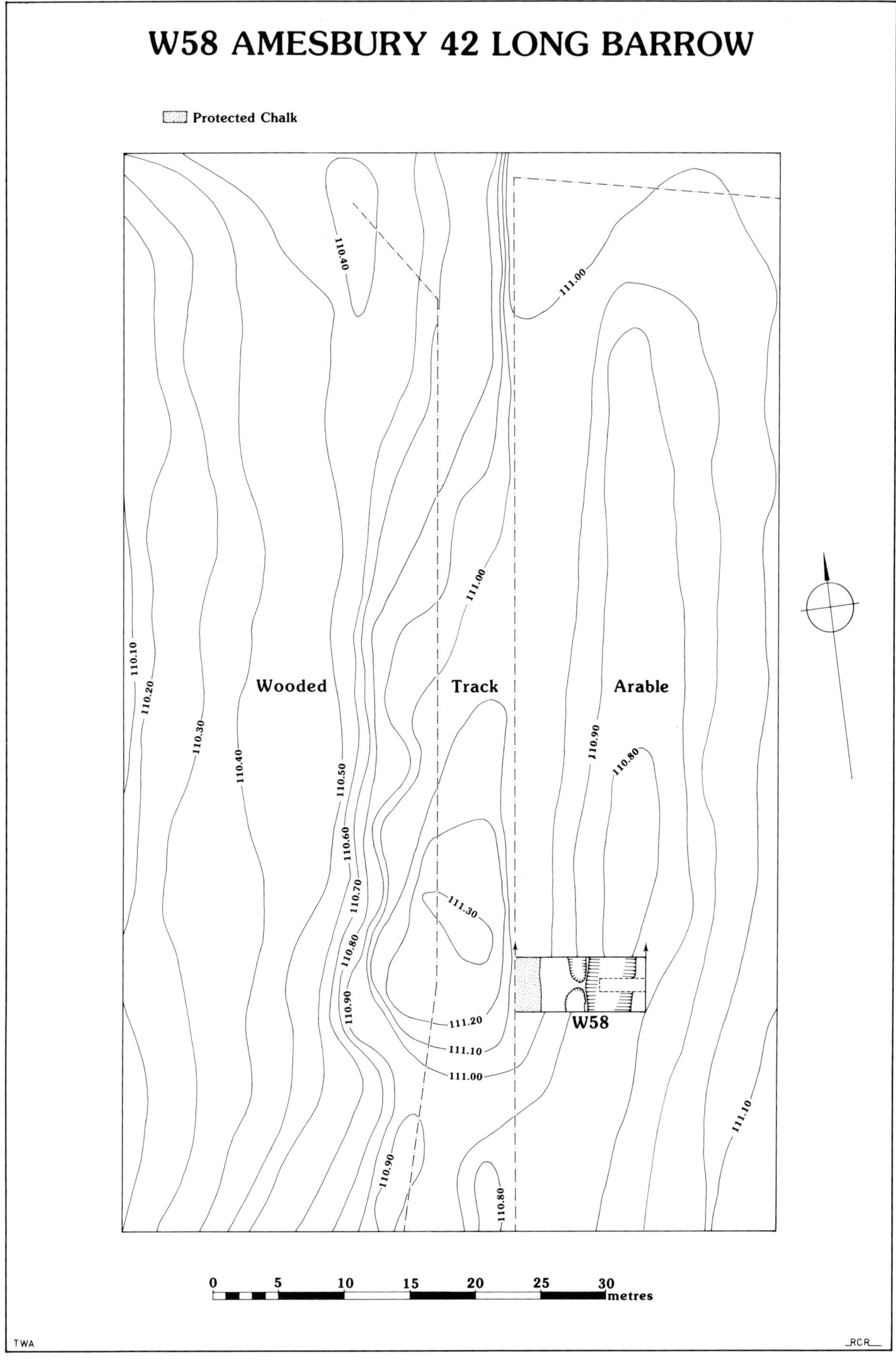

Fig 64 W58 Amesbury 42 long barrow: contour plan and trench location

vated area had been totally destroyed with the consequent loss of the buried soil.

Excavation

The sample excavation was to examine the surviving structure of the cultivated flank of the barrow by means of a single trench, the location of which is shown on Figure 64. Within the excavated area, 10m long and 4m wide, both the modern ploughsoil and the upper colluvial ditch fill, interpreted as an underlying ploughsoil, were excavated on a 1m grid, with a 20% sample dry-sieved through a 4mm sieve.

Excavation confirmed that all trace of the mound and buried soil had been removed, although the extent of the former was indicated by a 2m wide area of protected chalk, within which two stakeholes were recorded. However, the section at the junction of the cultivated area and the track border did preserve sporadic traces of both the mound and its buried soil, the former a maximum of 0.15m thick and penetrated by numerous root channels. The buried soil, a shallow rendzina overlying a sorted horizon, was sampled for molluscan analysis in two places, but produced very few shells. On pedological grounds, however, it can be suggested that the buried soil had supported grassland for some time prior to the construction of the mound (Entwistle, this vol, 4.7 e).

The excavation of the ditch provided unexpected evidence for two phases of construction. The sequence described and the contexts referred to are those shown in Figure 65, the northern main section. Data relating to aspects of the ditch sequence may be from contexts equivalent to those shown on this figure.

Phase 1 consisted of two terminals of a round-bottomed ditch (cut 111), separated by a causeway approximately 0.4m wide (Fig 66). The dimensions of the ditch were difficult to ascertain owing to the truncation of the profile by the eroded edge of the phase 2 ditch, but the width can be suggested as a maximum of 1.40m. The recorded depth was approximately 0.70m, but the level of the natural chalk surface from which this ditch was presumably cut suggests that the original depth may have been nearer to 1.30m. The filling of the phase 1 ditch, which contained no datable artefacts, suggests a largely natural accumulation, the eccentric profile of elements within context 96 suggesting an associated bank to the west. Context 84 may, however, be associated with a more deliberate episode of filling of the partly silted ditch, possibly at the time of the phase 2 enlargement.

A small nucleated scatter of *in situ* flint knapping debris was recovered from the base of the northern terminal of the phase 1 ditch. The location of this scatter, produced apparently by a single knapper working within the ditch, is shown in Figure 67. Small flint nodules, possibly obtained in the course of excavating the ditch, were utilised, at least in one case, for the production of a series of ridged flakes. In this case a

Fig 66 W58 Amesbury 42 long barrow: excavated phase 1 causewayed ditch and surviving structure of barrow mound (nearest scale 2m)

simple blade core technique was used (Harding, this vol, 4.7 b).

The phase 1 ditch described above was cut by a co-linear, but considerably larger ditch, cut 133. The phase 2 ditch was flat-bottomed, 1.5m wide at its base and approximately 4.0m wide at the surface. The maximum recorded depth was approximately 2.2m.

The filling of the phase 2 ditch shows an apparently natural silting sequence with vacuous primary rubble layers containing occasional lenses of humic soil overlain by increasingly fine calcareous colluvial deposits. The primary fills below context 94 are devoid of datable artefacts, despite containing considerable quantities of worked flint, the majority apparently primary knapping debris, including at least two further clusters with refitting potential. Positive dating evidence from the sequence first appears in context 94 where pottery of Beaker fabric is associated with occasional bone fragments. Context 90 contains greater quantities of Beaker/Collared Urn pottery, together with animal bone, identifiable fragments of which appear to be primarily cattle and pig.

The environmental sequence, which suggests that the monument was constructed in relatively open conditions, indicates an increase in shade during the Beaker period.

Above this, contexts 88 and, to a greater degree, 76, produced pottery of Roman date; context 88 also marked the first occurrence of sheep/goat bones within the sequence.

Both ditch sequences produced substantial quantities of worked flint, within which there were few tools/retouched pieces, and a high proportion of cores, suggesting a resumption of the primary industrial activity represented within the phase 1 ditch. The occurrence of additional, but inevitably less discrete areas of refitting knapping debris within the lower fills of the phase 2 ditch has already been noted. A preliminary assessment of this material suggests an element of blade/bladelet production. The flint assemblage from this site will be reported on in more detail in a further publication (Richards in prep b).

Discussion

The excavation of a relatively small sample of the flank of Amesbury 42 long barrow, while introducing the complication of a second phase of construction, has provided only limited indications of the morphology of the two individual phases of the monument. Considered in isolation, phases corresponding to those recovered from other complex long barrows, for example Waylands Smithy (Atkinson 1965), could perhaps be suggested, but Amesbury 42 must be considered in the light of its topographical and possibly physical relationship with the eastern terminal of the Stonehenge Cursus.

The discrepancy between Stukeley's drawn and engraved record of that relationship has already been noted, and on balance it appears that the long barrow mound was recorded as separate from the terminal ditch of the cursus. Magnetometer survey carried out in 1987 (Gater, this vol, MFI D12) confirms the position of a north–south terminal ditch in the position formerly suggested, approximately 20m west of the long barrow (Richards in prep b). The area between the terminal and the long barrow is unsuitable for detailed magnetometer survey but scanning in 1988 suggests the existence of a flanking ditch on the west side of the barrow (Ancient Monuments Laboratory, pers comm). Clarification of the relationship between these two monuments may only be resolved by further research.

4.7 b Lithics

The sample excavation produced a total of 3250 pieces of worked flint (Table 115), primarily from accumulative deposits within both the phase 1 and phase 2 ditches. The stage one assessment demonstrated refitting potential within several discrete deposits from the phase 2 ditch sequence, in addition to the knapping cluster from the base of the phase 1 ditch recognised during excavation (see below). The further analysis of this substantial assemblage was not seen as a priority within the initial lithic research programme. However, the subsequent recovery of a lithic assemblage from the western terminal of the Stonehenge Cursus has provided a comparative sample and both groups of material will be reported in more detail in a future publication (Richards in prep b).

This report is consequently concerned with the detailed analysis of a single well-stratified group of worked flint, selected for its spatial and stratigraphic integrity.

The analysis of a sealed knapping deposit from the phase 1 ditch

by Philip Harding

The excavation of the phase 1 causewayed ditch revealed *in situ* knapping debris in the compacted primary chalk silts. Given the constraints of excavation time, the excavation of individual pieces and intensive *in situ* cleaning was not possible. After definition,the assemblage was therefore excavated in units of 0.10m, with the total contents of each square bagged separately and all soil residue wet-sieved through a 60 micron mesh.

The cluster of knapping debris was oval in plan, approximately 0.50–0.60m N/S by 0.30m E/W with a central accumulation 0.20m in diameter (Fig 67). It lay horizontally against the eastern ditch edge in fine primary silts, which had accumulated from the west. There was no indication of subsequent horizontal or vertical movement. The material was lifted in a single shallow spit. The distribution by weight is shown in Figure 67.

The method of recovery was designed to facilitate subsequent refitting and analysis which it was hoped would:

i establish if the assemblage represented *in situ* knapping or resulted from dumping
ii establish the presence of a stratified sequence of cores
iii reconstruct the knapping techniques
iv clarify the function of individual flake types

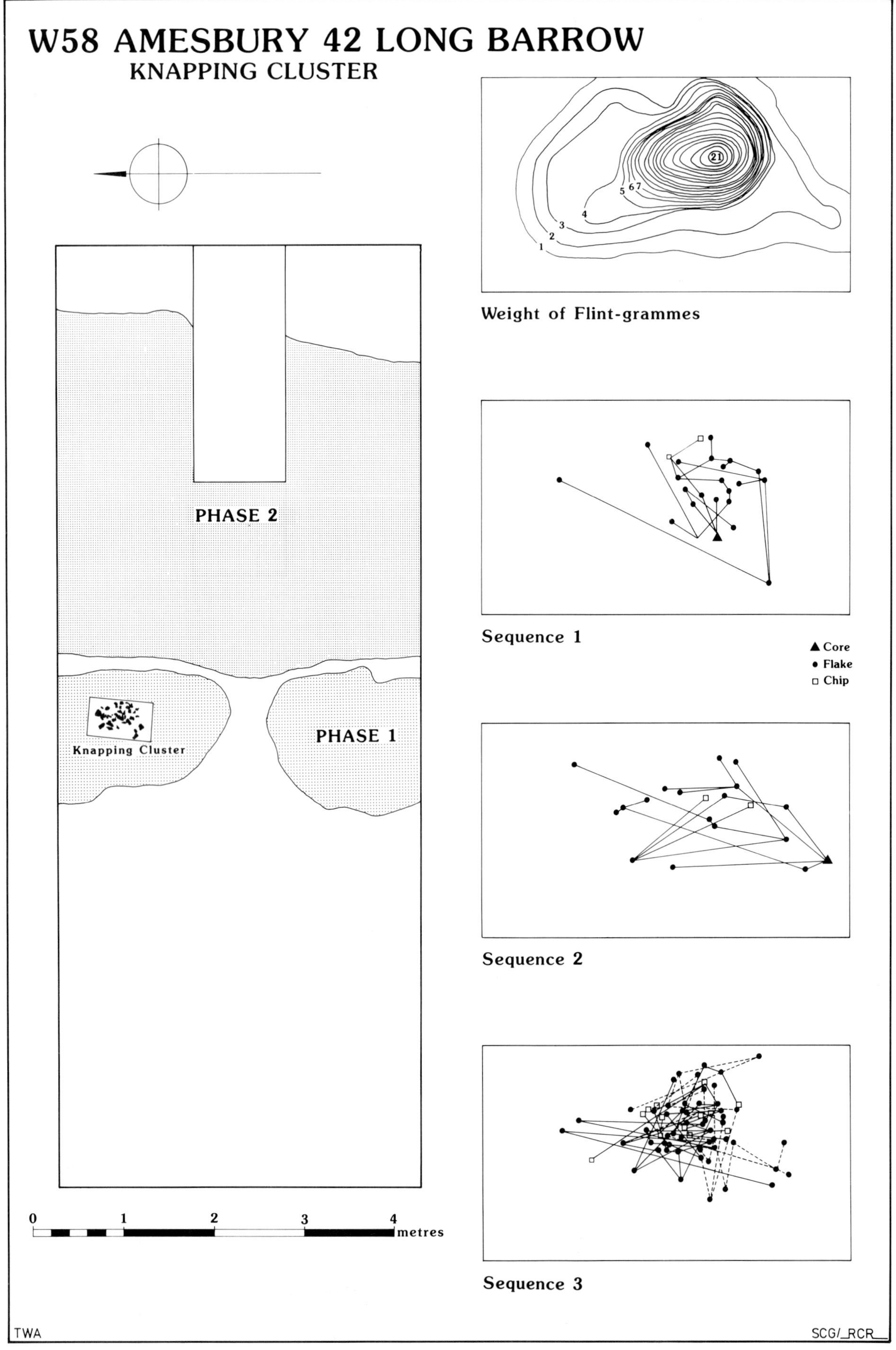

Fig 67 W58 Amesbury 42 long barrow: location plan and refitting sequences of phase 1 ditch flint knapping cluster

v provide comparisons with experimentally produced knapping clusters.

Raw material

The refitted nodules are rounded or subangular and weigh between 200g and 400g. Three unworked pieces which average 140g may have been too small for use. Nodule size results in the production of small flakes and good core control is essential to maximise production.

The results of refitting are shown in Figures 68 and 69. The three reconstructed sequences comprise two with cores which themselves refit to form a single nodule and one sequence with no core. A third nodule is represented by two small groups of refitting cortical flakes which were removed by alternate flaking. These probably represent platform preparation of a core

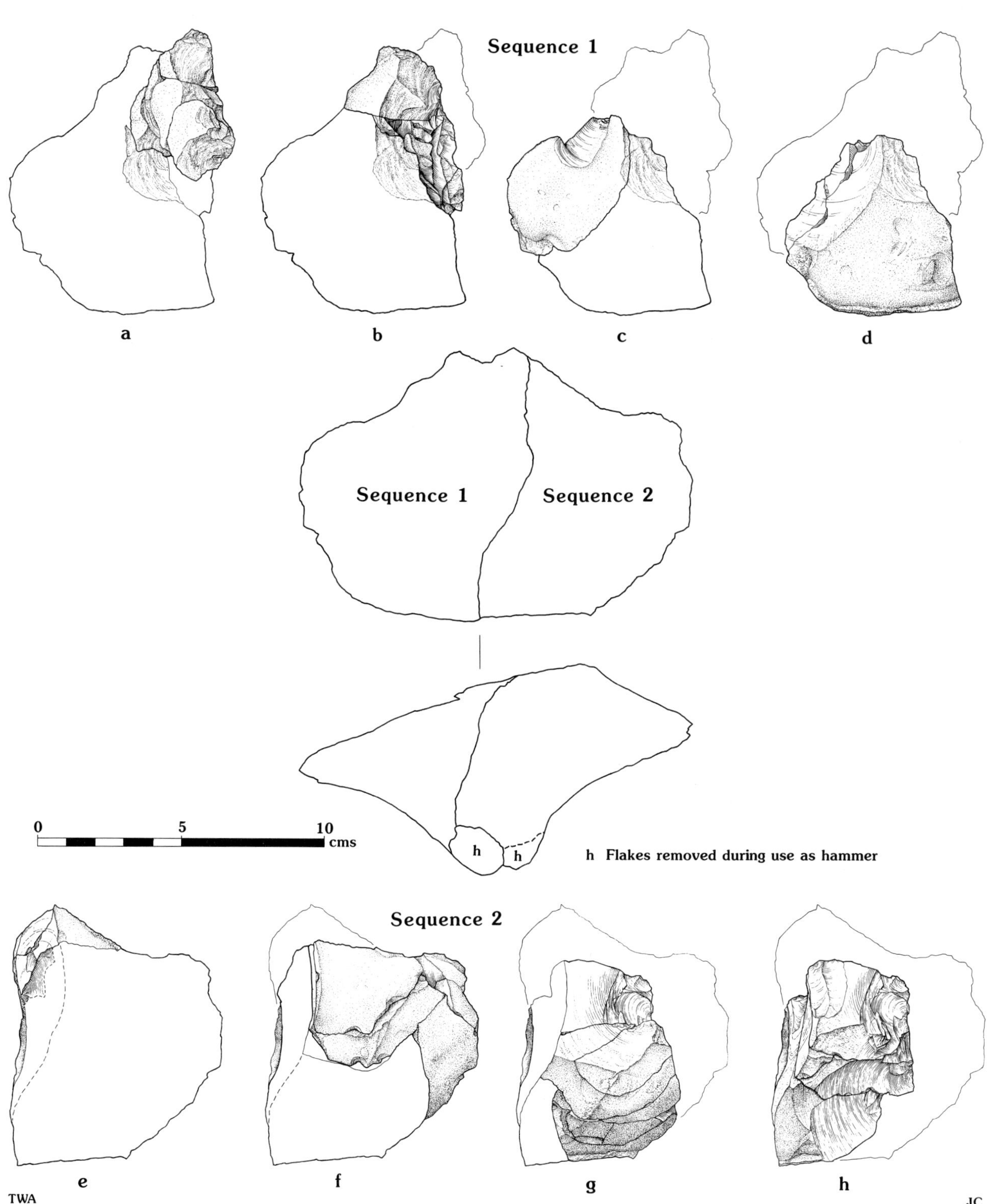

Fig 68 W58 Amesbury 42 long barrow: refitting flint 1

which was taken away. There are 12 miscellaneous flint flakes. The three major sequences can be summarised as follows.

Sequence 1, core 1

This failed core demonstrates core preparation and core orientation. Seventeen pieces plus two chips were refitted to two striking platforms and their flaking surfaces. Five flakes were reconstructed from broken pieces. The debris was contained within an area of approximately 0.20m by 0.20m, although two pieces of a flake were found 0.45m apart. The raw material was a nodule which had split along a thermal fracture. The rejected core which refits to core 2 was found on the western edge of the cluster.

Striking platform 1 (Fig 68a). Cortical flakes (two refitted) were removed to prepare a striking platform for the production of ridged flakes down the front of the core. Production failed and the striking platform was reprepared over a wider surface before production resumed.

Flaking surface (Fig 69b). Two unridged flakes were removed from the side of the flaking surface, possibly to accentuate subsequent guiding ridges. The five remaining flakes are ridged, the first flake being guided by a natural cortical ridge. They have cortical distal ends. No usable flakes were produced.

Striking platform 2 (Fig 68c). This was prepared by removing a flake adjacent to the first striking platform using the flaking surface as a striking platform.

Flaking surface (Fig 68d). Two large overlapping decortication flakes and one miss-hit flake were removed at right angles to the first striking platform before the core was abandoned.

Sequence 2, core 2

This failed core shows part of the core preparation sequence. Eighteen flakes plus three chips were refitted to two striking platforms and their flaking surfaces. One broken flake was reconstructed. Four flakes were found during initial cleaning, implying that sequence 2 was stratified above sequence 1 and possibly above sequence 3. There is also an area of battered cortex on one corner which undoubtedly results from use as a hammer. Three cortical flakes were refitted to this corner. The points of percussion on sequence 3 indicate a soft hammer mode. Ohnuma and Bergman (1982, 166) have demonstrated that cortical surfaces produce characteristics which are indistinguishable from other soft hammers.

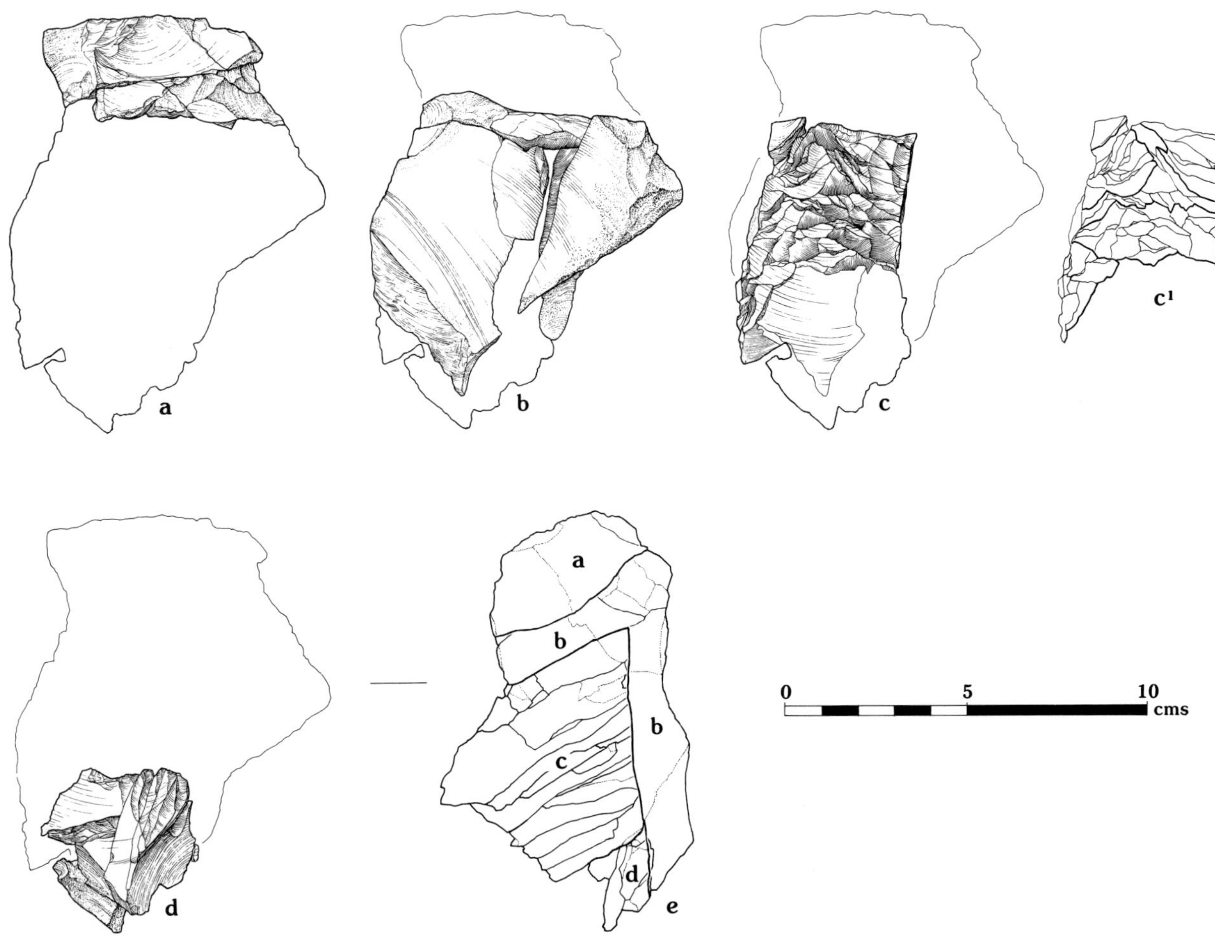

Fig 69 W58 Amesbury 42 long barrow: refitting flint 2

The debris from sequence 2 has a slightly more dispersed oval pattern with a maximum spread of 0.5m NE–SW. The core was abandoned in the south-west corner of the cluster, approximately 0.2m from core 1. They are of a similar type.

Striking platform 1 (Fig 68 e). Two flakes were removed to prepare this striking platform which cuts the area of hammering.

Striking platform 2 (Fig 68 f). Five flakes were removed by alternate flaking to prepare this striking platform at right angles to the first striking platform, as in core 1.

Flaking surfaces (Fig 68 g). Five overlapping decortication flakes were removed from the flaking surface of the second striking platform. This flaking surface was abandoned following severe crushing of the edge. The core was then rotated (Fig 68h) to utilise the first striking platform. This flaking surface also became unworkable when percussion angles became too steep. The penultimate flake is a 'crested rejuvenation flake', which results from rejuvenation by rotating the core. The position of this flake in the sequence also illustrates that such flakes do not necessarily represent deliberate attempts to rejuvenate the core. The core was abandoned after the second striking platform was rejuvenated. This flake is missing but was largely cortical and terminated in a hinge fracture. No further flakes were produced.

Sequence 3

This sequence, which demonstrates phases of core preparation and production, is the most complete in the assemblage. Its stratigraphic relationships with the other refitted groups are uncertain. A total of 46 flakes plus 12 chips and one broken core fragment were refitted. Five flakes were reconstructed from broken pieces and only one flake was not located *in situ*. The group was approximately 0.40m N–S by 0.30m E–W. It has a similar overall distribution to the other groups, but flakes removed during the later stage of the sequence are proportionally more common in the southern part of the scatter (Fig 67, shown by broken line). This may indicate a slight shift in the knapper's position during production. The nodule, which was worked to exhaustion, is subrectangular, weighing approximately 300g; it had cortical and thermally fractured surfaces.

Preparation. A striking platform was prepared by removing four thick, broad flakes which truncated one end of the nodule (Fig 69a). This platform was modified by alternate flaking which removed thick, elongated cortical flakes to prepare a possible flaking surface parallel to the long axis of the nodule (Fig 69b).

Production. Usable flakes were not removed from this flaking surface. The removal of a rejuvenation tablet with a plunged distal end led to the adoption of the flaking surface as a striking platform. A simple blade core technique was employed to remove a clear sequence of overlapping ridged flakes from the corners of this new flaking surface. This continued until the front of the core became flattened, butts became wider and core control was lost (Fig 69c, d). Most of the flakes/blades have cortical distal ends, some with hinge fractures. Approximately 23–25 pieces were removed in this way, although precise numbers cannot be ascertained owing to miss-hits and some double removals. The core was then rotated and the flaking surface used as the striking platform (Fig 69e). This stage is associated with the assumed shift of the knapper's position. Approximately five more small flakes, the first guided by a natural ridge, were removed before rejuvenation was necessary. This process split the core along a thermal fracture. A striking platform was then prepared by alternate flaking and two small flakes were removed from the original flaking surface. The exhausted core was probably discarded. Platform abrasion or faceting were absent throughout.

Flake analysis

Despite a high representation of smaller flakes, which are not normally present in archaeological collections, the total assemblage is too small to be statistically meaningful. However, the results of the flake analysis, shown by the breadth/length and flake class histograms, show similarities with the other analysed assemblages, particularly that from W83. The refitting at W58 therefore appears to demonstrate a technology that produces flakes similar to those seen at other sites and which may be representative of the prevailing earlier Neolithic technology in the Stonehenge area.

The flakes have also been grouped according to their position or function on the core. Four categories have been recognised and tentative characteristics suggested for each category.

- i Platform preparation flakes: preparation and side trimming flakes (see above). Twenty-eight per cent of the measured flakes, 17% of sequence 3. These have the widest size range in the assemblage, and include the largest butts. They are squat to broad in shape, include large areas of cortex or thermally fractured surface, and are generally unridged. They may include the highest incidence of multidirectional flake scars.
- ii Decortication flakes: preparation and side trimming flakes (see above). Fifteen per cent of the measured flakes, 15% of sequence 3. These flakes were classified as flakes to remove cortex or thermal surfaces, struck parallel with the flaking surfaces of the core. They are also cortical flakes but are distinguished in sequence 3 by being more elongated and ridged than the platform preparation flakes.
- iii Miscellaneous trimming: 16% of the measured flakes, 6% of sequence 3. These flakes were particularly prevalent in cores 1 and 2, both unproductive. Assuming that the product of the industry was long flakes/blades, the miscellaneous trimming flakes appear to be by-products of the process to prepare or modify the shape of the core. They are notably broader and less well ridged with less cortex cover. They may include a proportion of failed blanks.
- iv Flakes from the main production face: 40% of the measured flakes, 59% of sequence 3. These pieces were not removed from the site although it is likely that they were the intended end-product. Most exceed 20mm in length although some are extremely small. The absence of platform preparation indi-

cates that they are not abrasion chips. The reduction of cores to their minimum size has been noted before in the Neolithic (I F Smith 1965, 87) and is seen here in practice. The flakes are ridged, have minimal cortex and include some blades. They also possess the narrowest butts. Flakes from sequence 3 include a large proportion with cortical distal ends (distal trimming flakes, see above).

Siret fractures (accidental breakages, Bordes 1979, fig 4:2) are rare amongst all groups although at least 30% (15 flakes) terminate in hinge or step fractures, largely as a result of cortex.

Chips

The chips were recovered from the sieved residue and weighed. Total numbers are not given, but the presence of very small chips indicates that the assemblage is not likely to be dumped material. The horizontal distribution conforms to that of the flakes but the vertical relationship (Newcomer and Karlin 1987, 36) could not be established owing to the compacted nature of the fills. Most chips are broken, and, with the exception of bulbar scars, too small for classification. Most were probably produced around the point of percussion upon impact. There are no apparent retouch chips, nor is there evidence for the regular use of platform abrasion or faceting. This is confirmed by the absence of substantial gaps between the proximal ends of most of the refitted flakes. The absence of these specialist activities which produce more chips also explains why the total number of chips might appear to be under-represented.

Flake scatter formation

It has been demonstrated that the three groups were probably superimposed and a relationship has been suggested for cores 1 and 2. This, together with similar relationships between individual pieces within groups, the near total recovery of material, the presence of a complete range of chips, and the density of the spread, argues that the assemblage represents *in situ* knapping debris rather than dumped waste. Flake scatters of this type have been reconstructed experimentally (Newcomer and Sieveking 1980; Barton and Bergman 1982). These experiments have demonstrated the influence of knapping position, particularly the height above the ground, and flaking technique in the formation of flint scatter patterns. Groups of similar dimensions and density result from a sitting or squatting position on, or very close to the ground (Newcomer and Sieveking 1980, figs 5 and 7; Barton and Bergman 1982, fig 15b). This technique is very common amongst ethnographic stone-using cultures and might be expected of a knapper working within the shelter of the ditch. Flakes may be caught in the hand and dropped between the legs, or allowed to fall naturally. Newcomer and Sieveking (1980) also recorded that in superimposed groups the height of the debris increases but that the diameter does not.

The type of hammer mode made no difference to the flake scatter.

Discussion

This small assemblage has provided a unique opportunity to excavate and reconstruct a complete *in situ* Neolithic knapping scatter. Invaluable information which is not normally available has been obtained by detailed recording following immediate identification of the scatter in excavation. It cannot be assumed that this represents the typical form of technology because the work represents the output of one knapper of unknown ability over a very short period of time. It has been shown, however, that this technology produces flakes which are comparable with those of assemblages where flakes have not been refitted and many of the technological features of core control are also comparable.

The overall technology is very basic. There are none of the features, for example core shaping/preparation and cresting, which might be expected of a specialised blade industry. It was also not automatic to construct a second striking platform during the initial platform preparation. Platform abrasion is absent here, although its use at W2 (1981) may be a feature associated with productive flaking surfaces. Evidence for faceting is also absent. There is a consistent understanding, particularly in sequence 3, that guiding ridges control the length of the flake. Alternate flaking was clearly important to establish the first striking platform, and as a form of core rejuvenation. Rotating the core provided a suitable alternative.

Striking platforms were rarely more than 90° from each other; therefore multidirectional or opposed flake scars are absent from the dorsal surfaces of flakes.

Hammerstones were probably selected at random and appear to confirm the effect of cortex as a soft hammer.

4.7 c The prehistoric pottery (Fig 85)

by Frances Raymond

A total of 29 prehistoric sherds, representing a minimum number of five vessels, were recovered. In the absence of detailed information concerning form and decoration, the identification of individual pots has been restricted to differences in fabric. The proportion of sherds belonging to ceramic and fabric groups is shown in Figure 70 and Table 47, MF1 E2.

The assemblage, recovered from the secondary ditch silts of the long barrow, appears to represent intermittent activity during both the earlier and later Bronze Ages and the Romano-British period.

Details of the Romano-British pottery, which comprises 72% of the assemblage by weight, are contained within the archive.

Beaker/Collared Urn

A minimum of three vessels are represented, two Beakers and a third vessel with fairly thick walls (8–12 mm) which may either be a Collared Urn or a heavier Beaker. Unfortunately the nine sherds which represent this vessel (feGS:CU/1) are undecorated and too small to convey sufficiently detailed information concerning form. Three of the 26 Beaker/Collared Urn sherds are decorated and two motifs are represented. These are

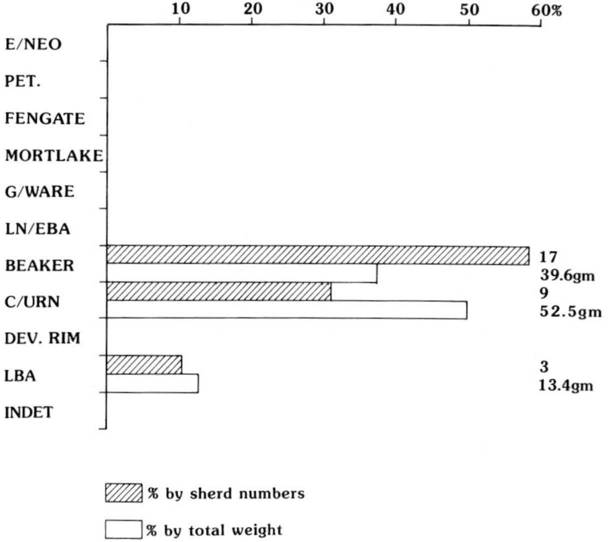

Fig 70 W58 Amesbury 42 long barrow: prehistoric pottery fabric histogram

exclusive to a single fabric group (feGS:Bkr/5) and consist of two sherds with sub-square impressions (of which P268 is the only illustrated example) and one sherd with a possible comb impression which is heavily abraded (not illustrated). None of the Beaker/Collared Urn fabrics found at Amesbury 42 occur elsewhere within the study area.

Late Bronze Age

A minimum of two vessels are represented, the first by a single sherd (CFV:LBA/1), the second by two sherds (FfeS:LBA/5). Although there is little information concerning their form, the fabrics are entirely consistent with the relatively undecorated jars of the post-Deverel-Rimbury complex.

Illustrated pottery (Fig 85)

Beaker

P268 Context 123
feGS:Bkr/5. Body sherd. Two sub-square impressions.

4.7 d Animal bones

by Mark Maltby

A total of 268 animal bones were retrieved from the topsoil and the two ditch sections. The species identified are shown in Table 48. Most of the bone was found in fills associated with Bronze Age and Roman pottery in the upper levels of the ditches. Only one bone, a cattle calcaneus, was found in a primary fill in the south section. Cattle were the most commonly identified species, followed by sheep/goat. Most of the sheep/goat fragments, however, were found in the topsoil or in the top of the ditch fills, and were absent

Table 48 W58 Amesbury 42 Long Barrow: animal species represented by context

Species	*Topsoil*	*Ditch fill* South section	*Ditch fill* North section	*Total*
Cattle	2	12(10)	41(7)	55(17)
Sheep/goat	3	14(6)	2	19(6)
Pig	–	–	8	8
Horse	–	2(2)	1(1)	3(3)
Red deer	–	1(1)	2(1)	3(2)
Roe deer	–	1	–	1
Fox	–	1	1	2
Unidentified large mammal	3	30(21)	49(2)	82(23)
Sheep-sized mammal	2	17(11)	24(11)	43(22)
Unidentified mammal	2	24(17)	26(11)	52(28)
Total	12	102(68)	154(33)	268(101)

( ) number found in 1mm wet-sieved sample

from contexts 90 and 91, from which all but one of the pig fragments was recovered. Horse bones were only identified in sieved samples from the top fills of the ditches. This tenuous evidence again points to the scarcity of sheep and horse bones amongst Neolithic material.

Red deer were represented by two fragments of antler and a tibia. A metatarsus fragment of a roe deer and two fox humeri were also recorded. The fragments represented in the samples of the other identified species and the unidentified categories are given in Table 49, MF1 E3. The poor preservation of the sample is reflected by the high proportion of loose teeth in the assemblage. The large percentage of unidentified fragments is a reflection both of poor preservation and of the types of bone recovered in the 1mm wet-sieved samples.

Most of the fragments (235) were eroded, many of them severely. Only one fragment was burnt. Six bones bore gnawing marks. Metrical ageing data were recorded where possible, but further analysis was considered inappropriate.

4.7 e Land mollusca

by Roy Entwistle

A column of 16 contiguous samples was taken from the northern section of the eastern ditch excavation (Fig 71). In order to provide a synopsis of the main environmental episodes nine samples, one from each of the main stratigraphic divisions, were selected for immediate analysis (Fig 72). A further 11 samples were taken from the buried soil beneath the barrow. This was clearly visible at the edge of the arable field where ploughing was gradually cutting into the side of the barrow. The mound itself was greatly reduced in height, surviving at the point of sampling as a thin cover of loose, root-penetrated chalky rubble with a maximum thickness of 0.15m.

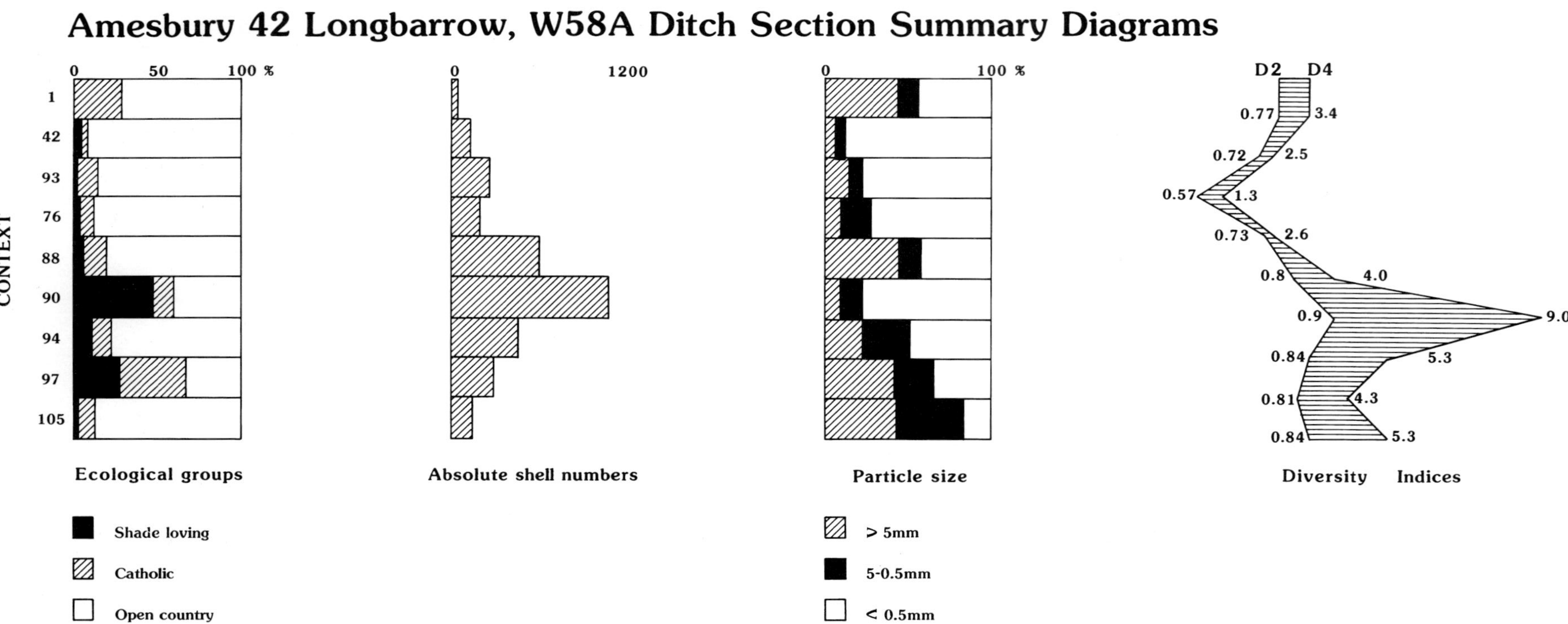

Fig 71 W58 Amesbury 42 long barrow: ditch section summary mollusc diagram

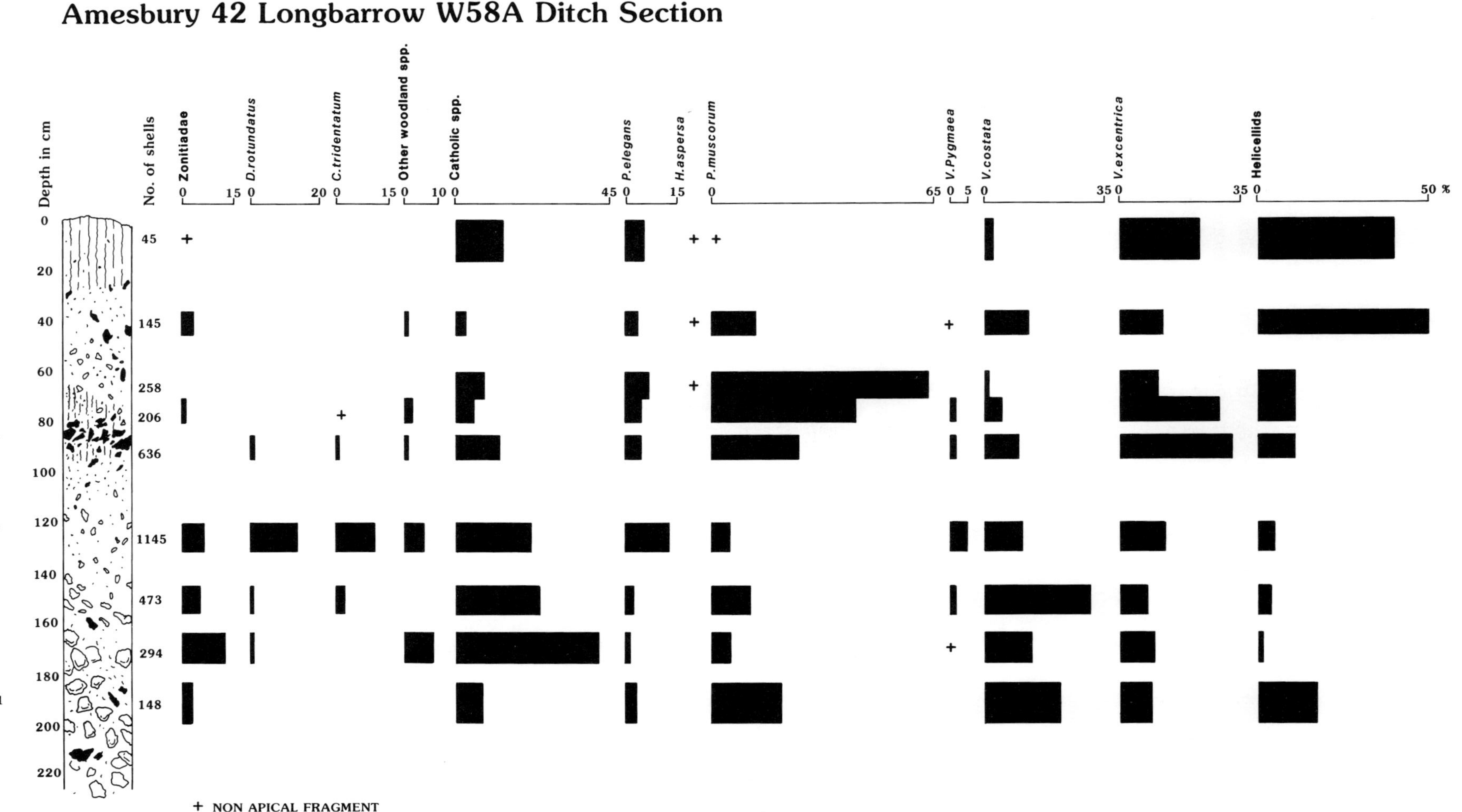

Fig 72 W58 Amesbury 42 long barrow: mollusc diagram

The buried soil

Very few shells were recovered from the buried soil (Table 51, MF1 E5), therefore little can be said about the pre-barrow environment. Samples 0.17–0.19m and 0.19–0.21m represent the A horizon of what appears to be a typical shallow rendzina soil. Beneath this a sorted horizon, samples 0.21–0.24m and 0.24–0.26m, directly overlies Coombe Rock (Table 50, MF1 E4). At present, rendzinas are widespread over the chalk of southern England, supporting the characteristic grassland of the Downs. On pedological grounds, there seems little reason to doubt that the buried soil beneath Amesbury 42 had supported grassland for some time prior to the construction of the mound.

The snail shells are too sparse to contribute very much detail, with the exception of those from two samples from the upper part of the buried soil profile. This is dominated by *Vallonia costata*, *Vallonia excentrica*, *Helicella itala*, and *Pupilla muscorum*, all of which are grouped as open country species (Evans 1972). The presence of *Pupilla muscorum* and *Helicella itala* reinforces the pedological evidence for a grassland environment, whilst relatively stable conditions are suggested by *Vertigo pygmaea*. The early Flandrian succession is not preserved, since no subsoil hollows were located, but it seems reasonable to assume that the transition from woodland to more open conditions followed a similar chronology to the succession at Durrington Walls (Evans 1971, 329–37).

The ditch sequence

The species from the ditch section are shown in Table 52, MF1 E6. Sample 2.2–2.5m from context 101, from the primary fill of the ditch, was devoid of shells. However, the open conditions suggested by the buried soil fauna may have still been present during the earliest stages of ditch silting. Sample 1.85–2m, context 105, was a lens of humic sediment within the upper part of the primary fill, thought to represent a turf fallen in from the eroding lip of the ditch. It contained an assemblage dominated by the xerophyllic species *Pupilla muscorum* and *Helicella itala*, which is entirely consistent with a continuation of the open conditions of the pre-barrow environment.

The values of diversity indices from the fallen turf (sample 1.85m–2.00m) in the primary silt are D2:0.84 and D4:5.28 (Fig 71, Table 53, MF1 E7). These values closely resemble those of D2:0.85 and D4:5.74 from a similar grassland phase in the upper horizon of the soil profile at Durrington Walls (Evans 1971, fig 107, DW 1), and of D2:0.85 and D4:5.7 from the upper horizon of the buried soil at Woodhenge (Evans and Jones 1979, 190–213).

In contrast, the values for the W58 buried soil are much lower, D2:0.70 and D4:2.37 (calculated for sample 0.17–0.19m). The discrepancy between these and the values from sample 1.85–2m in the ditch primary silts is difficult to explain. There would only be a short chronological gap between the aspect revealed by the mollusc assemblage in the upper horizon of the buried soil and that from the fallen turf, context 105. Two or three years at the most would have been sufficient time for weathering to undermine the subsoil at the ditch edge, producing a scree in the bottom of the ditch, incorporating humic sediment and fallen turves (Jewell and Dimbleby 1966, 313–24, Crabtree 1971). Spatial variation in the composition of snail populations is known to occur even over short distances especially when the environment offers a diversity of habitats (Evans 1972, 111–18). Lateral population variation would seem to be the most likely explanation for the differences in faunal diversity between these two apparently contemporary assemblages, although other factors such as pre-construction activity may have been influential.

As the secondary silts accumulated conditions became progressively more shaded; at 1.65–1.75m there appears to be a minor disturbance, but the trend continues, culminating in a peak at 1.2–1.3m (Fig 71). The species diversity indices reach a maximum at this level as a wider range of species exploit the more complex mosaic of micro-habitats. Shade-loving species such as *Carychium tridentatum*, *Discus rotundatus* and others of the family Zonitidae increase, but this trend is also accompanied by a slight increase in some open country species, principally *Vertigo pygmaea* and the Helicellids. This suggests a localised scrub vegetation cover within the ditch with more open conditions close by. Exposures of loose friable earth derived from slowly accumulating silts favoured *Pomatias elegans* which is well represented. The effect on the two Vallonia species is interesting: the numbers of *Vallonia excentrica* increase slightly, but there is a sharp decline in the *Vallonia costata* population, perhaps reflecting the ability of the former to exploit more successfully the changes in habitat diversity. This phase is associated with Beaker pottery and is probably homologous with a similar episode at W2, Coneybury Henge (Bell and Jones, this vol, 4.9 g). There are resemblances between the two, both in the species composition of mollusc assemblages and in the chronology of the environmental succession. Both sites witness a slight increase in shady conditions during the Beaker period, although at Amesbury 42 the trend is less strongly represented and is preceded by much more open xerophilous conditions than at W2. Evidence from the ditch sequence at Stonehenge reveals a similar phase of scrub regeneration (Evans 1984), suggesting that this may be a more general phenomenon. There are no environmental data from the Durrington Walls ditch silts, but land snail analysis of silts from the nearby monument of Woodhenge shows that open conditions prevailed throughout the period of secondary silting dated to the last quarter of the third millennium BC.

Above 1.2–1.3m clearance takes place, possibly followed by cultivation, which has brought some Beaker sherds into the upper stratigraphy, but by 0.85–0.95m (context 88) conditions have stabilised, enabling a soil profile to develop. This is clearly reflected in the particle size histogram where context 88, a sorted horizon, is shown to contain an increased percentage of stones larger than a 5mm mesh. At 0.7–0.8m (context 76) the sharp decrease in the frequency of larger stones reflects the relatively stone free A horizon of the buried soil (Fig 71). The trend of decreasing faunal diversity beginning in context 90 continues during this phase, with *Pupilla muscorum* and *Vallonia excentrica* as the predominant species, followed by the Helicellids. A minor shade element persists, indicating that some taller vegetation must have been present nearby. The Zonitidae and *Carychium tridentatum* are known to inhabit tall ungrazed grassland (Cameron and Morgan-Huws 1975; Bell and Jones, this vol, 4.9 g), but not *Discus rotundatus* which is present in very small numbers, perhaps indicating that scrub was growing in the ditch or in the barrow mound. However, the presence of sheep bones at this level in the stratigraphy strongly suggests that the open aspect, reflected in the environmental sequence, was maintained by grazing. Most likely the barrow was located on the margin of a pastoral zone, where taller vegetation was able to survive undisturbed. The snail assemblage therefore reflects two ecological settings: that of the barrow and the vegetation in its proximity and, secondly, the wider environmental trends in the vicinity of the barrow.

Above this level, context 93 represents a mixed horizon formed as ploughing spreads over the ditch disturbing the buried soil. It is here that the first shell fragments of *Helix aspersa* appear. The occurrence of this species provides a *terminus ante quem* for this horizon, since it is thought to have been introduced around the first century AD. The buried soil contains large quantities of Romano-British pottery which is chronologically consistent with the dating suggested by the appearance of *Helix aspersa*. Above context 93 a bi-sequential ploughsoil, represented by contexts 42 and 75, accumulated in the top of the ditch. There is no direct dating evidence for either episode, but the earlier phase could be Roman. Subsequent ploughing, leading to the accumulation of context 75, may be medieval, although the historical evidence for arable cultivation mainly comes from eighteenth- and nineteenth-century sources.

During the earlier part of this period the monument stood outside the open fields of West Amesbury, on Countess Court Down, but records show that from the eighteenth century onwards much of this land was being taken into arable cultivation (RCHME 1979, xvi–xvii). The land use map prepared by the Royal Commission (RCHME 1979, map 3), based mainly on the Tythe Maps for the period 1839–*c* 1850, shows the extent to which cultivation had spread on to the former downland. It is most likely that by this time ploughing was actually encroaching on the mound itself, gradually reducing it to the present height.

The sequence of ploughwash preserving the fossil ploughsoils contains progressively declining numbers of shells, but is accompanied by increasing faunal diversity. There is a decline in the numbers of *Pupilla muscorum* and *Vallonia costata*, perhaps reflecting their tolerance of agriculture (Evans 1972). *Helicella itala* numbers increase in the fossil ploughsoil, becoming less frequent in the modern ploughsoil. This may reflect an intolerance of modern agriculture, but could also be the function of the variable distribution of snail populations.

4.8 W59, the evaluation of a Neolithic flint scatter on the King Barrow Ridge

4.8 a Site description

Pioneering surface collection work carried out during the 1930s (Laidler and Young 1938) identified an extensive surface flint industry on the King Barrow Ridge to the east of Stonehenge. Material collected, centred on SU 135426, included a range of core tools, fabricators, scrapers, and arrowheads suggesting a broadly Neolithic date, with an apparent bias towards the later part of this period. Since this early fieldwork was carried out, the fields to the west of the track running along the King Barrow Ridge have been taken out of arable cultivation, restricting the area available for surface collection to those east of the Ridge. Extensive collection here (57) during the winter of 1981/2 produced further evidence of the activity first recorded by Laidler and Young and also provided some concept of its easterly extent.

The distribution within areas of surface collection examined in 1980 and 1981/2 suggested some emphasis on the flat crest of the ridge, certainly within the area to the east and north of the New King Barrows linear round barrow cemetery (Fig 73). This is demonstrated by the distribution map of all flint tools from surface collection (Fig 14), which shows high densities continuing to the south on to Coneybury Hill (51). This pattern, which on the King Barrow Ridge shows no direct correlation with higher densities of both flake and core material (Figs 12, 13), contrasts with the majority of the areas producing concentrations of tools, which are generally associated with a greater density of cores and flakes. Preliminary analysis of the material from extensive surface collection on the King Barrow Ridge suggested that levels of both tools and retouched material were exceptionally high when considered as a proportion of the total flint assemblage. While not initially perceived as a direct comparison with the Wilsford Down 'industrial' flint scatter (W31, this vol, 4.10), the sample excavation of an element of the King Barrow Ridge Neolithic 'domestic' zone was seen as having the potential to provide a series of analytically valuable comparisons.

Pre-excavation survey

The pre-excavation surveys and excavation strategy employed at the King Barrow Ridge represent the project's most developed methodological approach. The total approach has already been discussed (Richards 1985a), and a preliminary interpretation of the results offered (Entwistle and Richards 1987).

The preliminary analysis of material from extensive surface collection suggested some nucleation within a broad tool scatter, the overall extent of which is shown in Figure 14. The nucleated element identified for further evaluation was centred on SU 135425, immediately north of the ploughed-out course of the Stonehenge Avenue. The scatter contained a high proportion of tools, primarily scrapers but with some transverse arrowheads, fabricators and core tool fragments includ-

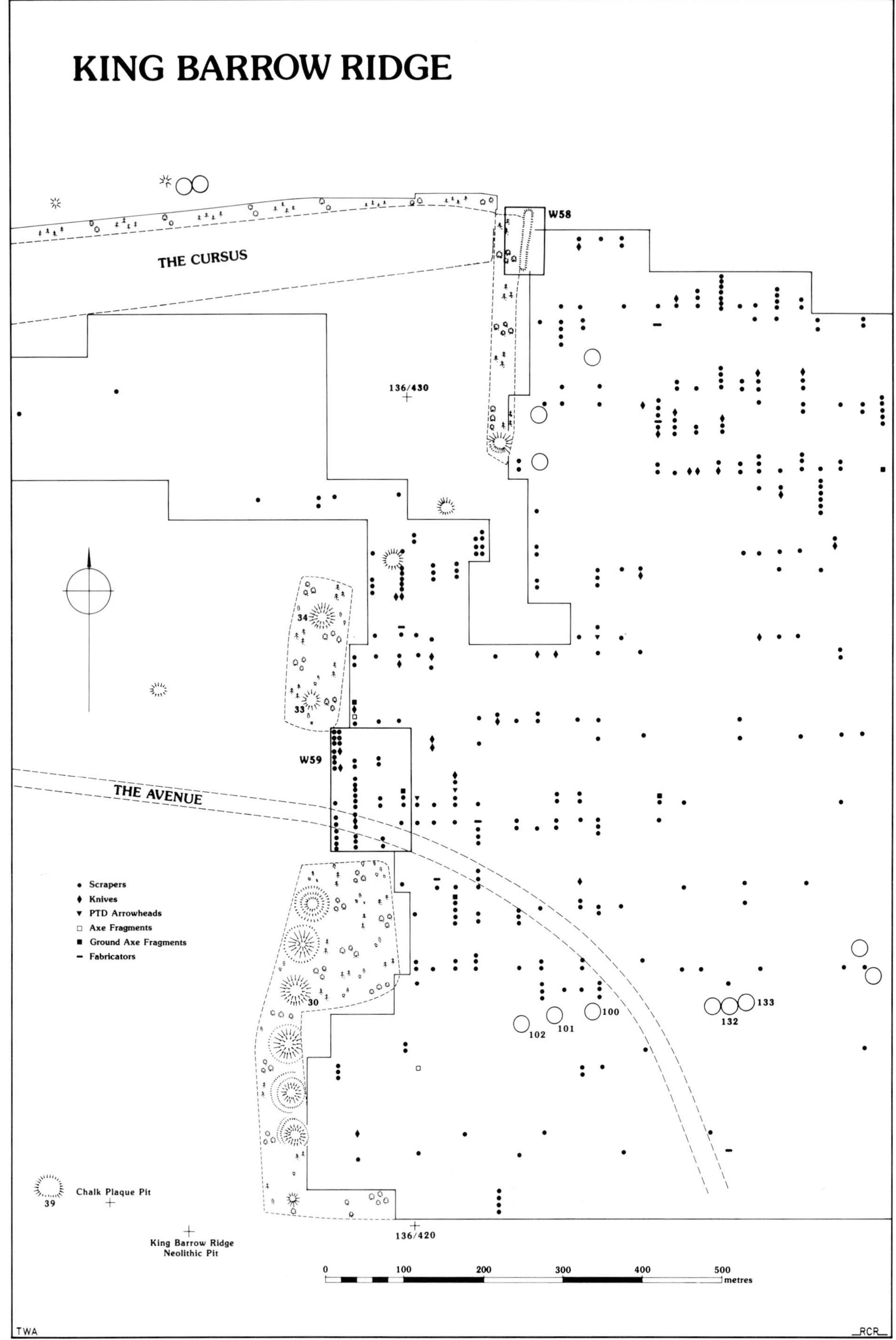

Fig 73 W59 King Barrow Ridge: all monuments and distribution of flint tools from surface collection

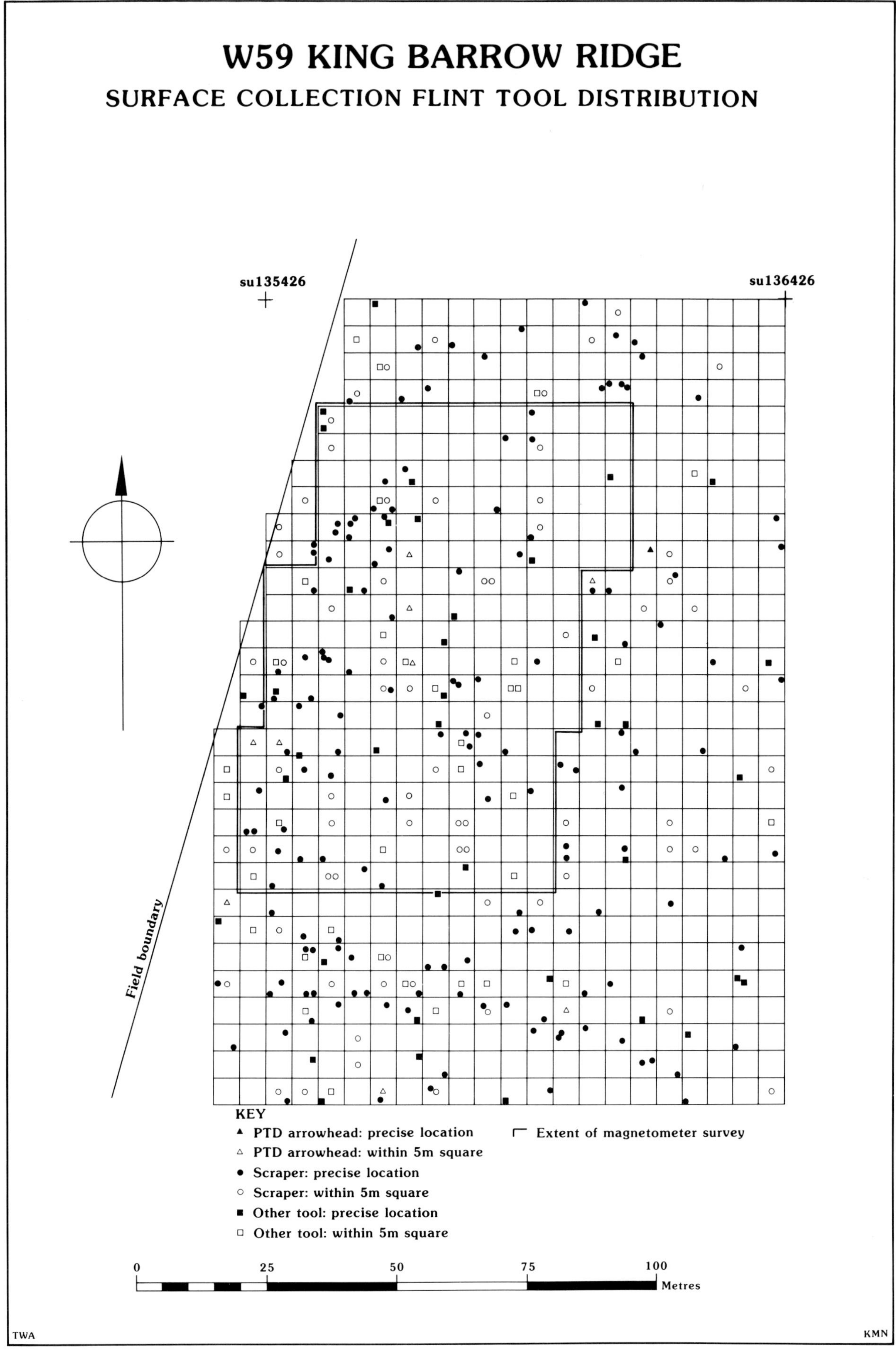

Fig 74 W59 King Barrow Ridge: distribution of flint tools from intensive surface collection

ing ground flint axes. On the basis of the diagnostic tool component it was assumed that the main phase of activity to be examined was of later Neolithic date.

Intensive surface collection

The second stage of surface evaluation, a gridded total collection designed to assess the internal spatial characteristics of the scatter, was carried out in spring 1983. An area of 1.585 hectares was examined on a 5m by 5m grid, within which all 'bulk' finds (worked flint, burnt flint, and sarsen) were collected by 5m grid unit. In the field, all identified flint tools, worked or other types of foreign stone, and pottery were individually recorded and precisely plotted.

Surface artefact levels (all per 5m square) range up to 26 pieces of worked flint, 0.534kg of burnt flint, 1.300kg of sarsen and four flint tools. No pottery of prehistoric date was recovered, but as the sample area lies within a zone subject to considerable post-medieval agriculture this was not unexpected. The exclusive survival in the ploughzone of more robust artefact types was subsequently confirmed by excavation.

The distributions of the classes of recovered artefacts (in archive) provided little clarification of the internal structure of the sampled area, although the strongly nucleated distribution of fragmentary hard sarsen (subsequently sampled by excavation, see below, area D) hinted at a type of activity hitherto not considered within the context of the site. The distribution of flint tools (Fig 74) was, however, employed in the definition of a more restricted area for geophysical survey.

The pre-excavation surface survey was concluded, immediately prior to excavation, with a magnetometer survey, carried out by the Ancient Monuments Laboratory. An area of 0.54 hectares (six 30m by 30m sample squares, Fig 75), was selected so as to impinge only slightly on the line of the Stonehenge Avenue. As this was a Scheduled Ancient Monument, and could also be suggested as being of later date than that assumed for the flint scatter, it was consequently excluded from the potential excavation sample frame.

The magnetometer survey (Bartlett, this vol, MF1 E8–9; Fig 76, MF1 E10) clearly defined the northern ditch of the Stonehenge Avenue and approximately 20 pits, many of which could be identified from the initial field chart at the time of survey, and which were incorporated into the overall sampling strategy. The most striking feature of the distribution of possible features is a cluster of three pits, subsequently confirmed by excavation (areas J/K, see below), partly surrounded by an arc of pits to the north and north-east. The survey plot also indicated that the central pit cluster lies within a relatively 'quiet' area, surrounded not only by pits but by potentially disturbed areas.

Table 54 W59 King Barrow Ridge excavation sampling strategy

Area	*Reason for sampling*
A	random
B	random
C	random
D	sarsen scatter
E	tool cluster/magnetometer anomaly
F	random
G	random
H	random
J	magnetometer anomaly
K	magnetometer anomaly
L	random
M	random

Sampling strategy

The excavation sampling strategy was designed to examine a number of varying aspects of the scatter, the majority derived from surface collection or geophysical survey but incorporating a random component intended to provide context for the more defined elements (Table 54).

The scatter was sampled by means of a series of 5m by 5m squares, areas A to M, directly related to surface collection units, within which all topsoil was hand excavated on a 1m grid. Following by this time established practice, a 20% sample of individual 1m squares were dry-sieved through 4mm mesh. Within the excavated areas phosphate samples and magnetic susceptibility readings were taken corresponding to individual 1m squares. Beyond the excavated areas, but within the magnetometer sample frame, samples and readings were taken at 5m intervals with the intention of providing a overall context for the more specific data sets (Fig 77, MF1 E11).

Ploughsoil artefact assemblages

Three types of material of a more robust nature were recovered from the ploughsoil: worked flint, including tools, burnt flint, and sarsen. Their distribution is shown in Figures 78–81, MF1 E12–F3. This material, and the associated magnetic susceptibility and phosphate data, has been discussed extensively in a previous paper (Entwistle and Richards 1987). This paper, prepared before radiocarbon dates were available for two of the excavated pits, made the assumption that the subsoil features and the majority of the ploughsoil assemblage were contemporaneous. This may not be the case, and in the light of this uncertainty it is perhaps unwise to offer a revision of the broad conclusions offered in this earlier paper.

The sample excavation of an area from which the surface artefacts had been collected gave the only opportunity within the project to examine the relationship between artefact levels on the surface and from the ploughsoil. This comparison was facilitated by the use of a common grid for both surface collection (Fig 74) and for excavation (Fig 75), and was restricted to three classes of durable material: worked flint, burnt flint, and sarsen. Total quantities (surface plus topsoil) were calculated for each of the excavated sample areas, and Figure 82 shows the percentage of each class of material recovered by surface collection, by area. Area H shows the effects of exceptionally efficient surface collection. The remainder of the sample areas show some uniformity in worked flint values which lie between 1.2 and 2.7%. In contrast, those for burnt flint and sarsen show considerable variation, although values for classes of material expressed as weight can be considerably af-

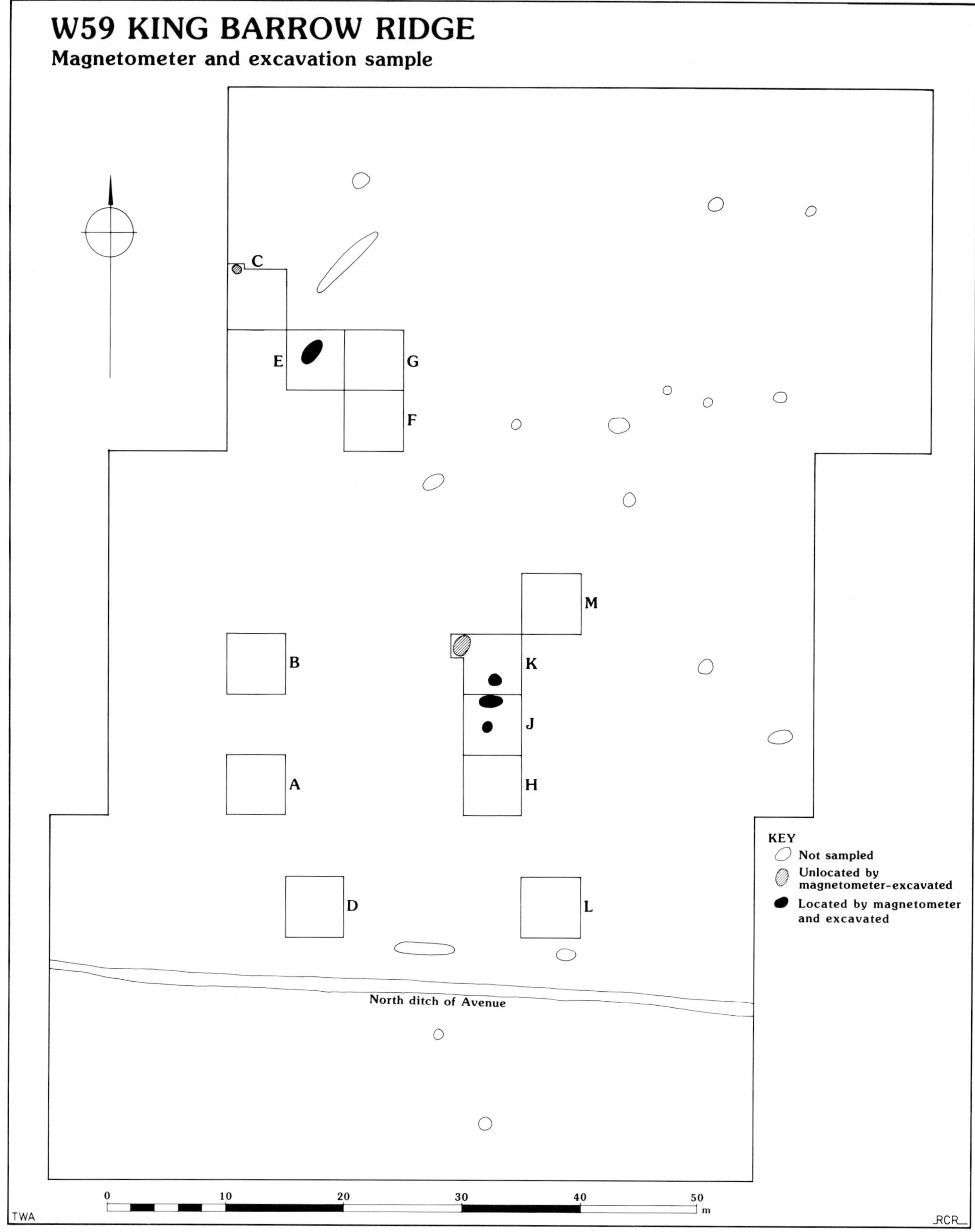

Fig 75 W59 King Barrow Ridge: magnetometer and excavation sample

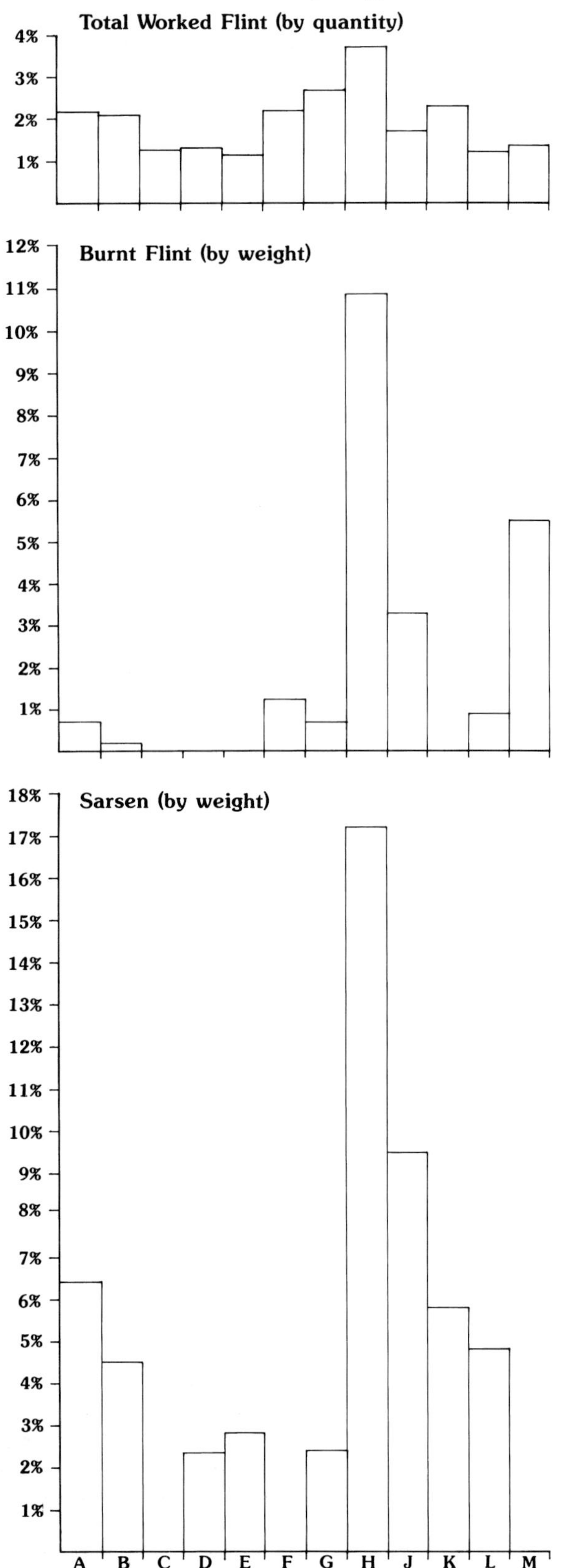

Fig 82 W59 King Barrow Ridge: comparative surface/ ploughsoil artefact densities

fected by the recovery of single, anomalously large pieces.

Excavated features

The removal of ploughsoil from the sampled areas revealed a number of stakeholes and pits. The former may be of relatively recent origin, although some spatial association with aspects of Neolithic activity can tentatively be suggested (see below, area L). The latter contained small and somewhat ambiguous assemblages of artefacts which initially suggested a strong association with the major emphasis of the surface flint scatter. Subsequently available radiocarbon dates and a consequent reappraisal of the stratified pottery now suggest that the association is at best tenuous. It is consequently more appropriate to discuss the nature and distribution of the subsoil features independently, before considering their potential association with activities suggested by the ploughzone data.

Pits occurred within two excavated areas: a single example within area C, at the northern limit of the area examined, and a cluster of four within adjoining areas J and K (see Fig 83 for plans and sections).

Area C, pit 418 was 0.70m by 0.80m in size and between 0.45 and 0.50m deep, with vertical sides, undercut in places, and a flat base. The upper fill was a mid-brown soil of colluvial appearance, and included quantities of natural small flint and chalk. In contrast, the lower fill had a dark 'ashy' appearance, very fine and grey in colour with few larger particles. In appearance it resembled the primary deposit recorded at W2 (1981), the Coneybury 'Anomaly' (this vol, 4.1), a similarity reinforced by a phosphate level of 260ppm (average value of 280ppm from W2 (1981)). A similar 'ashy' fill was recorded in one of the earlier Neolithic pits at W83, Robin Hood's Ball (data in archive). Pit 418 produced the largest number of animal bones (Table 61), with identifiable fragments heavily biased towards pig bones. At least four pigs are represented, mainly by head and feet bones, these being of lower meat value. A sample from context 523 (equivalent to 498, Fig 83) produced a radiocarbon date of 3650–3340 BC (OxA 1396). Grooved Ware pottery (P261–262) predominates in this pit, and shows closest affinities with the thin-walled cordoned vessels of Woodlands style (Wainwright and Longworth 1971). Several flint cores were recovered from the lower fill of this pit, the majority produced by alternate flaking showing no careful preparation or shaping. The deposition of exhausted or failed cores within subsoil features appears to be a characteristic of this site and is most convincingly demonstrated from pit 418.

Within areas J/K four pits were recorded. Three of these lay in a tight cluster, no more than 1m apart, while the fourth example lay approximately 4m away, partly beyond the edge of the original sample square.

Pit 430 was well cut and bowl-profiled, 1.20m by 1.15m in size and 0.60m in depth.

Pit 432 was approximately 1.30m in diameter and 0.50m deep. The profile was slightly irregular owing to animal disturbance and the fact that the pit was partly cut into a pocket of softer natural coombe rock.

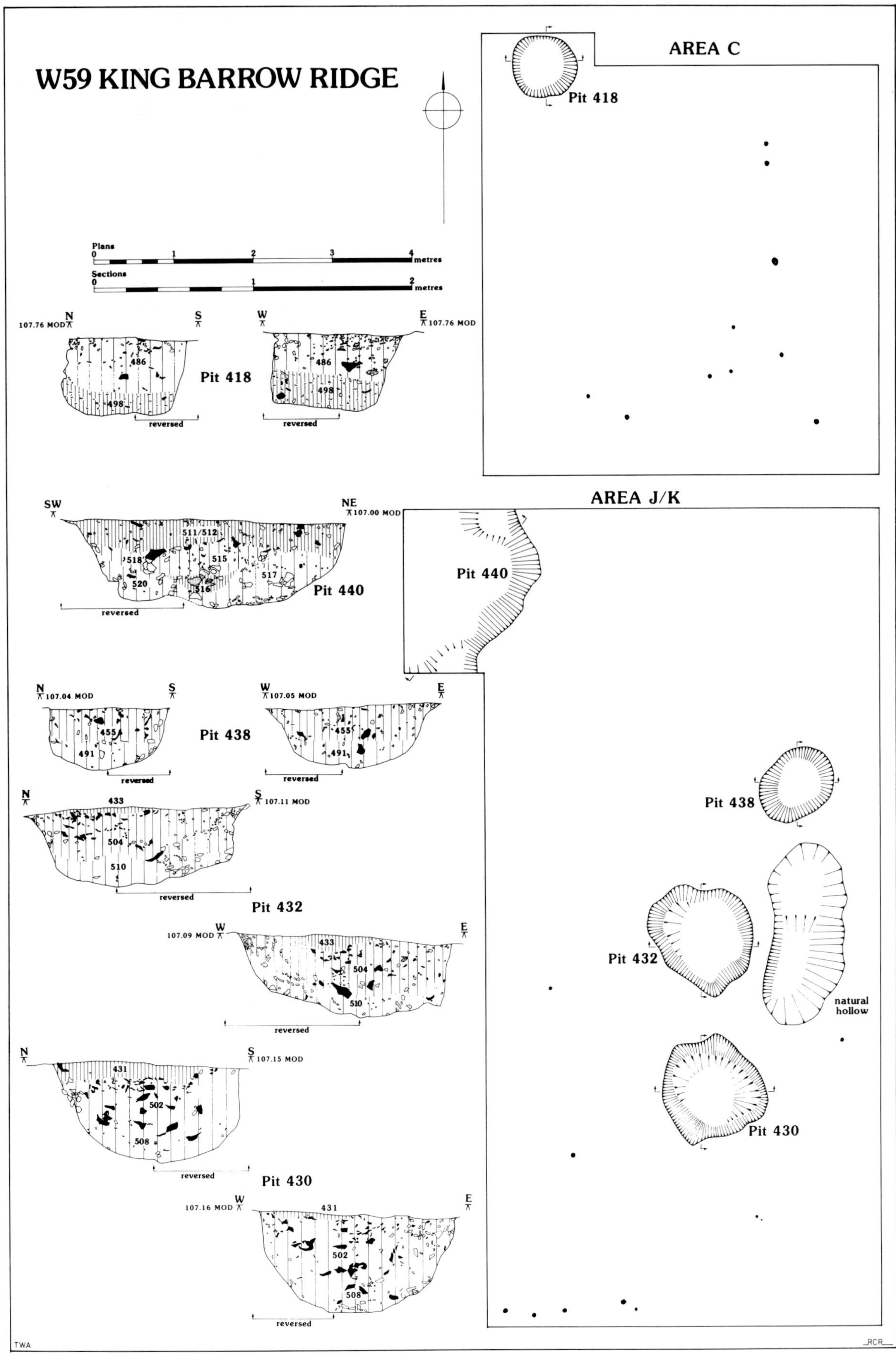

Fig 83 W59 King Barrow Ridge: plans and section of Neolithic pits

Pit 438 was oval and very well cut, 1.00m by 0.75m in size and 0.70m deep, with vertical sides on its short axis.

Pit 440 was much more irregular in shape, a maximum of 1.70m by 1.20m, and 0.55m in depth. The irregularity appears to be the result of the pit being cut into an area of unstructured chalk rubble. A large sample of this was excavated and sieved, proving to be devoid of artefacts, and it can be suggested that the 'pit' 440 may be the deposition of a rubbish deposit into an available tree throwhole (caused by the root ball of a falling tree tearing out a section of subsoil).

The filling of the three more regular pits (430, 432, and 438) was very similar, predominantly brown chalky soils, becoming paler with depth and including quantities of small natural flint. Only pit 438 suggested an element of deliberate filling.

Pit 440 in contrast showed a more complex sequence, at least parts of which appear deliberate. The upper fill (context 512) appears to be a localised colluvial deposit overlying a layer of redeposited chalk (contexts 515/518). This pottery from the upper fill consisted predominantly of plain sherds in Peterborough Ware fabrics, with one Grooved Ware sherd, P264. Below this was a 'rubbish' deposit (contexts 516/519), a thin dark layer which incorporated articulated cattle vertebrae and additional bones of sheep/goat, pig, red deer, and wild cat. Despite its 'organic' appearance this deposit produced a phosphate value of only 10ppm. Bone from this deposit produced a radiocarbon date of 3370–2930 BC (OxA 1397). The lower fill was chalky and devoid of artefacts.

The animal bones from this pit provided a contrast to those from the other pits within this area, all of which produced very small numbers of bones, with cattle, sheep/goat, pig, and red deer represented (Table 61).

In contrast to the deliberately excavated pits, the associations of which appear to be with Grooved Ware, if only in small quantities, area L appears to demonstrate an association between stakeholes and Peterborough Ware. Here, in contrast to the occasional stakeholes recorded from within other sample areas, a total of over 60 positive examples were recorded from the 5m by 5m square. These, although undated, were associated with two shallow and amorphous features, cuts 479 and 600 (Fig 84), possibly of natural origin, but which contained Late Neolithic pottery, predominantly of Peterborough type (P257, P259, P260, and P265).

Although the occurrence of this pottery may be a reflection of differential survival within even very shallow subsoil hollows, it may represent, in association with the stakehole clusters, a contrasting activity to that represented by the pits and their contents.

Discussion

The excavation at W59 demonstrated the problems of sampling and consequently of interpretation of a surface scatter which may be part of an extensive palimpsest rather than a chronologically and spatially discrete area of activity. Caution in the interpretation of the ploughsoil data is certainly required in such circumstances, but nevertheless, the excavation provided important positive data, particularly from the stratified pit groups.

The excavated pits, particularly if part of a more extensive and potentially structured cluster (Fig 75), may be interpreted as representing sedentary activity. The extensive use of flint tools is represented within the ploughsoil assemblage, and pottery and animal bone from sealed contexts suggests a range of domestic activities. The contents of the pits also provide a contrast to those from potentially 'special' examples, the 'Chalk Plaque Pit' (F de M Vatcher 1969; Harding 1988), and those from Woodlands, close to Woodhenge (Stone and Young 1948; Stone 1949).

4.8 b Lithics

by Philip Harding

The excavation of the ploughsoil within the 12 sample areas (A–M) produced a total of 7128 pieces of worked flint (Table 55). This assemblage of worked flint was initially examined for the production of a stage 1 catalogue to enable basic spatial analysis to be carried out.

More detailed analysis has been carried out on the smaller groups of material stratified within pits,

Table 55 W59 King Barrow Ridge: composition of the ploughsoil flint assemblage

	Cores		*Flakes*				*Scrapers*	*Other*	
Area	*complete*	*fragments*	*complete*	*broken*	*burnt*	*retouched*		*tools*	*Total*
A	14	22	364	254	62	38	10	4	768
B	17	11	331	168	35	33	10	4	609
C	8	14	293	168	32	18	13	6	552
D	6	2	252	141	16	8	10	0	435
E	9	8	362	174	34	12	17	7	623
F	19	4	321	141	34	16	11	6	552
G	11	4	331	173	44	19	6	4	592
H	6	0	278	173	25	10	7	7	506
J	9	3	416	177	23	10	7	6	651
K	16	3	412	188	39	16	7	5	686
L	9	2	322	160	31	10	11	3	548
M	13	0	354	171	42	9	8	9	606
Totals	137	73	4036	2088	417	199	117	61	7128

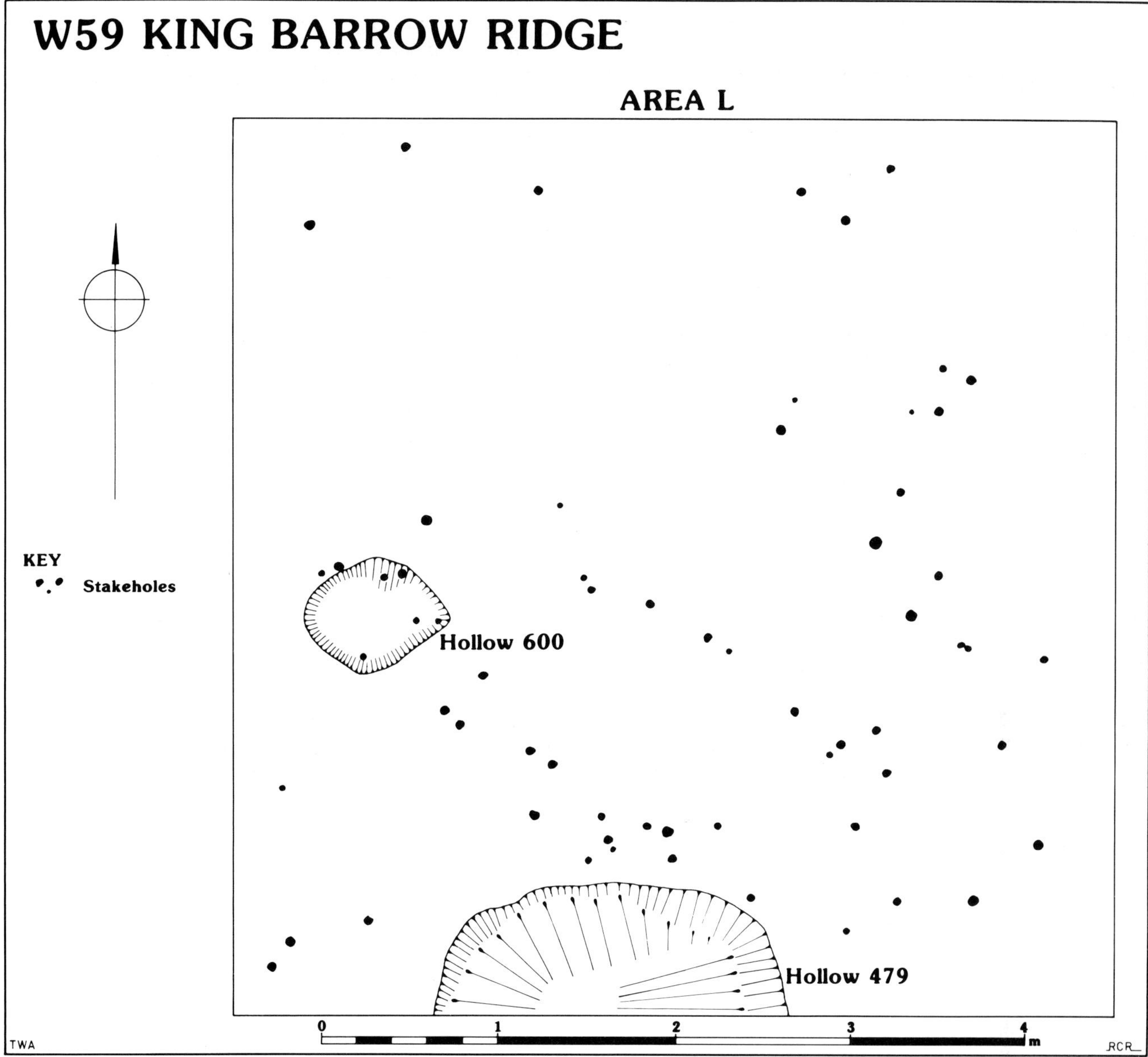

Fig 84 W59 King Barrow Ridge: area L plan

together with a reappraisal of the immediately adjacent ploughsoil material, specifically the tool component.

The assemblage from W59 is small (Table 116), although it probably represents a homogeneous industry. Most of the stratified material was contained in the upper filling of a series of pits, which despite the presence of refitting material may also include a small residual element. The majority of the technological conclusions have been drawn from the analysis of pit 418, the lower fills of which included a number of cores.

The industry is based on flake production with no predetermined tool blank form. A large flake from pit 418 and an assortment of surface tools suggest that some products from specialised industrial sites are present, but it cannot be established whether they were transported as finished tools, blanks, or cores.

Limited refitting, indicative of on-site knapping, has been possible. The quantity of flint in the pits suggests that much of it has gradually accumulated rather than being the product of specific dumping. Some vertical movement of pieces may have taken place within the relatively homogeneous pit fills.

i Recovery and condition

The pits were hand excavated and finds were bulk recorded by context from individual quadrants. All implements and most cores were three-dimensionally recorded. All pit fills were dry-sieved through 4mm mesh with smaller (10–12 litre) samples sieved through 1mm mesh. These differences are reflected in the quantities of chips recovered, the results of which are contained within the archive.

The flint from pit fills is in mint condition, although that from the ploughsoil shows considerable battering and edge damage. Flaked surfaces have developed a white/light grey patina. Calcium carbonate concretion is rare, even on objects from within the pits.

ii Raw material

Most flint for use was selected from surface nodules, this source being of sufficient quality to provide flint for the majority of productive needs. It is possible that this supply was supplemented by flint obtained during the excavation of pits or ditches. In general nodules are irregular in shape, weigh between 200g and 400g, and are covered in a chalky cortex up to 12mm thick. Internally the flint is black in colour with grey cherty inclusions and some thermal lines of weakness.

Some flakes and tools from this site also suggest that flint from the south of the study area was also used. This flint occurs in larger nodules and was probably exploited both for domestic flake tools and for core tools. The exploitation, which appears to have taken place during the later Neolithic, may represent a local form of industrial activity paralleling that from Grimes Graves in Norfolk (Saville 1981). However, insufficient material has been found to study this aspect of the flint industry at W59 in detail.

The flakes suggest that the majority were removed by hard hammer. There is no evidence of imported hammerstones and it is likely that flint nodules and cores were used for this purpose.

iii The flint industry

The industry from W59 is predominantly a flake industry and although blades formed 15% of the total, blade cores were absent. There was no evidence of core tool manufacture on site despite the presence of flakes which resembled thinning flakes (see below). The quantity of material is insufficient to represent waste from large-scale industrial knapping.

Table 56 shows the ratio of all flakes to cores and of whole and burnt flakes to cores. The results from the stratified pit deposits show a higher ratio of flakes to cores than at other examined sites. In addition Table 56 shows a strong contrast between the ratio derived from the material within pits and that from associated excavated ploughsoil squares. This would appear to suggest the deliberate deposition of exhausted or failed cores within subsoil features.

Cores

Thirty-one flake cores were found (Table 57), of which 13 (42%) weighed between 50g and 99g. The analysis suggests that both failed and productive cores are present. No complete knapping sequences have been reconstructed to demonstrate how flakes were produced.

The multi-platform cores are less systematic in their production than other types and rely on rotating the core for rejuvenation. These cores rarely show a consistent orientation but utilise random ridges to produce elongated flakes. Pit 418 contained several cores produced by alternate flaking which show no careful preparation or shaping but which do possess one surface with semi-convergent flaking. Discoidal cores have been recorded from surface collection material. Evidence of the Levallois technique is restricted to one flake from a ploughsoil context, which may be regarded as a product of a more industrial site.

Flake production was maintained by faceting to modify the flaking angle, and by platform abrasion to strengthen the edge of the core before percussion. Rejuvenation flakes removed during alternate flaking and crested flakes which result from rejuvenation by rotating the core indicate an attempt to prolong the productive capability of the core. Measurement of the longest complete flake scar indicates that these cores were of sufficient size to have provided blanks for the scrapers on the site.

Core rejection is predominantly a result of an increase in the flaking angle (30%), although this is infrequently accompanied by edge recession (6%), the result of continuous percussion of the core edge. The point at which a core becomes exhausted or has no potential for re-preparation and production are factors of size and shape. These factors are difficult to assess, particularly if small tool blanks are required. A subjective assessment suggests that 'potential', size, and exhaustion each accounted for approximately 13% of the rejected cores, with an additional 13% caused by flawed raw material.

Flakes

Table 116 shows totals of measured flakes, broken flakes, burnt flakes, and chips. All complete flakes were analysed using the system adopted for the South Dorset Ridgeway (Harding 1986). Results are shown in Figure 149 and details are contained within the archive. Most flakes have been classified as by-products of core trimming and preparation, although unretouched flake tools may also be present. On the basis of the sample analysed, blades appear to have formed 16% of the production of W59.

The results of the analysis from W59 show that despite being marginally squatter the industry most closely resembles that from W83. Flake length and breadth are similar, as are percussion angles, butt widths, flake class, planform, and scar pattern. Plain butts predominate (61% from pit 418), although 17% were faceted.

Occasional broad flakes with feathered edges, multidirectional flake scars, and dipping profiles resemble Newcomer's (1971) definition of thinning

Table 56 W59 King Barrow Ridge: flint flake/core ratios from analysed groups

Area/context		*Total flakes/core*			*Whole and burnt flakes/core*		
C	418	(63)	15		(40)	10	
HJK	432		18			10	
HJK	430	(56.5)	29	average 19.75	(38.4)	17	average 12.75
HJK	438		23			13	
HJK	440		9			11	

Figures in parentheses refer to data from ploughsoil square excavation

Table 57 W59 King Barrow Ridge: flint core classification

Clarke typology (1960)	*Number*	*Percentage*
Single platform (A)	6	19
Double platform (B)	2	6
Multi platform (C)	12	39
Alternate flaking (D)	4	13
D/E	2	6
Miscellaneous	5	16
Total	31 examples	

flakes. The lack of evidence for core tool production and the general rarity of these flakes suggest that they are probably by-products from biconical or discoidal cores. Chips of similar form are also present, which may result from faceting or retouch.

Platform abrasion persists at W59, where 16% of the measured flakes have abraded butts. This aspect of the technology correlates closely with the analysed sample from W83. Some faceted butts may also result from alternate flaking of cores with abraded platforms.

Of the measured flakes, 11.9% have hinged and 1.1% plunged distal ends. Siret fractures (accidents of debitage, Bordes 1979, fig 4.2) are present in 12% of broken flakes.

Chips

The chips (Newcomer and Karlin 1987) from each context have been examined. Total numbers from each context vary according to the sieve mesh used, but generally substantiate conclusions made about the waste flakes. Abrasion and faceting chips are present, although retouch chips have not been identified with certainty. Bulbar scars, which indicate debitage phases, are also present.

Scrapers

The distribution of ploughsoil scrapers is shown in Figure 79, MFI E13. The sample examined included 106 examples, although five were burnt and were excluded from the analysis. In contrast to both W2 (1981) and W83, where the majority of the scraper sample was derived from stratified contexts, the majority of the scrapers from W59 are from topsoil contexts. This must inevitably place some reservations on the conclusions although the accompanying diagnostic surface material suggests strongly that the assemblage is broadly homogeneous and may represent one phase of activity.

Scrapers are again the most common tool type, forming 45% of retouched material. They are made on flakes often with a slightly dipping profile, although plunged flakes were avoided. Hinged flakes were naturally unsuitable, although one side scraper was made on a hinged flake. Two scrapers are made on fragments, 19 are broken and one was made on a re-used patinated flake. Results of the analysis of blank form (Fig 150) show a consistent selection with blanks of a more elongated form than those from W83, and less elongated than the group from W31. The scrapers are also thinner than those from W83, and in this aspect show greater similarity with those from W31. Dorsal surfaces are more ridged than at W83, a feature which is consistent with the more elongated flake form at W59. Flake butts are broader than the waste flakes and include a number with faceting.

Some scraper blanks were undoubtedly removed from cores produced on site, but others, particularly those utilised to make larger, well-made scrapers, may have been introduced from industrial sites.

Blanks were normally modified by direct retouch (92%). Figure 151 shows the distribution of retouch on 78 scrapers. This shows that most retouch occurs around the entire distal end. Retouch which extends partially around the sides is more often on the right edge than the left as at W83. Additional retouch is rare. Figure 151 shows the relationship of scraper blade length to scraper blade angle. Comparisons with W83 show that both sets of scrapers are remarkably similar, although at W59 the angle of retouch is marginally higher. Scraping edges appear to be more irregular with some undercutting. Retouch often removes cortex from the distal end of the flakes. No refitting retouch chips were found.

Arrowheads

Table 58 shows the breakdown of arrowheads from excavation. The chisel arrowheads, none of which were recorded from strictly stratified contexts, have been examined and show remarkable similarities with those from W31. Blank forms and scar patterns imply the use of similar types of flakes, although controlled and systematic blank production has not been demonstrated.

The form and location of retouch are also similar. Bifacial retouch is most often used to thin the proximal end (15 out of 21 examples) but was less common at the distal end (9 out of 20 examples) where direct retouch (6 out of 20) was often sufficient. There is no evidence that an anvil was used to support the blank. Most truncations converged on the left side (12 out of 21 examples) rather than on the right (5 out of 21 examples) when looking at the dorsal surface. Overall size is again comparable: 13 out of 18 measured examples are between 20 and 29mm measured along the axis of percussion of the blank. Ten were 20–29mm wide and 12 were 5–7mm thick.

4.8 c *The prehistoric pottery (Fig 85)*
by Frances Raymond

A total of 174 sherds, representing a minimum of 14 vessels, was recovered. With the exception of seven unidentifiable fragments, all the pottery is of later Neolithic date, belonging either to the Peterborough or Grooved Ware ceramic traditions (see Figure 86 and Table 59, MF1 F4). In view of the relative fragility of the Grooved Ware fabrics, direct quantitative comparisons between the two groups are inappropriate. Problems of survival would tend to cause an obvious bias in favour of the more durable Peterborough Ware, illustrated clearly by the recovery of only two sherds of Grooved Ware from the excavation of the topsoil. With the exception of pits 430 and 432 (area J/K), which produced only plain sherds in Grooved Ware fabrics, and a shallow hollow, cut 600 (area L), which produced only Peterborough Ware (P257–P260), the ceramic assemblage from the pits was mixed, although in all cases weighted towards one of the two traditions. Grooved Ware predominated in pits 418 (P261–P262, with the flat piece P263, and one small decorated Peterborough Ware sherd in fabric FS:Pet/2), 430 (plain sherds only), and 438 (plain sherds only), while greater quantities of Peterborough Ware occurred in pit 440 (plain sherds in Peterborough Ware fabrics with one Grooved Ware

Table 58 W59 King Barrow Ridge: flint arrowheads

Arrowheads					
Chisel	*Oblique*	*Uncertain*	*Leaf*	*Barbed & tanged*	*Total*
21	2	6	2	1	32

sherd – P264), and in the shallow feature 479 (plain Peterborough Ware sherds with one Grooved Ware sherd – P265). Unfortunately the combination of the insecure dating evidence for later Neolithic pottery and the small available sample makes impossible the interpretation of intra-site activity on ceramic evidence alone.

Peterborough Ware

A minimum of four vessels are represented, based entirely on fabric distinctions. The low average sherd weight of 2.5g makes the reconstruction of form difficult. Excluding the Mortlake Ware pot found in context 600, area L (P259 and P260), the assemblage is mainly undecorated. Under these circumstances individual fabrics may well represent more than one vessel. Sherds using the same clay paste occurring widely scattered across the site cannot, therefore, be used to chart the movement of material from individual pots.

All fabrics, with the exception of FM: Pet/2, used to produce the Mortlake Ware vessel, are exclusive to W59. The presence of mica within the clay paste in this example may be indicative of contacts extending beyond the immediate study area (see W31, Peterborough Ware, this vol, 4.10 c).

Grooved Ware

A minimum of eight vessels are represented. Only 6 of the 35 sherds are decorated (all illustrated). The Grooved Ware from pit 418 in area C shows closest affinities with the thin-walled cordoned vessels of Woodlands style (Wainwright and Longworth 1971). An identification of the type of shell (freshwater, marine, or fossil), which occurs as a major intrusive element within the clay paste used to produce this pottery, could be crucial in identifying its possible origin and, by association, the contacts of its users. With the exception of three sherds, shell is a common inclusion in all the Grooved Ware from the King Barrow Ridge. Neither the form nor the decoration of the remaining sherds is isolated to a particular substyle.

The extremely unusual piece P263, also from pit 418, although in a fabric which shows some similarity to the fabrics of P261 and P262, is coarser and contains larger shell fragments. It also shows some similarity to the sherds containing sand and shell from W2 (1981), the Coneybury 'Anomaly' (fabric SSh:Indet/1). The sherd is completely flat and shows no curvature in any direction. It has been suggested (I F Smith pers comm) that it may be allied to certain unusual pieces found very occasionally in earlier Neolithic contexts (cf P137 from Carn Brea, I F Smith 1981). Dr Smith has noted a flat plate edged with a cordon at Helman Tor, although in that case the plate is rectangular, and the cordon is around the edge. The form of P263 seems to suggest an

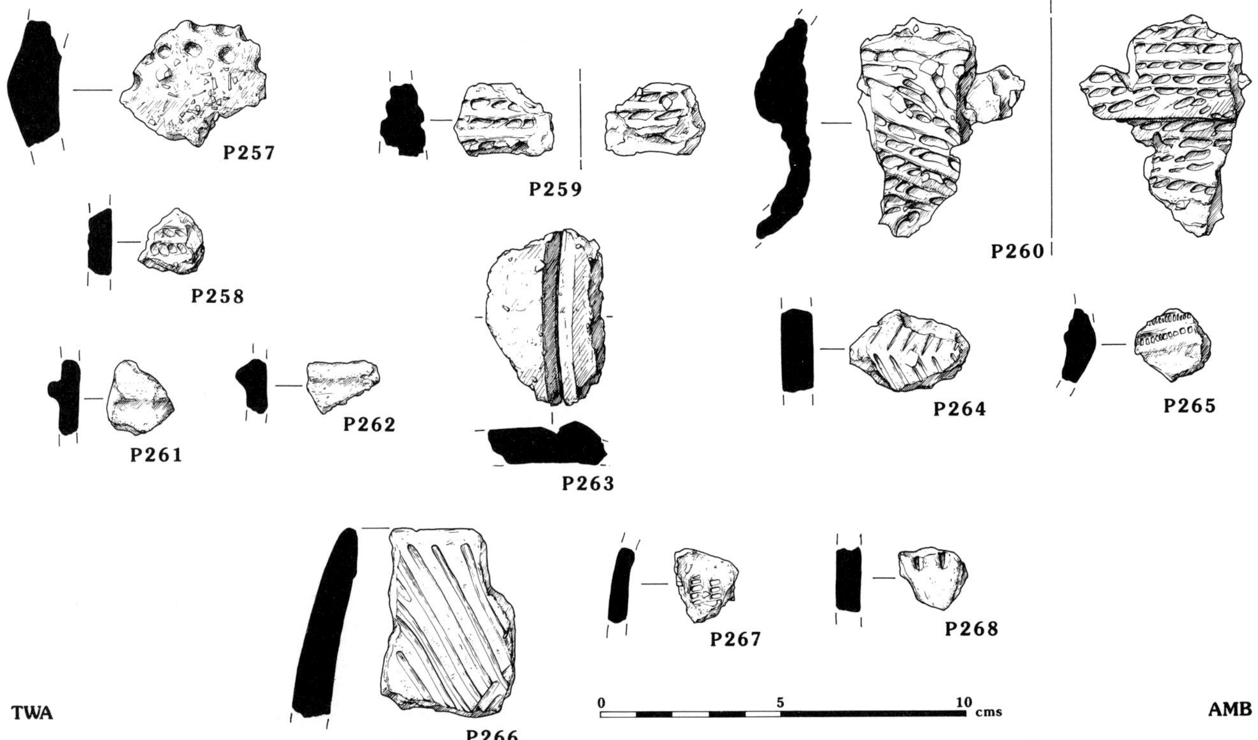

Fig 85 W59 King Barrow Ridge: prehistoric pottery (P257–P265), W58 Amesbury 42 long barrow prehistoric pottery (P267–P268), and King Barrow Ridge occasional find 1 (P266)

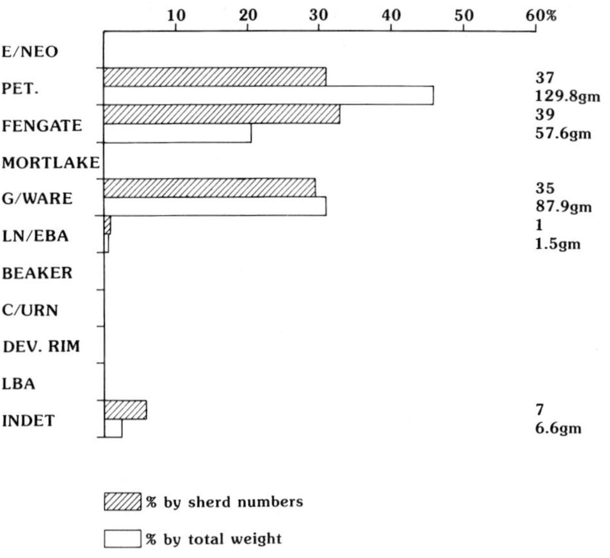

Fig 86 W59 King Barrow Ridge: pottery fabric histogram

oval platter, with a cordon set in slightly from the edge (I F Smith pers comm). The radiocarbon date from the primary deposits in pit 418 is more appropriate for P263, if it is related to earlier Neolithic assemblages, than for the Grooved Ware, which may be expected to date no earlier than the second quarter of the third millennium BC.

The unstratified find, P266, which was recovered from a rabbit scrape in the surface of barrow Amesbury 34, is a rim sherd, probably from a Durrington Walls style vessel similar to P323 from the type site (Wainwright and Longworth 1971).

Illustrated pottery (Fig 85)
(See Table 32, MF1 C1–14, for fabric descriptions)

Peterborough

P257 Area L, context 601
FfeM:Pet/3. Body sherd. Subcircular impressed motif.

P258 Area M, context 309
FS:Pet/2. Body sherd. Twisted cord impressions arranged in two parallel rows.

Mortlake

P259 Area L, context 642
FM:Pet/2. Body sherd. Twisted cord motif arranged in two parallel rows.

P260 Area L, context 642 (same vessel as P259)
FM:Pet/2. Collar. Twisted cord motif.

Grooved Ware

P261 Area C, context 497
Ssh:GW/1. Body sherd with cordon.

P262 Area C, context 497
Ssh:GW/1. Body sherd with cordon.

?Earlier Neolithic

P263 Area C, context 498
Ssh:GW/1. Sherd of ?platter, with cordon.

Grooved Ware

P264 Area K, context 515
fe:GW/1. Body sherd. Incised linear motif arranged in a herringbone pattern.

P265 Area, L context 480
feSV:GW/1. Body sherd with cordon. Two comb impressions running parallel to and on one side of the cordon.

P266 Occasional find 1 (barrow Amesbury 34 U/S)
-:GW/1. Rim sherd. Parallel grooves running obliquely below the rim; one or two grooves can be seen running at an angle in one corner, and must represent a complex pattern of decoration.

King Barrow Ridge (intensive surface collection)

Peterborough

P267 135425/547
FS:Pet/9 Body sherd. Two parallel whipped cord impressions.

4.8 d Animal bones
by Mark Maltby

The five pits located by sample excavation produced a total of 510 animal bone fragments. The bones represented for all species from the site are given in Table 60 and the species represented in each pit are given in Table 61. These totals include 248 fragments recovered from 1mm wet-sieved samples (Table 62, MF1 F5), the majority of which came from pit 418.

Pit 418 (Fig 83) produced by far the largest quantity of bones (Table 61) and was dominated by pig and sheep-sized mammal fragments. The pit produced all the pig fragments identified, apart from a calcaneus and loose tooth from pit 432, and a mandible, humerus, scapula, and another loose tooth from pit 440. It appears that the bones from several pigs were dumped in pit 418. At least two immature pigs were represented by several parts of the skeleton and, in addition, at least one neonatal mortality or foetus was represented by a calcaneus and a metatarsal. On the other hand, a femur with its distal articulation just fusing belonged to an older animal. This was a large bone (maximum distal breadth 56.6mm), comparable in size to one of a wild boar (*Sus scrofa*). At least four pigs were therefore represented in pit 418, but most of the bones could have derived from two carcases and the fragmentary nature of the assemblage limits further conclusions.

The contents of the pig assemblage were biased towards the bones (and teeth) of the head, metapodials, and phalanges. This is partially the result of fragmentation and the relative abundance of different bones in the pig skeleton. However, the vertebrae and major meat-bearing upper limb bones (scapula, os coxae, humerus, radius, ulna, femur, and tibia) were not as

Table 60 W59 King Barrow Ridge: fragments of major animal species represented

	Cattle	*Sheep/goat*	*Pig*	*Red deer*	*LM*	*SM*	*UM*
Skull fragments	3	–	11	–	3	29	2
Antler	–	–	–	2	–	–	–
Mandible	2	–	10	–	1	–	2
Loose teeth	10	1	14	–	3	–	4
Scapula	1	–	3	–	–	–	–
Humerus	1	–	1	–	–	–	–
Radius	–	2	2	–	–	–	–
Os Coxae	2	–	1	–	–	–	–
Femur	–	–	2	1	–	–	1
Tibia	1	–	–	–	–	–	–
Fibula	–	–	2	–	–	–	–
Carpals	–	–	1	–	–	–	–
Calcaneus	–	–	2	–	–	–	–
Astragalus	1	–	–	–	–	–	–
Other tarsals	–	–	1	–	–	–	–
Metacarpals	1	–	5	1	–	–	–
Metatarsals	2	–	2	–	–	–	–
Lateral metapodials	–	–	8	–	–	–	–
Metapodials	–	–	2	–	–	–	–
1st Phalanx	–	–	6	–	–	–	–
2nd Phalanx	1	–	7	1	–	–	–
3rd Phalanx	–	–	2	–	–	–	–
Ribs	2	–	2	–	4	2	1
Cervical vertebrae	6	–	2	–	–	–	–
Thoracic vertebrae	5	–	1	–	–	–	–
Lumbar vertebrae	1	–	3	–	–	–	–
Unidentified vertebrae	–	–	–	–	–	2	–
Longbone fragments	–	–	–	–	10	25	1
Unidentified fragments	–	–	–	–	27	115	127
Total	39	3	90	5	48	173	138

LM unidentified large mammal
SM sheep-sized mammal
UM unidentified mammal

well represented, nor were the tarsals and metatarsals. It is possible that most of the major meat-bearing bones of these animals were deposited elsewhere and the assemblage in this pit was consequently biased towards bones of lower meat value dumped after initial butchery. Surface erosion on the bones made observations of butchery difficult, but one mandible fragment did have knife cuts on the lateral aspect of the ramus close to the posterior condyle. These would have been made during the disarticulation of the mandible from the skull.

Two pig mandibles from pit 418 bore evidence of tooth eruption. The older specimen had its second and third permanent premolars just in wear and probably belonged to an animal aged between 18–36 months old. The younger mandible belonged to a sow. In this specimen, the deciduous incisors were still in wear and the permanent canine was just coming into wear. This animal may have been killed between 12–18 months of age (by analogy with tooth eruption data presented by Bull and Payne 1982). Both maxillae, which may belong to the same animal, had their deciduous molars still in wear and probably belonged to pigs under 18 months of age. Apart from the distal articulation of a lateral metapodial and an acetabulum, all the surviving articulations of pig limb bones were unfused. Several unfused epiphyses of phalanges were also recovered, which would support the impression that most of the bones belonged to immature animals of a similar age to those represented by the mandibles and maxillae, and possibly to the same animals.

Ageing data for pig from the rest of the pits were limited to the presence of a humerus of a neonate mortality, a scapula with a fused distal articulation, and a mandible in which the deciduous fourth molar was still present.

Pig bones were generally less well represented than cattle bones apart from pit 418. In pit 440 the 39 cattle fragments included several articulated vertebrae. The nine cattle bones in layer 516 consisted of the last two cervical vertebrae and the first two thoracic vertebrae of one animal. A further set of three thoracic vertebrae and two ribs in this layer may also have belonged to the same animal. In addition, layer 520 contained the second-fifth cervical vertebrae of one animal, probably the same one as described above. Their precise location within the pit was recorded during excavation and would support the belief that an articulated section of

Table 61 W59 King Barrow Ridge: animal species represented in pits

Species	*Pit* 418	420	430	432	438	440	*Other*	*Total*
Cattle	10	1	3	1	5	16	3	39
Sheep/goat	–	–	–	1	1	1	–	3
Pig	84	–	–	2	–	4	–	90
Red deer	2	–	–	–	1	2	–	5
Wild cat	–	–	–	–	–	1	–	1
Unidentified large mammal	22	5	3	7	2	8	1	48
Sheep-sized mammal	135	–	6	9	11	12	–	173
Unidentified mammal	82	3	11	15	18	9	–	138
Unidentified rodent	10	–	–	1	–	–	–	11
Frog/toad	2	–	–	–	–	–	–	2
Total	347	9	23	36	38	53	4	510

thoracic and cervical vertebrae was deposited in this pit.

A few cattle bones, including ten loose teeth, were found in each of the pits. They included a large tibia (maximum distal breadth 71.3mm) in pit 418, which either belonged to a very large domestic animal or possibly to an aurochs. Other measurements fell within the range usually attributed to domestic cattle. No bones of young calf were represented in this small sample and the only cattle bone that could be assigned to an immature animal was a metatarsus with an unfused distal articulation in pit 420.

Three pits each produced a single fragment of sheep/goat. The radius in pit 440 definitely belonged to a sheep, and possessed a fused proximal articulation. Another radius and a lower incisor were found in the top fills of pits 432 and 438 respectively.

The five fragments of red deer included fragments of a metacarpus and femur in pit 418. A substantial part of an antler base and brow tine was found in pit 440. This antler, which had not been cast, had a coronet breadth of 53.5mm and a depth of 68.4mm. The red deer assemblage was completed by a second phalanx of an immature animal (proximal epiphysis just fusing) in pit 438.

The upper fill of pit 440 produced a canine tooth of a wild cat (*Felis sylvestris*). Roe deer, beaver, and dog fragments were not identified in this collection. Several bones of rodents and amphibians were recovered from the sieving programme but none could be identified to species.

The unidentified portion of the assemblage was dominated by sheep-sized mammal fragments, reflecting their abundance in the sieved samples, in particular those from pit 418. Eighteen of the pig fragments in that pit were also found in the sieved samples and consisted of six loose teeth, two skull fragments, two second phalanges (one lateral), three epiphyses of phalanges, a carpal, the distal epiphysis of a metapodial, a fragment of a lateral metapodial, and two bones of newborn or foetal pigs.

Although sieving of these deposits produced mainly unidentifiable fragments, it did add to the information gained from manual recovery methods. Sieving strengthened the impression that pit 418 was dominated by pig fragments, and that bones of the limb extremities were common in the assemblage. It also produced the only evidence for the presence of foetal or neonate animals, rodents and amphibians in that pit. Sieving also increased the proportion of burnt bones represented as 62 out of a total of 83 charred and calcined fragments (75%) were found in the sieved samples. A total of 413 fragments (excluding loose teeth) were eroded. Bones from the upper fills of the pits tended to have suffered more from such surface erosion. Only one bone, from pit 440, was recorded as gnawed.

Worked bone (Fig 87)

A bone point, SF265, approximately 90mm long, was recovered from context 498 in pit 418.

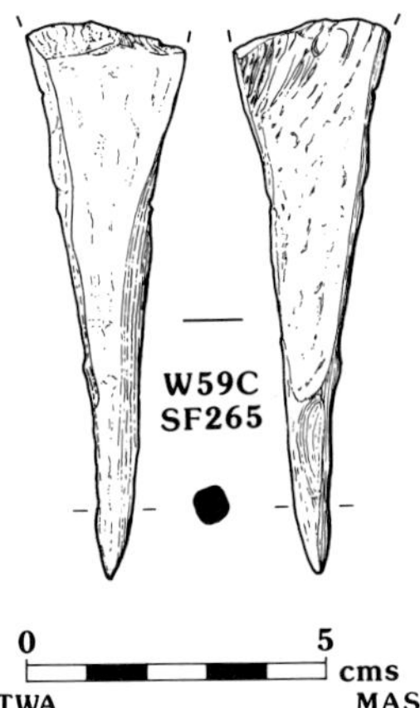

Fig 87 W59 King Barrow Ridge: area C, bone point SF265

4.9 W2, Coneybury Henge

4.9 a Site description

Until relatively recently, the cropmark enclosure on Coneybury Hill (SU 13424169) was recorded as a large, ploughed-out round barrow, although no extant barrow had been recorded by either Stukeley or Colt-Hoare. The morphology of the site was clarified by aerial photographs taken during the 1950s (see, for example, CUAP NP 44–7, QF 90, 92: RCHME 1979, plate 10), which clearly showed an oval enclosure with a single, north-east facing entrance. This new evidence, and the suggestion from bare soil marks of an external bank, led to the reclassification of the site as a small Class 1 henge monument (King 1970), and to its addition to the Schedule of Ancient Monuments for Wiltshire (AM 898).

Throughout the 1970s the site remained under annual arable cultivation and in 1979 the RCHME suggested the need for investigation by means of both geophysical survey and test excavation (RCHME 1979, xv (e)). This specific research recommendation, and the need to provide data for the formulation of a management plan, led to the evaluation excavation carried out in the autumn of 1980 as the first stage of the Stonehenge Environs Project.

The excavation was carried out in order to determine the nature and extent of surviving internal features and stratigraphy, and to assess the effect of continuing cultivation on these elements of the site. The excavation sample design assumed that the bank and any associated environmental potential had long since been removed by cultivation. The ditch deposits, unlikely to be subject to destructive processes, were to be sampled in order to provide both an environmental and chronological framework for the site.

Pre-excavation survey

Intensive surface collection. Artefacts were collected on a 5m grid over an area 80m by 70m, centred on the enclosure. This aspect of survey, details of which are contained within the archive, produced 550 flint artefacts: five scrapers, two rods, 17 cores, and 526 flakes. The highest density of worked flint was recovered from an area to the south-west of the henge monument.

Geophysical survey

Prior to excavation, geophysical surveys were carried out by the Ancient Monuments Laboratory. These included magnetometer, resistivity, magnetic susceptibility (field coil and soil samples), and phosphates (Bartlett, this vol, MF1 F6–12). Reports on the Coneybury survey have already been included in two publications by Dr A J Clark (1983; 1986).

After scanning to ascertain the approximate position of the henge ditch, an area 60m by 60m was surveyed using a magnetometer (located on Fig 88, MF1 F13). The ditch of the henge provided an exceptionally clear magnetic response, as did a substantial pit to the north (W2 (1981), this vol, 4.1). Features within the henge did not respond very clearly to the survey, although there is perhaps some correlation between the pattern of weak anomalies near the centre of the site and the cluster of pits found in excavation. The density plot (Fig 89, MF1 F14) shows the ditch surrounded by a band of low readings, which most probably correspond with a reduced topsoil depth over the former position of the bank.

The results from the resistivity survey were not as informative as those from magnetic survey (Fig 90, MF1 G1).

Magnetic susceptibility readings were taken with a field coil in an area of 45m by 31m within the centre of the henge, and a more restricted set of samples were also taken for laboratory measurement. Initial susceptibility data suggested a strong correlation between positive anomalies and higher levels of burnt flint recovered from ploughsoil excavation (A J Clark 1983, 133). Further processing of both susceptibility and ploughsoil artefact data has, however, somewhat blurred the still positive correlation (Figs 91, 92, MF1 G2–G3, discussed below).

Phosphate samples were also taken; the plotted results are shown in Figure 93, MF1 G4.

Contour survey

A contour survey was carried out across the whole site on a 1m grid. This demonstrated that the whole site sloped down very gently to the south and that no traces of the earthworks of the henge survived.

The sample design and topsoil excavation strategy

The magnetometer survey provided a clear indication of the layout of the ditched enclosure, enabling a tightly defined and therefore minimally destructive excavation sample to be applied. The overall sample of the site, which owes much to the ideas of Stephen Shennan (pers comm), was designed to examine a number of aspects of the site by means of a single trench. This incorporated two linked segments (areas C, D, and E) radiating from the long axis of the enclosure, representing approximately 25% of the interior of the enclosure. The two ditch cuttings (areas A, B, and F) incorporated in the sample together represent less than 8% of the area of the ditch and also include a sample of the exterior (Fig 94; Table 63).

Within the excavated area, ploughsoil (overall context 1), was treated as an integral part of the physical record of the site, and was consequently hand excavated on a 1m grid (contexts 2 to 537). In order to control ploughsoil artefact recovery, a programme of sieving was initiated. A series of nested sample fractions (10, 20, 25, and 50%) was calculated for each site subdivision (Fig 94), the intention being to provide the sieving programme with some flexibility. Eventually, 50% of the ploughsoil was dry-sieved through 4mm mesh, with all residues sorted on site by a restricted team in order to standardise this aspect of the process.

The removal of the modern ploughsoil, approximately 0.18m in average depth, revealed a 'lower ploughsoil' (overall context 538), a localised colluvial deposit overlying the ditches and the majority of the interior of the enclosure. The nature of this deposit, and its varying depth, suggest that the interior of the enclosure when constructed was scarped back into the hillside in order to create a level interior platform on the shallow slope. Context 538 was also removed on a 1m grid (contexts 539 to 910), and again 50% of these contexts were dry-sieved through 4mm mesh.

The distribution of artefacts from the ploughsoils

The artefacts recovered from the topsoil/subsoil excavation have no vertical stratigraphic integrity, although the degree of mixing may be small. Table 64 clearly demonstrates that the majority of the prehistoric pottery was recovered from context 538, and that over 89% by weight of the medieval and later pottery was recovered from context 1. Within area C, ploughing had penetrated almost to the surface of the chalk with a consequent destruction of any vertical relationship. However, it does appear that within the enclosure there had been little horizontal movement of soil, and thus of artefacts, enabling spatial analysis of both artefacts and geophysical data to be carried out with some confidence.

The following groups of artefacts were recovered: worked flint, burnt flint, non-local stone, and ceramic material. Of these, only worked flint, and then only elements of the overall assemblage, can be suggested as related directly to phases of construction and use of the enclosure. Both burnt flint and non-local stone carry no chronological indicators when unstratified (although the presence of a rhyolite (bluestone) flake from context 538 should be noted here), and the ceramic

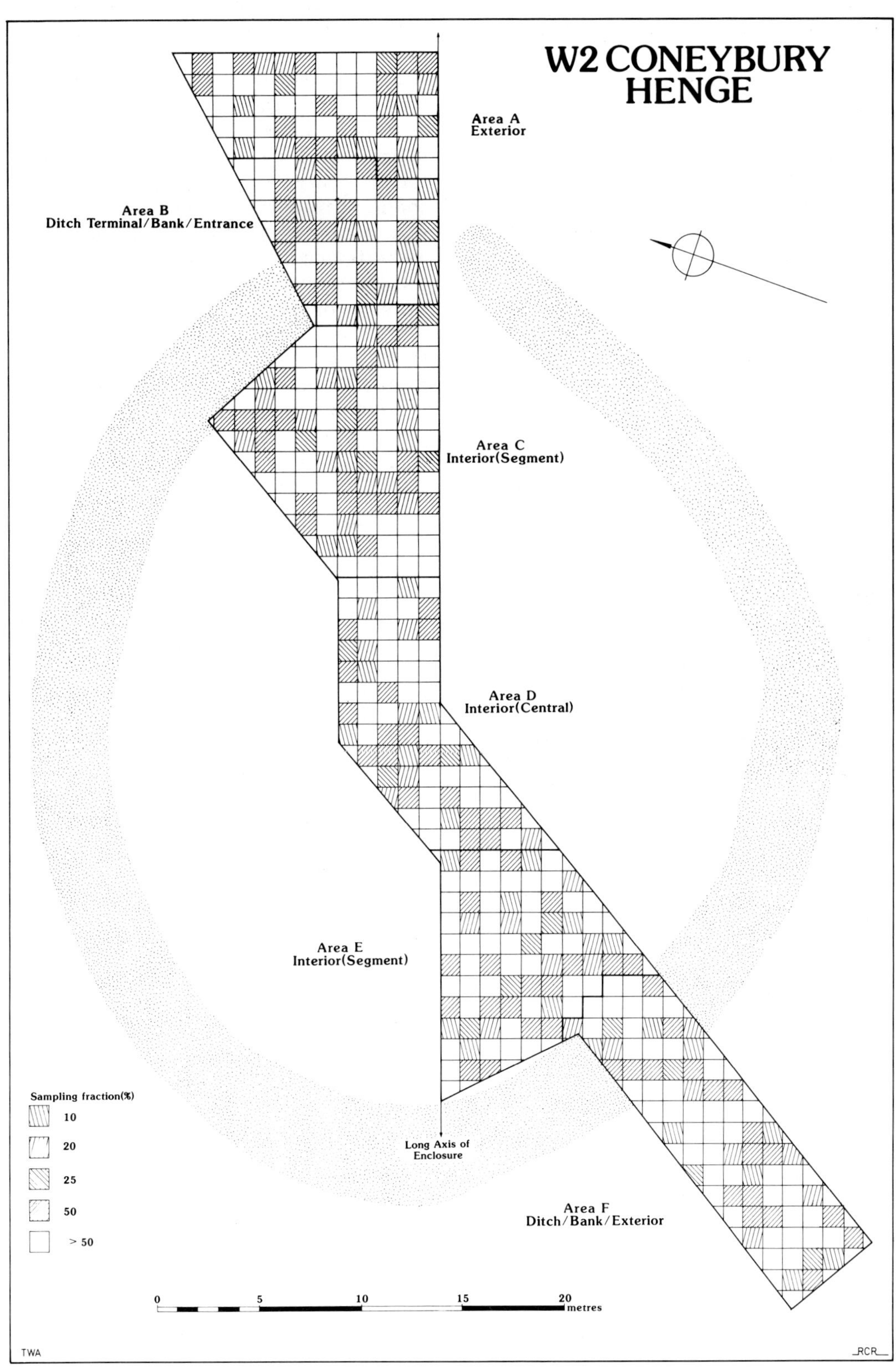

Fig 94 W2 Coneybury Henge: excavation sample design

Table 63 W2 Coneybury Henge: excavation sample design

Zone sampled	*Area*	*Size m^2*
Interior		
Centre	D	73
Segment (north)	C	104
Segment (south)	E	79
Entrance	B	16
Ditch	F	54
Ditch terminal	B	35
Exterior		
North	A	58
South	F	33

material recovered was primarily of Roman or later date (Table 64).

The distribution plans (Figs 95, 96) combine data from overall contexts 1 and 538.

The most obvious feature of the distribution of worked flint is the reflection, by low values (0–17 pieces per m^2) of the former position of the exterior bank in area F and of the bank terminal in area B. More positive aspects of the distribution are less easy to discern, although some clustering of values above 38 pieces per m^2 can be suggested in two areas, both within the enclosure and immediately adjacent to the inner edge of the ditch. Both of these apparent concentrations may be enhanced by the increase in depth, and in consequence of potential flint content, of the soils over the ditch. The distribution of flint tools, both scrapers and other types (Fig 96), shows a strong correlation with that suggested for total flint numbers, but in this case cannot be explained as a product of the enhancing effect of localised colluviation. In both areas scrapers and other tool types, particularly knives, occur in greater numbers than within the central area of the enclosure. The evidence from animal bones within the partly filled ditch terminal suggests that some form of carcase dressing or cooking activity may have taken place in the near vicinity, activities with which the flint tools and an element of the unretouched flake assemblage may be associated. This potential focus of activity is secondary to the construction of the enclosure, the evidence for butchery coming primarily from contexts 1486 and 1501 (Fig 100), where it is associated with Beaker pottery, not of a particularly early type. It is possible that the comparable tool and total flint cluster adjacent to the southern ditch cutting may be more strongly associated with the construction and primary use of the enclosure, as the ditch here lacks deposits of the type recovered from the terminal cutting.

The distribution of burnt flint within the enclosure provides an element of solid comparison for the data generated by the magnetic susceptibility survey (Bartlett, this vol, MF1 F6–12). A positive correlation between high densities of burnt flint in the topsoil and areas of high magnetic susceptibility has been demonstrated by A J Clark (1983, 133, and 1986, fig 7), although this interim interpretation was based on data available from the upper ploughsoil (context 1) only. The combined distribution from contexts 1 and 538 shown in Figure 95, while again emphasising the former bank positions, fails to produce such a positive and interpretable distribution as that published in the interim statement (A J Clark 1986). The weights of burnt flint are relatively low (compare, for example, those from an 'occupation' site, W59, Fig 80, MF1 F2), and produce a patchy and uninterpretable distribution.

The structure of the enclosure (Figs 97–99)

Two sections were excavated across the enclosure ditch, one across the ditch to the south and the other across the western terminal.

The section to the south (Fig 99) was 5m long and revealed a ditch (cut no 934, Figs 100, 101) which was *c* 2.5m deep and 5m wide with an irregular, V-shaped profile. After removal of contexts 1 and 538 the ditch was excavated in two sections, each 2m wide, leaving a 1m central baulk which was subsequently removed. The baulk was used to provide a sieved control sample for the ditch stratigraphy.

Three components to the tertiary fills were distinguished. The uppermost fill (context 1065) was chalky and showed evidence of sorting, becoming progressively stonier with depth. This overlay a layer of compressed chalk rubble (context 1421), which may represent bank material deliberately deposited in the partly filled ditch. The tertiary fills contained three sherds of prehistoric pottery (two sherds of earlier Neolithic and one sherd of mid/Late Bronze Age).

A period of stabilisation at the top of the secondary fills is represented by a thin layer of stone-free, silty clay loam (context 1444) which overlay a deep layer of relatively stone-free ploughwash (context 1487). Context 941 (equivalent to the junction between contexts 1444 and 1487) produced a small sample of burnt human bone, possibly representing one individual older than 12 years (Henderson, this vol, 4.9 f). The secondary fills contained over 50 sherds of Beaker pot-

Table 64 W2 Coneybury Henge: pottery from ploughsoil contexts

	Prehistoric		*Roman*		*Medieval*		*Post-medieval*		*?*	
	no	*wt(g)*	*no*	*wt(g)*	*no*	*wt(g)*	*no*	*wt(g)*	*no*	*wt(g)*
Context 1	2	10	36	116	34	181	41	249	18	81
Context 538	23	118	81	405	10	43	3	9	15	60
Totals	25	128	117	521	44	224	44	258	33	141

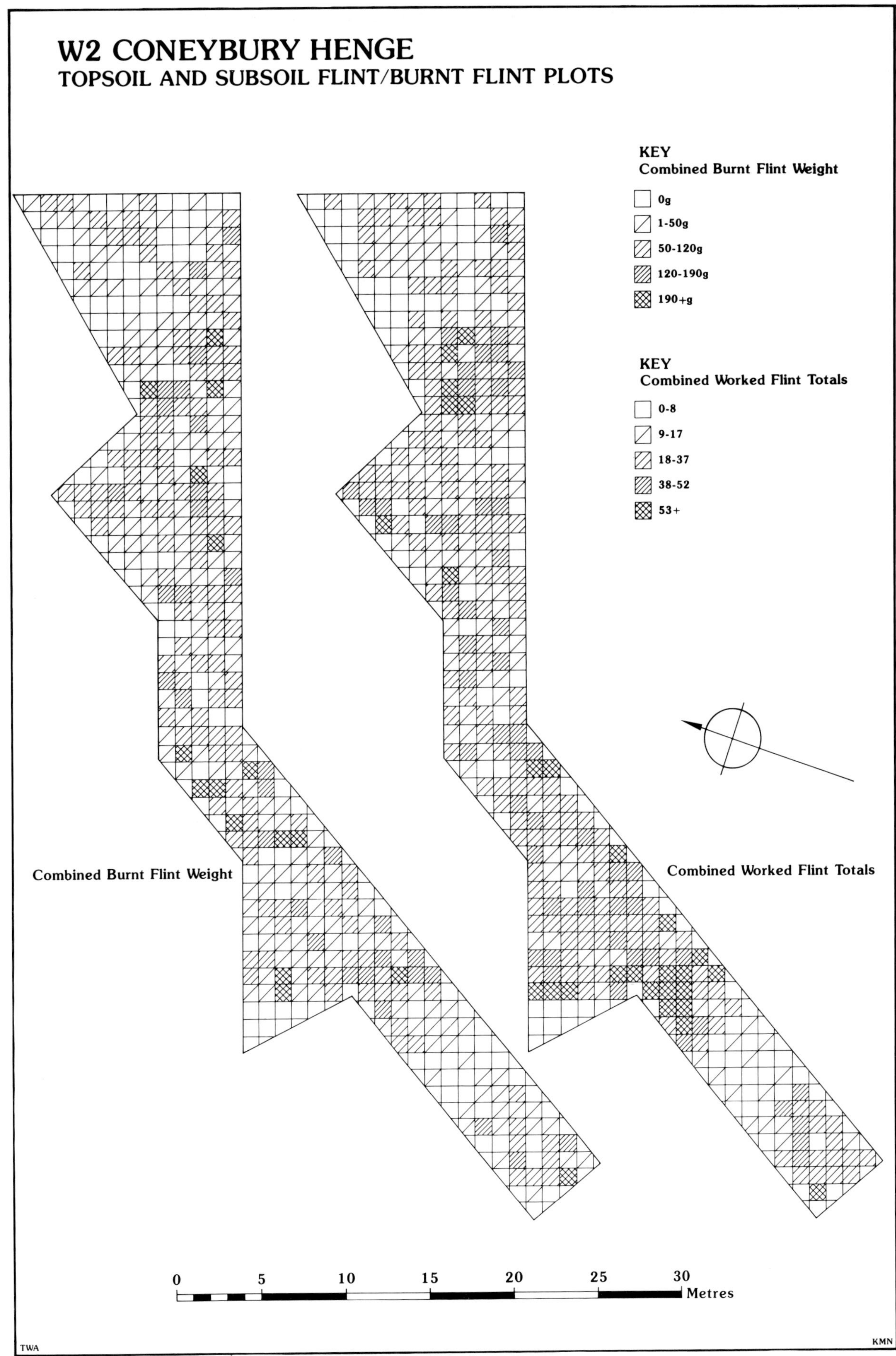

Fig 95 W2 Coneybury Henge: distribution of burnt and worked flint from ploughsoil excavation

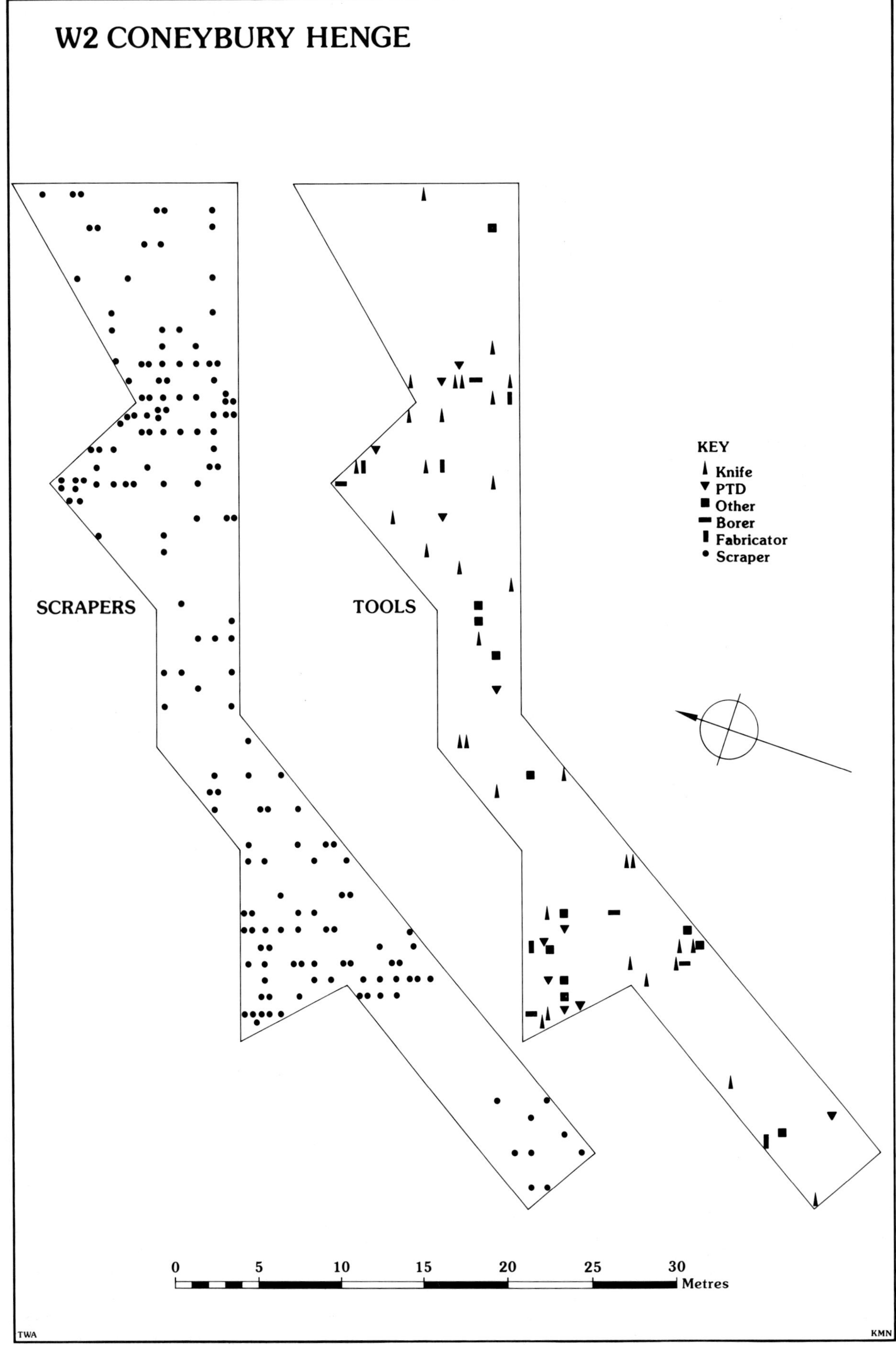

Fig 96 W2 Coneybury Henge: distribution of flint scrapers and other flint tools from ploughsoil excavation

tery, a considerable proportion of which (P77, P78, and P79, for example) may belong to a single vessel of the Late Style (Ellison, this vol, 4.9 c).

The primary fills consisted of a heavily cemented chalk wash (context 1420) above vacuous chalk rubble with a humic component (contexts 1445, 2305, and 2306). Stratigraphically, the cemented component of the primary fills can be suggested as essentially the same context as 1445; below this was a thin layer of fine, rain-washed primary silt. The upper part of the primary fills produced two sherds of Late Neolithic pottery (one sherd of Peterborough Ware and one sherd of Grooved Ware, none illustrated), and two sherds of Beaker pottery. The illustrated Beaker sherd (P82) is a base angle from a vessel with a plain zone at its base, and therefore cannot be assigned to a particular style.

Worked flint from the lower ditch fills exhibits a predominantly industrial character, with evidence of core production in the form of primary flakes. This character, emphasised by a lack of retouched material (only 1.9% of all flakes), may represent the immediate exploitation of flint nodules recovered during ditch quarrying (Pollard, this vol, 4.9 b).

The primary fills of the ditch produced 13 bones of a large bird, identified as a white-tailed sea eagle, and the dispersed part skeleton of a male dog (Maltby, this vol, 4.9 e). The 52 bones which represented this animal were found in the lower part of context 1420 and in 2306. Bone from context 2306 produced a radiocarbon date of 2917–2615 BC (OxA 1408).

The base of the ditch in this cutting showed a markedly irregular 'gang-dug' profile. The excavation of the lower levels of the ditch, where the chalk edge had been protected by rapidly accumulating primary chalk rubble, showed that the natural bedding planes of the chalk had been followed, creating a stepped profile. Two basal 'terminals' were identified, the line of which did not correspond exactly, and the lowest levels of which differed by up to 0.35m. Little attempt seemed to have been made to create a regular ditch at the point examined.

A column for molluscan analysis was taken from the west face of this section (Bell and Jones, this vol, 4.9 g).

The northern section exposed a 5m length of the western ditch terminal (cut 1500, Fig 98). After removal of contexts 1 and 538, a 1m section of the ditch was excavated adjacent to the north-west section. Subsequently, the excavation of the terminal commenced as a series of radiating cumulative sections, with all artefacts three-dimensionally recorded. This excessively time-consuming strategy was rapidly abandoned and eventually only the northern half of the longitudinal section of the terminal was fully excavated.

At the point sectioned, the ditch was *c* 2.4m deep and 4.5m wide (Figs 100, 102). It had a U-shaped profile and a flat bottom. The tertiary fill contained two sherds of Peterborough Ware and four sherds of mid/Late Bronze Age pottery. The secondary fills consisted of a deep localised colluvial layer (context 1501), containing a large amount of animal bone, predominantly of cattle, with pig the only other species commonly represented. The accumulative nature of context 1501 is emphasised by the pottery it contains, ranging from earlier Neolithic (P57), Beaker (P71 and P72), and Collared Urn (P86) to Middle Bronze Age (P87 and P89) in its upper levels. A layer of dark brown material (context 1486), containing charcoal, burnt flint, and animal bone was subsequently recognised in section to have filled a recut (cut 2301) in the top of the secondary fills. The nature of context 1486 suggests a midden deposit, on the basis of the pottery that it contained, dating to the late Beaker period. The bones from this context, again from relatively good meat bones, reflect the patterns observed in context 1501, but with a considerable degree of scorching and fragmentation. Maltby suggests (this vol, 4.9 e) that the bones from the Beaker horizons within the ditch terminal represent dumping, particularly of cattle bones, over a considerable timespan. This apparent continuity of deposition may, in association with the evidence for both burning and flint tool use recorded within the enclosure adjacent to the entrance, suggest an area where both carcase preparation and cooking were taking place.

Within this ditch cutting the greatest proportion of worked flint was recovered from contexts 1486 and 1501, which together produced over 88% of the entire flint assemblage from the terminal. Although the emphasis again appeared to be on the production of cores, the recovery of scrapers and other tools from 1501 suggests that a wider variety of more 'domestic' tasks may be represented. The concentration of flint implements recorded from the ditch terminal can be paralleled in other Wessex henges, including Durrington Walls (Wainwright and Longworth 1971), and at the western terminal at site IV, Mount Pleasant (Wainwright 1979).

Further evidence of Beaker activity associated with the enclosure is attested by the presence of a small pit (cut 2115) located within area K (the area excavated in order to examine a magnetometer anomaly lying beyond the henge, W2 (1981), this vol, 4.1). Lying approximately 15m to the north of the enclosure, this pit, 0.95m in diameter and 0.5m deep (Fig 97), contained fragments of antler and animal bone and a comb-impressed Beaker rim sherd (P74).

Within the ditch a period of stabilisation at the top of the primary filling was marked by a possible turf line (context 2300). Below this were layers of chalk wash (context 1502) and vacuous chalk rubble (context 1422), overlying a layer of primary silt (context 2099) at the bottom of the ditch. Context 1422 contained a sherd of Grooved Ware (P64).

The two ditch sections, while exhibiting some similarity in broad stratigraphic sequence, were very different in both plan and profile. The southern ditch had an irregular 'gang-dug' appearance, and the profile at the base was narrow and V-shaped, with no evidence of recutting. The fresh-looking edges of the ditch and the homogeneous vacuous chalk rubble and humic lenses of the primary fills, suggest that the initial filling of this part of the ditch occurred as a single episode.

The terminal ditch, in contrast, was wider, flat-bottomed, and had very smooth sides, into one of which (the interior side) a step was cut. This appearance, together with the primary silts and chalk wash at the bottom of the ditch, suggests that the ditch here may have been cleared out at least once before being allowed to silt up naturally.

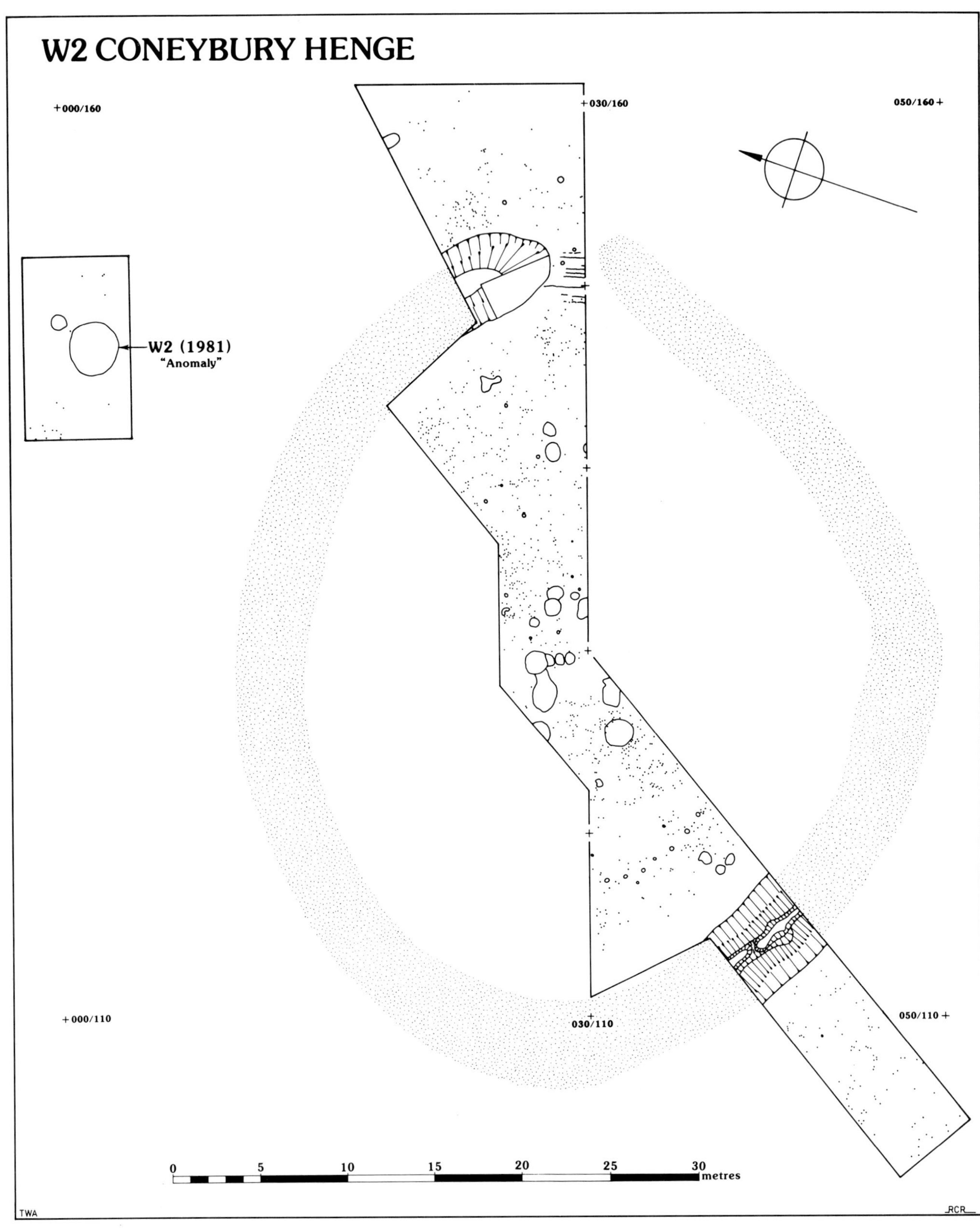

Fig 97 W2 Coneybury Henge: overall excavation plan

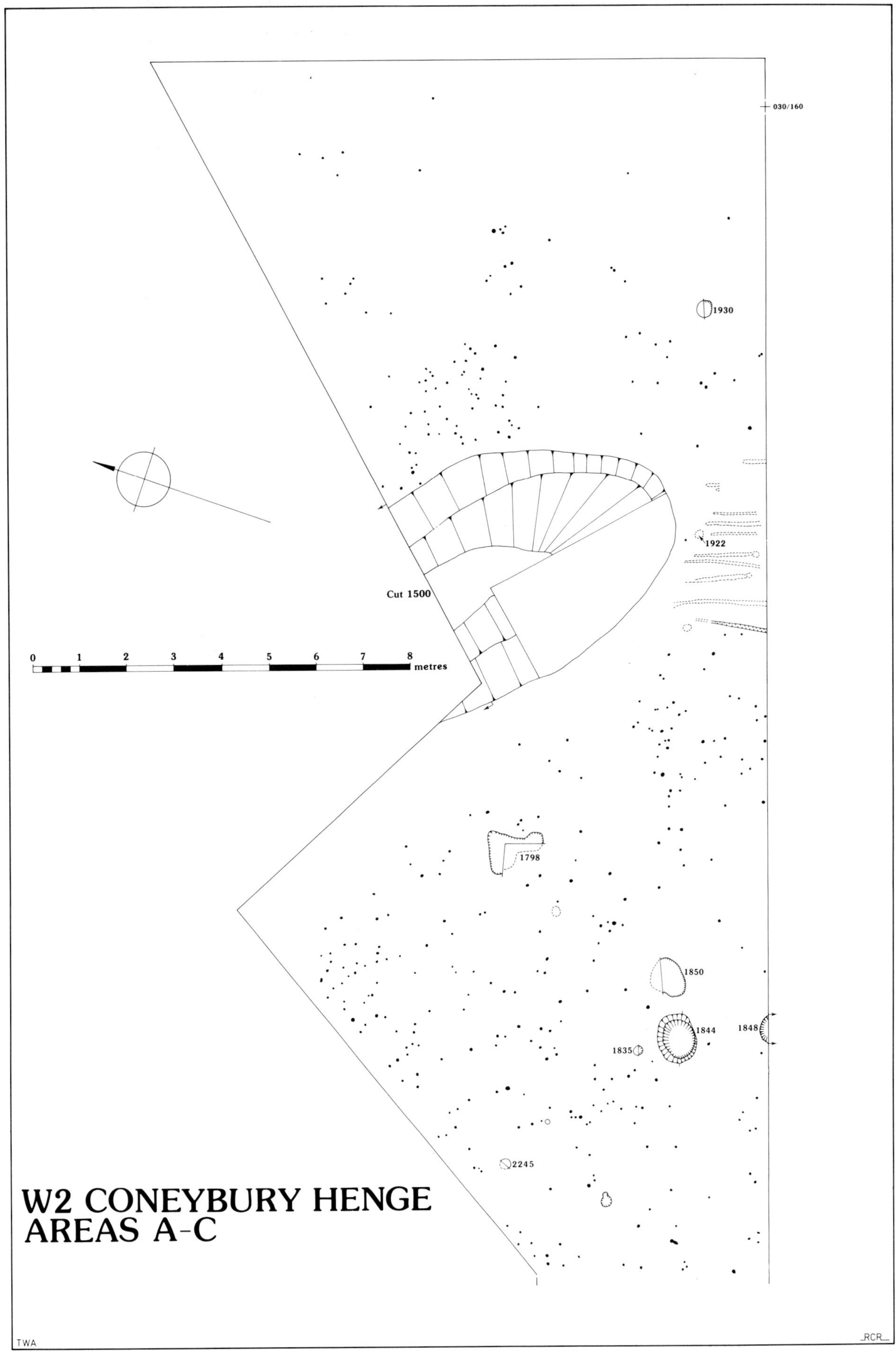

Fig 98 W2 Coneybury Henge: detailed plan of areas A–C

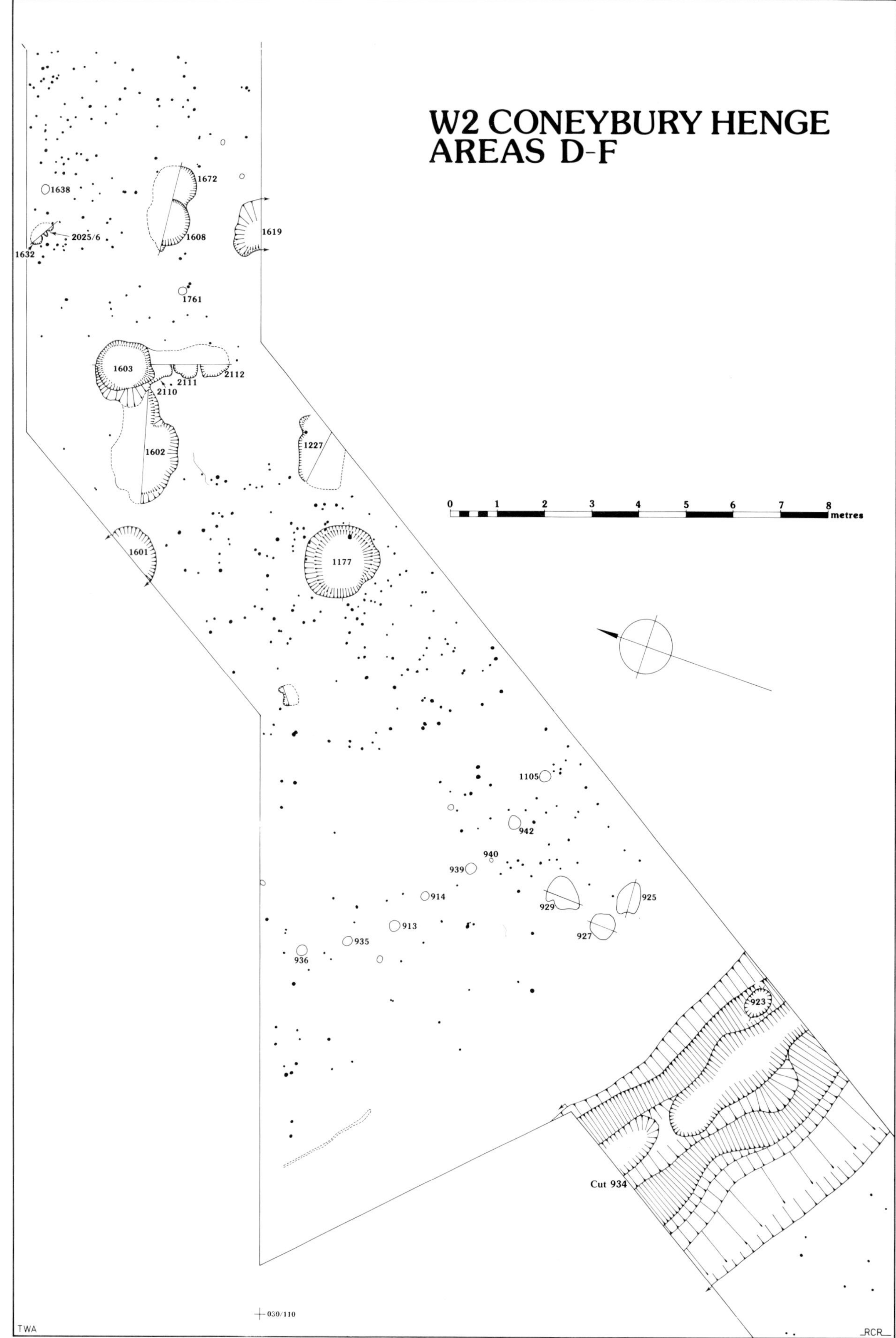

Fig 99 W2 Coneybury Henge: detailed plan of areas D–F

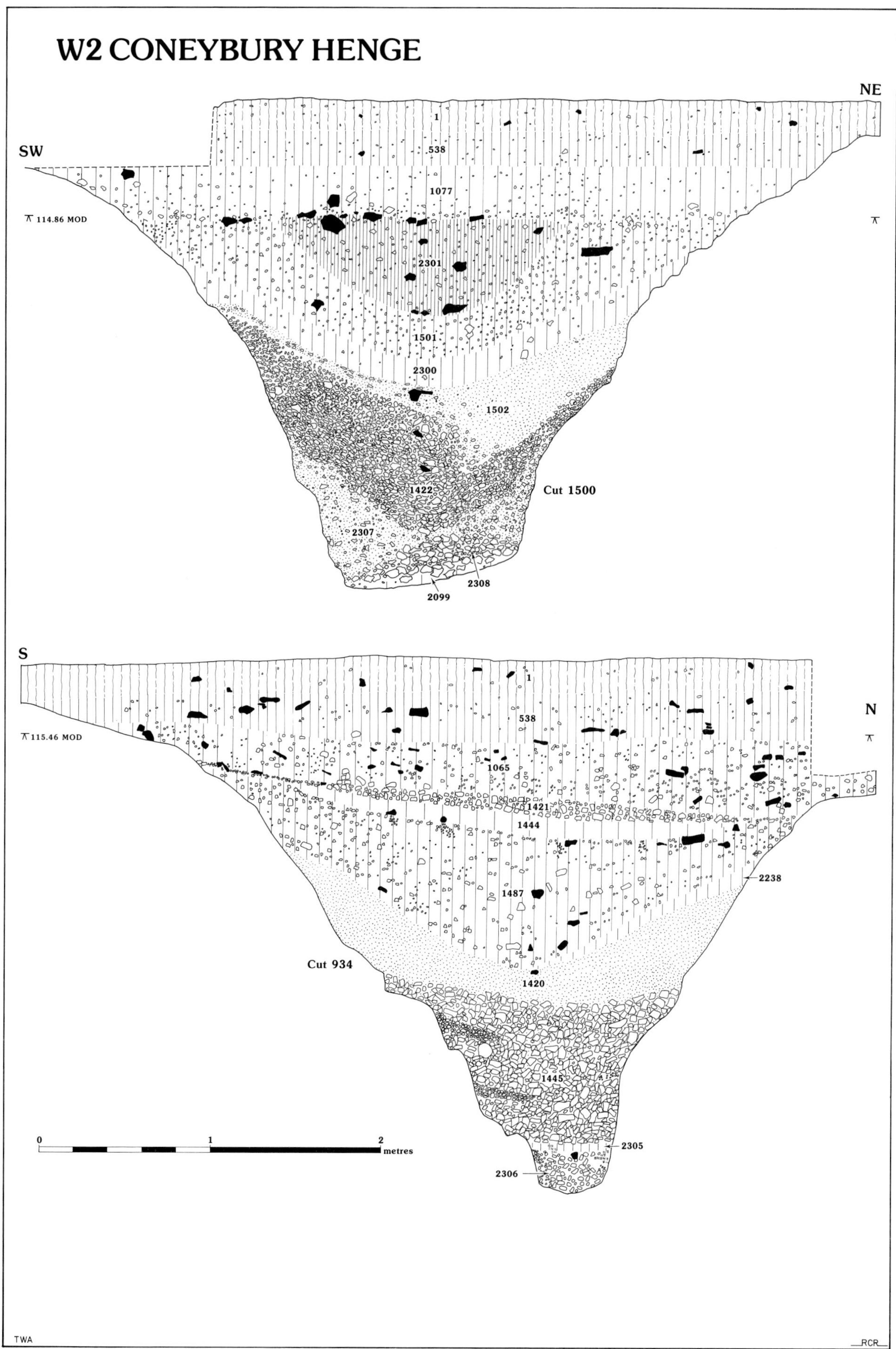

Fig 100 W2 Coneybury Henge: ditch sections

Fig 101 W2 Coneybury Henge: southern ditch section from west (scale 2m)

The internal features

The excavation revealed a number of different types of feature in the interior of the henge which, as far as can be ascertained from the area examined, seemed to have some form of spatial integrity. Figure 97 and the detailed Figures 98 and 99 show three zones of features inside the enclosure. The dimensions and profiles of all of the pits and postholes described below are given in Table 65, and Figure 103 shows section drawings of the larger pits.

The features discussed contained few artefacts, and the majority of those recovered were from the upper localised colluvial fills and need not necessarily be associated with the use or immediate disuse of the feature. The bone assemblage from these features was small and generally fragmentary, with cattle being the most common species represented (Maltby, this vol, 4.9 e). Pit 1619 contained a bone, possibly of an aurochs, from context 1398.

Although some variation in assemblage composition between individual features can be observed, the overall flint assemblage from the interior pits (Table 67, MF1 G6) is too small for any positive assessment to be made concerning the nature of production or use of lithic resources. In comparison with the levels of worked flint recovered from the horizontal deposits within the enclosure, such paucity of flint from features suggests, with few exceptions, that they were deliberately and rapidly backfilled, possibly prior to any extensive interior activity.

In the centre of the enclosure was part of a possible circle of pits/post pits. The largest complex of features, *c* 3m from the estimated centre of the enclosure, comprised a pit (cut 1603) flanked by a shallow depression to the west (cuts 1602 and 1242) and three postholes (cuts 2110, 2111, and 2112) to the south. Part of the lower fill of cut 1603 (2239) appeared to be a deliberate tip of material, the rest (2109) was very chalky. The only pottery from this complex of features was a small sherd of (probably) Neolithic pottery from the posthole cut 2112. The relationship between all of these features remained unclear, both in plan and section, but it could be suggested that they are the result of levering or packing during the process of erecting an upright into the pit.

Two pits lay *c* 2m to the east of these features. The top fill of cut 1608 was cut by a smaller pit, cut 1672. The fills of the larger pit contained a large proportion of chalk. All of the pottery from this larger pit was

Fig 102 W2 Coneybury Henge: ditch terminal section from south-west (scale 2m)

Table 65 W2 Coneybury Henge: dimensions and profiles of interior pits

Zone	*Cut no*	*Diameter(m)*	*Depth(m)*	*Profile*
Central	1603	1.12	0.95	steep sides, flat bottom
	1602 & 1242	–	0.30	irregular
	2110	0.35	0.26	shallow, U-shaped
	2111	0.44	0.20	shallow, U-shaped
	2112	0.53	0.24	shallow, U-shaped
	1608	0.92	0.66	steep sides, flat bottom
	1672	0.79	0.21	shallow, U-shaped
	1619	1.00	0.60	steep sides, flat bottom
	1227	–	0.20	irregular
	1177	1.35	0.80	steep sides, flat bottom
	1601	1.20	0.90	steep sides, flat bottom
Entrance	1844	0.75	0.45	rounded bottom
	1835	0.19	0.06	flat bottom
	2245	0.24	0.10	rounded
Interior South	1105	0.17	0.10	rounded
	945	0.23	0.07	rounded
	939	0.29	0.23	rounded
	914	0.20	0.21	rounded
	913	0.30	0.19	rounded
	935	0.27	0.24	rounded
	936	0.23	0.20	rounded
	925	0.24	0.09	shallow, U-shaped
	927	0.20	0.06	shallow, U-shaped
	929	0.35	0.10	shallow, U-shaped

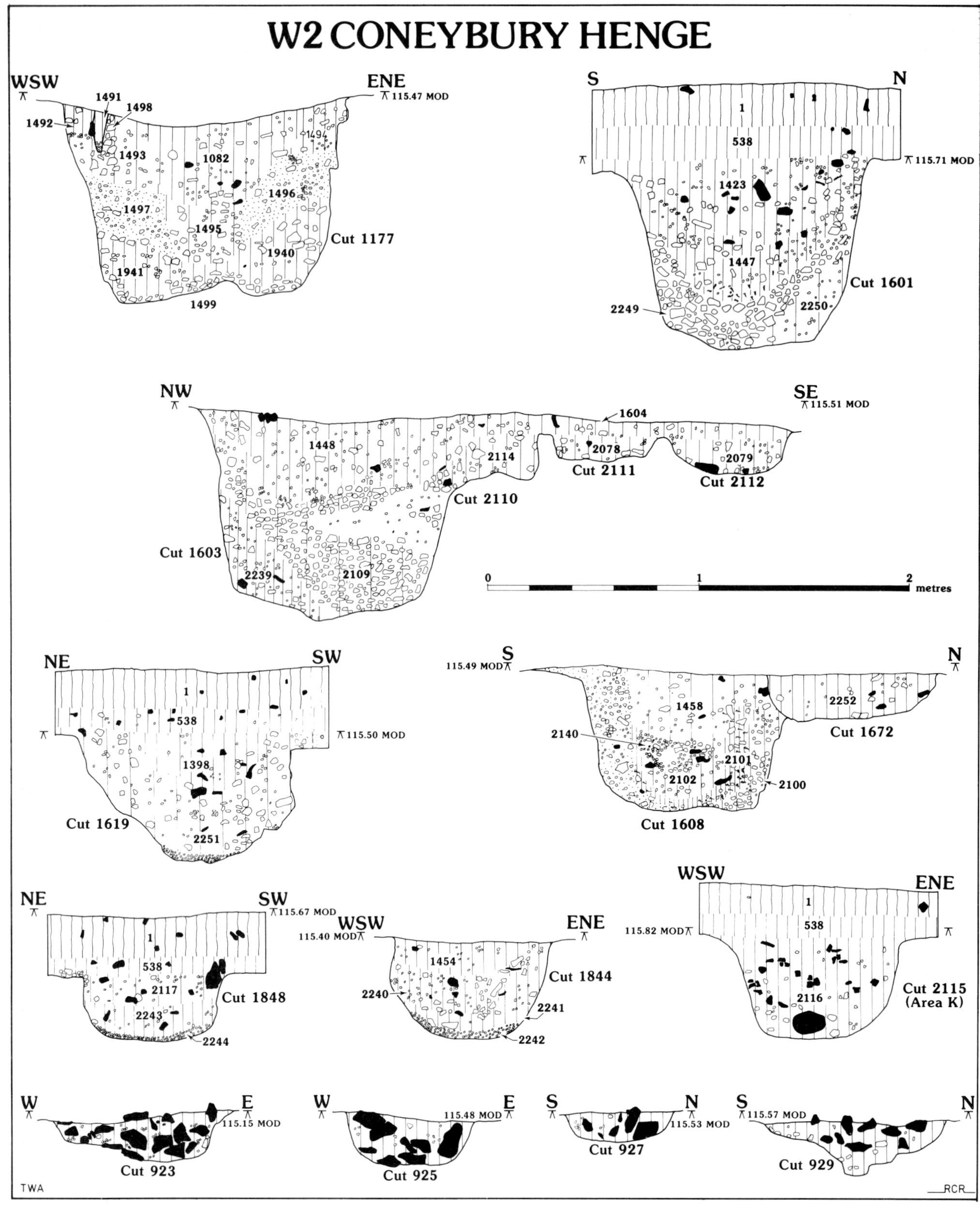

Fig 103 W2 Coneybury Henge: sections of interior features

Grooved Ware (including P62), while both Grooved Ware (seven sherds including P61, P63, and P65) and Beaker (two sherds, one of which, P70, is of Case's Middle Style) were recovered from the smaller pit. A posthole, cut 1606, lay *c* 1m west of this pit.

Approximately 1m to the south of these two pits lay a single pit, cut 1619. This was rather irregular in comparison to those already described, with evidence for weathering back of the sides and a more humic fill. A single sherd of Grooved Ware (P60) was recovered from context 1398, the upper pit fill, and the lower fills produced some animal bone, three fragments of which were identifiable as cattle. A posthole, cut 1610, lay just to the north of the pit. Four metres west of this pit was a feature which may have been natural in origin; it contained no artefacts and the portion excavated was irregular in profile. It compared to the shallow depression associated with cut 1603 described above, but, as its complete excavation was not possible, it is not known whether it is associated with other features.

A large pit, cut 1177, lay *c* 1m to the west of this feature (Fig 104). The top fill of the pit was cut by a stakehole and the lower fills were chalky. It contained a small sherd of unidentifiable pottery and some cattle bone. Another pit, cut 1601 lay *c* 3.5m to the north; part of it lay outside the area sampled by excavation. In section it appeared to be similar to the fill of cut 1603, with a deliberate tip of material (context 2250) and a chalky lower fill (context 2249). The upper fill contained six sherds of Grooved Ware (none illustrated), and animal bone from context 1447 produced a radiocarbon date of 3254–2911 BC (OxA 1409).

The lower fills of all of the large pits in this group had a high chalk content and a proportionately low humic content, suggesting that they had been deliberately backfilled, either partially or totally.

The southern excavated segment of the interior of the enclosure (area E) revealed an arc of seven postholes (contexts 913, 914, 935, 936, 939, 942, and 1105), running concentric to the inner edge of the enclosure ditch. These features were evenly spaced and were also all of similar dimensions and profiles (Table 65). The survival of such shallow features within this part of the enclosure is largely an effect of the scarped interior. Here, within area E, both the lower and upper ploughsoils were deeper and offered protection from the effects of later cultivation. Within the corresponding northern segment of the enclosure (area C), it is likely that plough damage and chalk solution may have combined to remove similar relatively shallow features. Certainly the chalk surface within area C showed traces of physical damage in the form of plough scoring, and fewer small features were recorded. Within area C, however, two slightly more substantial pits, cuts 1844 and 1848, lay on the projected line of the post circle, *c* 10m west of the entrance. The pits appeared to flank the 'axis of symmetry' of the enclosure, the long axis aligned through the single entrance. The majority of pit 1848 lay just outside the sample trench and it was consequently only partly examined. The other, cut 1844, was

Fig 104 W2 Coneybury Henge: pit 1177 with surrounding stakeholes (horizontal scale 2m)

fully excavated and was shown to be a fairly shallow, round-bottomed pit, containing seven sherds of Grooved Ware (including P58, P59, P66, and P67), and one sherd of Beaker pottery (P83), all of which was recovered from the upper fill of the pit. Despite the plough damage noted above, two smaller features were located on the projected line of the post circle, postholes cuts 1835 and 2245. These were both similar in size to those in the southern section of the interior (Table 65). The other features in this area (cuts 1807 (not on plan) and 1798) were found on excavation to be shallow in depth and irregular in shape. Molluscan analysis (Bell and Jones, this vol, 4.9 f) suggests that feature cut 1798 is a former tree hole, probably the result of minor scrub growth in post-Neolithic times.

In the southern segment of the interior, three pits (cuts 925, 927, 929) lay between the post circle and the inner edge of the enclosure ditch. They were all of a similar size and shape, and were packed with flint nodules, all of which were examined but showed no signs of utilisation. A similar feature, cut 923, was cut into the weathered upper edge of the ditch (Fig 99). None of these features contained any datable artefacts and their function must remain uncertain.

The chalk causeway marking the entrance to the enclosure, which appears, based on excavated and geophysical data, to be only 3m wide, was noticeably lower than the surface of the surrounding chalk natural. The lowering presumably results from wear, most likely from the use of the single entrance causeway across which a number of longitudinal striations were observed during excavation. When examined in detail these parallel striations were found to be shallow, irregular in profile, and filled with the same colluvial soil which covered the entire causeway. They were originally suggested as plough/ard marks, an interpretation which now seems unlikely in view of their position and relationship to the silted-up ditch terminals. An alternative suggestion is that they may represent traces of attempts to protect the surface of the narrow causeway. A horizontal wooden structure placed on the causeway surface, presumably devoid of soil cover, would have served to prevent erosion beyond that evident from the lowered level of the causeway.

Outside the entrance, *c* 4m to the east, lay a large, flat-bottomed posthole, cut 1930. Apart from the numerous stakeholes described below, this was the only feature recorded in both of the immediate exterior sample areas. The two pits recorded in the separate excavation area to the north-west (this vol, 4.1) cannot be suggested as being integrated with the structure of the enclosure.

Where sampled, both the interior and the exterior of the enclosure revealed dense clusters of stakeholes, over 730 in total. The hard and structured nature of the chalk bedrock and the ideal conditions during excavation mean that within the sampled area the overall stakehole plan can confidently be assumed to be complete. Not all stakeholes were fully excavated, but all identified examples were initially probed with a surveyor's arrow to confirm an acceptable depth. This was generally taken as a minimum of 5cm although examples up to 20cm in depth were recorded. Subsequently a sample were fully excavated and a small number were box-sectioned to examine base profile. The excavated sample, the filling removed with a plastic spoon attached to the end of a surveyor's arrow, showed considerable uniformity in diameter, the majority lying between 6cm and 7cm (overall range 4cm to 8cm, Fig 105). As the stakeholes were recorded from a sample of the site, no attempt has been made to carry out any detailed spatial analysis, although some patterns can be observed from within the available sample. Although essentially undated, the distribution of the stakeholes, in relationship to both the enclosure as a whole and to specific internal elements, suggests that many of them may be associated with the phases of Neolithic and Bronze Age activity. Their absence immediately adjacent to the edges of the ditch is due entirely to weathering back of this area, leaving an apparently genuine contrast between the relatively small numbers recorded outside the enclosure and the dense clusters within. In the interior stakeholes appear to cluster around some of the larger features, specifically pit cut 1177, which may have several concentric stake circles focused on it (Fig 104). The central cluster of pits appears to define an area within which there are few stakeholes and there also appears to be a narrow zone relatively devoid of stakeholes concentric with the inner edge of the post circle in area E.

Sequence, dating, and interpretation

Dating evidence for the construction of the enclosure and for the excavation of the majority of the enclosed features depends on the stratified ceramic material and on the available radiocarbon dates. Very small quantities of Grooved Ware occur in a primary position in both ditch sections. Grooved Ware occurs in some of the interior pits, but generally from their upper fills, where in two cases it is associated with Beaker pottery. Ellison suggests, on ceramic grounds (this vol, 4.8 c), that the initial digging of the pits may predate the enclosure, a suggestion which the radiocarbon dates, although statistically indistinguishable, appear to support.

The excavation demonstrated that many of the elements of internal structure previously recorded from the excavation of small henge monuments, and consequently incorporated within the sampling strategy, were present at Coneybury.

The features recorded from within the interior sample area demonstrate a high degree of spatial organisation related to the enclosure ditch and its entrance. This would appear to suggest that although there may be an element of sequence in the digging of the internal pits and of the enclosure ditch, the length of time between these activities may be relatively short. Spatial interpretation beyond the excavated area is made difficult by the weakness of the magnetic response from even the larger internal features.

The similarity in profile between pits 1844 and 1848 (Fig 103) suggests an element of 'pairing', and their position astride the long axis of the enclosure has already been noted. These two features appear to be integrated with the suggested post circle, although the recorded depth of the excavated postholes (Table 65) suggests that they may not have been capable of hold-

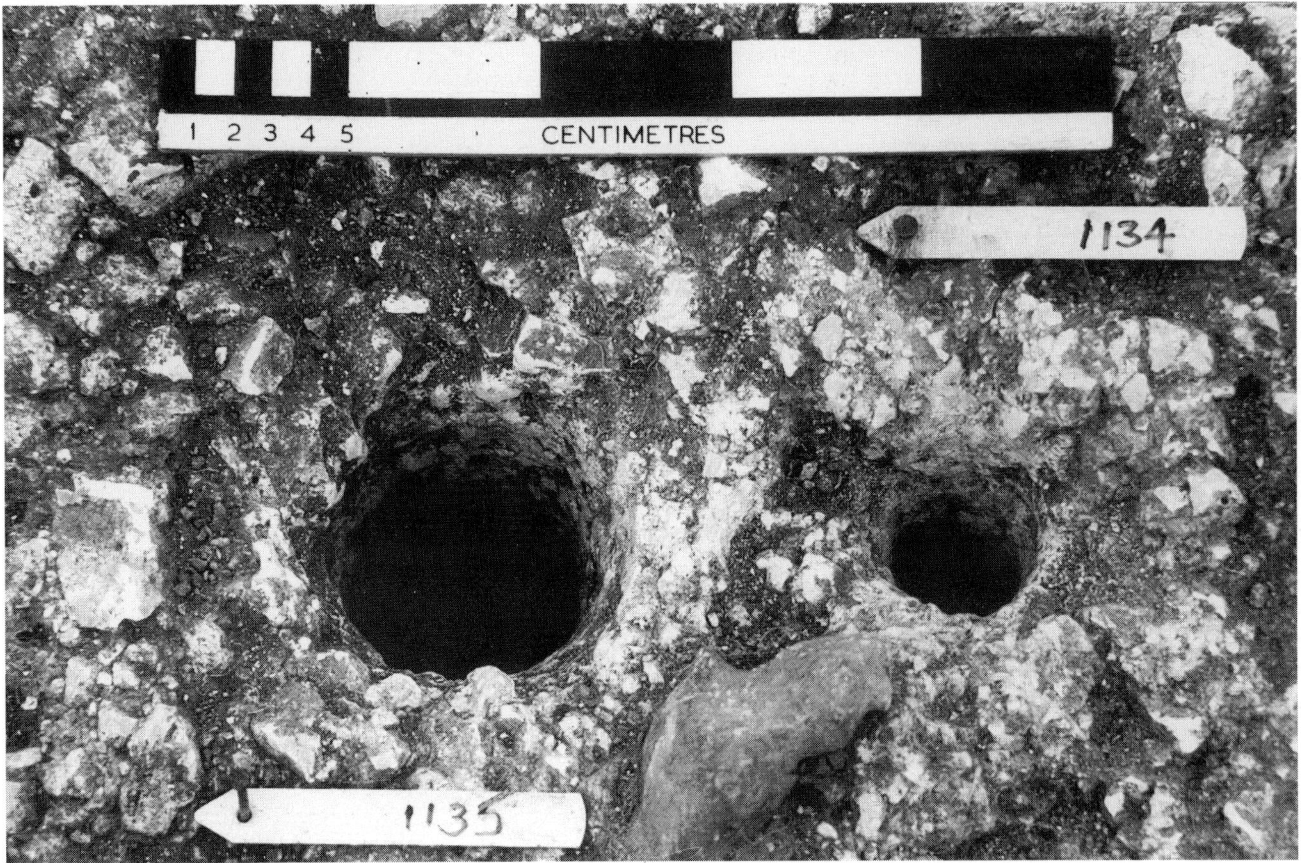

Fig 105 W2 Coneybury Henge: stakeholes 1134 and 1135 (scale 25cm)

ing free-standing uprights of any length. In no case was any packing or post-pipe observed, and the lack of artefacts from their fills makes their interpretation as miniature 'Aubrey Holes' (Atkinson 1979) untenable.

The uniformly good preservation in Area E, the southern quadrant, provides some indication of a band, relatively devoid of stakeholes, immediately inside the post circle (Fig 99). A similarly stakehole-free area can be noted within the central pit cluster, the individual components of which fail to exhibit the uniformity of the postholes discussed above. The pit fills show little evidence for gradual accumulation, suggesting, in their high chalk content and the incorporation of lenses of humic material, rapid and deliberate backfilling. The eccentric primary fills of pits 1601 and 1603 (Fig 103) suggest that these particular features may have held uprights, subsequently removed, although no indication of the former position of uprights was recovered from the chalk base of either of these pits. The fill of pit 1608 also suggests either a substantial and deep recut, or the position of a removed upright. The shallow features adjacent to pits 1603 and 1608 are more difficult to interpret, although the function of the group of three adjacent to the former pit could have been associated with leverage, either in erection or removal of a substantial timber or stone upright.

4.9 b Lithics

by Julian Richards and Joshua Pollard

The sample excavation produced a total of 14,760 pieces of worked flint. These were recovered from four broad contextual groups: the ploughsoil/subsoil, the ditch terminal cutting (cut 1500), the southern ditch cutting (cut 934), and the interior features, including pits and postholes. The breakdown of the total assemblage by context group is shown in Table 66.

Over 81% of the entire assemblage was recovered from the ploughsoil/subsoil excavation, with only 4.5% recovered from the interior features. Both ditch cuttings produced broadly comparable quantities of worked flint in relation to the varying size of the two cuttings, although the nature of these two assemblages varied considerably. Table 67 (MF1 G6) shows the composition of the assemblage from the interior pits.

Although the total assemblage is large, the bias towards the unstratified element suggested that detailed analysis, within the framework of the lithic research design, was not an appropriate first step. An awareness, based on ceramic studies (Cleal, this vol, 4.1 c; Ellison, this vol, 4.9 c), that activity both in and immediately around the sampled henge enclosure spanned the period from the Early Neolithic to the later Bronze Age, suggested that the bulk of the lithic assemblage was also likely to be mixed. The material from the ditch cuttings, although considered 'stratified', was also considered likely to include a residual element. Analysis of the assemblage therefore initially involved the prepara-

Table 66 W2 Coneybury Henge: composition of the flint assemblage

Area	Cores		Flakes				Scrapers	Other tools	Total
	whole	*fragments*	*whole*	*broken*	*burnt*	*retouched*			
Ploughsoil	70	92	6451	4549	395	140	182	93	11972
Cut 934 (South Ditch)	17	22	555	678	93	20	7	3	720
Cut 1500 (Ditch terminal)	8	7	345	243	89	19	4	5	1385
Interior features	13	11	201	290	147	6	2	3	673
Total	108	132	7552	5760	724	185	195	104	14760

tion of a stage 1 catalogue incorporating a number of observations relating to technology and assemblage curation.

Data from this initial analysis, carried out by Mark Edmonds, details of which are contained within the archive, are used as part of the analysis of the sites ploughsoil record, discussed above. The flint scrapers and arrowheads of petit tranchet derivative form have also been examined as part of overall project studies (Riley, this vol, 5.3).

A subsequent, more detailed analysis, primarily directed towards the stratified lithic groups, was undertaken by Joshua Pollard as undergraduate research at Cardiff University. The results of this subsequent stage of analysis are reported below.

Raw material

Examination by eye suggests that four types of flint are present:

i Tabular flint, probably derived from the digging of the ditch or from local surface deposits. Often of a very poor or moderate quality, with numerous internal flaws leading to irregular fracturing.

ii Nodular flint, of moderate to good quality, probably derived from surface deposits in the vicinity of the site. The cortex is usually thin and weathered, with a light brown colour. Occasional crystalline and cherty inclusions, along with internal fracture lines, are sometimes present.

iii Gravel flint, rarely used, but of good flaking quality. The cortex is usually thin and battered, patinated a grey/blue-grey colour with occasional ochreous patches. Such flint was probably obtained from the river gravels of the River Avon 0.7km to the south-east.

iv Freshly extracted nodular flint of good quality with few impurities, distinguished by its thick, white, unweathered cortex. Flakes and cores of such flint occur almost exclusively in the primary fills of both ditch sections, suggesting that it is material obtained during the digging of the ditch which has been immediately exploited.

Flint of types i and ii was used quite extensively, probably reflecting its ease of availability, in contrast to the river gravel and freshly extracted material which has a more restricted usage. It is interesting to note however, that residual flakes of probable earlier Neolithic date are often of gravel flints.

Prehistoric contexts

Flakes

The distribution of unmodified flakes by feature group is shown in Table 66. Metrical analysis was not undertaken. With very few exceptions, the character of the waste material is entirely in keeping with Late Neolithic and Beaker industries, the majority of flakes exhibiting wide, unfaceted butts, prominent bulbs of percussion, a high incidence of hinge fractures (around 20%), and a squat, thick appearance. Such features are the result of a more or less random core reduction strategy, as opposed to the careful production of blanks for conversion to tools noted in Mesolithic and Early Neolithic industries (Pitts 1978). Greater emphasis is instead placed on intensive shaping through secondary working to produce finished tool forms. Hammerstones were invariably employed during all stages of core reduction, as evidenced by the prominent conchoidal features visible on most flakes.

Approximately half the flakes are broken (Table 66). As the broken flake surfaces are all patinated, this seems to be the result of depositional or pre-depositional factors. Flaws in the raw material, particularly in the tabular and nodular flint, may be a major cause of flake breakage.

Cores

Cores were particularly numerous in the secondary fills of the ditch. Complete examples are predominantly single or multi-platform, with two discoidal and three miniature forms, both confined to the secondary fill of the southern ditch section. Miniature cores appear impractical, as the final removals seem useless as blanks for conversion into tools. A large proportion of other cores have been worked beyond a stage of producing apparently usable flakes, a feature common in the West Kennet and Windmill Hill assemblages (I F Smith 1965, 87, 236–7). Miniature cores may be seen as part of this phenomenon. The high frequency of broken cores and shatter fragments (Table 66) is largely due to the poor quality of the flint, particularly the tabular type.

All but one of the cores had been used to produce flakes, corresponding to the lack of deliberate blade production seen among the waste flakes. Most cores were quite persistently worked down, 80% retaining less than 50% cortex. This is also reflected by the weight of discarded cores, which is remarkably uniform across the site, with means of 144g from the south section of the ditch, 114g from the ditch terminal, and 118g from internal features.

Two cores and a core fragment show signs of trimming to one or more face. This was probably carried out in order to remove spurs or ridges between flake scars, rather than being a form of retouch (Healey and Robertson-Mackay 1987, 97). With the exception of the two discoidal cores, there is no evidence for platform or core face preparation.

Three cores and an unworked flint nodule had been utilised as hammerstones or pounders.

Micro-debitage (chips)

Over 640 chips (here taken to be pieces under 1.5cm along the maximum axis) were recovered from the excavation of the two ditch sections and internal features, the majority derived from sieved samples. From these four basic categories of flint chip could be identified:

i burnt fragments, most deriving from larger chunks and flakes

ii irregular, heterogeneous chips, shatter fragments, and pieces of larger flakes, often showing little indication of intentional fracture. This is the most common form of micro-debitage present in the assemblage; approximately 50% of the chips examined fell within this group

iii tiny flakes displaying characteristic features of conchoidal fracture such as striking platforms and bulbs of percussion

iv retouch chips. Unlike other forms of flint chip, these generally display very small or negligible butts, multiple small flake scars on the dorsal face; almost invariably they lack cortex. Both squat and elongated forms are present, the edges of which are usually irregular with occasional feathering.

Eleven chips from the secondary fill of the ditch terminal and two small flakes from pits within the interior could be recognised as the by-products of preparing or rejuvenating scraper edges. Such chips possess a very stepped profile to the proximal end of the dorsal face due both to use and the removal of tiny spalls forming a blunt, scraping edge. The distal end tends to terminate in a pronounced hinge fracture, often taking the form of a lip extending along the ventral surface. Two chips in particular exhibit very worn 'flake' facets on the dorsal side and are therefore likely to be the result of scraper edge rejuvenation.

As flint chips are unusable waste, which is seldom transported far, they are a useful indicator of the location and nature of areas of flaking activity (Newcomer and Karlin 1987).

All four forms of chip occurred in both the ditch sections and interior features. However, scraper retouch and rejuvenation chips were almost completely restricted to the secondary fill of the ditch terminal. Since this coincides with a high proportion of scrapers in fresh condition, it is strongly suggestive of scraper manufacture.

The occurrence of chips in the secondary ditch fills similarly implies that core reduction was carried out within the immediate vicinity of the ditch edge or that chips were scooped up along with other waste and dumped in the ditch.

Core rejuvenation flakes

As in other Late Neolithic and Early Bronze Age assemblages, evidence for intentional core rejuvenation is limited, being confined to trimming flakes, which result from the renewal of a core face when it becomes step-fractured and unworkable. Contexts within the ditch produced 40 examples, with a further four from interior features.

Core tablets and keeled flakes, both usually associated with blade production, are present in small numbers. Given the technology of the collection, however, they may be best considered as debitage resulting from the random flaking of multi-platform cores, rather than as deliberate attempts at core rejuvenation.

Implements

Implement forms present are, in order of frequency: scrapers, knives, notches, and transverse arrowheads, denticulates, fabricators, and microdenticulates, together with one borer and a microlith.

Scrapers

With the exception of one example, all the scrapers had been produced on hard hammer struck flakes with unfaceted butts. Complete examples were measured for length, breadth, and thickness. Only two have a length–breadth ratio greater than 2:1, although truly squat forms are noticeably rare. The angle and quality of retouch vary considerably, from crude and abrupt to almost flat and invasive. It remains possible that functional variability may in some way be reflected both in form and edge angle. Condition also varies, with some scrapers broken or showing signs of damage, while examples from the secondary ditch fills tend to be quite fresh, often with little apparent sign of utilisation.

There was a noticeable concentration of scrapers in the ditch terminal.

Knives

This category includes a plano-convex form from the secondary silts of the southern ditch section.

Arrowheads

Arrowheads from securely stratified contexts comprise two oblique forms, respectively attributable to J G D Clark's (1934) classes G and F, with perhaps a third atypical example and a fragment of a fourth. With one possible exception, all appear to have been produced from locally available flint of moderate quality.

Fabricators/rods

Two examples were recovered from the southern ditch section. One has a straight 'scraper-like' proximal end with indications of damage/wear on both lateral edges. The other exhibits considerable wear in the form of a distinct smoothing, together with a slight discoloration on the distal end.

Microdenticulates

Two microdenticulates were recovered from the southern ditch section. Serrations run along the entire edge (with the exception of the proximal end) of one example. They have been produced by the careful removal of single spalls of flint from the ventral face at a spacing of approximately one per millimetre. Slight traces of wear are visible towards the distal end.

The second specimen has been produced on a flake of fine-grained grey chert. Serrations, approximately six per 10mm are largely confined to one edge of the dorsal face and show little sign of wear.

Denticulates

Three coarse denticulates were recovered from the southern ditch section. Two examples are fragmentary, the patinated broken surfaces suggesting that breakage could have occurred during use. An exceptionally large specimen had been produced by removing a series of small flakes from the dorsal surface to form each denticulation. The 'teeth' show considerable signs of wear and a slight gloss is also visible, suggesting it was utilised to cut a relatively compact material, possibly wood.

Miscellaneous retouched flakes

Measurement of complete examples showed a preference for slightly elongated flakes. Selection is also indicated by the frequency of flakes with less than 25% cortex, which form well over half of this class.

A small flake of fine-grained grey chert, from the secondary fills of the ditch terminal, has evidently been removed from a multidirectional, possibly discoidal, core. Both the retouch and two areas of breakage show a distinct gloss, which does not extend on to the remainder of the flake. This may indicate deliberate or accidental heating prior to secondary working.

Utilised flakes and blades

Macroscopic identification of use wear is uncertain and incomplete even in the best-preserved collections. Here, the probability of depositional or pre-depositional breakage, indicated by patinated breaks, suggests that ancient edge damage, unrelated to use, may also have occurred.

Within these limitations, it appears that blades and blade-like flakes, rare in the collection as a whole, were preferred for utilisation as they were for retouch. The straight edges of blades make them ideal as cutting implements, often without any need for secondary working.

Conjoined flakes

The fresh nature of much of the debitage, particularly from the primary and secondary ditch fills, suggested that it had not accumulated through natural processes, but represented freshly knapped and deliberately deposited material. No distinct concentrations of lithic debitage were noted during the excavation, arguing against the occurrence of *in situ* knapping debris, but rather dispersed deposits of dumped material, probably thrown from the ditch edge.

Attempts at refitting not only confirmed these initial suggestions but provided further limited information on the technology of the assemblage, the nature of the ditch fills and patterns of activity.

Efforts were largely concentrated on debitage recovered from the primary and secondary fills of the southern ditch section, which presented a clear and well-recorded sequence. The aim of the refitting exercise was not complete reconstruction, but to assess the refitting potential within each context.

Dorsal/ventral refits consist of 32 individual pieces. The number of refits in each group is shown in Table 68, MF1 G7.

In addition, three flakes, one of which was burnt, have been reconstructed from broken halves. Breakage would appear to have occurred during flaking in at least two instances.

Technology

The small amount of material refitted provides a limited degree of information on the technology of the assemblage (Table 69, MF1 G8). All the flakes conjoined are hard hammer struck and, with a single exception, possess plain butts and a high proportion of hinge fractures. Four groups show a change in striking platform between removals; one in particular has indications of a minimum of three successive platforms (Fig 107, MF1 G10, R5), illustrating the extent to which a core can alter during knapping. No clear reduction strategy can be discerned.

In one instance a blade has been produced through the creation and subsequent removal of a keel/ridge on the core face (Fig 106, MF1 G9, R1), though it is uncertain whether this was deliberate.

Contextual analysis

The evidence of refitting, studied in conjunction with a detailed assessment of the condition and homogeneity of the lithic material from each context, provides further information on both ditch sediment formation processes and patterns of behaviour. It must be emphasised that the conclusions reached are based upon the analysis of material recovered from the excavation of approximately 8% of the ditch deposits and are hence unlikely to be applicable to the site as a whole. In addition, the study is necessarily limited to the secondary fills of the two ditch sections which provided the only refittable material.

A description and interpretation of the flint waste products from each context of the secondary ditch fills is given in Table 70, MF1 G11–12).

Within the southern ditch section (cut 934) a recurrent pattern of deposits of flint debitage and tools can be discerned. In at least three instances the debitage is the product of a single knapping event, the homogeneity of the flakes suggesting in each case that they derive from the same nodule. However, cores often seem unrelated and over-represented (for example, within context 1444), indicating an independent history from flakes and other waste. The two contexts where refitting has proved unsuccessful (contexts 1061 and 1063) incorporated deposits of unworked flint nodules, perhaps the result of clearance activities.

Within the ditch terminal section (cut 1500) quantities of burnt material were noted from two contexts. Neither of these appear to represent *in situ* burning. Context 1486 included a large quantity of burnt and heat-affected worked flint which, although giving the appearance of burnt knapping debris, seems to have little refitting potential.

The condition of lithic material from 1501 varies greatly, flakes from the lower part of the layer being fresh and, in some instances, conjoinable, in contrast to the often rolled appearance of the flint from higher levels. It may be justifiable to suggest that the upper part of this context consists of colluvial material attributable to later activity (a point reinforced by the presence of later Bronze Age sherds).

Disposal of lithic material in the semi-silted ditch may reflect little more than a need to remove sharp and potentially harmful debris from living or activity areas. However, this fails to explain the presence of large quantities of worked flint in the interior of the enclosure, a proportion of which is likely to be contemporary with the ditch deposits. Although the former could derive from a series of middens within the interior, such as that excavated at Durrington Walls (Wainwright and Longworth 1971, 38–41), it does not explain the duality of deposition.

Ploughsoil

The large quantity of material involved (Table 66) did not allow a detailed assessment to be made in the limited time available. Distinctive tool forms were, however, examined in varying detail, and are described below.

Implement forms present are, in order of frequency: scrapers, knives, transverse arrowheads, fabricators, bifacial forms and borers, barbed and tanged arrowheads, backed flakes, discoids, Y-shaped tools, and points together with single examples of a denticulate, a chisel or axe, and a microburin.

Scrapers

As on other sites of this period, short end/side and 'thumbnail' varieties predominate; long end forms are noticeably rare, reflecting a scarcity of narrow flake/blade blanks.

One hundred and five undamaged examples were measured for length, breadth, and thickness; 59% were between 31 and 50mm in length, compared with 25% between 0 and 30mm and 16% in excess of 50mm. This contrasts markedly with the Durrington Walls assemblage, where 54% of the scrapers are longer than 50mm (Wainwright and Longworth 1971, 167). The preferred breadth for the Coneybury scrapers falls between 21 and 40mm (73%); with only 13% in excess of 40mm, compared with 60% from Durrington. The marked contrast in size between the Coneybury and Durrington examples could well be related to differences in the quality and size of the raw material utilised.

Cursory examination suggests that scrapers possessing a moderate or shallow angle to the working edge (*c* 70–30°) are more numerous than examples with acute retouch (70°+). The angle and extent of the working edge may reflect implement function: steep-edged scrapers often display visible signs of wear, suggesting a scraping or burnishing action on a hard material such as dry animal hide, while shallow working edges would tend to fracture and abrade rapidly under such pressure and would be better suited to processing softer materials such as greasy skins and plant fibres (Gardiner 1987b).

Arrowheads

Chisel and petit tranchet forms account for 10 of the 18 arrowheads. There are only four oblique forms from ploughsoil deposits, despite the fact that they are the only variety of arrowhead from the fills of the cut features. Three large and finely-worked chisel arrowheads and a single oblique example have been manufactured from a good quality speckled flint, probably gravel flint; the remainder are of local material.

Chisel arrowheads have been produced on flake or blade segments which in some instances appear to be intentionally broken; two examples exhibit negative cones of percussion on the break surface consistent with the use of a hammer or anvil (Fischer *et al* 1984). Most exhibit damage consistent with utilisation, although differentiation between post-depositional breakage and genuine use-related wear is difficult.

Four fragmentary barbed and tanged arrowheads were recovered from ploughsoil contexts, the three more complete examples being of Green's (1980) Sutton class. One has been manufactured from a distinctive blue-grey, lustrous flint.

Axe/chisel

An end-ground implement 84mm long is of axe-like form, despite its small size. It is made of local flint which is quite cherty in places.

Discoids

Two bifacially flaked discoidal objects appear too crudely worked and rather thick to be finished implements and may belong to a class of Levallois cores related to the production of blanks for the production of petit tranchet derivative arrowheads (Manby 1974). In both instances shallow flaking covers each face, which has been worked until almost flat.

Fabricators

Two of the five examples show slight wear or polish.

Y-shaped tools

One example, produced on a thermally fractured fragment, is probably related to Gardiner's class of '*tranchet* tool' (Gardiner 1987a). Two of the sides are concave with steep, blunting retouch, whilst the third is formed by a straight tranchet cutting edge. Similar implements are known from Late Neolithic contexts at Grimes

Graves, Norfolk (Saville 1981, 54–5), and the Dorset Cursus (Gardiner 1985). A second example is less certain and may have functioned as a concave scraper.

Dating

Evidence for earlier Neolithic activity in the immediate vicinity of the henge is provided by the Coneybury 'Anomaly' (W2 (1981), this vol, 4.1) and by sherds of plain bowl pottery from the henge ditch terminal (Ellison, this vol, 4.9 c). Surprisingly, there is little indication of distinctive earlier Neolithic flintwork from the ploughsoil. The former position of the henge bank, so strongly reflected by low values of lithic artefacts (Figs 95, 96), tends to imply that the old land surface was relatively free of cultural debris when the enclosure was constructed.

The majority of the tool assemblage can be suggested as having Late Neolithic and Early Bronze Age associations. Chisel and oblique arrowheads are strongly related to Late Neolithic ceramic styles, notably Grooved Ware, and have a particular association with henges (Green 1980, 235, 238). Y-shaped and tranchet tools and bifacially flaked discoidal objects are also distinctively Late Neolithic (Gardiner 1985; Saville 1981, 48, 54–5). A Beaker and Early Bronze Age element in the assemblage is indicated by the presence of four barbed and tanged arrowheads and a high proportion of invasively flaked 'thumbnail' scrapers. The comparative invisibility of earlier Neolithic material may in part be due to differences in deposition. Healy (1987) has argued that the disposal of lithic debris in pits and other subsoil features was common practice throughout the Early Neolithic, worked flint rarely occurring in surface deposits. Late Neolithic and Early Bronze Age material, in contrast, often dominates surface scatters, but rarely occurs in pits. Coneybury would fit this pattern.

Intra-site variations

A high percentage of flakes with more than 75% cortex (Table 71, MF1 G13) and the scarcity of tools and retouched flakes (1.9%) from the primary fills of both ditch sections are consistent with core preparation activities; presumably the exploitation of flint nodules recovered during the cutting of the ditch. This is a marked contrast with the domestic nature of the lithic material from the secondary fills, which includes a higher proportion of implements (5.5%), quantities of worked-down cores, and, in the ditch terminal, a high proportion of flakes with less than 25% cortex (Table 71, MF1 G13).

Greater variation is evident in the worked flint from the interior features, although this may in part result from the small numbers of artefacts present in some of them. Pits 1844, 1601, and 1672 have a low proportion of implements (Table 67, MF1 G6), but comparatively few flakes with more than 75% cortex (Table 71, MF1 G13). In contrast, pits 1603, 1608, and 1177 were relatively rich in tools, though the waste flakes possess both an industrial (1608) and domestic (1603) character.

Scrapers were more numerous in the secondary fills of the ditch terminal than in the southern section and interior features, while scraper rejuvenation chips are almost exclusively limited to the ditch terminal. The range of tool types present also shows a marked distinction between the two sections, a distinction reflected in the ploughsoil material. The restricted range of implements from the ditch terminal, consisting largely of scrapers, utilised flakes, knives, and miscellaneous retouched flakes, is echoed in the limited tool repertoire present in the overlying ploughsoil (scrapers, knives, borers, and fabricators). Conversely, a wider and slightly more elaborate range of artefacts was recovered from the southern ditch section and its immediate environs, though tools and utilised pieces form a lower percentage of the material from this area.

On a narrower scale, variations between individual contexts can be noted. Layers 1444 and 1061 for instance, produced an abnormally high ratio of cores to flakes – 1:8.25 and 1:3.25 respectively. Attempts at refitting have shown that cores from the secondary ditch silts are often unrelated to other waste products from the same deposits, indicating an independent cycle of movement and discard. Tools and utilised flakes would similarly have been subjected to a process of transportation, use, and rejuvenation, with disposal often occurring away from the place of manufacture.

Inter-site comparison

Within the Stonehenge area, the three henge sites of Durrington Walls (Wainwright and Longworth 1971), Woodhenge (Cunnington 1929), and Coneybury, share a similar range and balance of debitage and implement types, except for the presence at Durrington Walls of a number of heavy woodworking tools, which it is tempting to link with the large timber structures which stood within the enclosure. Transverse arrowheads occur at all three henges, as well as in the Woodlands pits (Stone 1949), and are a feature of surface scatters on the King Barrow Ridge (W59, this vol, 4.8), perhaps stressing the importance of this area during the later Neolithic. Oblique arrowheads noticeably outnumber chisel forms at both Durrington Walls and Woodhenge, and include a significant number of finely-worked ripple-flaked variants, the majority of which were found in direct association with the timber circles and appear to be from formal deposits. It is impossible to be certain whether the variation in the frequency of different transverse arrowhead forms between these sites and Coneybury is chronological or cultural.

Durrington Walls, Woodhenge, Stonehenge, and Coneybury all possess evidence of subsequent Beaker activity, although its scale and nature vary considerably. That represented at Coneybury is notable for the quantity of flintwork occurring in Beaker/Early Bronze Age contexts, implying substantial renewed or sustained interest in the site. In this respect, although the nature of activity is clearly quite different, it provides a similarity with contemporary interest in Stonehenge.

4.9 c The prehistoric pottery (Fig 108)

by Ann Ellison

The sample excavation carried out in 1980 produced a total of 199 sherds of Neolithic and Bronze Age date.

This total excludes the pottery from the Early Neolithic pit (W2 (1981)) located outside the henge monument. This assemblage is considered within a separate report (Cleal, this vol, 4.1 c). Pottery from the henge represents all phases of the Neolithic and Bronze Age, with sherds found within the pits and postholes located inside the enclosure (30 and 2 sherds respectively) as well as within the ditch deposits (32 sherds from the ditch terminal, cut 1500, and 103 from the southern section, cut 934). Only 32 finds of early prehistoric pottery were made in the upper levels of the site.

Seventeen fabrics were defined. Their main characteristics are summarised in Table 72 and full descriptions may be found within the archive. The distribution of fabrics amongst the main context groups is shown in Table 73. Early Neolithic fabrics occurred mainly in the ditch terminal section, where they can be considered as residual. Sherds of Late Neolithic wares were found within the upper fills of the interior pits and were also represented throughout the ditch fills (especially the southern section 934). Within the ditch fills Beaker sherds first appear in the upper part of the primary fills while later Bronze Age sherds were found only in the upper levels of the ditch deposits. Both earlier and later Neolithic sherds were present in the ditch sequences, but in small quantities only.

Illustrated sherds (Fig 108)

Neolithic

P57 Ditch terminal, context 1501
Rim sherd from plain bowl. Fabric 1 (3SS). Early to Middle Neolithic.

P58 Pit 1844, context 1454
Body sherd with vertical applied plain cordon. Fabric 16 (2MG; 2M/LSh; 1S). Grooved Ware.

P59 Pit 1844, context 1844
Body sherd decorated with widely spaced vertical applied plain cordons. Fabric 16 (2MG; 2M/LSh). Grooved Ware.

P60 Pit 1619, context 1398
Body sherd decorated with evenly executed diagonal incised lines bordered by an applied serpentine strip surmounted by a single applied plain pellet. Fabric 19 (1G; 1SSh; 1SF). Grooved Ware.

P61 Pit 1672, context 2015
Body sherd decorated with fairly widely spaced applied plain vertical cordons bordering a panel of irregular fingernail-impressed rusticated ornament. Fabric 16 (2MG; 2M/LSh; 1S). Grooved Ware.

P62 Pit 1608
Body sherd decorated with diagonal incised lines partially obscured by a thumb-smoothed semicircular zone (which might represent the expanded and flattened termination of an applied vertical cordon). Fabric 19 (1G; 1SSh; 1SF). Grooved Ware.

P63 Pit 1672, context 2015
Body sherd decorated with diagonal incised lines and incised ladder motif. Fabric 16 (2MG; 2M/LSh; 1S). Grooved Ware.

P64 Ditch terminal, primary chalk rubble, context 1445
Body sherd decorated with diagonal incised lines. Fabric 16 (2MG; 2M/LSh; 1S). Grooved Ware.

Table 72 W2 Coneybury Henge: summary of prehistoric pottery fabric descriptions

Fabric no	*Hardness*	*Texture*	*Inclusions*	*Type*	*Date*
1	very hard	sandy	3SS	bowl	Neo
2	soft	v. sandy	3SS	bowl	Neo
3	hard	sandy	2SS; 1M/LF	bowl	Neo
4	hard	sandy	1SS; 2S/MF	bowl	Neo
5	hard	sandy	2SS; 3M/LF	bowl	Neo
6	soft	soapy	G, 1S/LF (angular)	Peterborough Ware	Late Neo
7	soft	sandy	1M/LF (angular)	Peterborough Ware	Late Neo
16	soft	soapy	2MG; 2M/LSh; 1S	Grooved Ware	Late Neo
19	hard	smooth	1G; 1SSh; 1SF	Grooved Ware	Late Neo
8	hard	sandy	1S	Beaker (Vessel A)	L.Neo/EBA
9	very hard	sandy	3S	Beaker	L.Neo/EBA
10	soft	sandy	S and G	Beaker (Vessel B)	L.Neo/EBA
18	hard	sandy	1SF; G	Beaker (Vessel C)	L.Neo/EBA
11	soft	soapy	S, Sh, G	urn	EBA
12	very soft	soapy	3MG	urn	EBA
13	very hard	rough	3S/MF	urn	MBA
14	soft	chalky	2MSh	urn	MBA
15	very hard	rough	2S/MF	urn	MBA
17	very hard	sandy	1MF, 1MG, 3S	jar	?LBA

Abbreviations used
Size: S small, M medium, L large
Density: 1 sparse, 2 medium, 3 dense
Inclusions: F flint, G grog, S sand, Sh shell

Table 73 W2 Coneybury Henge, the distribution of prehistoric sherds by fabric

Context group	*Early Neolithic*					*Late Neolithic*				*Beaker*				*EBA*		*M/LBA*			
Fabric	1	2	3	4	5	6	7	16	19	8	9	10	18	11	12	13	14	15	17
Northern ditch section (934)	2	1	2			2	2	1		55	13	17			6		2		
Ditch terminal (1500)	1					2	5	1				8	2	2	1	6	1	1	2
Pits							1	19	5			3	2						
Post-holes	1											1							
Later levels			2				3	2		3		5	4	1	3	1	2	4	2
Totals	4	1	4			4	11	23	5	58	13	34	8	3	10	7	5	5	4
Grand total																			199

P65 Pit 1672, context 2015
Body sherd decorated with diagonal incised lines, probably arranged to form alternate filled triangles. Fabric 16 (2MG; 2M/LSh; 1S). Grooved Ware.

P66 Pit 1844, context 1454
Body sherd decorated with a drilled circular pit. Fabric 16 (2MG; 2M/LSh; 1S). Grooved Ware.

P67 Pit 1844, context 1454
Rim sherd from plain bowl. Fabric 16 (2MG; 2M/LSh; 1S). Grooved Ware.

Beaker

P68 and P69 Ditch cutting 934, contexts 1444 and 1487
Two body sherds decorated with zones of horizontal lines and herringbone executed in square-toothed comb impressions. Fabric 10 (sandy with sand and grog inclusions). Both have a distinctive red surface colour.

P70 Pit 1672, context 2015
Body sherd decorated with extremely worn horizontal lines bordering a zone of diagonal lines, all executed in fine square-toothed comb impressions. Fabric 10.

P71 Ditch terminal 1500, context 1501
Two wall sherds (one not illustrated) decorated with horizontal lines of rectangular-toothed comb impressions bordering a row of neatly executed fingernail impressions. Fabric 18 (hard; 1SF; G).

P72 Ditch terminal 1500, context 1501
Body sherd decorated with four horizontal rows of rectangular-toothed comb impressions defining a zone of cross-hatching executed with a square-toothed comb. Fabric 18.

P73 Ditch cutting 934, context 1062
Body sherd decorated with zones of impressed 'ermine' motif and cross-hatched rectangular-toothed comb impressions, both defined by one row of very fine-toothed comb impressions, very worn. Fabric 10.

P74 Pit 2115 (area K), context 2116
Rim sherd decorated below the rim with three lines of rectangular-toothed comb impressions above a zone of cross-hatching. Fabric 10 (plus some shell inclusions).

P75 Ditch cutting 934, context 1487
Body sherd showing part of a cross-hatched zone executed in square-toothed comb impressions, very worn. Fabric 9.

P76 Ditch cutting 934, context 1062
Body sherd decorated with equally spaced lines of rectangular-toothed comb impressions, and between two of them, vertical fingernail impressions, worn. Fabric 9.

P77 Ditch cutting 934, context 1444
Two joining rim sherds decorated below the rim with two lines of rectangular-toothed comb impressions above reserved bar chevron defined with similar impressions. Fabric 8 (sandy) (P77–P80, with 50 other body sherds, probably belong to a single vessel).

P78 Ditch cutting 934, context 1444
Body sherd decorated with lines of rectangular-toothed comb impressions defining bands alternately reserved and filled with vertical incisions.

P79 Ditch cutting 934, context 1444
Shoulder sherd decorated with lines of rectangular-toothed comb impressions above which is a reserved chevron against a background of vertical incisions. Below are horizontal bands alternately reserved and filled with vertical incisions. Fabric 8 (sandy).

P80 Ditch cutting 934, context 1487
Body sherd with rectangular-toothed comb impressions and vertical incision. Fabric 8 (sandy).

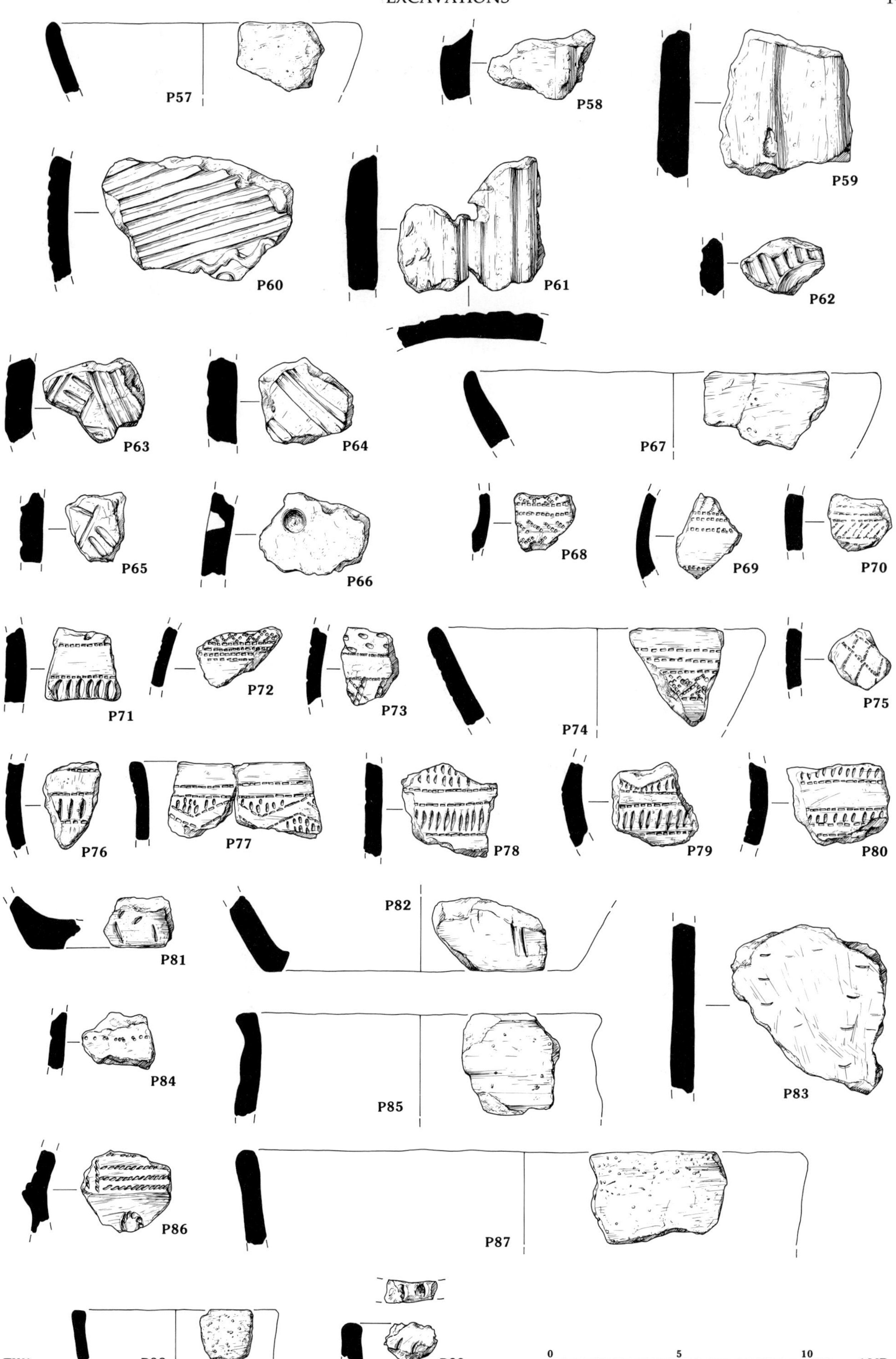

Fig 108 W2 Coneybury Henge: prehistoric pottery (P57–P89)

P81 Ditch cutting 934, context 1062
Base angle decorated with irregular fingernail impressions. Fabric 9.

P82 Ditch cutting 934, context 1420
Base angle from vessel with plain zone at base. Fabric 9.

P83 Pit 1844, context 1454
Body sherd decorated with two widely spaced diagonal rows of faint finger-nail impressions. Fabric 10.

Early Bronze Age

P84 Ditch cutting 934, context 1062
Body sherd decorated with irregular circular-tooth comb impressions forming a rough horizontal line. Fabric 12 (3MG). Possibly from the upper part of a Biconical Urn.

P85 Ditch cutting 934, context 1062
Rim sherd and wall sherd (not illustrated) with two horizontal ridges below rim. Fabric 12. Food Vessel.

P86 Ditch terminal 1500, context 1501
Body sherd from base of collar. Decoration: three rows of twisted-cord impressed horizontal lines above collar and inverted twisted-cord-impressed horseshoe below, all extremely worn. Fabric 12. Collared Urn.

Later Bronze Age

P87 Ditch terminal 1500, context 1501
Plain rim sherd. Fabric 13 (3S/MF). Globular Urn.

P88 Ploughsoil, context 1442 (area K)
Plain rim sherd. Fabric 13. Late Bronze Age cup.

P89 Ditch terminal 1500, context 1501
Rim sherd decorated with row of fingertip impressions on top of rim. Fabric 13. Middle Bronze Age bucket Urn.

Discussion

Earlier Neolithic

Only nine sherds are in fabrics likely to be earlier Neolithic in date. A single rim in Fabric 1 (3SS) belongs to a cup which is comparable to those in the Coneybury 'Anomaly' (W2 (1981)) assemblage (Cleal, this vol, 4.1 c). The earlier Neolithic sherds from the henge are presumably residual material derived from the episode of occupation represented by the 'Anomaly'.

Grooved Ware

The decoration on most of the 28 sherds found at Coneybury comprises grooved lines executed before firing with a blunt instrument. The motifs include filling of probably triangular patterns (P62, P64, and P65) and a more complex ladder pattern (P63). These probably derive from the portions of vessels between the rim and cordon and can be compared with the motifs common to the Durrington Walls substyle (Wainwright and Longworth 1971, 68, fig 27). The vertical applied plain plastic cordon, displayed on sherds P58, P59, and P61, are also very typical of the Durrington Walls substyle, although the panel of rusticated decoration on P61, can better be matched at Woodhenge (Cunnington 1929, plate 37, no 85) rather than at the type site itself. The wavy cordon on P60 is a rare variant, but one vertical example of this type of cordon occurs at Durrington Walls (Wainwright and Longworth 1971, P58) on a vessel of the Durrington Walls substyle. However, applied pellets, although occasionally occurring on vessels of the Clacton and Rinyo substyles (Wainwright and Longworth 1971, fig 93), are most common in the Woodlands substyle (Wainwright and Longworth 1971, 90), where they typically occur at the junction of cordons which run diagonally across the vessel wall. Because fairly little of P60 survives it is not possible to determine whether the pellet was situated at a junction, and the curvature of the wall suggests that the pot was of a form not typical of Woodlands style Grooved Ware, which is normally represented by tub-shaped vessels with straight walls.

It is possible that the motif represented by the smooth semicircular zone on P62 is part of a circular motif similar to that on P471 at Durrington Walls (Wainwright and Longworth 1971). So little survives of the motif that it is difficult to estimate its likely diameter, but it appears not to be as large as that on P471 (which is approximately 70mm).

Peterborough Ware

Fifteen sherds possibly of Peterborough Ware were isolated on the grounds of fabric. They were all small in size and no decorative motifs could be detected. In view of the complete lack of decorated sherds the identification as Peterborough Ware must be regarded as extremely tentative.

Beaker

A total of 113 sherds of Beaker represents a minimum of 11 vessels. No cord-decorated sherds were recovered, but P70 and P68/P69, decorated with the Basic European motif 3 (herringbone zone) executed in square-toothed comb impressions, may belong to Clarke's European (E) group, or the Wessex/Middle Rhine group (W/MR) and thus to the Middle Style defined by Case (Clarke 1970; Case 1977, 72); P68/P69 in particular have a distinctive red, smooth surface which suggests that they belong to a W/MR rather than an E Beaker. P72, P73, and P74 probably derive from vessels of the W/MR group, and therefore also belong to the Middle Style. These sherds bear comb-impressed and reserved zones and the motifs include diagonal lines (Basic 3) and cross-hatched zones (Basic 4). P72 also possesses the fine, smoothed surface characteristic of this class of vessel. Two vessels of the Late Style are clearly represented, one by P76, bearing comb and incised decoration, and the other by P77–P79 which bears reserved bar chevron motifs (Southern British motif 32ii) as well as Basic European motif 5. Both vessels fall within Clarke's Southern 2 to 3 typological groups. Fingertip rusticated vessels are also represented by P81 and P83.

Collared Urn

One sherd, P86, displaying the base of the collar and a portion of the body, probably derives from a Secondary Series Collared Urn. It carries Longworth's decorative motif M (miniature horseshoes executed in cord technique) just above the shoulder (Longworth 1984, fig 9). This motif is common on urns of the South-East Style.

Food Vessel

The rim (P85) and upper body of a Ridged Vase is represented.

Biconical Urn

A single sherd P84 may derive from the upper body of a Biconical Urn of Ellison Type A (Ellison 1975), similar to those from Cherhill 1 (Oldbury Hill) (I F Smith 1961, 104, and fig 23) and from near Dorchester, Dorset (Warne 1866, pl VIII, no. 12).

Globular Urn

The rim sherd P87 derives from a Globular Urn of Type I (Ellison 1975), according to its fabric. The vessel may have been either plain or decorated.

Bucket Urn

One rim sherd, P89, was decorated with a row of fingernail impressions on top of the rim.

Late Bronze Age

The rim of a small cup, P88.

Conclusions

The prehistoric pottery assemblage suggests that the site was occupied from the earlier Neolithic to the Middle Bronze Age. The concentration of Grooved Ware within the interior pits might suggest that they were earlier than the enclosure ditch, a suggestion which the radiocarbon dates now appear to support. The two sherds of Grooved Ware found in the ditch fillings could therefore be residual, although there is no later pottery from most of the primary fill, Beaker only appearing in its uppermost part. In the upper ditch fills there is only Beaker and later pottery. However, the pits also contained the two largest Beaker sherds recovered during the excavations: neither was abraded and one of them, P74, was definitely not of early style and date. Within the ditch deposits, Beaker sherds from vessels belonging to both the Middle and Late Styles were found intermixed in broad stratigraphic units which may represent long periods of gradual accumulation. This echoes the analytical results relating to the Beaker assemblage from Mount Pleasant (Longworth and Wainwright 1979, 90), which suggested that there was some degree of contemporaneity between groups previously allocated to the Early, Middle, and Late Styles. The results from Coneybury cannot, however, be used to support this hypothesis. The deposits containing sherds of Middle- and Late-Style Beakers at Coneybury also included most of the items assignable to the Early Bronze Age, but later Bronze Age ceramics were only found in subsequent deposits. A plot of all featured sherds from the ditch fills, projected on to the sections, is in the archive.

4.9 d Copper alloy objects (Fig 109)

SF125 Context 1444 (southern ditch cutting)
Disc-headed pin, overall length 90mm, diameter of head 14.5mm. Perfect smooth blue-green patina. This pin is of Heathery Burn type (Britton 1967) and can be regarded as dating from the later Bronze Age. A similar, but more elaborate, example was found in the ditch of barrow 56 at Shrewton (Green and Rollo-Smith 1984, 281, 307, and fig 27 Ae I), here associated with later Bronze Age pottery.

SF778 Context 6 (ploughsoil)
Small circular disc, maximum diameter 21mm. Chased and punched curvilinear decoration retaining traces of gilding (originally totally gilt?). No trace of attachment. Saxon.

SF99 Context 1409 (ploughsoil, area K)
Annular brooch. External diameter 14mm, width irregular (2–3mm), approximately 1.5mm thick. Pin made from circular section wire.

SF52 Context 671 (lower ploughsoil)
Strap end, overall length 19mm, maximum width 10mm, 3mm thick. Consists of two flat plates joined by a single circular section rivet.

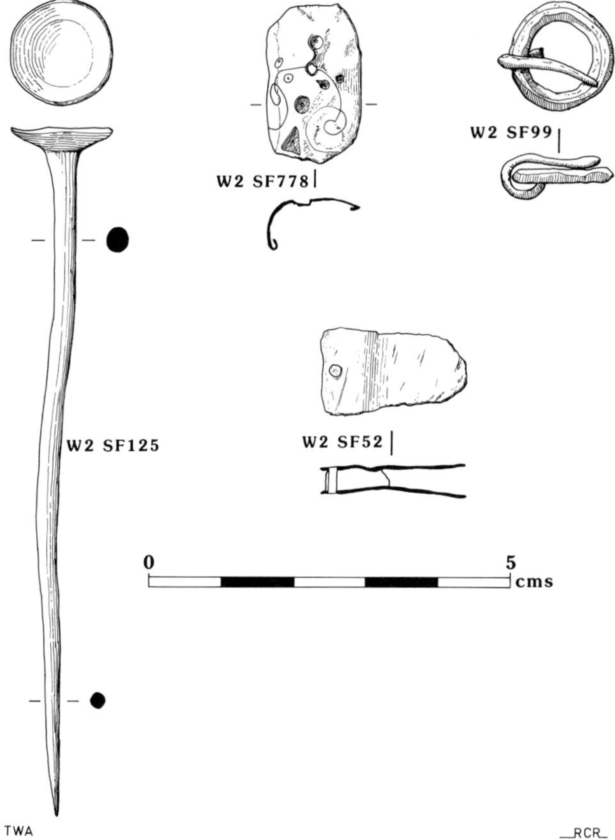

Fig 109 W2 Coneybury Henge: copper alloy objects

4.9 e Animal bones

by Mark Maltby

The excavation produced 1797 animal bone fragments which have been divided into four main groups for analysis: the ditch terminal section; the southern ditch section; the interior features; and the topsoil. The fragments from each of these groups are shown in Table 74, which demonstrates that the majority of the bones came from the two ditch sections. In contrast the pits and the topsoil produced samples of less than 100 fragments. The 1mm wet-sieved samples produced 656 of the bones, many of which came from context 1486 in the ditch terminal.

The ditch terminal section

This section produced the majority of the bones from the excavation. The 1301 fragments included 570 recovered from the 1mm wet-sieving of samples from context 1486. The fragments recovered from each layer are shown in Table 75, together with the number of observations of surface erosion, burning, and gnawing on the bones. The bone condition data show how surface erosion became less common on fragments in the lower fills of the ditch and also reveal that context 1486 contained a very high proportion of burnt fragments. These consisted principally of small unidentifiable fragments recovered in the sieved samples, but burning and scorching marks were found on several identifiable bones as well. Fourteen of the cattle fragments in context 1486 showed evidence of burning (3 humeri, 8 radii, 2 ulnae, and 1 tibia). Although none of the identified pig bones were burnt, several sheep-sized mammal fragments did show evidence of burning and, in the absence of sheep/goat and roe deer bones in this layer, it is probable that these belonged to pig.

The lowest fills of the ditch produced a greater proportion of gnawed bones, but the numbers of bones from these layers were low compared to those from contexts 1486 and 1501. Context 1501, recognised in excavation as containing a recut filled with context 1486, appears to be a 'midden deposit' of Bronze Age date. In the ditch terminal section cattle bones predominated amongst the identifiable fragments, with pig the only other species commonly represented. The dominance of cattle is supported by the high proportion of large mammal fragments amongst the unidentifiable categories in the assemblage.

The elements represented in the cattle assemblage are shown in Table 76. This shows that the different skeletal elements were not equally represented. The major bones of the upper limbs (humerus, radius, ulna, femur, and tibia) were much better represented than the skull, mandible, vertebrae, and bones of the limb extremities, particularly within contexts 1501 and 1486. The minimum number of animals represented by each skeletal element is also given in Table 76, in which figures were calculated taking into account the size of the body, and data relating to fragmentation and ageing. No account was made of the contexts in which the bones were found and it was assumed for these purposes that bones in different contexts could have belonged to the same animal. The results confirmed the bias towards upper limb bones with the highest counts obtained for the humerus, radius, and tibia. In contrast, only one animal was represented by the mandible, which is usually one of the most common elements represented in excavated cattle samples. The bias, therefore, cannot be attributed to differential preservation of the bones and suggests that this area of the

Table 74 W2 Coneybury Henge: animal species represented

Species	*Terminal Ditch*	*South Ditch*	*Pits*	*Topsoil*	*Total*	*(1mm)*
Cattle	167	48	16	6	237	(10)
Sheep/goat	7	5	–	2	14	(–)
Pig	49	20	7	3	79	(12)
Horse	–	1	–	–	1	(1)
Dog	3	52*	1	–	56	(–)
Red deer	–	–	1	–	1	(–)
Roe deer	4	1	–	–	5	(1)
Unidentified large mammal	634	113	36	7	790	(219)
Sheep-sized mammal	82	36	9	16	143	(70)
Unidentified mammal	348	55	25	18	446	(333)
Sea eagle	–	13*	–	–	13	(–)
Lapwing	–	–	–	1	1	(–)
Unidentified bird	1	–	–	2	3	(3)
Short-tailed vole	1	–	–	–	1	(1)
House mouse	–	1	–	–	1	(1)
Unidentified rodent	–	1	–	–	1	(1)
Frog/toad	5	–	–	–	5	(5)
Total	1301	346	95	55	1797	(656)

1mm: number of fragments in total from 1mm wet-sieved samples
* articulated bones

Table 75 W2 Coneybury Henge: animal species represented in ditch terminal section

Species	*1077*	*1501*	*Context* *1486*	*1488*	*1422*	*Total*	*(1mm 1486)*
Cattle	1	80	55	19	12	167	(8)
Sheep/goat	–	7	–	–	–	–	(–)
Pig	1	28	14	4	2	49	(7)
Dog	–	2	1	–	–	3	(–)
Roe deer	–	3	–	1	–	4	(–)
Unidentified large mammal	2	84	502	24	22	634	(206)
Sheep-sized mammal	1	24	57	–	–	82	(50)
Unidentified mammal	2	30	309	6	1	348	(292)
Short-tailed vole	–	–	1	–	–	1	(1)
Frog/toad	–	–	5	–	–	–	(5)
Unidentified bird	–	–	1	–	–	1	(1)
Total	7	258	945	54	37	1301	(570)
Slightly eroded	–	98	63	9	3	173	(37)
Moderately eroded	–	53	46	3	–	92	(39)
Severely eroded	7	46	39	–	–	92	(39)
Charred/calcined	–	6	562	15	–	583	(294)
Gnawed	–	–	6	4	6	16	(2)

1mm 1486: number of fragments from 1mm wet-sieved samples from context 1486

ditch was preferred for the dumping of upper limb bones. These are relatively good meat bones and offer a contrast to limb bones of poorer meat quality which were rarely represented in this section. Those may have been removed during primary butchery and deposited elsewhere.

The cattle bones in the ditch terminal, therefore, may mainly represent waste from a later stage in carcase processing, and it is possible that some form of carcase dressing or cooking activities took place nearby. The occurrence of a large number of burnt bones in context 1486 suggests an association with cooking activities. Several of the cattle bones bore only slight traces of scorching and it is possible that such marks were made during the roasting of the meat on the bone. Although traces of burning were relatively rare in other layers, the composition of the cattle assemblages was similar. Unless the fills were formed over a relatively short period, this implies that there was some sort of continuity or tradition in the dumping of cattle bones in this area of the ditch over a considerable timespan.

Table 77 (MF2 A5) gives the fragmentation data for the major upper limb bones of cattle recovered from the ditch terminal. Fragmentation of these bones was due to a combination of factors. A few bones had been partially destroyed by gnawing and several had breaks in the shafts probably made during marrow processing. The relatively high number of small radius and ulna fragments in the sample partly reflects the occurrence in context 1486 of small completely charred fragments, several of which may have belonged to the same bones. The sturdier bones (particularly the humerus and tibia) tended to survive in a more complete condition.

Although surface erosion occasionally hindered observation, surprisingly few knife cuts or chop marks were observed on these bones. Only one bone, a tibia from context 1501, bore knife cuts on the anterior of its shaft, possibly made during the removal of meat from the bone. The only other observation of butchery marks on cattle bones from the excavations was made on a fragment of rib from context 1422, which appeared to have been chopped superficially near its articulation with the vertebra. Such marks can be made during the disarticulation of the flanks of the animal from the vertebral column. The lack of butchery marks near the distal articulation of the humerus and the proximal articulation of the radius may suggest that these bones were not disarticulated at this point and thus formed part of one joint.

The relatively low number of ribs and vertebrae amongst the cattle (and indeed the unidentifiable large mammal assemblage, Table 79, MF2 A7) is perhaps surprising, since they can also be associated with good meat joints. However, this depends largely on how the carcases were butchered, and there are methods in which the vertebrae in particular are deposited as waste during the early stages of carcase processing. In addition, it is possible that these bones may have been more susceptible than limb bones to destruction by canine scavenging or other processes.

The ditch terminal produced 49 fragments of pig, mainly from the upper fills (Table 78, MF2 A6). The figures obtained for the minimum number of individuals were highest for some of the upper limb bones (humerus, femur, and tibia), again suggesting that there was a bias in the assemblage towards good meat bones. However, the pig sample is small and such conclusions are tentative. No butchery marks were observed on any of the bones, although most of the limb bones seem to have been broken open for marrow extraction.

Table 76 W2 Coneybury Henge: fragments of cattle represented in ditch terminal section (cut 1500)

Cattle	*1077*	*1501*	*Context* *1486*	*1488*	*1422*	*Total*	*MNI*
Skull fragments	–	–	2	6	2	10	1
Mandible	–	2	–	1	1	4	1
Loose teeth	–	10	3	–	1	14	2
Scapula	–	3	1	–	–	4	2
Humerus	–	14	8	1	1	24	8
Radius	–	12	12	2	1	27	7
Ulna	–	7	7	2	1	17	5
Os Coxae	–	2	5	–	1	8	4
Femur	–	6	5	4	–	15	4
Tibia	1	4	8	2	–	15	7
Carpals	–	2	–	–	–	2	1
Calcaneus	–	1	–	–	–	1	1
Metacarpal	–	1	–	–	–	1	1
Metatarsal	–	4	1	–	–	5	4
Metapodial	–	1	–	–	–	1	1
1st Phalanx	–	1	1	–	–	2	2
2nd Phalanx	–	1	–	–	–	1	1
Ribs	–	–	–	–	2	2	1
Cervical vertebrae	–	3	1	–	1	5	2
Thoracic vertebrae	–	3	–	1	–	4	1
Lumbar vertebrae	–	1	1	–	1	3	2
Sacrum	–	2	–	–	–	2	1
Total	1	80	55	19	12	167	

MNI minimum number of individuals represented

All seven sheep/goat fragments came from context 1501. The absence of such bones in the lower fills suggests that sheep may have been exploited only rarely during the earlier period of the henge's development. The bones represented consisted of two fragments of mandible, a loose tooth, and a single fragment each of radius, femur, tibia, and cervical vertebra.

Dog was represented by three fragments in the terminal cutting. Context 1501 produced a fragment of scapula and an acetabulum, and a fragment of ilium came from context 1486. Four roe deer fragments were recovered: context 1501 included a scapula and two fragments of humeri (which may have belonged to the same bone), and context 1488 produced a femur fragment. The sieving produced a tooth of short-tailed vole and five bones of frog or toad in context 1486. A tibiotarsus fragment of an unidentifiable passerine was also recovered from the sieved samples.

The number of fragments represented in the unidentifiable large mammal and sheep-sized categories in each layer of the ditch terminal section are shown in Table 79 (MF2 A7). Most of the sheep-sized mammal fragments were small fragments recovered from the sieved samples. The large mammal assemblage was also dominated by small unidentifiable fragments, often burnt, from the sieved samples. Apart from these, the relative number of longbone fragments is higher than usually encountered in archaeological samples.

The southern ditch section

The number and density of animal bones were significantly smaller in this section than in the ditch terminal. Only 346 bones were recorded, of which 65 belonged to partial skeletons of dog and white-tailed sea eagle. Table 80 lists the identifications made in the various fills of the ditch which, for the purposes of this analysis, were grouped as follows (context numbers refer to Fig 100, and equivalent contexts):

1065 and 1421 final ditch fill and redeposited bank material
1444, 938, and 1441 stone-free grassland soil
941 and 1063 upper ditch fills
1062 and 1487 upper colluvial ditch fills
1072, 1472, and 2238 lower colluvial ditch fills
1420 cemented chalk wash
1445 primary chalk rubble
1446 and 2306 chalk wash and primary ditch fill.

Table 80 also summarises the observations of bone condition from each of these groups. In general, the assemblage was much more severely eroded than that from the ditch terminal, and in contrast only a few fragments were burnt. Only four observations of gnawing and none of butchery were made, but erosion may have destroyed such marks in many cases. Once again, the severity of the erosion on the bones tended to decrease in the lower fills, and the few bones from the primary fills were well preserved. The high proportion of unidentifiable fragments is also indicative of the relatively poor preservation of much of this sample.

Cattle fragments were the most commonly identified (excluding articulated bones), although nearly all of them were found in the colluvial and other upper fills of the section. The skeletal elements represented of all the principal mammals are given in Table 81 (MF2 A8). In the cattle sample, although fragments of the upper limb bones were more common than those from other parts of the skeleton, the bias towards such bones was by no means as marked as in the ditch terminal. The sample was too small to draw further conclusions.

All 20 of the pig fragments, primarily of loose teeth (Table 81, MF2 A8), were found in the colluvial fills, in the lower parts of which they outnumbered cattle fragments.

The five sheep/goat fragments were found in the upper fills of the section. Once again, they were absent from the primary fills and may not have been exploited at that period. A fragment of horse, third metacarpal, was found in context 938. Both the house mouse maxilla and the unidentified rodent incisor in context 1444 could have been quite modern intrusions into the fills. A roe deer tooth was found in the same context.

The 52 dog bones consisted of a series of articulated sets of bones from contexts 1420 and 2306. These all appear to have belonged to the same animal, the skeleton of which had become separated in the lower ditch fills. The sets of lumbar vertebrae from the different contexts are a good match and the astragalus found in context 1420 articulates with the right tibia recovered from context 2306. The bones belonged to an adult male dog (the baculum was recovered), which had suffered from severe pathology to its left hindlimb. Both the femur and tibia were malformed and the latter appears to have been fractured at some stage in the animal's life. The femur was also distorted towards its distal articulation and the limb would have been substantially shorter than its counterpart. The fracture had healed, but the animal is likely to have hobbled around for a considerable part of its life.

The 13 bones of white-tailed sea eagle consisted of bones from the left wing and some vertebrae, probably from the same individual. Context 2306 contained the distal half of the humerus and fragments of the proximal parts of the radius and ulna, and 1445 contained fragments of the distal halves of the radius and ulna, the metacarpus, the ulnare, and six vertebrae. The humerus had suffered quite severely from a pathological condition which resulted in the distortion of the shaft, exostosis and pitting.

Interior features

Pits 1177, 1458, 1608, 1619, 1672, 1844, 1848, 2112, and 2115, together with the stakehole 976, produced 95 bones. Only pits 1844 (29 fragments) and 1619 (15 fragments) produced over ten bones. The bones identified are listed in Table 74 and the elements represented are shown in Table 82 (MF2 A9).

The assemblages from these shallow features were generally poorly preserved. Of these fragments, 38 were severely eroded, 38 moderately eroded and 16 slightly eroded. Eight fragments showed evidence of burning and at least 11 had been gnawed. Consequently there was a high proportion of unidentifiable fragments, with only cattle and pig identified in more than one pit. Cattle bones were found in five pits and pig in three. Bones of sheep/goat and roe deer were not identified. Context 1398 contained the proximal articulation of a radius, which, in view of its extremely large size, may have belonged to aurochs (*Bos primigenius*).

Table 80 W2 Coneybury Henge: species represented in southern ditch section (cut 934)

	Contexts:								
Species	*1065/ 1421*	*938/ 1444*	*1072/ 941/ 1063*	*1062/ 1487*	*1472/ 2238*	*1420*	*1445*	*1446/ 2306*	*Total*
Cattle	3	8	3	20	9	3	–	2	48
Sheep/goat	–	–	2	3	–	–	–	–	5
Pig	–	–	–	7	13	–	–	–	20
Horse	–	1	–	–	–	–	–	–	1
Dog	–	–	–	–	–	15	–	37	52
Roe deer	–	1	–	–	–	–	–	–	1
Large mammal	3	18	6	65	11	5	1	4	113
Sheep-sized mammal	–	9	6	6	11	–	4	–	36
Unidentified mammal	6	14	3	16	13	1	–	2	55
House mouse	–	1	–	–	–	–	–	–	1
Unidentified rodent	–	1	–	–	–	–	–	–	1
Sea eagle	–	–	–	–	–	–	10	3	13
Total	12	53	20	117	57	24	15	48	346
Slightly eroded	–	6	–	4	23	6	–	1	40
Moderately eroded	–	12	3	23	12	–	–	2	52
Severely eroded	9	30	15	80	13	–	4	–	151
Charred/calcined	–	6	–	2	–	–	1	1	10
Gnawed	–	–	–	1	2	1	–	–	4

A fragment of the top of a red deer antler was found in pit 2115, a Beaker period pit outside the henge. Finally, a radius of a dog was recovered from context 1672.

Topsoil contexts

Fifty-five fragments of animal bone were recovered from the topsoil, several of which (including three bird bones) had a modern appearance and may have been relatively recent intrusions into the deposits. Table 74 lists the species represented. All of the fragments identified to cattle, sheep/goat, and pig consisted of loose teeth, apart from a fragment of pig mandible. Most of the remaining fragments were eroded and seven bore some degree of burning.

Discussion

Interpretation of the faunal assemblage from Coneybury Henge must rely heavily on the evidence from the ditch terminal, which may not have been typical of the rest of the site. It seems clear that the upper fills of that section of the ditch contained the bone debris derived mainly from a particular stage in cattle carcase processing. That stage was one in which meat from the upper limb bones was processed and possibly in some instances roasted on the bone. Such processing may have taken place close to the entrance of the enclosure. Unfortunately, samples from the rest of the excavation were too small to test whether the waste from such processing was restricted to that area of the ditch, or whether there were other contemporary discrete concentrations of particular bone elements. It is possible that the pig assemblage was also derived principally from a similar stage of processing but the sample was again too small to be certain.

Cattle and pig were the only two species eaten in any numbers. Most of the cattle bones appear to have belonged to fully grown animals, as only five porous bones belonging to young calves were identified. The epiphysial fusion evidence (Table 83, MF2 A10) supports this as nearly all the articulations, even those of late-fusing age, were fused. Even allowing for the fact that unfused specimens are likely to be under-represented because of their greater susceptibility to destruction, it does appear that most of the cattle represented in this sample were over four years of age, and in some cases may have been considerably older. The absence of tooth eruption makes it impossible to gain a more detailed impression of cattle mortality patterns. In contrast, the pig bones included a greater proportion of immature specimens (Table 83, MF2 A10).

It was possible to gain some impression of the size of the cattle represented at the site. Table 84 (MF2 A11) summarises the more common measurements which generally fall within the size range of animals represented in the larger sample from Durrington Walls (Harcourt 1971). The mean of the distal humeri measurements at Coneybury was slightly greater than at Durrington Walls (*c* 71.8mm) but smaller than the mean obtained from specimens from Windmill Hill (75.4mm: Grigson 1965, 155). Most of the Coneybury specimens were larger than those represented in the Middle Bronze Age deposits at Grimes Graves (Legge 1981b, 84). The decrease in size of cattle from the Neolithic period to the Iron Age has been noted for some time (Jewell 1963), and the results from Coneybury correspond with this trend.

The absence of sheep/goat bones from any of the primary fills of the deposits may indicate that they were not exploited in the early phases of the development of the henge. Deer bones were also comparatively rare compared to their abundance in the earlier bone assemblage from W2 (1981), the Coneybury 'Anomaly' (Maltby, this vol, 4.1 d).

4.9 f *Land mollusca*

by Martin Bell and Julie Jones

Surviving archaeological deposits were restricted to those within the ditch and within subsoil features, no trace of a bank and corresponding buried soil surviving. This meant that analytical work was restricted to a major column of samples from the ditch and three spot samples from subsoil features.

The methods of mollusc analysis employed are basically those outlined by Evans (1972) and the nomenclature follows Walden (1976). The molluscs were generally in a good state of preservation although somewhat encrusted by a calcareous deposit. The results are shown in Tables 85–87 (MF2 A12–14) and as histograms of relative abundance (Fig 110), in which each species is plotted as a percentage of the total individuals, excluding the burrowing species *Cecilioides acicula*, which is plotted as a percentage over and above the rest of the assemblage.

During the course of mollusc analysis the sediments were divided into various sieve fractions. These fractions have been grouped into three: particles larger than 5.6mm; particles between 5.6mm and 0.5mm; and particles smaller than 0.5mm. When plotted graphically (Fig 111), this provides a crude index of the extent of physical weathering and sorting within the ditch sediments. Also represented on the same diagram are the numbers of molluscs per kilogramme of soil, which, by comparison with the sedimentological sequence, helps to provide some indication of the speed with which the various layers accumulated and the extent to which conditions at the time favoured molluscan life.

The southern ditch section

A full description of the ditch sediments at the point sampled is contained in the detailed soil report (Keeley, this vol, MF2 B2–4). An abbreviated outline of the main layers is given in Table 88 (MF2 B1). The primary fill contained very few molluscs (generally less than ten per sample) and these samples have been omitted from the histograms (Fig 110). In any case, the molluscs concerned were probably weathered from the ditch sides and are of little value for interpretation. Of more interest is the soil lens at 2.72–2.78m, which was interpreted in the field as a possible collapsed turf. Analysis did not, however, support this interpretation since a large soil sample weighing 3.5kg contained only 58 molluscs, far fewer than one might expect in topsoil. More probably the lens represents subsoil from the pre-henge soil profile which has fallen, or been washed, into the ditch. *Pomatias elegans* is the most abundant species. It is often found in conditions of clearance and broken ground such as probably accompanied construction of the henge; alternatively its importance here may be explained by its tendency to become concentrated in subsoil horizons. The other species present include *Carychium tridentatum, Acanthinula aculeata, Vitrina pellucida,* the Zonitidae, and *Clausilia bidentata,* which generally prefer shady conditions. With these, however, are *Vallonia excentrica* and *Helicella itala,* which like open conditions. Interpretation is made difficult both by the small number of individuals and by a degree of uncertainty as to whether they were all derived from the same horizon in the pre-henge soil. All we can do is to record the presence of shade-loving and open country elements and see how this compares to the assemblages from overlying horizons.

The secondary fill between 1.1m and 1.76m produced much larger numbers of molluscs and a more diverse assemblage than the other layers. Clearly, the sediments accumulated relatively slowly and conditions were highly favourable for molluscan life. Throughout this period the assemblage is characterised by an abundance of *Carychium tridentatum,* accompanied by large numbers of *Discus rotundatus, Aegopinella pura, Vitrea contracta,* and *Vallonia costata*. There is also evidence for a small degree of ecological change through the secondary fill. *Helicella itala* and some catholic species are more abundant at the base, as are *Punctum pygmaeum* and *Nesovitrea hammonis,* which Evans reports as abundant in the early stages of ditch colonisation by plants (1972, 331).

Subsequently, towards the middle of the secondary fill, *Pupilla muscorum, Vallonia costata,* and *Helicella itala* decrease and there is a corresponding increase in the proportions of *Carychium tridentatum, Discus rotundatus,* and, to a lesser extent, *Oxychilus cellarius* and *Aegopinella nitidula,* which suggests some further increase in shade. The trend is a minor one, however, and throughout the secondary fill the assemblage is predominantly one of shade-loving species which account for a mean of 63% using the categories of Evans (1972, 194). Associated with these are some 15% of species in the open country category. The only one of these which is consistently important is *Vallonia costata,* which does occur at similar levels of abundance in open woodland. This is not the case, however, with *Helicella itala,* which has been described as 'the most characteristically open country species' (Evans 1972, 180) and occurs in small proportions in all samples.

It must now be considered to what extent the predominantly shade-loving assemblage in this layer reflects a more shady micro-environment in the ditch as opposed to general site conditions. If the assemblage had been the result purely of shade and lush vegetation in a ditch set within an otherwise open landscape one could have predicted, on the basis of sites where it is possible to compare palaeosol and ditch assemblages, that there would be a much greater proportion of open country species (K D Thomas 1982). It might also be anticipated that the lower part of the secondary fill would produce a largely open assemblage and that the proportion of shade-loving species would increase as vegetation colonised the ditch. Instead, it is evident that a plant cover creating shady conditions was already present when the secondary fill began to accumulate.

More problematical is the nature of the plant community. Tall ungrazed grassland has, for instance, been shown to support faunas similar in some respects to those from woodland (Cameron and Morgan-Huws 1975). Such faunas tend to be rich in *Carychium tridentatum, Vitrea contracta,* and *Aegopinella pura,* which are all abundant in these samples. Tall grassland faunas do not, however, contain *Discus rotundatus, Aegopinella nitidula, Acanthinula aculeata, Oxychilus cellarius,* and the Clausiliidae, which are present here. Further evidence that the relatively rich assemblage is not purely the result of lush grass in the sedimenting ditch comes from the sediments themselves. Lush grass implies stable conditions but the 0.66m of poorly sorted sediment clearly suggests conditions which were far from stable. Taken in aggregate, the evidence indicates that during the Beaker period shady conditions were created at least partly by shrubs and trees. Leaf litter accumulating in the ditch would account neatly for the large numbers of *Carychium tridentatum*. Patches of bare ground are implied by the sediments and those on the weathered bank could have created a favourable niche for *Helicella itala*.

A further aspect of the secondary ditch fill assemblage which deserves mention is the occurrence of a single example of *Oxyloma pfeifferi* at 1.1–1.15m. This is anomalous because the species is one of fens, marshes, and wet places (Kerney and Cameron 1979, 60). Suitable habitats would almost certainly have existed in the Avon Valley 0.7km to the south-east. A solitary individual might have been brought here by a bird or mammal or imported by man along with reeds or some other raw material from the valley.

At the very top of the secondary fill and into the stone accumulation zone of the overlying stabilisation horizon an abrupt change occurs. There is a minor peak in mollusc numbers, as one would expect in a stabilisation horizon, but a decrease in the number of species. All the shade-loving species decline rapidly and never achieve major representation again. In the early stages of this decline there is a minor peak of *Pomatias elegans,* which is favoured by clearance episodes and disturbed conditions. Following this is a rapid increase in open country species: *Pupilla muscorum,* the Vallonias, *Helicella itala,* and *Vertigo pygmaea*. From these species we can infer that conditions at the time of the stabilisation were open, dry, and probably short grassland. The reasonably large number of molluscs per kilogramme (up to 900) is probably more an indication that the layer formed over a long period than evidence that the environment was particularly favourable for molluscs.

It was, therefore, probably some considerable time after the removal of woody vegetation that a second aspect of clearance occurred. This is represented by the sedimentological evidence for levelling of the bank into the ditch to form the chalk lens at 0.78–0.89m. Then followed the deposition of 0.78m of colluvial soil, during which time there was a gradual decrease in mollusc numbers and diversity. The assemblage is a restricted one dominated by *Pupilla muscorum,* Limacidae, the Vallonias, and *Helicella itala*. Some parallels can be seen

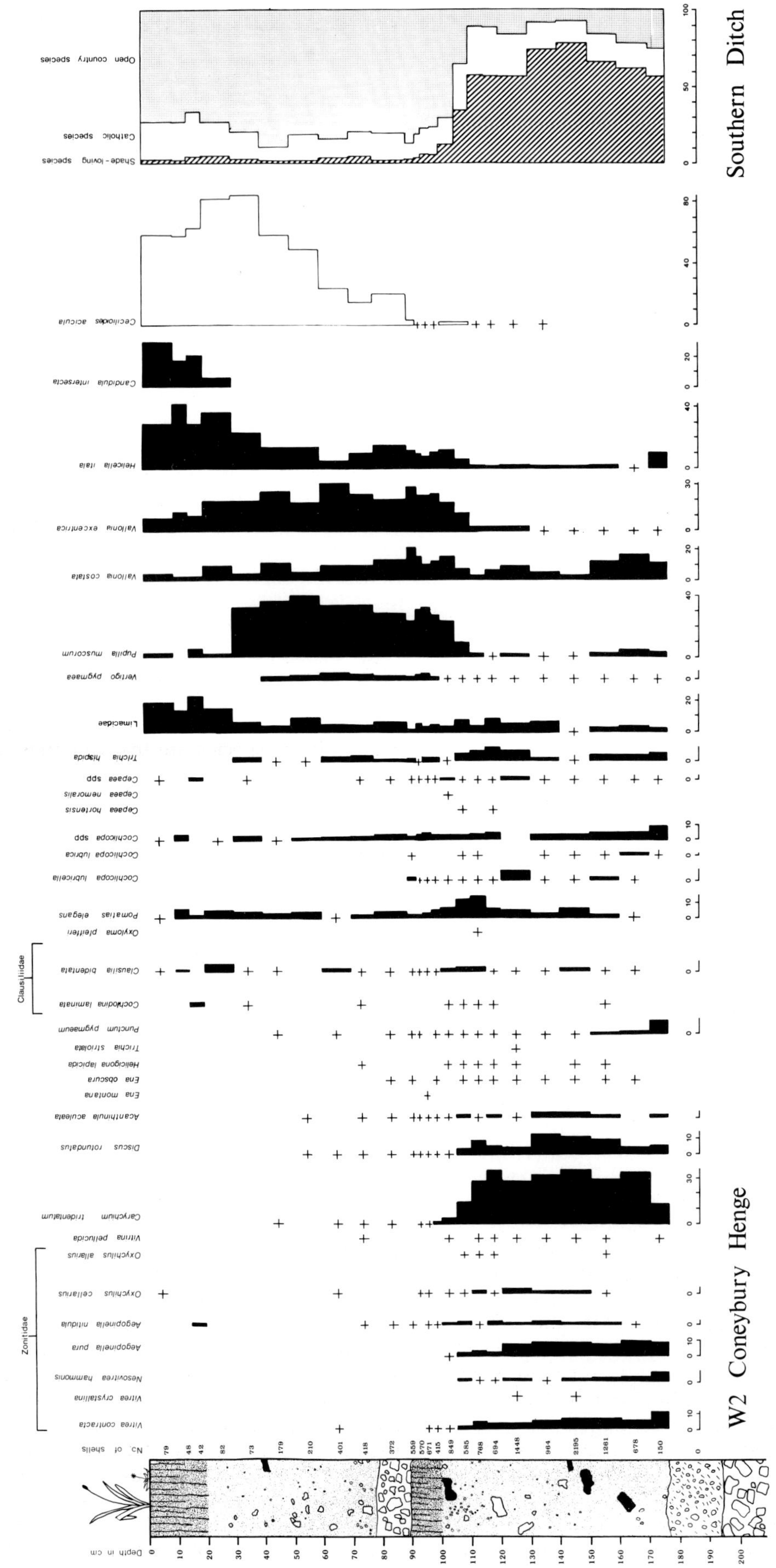

Fig 110 Coneybury Henge: mollusc diagram

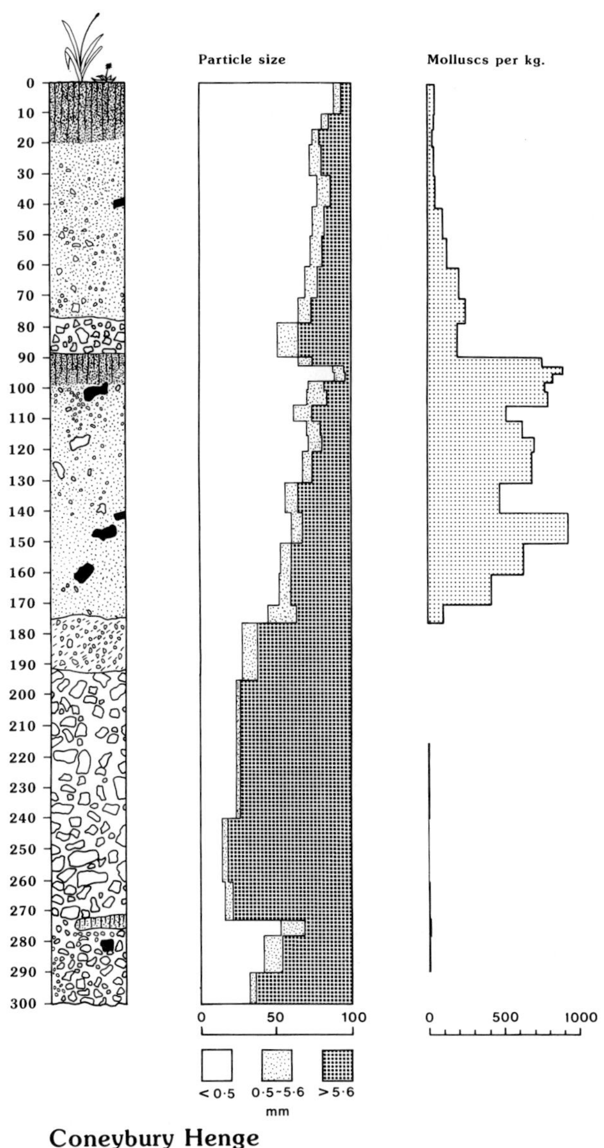

Fig 111 W2 Coneybury Henge: southern ditch sediment diagram

with assemblages in lynchet deposits (Evans 1972, 319; K D Thomas 1977, 262) and colluvial valley fills of arable origin (Bell 1981a). These generally have large numbers of Vallonias, with *Vallonia excentrica* predominating over *Vallonia costata* as in this case. Where they differ from the present sediments is in having more *Trichia hispida* and smaller numbers of *Pupilla muscorum*, which seems to shun intensive agriculture (Evans 1972, 146). This could suggest that brief grassland episodes interrupted the arable activity represented by the tertiary fill. If so, the horizons in question must have been mixed during subsequent cultivation, for there is no hint of stabilisation horizons either from the sediments or the histogram of mollusc abundance.

At *c* 0.3m the situation changes; *Pupilla muscorum* declines very suddenly and almost vanishes, and there is a corresponding increase in Limicidae, *Helicella itala*, and *Candidula intersecta*. This change is probably the result of drier and more intensive arable conditions during comparatively recent times, since *Candidula intersecta* is a medieval introduction (Kerney 1966).

W2 (1981) Coneybury 'Anomaly' (this vol, 4.1)

One sample was examined from a soil layer within the fill of the Early Neolithic pit (context 2507) in an attempt to obtain evidence about the pre-henge environment. Interpretation of feature fills of this kind is hazardous as clearly most of the molluscs did not actually live in the features but were derived from possibly multiple contexts round its periphery. These might easily have included earlier subsoil features. The assemblage does, however, have a close general similarity to that from the secondary fill of the ditch. In terms of Evans's (1972, 194) ecological groups, 51% are woodland species, 23% of catholic ecological preferences, and 25% open country. Thus the proportion of open country species and particularly of *Helicella itala* is slightly greater than all but the very basal sample of the secondary fill. It can be inferred from this that there is no evidence that the Early Neolithic environment was dramatically different from that of the later Neolithic and Beaker period and that areas of shade are likely to have existed.

Interior features

Within the henge, two shallow subsoil features of irregular shape were tentatively interpreted in the field as former tree holes possibly relating to an earlier woodland episode. Analysis did not support this hypothesis. In the sample from context 1602/1242, the predominant species are the Vallonias, *Helicella itala*, and *Pupilla muscorum*; together, open country species comprise 47% of the assemblage, with shade-loving types, particularly *Discus rotundatus*, forming 31%. The closest match with the ditch sequence is with the bottom of the stabilisation horizon. The second subsoil hollow (context 1798) produced a smaller number of species, an assemblage similar to that in the tertiary fill of the ditch. The main species were *Helicella itala*, the Vallonias, and the Limacidae. These features are not, therefore, the eroded relics of climax woodland, but more probably the result of minor scrub growth in post-Neolithic times.

Conclusions

The absence of a pre-henge soil is unfortunate. The only evidence we have for the pre-henge environment comes from two isolated samples: one from the Coneybury 'Anomaly', the other from the soil lens at 2.73–2.78m in the primary ditch fill. Unsatisfactory as these two contexts are for mollusc analysis, they do hint at the existence of some shade in the pre-henge environment. More satisfactory evidence pointing in the same direction comes from the base of the secondary fill, since most of the woodland species were clearly on hand to colonise the site, and form the predominant aspect of the assemblage at the lowest level of the secondary fill. Some importance is therefore attached to the timescale for accumulation of the primary fill. Within this fill were four bands of coarse angular chalk rubble separated by bands of small chalk pieces. Experimental earthwork evidence at Overton Down

(Crabtree 1971) and Butser (P J Reynolds pers comm) suggests that paired coarse and fine bands represent annual increments and there is evidence of such banding in the primary fills of a number of prehistoric features on the chalk (Bell 1983). An implication of this is that the secondary fill began to accumulate within a few years, perhaps less than a decade, of construction. Since molluscs indicative of shady conditions were present by this stage, it implies that any cleared area round the henge may not have been extensive.

It cannot, however, be assumed that the monument was constructed in woodland. A warning against making this assumption comes from the Mount Pleasant henge (Evans and Jones 1979), where evidence can be compared from the old land surface and ditch. The old land surface showed that the monument had been constructed, following woodland clearance, in a grassland environment. However, a stabilisation horizon at the base of the secondary fill had a shade-loving assemblage which contained little clear indication of the foregoing grassland episode. This indicates that, had the Coneybury Henge been constructed in a clearing which then became overgrown, it is by no means certain that the episode would register at the base of the secondary fill. What can be said is that if the henge was constructed in a cleared area then that area is likely to have been of small size and seems to have become overgrown in less than a generation. Shady conditions certainly obtained at the time of the site's Beaker utilisation.

It remains to compare the Coneybury sequence with that from other henges. Most were constructed after forest clearance in an open grassland environment, often of fairly long standing. No evidence has survived to show that this was the case at Coneybury and the speed of colonisation by shrubs and trees implies that shade survived not far away in the pre-henge environment. Other henges in the study area have produced molluscan evidence that they were constructed in grassland; this was the case at Durrington Walls (Evans 1971) and Woodhenge (Evans and Jones 1979). The Stonehenge old land surface lacked contemporary molluscs (Evans 1984). Beyond the study area pre-henge grassland environments have been demonstrated at Avebury (Evans 1972), Mount Pleasant (Evans and Jones 1979), and Priddy (Dimbleby 1967). Only at Condicote on the Cotswold limestone is there a ditch assemblage with a predominantly shade-loving fauna in the primary fill, which implies that the monument may have been constructed in woodland (Bell 1983). Fewer post-construction ditch sequences have been obtained. An entirely open landscape was maintained at Woodhenge. However, at Stonehenge, Evans (1984) has found evidence for a later phase of scrub or woodland development. This is of considerable archaeological importance because it implies a period of abandonment after Stonehenge I. That episode is roughly contemporary with the evidence for woodland conditions from the secondary fill of the Coneybury ditch only 1.2km away, so we may be looking at a regeneration episode affecting a much larger area than the individual sites. Other henges outside the study area where there is evidence in the secondary fill for scrub and woodland are Condicote and Mount Pleasant. The question is whether these episodes represent a reduced level of land utilisation in Late Neolithic/Beaker times as hypothesised more widely by P J Whittle (1978). This sequence may also reflect a more complex mosaic of vegetation types on the chalk in the Neolithic and Early Bronze Age than we have come to infer from the basically short grassland environments associated with some of the major Wessex Neolithic monuments. The Coneybury Henge does not seem to have been constructed in a totally cleared landscape and to that extent it contrasts with the Durrington Walls/Woodhenge area some 2km to the north-east. This emerging picture of some landscape diversity round Stonehenge is interesting in the context of recent evidence for the Neolithic and later survival of woodland on other areas of the chalklands (K D Thomas 1982; Waton 1982).

Acknowledgements We are grateful to Dr John Evans for his comments on an earlier draft of the report, and to Dr David Maguire for assistance with computing the molluscan data.

4.9 g Human bone

by Janet Henderson

Context 941 (southern ditch cutting)

A small sample (weight 300g) of burnt human bone. No evidence for more than one individual. Very little of the material was identifiable but it was noted that there were fragments of skull and tooth roots present. Since the tooth roots came from the permanent dentition it can be suggested that the individual was a sub-adult or an adult (older than 12 years). No further comment was possible. (See also MF1 G5 for human bone catalogue.)

4.10 W31: the sample excavation of a flint scatter on Wilsford Down

4.10 a Site description

Extensive surface collection on Wilsford Down over the winter of 1981/82 located a large and apparently nucleated scatter of worked flint at the south-eastern end of The Diamond (59). The scatter lay on a gentle south-east facing slope, primarily within hectare SU 107408 in a field known colloquially as the 'Stony Diamond'. Initially recorded densities averaged 97 pieces of worked flint per 50m run with a maximum value of 184 pieces. As the scatter lay immediately above the nodule-strewn floor of a small dry valley it was initially interpreted as an area of primarily industrial activity exploiting a nearby surface outcrop of flint. Within this suggested industrial area, however, 15 scrapers and 12 other tools from the initial sample suggested an additional domestic component. At this stage the nature of the recovered tools was taken to suggest a date in the later part of the Neolithic.

After its initial location, the scatter was further examined in the spring of 1982. In order to design an appropriate excavation sampling strategy the extent of the scatter needed to be defined more closely. Total collection of an extensive area was rejected on logistical grounds, and an alternative approach was formulated.

This involved a small team walking on and off the scatter as originally recorded, observing and noting varying levels of surface flints. The general limits of the scatter defined by broad consensus were then plotted (Fig 112). During the course of this definition a number of individually diagnostic flint tools were noted, plotted, and recovered. These, including a fabricator and a discoidal knife, again suggested a broadly later Neolithic date.

Sampling strategy

The excavation sampling approach adopted for the defined scatter was based on a topographically aligned transect, running down the slight south-easterly slope, across the scatter and towards the assumed flint source. The transect, 190m long and 30m wide, was divided into two zones: the main scatter and the uphill (north-westerly) 'edge', and beyond. Prior to excavation the Ancient Monuments Laboratory carried out a magnetometer survey over the whole transect. This confirmed the existence of an element of the extensive Wilsford Down linear ditch system at the south-easterly (downslope) end of the transect (Fig 112, cropmark 970, sampled in area M, this vol, 4.13), and suggested a number of additional anomalies, primarily towards the upslope edge of the scatter (Figs 113–115, MF2 B8–10). A magnetic susceptibility survey was also carried out using equipment loaned by the Ancient Monuments Laboratory, and in 1985 the transect was retrospectively sampled on a broad basis for soil phosphate analysis. Results from the magnetic susceptibility survey were subsequently processed by the Ancient Monuments Laboratory (Bartlett, this vol, MF2 B5–7).

Within the overall transect a total of 16 sample squares, each 5m by 5m, were selected for excavation (Fig 112, areas A–L and N–T). The squares were selected partly in order to sample magnetometer anomalies and partly on a random basis (Table 89). Area M was excavated in order to examine the relationship of the linear ditch to the flint scatter. Located beyond the main transect and not aligned on the main excavation grid, this area was only 3m wide and 2m long. Within the individual excavation squares, all topsoil was excavated by hand on a 1m grid with a 20% sample dry-sieved through 4mm mesh.

Topsoil artefact patterning

The topsoil excavation produced considerable quantities of worked and burnt flint, together with smaller quantities of foreign stone and ceramic material. Figures 116 and 117 show objective distribution plots of various categories of worked and burnt flint and pottery. These plots were used in conjunction with a preliminary assessment of data from the phosphate and magnetic surveys in the production of an interim data profile for the excavated transect (Entwistle and Richards 1987, fig 3.3). This profile served to demonstrate the general relationship between varying elements of the solid, chemical, and magnetic record of the sample transect, but necessitated the lateral compression of the data from individual squares. The data is consequently now presented in plan view, and some reinterpretation offered in the light of refined geophysical data.

The excavated areas provide a 7% sample of the overall transect, itself representing no more than a 30% sample of the total scatter. The size of this sample inevitably places limitations on the potential level of interpretation. However, the composition of the ploughsoil artefact assemblages from each of the sample squares does vary sufficiently to suggest a potential range of activities. As suggested in the interim interpretation (Entwistle and Richards 1987), the association of high total flint numbers and a higher level of burnt worked flint suggests activity of an essentially domestic nature. Following this model, areas E and J/K/L can be suggested as fulfilling the necessary criteria. Area K/L, having relatively low core numbers, reinforces the idea of the localised curation of elements of an assemblage, but is also one of the areas in which refitting material from a subsoil hollow demonstrates *in situ* knapping (Harding, this vol, 4.10 b). Areas R and T, the other areas showing evidence of this type of more industrial activity, appear peripheral to the identifiable 'domestic' zone.

The south-eastern end of the transect produced the highest recorded number of cores, in the case of area E associated with concentrations of both flakes and tools. The overall pattern in this part of the transect is far from coherent, suggesting a zone of more sporadic activity, perhaps associated with the topographical break, later marked by the linear ditch.

The magnetometer survey (Fig 114, MF2 B9) identified a number of localised anomalies, interpreted as potentially pits or short lengths of ditch. Their distribution was rather sparse, and where examined, with the exception of the ditch (area M), they proved to be of natural, rather than archaeological, origin.

The results of the susceptibility survey (Fig 115, MF2 B10) are more difficult to interpret, primarily owing to the lack of precedent for extensive and close-spaced susceptibility surveys. Consequently, factors such as slope and the direction of ploughing, both current and historic, may be factors affecting the observable trends in the data. Bartlett (this vol, MF2 B5–7) suggests that the data may not allow for interpretation beyond suggesting a palimpsest of activities. The activity at W31, however, results in a mean level of susceptibility considerably higher than that recorded at W2, Coneybury Henge (W31, mean 55×10^{-8} SI/kg], standard deviation 17; W2, values 37 and 4 respectively). Both the interim data transect (Entwistle and Richards 1987, fig 3:3), and

Table 89 W31 Wilsford Down: excavation sampling strategy

Area	*Zone*	*Reason for sample*
A	Main scatter	Geophysical anomaly – pit?
B–J	Main scatter	Random
K	Main scatter	Geophysical anomaly
L	Main scatter	Geophysical anomaly
M	N/A	Geophysical anomaly – linear ditch
N	'Edge'	Random
P	'Edge'	Random
R	'Edge'	Geophysical anomaly – pit and ditch?
S	'Edge'	Random
T	'Edge'	Geophysical anomaly – ditch?

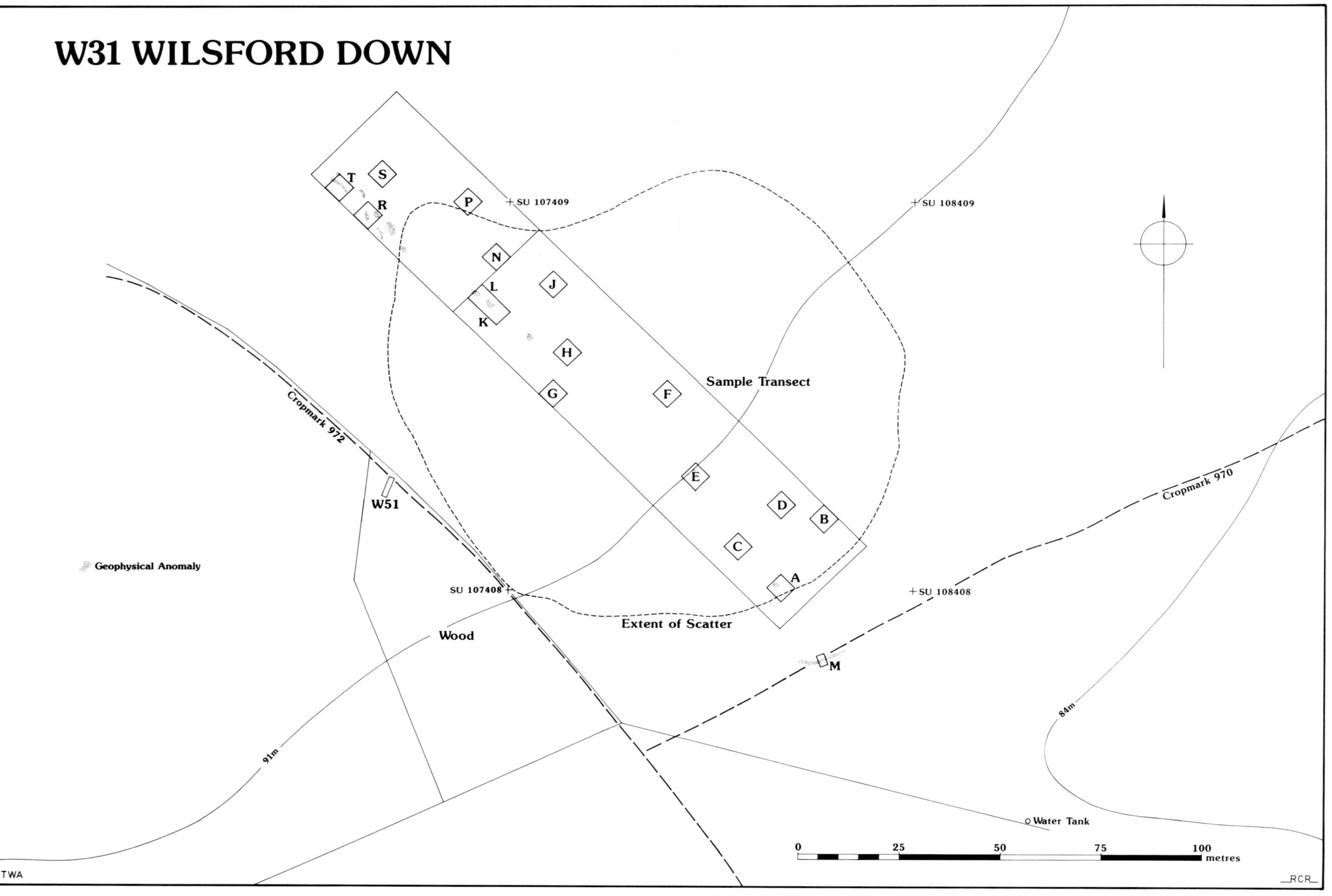

Fig 112 W31 Wilsford Down: location plan and sample transect

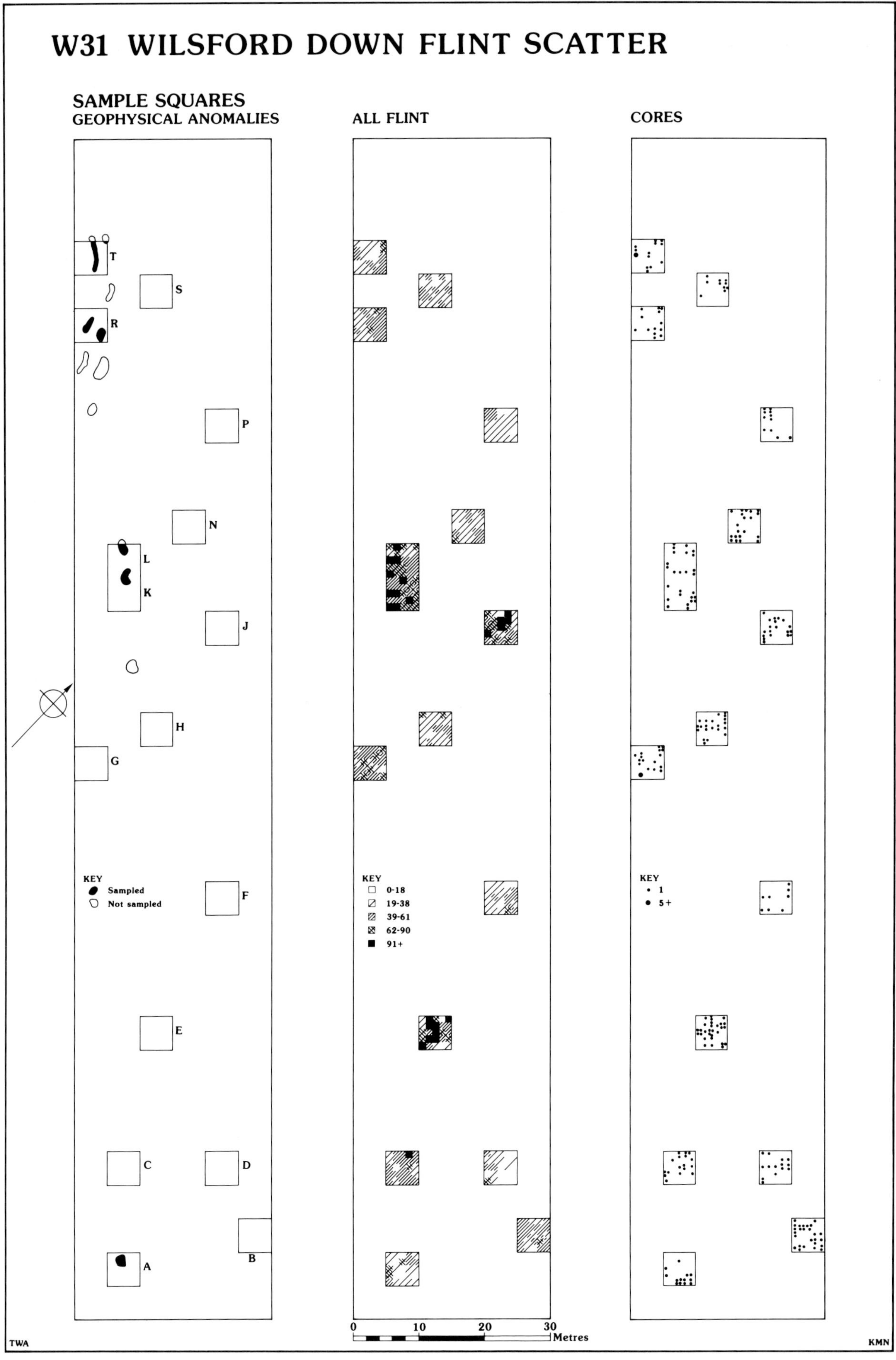

Fig 116 W31 Wilsford Down: sample transect, geophysical anomalies, distribution of all worked flint and flint cores

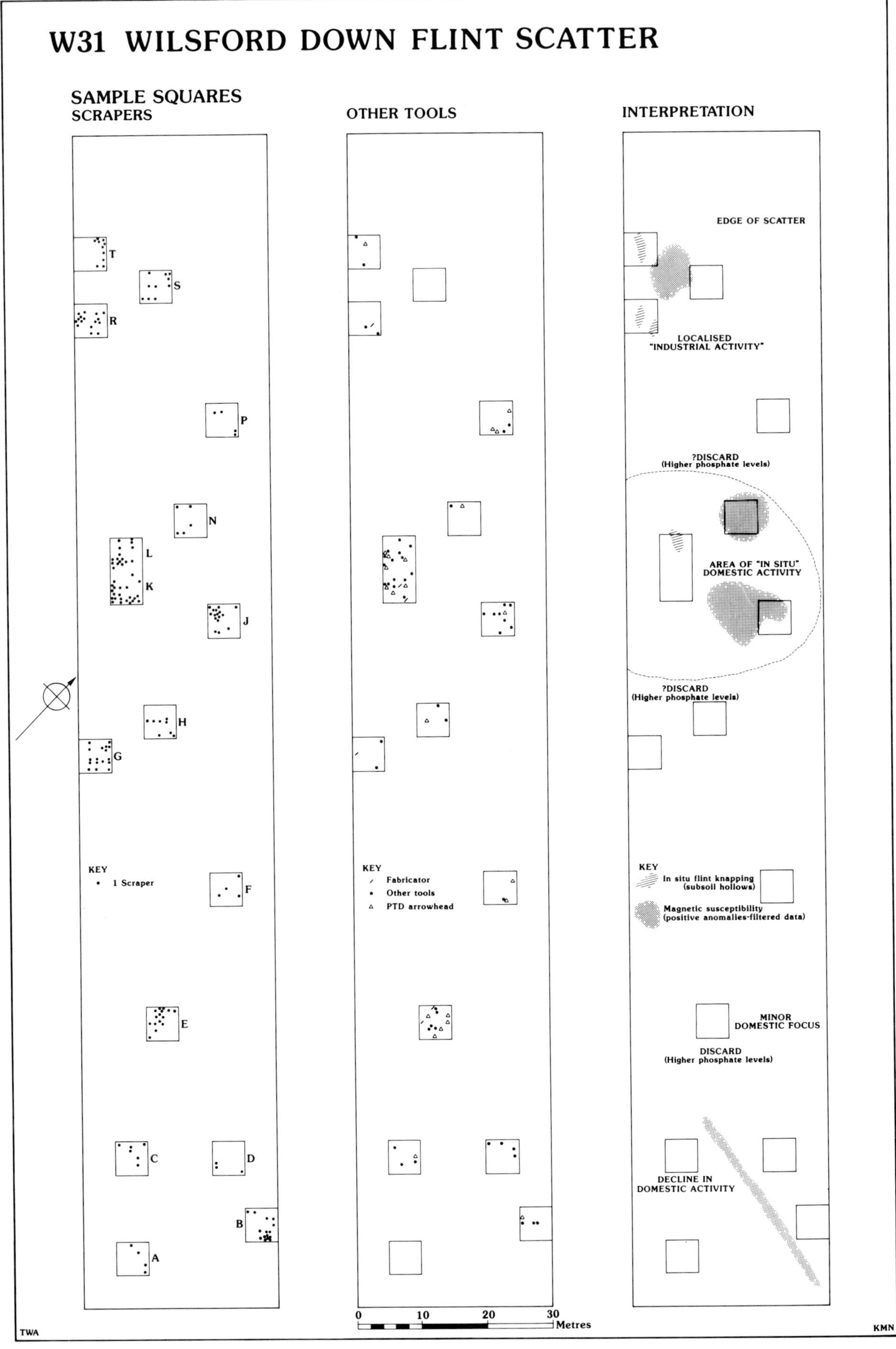

Fig 117 W31 Wilsford Down: sample transect, flint scrapers, other flint tools, and overall interpretation

the initial data plot (Fig 115, MF2 B10) appear to show a strong correlation between the edge of the flint scatter, in terms of flint distribution, and an area of enhanced susceptibility. The suggestion that this enhancement, associated with higher levels of phosphates, may represent peripheral disposal of organic material (Entwistle and Richards 1987, 28), cannot be dismissed.

If the sampled scatter is to be considered chronologically discrete, and the evidence, although limited, suggests a major phase of activity in the later Neolithic, then some zoning of activity can be tentatively identified and characterised. A suggested scheme is offered in Figure 117.

Subsoil features

Within all the excavated squares modern ploughsoil directly overlay the abraded surface of the natural chalk. With the exception of the linear ditch examined in area M (described together with W51, Wilsford Down linear ditch, this vol, 4.13), only one apparently archaeological feature was recorded. This was a small pit, cut 448, lying partly beyond the edge of area S and therefore not fully excavated. It appeared to be considerably disturbed by rabbit burrowing and contained a chronologically mixed assemblage of artefacts. A small group of worked flint included a leaf-shaped arrowhead, suggesting an earlier Neolithic date, although the only pottery from the feature was a rim sherd of later Neolithic or Early Bronze Age date (P117).

Within the gently sloping area of the transect, between areas A and G, the natural surface of the chalk showed pronounced downslope periglacial stripes, most coherent in area A. One irregular linear subsoil hollow in area G contained five sherds of Peterborough Ware fabric including one decorated sherd (P93).

Upslope, beyond area G, no periglacial stripes were recorded, and the removal of topsoil revealed a series of irregular subsoil features, many of which had appeared as anomalies on the magnetometer survey (Bartlett, this vol, MF2 B5–7). On excavation they demonstrated a consistent sequence, the upper fills stone-free and overlying a densely packed sorted horizon. In many cases, specifically within features 454 and 460 (area L), 480 (area R), and 462, 464, and 466 (area T), this sorted horizon contained, within a matrix of naturally broken flint, considerable quantities of worked flint in fresh condition. Refitting potential could be recognised on site and this material has subsequently been examined in some detail (Harding, this vol, 4.10 b). This analysis suggests that flint working was taking place in the immediate vicinity of the subsoil hollows and includes the manufacture of core tools (Fig 118, for example).

Within some of the sampled areas (F, G, K/L , R, and T), the upper levels of the subsoil features also contained small quantities of prehistoric pottery (Raymond, this vol, 4.10 b; Fig 119 for illustrated examples). Some correlation between material from subsoil hollows and that recovered from associated ploughsoils is apparent. The two adjoining squares, area K/L, contained together 32% by weight of the total prehistoric pottery assemblage. Within this combined area, the ploughsoil contained 31% by weight of the total ploughsoil prehistoric pottery assemblage and included sherds of Peterborough Ware (P94, P95, P102, P103). Area T produced 26% by weight of the total prehistoric pottery assemblage, and 16% by weight of the total prehistoric pottery assemblage from the topsoil. Decorated sherds from the ploughsoil included those of probable Mortlake Ware (P99), of indeterminate Peterborough Ware (P98), and of less specific Late Neolithic/Early Bronze Age type (P107).

Excavation of the features below the level of the sorted horizon described above showed their lower filling to be devoid of artefacts. This, and the very irregular profile of the bases of the features, rapidly led to the realisation that they were not anthropogenic, although whether isolated solution features or parts of more extensive polygons cannot be determined. In this context it is perhaps worth noting that close to W31, round barrow Wilsford 54, excavated by Ernest Greenfield, may have originated as a natural polygonal feature. The 'ditch' is described as a ring of shallow soil-filled hollows, not centred on the grave (RCHME 1979, 6) and the description of the soils also tends to suggest a natural origin (Isobel Smith pers comm).

At W31, the occurrence of groups of artefacts in the upper fills of the periglacial features can be explained solely as a product of sorting, although the quantity of lithic material contained within a limited area of sorted horizon considerably exceeds the quantity from adjacent ploughsoils. The occurrence within the subsoil features of the groups of conjoining flints suggests that while the material may not be strictly *in situ* it must have been worked very close by. The fact that the subsoil features contained nearly 47% by weight of the total prehistoric pottery assemblage can be explained as resulting from the differential survival of a fragile class of artefact.

The lower fills of the features showed no evidence that they had been utilised for the extraction of flint nodules, a seam of which lay at a depth of between 1.0–1.2m below the surface of the natural chalk in the immediate area of the excavation. Analysis of the flint assemblages from the features confirms that the larger and relatively easily available nodules were not utilised as a major source of raw material (Harding, this vol, 4.10 b).

With the exception of intrusive rabbit bones, the identifiable animal bone from this excavation consists of one slightly charred pig tooth from feature 481 in area R.

Discussion

The interpretation of what was initially considered to be a coherent and relatively well-defined area of activity is inevitably constrained by the absence of strictly stratified deposits and an awareness of the limitations of the sampling strategy. Subsequent fieldwork has also demonstrated the extent of the type of activity initially thought to be focused on the area sampled.

Despite the caveats noted above, it is possible to offer some interpretation of the nature and date of the activity represented at Wilsford Down. The area was initially suggested as being one solely concerned with the industrial side of prehistoric flint technology (Richards 1984b, 183) and the overall assessment of activity recorded by surface collection clearly emphasises the zone within which the sampled area lies (Figs 12 and 13). A more detailed interim statement (Entwistle and Richards 1987) suggested that the area sampled also included a strong domestic component, identifiable not only within the solid components of the excavated assemblage, but also within the magnetic and chemical record of the site's ploughsoil.

In the absence of environmental and economic data, the potential for defining the range of activities represented by the sampled area of W31 is inevitably restricted. The nucleated nature of the overall scatter, at least one edge of which appears to have been confirmed by the excavation, suggests a preferred location, possibly associated with the available flint source. The availability of water may be an additional factor influencing site location. Within the adjacent dry valley, bourne streams may have run, and areas persistently holding water, even in dry weather, have been recorded recently until drained as obstacles to present cultivation.

The evidence from both extensive and more restricted data suggests that the use of the lithic resources ranged from primary working through all stages of production to the use and discard of tools. Spatially, many of these activities appear to cluster around the upslope 'edge' of the defined scatter, and beyond. With the exception of the one pit, possibly of earlier Neolithic date, and the linear ditch, assumed on association with settlement data (Winterbourne Stoke Crossroads, this vol, 4.15) to date to the Late Bronze Age, the activity appears to date to the Late Neolithic/Early Bronze Age. This relatively restricted date range is suggested both by the small pottery assemblage (Raymond, this vol, 4.10 c) and by the range of chronologically diagnostic lithic artefacts, specifically arrowheads of petit tranchet derivative type (Harding, this vol, 5.2; Riley, this vol, 5.3).

4.10 b Lithics

The sample excavation produced a total of 21,343 pieces of worked flint. With the exception of those groups recovered from sealed subsoil contexts (below), all of the worked flint was recovered from the programme of ploughsoil excavation. This material, amounting to over 86% of the total site assemblage, has not been examined beyond the production of a stage 1 catalogue. The data from this catalogue have been employed in the production of a series of sample area distribution plots (Figs 116 and 117) from which elements of activity zoning within the overall sample transect can be suggested.

The composition of the flint assemblages from the individual sample areas is shown in Table 90.

The flint scrapers from this site have been examined separately as part of an overall project study (Riley, this vol, 5.3), as have the broader typological aspects of the petit tranchet derivative arrowheads. A technological study of these arrowheads also forms a part of Harding's study (this vol, 5.2).

Sealed flint assemblages

by Philip Harding

This report describes the analysis of groups of worked flint recovered from a series of sealed subsoil features. The features appear to be periglacial in origin, but many included sorted horizons in their upper levels,

Table 90 W31 Wilsford Down: ploughsoil flint assemblage

	Cores		*Flakes*						
Area	*complete*	*fragments*	*complete*	*broken*	*burnt*	*retouched*	*Scrapers*	*Other tools*	*Total*
A	13	18	492	304	17	–	5	1	850
B	27	11	538	500	3	–	12	3	1094
C	17	12	634	572	11	1	6	4	1257
D	14	11	271	274	23	–	3	3	599
E	29	9	861	702	32	3	14	9	1659
F	8	18	487	260	7	–	4	2	786
G	36	22	611	565	16	11	19	5	1285
H	21	6	372	400	20	5	9	2	835
J	19	14	688	828	51	7	16	9	1632
K	12	22	793	962	60	15	21	11	1896
L*	14	2	608	884	61	23	16	14	1622
M	7	6	223	183	3	1	3	3	429
N	20	2	479	344	8	5	5	2	865
P	11	2	354	386	14	3	4	5	779
R*	13	5	545	609	11	10	18	8	1219
S	10	8	306	395	15	5	10	2	751
T*	17	3	326	437	26	2	17	11	839
Sealed	78	16	1174	1382	237	59	(within total count)		2946
Totals	366	187	9762	9987	615	150	182	94	21,343

* area with sealed flint assemblage (Harding, this vol, 4.10 b)

horizons which contained substantial groups of worked flint. The condition of this material, together with refitting potential recognised during excavation and the occurrence of numerous chips, suggests that the contents of the subsoil hollows represent a homogeneous industry.

Excavation was undertaken manually, with all stratified contexts (as defined above) dry-sieved through 4mm mesh and a sample from one specific context (489) wet-sieved through 1mm mesh.

Table 91 shows the composition of the analysed flake assemblages recovered from undisturbed subsoil contexts.

Distribution

The density of flint recovered from topsoil excavation at W31 is plotted on Figure 116. This demonstrates the approximate extent of the flint scatter, largely confirming that suggested by surface collection and observation.

Refitting of material from adjacent subsoil contexts suggests that some mixing of material may have taken place. Refitting, the potential of which has probably not been exhausted, has been used wherever possible in reconstructing knapping sequences, and has demonstrated that the deposits are *in situ*. It has also indicated core tool manufacture and has clarified many technological details. Much of the refitting is from core preparation, correction, and rejuvenation, implying the removal of successful blanks from the site. The remaining material, therefore, can probably with justification be classified as waste.

Condition and raw material

The material, which was in mint condition, had developed a white/mottled light blue patina.

The immediate area of the site is a rich source of flint. Large nodules weathered from the chalk lie on the surface and extend down into the dry valley to the east. A thick seam of flint outcrops at approximately the same height as W31, above which the amount of knapping debris diminishes. There is, however, no indication that this seam was exploited, surface flint probably serving as raw material. In addition there seems to have been no preference for larger nodules. Core and flake size suggest that smaller and consequently more manageable pieces were used, or that fragments from larger broken nodules were flaked, especially for the production of small blanks. It is uncertain whether these larger blocks, many of which exhibit thermal fractures, were broken deliberately.

Table 91 W31 Wilsford Down: analysed flint flake groups

Area L contexts 454, 460	444 flakes (66% of all unbroken flakes)
Area R context 480	69 flakes (42% of all unbroken flakes)
Area T contexts 462, 464, 466	285 flakes (84% of all unbroken flakes)

This represents 68% of all unbroken flakes from areas L, R, and T

The flint industry

The waste from W31 is derived from a flake industry with some subsidiary blade/bladelet and core tool production. Retouch phases are indicated by apparently unfinished and rejected tools. The flake blanks are difficult to identify as no predetermined forms appear to have been produced. Evidence for blade/bladelet production is restricted to waste from context 454 and core rejuvenation tablets showing signs of platform abrasion; the absence of failed and broken blade/bladelets suggests that they formed an insignificant part of the production of the site.

Evidence of core tool production is limited to one refitted sequence assumed to represent a core tool roughout and a broken roughout from the surface collection. Such small numbers of roughouts and thinning flakes (Newcomer 1971) do not suggest the production of core tools on any scale.

Table 92 shows the ratio from each context of all forms of flake to cores, and of complete and burnt flakes to cores. The results suggest that cores are under-represented and, given the limitations of the excavation sampling, it can be suggested that they may have been removed from site. The absence of some cores is substantiated by the presence of waste and rejuvenation flakes of a distinctive flint for which there are no apparent cores. The most productive core, calculated from refitted flakes, showed a minimum of 25 flake removals. This number must be reduced for many of the remaining cores which are either failed or unproductive examples. Rejuvenation flakes and the proportion of preparation flakes, however, suggest that core preparation was not the main function of the site.

Cores

The 58 cores were dominated by flake cores and although some blades/bladelets were produced, there appears to have been no effort made to predetermine the end product. The cortex on flakes and the weight of residual cores (87% less than 199gm) suggest that raw material was probably selected at random from the abundant surface flint rather than from the large fresh flint which outcrops at the site. The correlation of flake size with other assemblages which use small raw material substantiates this.

Complete knapping sequences based on refitting cores are absent, so precise details of knapping techniques are unclear.

Table 92 W31 Wilsford Down: flint flake/core ratios from analysed groups

Context	*Flakes, broken flakes burnt flakes to core*	*Flakes, burnt flakes to core*
454	29	13
460	24	12
462	17 average 49	9 average 23
464	74	38
466	52	30
480	97	39

Table 93 W31 Wilsford Down: flint core classification

Clarke typology (1960)	*Number*	*Percentage*
Single platform (Aii)	20	34
Double platform (B)	12	21
Multi platform (C)	6	10
Alternate flaking (D)	8	14
Miscellaneous	12	21
	Total 58 examples	

Table 93 shows that most cores have a single striking platform (34%), the miscellaneous examples (21%) mainly being failed pieces. Such pieces are characteristic of industrial sites of all periods and representing all technologies.

Most cores lack deliberate or careful preparation of the striking platform or shaping of the back and base of the core to influence the form of the blank. Table 94 shows that 62% of all platforms show only basic preparation of the striking platform or utilise a negative flake scar as a platform. Most of the remainder were used unmodified. Some of the thermal striking platforms have a similar patina to the flake surfaces and may have been fresh surfaces at the time of knapping. This implies that pieces of broken nodules were sometimes selected for use. Two small cores which refit to a waste fragment could only have been worked after the nodule had broken. It is not certain whether these nodules were smashed deliberately.

Blank production can be divided into two types: bladelets and flakes. The bladelets constitute a minor part of the production and their manufacture is based entirely on the evidence of cores. The end product may have fulfilled a need for small blanks for inclusion in composite tools. They were produced from simple, unprepared single- and double-platform cores, the platforms of which were commonly abraded and represent a continuity of earlier Neolithic technology. The flakes were removed from single-platform or multi-platform cores, cores produced by alternate flaking (Fig 118), and from semi-discoidal cores. The illustrated example was produced by a similar technique to one from an Early Neolithic context at Rowden, Dorset (Harding 1986). The form of this core, which had been removed, was reconstructed by refitting the waste flakes. The technique was similar in all respects except flakes from Rowden had been prepared by faceting.

Table 94 W31 Wilsford Down: flint core platform analysis

Platforms	*No of platforms*	*Percentage*
Modified		
Negative facet	14	18
Prepared	34	44
Thermal	21	27
Unmodified		
Natural patination	3	4
Fracture surface	3	4
Unknown	2	3

Faceted butts and faceting chips show that, at W31, striking platforms were sometimes modified in order to maintain production. However, faceting to remove prepared flakes is rare and some faceted butts were probably accidental. Refitting showed that one resulted from rotating the core during rejuvenation, while others have lower percussion angles than might result from deliberate faceting to modify the flaking angle.

Flakes are also present which show the occasional use of platform abrasion to strengthen the front of the core before the flake is detached. Many of the flakes have broad butts, which require no abrasion, and which leave the striking platform with a coarse sinuous edge.

Cores were occasionally rejuvenated during their productive stages by the removal of a rejuvenation tablet. Most cores, however, were rejuvenated by rotating the core or by alternate flaking.

Estimated flake productivity, based on visual assessment, suggests that 20% of cores produced usable blanks. Many cores were rejected during initial preparation because an unsatisfactory angle of percussion had been produced. Such an increase in the flaking angle caused 57% of core rejection. This problem was probably understood as only 9% of cores show edge recession of the striking platform caused by continuous percussion. An assessment of additional potential of each core is difficult to make as the core may not produce sizeable blanks after additional wastage for preparation or rejuvenation. The fact that some cores were designed to produce small flakes causes additional problems. Subjective assessment suggests that over 50% of the cores have little or no potential. Flaws in the raw material have affected 26% of the overall core population.

Flakes

Figure 116 shows flake totals from W31. Samples were analysed using the system adopted for Rowden, Dorset (Harding 1986). Amalgamated results are shown in Figure 149 and detailed results are contained within the archive.

Comparisons with the assemblage from W59, King Barrow Ridge (this vol, 4.8 b), where an apparently smaller, less abundant raw material was used, shows an overall similarity in flake size. This may confirm the suggested selection of small nodules or the quartering of larger ones at W31. The results of flake scar pattern also show an increase in the amount of thermal surface on flakes from W31. The two industries are, however, remarkably similar in most respects. The W31 flakes are marginally broader and therefore squatter overall, a trend which typifies Late Neolithic industries. The more elongated flakes at W59 may relate to site function, flake selection, or be a function of chronology. The W31 breadth:length shape histogram contains the broadest flakes examined within the present study and compares most closely with the data from Durrington Walls (Wainwright and Longworth 1971, fig 68). This broadness at W31 may be a result of site function, affected by the readily available raw material and by elements of industrial production. The broad shape of the flakes is confirmed by the flake class analysis (classes defined in Gingell and Harding 1979), where

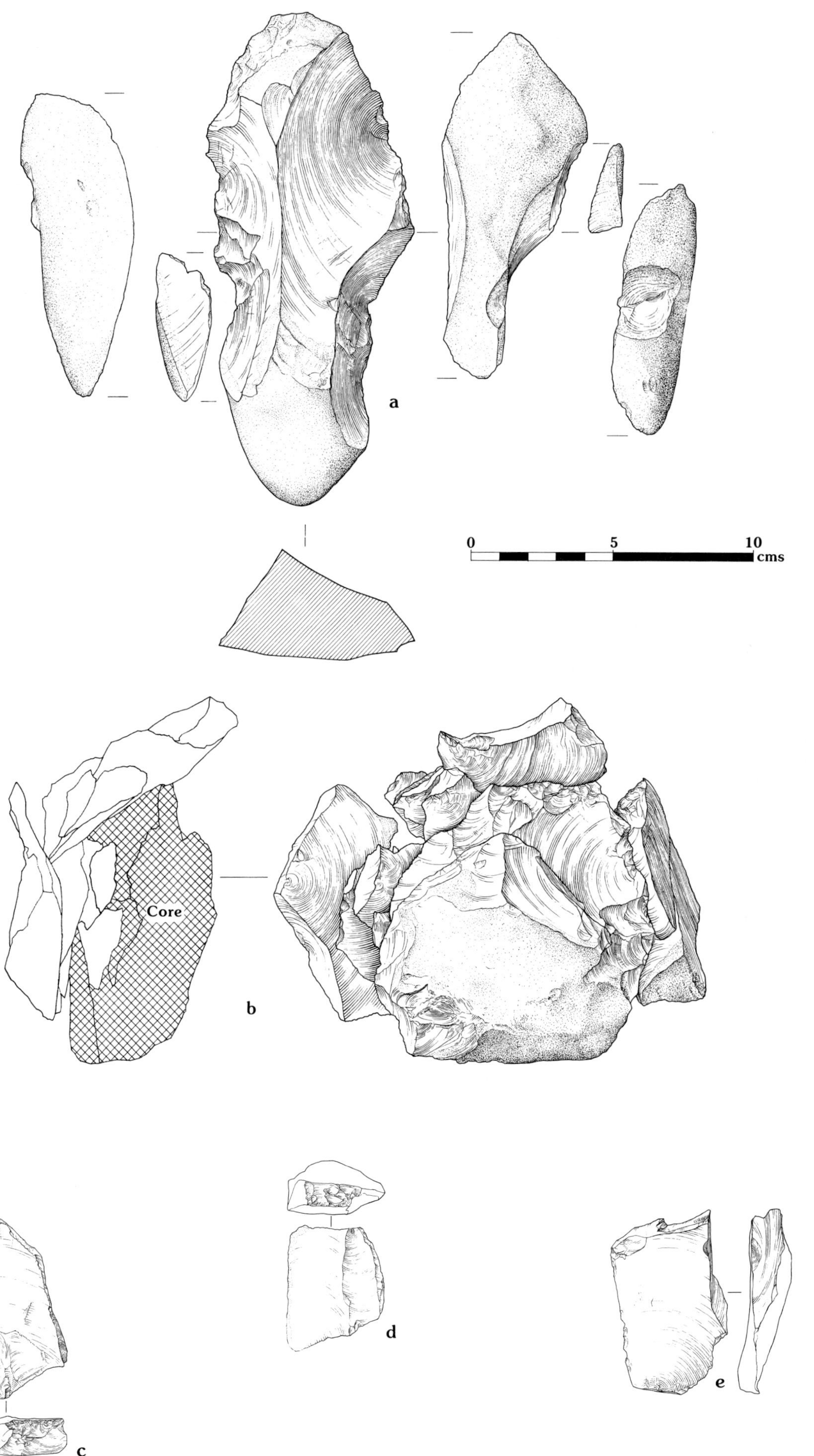

Fig 118 W31 Wilsford Down: flint blade cores and refitting material

approximately 40% can be classified as class 3 or miscellaneous.

Despite the presence of core tool manufacture, recognisable thinning flakes are rare. The flakes associated with the core tool roughout (Fig 118) are amongst the broadest flakes analysed, and also exhibit some of the lowest angles of percussion. Thinning flakes produced by hard hammer percussion during the production of an axe of this type may not exhibit the broad, invasive characteristics associated with soft hammer struck hand axe flakes (Newcomer 1971). They may, therefore, not have been recognised.

Flake butts at W31 are also generally broader than at other sites in the study area. Platform abrasion is present on only 4.5% of flakes of which 66% are miscellaneous trimming flakes. The absence of faceting as a deliberate technique may also be notable. Plain butts predominate and the increase in 'other' butt forms probably includes more dihedral butts from the multi-platformed cores and those worked by alternate flaking.

Eleven per cent of broken flakes have Siret fractures (accidental breakages, Bordes 1979, fig 4:3), and 7% have hinged distal ends. The measured flakes showed that 15% have either hinged or plunged distal ends, of which 83% are hinged. Preparation flakes showed the greatest susceptibility to hinge fracture (26%), and distal trimming flakes possessed more plunged distal ends (45%). These results are in general agreement with similar observations at Rowden (Harding 1986).

Chips

Numbers of chips from each area are shown in Table 116. Most are undiagnostic and probably result from impact around the point of percussion. There are, however, diagnostic chips which confirm features of the technology outlined above. These include faceting chips; abrasion chips, particularly those with abraded butts in their own right; and bulbar scars, denoting debitage stages (Newcomer and Karlin 1987). There is, however, an apparent absence of identifiable retouch chips, which is contrary to the evidence of unfinished tools that blanks were retouched at the site. One Janus flake, indicating bulb removal, was identified.

Retouched material

Tool totals are shown in Table 123. Analysis was restricted to those from the examined squares, both stratified and unstratified contexts, although all arrowheads were examined in order to maximise the sample. A residual element is suggested by the presence of leaf arrowheads while visible wear traces on some tools suggests their use as well as manufacture.

Scrapers

The 67 scrapers form the largest single retouched tool type from the analysed squares (36%). They include two burnt examples and three apparently made on cores or natural fragments. The undisturbed subsoil hollows however produced only ten scrapers, a ratio of 199 flakes for each scraper. This is the lowest ratio for any of the sites from the project area and reflects the industrial nature of activity within the subsoil hollows and perhaps within specific zones within the overall scatter.

Most scraper blanks were required to have a dipping profile, and distal trimming flakes, where this feature is most common, therefore predictably account for 20% of flakes selected. Flakes with hinged or plunged distal ends appear to have been avoided, presumably owing to the difficulty of retouching such a profile. Results of blank form analysis are shown in Figure 150. Comparison with blanks from W2 (1981), the Coneybury 'Anomaly' (this vol, 4.1 b), and from W83, Robin Hood's Ball (this vol, 4.2 b), show that the blanks at W31 are longer and narrower. They are also thinner, a feature noted for Late Neolithic scrapers at Durrington Walls (Wainwright and Longworth 1971, 168, fig 72) and the West Kennet Avenue (I F Smith 1965).

Comparison with sites on a wider scale can be made with published material. Groups at Durrington Walls, Windmill Hill, the West Kennet Avenue, and Hurst Fen (J G D Clark 1960) all averaged 40–45mm in length, as do those from the analysed Stonehenge Environs groups. The latter, however, have a greater average breadth than those from Durrington Walls.

Retouch location has been plotted but the results are inconclusive. All groups examined are dominated by end scrapers, often – for example W31 and W59 – with retouch extending round the right edge. This seems to result from manufacture or use rather than to indicate cultural differences. Scraper blade angle also differs insignificantly.

Arrowheads

Initial assessment of the 17 chisel arrowheads from W31 suggested that they formed a coherent group. They were consequently examined in some detail for consistent elements of manufacture.

Most butts have been removed by retouch, although some examples suggest that the blank originally had a crushed, linear, or punctiform butt, some of which were probably accidental. Flat, broad, unridged blanks with an upright profile were selected which have proportionally more scars at right angles to the axis of percussion (50%) than miscellaneous trimming flakes. This suggests that some blanks were more suitable than others. There is no evidence of employment of a Levallois technique (Manby 1974, Gardiner 1984), nor of deliberate blank manufacture. Selection could therefore have been made from the waste produced from discoidal cores, core tools, or from rejuvenation flakes.

Blanks were converted into arrowheads by retouching the ends, most commonly with straight or oblique truncations. The proximal end often required bifacial thinning (11 out of 13 examples), but the distal ends, which required less modification, were retouched either by direct flaking (6 out of 13 examples) or by bifacial flaking (6 out of 13 examples). There is no evidence that an anvil was used to support the blank. A disproportionate number of pieces were noted where the truncations converge on the left edge of the flake (13 out of 17 examples) to those on the right (2 out of 17 examples). The chisel arrowheads examined show consistency in size: 14 are between 20mm and 29mm in length (measured along the axis of percus-

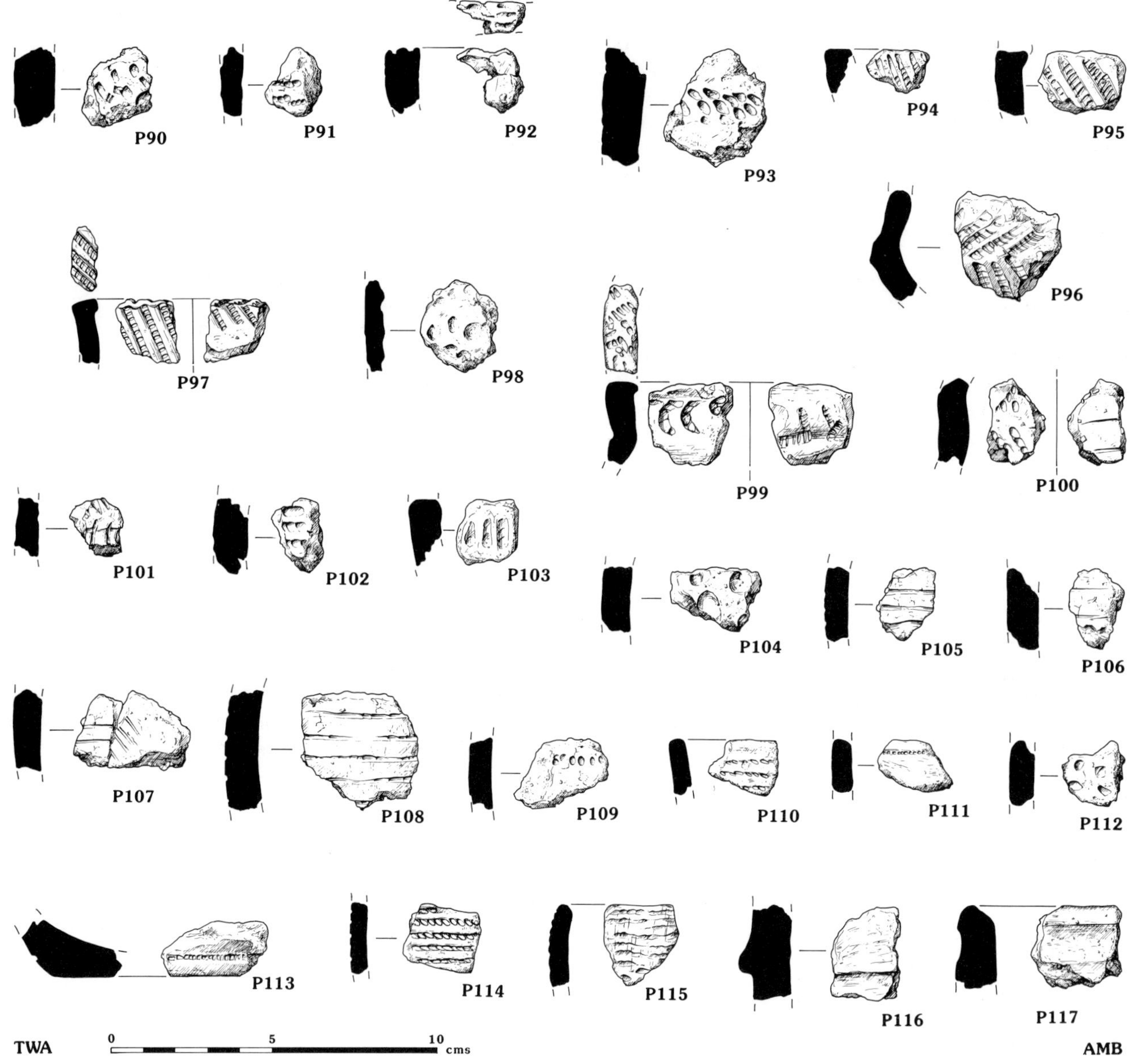

Fig 119 W31 Wilsford Down: prehistoric pottery (P90–P117)

sion), 9 are 30mm–39mm broad, and 9 are 5mm–7mm thick.

'Burins'

Eleven retouched pieces which appear to have been modified by a burin blow deserve comment (see Fig 118 for examples). The precise sequence of removals is occasionally unclear so that this may represent a maximum number. A truncation has been used in at least five pieces as deliberate preparation. Although the technique of manufacture seems to be consistent, their function as burins is doubtful and they can probably be regarded as representing a simple method of producing bladelets.

4.10 c The prehistoric pottery (Fig 119)

by Frances Raymond

A total of 161 sherds representing a minimum of 27 vessels was recovered. The degree of preservation exhibited by pottery from topsoil contexts is directly comparable with the more deeply stratified sherds from the sub-surface hollows. This reflects the nature of the deposits within these features which are not strictly stratified, but may represent a process of pedalogical sorting. The fragmentary condition, indicated by an average sherd weight of 2.15g, combined with the surface abrasion characteristic of this assemblage, seems likely to represent the effects of post-depositional attrition and modern agricultural activity. The Peterborough Wares in particular are far from robust, the clays being both insufficiently combined and poorly fired, factors which lead to laminar fracture and fairly rapid degradation under disturbed conditions.

With the exception of two Late Bronze Age sherds, the pottery can be attributed to the later Neolithic and Early Bronze Age. The fabrics of undiagnostic sherds, grouped together under the heading 'indeterminate', are broadly comparable with the Peterborough series, and are unlikely to include a later element. Although Peterborough Ware, Beaker, and Collared Urn occur within the same contexts, this is more likely to be indicative of the derived nature of the ploughsoil than of strict contemporaneity.

Numbers of decorated and undecorated sherds belonging to each ceramic group are shown in Figure 120, while Table 95 (MF2 C1–6) gives details of the division of each group into individual fabrics. The condition of the assemblage precludes comments concerning overall design configuration or vessel shape and, while individual rim forms have been illustrated, their size prevents an accurate assessment of diameter.

Peterborough Ware

A minimum of ten vessels are represented, all of which are likely to belong to the Ebbsfleet or Mortlake substyles. The unthickened rim forms of P97 and P99 are more typical of the Ebbsfleet substyle, although crescentic twisted cord impressions, such as those on P99, are normally found only on Mortlake Ware.

Two of the fabrics (FfeM:Pet/1 and FfeM:Pet/2) are unusual in the inclusion of mica within the clay paste. This also occurs in one of the Beaker fabrics (feGM:Bkr/2) and in a sherd which is of unusual form but likely to be of later Neolithic or Early Bronze Age date (P115 in M:Bkr/1).

The fabrics of the Peterborough Ware are mainly confined to W31, Wilsford Down, and The Diamond (59), the associated area of surface collection. The exception to this is fabric Ffe:Pet/1, which has a rather wider distribution within the Stonehenge area, occurring at W32, North of the Cursus (52), and at W53, adjacent to Robin Hood's Ball (Richards in prep a).

Later Neolithic/Early Bronze Age

A minimum of five vessels, each with a distinctive fabric, are represented. In the absence of any indication of form it was not possible to assign them with certainty to a specific ceramic group. CFfe:LN/EBA/1 shows greater affinities in fabric terms with Peterborough Ware, while the presence of grog in three of the fabrics (feG?:LN/EBA/1, feGS?:LN/EBA/1 and feGSV: LN/EBA/1), together with their general appearance, could be taken to indicate that they are more likely to belong to the Beaker than to the Peterborough series. In particular, P105 and P106 almost certainly belong to Beakers. The rim sherd P115 is unusual both in form and decoration, and does not appear to fall into either the Peterborough or Beaker traditions: the slightly inturned rim form and irregular grooved decoration is certainly not easily paralleled in either tradition, but the fabric may be later Neolithic or Early Bronze Age.

The question mark used in feG?:LN/EBA/1 and feGS?:LN?EBA/1 refers to the identification of crushed bluestone within the clay paste which requires confirmation by thin-sectioning.

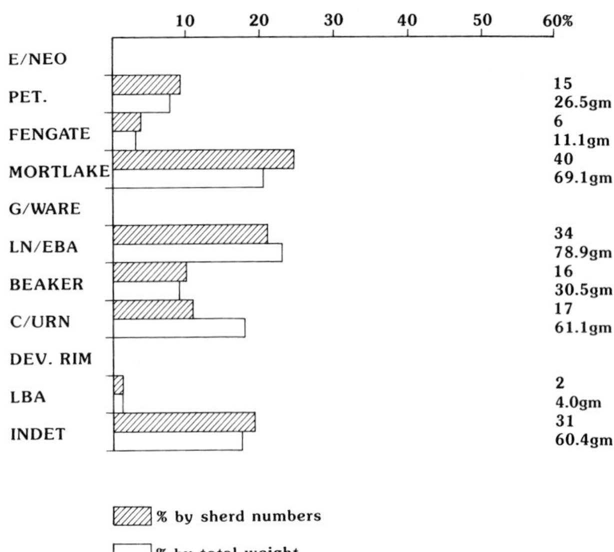

Fig 120 W31 Wilsford Down: prehistoric pottery fabric histogram

Beaker

A minimum of five vessels are represented, one of which belongs to the All Over Cord (AOC) subgroup (Clarke 1970). The size of sherds attributed to the remaining four vessels is only sufficient to allow for the identification of decorative technique and does not allow for classification to a particular Beaker style. However, the same fabrics (feG:Bkr/1 and feGM:Bkr/2) are found widely within the Stonehenge area at W32, W34, 55, Fargo Road (63), North of the Cursus (52), Cursus West End (62), Horse Hospital (64), and at W53 (Richards in prep a).

Collared Urn

One vessel is certainly represented by P116, which appears to be the base of a collar. P117, which is in the same fabric as P116, is of a form which it is not easy to envisage as part of a Collared Urn, but is almost certainly of later Neolithic or Early Bronze Age date.

Illustrated pottery (Fig 119)

Peterborough

P90 U/S
F:Pet/1. Body sherd. The decoration is indistinct but appears to be an impressed triangular motif.

P91 Area L, context 454
FfeM:Pet/2. Body sherd. Twisted cord impressions.

P92 Area L, context 460
FfeM:Pet/1. Rim sherd. Flattened top. Two abraded parallel linear impressions running along the top of the rim.

P93 Area G, context 310
Ffe:Pet/1. Body sherd. Six parallel crescentic twisted cord impressions arranged in a single narrow band.

P94 Area K, context 246
Ffe:Pet/1. Rim sherd. Expanded with flattened top. Five parallel twisted cord impressions set on a diagonal axis to the top of the rim.

P95 Area L, context 267
Ffe:Pet/1. Body sherd, probably from just below the shoulder. Three parallel whipped cord impressions.

P96 Area L, context 454
Ffe:Pet/1. Shoulder. Parallel whipped cord impressions arranged to produce a herringbone pattern.

P97 Area L, context 454
F:Pet/2. Rim sherd. Expanded with flattened top. Parallel whipped cord impressions set on a diagonal axis on the interior and exterior of the vessel and on the top of the rim.

P98 Area T, context 429
CFS:Pet/1. Body sherd. Sub-circular impressed motif.

P99 Area T, context 438
CFS:Pet/1. Rim sherd. Flattened and expanded internally. Whipped cord impressions arranged in an uneven herringbone or chevron pattern on the exterior of the vessel and on the top of the rim. Four parallel crescentic twisted cord impressions arranged in a narrow band on the interior of the vessel. The decoration on the top of the rim may change around the circumference as there appears to be at least one crescentic impression.

P100 Area T, context 466
CFS:Pet/1. Sherd from the concave neck of a vessel. Abraded linear impressions arranged in a herringbone pattern on the interior.

P101 Area T, context 466
Ffe:Pet/1. Body sherd. The decoration is of very fine twisted cord impression.

P102 Area K, context 257
F:Pet/3. Body sherd. Three parallel oblique twisted cord impressions.

P103 Area K, context 258
F:Pet/3. Body sherd. Four parallel twisted cord impressions arranged in short lengths.

Late Neolithic/Early Bronze Age

P104 Area F, context 142
feGS?:LN/EBA/1. Body sherd. Three sub-circular impressions, possibly the result of fingertipping.

P105 Area R, context 478
feG?:LN/EBA/1. Body sherd. Parallel linear incisions. Probably Beaker.

P106 Area R, context 480
feG?:LN/EBA/1. Body sherd. Parallel linear incisions. Probably Beaker.

P107 Area T, context 433
feG?:LN/EBA/1. Body sherd. Parallel linear incisions possibly arranged in a herringbone pattern.

P108 Area T, context 466
CFfe:LN/EBA/1. Body sherd. Five parallel incised lines.

P109 Area T, context 466
feG?:LN/EBA/1. Body sherd. Six circular stabbed impressions arranged to form a row.

Beaker

P110 Area A, context 22
feGS:Bkr/1. Rim sherd. Rounded with slight internal bevel. Three parallel horizontal twisted cord impressions. All Over Corded.

P111 Area C, context 67
feG:Bkr/1. Body sherd. Very small square-toothed-comb impressions.

P112 Area E, context 129
feGM:Bkr/2. Body sherd. Paired non-plastic fingernail impressions; orientation of the sherd is not certain.

P113 Area E, context 169
feGM:Bkr/2. Base sherd. Square-toothed-comb impressions.

P114 Area L, context 265
feGS:Bkr/1. Body sherd. Five parallel twisted cord impressions. All Over Corded.

Late Neolithic/Early Bronze Age

P115 Area T, context 526
M:Bkr/1. Rim sherd. Asymmetrically rounded. Eight parallel horizontal lines in irregular grooving.

Collared Urn

P116 Area D, context 33
CfeG:CU/1. Sherd probably from the base of a concave collar.

Late Neolithic/Early Bronze Age

P117 Area S, context 449
CfeG:CU/1. Rim sherd. Rounded with internal bevel and concave external surface below the lip of the rim.

4.10 d Animal bones
by Mark Maltby

Only two contexts produced animal bones. Six bones of a rabbit (os coxae, both femora and tibiae, and a metatarsal) were recovered from context 302. These were modern intrusions into the deposits. An upper tooth of a pig and a severely eroded unidentifiable fragment of a large mammal were found in context 542. Both fragments were recovered from 1mm wet-sieving and both were slightly charred. The bones from this site were not computer-recorded.

4.11 W57, Durrington Down round barrow and its immediate environs

4.11 a Site description

Surface collection in Fargo Road (63) during December 1982 produced a nucleated scatter of Middle to Late

Bronze Age pottery at SU 11424432, immediately adjacent to round barrow Durrington 7. The barrow, previously recorded as destroyed and of indeterminate size (Wilts SMR 14 SW 625), appeared at the time of field survey as an almost imperceptible rise in the surface of the arable field, coincident with a dense scatter of flint nodules. The scatters of both pottery and of flint nodules were sketch plotted at this time and a wide and shallow depression to the north-east of the 'mound' was also noted. As this did not appear to encircle the scatter of flint nodules it was assumed not to be an associated ditch.

Prior to excavation the extent of the flint nodule scatter was plotted at the same time as the area of the barrow was contour surveyed (Fig 121).

Sample design

The sample excavation was originally designed to examine only the pottery scatter, initially interpreted as representing an urnfield, an unusual occurrence within the immediate environs of Stonehenge. This was to be sampled by means of a single trench (area A), 12m by 7m in size. However, during the course of excavation the sample was extended to include both elements of the barrow itself and the adjacent depression (area B). This single sample trench was initially placed to examine one segment of the mound and the adjacent hollow, but was later extended to examine the central area and southerly limits of the former. A wider contextual sample was provided by means of ten randomly selected squares, each 2m by 2m (areas C–M), intended to examine the immediate context of the barrow mound and 'urnfield' area. The overall sampling and topsoil sieving strategy is shown in Figure 121.

The ploughsoil within all areas was hand excavated on a 1m grid, with a 25% sample, applied by area, sieved through a 4mm sieve. This ploughsoil excavation programme produced the range of artefacts discussed below.

Ploughsoil artefact distributions

Pottery

Area A produced considerable quantities of pottery, primarily of Middle to Late Bronze Age date, but including small quantities of Saxon material (Raymond, this vol, 4.11 c). The comparative distributions by weight of Middle to Late Bronze Age pottery and of individual sherds, including Late Neolithic/Early Bronze Age and Saxon material, is shown in Figure 122. Within the areas sampled, data both from area B and from the random contextual sample confirm the restricted distribution of the main Bronze Age pottery scatter, clustered to the north-north-west of the barrow mound.

Although only six sherds of Late Neolithic/Early Bronze Age pottery were recovered, their distribution, in contrast to the later material, is exclusively within an area to the west, south-west, and south of the barrow, and includes one sherd on the barrow mound. This pottery, which may be associated with phases of construction and primary use of the barrow (see below, primary burial) cannot be assigned with any certainty to any particular style (Raymond, this vol, 4.11 c).

The distribution of the Saxon pottery (total weight 63g) is entirely coincident with that of the main scatter of Middle to Late Bronze Age pottery centred on area A.

Lithics

The majority of the flint assemblage (approximately 5000 pieces) was recovered from the ploughsoil, where recorded numbers were generally low and, within the sampled areas, showed little spatial variation (Fig 123, MF2 C7). One low level concentration can be suggested in the southern part of area A and to the south, where higher levels of total flint are associated with flint tools. The other, more defined, concentration lies on the edge of the barrow mound within area B. Here, flake levels of over 100 pieces per m^2, including a small number of tools, may suggest that the flint cairn has been exploited as a source of raw material. Although there is a potential circularity of argument in the identification of a similar raw material for both cairn construction and knapping, the association has previously been recorded (Fasham and Ross 1978) and, at W57, the clustering of knapping activity appears to support the suggestion.

Burnt flint

Little specific patterning is evident with the exception of a small cluster of values over 300g per m^2 on the northern edge of the surviving barrow mound (Fig 124, MF2 C8).

Burnt bone

Small quantities of burnt bone, some positively identified as human (Henderson, this vol, 4.11 e), were recovered from ploughsoil excavation. The distribution of burnt bone, major elements of which demonstrate a very positive association with pit 225, is shown in Figure 129. Pit 225, which contained a large sample of burnt bone, was undisturbed by agricultural activity and therefore not responsible for the scatter of burnt bone within the nearby ploughsoil. Other, more minor, occurrences of burnt bone cannot positively be identified as human but suggest the possibility of a number of token deposits both on and around the barrow.

Sealed deposits

As no subsoil features were recorded within either area A or any of the 2m random sample squares, the discussion of stratified deposits refers only to area B. Here the removal of modern ploughsoil revealed both elements of the barrow structure and burial features which, in the absence of stratigraphic relationship, are suggested as secondary to the construction of the barrow.

The structure of the barrow

The central area of the barrow mound, originally defined by both contour survey and the greatest density of surface flint nodules, appeared, on removal of the ploughsoil, as a small patch of *in situ* flint nodules (Fig 125). The surviving pattern of the nodules, further

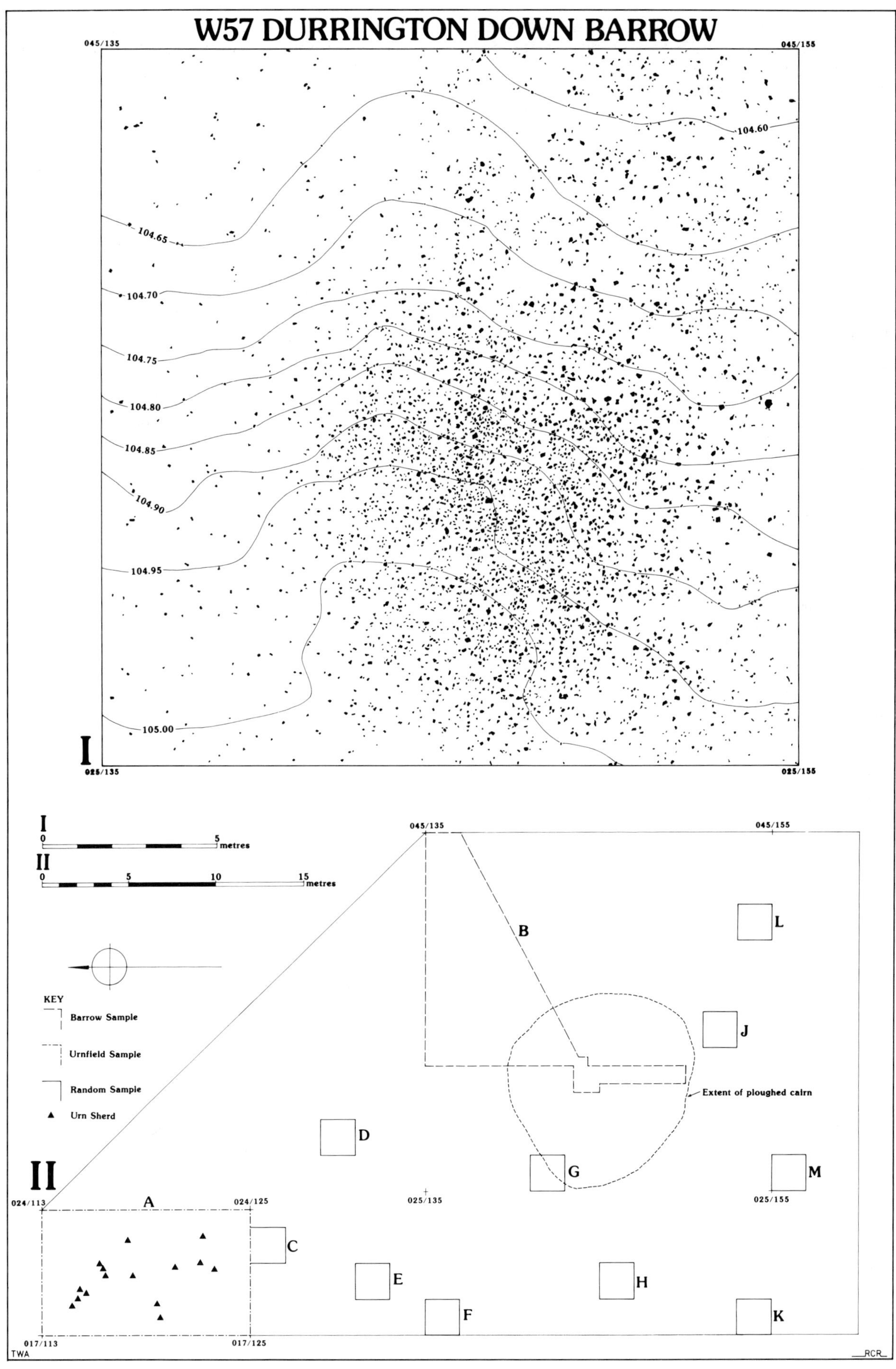

Fig 121 W57 Durrington Down barrow: pre-excavation contour and flint nodule plan, and sample design

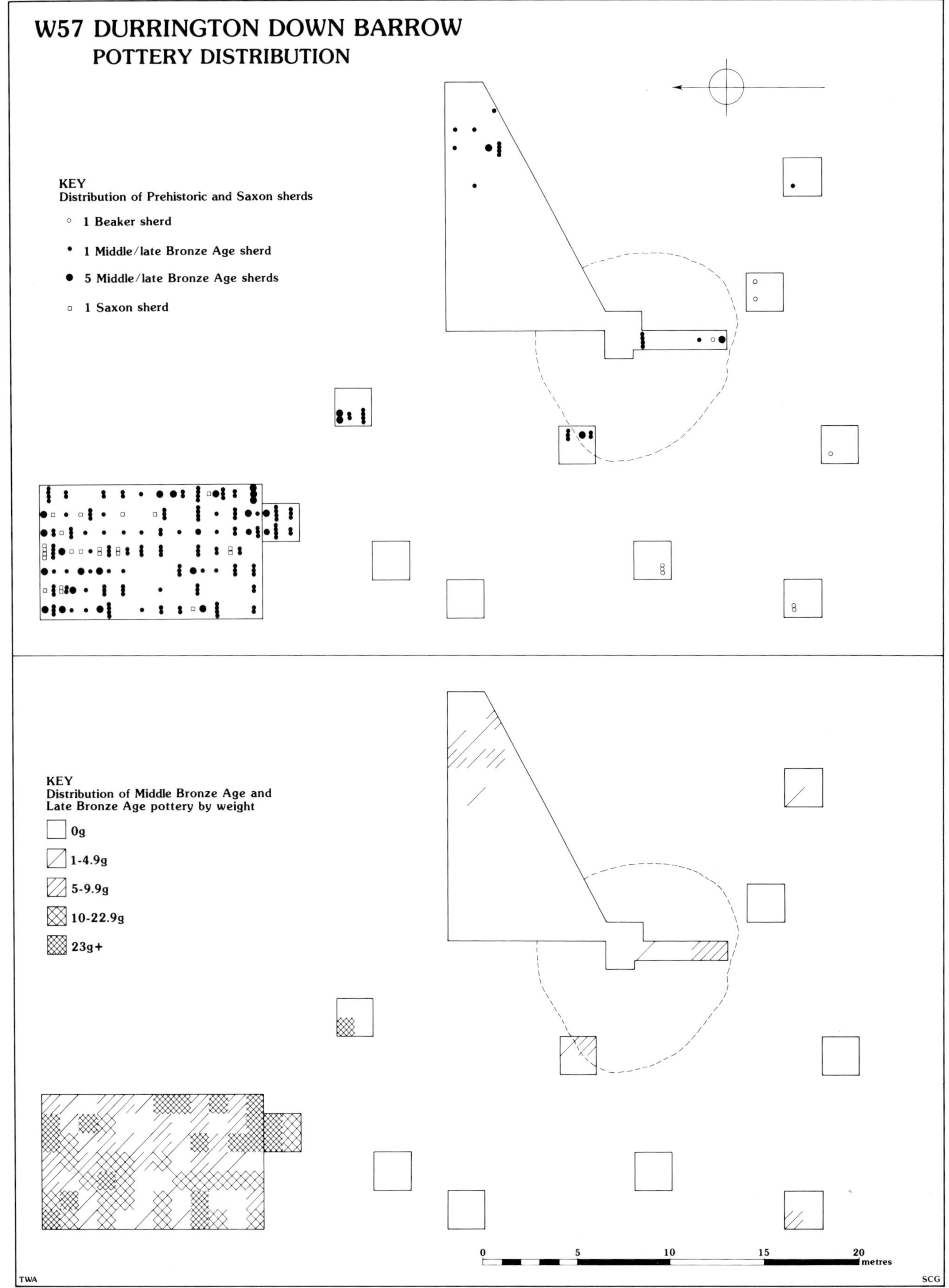

Fig 122 W57 Durrington Down barrow: distribution of prehistoric and Saxon pottery from ploughsoil excavation

defined by the extension of area B to the south, suggested a circular arrangement, approximately 8m in overall diameter. The nodules which survived *in situ* surrounded a relatively flint-free area approximately 3m in diameter. This was initially interpreted as the product of more abrasive ploughing of the summit of the mound, but may equally suggest that the original form of the flint cairn was annular.

The removal of the remains of the flint cairn revealed a corresponding area of reddish-brown clay silt buried soil (context 240), on which were three sherds of pottery (one Late Neolithic/Early Bronze Age and three Barrel Urn fabric), together with small deposits of burnt bone, none of which could be positively identified as human (Henderson, this vol, 4.11 e). The extent of context 240, at least 11m in diameter, may provide a more realistic estimate of the original overall dimension of the barrow structure.

The initial appearance of the buried soil suggested that the fragmentary deposits of both pottery and burnt bone may have represented all that remained of the primary burial record of the barrow. However, repeated cleaning revealed the edges of a substantial oval feature, cut 251, lying only partly within the excavated area. The difficulty of recognising the edges of this feature may suggest an alternative interpretation for the structure of the flint cairn, that the central flint-free area represents an unrecorded antiquarian central excavation which stopped at the old ground surface.

On excavation the central feature proved to be a substantial and steep-sided oval grave pit, approximately 2.5m long, 1.5m wide, and 1.4m deep (Fig 125). The pit fill consisted of a mixture of redeposited clay soil, coombe rock, and chalk, within which were a large cattle lumbar vertebra and a fragment of antler (Maltby, this vol, 4.11 d). The grave appeared disproportionately large for the burial it contained (Figs 125 and 126), the crouched inhumation of a juvenile, sex not assessed (Henderson, this vol, 4.11 e). A sample of bone from the inhumation produced a radiocarbon date of 2275–1958 BC (OxA 1398). Buried with its head to the east, and with knees and one arm flexed, the inhumation was accompanied by a deposit of burnt bone (context 254) in a restricted area to the rear of the pelvis and by objects of antler and bone approximately 0.15m from the feet. The burnt bone represents the apparently complete and well-cremated remains of a further juvenile, aged approximately five to ten years. No assessment was made of sex (Henderson, this vol, 4.11 e). The closely defined area within which the cremated bone lay may suggest that it was deposited in an organic container. The objects of bone and of antler, both somewhat unusual, appear to be deliberate deposits within the grave. The bone (SF189) is a thoracic vertebra from an animal comparable in size to an aurochs (Maltby, this vol, 4.11 d) and the object of red deer antler (SF190), a portion of the stem and the base of the trez tine, appears to show signs of use or wear (Fig 132). In the absence of any obvious function, and in the light of the age of both the individuals within the grave, it seems reasonable to suggest that the antler object may have been a toy.

Secondary features

Three subsoil features were located to the north-east of the barrow mound within area B. These features are located on Figure 129, with sections on Figure 127, and will be described in context order.

Pit 225 was circular and bowl-profiled, approximately 1.0m in diameter and 0.4m deep. The fill, a fine brown soil (context 226), overlay a deposit of burnt bone (SF175), weighing 2950g. This deposit appears to represent a minimum number of three individuals: two adults, one possibly male, and a juvenile (Henderson, this vol, 4.11 e). The deposit of burnt bone appeared to be intact and undisturbed by either ploughing or animal activity.

Pit 230 originally appeared as a circular feature, approximately 1m in diameter, the upper fill of which was a brown silty soil, context 231. Below this the pit fill consisted of a deep deposit of flint nodules, context 235, in a silty clay soil matrix. This flint packing contained a cattle skull (SF174), from an animal considerably smaller than that represented by the vertebrae in the primary burial. The removal of context 235 showed the pit to be approximately 0.9m deep with edges slightly undercut in part. At the base of the pit lay the crouched inhumation of an adult male (Fig 128), aged about 35–45 years and showing little evidence of joint disease (Henderson, this vol 4.11 e). The uncomfortably compressed nature of this burial, a feature more of inadequate grave-pit size than apparent trussing, contrasts strongly with the more spacious primary grave.

Pit 241 lay immediately adjacent to the northern edge of area B. It appears that it may be a roughly circular feature, approximately 0.75m in diameter and a maximum of 0.4m deep, with its eastern side cut through a natural feature. This resulted in the somewhat irregular profile shown in Figure 127, where the maximum east–west dimension is approximately 1.2m. The fill of this feature, context 242, consisted of a brown soil with an admixture of both natural flints and of 'pea gravel', natural small rounded chalk lumps. This feature also contained the top of a red deer antler (SF179).

Discussion

The original morphology of the barrow is difficult to reconstruct from the excavated sample of its much abraded remains. The primary phase, however, appears to consist of an unditched cairn of flint nodules, either annular or circular in form, lying adjacent to an apparently natural subsoil hollow, the position of which would have enhanced the apparent height of the cairn. This form of construction is unusual for the Stonehenge area, where earthen round barrows, either ditched or unditched, are the norm. The cairn at W57 may be suggested as embodying two linked functions, the definition of a funerary site, and potentially an element of clearance for cultivation purposes. Evidence from aerial photographs suggests that the barrow is integrated with elements of 'Celtic' fields (RCHME 1979, map 1).

The dating of the primary burial is consistent with the few radiocarbon determinations previously obtained for Early Bronze Age burials from the area (Figure 155),

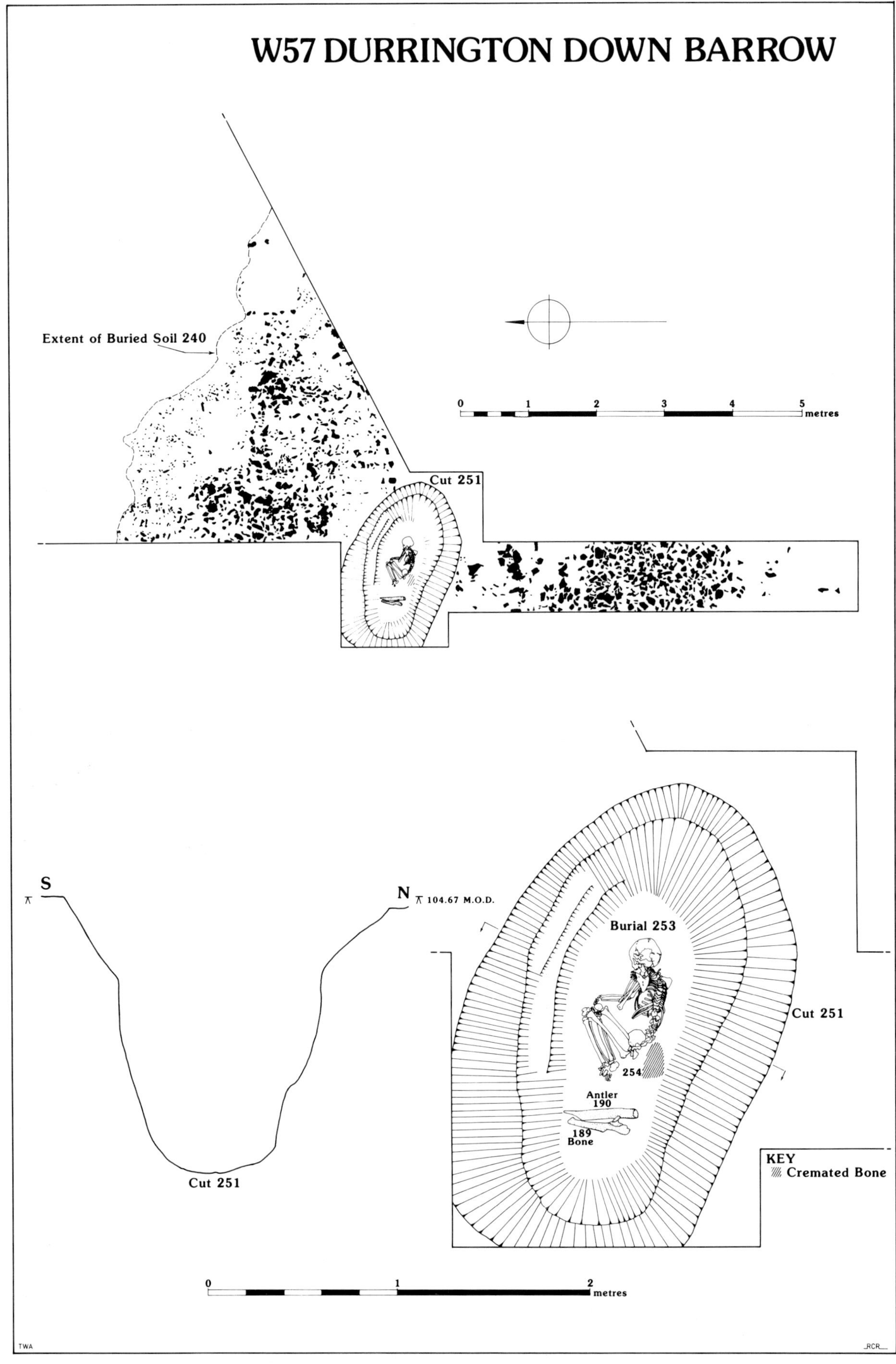

Fig 125 W57 Durrington Down barrow: plan of surviving barrow elements and detail of primary inhumation

Fig 126 W57 Durrington Down barrow: primary inhumation and associated cremation deposit (scale 30cm)

both those from beneath barrows and the example from the Stonehenge ditch.

The primary grave group, while not unusual in its association of inhumation and cremation, included what must be regarded as deliberately deposited objects of unusual type (see below and Fig 132). A combination of the requirements of nineteenth-century excavation, and the lack of more recent work, may, however, be factors in determining the rarity of such items.

The excavation of the ploughsoil has introduced a range of otherwise irrecoverable potential events and activities into the overall site record. The discussion below of the sealed deposits demonstrates, from the small excavated sample, the potential for the recovery of secondary activity centred on round barrows. In many cases there appears to be no direct correlation between the activities suggested by the two differing elements of the site record.

Within area A and immediately adjacent sample areas, the material within the ploughsoil constituted the entire record. Here, the concentration of pottery was unassociated with either positive evidence for secondary burial, or with burnt bone from the ploughsoil. In the absence of evidence which may suggest a more domestic explanation for this material, the area may be suggested as one reserved for the surface deposition of pottery potentially with funerary associations.

Within area B the record from the ploughsoil is both more complex and must be assessed together with the data from sealed deposits discussed above. Figure 129 shows the features from this area, together with an interpretation of the combined ploughsoil artefact distributions. The ploughsoil immediately adjacent to pit 225 produced both pottery of Middle/Late Bronze Age date and additional burnt bone. This association may suggest the potential ploughsoil record of a disturbed inurned cremation.

4.11 b Lithics

The excavation produced a total of 4896 pieces of worked flint (Table 96), over 95% of which was recovered from the ploughsoil. In the absence of stratified groups, material has only been examined for the production of a Stage 1 catalogue (carried out by Mark Edmonds), including observations which are incorporated within this summary.

The breakdown of excavated lithic material by sample area is shown in Table 96, which shows variation within the 2m by 2m sample squares (areas C to M) of between 30 and 101 pieces.

Within the two more extensive sample areas some distinction can be noted between the material from area A (originally defined as the 'urnfield') and that from area B, the barrow mound and its immediate context.

Within area A, a small number of broken blades were noted, none showing any evidence of reworking (for example, breaks through patina). These may suggest a small residual Neolithic element within what appears to be a much later industry, potentially late within the Bronze Age. Flakes show a high incidence of hinge fractures and virtually no evidence of platform preparation. Numbers of tools, particularly scrapers, are high from this area, but their production appears to have been on an expedient basis, with little control exercised over final form.

A similar potentially residual element was recorded within area B, again largely characterised by broken blades, but here associated with core trimming flakes and platform preparation flakes. Some evidence of knapping involving the exploitation of nodules incorporated into the barrow cairn was recorded. This exploitation appears largely to involve the testing of nodules and, in the absence of specific core preparation, can be suggested as considerably postdating the primary construction of the barrow.

Although some limited refitting potential was identified within the assemblage from area B, a subsequent stage of analysis was considered inappropriate as part of the initial stage of project lithic analysis.

4.11 c The prehistoric and Saxon pottery (Fig 130)

by Frances Raymond

A total of 373 sherds, representing a minimum number of 18 vessels, was recovered. The nature of this ceramic group is likely to have contributed to the low estimate of vessel numbers. Only 7% of the assemblage comprises featured sherds (a total of 25, of which 17 are illustrated), while each piece has a relatively low average weight of 4g. The calculations made to determine the minimum numbers of vessels are, therefore, based upon fabric differences (16); vessel thickness FfeS:DR/1 was used to produce at least two vessels, the first with walls measuring 4–8mm; and the second with walls measuring 9–14mm); and rim form FSV:DR/1 was used to produce at least two vessels, the first with a flattened top and convex external surface (P246, P247, and P252), and the second with a rounded top, an internal bevel, and a convex external surface (P250).

The assemblage comprises four ceramic groups (Fig 131 and Table 97, MF2 D1–8), which include Beaker, Deverel-Rimbury, Late Bronze Age, and Saxon, each of which is discussed below.

Later Neolithic/Early Bronze Age

This is represented by a total of six very abraded sherds, which may come from a single vessel with a wall thickness of between 6 and 11mm. The sherds have a very low average weight of 3.8g and provide little information concerning form, while abrasion of the outer surface has obscured details of decoration. Although the type of fabric, as well as the colour and feel of the sherds, would be quite acceptable as Beaker, the pointed rim and the position of the decorative motif distinguishes P240 from comparable Beaker material discussed in this volume. In addition, although twisted cord impression does occur on Beakers, the thickness of the cord used in this case is quite unlike the fine cord normally used on AOC Beakers. A similarity with Food Vessels can be suggested, but not confirmed. The absence of any grog within the fabric (feM:Bkr/1) is also unusual. The occurrence of mica within Beaker fabrics

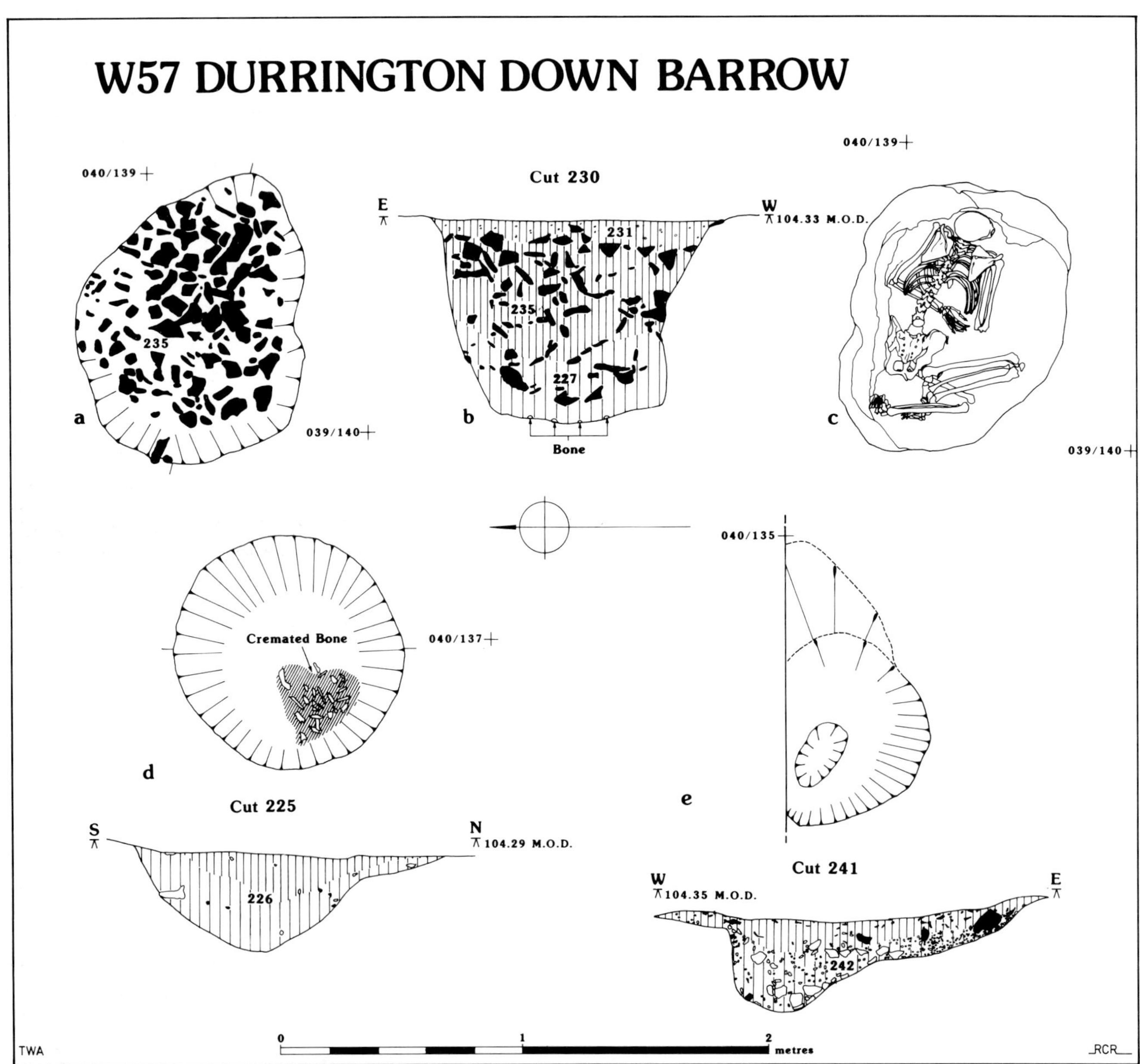

Fig 127 W57 Durrington Down barrow: plans and section of associated burial features

Fig 128 W57 Durrington Down barrow: secondary inhumation (scale 30cm)

has been noted at a number of sites within the Stonehenge Environs Project area.

The sherds within this group have a limited distribution within the excavated areas, occurring within areas B, H, J, K, and M (Fig 122).

Deverel-Rimbury

The Deverel-Rimbury pottery consists of a total of 334 sherds representing a minimum number of 12 vessels. Only 6% of this assemblage comprises featured sherds, while body fragments with an average weight of 3.3g provide a restricted range of information concerning form.

The fabrics (Tables 31, 97, MF1 B9–12, MF2 D1–8) are used to produce relatively thin-walled vessels with measurements which range between 4mm and 10mm. The exception is FfeS:DR/1, which is also used for vessels with walls up to 14mm thick. There is no information concerning the form of vessels represented by fabrics FfeV:DR/1, FV:DR/1, feSV:DR/1, and Ssh:DR/1, which compare most closely with the clay pastes used to produce Deverel-Rimbury ceramics.

Of the Deverel-Rimbury assemblage, 45% is composed of sherds belonging to the fabric group FSV:DR/1. As might be expected, this group includes the largest number of featured sherds. These indicate at least two vessels, distinguished from one another by variations in rim form. One example has a flattened top, a very slight internal bevel, and a convex external surface (P246); the second (P250) has a rounded top, a more pronounced internal bevel, and a convex external surface (a similar rim form also occurred in a vessel, P254, made from the fabric FfeS:DR/2). These rim forms are accompanied by sherds made from the same fabric, but with horizontal cordons. The proportion of the body of the vessel surviving on either side of the cordon is sufficient (in a few examples) to suggest that this type of decoration was applied to pottery which appears to be characterised by one of two profiles. The first is more typical of thin-walled Barrel or Bucket Urns with straight and upright profiles (eg P243), which have been noted on other sites in central Wessex. The second (eg P249) is allied with the plain ware tradition of Class 1 jars discussed below. Unlike the Late Bronze Age assemblage from Fargo Wood II (W34), however, the fabrics used are particularly vesicular. The general impression is of a ceramic group which occupies a transitional position between classic Deverel-Rimbury forms and the Class 1 jars characteristic of the Late Bronze Age. The remaining rim forms, illustrated in Figure 130, support this suggestion.

Of the pottery belonging to this ceramic group, 80% (calculation based on sherd weight) was recovered from area A, 9% from area B, 7% from area C, and smaller quantities from areas D, G, K, and L. The decrease in quantity is accompanied by a decrease in the number of fabrics represented within each area: eight in area A, three in area C, and one each in areas D, G, K, and L. For detailed information concerning the distribution of the fabric groups by context see Table 97 (MF2 D1–8).

Table 96 W57 Durrington Down barrow: composition of the flint assemblage

Area	*Cores*	*Core fragments*	*Flakes*	*Broken flakes*	*Burnt worked flint*	*Retouched flakes*	*Scrapers*	*Other tools*	*Total*
A	6	21	573	296	6	43	12	6	963
B	71	67	1867	1245	49	67	19	5	3390
C	1	1	46	20	–	2	1	1	72
D	2	1	25	17	1	4	1	–	51
E	1	1	29	15	3	1	–	1	51
F	–	3	24	5	–	–	–	–	32
G	1	1	58	33	–	1	–	–	94
H	1	–	20	11	–	–	–	–	32
J	1	–	24	8	1	–	–	1	35
K	–	4	50	27	16	2	1	1	101
L	2	–	12	13	3	–	–	–	30
M	–	2	33	6	3	1	–	–	45
Total	86	101	2761	1696	82	121	34	15	4896

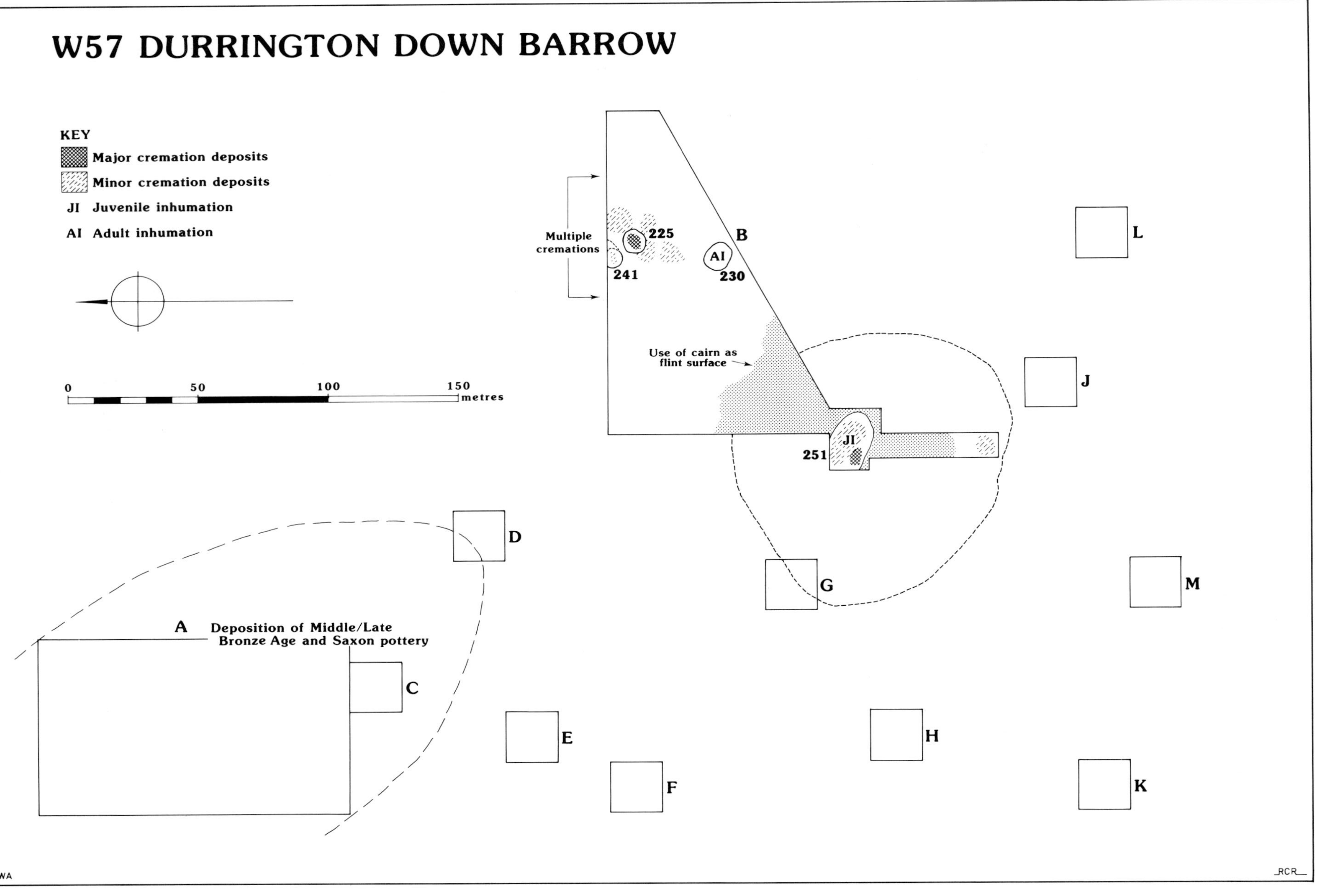

Fig 129 W57 Durrington Down barrow: overall interpretation plan

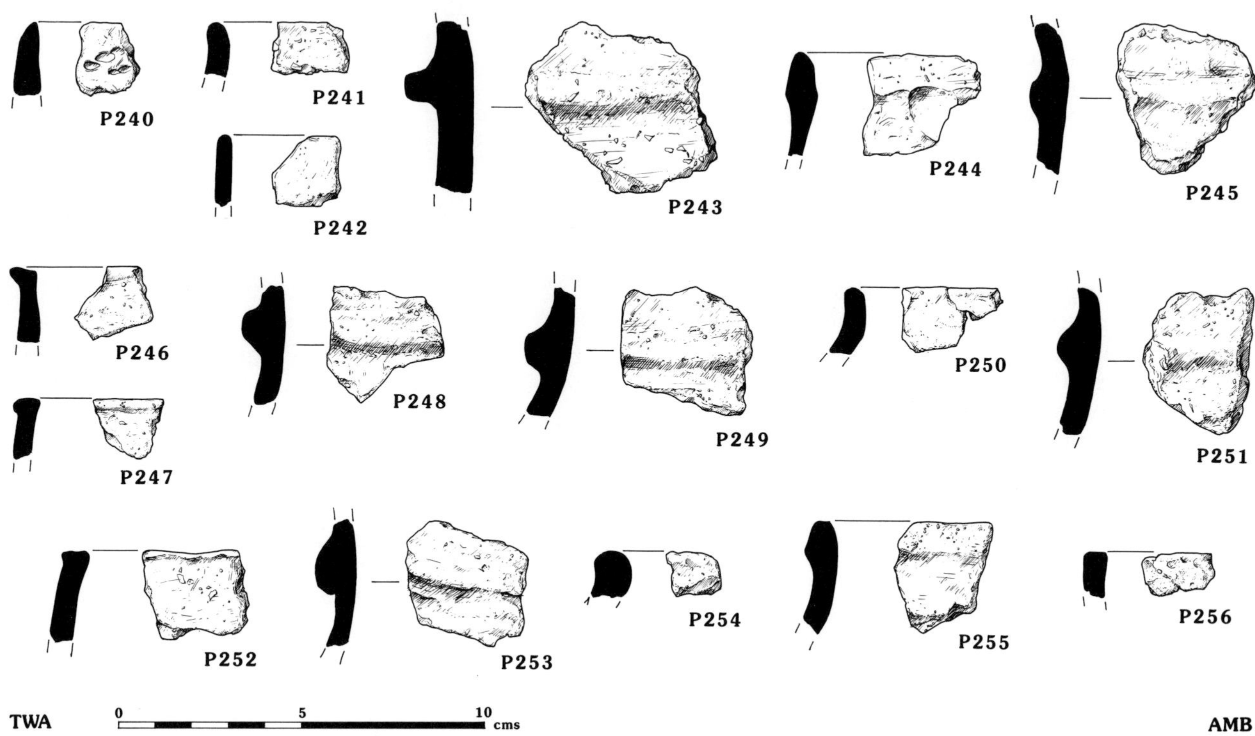

Fig 130 W57 Durrington Down barrow: prehistoric and Saxon pottery (P240–P256)

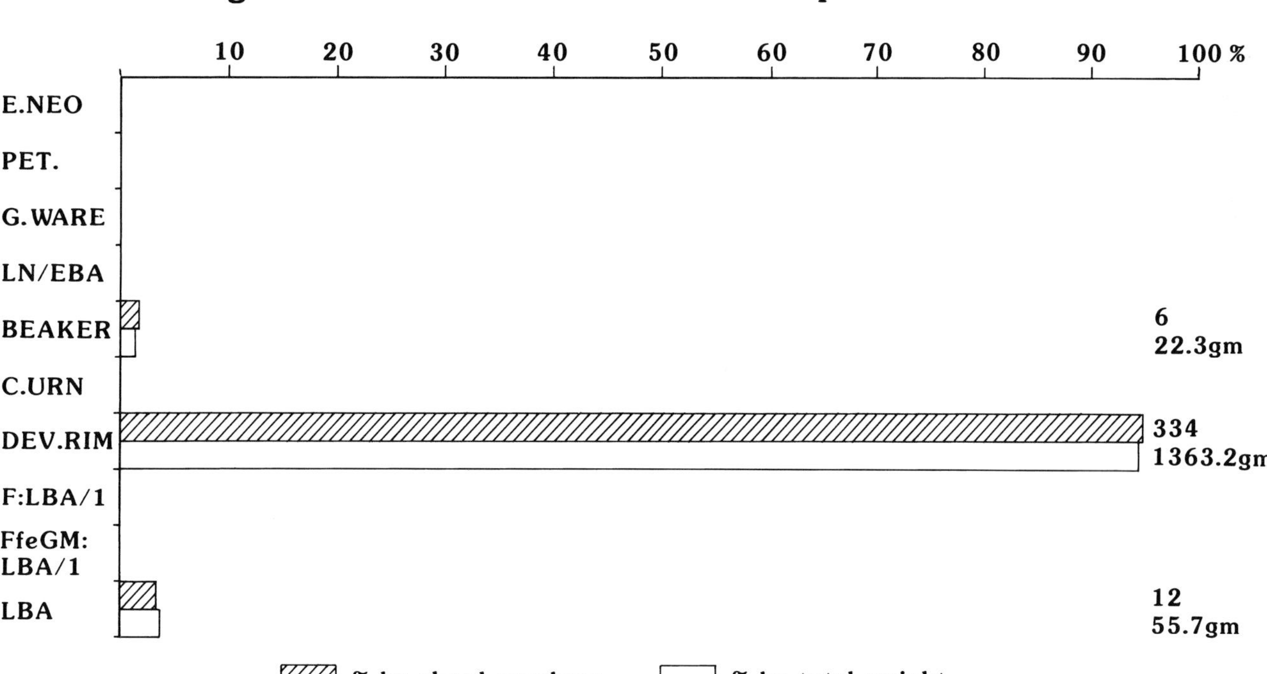

Fig 131 W57 Durrington Down barrow: prehistoric and Saxon pottery fabric histogram

Late Bronze Age

This group comprises a total of 12 sherds which represent a minimum number of four vessels. Each vessel is distinguished purely on the grounds of fabric differences. With the exception of one rim fragment (P255), the sherds are featureless and provide little information concerning vessel form. Fortunately, they are paralleled by identical fabrics at W34 Fargo Wood II (this vol, 4.14 c), which are used to produce jars typical of the Late Bronze Age plain ware assemblages identified by Barrett in the Thames Valley (1980). In Wessex comparable assemblages are poorly researched and the chronology is uncertain. On some sites Late Bronze Age ceramics are found in conjunction with Deverel-Rimbury pottery (Barrett and Bradley 1980, 199), a pattern which is repeated at W34. All of these examples, however, including W34, involve pottery from unstratified (usually ploughsoil) contexts and the degree of contemporaneity is therefore uncertain.

The fabrics used to produce this pottery (FfeSV: LBA/2, FS:LBA/3, FSV:LBA/1, and FV:LBA/1) are well fired and robust, while the interior and exterior surfaces appear to have been highly smoothed. Two of the clay pastes (FfeSV:LBA/2 and FSV:LBA/1) are distinctive in the inclusion of large quantities of finely crushed flint as a filler.

The distribution of the Late Bronze Age pottery is confined to area A.

Saxon

This is represented by a total of 22 sherds with an average weight of 2.8g and a wall thickness of between 4mm and 8mm. The variation in these measurements can be accounted for by changes in the width of the vessel at different points in its profile, and by the nature of handmade pottery. In the absence of evidence to the contrary, it is assumed that these sherds represent a single vessel.

Apart from a slight curvature on one of the larger body sherds there is no information concerning form. A single rim with a flattened top (P256) accounts for the only featured sherd.

All of these sherds are made from a single fabric (feMV:Saxon/1). Both surfaces of the pottery are crossed by a series of grass/stalk impressions, while numerous voids seen in section imply that a similar vegetable filler occurs throughout the clay paste. The occurrence of mica within the clay paste implies that the vessel was produced outside the immediate locality.

The distribution of the fabric feMV:Saxon/1 is confined to area A.

Illustrated pottery (Fig 130)

Later Neolithic/Early Bronze Age

P240 Area , context 214
feM:Bkr/1. Rim sherd. Pointed. Twisted cord impression set obliquely below rim.

Deverel-Rimbury

P241 Area A, context 12
FfeS:DR/1. Rim sherd. Rounded. Barrel Urn related vessel.

P242 Area A, context 18
FS:DR/1. Rim sherd. Flattened top. Barrel Urn related vessel.

P243 Area A, context 21
Ffe:DR/1. Body sherd with cordon. Barrel Urn related vessel.

P244 Area A, context 45
FfeMV:DR/1. Rim sherd. Pointed with internal bevel. Barrel Urn related vessel. Exterior badly abraded.

P245 Area A, context 49
FSV:DR/1. Body sherd with cordon. Barrel Urn related vessel.

P246 Area A, context 53
FSV:DR/1. Rim sherd. Flattened top with a slight inward slope and convex external surface. Barrel Urn related vessel.

P247 Area A, context 60
FSV:DR/1. Rim sherd. Flattened top with convex external surface. Barrel Urn related vessel.

P248 Area A, context 60
FSV:DR/1. Body sherd with cordon. Barrel Urn related vessel.

P249 Area A, context 67
FSV:DR/1. Body sherd with cordon. Barrel Urn related vessel.

P250 Area A, context 83
FSV:DR/1. Rim sherd. Rounded with internal bevel and convex external surface. Barrel Urn related vessel.

P251 Area A, context 84
FSV:DR/1. Body sherd with cordon. Barrel Urn related vessel.

P252 Area C, context 170
FSV:DR/1. Rim sherd. Flattened top with convex external surface. Barrel Urn related vessel.

P253 Area C, context 172
FfeS:DR/2. Body sherd with cordon. Barrel Urn related vessel.

P254 Area C, context 172
FfeS:DR/2. Rim sherd. Rounded with internal bevel and convex external surface. Barrel Urn related vessel.

Later Bronze Age

P255 Area A, context 12
FfeSV:LBA/2. Rim sherd. Everted with flattened top and external bevel.

Saxon

P256 Area A, context 10
feMV:Saxon/1. Rim sherd. Flattened top.

4.11 d Animal bones and worked bone
by Mark Maltby and Julian Richards

The 73 animal bone fragments which were recovered are shown in Table 98. The bones from the topsoil are best discounted, since many of them had a modern appearance and four had modern styles of butchery marks on them.

A few animal bones were recovered from features within area B. Context 225 contained a cattle metacarpus with an unfused distal articulation, a fragment of cattle horn core, and a sheep/goat tooth. Context 230, which contained the secondary inhumation, also produced the fragmented remains of a cattle skull, a fragment of ilium, and most of a thoracic vertebrae, also of cattle. The cattle skull belonged to a relatively small animal. Its horn core had a maximum width of 47.3mm and a basal circumference of *c* 125mm. This was smaller than any of the Neolithic horn core measurements of domestic cattle presented by Grigson (1982b, 28), although the skull belonged to an adult animal. Sheep/goat was represented by two loose teeth and the distal half of a maxilla. The two bones of water vole were probably intrusive. The only identifiable bones from contexts 241 and 245 were the top of a red deer antler and a small fragment of red deer antler tine respectively.

The primary grave fill, context 251, produced a small tip of an antler (with a modern break) and a much larger portion of the stem and the base of the trez tine of a red deer antler. It also contained a thoracic and lumbar vertebra of cattle. Both of these belonged to large animals, particularly when compared to the cattle sample from context 230. The thoracic vertebra was comparable in size to an aurochs (*Bos primigenius*).

Worked antler

Context 255, SF190 (Fig 132)

Object of worn and broken antler, accompanying the primary (central) inhumation (Figs 125 and 126). The lower end (as drawn) appears to have been snapped and also shows signs of scorching. The other end appears to have been at least partly sawn, resulting in a straight edge around *c* 40% of the circumference. This end also exhibits considerable wear, including a recessed diagonal groove. The function, if any, of this object is uncertain. That it was in some way significant appears to be suggested by its inclusion as the only object to be directly associated with the burial.

4.11 e The human bone
by Janet Henderson

Two skeletons and a number of samples of burnt bone were examined. Examination of the remains showed that both skeletons were nearly complete, but that with the exception of two samples (contexts 226 and 254) the material from the cremations was poorly preserved and present in very small quantity.

Observations were made on the skeletons for age, sex, stature, metrics, morphology, and pathology. On the cremations only age and sex could be assessed but, in addition, any evidence for cremation practice was noted.

The results of analysis are summarised below with details in microfiche (Henderson, this vol, MF2 D9–E1).

Table 98 W57 Durrington Down barrow: animal species represented by context

Species	*Topsoil*	*Feature* 225	230	241	245	251	*Total*
Cattle	5	2	3	–	–	2	12
Sheep/goat	1	1	3	–	–	–	5
Horse	4	–	–	–	–	–	4
Dog	–	–	3	–	–	–	3
Red deer	1	–	–	1	1	2	5
Rabbit	4	–	–	–	–	–	4
Water vole	–	–	2	–	–	–	2
Unidentified large mammal	21	–	3	–	–	–	24
Sheep-sized mammal	2	–	–	–	–	–	2
Unidentified mammal	8	–	2	1	1	–	12
Total	46	3	16	2	2	4	73

Primary inhumation (context 192)

Sex and stature not assessed; age 7–9 years. Nearly complete skeleton in good condition, all parts represented.

Secondary inhumation (context 177)

Male aged 35–45 years; stature *c* 1.72m. Nearly complete skeleton in good condition, all parts represented. Evidence for joint disease on this individual was slight and, as it is such as could be expected at this age, is of little significance. There is evidence for fairly marked dental disease including at least three carious lesions.

Cremations (Table 99)

A total of 14 samples were examined. In many cases a conclusive identification of the bone as human could not be made and these samples have been omitted from the following discussion and from the results shown in Table 99. This table shows the results for sex, age, and sample weight and suggests the minimum number of individuals as six. The finding that context 226 contained the remains of a minimum number of three individuals was perhaps the most surprising, given the sample weight. The average, fat-free skeleton weighs between 2–4kg (Krogman 1962) and the average cremated sample weighs *c* 1.6kg (Evans 1963).

Details of the bones present, and the colour and size of the bone fragments, may yield information concerning cremation practices. With this group it should be noted that there were only two samples of sufficient weight for these observations to be made (contexts 226 and 254), and therefore any comments apply to them alone. In these samples elements of all parts of the skeleton were found, which indicated that there was no discrimination made between specific bones, in favour of the skull for example. Most of the fragments

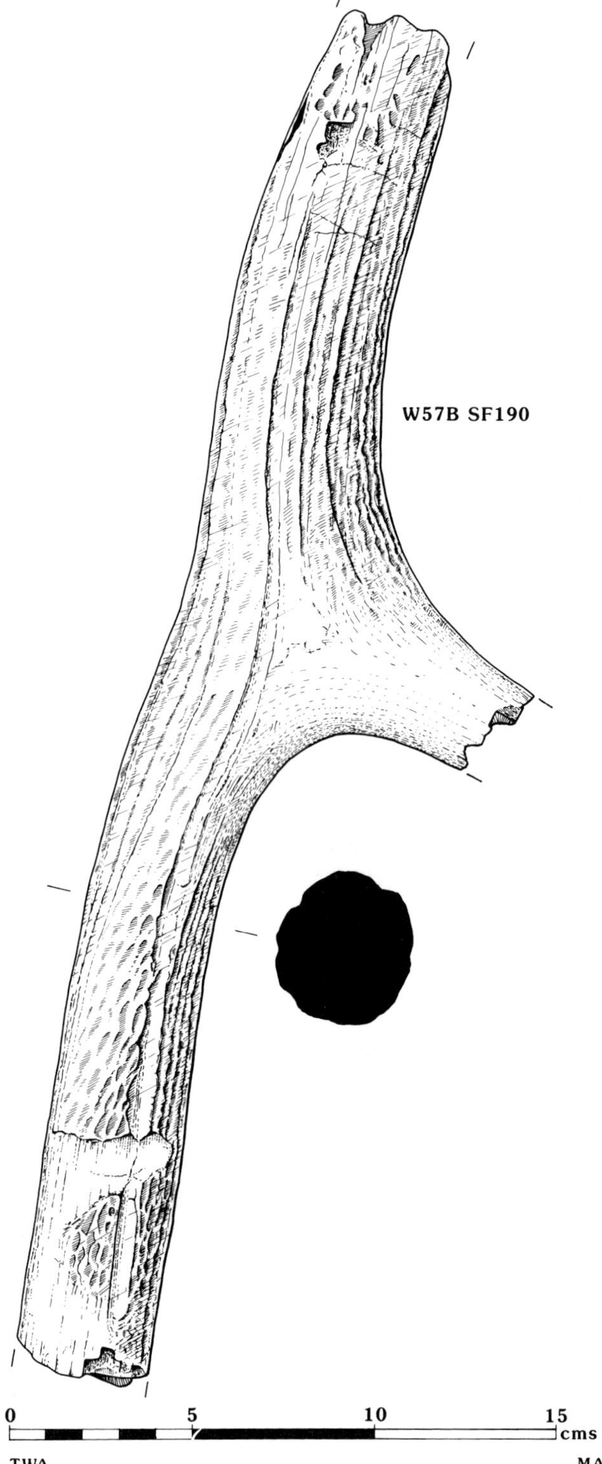

Fig 132 W57 Durrington Down barrow: area B antler object SF190

were white in colour and although some, particularly in context 226, were of a fair size, they were well broken up with some distortion evident. All of this would indicate that the cremation itself in both cases had been fairly complete, but does not show whether this was because the technique had been very efficient (and therefore quick), or simply that the pyre had been allowed to burn for a long time. It should be noted that the larger size of some of the fragments reflects the degree to which the bones were broken after cremation rather than the heat of the pyre.

4.12 W52: the sample excavation of the Wilsford Down North Kite

The Wilsford Down North Kite is a large three-sided earthwork enclosure, originally consisting of a bank with exterior ditch, enclosing an area of approximately 8 hectares (Fig 133). The enclosure lies on Wilsford Down, the east and west sides running down a moderate south-facing slope immediately north of the Lake barrow group. The northern side lies within Normanton Bottom, a narrow dry valley, and the southern side is open. Crawford and Keiller were able to observe the intact site within an area of old grassland (1928, 254), and, while suggesting a Romano-British date, repeated Colt Hoare's description of the enclosure as originally having a fourth side (Hoare 1810, pt 1). Since these observations, much of the earthwork has been levelled by ploughing, leaving only a short length of the western bank and ditch intact.

In 1958 Ernest Greenfield excavated a number of exploratory cuttings through both the extant and levelled areas of the earthwork (interim report, Greenfield 1959, 229). The location of these, and sections of cuttings A and D, are shown in Figure 133. Cutting A, located on the levelled eastern side, showed that a small ditch ran parallel to and outside the main earthwork ditch. This feature, which contained post settings and appears to be a palisade trench, was traced southwards beyond the suggested limit of the enclosure, and northwards for a distance of 137m. Cuttings were also made in an unsuccessful attempt to locate the fourth side to the enclosure. Of the cuttings made through the extant earthwork, one, cutting C, produced pottery of both later Neolithic and Early Bronze Age from beneath the bank, suggesting a construction date early in the second millennium BC.

More recently, the RCHME have suggested that barrows within the Lake Group, specifically disc barrow Wilsford 45b, overlie the western side of the enclosure, again suggesting a construction date in the earlier Bronze Age (RCHME 1979, 27 and fig 15).

Table 99 W57 Durrington Down barrow: cremated bone results for sex, age, and sample weight

Context	*Sample no*	*Sex*	*Age (years)*	*Sample weight (g)*
95	131	–	adult	35.5
246	–	–	adult	132.0
226	175	?male	adult	2950.0
		–	adult	
		–	juvenile	
254	–	–	5–10	810.0

(10 additional samples of burnt bone were examined but could not conclusively be identified as being of human origin. See Henderson, this vol, MF2 D9–E2 for catalogue)

4.12 a W52, the 1983 excavation (Fig 133 for location, Fig 134 for sections)

The 1983 excavation, within the area of surviving ditch and bank (Scheduled Ancient Monument Wilts AM 61), was positioned close to Greenfield's cutting C (Fig 133). The excavation was carried out in order to clarify the suggested date of the monument and to sample both ditch deposits and buried soil for molluscan analysis.

A single trench, 2m wide and 14m long, was hand excavated through the two major components of the earthwork: the ditch (area B) and its associated bank (area A).

The ditch was 2.5m wide at the chalk surface and a maximum of 1.2m deep from present ground level. The sides sloped shallowly down to a flat base 1.2m wide. Contexts 1, 3, 8, and 12 represent a series of essentially localised colluvial soils within which no evidence of stabilisation in the form of sorted horizons or established turf lines could be recognised. Below this, contexts 21 and 22, fine pale compact silts, overlie context 23, a fine chalk wash, and 25, the primary ditch silt. The compact nature and small particle size of both contexts 23 and 25 are unlike a rapidly formed primary silt, usually characterised by the angularity of the chalk component and the vacuous, but cemented, nature of the deposit. The absence of such primary fill, and the somewhat smoothed profile exhibited by the excavated ditch, suggest that it may have been scoured out before eventually being allowed to silt up. The filling of the ditch contained no pottery and the assemblage of worked flint included no individually diagnostic pieces. A column of molluscan samples was taken from the ditch fill (see Fig 134 for position); in the absence of dating it has not been analysed but is retained in reduced form within the project archive.

The bank (Fig 135), 6m wide and a maximum of 0.7m high from the old land surface, appeared to have been revetted at its western (ditch) edge by a substantial turf stack (context 24). This, 2.8m wide and a maximum of 0.3m high from the old land surface, may have served to retain the mass of ditch-derived chalk rubble (contexts 7 and 17) which forms the main bulk of the bank. The size of this turf stack, if this section is representative of the sequence along the length of the earthwork, suggests the removal of considerably more turf than would be produced from the area of the ditch. The occurrence, at the rear both of the turf stack and of the main chalk bank, of occasional substantial lumps of natural coombe rock, may represent marking out of the extent of the two bank elements prior to construction. Contexts 10 and 19, a mixed deposit of weathered chalk and humic soil, can be suggested as representing the type of deposit which would be derived from an episode of ditch scouring, here dumped at the rear of the bank. There is no indication of timescale for this addition to the bank, but experimental evidence suggests that primary silts accumulate and stabilise in a relatively short time (Jewell and Dimbleby 1966).

Both the main phase of bank construction and the suggested addition to the rear sealed a uniform buried land surface, overall context 20. An area 5.2m in length was examined, truncated at the tail (eastern) end by recent ploughing. The old land surface was found, on removal of the bank, to be an extremely compact and undisturbed strong brown soil. The surface appeared largely undisturbed by burrowing animals and at this stage of the excavation it became apparent that certain artefacts lay on the surface of the soil. As such these represented deposition or loss immediately prior to the construction of the bank. The artefacts included a substantial flint core, together with a small number of refitting flakes, the reduction sequence apparently abandoned, and a sherd of Developed Southern British Beaker. This sherd (P214), is in extremely fresh condition and, in view of its stratigraphic position, can be taken as providing a convincing *terminus post quem* for the bank construction.

On excavation, the buried soil exhibited a typical sorted profile, the compact upper stone-free horizon overlying a layer of larger particles immediately above the surface of the chalk. The excavation of the upper stone-free horizon was carried out without sieving, while the lower horizon was entirely wet-sieved through a 4mm sieve.

Artefacts recovered from within the buried soil profile included, for the restricted area examined, a surprising quantity of pottery, entirely of later Neolithic/earlier Bronze Age date (Raymond, this vol, 4.12 c). Specifically identifiable elements within the Peterborough assemblage include two vessels belonging to the Mortlake substyle (P208, P209, and P212). Beaker pottery includes small cord-decorated sherds (P223 and P226) although their size precludes their identification as being of AOC type. The extremely fresh and relatively large sherd (P214), decorated in Clarke's Southern Motif Group 4 (1970), has already been noted and probably belongs to the Developed Southern British Series S2. One sherd of Deverel-Rimbury pottery (not illustrated) was recovered from a ploughsoil layer (context 4) to the rear of the bank.

In addition to a small assemblage of worked flint, which included two petit tranchet derivative arrowheads, one of petit tranchet type, the other chisel (Riley, this vol, 5.3), three pieces of spotted dolerite (bluestone) were recovered from both manual excavation and sieving. Two of these, all of which are in very fresh condition, give the appearance of having been removed by percussion. While the circumstances of their deposition must remain uncertain, the recovery by Greenfield of a Group XIII (Preselite) battleaxe (Roe 1966, 238) from barrow Wilsford 54, only 400m to the east, is perhaps worthy of note (Greenfield 1959, 228–9).

The buried soil profile was sampled for molluscan analysis but unfortunately, on processing, was demonstrated to contain an inadequate number of snails for environmental assessment (Allen, this vol, 4.12 e). The sorted nature of the pre-bank soil profile may be taken to suggest a grassland environment. A small collection of poorly preserved animal bones were recovered from the buried soil (Table 101), of which only pig and cattle were positively identified.

Conclusion

The excavation carried out in 1958 provided the initial indication of a potentially earlier Bronze Age construction date for the North Kite. The 1983 sample, in addition to confirming Greenfield's observations, has

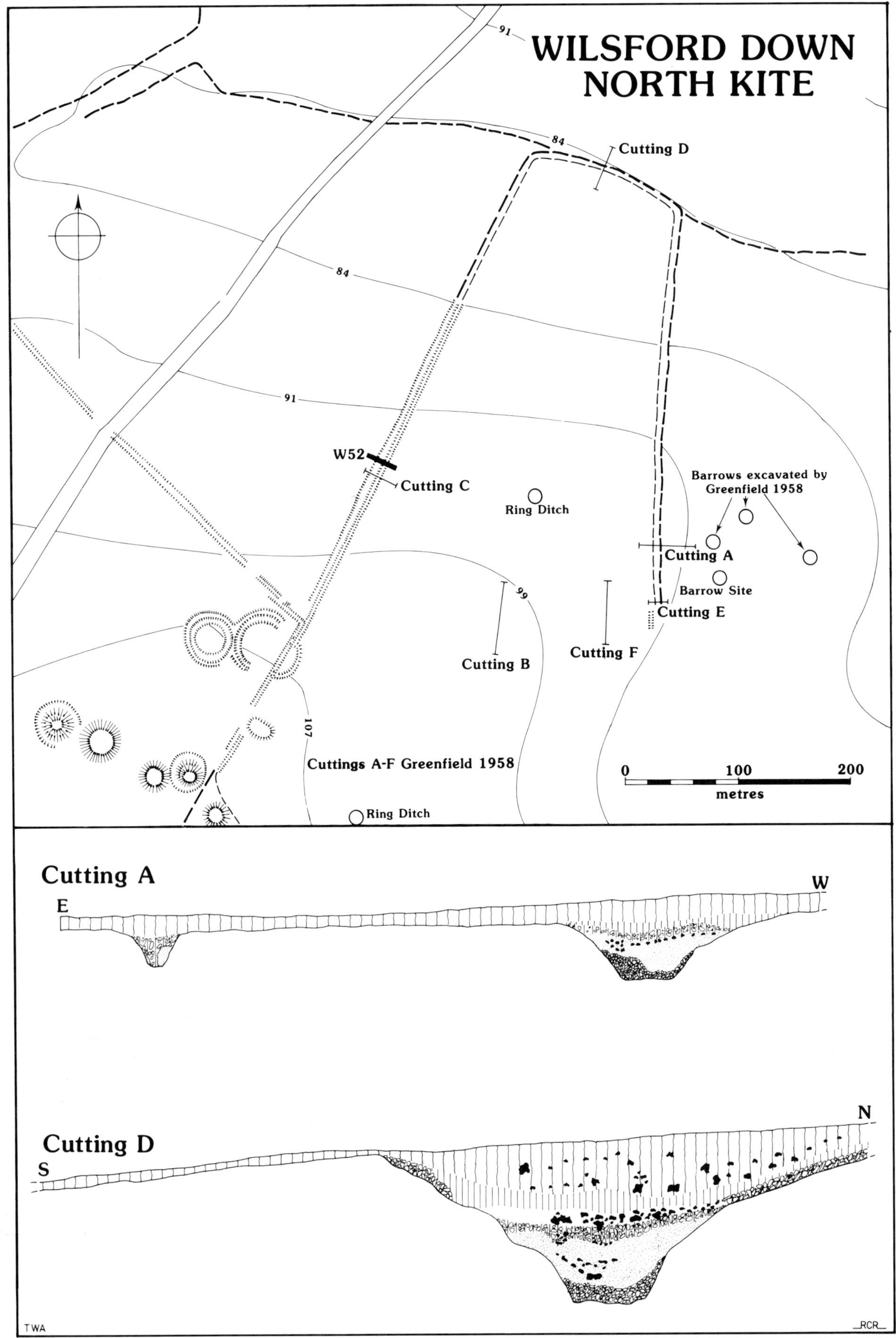

Fig 133 Wilsford Down North Kite: overall plan, location of cuttings, and sections of Greenfield's cuttings A and D

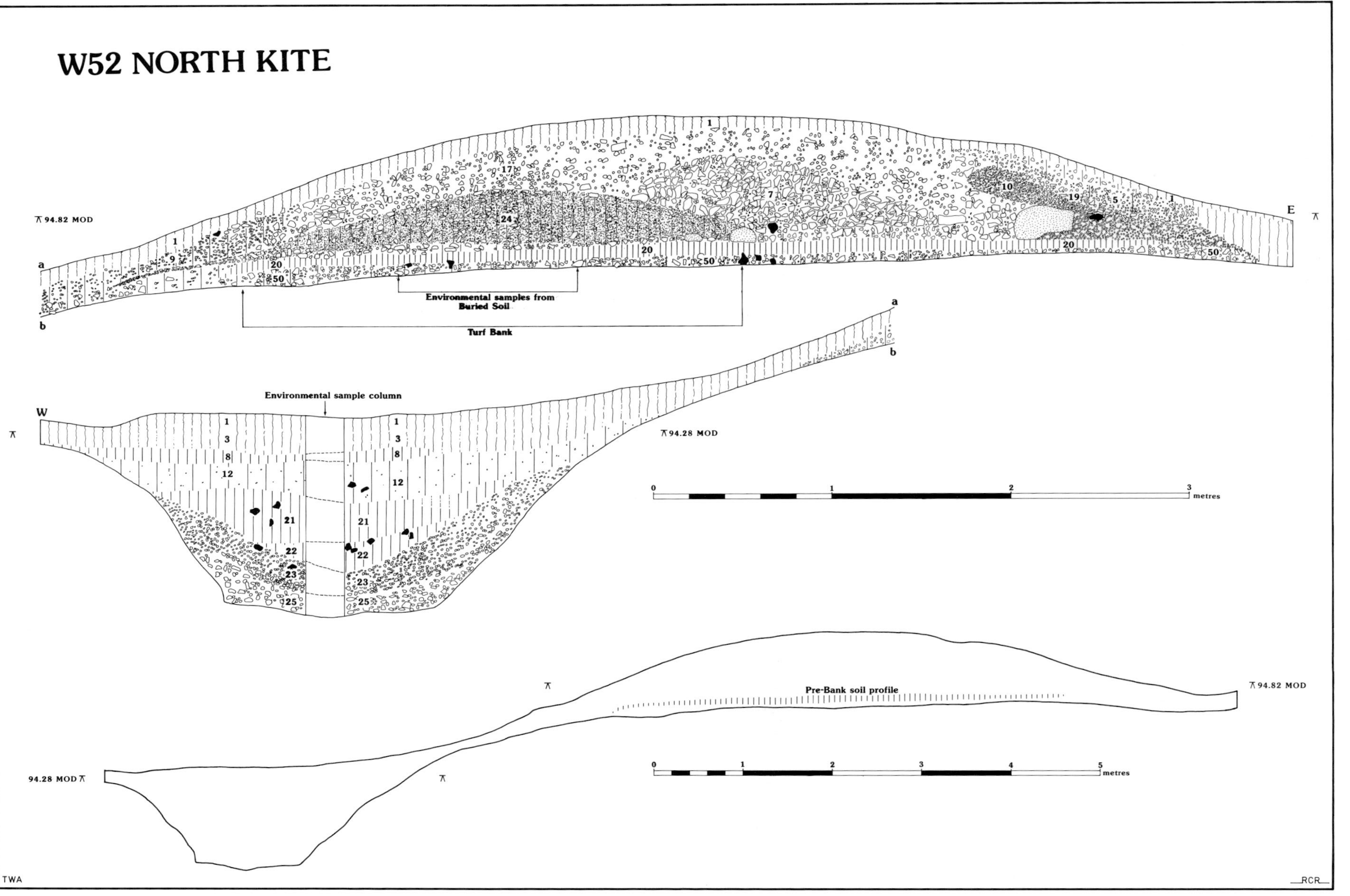

Fig 134 W52 Wilsford Down North Kite: sections

Fig 135 W52 Wilsford Down North Kite: general view of cutting from west showing bank structure and buried soil (scale 1m)

provided some refinement in separating potentially datable material from both on and within the buried soil sequence.

The North Kite is unique in the earlier Bronze Age in terms of both scale and morphology, although two examples of a series of enclosures in Sussex have recently produced middle to late Beaker pottery (M J Allen pers comm). These 'valley entrenchments', originally recorded by Toms (1926), enclose areas of up to 4 hectares, and occupy similar topographic positions to that of the North Kite.

No indication of the potential function of the North Kite is available, although it is certain that the enclosure was constructed in an area already much utilised. It is also clear that the enclosure, although potentially redundant, formed a focal element of the later Bronze Age linear ditch systems in the Wilsford Down area, influencing their morphology and subsequent development.

4.12 b *Lithics*

A total of 673 pieces of worked flint were recovered from the excavation of the ditch and buried soil. The

Table 101 W52 Wilsford Down North Kite: animal species represented by context

	Context			
Species	*Ditch*	*20*	*50*	*Total*
Cattle	–	3	3	6
Pig	–	1	4	5
Unidentified large mammal	1	5	3	9
Sheep-sized mammal	2	2	3	7
Unidentified mammal	–	9	5	14
Total	3	20	18	41

composition of this assemblage, which has not been analysed in detail, is shown in Table 115.

A large proportion (60%) of the assemblage from the ditch (area B), was recovered from contexts 21 and 22.

Within area A, 67% of the total assemblage from this area was recovered from the buried soil beneath the bank (overall context 20). The majority of this was recovered from within the soil profile, primarily from within the stony lower sorted horizon. This material reflected the mixed, but predominantly later Neolithic, emphasis within the ceramic assemblage, and contained two petit tranchet derivative arrowheads, one of chisel form and the other a true petit tranchet.

A substantial core, associated with over 20 flakes, was recovered from the surface of the buried soil adjacent to the southern section. Limited refitting has demonstrated that this appears to represent *in situ* knapping, perhaps corroborated by the recovery of numerous small chips from the top of the buried soil in the immediate area. The raw material utilised appears to be a nodule of fresh chalk flint, abundant sources of which are available in the near vicinity, and the sequence appears to represent abandonment at an early stage of core preparation. The nodule does contain both voids and flaws, and indications, in the form of hinge fractures, suggest that the knapping was carried out with little concept of predetermined end product. The more detailed study of this sequence was consequently not regarded as a priority within the overall programme of lithic analysis.

4.12 c *The prehistoric pottery (Fig 136)*

by Frances Raymond

A total of 74 sherds representing a minimum of 14 vessels was recovered. The buried soil contains both Peterborough Ware and Beaker, but the sorted horizon includes only Peterborough Ware and AOC Beaker. This confirms that they were present in the area some time before the Late Style Beakers. There had clearly been sufficient time for their incorporation in the sorted horizon before the construction of the bank. There is a marked variation in average weight between sherds belonging to different fabric groups. In the case of the Peterborough Ware this is a reflection of fabric resilience. The soft and loosely textured FV:Pet/2 has a low average weight of 1.4g in contrast to the average weights of 4.9g and 3.2g for the hard and closely textured fabrics Ffe:Pet/2 and FS:Pet/1 respectively. A similar explanation cannot be used to account for the high average weight of 4.8g for the Beaker fabric FfeGM:Bkr/1 which, in decorative terms, belongs to Clarke's Motif Group 4, Developed Southern British Series (Clarke 1970, 210, 427). Although the Beaker clay pastes are distinctive, as far as treatment and finish are concerned they are very alike and therefore might be expected to exhibit a similar degree of fragmentation. However, at W52, differences in sherd size amongst pottery from the same context may be a direct reflection of the length of time elapsing since deposition. The very fresh condition of the sherd probably from a Developed Southern British Beaker (P214) may be taken as providing a *terminus post quem* for the construction of the earthwork.

The proportion of sherds assigned to ceramic and fabric groups have been plotted in Figure 137 and Table 100 (MF2 E2) by total weight, while a more detailed discussion of the assemblage is given below.

Peterborough Ware

A minimum of four vessels is represented, including Fengate and Mortlake Ware. P199 is from the base of a Fengate Ware vessel, which is decorated with a curvilinear motif in twisted cord impression; P200, which is decorated in a similar fashion, may represent part of the same vessel, although this is not certain. At least one other vessel is represented by body sherds in fabric Ffe:Pet/2, but the substyle to which these belong is unclear. The remaining two vessels belong to the Mortlake substyle: P208 and P209 almost certainly belong to a single vessel, as do P210–P213. The fabrics used to produce one of the Peterborough pots (P202, P203, P204, and P206 – Ffe:Pet/2) and the Mortlake bowl (P210–P213 – FV:Pet/2) are exclusive to each vessel. This is not true of FS:Pet/1, which represents a minimum of three pots, of which only one is identifiable as Mortlake Ware (P208–P209).

Beaker

A minimum of eight vessels, mainly distinguished on the basis of fabric differences, are represented. Eleven of the 39 Beaker sherds are decorated and five separate motifs are represented. The incomplete nature of the assemblage has restricted the identification of specific style groups to the fabric FfeGM:Bkr/1, which is decorated in a manner typical of Clarke's Southern Motif

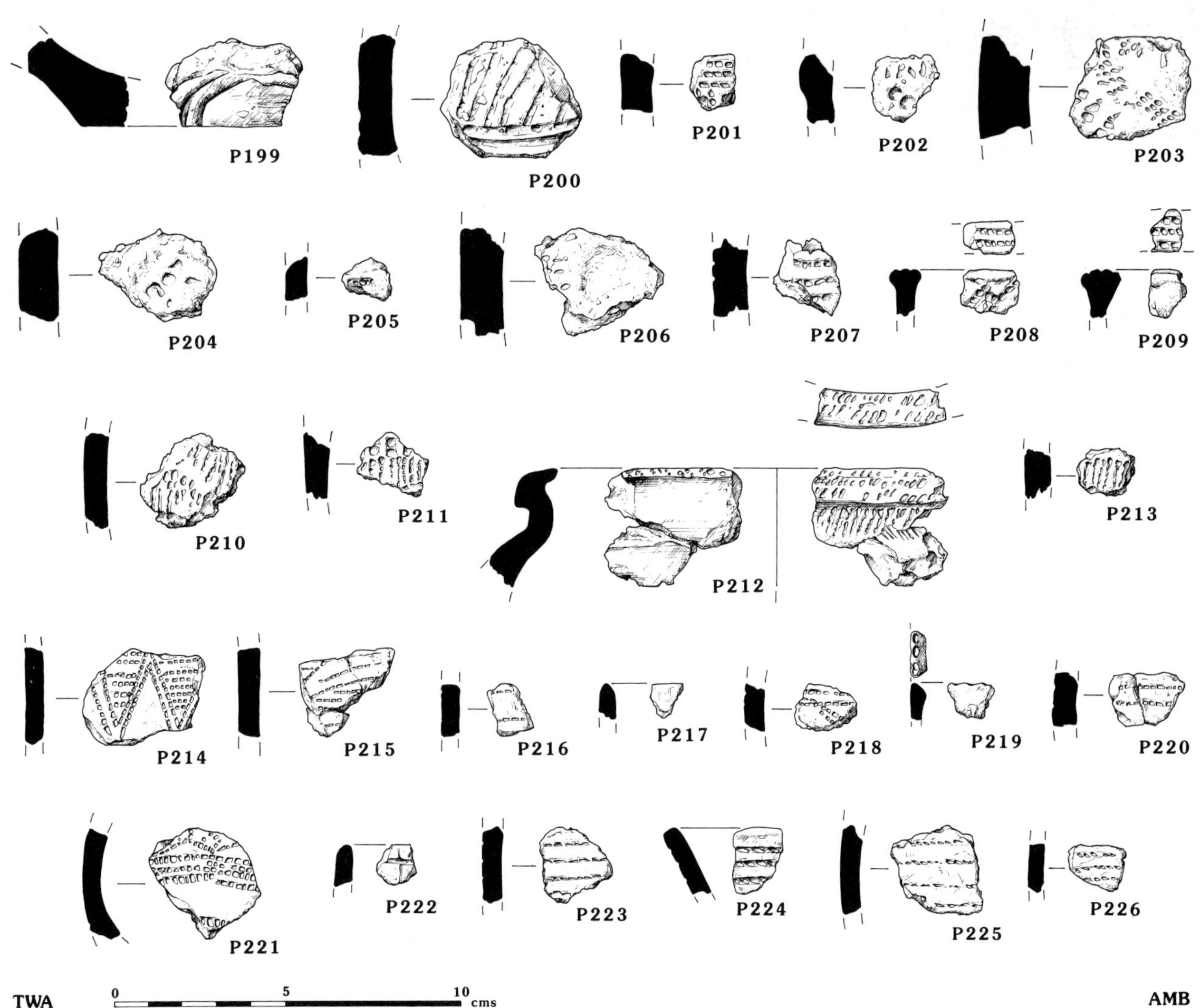

Fig 136 W52 Wilsford Down North Kite: prehistoric pottery (P199–P226)

W52 The North Kite Ceramic Groups

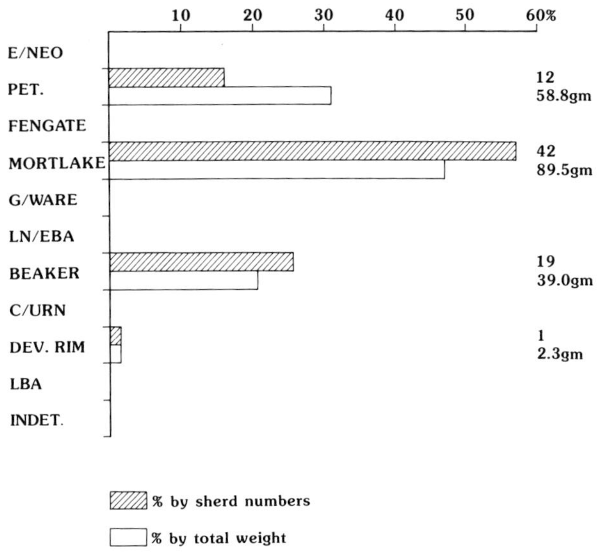

Fig 137 W52 Wilsford Down North Kite: prehistoric pottery fabric histogram

Group 4 and probably belongs to the Developed Southern British Series S2 (Clarke 1970). P221, a sherd from just above the base angle of a vessel, exhibits a bar chevron, filled with small vertical impressions, and may belong to the same vessel as P214. The decoration on P215 also appears to be part of a complex motif, possibly a bar chevron or a 'floating' motif of some type.

The absence of an undecorated zone beneath the rim on the exterior of P224 allow it to be placed in Lanting and van der Waals Step 1 and in Case's Early Style (Lanting and van der Waals 1972; Case 1977). The other cord-impressed sherds almost certainly belong to AOC Beakers, although no other rim sherds are present. All the Beaker fabrics occur elsewhere within the study area (see W32, this vol, Table 33).

Deverel-Rimbury

This consists of a single sherd in the lower ploughsoil (area A context 4 – not illustrated), the fabric identified as Globular Urn in preliminary examination of the pottery from W85, Netheravon Bake long barrow (Richards in prep a).

Illustrated pottery (Fig 136)

Fengate

P199 Area A, context 14
FS:Pet/1. Base sherd. Two parallel curvilinear twisted cord impressions. (Probably the same vessel as P200.)

P200 Area A, context 20
FS:Pet/1. Body sherd. Curvilinear twisted cord impressions. (Probably the same vessel as P199.)

Beaker

P201 Area B, context 25
FS:Pet/1. Body sherd. Three parallel comb impressed rows arranged to form a right angle with a fourth impression.

Peterborough

P202 Area A, context 29
Ffe:Pet/2. Body sherd. Impressed motif.

P203 Area A, context 33
Ffe:Pet/2. Body sherd. Short lengths of impressed twisted cord arranged in narrow bands.

P204 Area A, context 37
Ffe:Pet/2. Body sherd. Impressed motif.

P205 Area A, context 44
FV:Pet/2. Body sherd. Indistinct impression, probably cord.

P206 Area A, context 45
Ffe:Pet/2. Body sherd. Twisted cord impressions and one large indistinct impression.

P207 Area A, context 47
FS:Pet/1. Body sherd. Three parallel twisted cord impressions.

Mortlake

P208 Area A, context 20
FS:Pet/1. Rim sherd. Expanded with flattened top. Impressed twisted cord motif arranged in two parallel lines along the top of the rim and in a cross-hatched pattern on the exterior of the vessel.

P209 Area A, context 38
FS:Pet/1. Rim sherd. Expanded with flattened top. Impressed twisted cord motif arranged in three parallel lines along the top of the rim.

Mortlake Bowl

P210–213 are sherds from one vessel. In addition, three more rim sherds of this vessel (not illustrated) were found in contexts 43 (two sherds) and 47.

P210 Area A, context 16
FV:Pet/2. Body sherd. Impressed motif arranged in two narrow bands.

P211 Area A, context 45
FV:Pet/2. Body sherds. Parallel linear impressed motif used to infill area defined by a single horizontal impression.

P212 Area A, context 46 (three sherds illustrated)
FV:Pet/2. Rim sherd. Expanded with flattened top. Bird-bone impressions along the top and external surface of the rim; sub-circular impressions along the inner lip of the rim. Parallel linear impressions arranged in a herringbone pattern below the rim and above the shoulder of the vessel. The linear impressions may be segmented, but the detail is unclear.

P213 Area A, context 49
FV:Pet/2. Body sherd. Parallel linear impressed motif.

Beaker

P214 Area A, context 20
FfeGM:Bkr/1. Body sherd. Impressed comb motif arranged in pendants defined by two parallel lines, infilled with a series of horizontal impressions.

P215 Area A, context 24
feGSBkr/9. Body sherd. Six parallel comb impressions.

P216 Area A, context 28
feGS: Bkr/4. Body sherd. Two parallel comb impressions.

P217 Area A, context 28
G:Bkr/2. Rim sherd. Rounded with internal bevel.

P218 Area A, context 30/42
feGS:Bkr/9. Body sherd. Two double rows of comb impressions arranged on a diagonal axis to one another.

P219 Area A, context 31
FfeS:Bkr/1. Rim sherd. Asymmetrically rounded. Small impression around the top of the rim.

P220 Area A, context 36
feGS:Bkr/4. Body sherd. Two parallel comb impressions.

P221 Area A, context 37
FfeGM:Bkr/1. Body sherd. Impressed comb motif arranged in a zigzag pattern bounded by a narrow band of three closely set impressions. These display traces of the comb having been lifted and then replaced to continue the design. A fourth row occurs after a gap of 10mm.

P222 Area A, context 49
FfeGM:Bkr/1. Rim sherd. Rounded. Abraded impressed motif.

Sherds possibly from the same vessel

P223 Area A, context 33
feGS:Bkr/4. Body sherd. Twisted cord impressions arranged in four parallel rows.

P224 Area A, context 33
feGS:Bkr/4. Rim sherd. Rounded and everted. Twisted cord impressions arranged in three parallel rows on a horizontal axis.

P225 Area A, context 47
feGS:Bkr/4. Body sherd. Twisted cord impressions arranged in four parallel rows.

P226 Area A, context 48
feGS:Bkr/4. Body sherd. Twisted cord impressions arranged in three parallel rows.

4.12 d Animal bones
by Mark Maltby

A total of 41 animal bone fragments were recovered, of which 14 were found in the 1mm wet-sieving samples. The species represented are shown in Table 101. Only three bones, none of which was identifiable, were found in the fill of the ditch. The earlier Bronze Age layers 20 and 50 each produced a small collection of poorly preserved bones. Of these, 14 were collected in the 1mm wet-sieved samples. These contained four fragments of pig, two of cattle, two of sheep-sized mammal, and six small unidentifiable mammal fragments.

Five of the six cattle fragments were loose teeth and the other was a small fragment of the fused distal articulation of a metapodial. The five pig fragments consisted of three loose teeth, an unfused calcaneus, and a small fragment of a humerus. No other species was positively identified, although a small sheep-sized longbone fragment bore close similarities to the proximal articulation of a sheep/goat's metatarsus.

Twenty-one bones were observed to have suffered various degrees of surface erosion and 11 fragments (mostly from the sieved samples) were charred.

4.12 e Land mollusca
by M J Allen

Samples specifically for molluscan analysis were taken (by Roy Entwistle) from the buried soil and from the ditch deposits. In the absence of dating evidence from the ditch, the samples have been reduced to their sieve fractions and stored with the archive. The samples from the buried soil unfortunately yielded too few molluscs for any detailed interpretation to be offered with confidence.

However, two samples from the buried soil beneath the bank were taken (by M J Allen) for laboratory measurement of magnetic susceptibility, as a comparison with values from the modern soil (Allen 1986, 1988). Once this had been undertaken, 1.5kg air-dried sub-samples were analysed for land snails using the procedures outlined by Evans (1972) and mollusc nomenclature provided by Waldén (1976). The results are shown as histograms of relative abundance (Fig 138).

The upper portion of the buried soil (0–50mm) was well worm-sorted and almost stone-free, whilst the lower portion (50–120mm) contained common small to medium rounded chalk pieces. The upper stone-free horizon was observed to be patchy, in places occupying most of the profile, and elsewhere entirely absent. Both units of the buried soil were carefully sampled and the molluscan assemblages certainly reflect the observed variation.

The lower portion (50–120mm) produced relatively high numbers of molluscs and shell preservation was reasonable. The assemblage is mixed and is dominated by *Helicella itala*, *Trichia hispida*, and the Vallonias, indicating open country conditions. However, some shade-loving species were present, but with the exception of the robust species of *Discus rotundatus* and *Clausilia bidentata*, they are common in tall, ungrazed grassland as well as woodland (Cameron and Morgan-Huws 1975). The other point of note is the relative abundance of *Pomatias elegans*, which enjoys disturbed ground and is often taken as an indicator of bare loose earth created by clearance (Evans 1972). The open country molluscs are consistent with a grassland rather than arable context.

The upper sample (0–50mm) is impoverished and only 24 specimens were recovered. Nevertheless the assemblage is dominated by open country species (79%) typical of short grass downland or even arable contexts.

Discussion

Numbers of molluscs vary considerably throughout the buried soil profile and the assemblages represent significant change. The recovery of very low numbers of molluscs, noted above, may be explained in terms of the location of the sampling point, possibly where the stone-free horizon occupied the majority of the buried soil horizon.

Analysis indicates an episode of tall, ungrazed grassland, possibly with occasional shrubs which was later cleared and heavily grazed prior to the construction of the monument. The results of the magnetic susceptibility confirmed the similarity between the modern grassland and palaeosol environments (Allen 1986, 1988).

4.13 W31, area M, and W51: the sample excavation of linear ditches on Wilsford Down, 1982–3

4.13 a Site description

The linear earthwork research project was designed to investigate the potentially earlier Bronze Age date of elements of the linear ditch system within the Stonehenge area. Two sections were excavated, located on Figure 112, with sections and plans on Figure 139.

W31, area M

In 1982, a linear ditch adjacent to the Wilsford Down flint scatter was sectioned as part of the excavation strategy for that particular site (this vol, 4.10 a). The ditch (RCHME 1979, fig 14g) runs for a distance of 1.2km from a point to the north on Stonehenge Down at SU 11464171, approximately south-west to join the ditch described below (W51) at SU 10744075.

Where sampled at SU 10784078, the ditch, the location of which was confirmed by magnetometer survey (Fig 114, MF2 B9), was extremely shallow. A 2m length was hand excavated and was found to be approximately 1m wide, irregularly V-profiled, and only 0.5m deep. The position of the ditch in relationship to the local topography, running across a slope, may suggest that the profile has been somewhat truncated. The chalky lower fills, contexts 297 and 298, contained no datable artefacts. The sequence appears to include a recut, context 299, the fill of which, context 296, contained considerably more natural flint than the lower fills. Context 299 also contained two sherds of Beaker pottery, while a further similar sherd was recovered from the topsoil from within area M. The ditch sequence was not sampled for molluscan analysis.

W51

A single trench was hand excavated through the ditch of the linear earthwork (RCHME 1979, fig 14h) at SU 10674083. The ditch runs from SU 11094039 where it joins the west side of the North Kite (W52, this vol, 4.12) north-westwards for a distance of approximately 700m to SU 10594087.

The excavation was carried out at a point where no bank survived. A trench 4.8m long and 1.4m wide was excavated, showing the ditch to be 2.4m wide, 1.1m deep and V-profiled, with a narrow rounded base approximately 0.3m wide. The fill of the ditch suggests an uninterrupted silting sequence, with context 8 possibly representing a lower stabilisation horizon. The accumulation of natural flints at the base of context 7 may represent an episode of clearance and context 4 can be suggested as the remains of the sorted horizon reflecting more recent grassland land use. No datable finds were recovered.

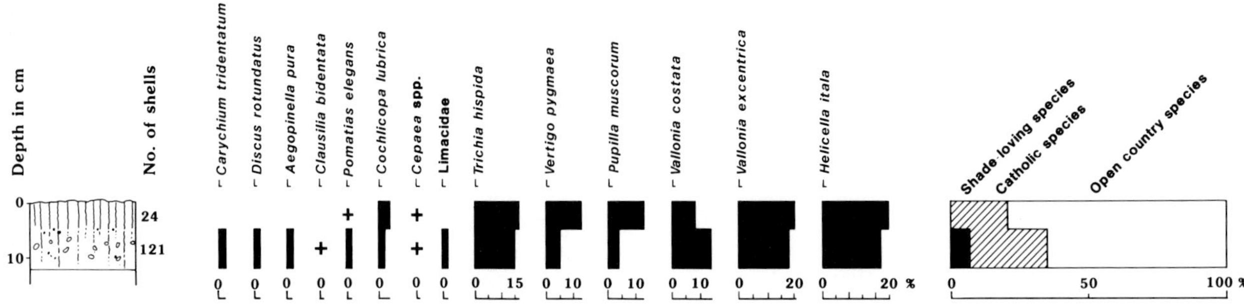

Fig 138 W52 Wilsford Down North Kite: buried soil mollusc diagram

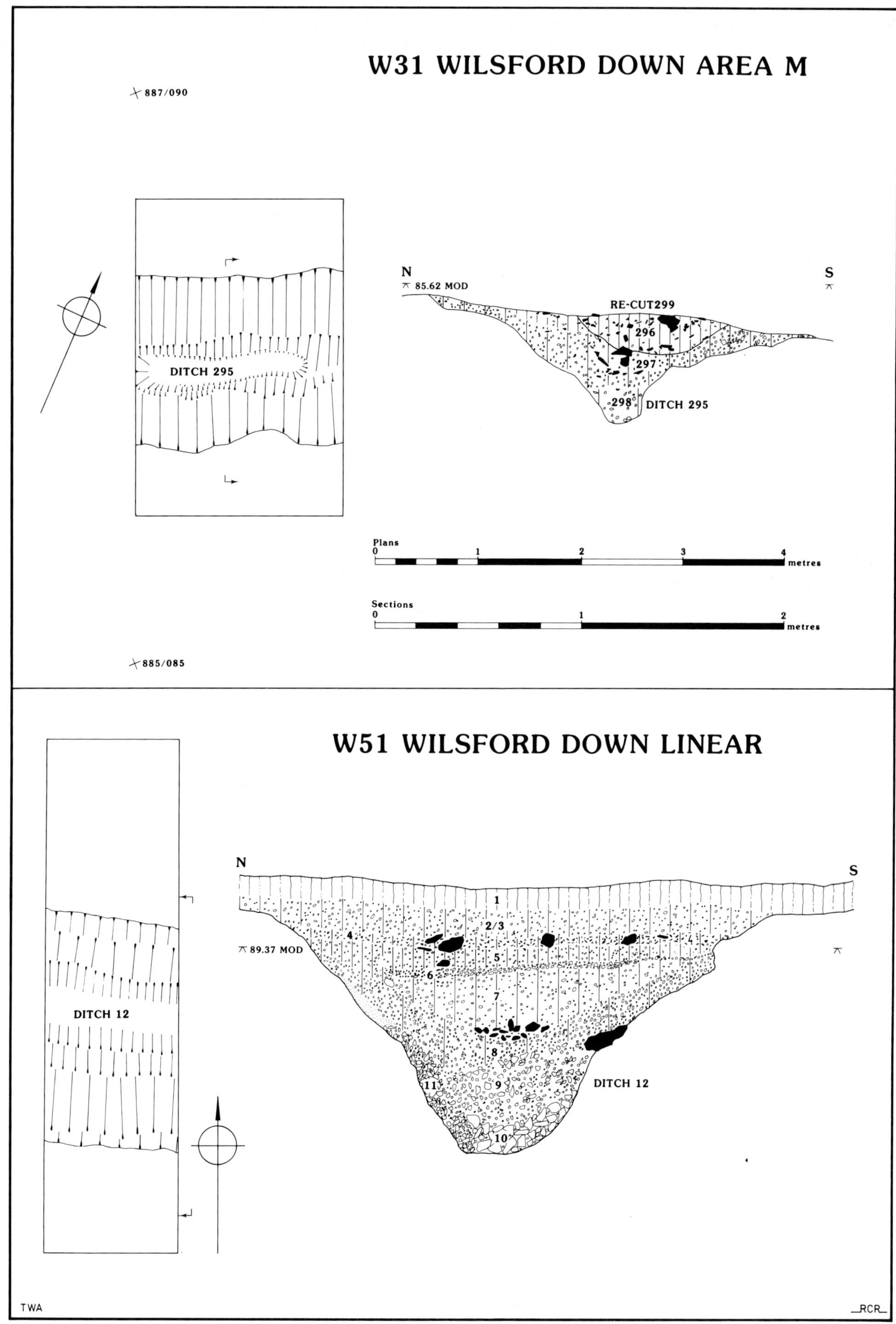

Fig 139 W31 Wilsford Down (area M) and W51 Wilsford Down linear ditch: plans and sections

4.14 W34: the sample excavation of Fargo Wood II later Bronze Age pottery scatter

4.14 a Site description

Extensive surface collection in the area north of the Stonehenge Cursus in the winter of 1980/81 suggested an area of later Bronze Age activity lying on the summit of a low ridge immediately adjacent to Fargo Wood (located on Fig 36). Centred on SU 11174318, the most obvious element of the surface scatter consisted of pottery, associated with large quantities of burnt flint and of burnt and broken sarsen, the latter including quern fragments. The visible extent of the pottery scatter was plotted in spring 1982, at which time it was also noted that slight surface depressions corresponded with an absence of surface artefacts. This suggested that conditions of preservation could be expected to vary considerably within the defined area of activity, and the sampling strategy adopted for the evaluation excavation consequently incorporated an awareness of such variables.

Pre-excavation survey and sampling strategy

Magnetometer and magnetic susceptibility surveys (located on Fig 37, MF1 B7) were carried out prior to excavation, the former producing few positive anomalies (Bartlett, this vol, MF2 E3–4; Figs 140, 141, MF2 E5, E6). A transect of phosphate samples was taken in order to examine the relationship between the areas of activity represented by W32 (this vol, 4.4) and W34 together with their overall context (see Entwistle and Richards 1987, fig 3.6).

The defined area of the surface scatter was sampled by means of an overall systematic sample of 1m squares, contexts 2–49, augmented by five squares, areas A–E (Fig 142), each 5m by 5m in size. The 1m systematic sample squares were all sieved through 4mm mesh, as was a 20% sample of 1m squares from areas A to E.

The ploughsoil artefact assemblages

The excavation of the ploughsoil produced considerable quantities of pottery, over 99% of which, both by weight and sherd number, was of Late Bronze Age date. The remaining pottery, a total of 34 sherds, included sherds of Peterborough Ware (P139, P140) and Beaker (P141–P151). The distribution by weight of later Bronze Age pottery from the ploughsoil is shown in Figure 142. This and other overall distribution plots from W34 combine data from the excavation of the present agricultural ploughsoil and, where such deposits were recorded, from underlying extensive deposits. The distribution of pottery, even allowing for the possible total destruction of elements of the assemblage within the more abraded areas of the site, shows a clear emphasis towards the northern end of the sampled area, most notably within area B. Here the majority of the pottery, and other classes of artefacts, were contained within a sealed sorted horizon, undisturbed by current agriculture. Beyond the obvious focus provided by area B the pattern is less consistent, although data from systematic sample squares lying between areas C and E may suggest an area of similar, but less intensive, activity.

More solid components of the artefact assemblage include very large quantities of both worked and burnt flint, and a range of non-local stones, many of which were also burnt.

The distribution of burnt flint (Fig 142), the recorded weight of which ranged from 7 to 27,988g per $1m^2$, is similar to that of both unburnt and burnt stone, suggesting a concentration of either *in situ* burning or the deliberate dumping of the solid residue from burning in a restricted area.

Data from the magnetic susceptibility survey suggests that the direction of modern cultivation may have some effect on the distribution of areas of enhancement. Some areas of higher readings can be identified, however (Fig 141, MF2 E6, iii, points a and b), although unfortunately these were not sampled by excavation and no direct correlation is possible. Overall, the mean susceptibility level of 47 (× 10–8 SI/kg), and the standard deviation of 11, are comparable with levels recorded at W31 (this vol, 4.10). Given the large quantities of burnt stone at W34, levels here might have been expected to be higher, if *in situ* burning is a direct cause of magnetic enhancement.

The non-local stone assemblage, primarily of sarsen and greensand fragments, also included 22 identifiable fragments of querns/rubbers, 12 of which were from area B, together with one complete saddle quern recorded from immediately beyond the sample area. The majority of these, the distribution of which is combined with that of burnt flint in Figure 142, are of saccharoidal sarsen, with only one example of ferruginous sandstone. The majority of such fragments of saccharoidal sarsen located within the study area may well be undiagnostic fragments of querns or rubbers. If this is the case then the size and composition of the non-local stone assemblage from W34 suggest a considerable emphasis on the use of querns, and by extension on the production of cereals. Unfortunately the stratigraphic record of the investigated areas of the site, even where sealed deposits were located, could not provide positive environmental support for this suggestion. Only one grain of emmer/spelt was recovered from a posthole (Carruthers, this vol, 8.1).

The excavation of the ploughsoil produced a substantial, but wholly unstratified flint assemblage, the composition of which is shown in Table 102. A preliminary analysis of the tool component suggested a potential range in date from the later Neolithic to the later Bronze Age, corresponding to that suggested by the ceramic evidence. Perhaps more in accord with the emphasis from the pottery, scrapers of types 9 and 10, which together form 29% of the total scraper assemblage (Riley, this vol, 5.3), may be considered as late types, as may borers/awls, of which 15 examples were recovered.

Preliminary assessment of the overall lithic assemblage suggests that it can be characterised by unsystematic cores utilising locally available flint, possibly surface nodules from the nearby clay-with-flint. Little core control seems to be employed and product appears to be unspecific. The overall percentage of re-

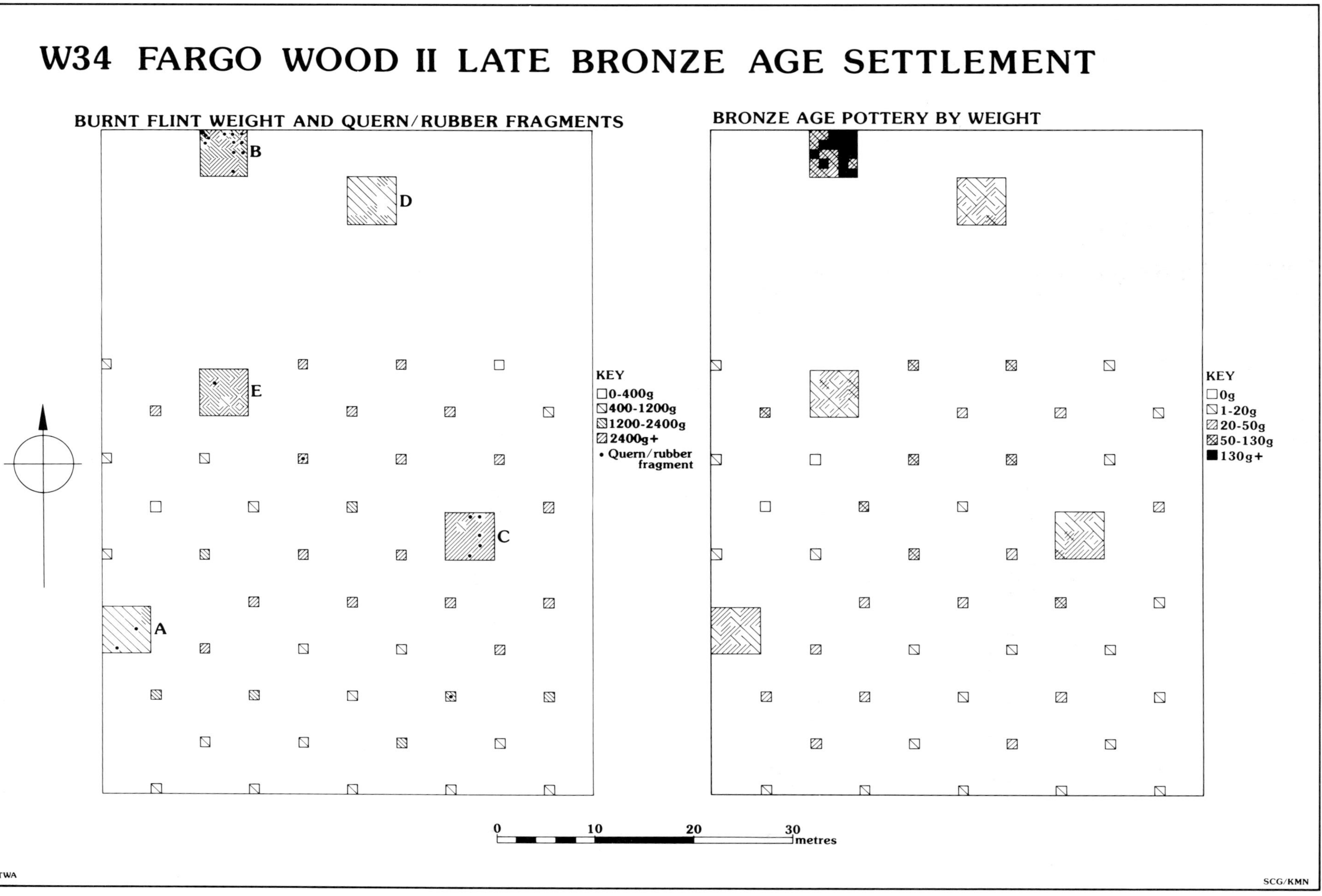

Fig 142 W34 Fargo Wood II Late Bronze Age settlement: distribution of burnt flint, querns/rubbers, and Bronze Age pottery from ploughsoil excavation

touched material is low (approximately 2%) and may suggest the expedient use of unmodified flakes for a range of tasks.

The distribution of total flint numbers and of flint tools is shown in Figure 143. These distributions, which include all worked flint, may be the least chronologically viable of those produced using the ploughsoil data. However, the reinforcement, particularly by the distribution of flint tools, of area B as an activity focus suggests that a large proportion of this artefact class may be associated with the other, more specifically later Bronze Age, artefacts.

A bronze awl (Fig 147, SF71) was recovered from context 42, part of the systematic sample.

Comparative discussion of the ploughsoil artefact assemblages

The data from the ploughsoil excavation sample suggest that the southern, and to a lesser degree the eastern, extent of the overall activity area has been ascertained. This is the case only if concentrations of artefacts are assumed to represent disturbed but essentially *in situ* activity, rather than a manifestation of selective disposal strategies. Interpretation is difficult in the absence of identifiable domestic foci within the area examined. However, the correspondence within area B of high levels of burnt flint, pottery, quern fragments, and flint tools, suggests either an area for rubbish disposal or of intensive *in situ* activity. If the traces of subsoil features recovered within this area (see below) are associated with the artefact concentrations, then the latter can be suggested. Some indication that this hypothesis is correct may be provided by the reflection in the negative distributions of pottery, quern fragments, and flint tools of the position of gully 267. In the absence of evidence for this gully having cut already formed midden deposits, it can be inferred that the discard of the items noted above may have taken place while this shallow feature was in use.

Sealed deposits

The removal of modern ploughsoil, varying in depth from 0.10m to 0.41m, revealed considerable variation in underlying deposits. The possibility of deeper deposits surviving beneath current plough depth, suggested initially by the microtopography of the site and also by the results from the systematic excavation sample, was confirmed in area B. Here an artefact-free topsoil overlay a dark horizon (overall context 269) containing a similar but considerably better preserved artefact assemblage to that recovered from the other examined areas. The size of sherds from this horizon is considerably larger and the analysis of the pottery assemblage suggests the possibility of differential fabric survival (Raymond, this vol, 4.14 c).

With the exception of one posthole (context 306) recorded within systematic sample square 40, and a possible pit within area A (context 177), no stratified deposits were recorded beyond area B. This area may, however, represent a sample of a much wider area of higher preservation potential, within which what may be a thin midden deposit appears to be associated with areas of *in situ* activity. These include the terminal of a possible shallow ditch or gully (context 267), within which was a dense concentration of burnt flint and charcoal. The charcoal was of a range of species (Gale, this vol, 8.2).

Discussion

Despite the limitations imposed by the sampling strategy, the comparative analysis of the ploughsoil artefacts has suggested a concentration of activity within a specific part of the sampled area. Some evidence has been recovered for the existence of hearths and possible ovens, while the one posthole recorded hints at the existence of post-built structures.

The combined data from W34 together suggest an increasing emphasis on arable cultivation. The site lies at the centre of an area of 'Celtic' fields, those to the north and to the west of Fargo Wood recorded by the RCHME (1979, map 1) and extending beyond the element examined in the excavation at W32 (this vol, 4.4). Late Bronze Age pottery from this excavation, perhaps not unexpectedly, provides a direct fabric link with elements of the W34 pottery assemblage (Table 32, MF1 C1–14). Under favourable conditions, traces of slight field banks can be seen on the ground to the south of the excavated area, extending to and overlying the Cursus. Evidence for the incorporation of the banks of the Cursus into this field system is provided by the sample excavation of the southern bank and ditch of

Table 102 W34 Fargo Wood II: composition of the flint assemblage

	Cores		*Flakes*				*Scrapers*	*Other*	*Total*
	complete	*fragments*	*complete*	*broken*	*burnt*	*retouched*		*tools*	
Systematic ($1m^2$) sample	66	39	1207	445	66	37	11	4	1875
Area A	26	13	655	214	34	20	9	8	979
Area B	88	60	1380	390	58	35	24	15	2050
Area C	37	19	946	246	41	20	6	8	1323
Area D	51	14	595	168	30	21	15	3	897
Area E	21	14	474	144	42	17	4	3	719
Totals	289	159	5257	1607	271	150	69	41	7843

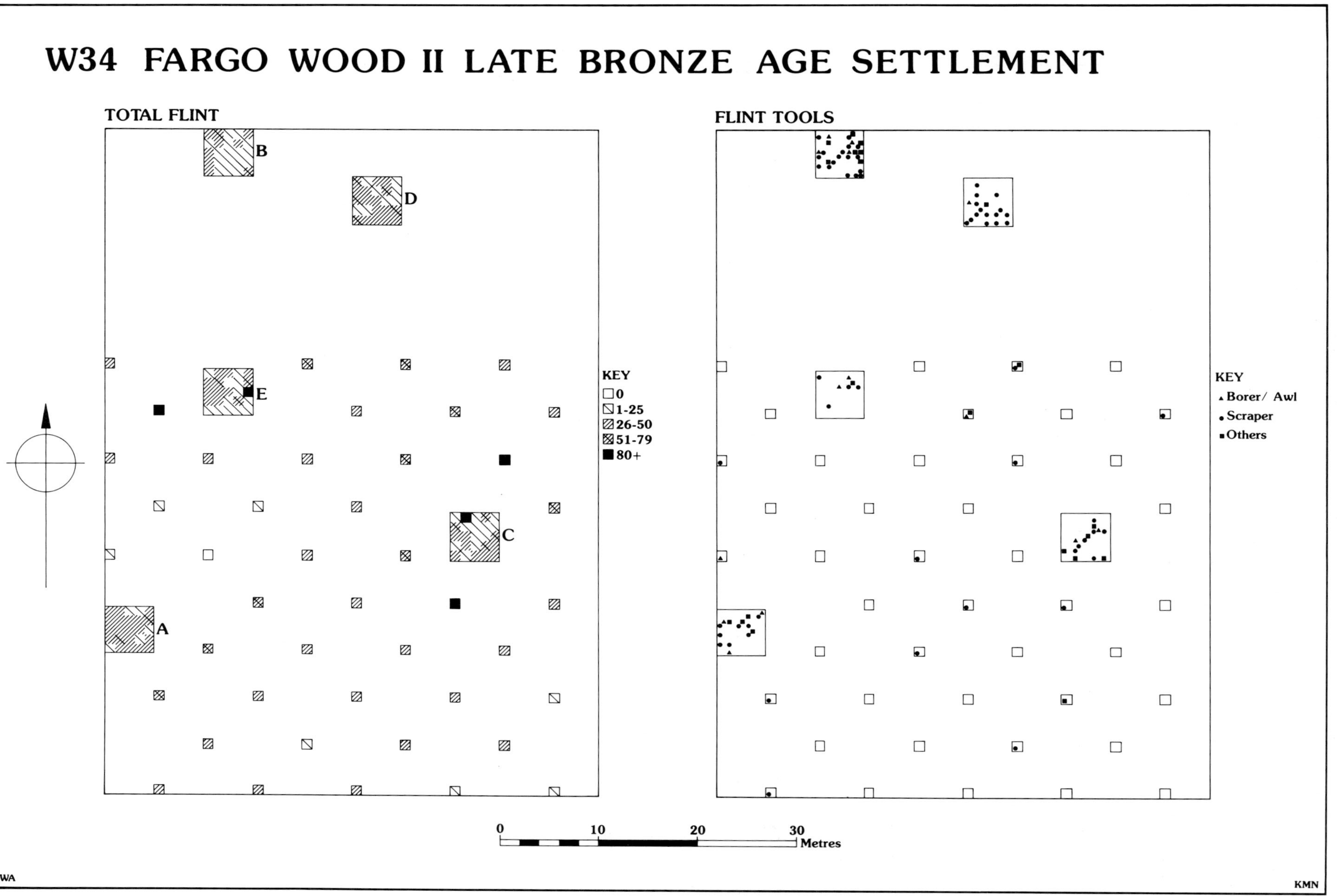

Fig 143 W34 Fargo Wood II Late Bronze Age settlement: distribution of all worked flint and flint tools from ploughsoil excavation

the Neolithic monument (W56 A, this vol, 4.6). The continuation of the field system as earthworks through Fargo Wood also provides a direct link with ploughed-out elements to the west of the wooded area. Here too, the traces of a cursus monument (W55, Lesser Cursus, this vol, 4.5), appear to have been used as the alignment for 'Celtic' fields and may also have been incorporated into the overall agricultural layout (Fig 159). Molluscan evidence for a phase of arable cultivation at the eastern end of the Lesser Cursus (W 55 B, Entwistle, this vol, 4.5 e) is here associated with pottery of both Beaker and later Bronze Age date. The latter provides a further direct association of fabric groups with those from W34 (Table 32, MF1 C1–14).

In the absence of stratified deposits, the environmental data from W34 are poor, and even the extensive animal bone assemblage of 1109 fragments is heavily biased towards more robust elements such as loose teeth (Maltby, this vol, 4.14 e). The overall assemblage suggests a dominance of sheep/goat and cattle, the type of association perhaps expected of a mixed agricultural regime. Pig are poorly represented and potentially exploitable wild animals such as deer are totally absent. This, in combination with the evidence for extensive fields, may suggest in the later Bronze Age a much diminished woodland cover in the vicinity of the sampled area.

W34 thus appears to be a small and nucleated area of later Bronze Age settlement, lying within an area of at least 40 hectares of regular fields within which some double elements suggest formal access routes.

In the discussion of the overall context of the settlement it remains only to point out the position of the single round barrow (Amesbury 113), which lies apparently on the periphery of the field system, approximately 200m to the east of the sampled area. Recorded initially as a small mound, it is now levelled and aerial photographic evidence suggests that it is a round barrow with an outer bank (Wilts SMR SU 14 SW 999). This funerary aspect of the complex can be suggested as providing the final element of the essentially self-contained later Bronze Age farming unit. It is this 'unit', viewed from the north, which formed the basis for the reconstruction of the Late Bronze Age landscape of the Stonehenge area (Richards 1985b, 20).

4.14 b Lithics

The sample excavation produced a total of 7843 pieces of worked flint (Table 102). With the exception of a small proportion from shallow subsoil features within area B, the assemblage was entirely recovered from unstratified contexts. These included both the modern ploughsoil and, in more restricted areas, a sorted horizon below present plough depth.

In view of the contextual insecurity of the assemblage, analysis has involved only the production of a stage 1 catalogue, data from which have been used in the production of the overall distribution plot shown in Figure 143.

Although the ceramic evidence suggests activity from the later Neolithic and throughout the Bronze Age, it can be suggested that the majority of the worked flint from W34 is in fact associated with the main phase of activity, here represented by a pottery assemblage predominantly of later Bronze Age date. Subsequent, more detailed analysis, beyond the brief of the present lithic research design, may serve to identify some of the elements suggested as typifying such late assemblages. At present, the preparation of the stage 1 catalogue has enabled some preliminary observations to be made.

Unfortunate characteristics of 'late' flint assemblages appear to include an unsystematic core technique, the expedient selection of tool blanks, and a variety of both position and type for retouch (Ford *et al* 1984). Such characteristics conspire to make either rapid assessment or a more detailed approach both difficult and potentially unrewarding. More recently Harding (forthcoming a) has suggested that Janus flakes may also characterise late industries, while Riley's scraper analysis (this vol, 5.3) re-emphasises the suggestion that 'expedient' or unclassifiable types may have later Bronze Age associations.

Assessment

The assemblage is all in a very fresh condition and exhibits a range of patination according to the localised soil conditions from which it was recovered. Areas with shallow, largely calcareous, soils produced flints with a pale patination, whereas those from areas of deeper deposits were a dark to mid-blue in colour. A chronological aspect of patination may be suggested by one anomalous systematic single-platform core, potentially of Neolithic date, which was patinated a pale blue/white colour. A small amount of retouch apparently cutting patination may also suggest the re-use of residual material.

The majority of the cores were unsystematic, with multidirectional flaking and considerable evidence for hinging and associated edge recession. In many cases successful flake removal appears minimal and the term 'bashed lump' seems a more appropriate term than the strict application of 'core'. The subsequent use of failed or exhausted cores as hammers was recorded on 13 examples. No attempt was made to quantify the occurrence of hinge or Siret (accidental breakage) fractures and only two Janus flakes were noted.

The overall percentage of retouched material (approximately 2%) appears low in comparison to earlier assemblages and may again suggest an expedient use, this time of unmodified flakes for a variety of cutting tasks. The proportion of burnt worked material may be under-represented owing to the large quantities of burnt flint recovered from the excavation (see Fig 142). This was all sorted and discarded on site, and while attempts were made to recover all burnt worked material, some loss may inevitably have occurred.

The data generated by the initial assessment have, within the restrictions of the sampling framework, enabled foci of activity to be identified (Fig 143). These are discussed above. The nature of the assemblage does not at present allow any more specific interpretation.

Further analysis of the assemblage should be dependent on the recovery of sealed comparative groups, ideally demonstrating stages of both production and utilisation.

4.14 c The prehistoric pottery (Figs 144, 145)

by Frances Raymond

A total of 4027 sherds, weighing 10,591kg, and representing a minimum of 85 vessels, was recovered. The assemblage includes ceramics typical of the Peterborough, Beaker, Deverel-Rimbury, and later Bronze Age 'plain ware' traditions. In all tables and figures the Deverel-Rimbury pottery is identified by the fabric codes F:LBA/1 and FfeGM:LBA/1; however, FfeGM: LBA/1 was also used in the production of vessels which are typical of later Bronze Age plain wares: this is discussed in more detail below. There is no evidence allowing for a stratigraphic separation of any of the ceramic groups, since most of the pottery was recovered from the topsoil and underlying sorted horizons within which sherds from vessels representing all periods were mixed (Table 103, MF2 E7–F8).

Spatial analysis failed to identify areas which only incorporate pottery from a single ceramic group, although some types tend to concentrate within specific areas. The majority of Beaker sherds occur in area B, with lesser concentrations in areas C and E. The distribution of Deverel-Rimbury pottery (F:LBA/1) forms a comparable pattern to the Beakers, although there is less in area E. A similar emphasis in area B is reflected by the remaining ceramics, with a second and smaller concentration of later Bronze Age 'plain wares' in area A (see Table 104).

The nature of the assemblage negates the interpretation of changing activity areas between different periods as the quantities of Peterborough Ware, Beakers, and Deverel-Rimbury (F:LBA/1) pottery are small, and fabric FfeGM:LBA/1 includes forms typical of both Deverel-Rimbury and later Bronze Age 'plain wares'. Since the majority of pottery assigned to FfeGM:LBA/1 comprises undecorated and fragmentary body sherds, it is rarely possible to separate the two ceramic traditions. Statements concerning changing discard patterns between phases when Deverel-Rimbury and later Bronze Age ceramics were in use are, therefore, inappropriate.

The following discussion provides details of the characteristics and distribution of each of the ceramic groups in chronological order. A general summary of all identified groups is given in Table 104, with detailed fabric descriptions in Table 32. In addition, Table 103 (MF2 E7–F8) describes the number and weight of sherds belonging to each fabric group by context.

Peterborough Ware

Two sherds (P139 and P140), weighing 11.3g and representing two vessels, were identified. Both are illustrated. The first vessel, P139, belongs to an indeterminate substyle and is too small to allow for an adequate fabric description. The clay paste, however, is very similar to F:Pet/1, used to produce the Fengate Ware vessel P140. This fabric is found elsewhere in the Stonehenge area, and at Wilsford Down (W31) it is used for Mortlake or Ebbsfleet vessels (eg P90). Both sherds from the vessels P139 and P140 are very abraded and neither is large enough to allow for an assessment of rim diameter.

Beaker

Thirty-four sherds, weighing 79.1g, and representing a minimum of 12 vessels, were identified. This represents less than 1% of the total ceramics (Fig 146). Cuts 267 and 270 contained significantly higher percentages of Beaker than elsewhere on the site. The sherds are fragmentary, so that the information on form is extremely limited. The assemblage includes a Wessex/Middle Rhine (W/MR) Beaker (P150); a sherd with a motif characteristic of Clarke's Southern Motif group 4 (P141); three 'rusticated' vessels, one with non-plastic fingernail impressions ((P149), and two of different thicknesses decorated with impressed triangles (P147, P150). Wessex/Middle Rhine Beakers are most characteristic of Case's Middle Style, although this type does continue into the Late stage. The other vessels could belong equally to the Middle/Late Styles.

Six fabric groups were identified (see Tables 103, 105, MF2 E7–F8, F9). Five of these are found on other sites within the Stonehenge area. The exception is CMS: Bkr/1, which is unique to W34. Two of the fabrics, FfeS:Bkr/1 and G:Bkr/2, are shared between sites in the Fargo Wood area and on Wilsford Down. In addition, sherds of feG:Bkr/1 were recovered from W53, the intensive collection site outside Robin Hood's Ball causewayed enclosure. Of the remaining fabrics, feGS:Bkr/3 occurs in the Stonehenge Triangle (54) and on Durrington Down (65), and feGM:Bkr/2 is found on a number of sites in the Fargo Wood area, including the Lesser Cursus (W55). The overall picture is of a similar sharing of fabrics between the north and south of the Stonehenge area, as occurred with the Peterborough Wares.

Within the W34 assemblage all the fabrics, with the exception of FfeS:Bkr/1 and G:Bkr/1 (represented by single sherds), are found within the same contexts. The distribution of fabrics by area is shown in Table 105, MF2 F9. The Beaker fabrics at W34 are not especially unusual and compare closely with examples found widely in the Stonehenge area. Although the inclusion of small quantities of chalk and flint is relatively rare, it has been noted in several other examples. Similarly the presence of moderate and sparse quantities of mica,

Table 104 W34 Fargo Wood II: spatial distribution of ceramic groups (expressed as a percentage of weight)

	A	*B*	*C*	*D*	*E*	*General*
Ceramic group						
Peterborough	–	50	–	50	–	–
Beaker	2	55	16	1	10	16
F:LBA/1	–	65	28	2	4	–
FfeGM:LBA/13	3	75	4	9	6	3
Later Bronze Age	15	42	7	5	9	22
Total pottery	11	54	7	6	8	14

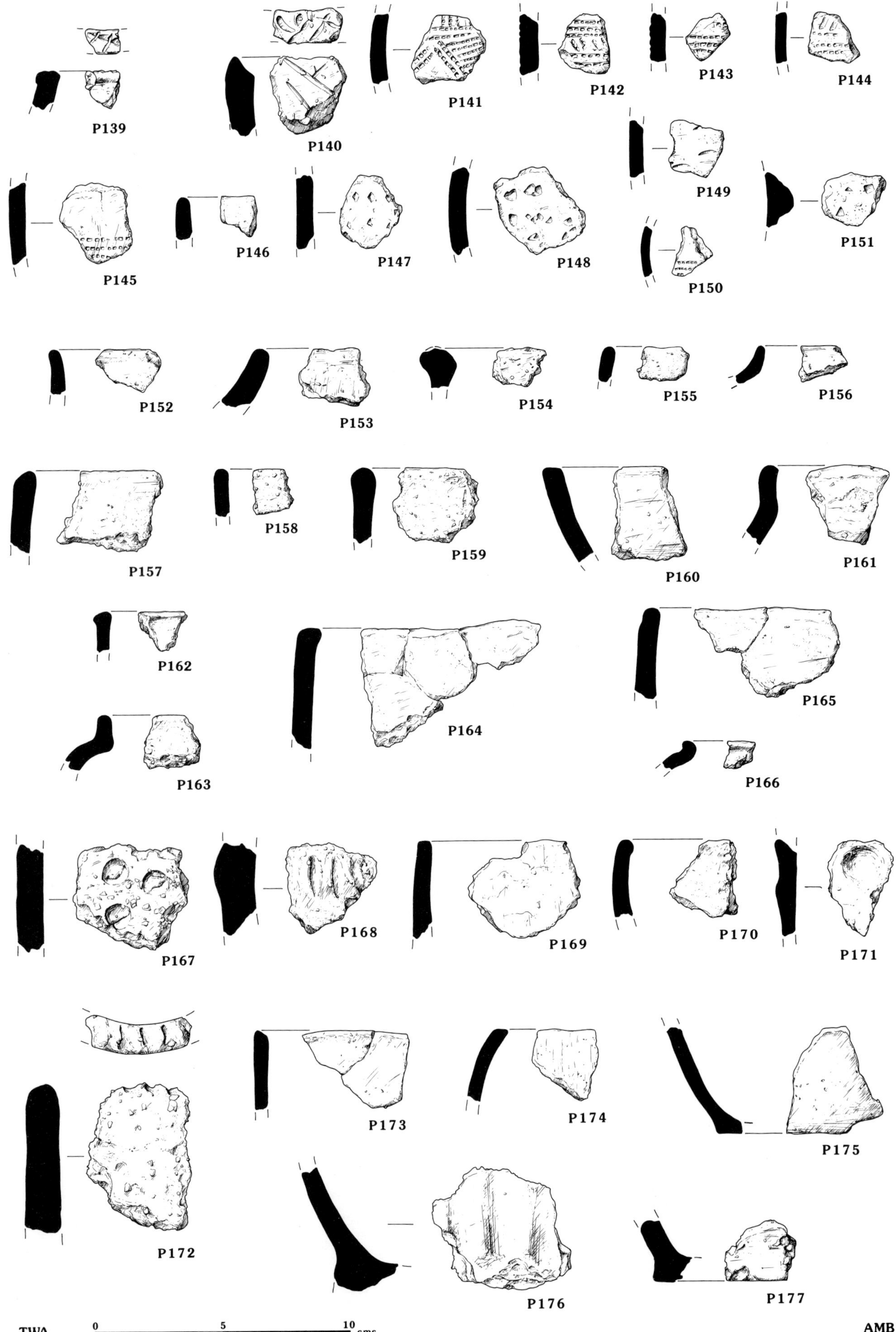

Fig 144 W34 Fargo Wood II Late Bronze Age settlement: prehistoric pottery (P139–P177)

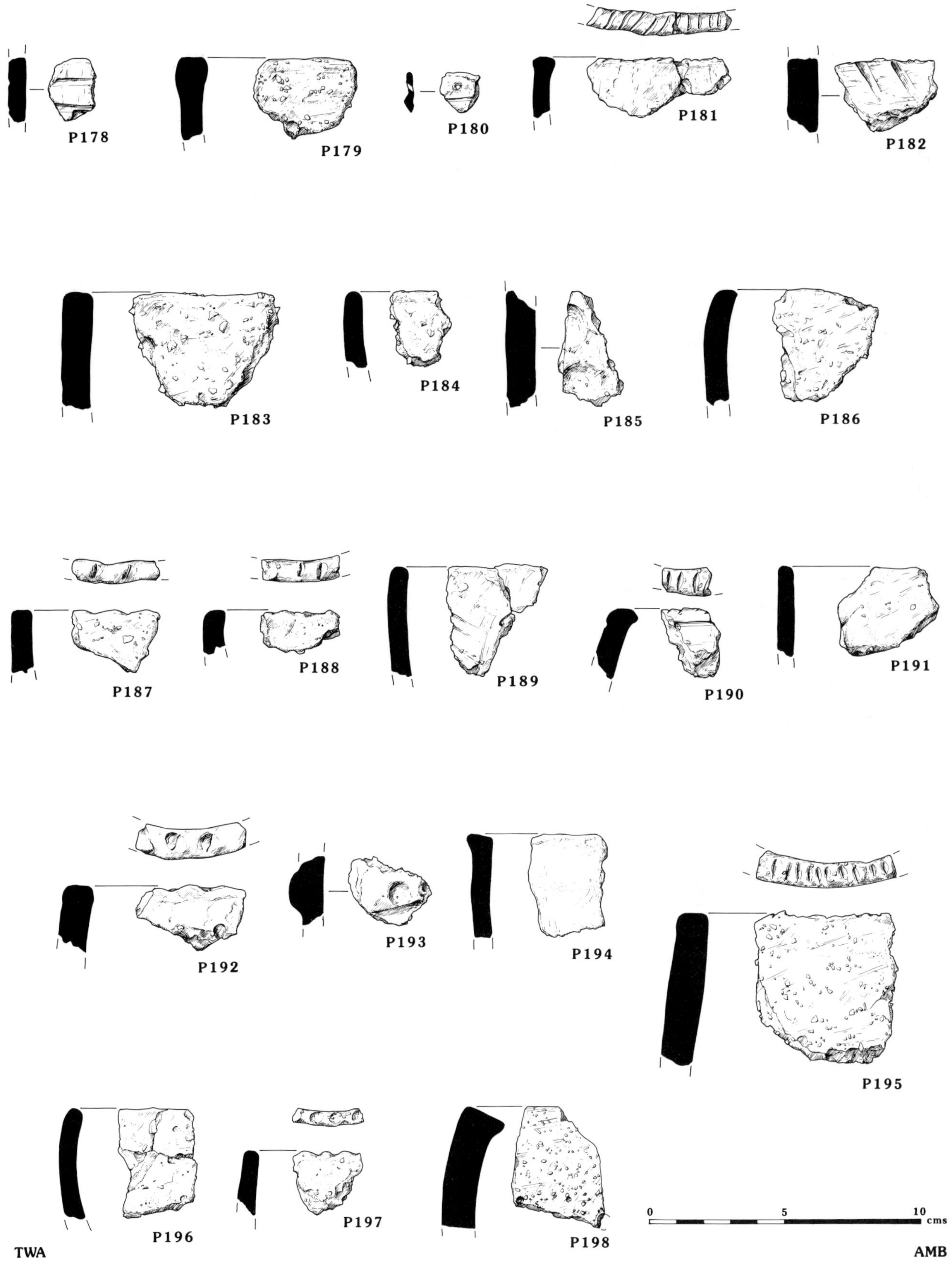

Fig 145 W34 Fargo Wood II Late Bronze Age settlement: prehistoric pottery (P178–P198)

which may have a source outside the Stonehenge area, is fairly characteristic of this ceramic group. As with most of the Beakers recovered by the project, ferruginous clays are favoured, while grog is the major tempering material. None of the other inclusions are likely to have been added deliberately. The particles of quartz sand show a very restricted size range, inconsistent with specially prepared tempers. Sandy clays are particularly common in riverine or floodplain locations, and may have formed a possible source for some of the pottery.

Several of the fabrics are shared between Beakers carrying a range of decorative motifs. An identical fabric, feGS:Bkr/3, is used to produce the Wessex/Middle Rhine Beaker (P150) and a comb-decorated vessel of indeterminate substyle (P144). At Durrington Down (65) this same fabric, but without the 'sealing wax red' finish, carries a comb-impressed infilled pendant, characteristic of Clarke's Southern Motif Group 4 (P287). Both comb- (P141, P142) and fingernail-decorated vessels (P149) occur in feG:Bkr/1, while feGM:Bkr/2 is used for vessels with comb (P143, P145) or triangular impressions.

The occurrence of 'rusticated' and comb-decorated vessels in identical fabrics has been noted on other sites in the Stonehenge area. Interestingly these include feGM:Bkr/2, which at Wilsford Down (W31) carries paired non-plastic fingernail decoration (P112), and infilled comb-impressed pendants at Fargo Wood I (W32, P120), the Lesser Cursus (W55, P232), and Horse Hospital (64) (P283, P284). Such associations support observations made elsewhere (Bamford 1982), that rustication is a feature most commonly associated with Middle/Late Style Beakers. The fabrics recovered by the project are all fine wares, in the sense that the tempers used are finely crushed and well combined, while the vessels appear to have been fired under very controlled conditions. Equal care was taken in the manufacture of these Beakers regardless of the decorative techniques employed.

The range of decorative motifs occurring on vessels at W34, while limited, are entirely consistent with the majority of Beakers recovered by the project, which fall within Case's Middle/Late Styles. The occurrence of

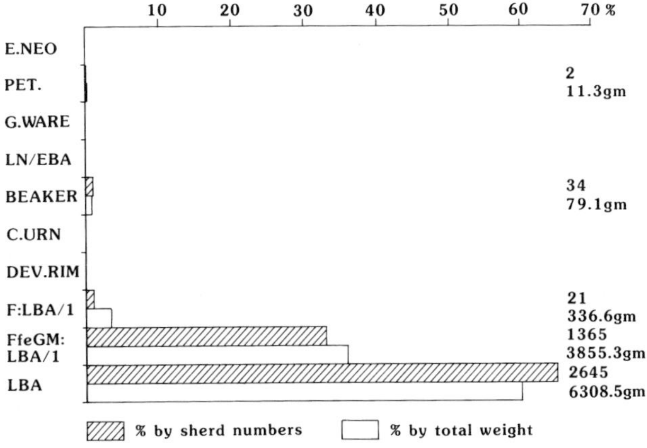

Fig 146 W34 Fargo Wood II Late Bronze Age settlement: prehistoric pottery fabric histogram

Wessex/Middle Rhine Beaker at W34 is mainly notable in terms of its context. Although there is a marked concentration in the distribution of this style in the Wessex region, it has been recovered mainly from burials. The sherds of Wessex/Middle Rhine Beaker on Easton Down (Stone 1933) are one of the few exceptions to this pattern.

Deverel-Rimbury (fabric F:LBA/1)

Twenty-one sherds, weighing 336.6g and representing a minimum of three vessels (P172, P195, P198), were identified. Apart from the illustrated rims, this assemblage includes two base sherds with thicknesses of 20mm. These are very small, and the body angle uncertain. The remaining sherds vary in thickness between 9mm and 12mm, and comprise undecorated body fragments.

The density and even distribution of the flint grits is typical of Deverel-Rimbury fabrics. The size range of the inclusions is wider than in comparable ceramics recovered by the project, giving an overall impression of coarseness. This is reinforced by minimal surface treatment of the vessels represented. The fact that the fabric is not particularly vesicular may indicate that it was being used to produce Bucket Urns.

Unfortunately the information concerning vessel size and form is extremely limited. The rim sherds are too small to allow for accurate diameter measurements. The form of P198 finds parallels at Eldon's Seat, Dorset (Cunliffe and Phillipson 1968, figs 11:10 and 11:11), where rims of this type are characteristic of sub-biconical and ovoid Bucket Urns. The shape of the vessels represented by the two remaining rims (P172, P195) is uncertain.

Deverel-Rimbury ceramics are represented in all areas at W34 with the exception of area A (Table 104). The largest number of sherds occur in areas B and C. They are frequently associated with later Bronze Age 'plain wares' (see Tables 106, 108, MF2 F10, G1–2), although there is insufficient evidence to allow for chronological separation.

F:LBA/1 does not occur on other sites in the area covered by the project.

Deverel-Rimbury/later Bronze Age

Thirteen hundred and twenty-five sherds, weighing 3855.3g and representing a minimum of ten vessels, were identified. Eight of these are illustrated (P179, P183, P184, P186–P198, P192), while the remaining two comprise rims which are identical to P159 and P174. It is not possible to assign the decorated sherds (P167, P168, P185, P193) to any of the identified rim forms. As with all of the pottery at W34, this group is dominated by plain body sherds. Featured fragments comprise less than 3% of the assemblage. These include 12 rims, 14 base angles, 2 decorated cordons, and 7 finger-impressed sherds (see Table 109, MF2 G3–5, for a complete list of featured sherds). The forms represented are characteristic of Deverel-Rimbury ceramics and of later Bronze Age 'plain wares', although in the majority of cases the attribution to a specific tradition is ambiguous.

This ambiguity is mirrored by the fabric FfeGM:LBA/1, which is used to produce vessels with wall thicknesses varying between 4mm and 12mm. Flint is the major tempering material, and as with the Deverel-Rimbury pottery (F:LBA/1) the size range is wide, giving an overall impression of coarseness. The major differences lie in the uneven distribution of these inclusions throughout the clay paste, and in their reduced density. In addition, some sherds display indications of surface treatment in the form of smoothing. This must have occurred at a time when the clay had dried sufficiently to prevent further shrinkage from the flint grits. While this fabric does not compare particularly well with the range of Deverel-Rimbury ceramics recovered by the project, it would not be out of place within assemblages attributed to this tradition. On the other hand, it also finds parallels with the fairly coarse pastes used for the larger 'plain ware' storage jars. The general impression is of the continued use of established technologies between periods when Deverel-Rimbury and later Bronze Age ceramics were being produced. This is not particularly surprising, especially in connection with the larger vessels, where body walls suffer increased stress due to shrinkage during drying. One solution to this problem is to include increased quantities of temper (Braun 1982).

At W34 the same fabric seems to have been used for vessels belonging to both traditions. The incised cordon (P168) is certainly Deverel-Rimbury in character, although the finger-impressed example (P193) could equally be later Bronze Age. Finger-decorated cordons are found most frequently on the larger storage jars within 'plain ware' assemblages. The rims represented by P179, P183, and P186, are consistent with examples found on Deverel-Rimbury urns, although identical forms to P183, from thinner-walled vessels, occur in later Bronze Age fabrics.

The rest of the featured sherds include forms which are characteristic of 'plain ware' vessels. Finger impressions across the tops of rims (P187, P188, P192) are recorded amongst these ceramics. Indeed, at W34 this form of decoration is also found on sherds in fabrics typical of the later Bronze Age (P181, P190, P197), while the square profile of P192 finds parallels in pottery of this period. Similarly, the finger-decorated sherd P167, is mirrored by an example in a later Bronze Age fabric, P171. The rims P184 and P189 have slightly curving profiles characteristic of 'plain ware' jars and indeed both forms occur in a wide range of fabrics attributed to this tradition. This is also true of the rims in FfeGM:LBA/1, which are identical to the illustrated sherds P159 and P174. Finally, three of the more complete base sherds are similar to P175 and P177, and are characteristic of later Bronze Age forms.

There is insufficient evidence at W34 to suggest that the assemblage might be transitional, with precedence over the main group of 'plain wares'. In the first place there is not enough information concerning form, and in the second, the stratigraphic associations are missing.

In area B the position of FfeGM:LBA/1 as the dominant fabric group (Table 104) is at its most marked. This dominance is maintained to a lesser degree within the sorted horizon in area C, and in the topsoil in areas D and E (Table 103, MF2 E7–F8). The figures for weight, however, tend to over-emphasise the importance of the fabric in areas C, D, and E, where greater sherd size causes a bias in its favour. A consideration of the number of sherds indicates equal and sometimes greater quantities of FS:LBA/3.

An analysis of the associations and distribution of sherds belonging to this fabric group demonstrates the mixed nature of the ceramic assemblage at W34. Sherds belonging to FfeGM:LBA/1 are associated with the rest of the 'plain wares' in each of the sample areas, as well as in the majority of the 1m systematic sample squares (Table 103, MF2 E7–F8). They are found with pottery representing all the identified later Bronze Age fabric groups (Table 108, MF2 G1–2).

FfeGM:LBA/1 occurs within every excavated area at W34, with a marked concentration in area B (Table 104), particularly in its north-eastern sector where the largest quantities of pottery from the 'plain ware' assemblages also cluster.

In contrast to F:LBA/1, FfeGM:LBA/1 is found more widely within the Fargo Wood area, at the Lesser Cursus (W55) and from Cursus West End (62). Although the number of sherds is low, their distribution coincides with the field system associated with W34 and does not extend to other parts of the Stonehenge area. This evidence is reinforced by the distribution of 'plain wares' from W34 (described below). Later Bronze Age ceramics recovered during excavation and fieldwalking all have very localised distributions.

Later Bronze Age

Sherds numbering 2645, weighing 6308.5g, and representing a minimum of 58 vessels, were identified. Featured sherds comprise only 3% of the assemblage and include 46 rims, three decorated rims, 29 base angles and four decorated body sherds (Table 109, MF2 G3–5), all of which are characteristic of later Bronze Age 'plain wares'.

Twelve fabrics can be identified (Table 103, MF2 E7–F8). All, with the exception of CFG:LBA/1, are used to produce vessels with body walls ranging in thickness between 3mm and 10mm. The size range represented by body sherds in CFG:LBA/1, at between 3mm and 8mm, is more restricted. There are fairly close similarities between several of the fabrics in terms of temper, and the surface treatment of the vessels which they form.

FfeSV:LBA/2 and FSV:LBA/1 both include high densities of finely crushed flint and quartz sand. The sand is of a restricted size range and may have been present within the raw clay. It is particularly common within deposits adjacent to rivers and their floodplains. Although the flint grits in FfeSV:LBA/2 and FSV:LBA/1 are visible from the surface, they do not stand out in relief, indicating that smoothing must have occurred when the vessels were almost dry. Both fabrics have very similar counterparts amongst Deverel-Rimbury ceramics, but at W34 are used for later Bronze Age vessels (P174, P175). This certainly supports suggestions for the continuation of established technologies between the two ceramic traditions. Indeed, a similar pattern has already been described in connection with FfeGM:LBA/1.

In contrast, both FfeS:LBA/3 and FV:LBA/1 include very little flint. They were also used to produce vessels rather similar in surface treatment, which involved careful smoothing of both surfaces, but particularly the exterior. FfeS:LBA/3 is especially notable in the almost polished appearance of a number of body sherds, although burnishing *per se* was not apparent.

A third and fairly obvious group consists of the four fabrics which include shell as a tempering material (feSsh:LBA/1, feSsh:LBA/2, fesh:LBA/1, and feV: LBA/1). This must have been derived from an area outside the immediate vicinity of W34. Both feSsh: LBA/1 and feSsh:LBA/2 incorporate sand as the dominant non-plastic inclusion. This has a restricted size range and is evenly distributed throughout the fabric. These factors, together with the uneven distribution of shell in feSsh:LBA/1, may indicate that the clay exploited already included sand as a major impurity. While the surfaces of the sherds in these fabrics show signs of finger-smearing, the finish is not as fine as in vessels made from fesh:LBA/1. Here the pottery is highly smoothed, with an almost polished appearance. The surface treatment of vessels made from feV:LBA/1 is no longer apparent, mainly because the sherds are all over-fired. Shell decomposes at temperatures in excess of 650°C, especially when starved of carbon dioxide (Shepard 1956). This appears to have occurred in the case of feV:LBA/1, leaving a very brittle ceramic with numerous voids.

The remaining fabrics represented at W34 (CFG: LBA/1, FS:LBA/1, feSV:LBA/1, and G:LBA/1) are all rather different, and do not fall within any of the groups defined above. Apart from variations in inclusion types and in densities of those inclusions, some of these fabrics display fairly distinctive surface finishes. Although there are large quantities of flint within CFG:LBA/1 smoothing must have occurred at a time when the clay paste was largely dry. The grits are pressed well into the fabric and do not stand out on either surface. In contrast FS:LBA/1 has a coarser appearance, although it contains lesser amounts of flint. There is a tendency for inclusions to stand out from the surface, even though there is ample evidence for finger-smearing on body sherds. The fabric feSV:LBA/1 is mainly distinguished by the common use of vegetable temper in conjunction with sand, while G:LBA/1 incorporates grog as a major inclusion. The surfaces of vessels made from feSV:LBA/1 do not appear to have received special treatment. Vertical finger-smearing occurs on sherds in G:LBA/1, where the orientation is apparent (eg P176).

The fabrics represented at W34, in terms of inclusion kind and combination, incorporate a fairly wide range of contrasting types. This suggests the development of clay pastes which met rather different functional requirements. Containers with specifically prepared fabrics are better suited to certain tasks. The most obvious example is in the case of cooking pots, which need to be resistant to thermal shock. One way of achieving this is to use inclusions with very similar expansions to the clay matrix (Braun 1982; Bronitsky and Hamer 1986). Grog and shell are obviously of value in this respect. Thinner body walls also increase thermal shock resistance (Braun 1983).

The range of fabrics at W34 may represent a refinement in the production of ceramics for different purposes during the later Bronze Age, a time at which there was a corresponding increase in the range of vessel shapes. Unfortunately, at W34, there is not enough information to allow for a correlation between varying forms and fabrics. Although the range of rim forms is wide (Table 109, MF2 G3–5), the fragmentary condition of the pottery and the low percentage of featured sherds negates detailed discussion concerning vessel shape, and does not allow for discussion of style and function. Only three fairly general forms are identifiable on this site. These include a series of jars with inturned rims (eg P170, P174, P196); jars with upright rims and convex body profiles (eg P152, P156, P161, P163, P166), and one possible bowl (P160).

An analysis of the distribution of each of the fabric groups identified at W34 suggests that some areas were being singled out for the deposition of specific wares (Table 110, MF2 G6). Although most fabrics are represented within every excavated area, there are marked concentrations in certain areas. Between 85% and 90% of the fabrics including grog (CFG:LBA/1 and G:LBA/1) are found in area B. Those incorporating flint as a tempering material also occur in greater numbers within the same area. In contrast there are high percentages of shell-tempered wares in area A, although they also occur in significant numbers in area B. In addition, there is a concentration of these fabrics in cut 175 in area A and in the layer below the sorted horizon in area B. At the same time, shell-tempered pottery is entirely absent in area D.

A consideration of the relative proportions of different fabric groups within each of the areas (Table 107, MF2 F11–14), indicates the dominance of FS:LBA/3 in areas C, D, and E. This same fabric occurs in roughly equal numbers with feSsh:LBA/1 in area A. In contrast, CFG:LBA/1 is the largest fabric group in area B.

The distribution of later Bronze Age 'plain wares' also extends across the area of the adjacent field system. They are represented at Fargo Wood I (W32), the Lesser Cursus (W55), Durrington Down barrow (W57), and from surface collection North of the Cursus (52), Cursus West End (62), and Fargo Road (63).

Summary

The general impression gained from the W34 ceramic assemblage is of fairly limited and intermittent activity during the later Neolithic and Early Bronze Age. The main occupation in the area is represented by the Deverel-Rimbury pottery and the later Bronze Age 'plain wares'. The character of the Deverel-Rimbury ceramics indicates that they may belong to a fairly late phase of that tradition. The rather limited evidence concerning the form of the group of pottery FfeGM:LBA/1 implies that it consists largely of later Bronze Age 'plain wares', with a minor Deverel-Rimbury element.

It has been suggested elsewhere (Gingell 1980) that Deverel-Rimbury and later Bronze Age 'plain wares' were in contemporary use on sites in Wessex (see Barrett 1980 for a summary). The evidence is ambiguous and remains so when the results of excavations at W34 are taken into account. Here, in the absence of stratigraphic association, it is not possible to discern the degree of contemporaneity between the Deverel-Rimbury pottery and the later Bronze Age assemblage. The use of the same fabric (FfeGM:LBA/1) for vessels belonging to both traditions does not necessarily mean they are the same age. It seems highly likely that successful technologies, once established, continued into the later period. This finds support in similarities between Deverel-Rimbury wares and the two fabrics, FfeSV:LBA/2 and FSV:LBA/1, used for later Bronze Age forms.

It is entirely possible that the pottery from W34 comprises the kind of transitional assemblage represented at Eldon's Seat in Dorset (Cunliffe and Phillipson 1968). Its occurrence would not be especially surprising on a site where occupation continued uninterrupted. In the light of the evidence from W34, however, this must remain purely conjectural. In any case, the production of such wares need not represent a particularly long phase in the history of the site. They could well have been replaced fairly rapidly by purely later Bronze Age forms.

The extrapolation of the chronology for 'plain wares' in the Thames Valley (Barrett 1980) for application in Central Wessex may be inappropriate. On the other hand, there is still a gap between the latest dates for Deverel-Rimbury ceramics and the earliest for Late Bronze Age decorated pottery. There seems little reason to deny that the 'plain wares' at W34 fill this hiatus. A shorter chronology for later Bronze Age pottery in Wessex might help to explain the relative infrequency of pottery assemblages of this date in comparison with the Thames Valley. The relative scarcity of such assemblages in Central Wessex may be more apparent than real, as they are certainly well represented in the area covered by the Stonehenge Environs Project. Their occurrence on the same sites as Deverel-Rimbury pottery may indicate little more than a greater continuity between the two periods in this area.

Illustrated pottery (Figs 144, 145)

Peterborough

P139 Area D, context 124
FS:uncertain (sherd too small to determine fabric). Rim sherd. Square with convex external surface. Cross-hatched impressed motif (possibly cord) along top of rim.

P140 Area B, context 224
F:Pet/1. Rim sherd of a Fengate Ware vessel with fingernail impression arranged as a lattice or herringbone design on the interior rim bevel. In addition there are end-to-end fingernail impressions on the exterior, apparently arranged in a complex pattern, with groups of lines running at an angle to each other.

Beaker

P141 context 23
feG:Bkr/1. Body sherd. Rectangular-toothed comb impressions arranged in pendants defined by two parallel lines infilled with horizontal lines.

P142 context 37
feG:Bkr/1. Body sherd. Closely set parallel comb impressions arranged in two narrow bands, filled with oblique comb impressions; all rectangular-toothed comb.

P143 Area A, context 83
feGM:Bkr/2. Body sherd. Four parallel rectangular-toothed comb impressions.

P144 Area B, context 109
feGS:Bkr/3. Body sherd. Two parallel linear impressions (probably comb) set on a diagonal axis to three comb-impressed rows: the impressions are worn but appear to be rectangular-toothed comb.

P145 Area C, context 124
feGM:Bkr/2. Body sherd. Three parallel comb impressions; the teeth vary in shape between square and rectangular.

P146 Area C, context 147
feG:Bkr/1. Rim sherd. Rounded and upright.

P147 Area B, context 210
CMS:Bkr/1. Body sherd. Impressed triangular motif.

P148 Area B, context 223
feGM:Bkr/2. Body sherd. Impressed triangular motif.

P149 Area E, context 247
feG:Bkr/1. Body sherd. Single non-plastic fingernail impressions; orientation of sherd not certain.

P150 Area B, context 268
feGS:Bkr/3. Body sherd. Two parallel comb impressions in square-toothed comb. This sherd is very thin-walled and fine, and has a distinctive red colour. Although it lacks the 'sealing wax' finish *senso stricto* this could be the result of erosion. The colour and fineness of the sherd alone strongly indicate that the vessel represented is of Clarke's Wessex/Middle Rhine group.

P151 Area B, context 268
CMS:Bkr/1. Body sherd. Impressed triangular motif.

Later Bronze Age

P152 context 21
CFG:LBA/1. Rim sherd. Rounded and everted.

P153 context 38
FS:LBA/3. Rim sherd. Rounded. From a vessel with an inward sloping neck.

P154 context 43
FS:LBA/3. Rim sherd. Rounded and everted with an internal bevel.

P155 context 47
FS:LBA/3. Rim sherd. Rounded.

P156 Area A, context 70
fesh:LBA/1. Rim sherd. Rounded with internal bevel. From a vessel with an inward sloping neck.

P157Area A, context 70
feSsh:LBA/1. Rim sherd. Rounded with external bevel.

P158 Area A, context 72
FS:LBA/3. Rim sherd. Rounded with internal bevel.

P159 Area A, context 73
fesh:LBA/1. Rim sherd. Rounded with convex external surface.

P160 Area A, context 74
fesh:LBA/1. Rim sherd. Flattened top, possibly from a bowl.

P161 Area A, context 76
CFG:LBA/1. Rim sherd. Inverted with a flattened top. From a vessel with an upright neck and a flaring body.

P162 Area A, context 87
fesh:LBA/1. Rim sherd. Flattened top with convex external surface.

P163 Area A, context 93
FS:LBA/3. Rim sherd. Rounded. From a vessel with an upright neck and a flaring body.

P164 Area B, context 101
G:LBA/1. Rim sherd. Variation in profile from rounded to rounded with a flattened and expanded internal surface.

P165 Area B, context 101
CFG:LBA/1. Rim sherd. Asymmetrically rounded.

P166 Area B, context 102
FfeS:LBA/3. Rim sherd. Everted with a flattened top. From a vessel with an inward sloping neck.

P167 Area B, context 108
FfeGM:LBA/1. Body sherd. Fingertip impressions.

P168 Area B, context 109
FfeGM:LBA/1. Body sherd with cordon, decorated with an incised linear motif. Deverel-Rimbury.

P169 Area B, context 112
CFG:LBA/1. Rim sherd. Flattened top with internal bevel.

P170 Area B, context 113
G:LBA/1. Rim sherd. Inverted and rounded with convex internal surface.

P171 Area B, context 117
FS:LBA/3. Body sherd. Fingertip impression.

P172 Area B, context 120
F:LBA/1. Rim sherd. Upright and rounded. Fingernail impressions set on a slight diagonal axis across the top of the rim. Deverel-Rimbury.

P173 Area B, context 120
FfeS:LBA/3. Rim sherd. Upright and pointed with internal bevel.

P174 Area B, context 121
FfeSV:LBA/2. Rim sherd. Inverted with a flattened top.

P175 Area B, context 121
FfeSV:LBA/2. Base sherd from a vessel with a rounded profile.

P176 Area B, context 121
G:LBA/1. Base sherd from a vessel with a rounded profile. There are traces of finger-smearing on the exterior surface.

P177 Area B, context 122
CFG:LBA/1. Base sherd from a vessel with a rounded profile.

P178 Area B, context 206
CFG:LBA/1. Body sherd. Incised linear motif arranged in two parallel lines.

P179 Area B, context 218
FfeGM:LBA/1. Rim sherd. Flattened top with convex external surface.

P180 Area B, context 220
G:LBA/1. Body sherd. Pierced. The sherd has lost most of both surfaces.

P181 Area B, context 221
CFG:LBA/1. Rim sherd. Flattened and expanded top with convex internal surface and external bevel. Decorated with fingernail impressions across the top of the rim set on an axis varying from diagonal to vertical.

P182 Area B, context 221
G:LBA/1. Body sherd. Two parallel linear impressions.

P183 Area B, context 223
FfeGM:LBA/1. Rim sherd. Upright with a flattened top.

P184 Area B, context 223
FfeGM:LBA/1. Rim sherd. Rounded with convex internal surface.

P185 Area B, context 223
FfeGM:LBA/1. Body sherd. Fingertip impressions.

P186 Area B, context 224
FfeGM:LBA/1. Rim sherd. Inverted and rounded with internal bevel.

P187 Area B, context 224
FfeGM:LBA/1. Rim sherd. Flattened top with internal bevel. Decorated with fingernail impressions set on a diagonal axis across the top of the rim.

P188 Area B, context 225
FfeGM:LBA/1. Rim sherd. Flattened top with convex internal and external surfaces. Decorated with fingernail impressions across the top of the rim.

P189 Area B, context 279
FfeGM:LBA/1. Rim sherd. Rounded.

P190 Area C, context 131
CFG:LBA/1. Rim sherd. Rounded and expanded with convex internal and external surfaces. Decorated with fingernail impressions across the top of the rim on a slightly diagonal axis.

P191 Area C, context 133
feSsh:LBA/1. Rim sherd. Flattened top.

P192 Area D, context 152
FfeGM:LBA/1. Rim sherd. Flattened top. Decorated with fingertip impressions along the top of the rim.

P193 Area D, context 154
FfeGM:LBA/1. Body sherd with cordon. Fingertip impressions.

P194 Area E, context 235
FfeS:LBA/3. Rim sherd. Flattened top with convex external surface.

P195 U/S
F:LBA/1. Rim sherd. Flattened top with convex external surface. Fingernail impressions across top of rim. Deverel-Rimbury.

P196 Area E, context 243
feV:LBA/1. Rim sherd. Rounded top with inward curve.

P197 Area E, context 245
FS:LBA/3. Rim sherd. Rounded with convex external surface. Decorated with fingertip impressions across the top of the rim.

P198 U/S
F:LBA/1. Rim sherd. Inverted with a slightly indented internal bevel. Deverel-Rimbury.

4.14 d Copper alloy and shale (Fig 147)

Context 42, SF71

Copper alloy awl; maximum length 55mm, maximum thickness 4mm. Square section, one end flattened, the other pointed. An ubiquitous Bronze Age find with many parallels.

Context 122, SF20

Incomplete copper alloy object (broken at both ends); length 83mm, circular section of maximum diameter 3.2mm, flattened at one end. ? Roman toilet spoon (cf Crummy 1983, fig 64).

Context 224, SF43

Copper alloy coin; indecipherable but assumed to be Roman (not illustrated).

Context 217, SF50, and context 213, SF58 (both area B subsoil)

Fragments of shale armlet; diameter appears to be approximately 80mm (internal), with a complete cross-section of approximately 7mm in diameter. Owing to the laminated state of these fragments it is not possible to ascertain whether they are lathe turned. They may therefore be of prehistoric or Roman date.

4.14 e Animal bones

by Mark Maltby

A total of 1109 animal bone fragments were recovered from the excavations. These were subdivided into the following groups:

Context 1	Topsoil from 1m sample squares
Context 71	Area A topsoil
Context 97	Area B topsoil; 206 Area B sorted horizon
Context 123	Area C topsoil; 180 Area C sorted horizon
Context 149	Area D topsoil
Context 232	Area E topsoil
Stratified	Contexts 175, 258, 262, 267, 269, 270

The bones found in each of these groups are shown in Table 111. The totals included 17 fragments from sieved samples. The number of bones from the sample squares tended to be greater in squares to the northern part of the sampling area. Of the 5m squares (areas A to E), area C produced the most fragments but these included most of the intrusive rabbit bones. Area E was the only 5m square to produce over 100 fragments. Area B appears to have preserved bones particularly badly. Only loose teeth survived and these had lost most of their calcification.

Amongst the identifiable bones, cattle and sheep/goat fragments dominated. Sheep/goat fragments outnumbered those of cattle in the 1m sample squares. In Areas A, C, and D cattle fragments narrowly outnumbered those of sheep/goat, whereas sheep/goat fragments were more common in area E. Such variations may not be very significant, given the small sample size and the extremely fragmentary nature of the faunal assemblage. The only bone positively identified to sheep was a fragment of metacarpus. There was no positive identification of goat.

Pig fragments were consistently poorly represented throughout the deposits. Three of the five horse fragments were teeth from area E that may have been from the same animal. Dog was represented by a single fragment of tibia. No bones of red or roe deer were identified.

The rabbit, hare, and water vole bones may all have been relatively recent intrusions into the deposits. Rabbit bones were found particularly in context 180 and in the cut 258/265, which supports the suspicion that this feature may have been a rabbit burrow and that area C in general was disturbed by rabbit activity.

The poor preservation of the assemblage is indicated by the high proportion of loose teeth in the assemblage: 84% of the cattle and 80% of the sheep/goat assemblages consisted of loose teeth (Table 112, MF2 G7). Although no bones were severely eroded, 477 had slight and 33 had moderate surface erosion (the total of eroded bones excludes loose teeth). The fragmentary nature of the assemblage can be attributed to weathering, trampling, shallow burial, and plough disturbance. As a result of these factors, a high percentage of the bones consisted of small unidentifiable fragments and, apart from loose teeth, only a few sturdy elements

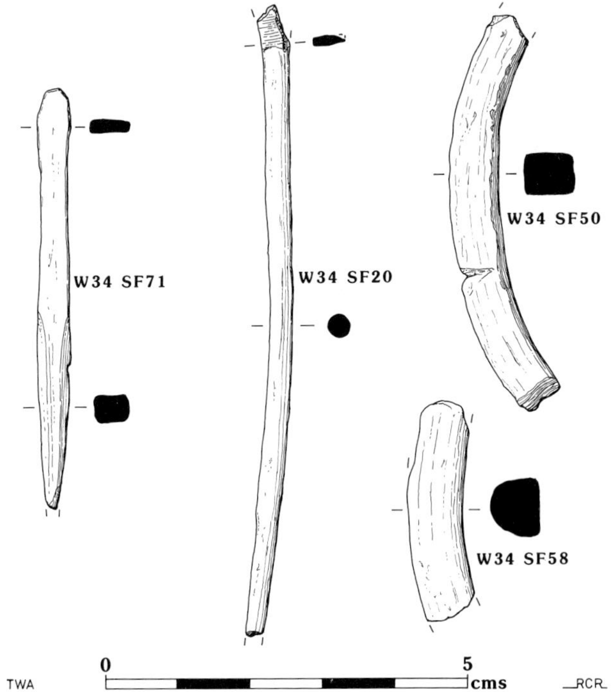

Fig 147 W34 Fargo Wood II Late Bronze Age settlement: copper alloy and shale objects

Table 111 W34 Fargo Wood II: animal species represented by context

	Context									
Species	*1*	*71*	*97*	*123*	*149*	*180*	*206*	*232*	*Other*	*Total*
Cattle	37	24	7	19	19	12	8	15	15	156
Sheep/goat	57	20	–	14	12	14	1	28	18	164
Pig	1	2	–	2	–	1	–	1	–	7
Horse	1	–	–	–	–	1	–	3	–	5
Dog	–	–	–	–	–	1	–	–	–	1
Rabbit	2	–	–	–	–	17	–	2	46	67
Hare	1	–	–	–	–	–	–	–	–	1
Water vole	–	–	–	–	–	1	–	–	–	1
Large mammal	115	10	1	22	22	30	–	32	7	239
Sheep-sized mammal	81	11	–	19	16	29	–	42	10	208
Unidentified mammal	94	3	1	5	8	14	–	44	1	170
Total	389	70	9	81	76	120	9	167	97	1019

survived in an identifiable state. Sixty-eight fragments bore evidence of burning; 13 of these were from area D, where they accounted for 17% of the fragments recorded.

Ageing evidence was sparse, despite the large numbers of loose teeth. There was little evidence for the presence of a significant number of young cattle in the assemblage, whereas the sheep/goat assemblage did include a few bones and teeth that belonged to young lambs.

Two observations of butchery were made. A cattle mandible had superficial chop marks on the medial aspect of the posterior of the ramus and a knife cut on the lateral aspect of the ramus near the posterior condyle. The latter mark was probably inflicted during the detachment of the mandible from the skull. An astragalus of a sheep/goat had knife cuts on the anterior aspect towards the distal articulation. These would have been made during the disarticulation of the lower hindlimb from the tibia. Both types of butchery have been commonly found on Iron Age specimens from southern England.

4.15 A Late Bronze Age settlement at Winterbourne Stoke Crossroads

In the course of a watching brief carried out in 1967 during the improvement of the A303, an area of settlement was located adjacent to the Winterbourne Stoke barrow group. The positioning of a new roundabout to the south-west of the end of the long barrow (Winterbourne Stoke 1) resulted in the stripping of a substantial area, within which a number of subsoil features were recorded and excavated (interim report, Vatcher and Vatcher 1968, 108). These were reported as four circular structures, probably of later Bronze Age date, shallow pits, and two stockade trenches thought possibly to be part of the settlement.

The material from which this brief report was compiled consisted of the artefacts together with an annotated field plan which was used for the compilation of Figure 148. The descriptions of features from the finds bags and boxes have been used to compile a context record, subsequently used in the identification of the finds. Details of identified contexts and finds are contained within the archive.

The structure of the site

The western side of the area examined, if not the extent of the settlement area itself, was defined by a linear ditch (one of the 'stockade trenches' referred to in the interim report). This was located in 11 separate cuttings and was sectioned in three places. There appear to have been no finds from any of these cuttings.

In the south-east quadrant of the examined area, the stripping of topsoil revealed a small cluster of pits, three of which, closely grouped, are recorded as containing sherds of both Middle Bronze Age urn, and of 'rusticated Beaker'. A short length of ditch to the west of these pits is not located on plan and is therefore not shown on Figure 148 A. The finds from this ditch included sherds of Roman pottery.

The majority of the settlement evidence was recorded in the north-east quadrant (detail in Fig 148 B). Interpretation of the available feature plan suggests at least three circular post-built structures. The density of structures within such a small area may indicate a sequence, irrecoverable from the available data, but suggesting a long period of occupation. Two of the structures, approximately 5m and 6.5m in diameter respectively, have clearly defined rectangular south-facing porches. The multiple postholes in the area of the porch on the most westerly example suggests replacement, and this structure also appears to have a roughly central, flint-packed posthole. The third and largest structure, approximately 8.5m in diameter, has a less coherent plan, although there is again some indication of a porch structure to the south/south-west. The incorporation of the 'working hollow' may suggest a non-domestic function.

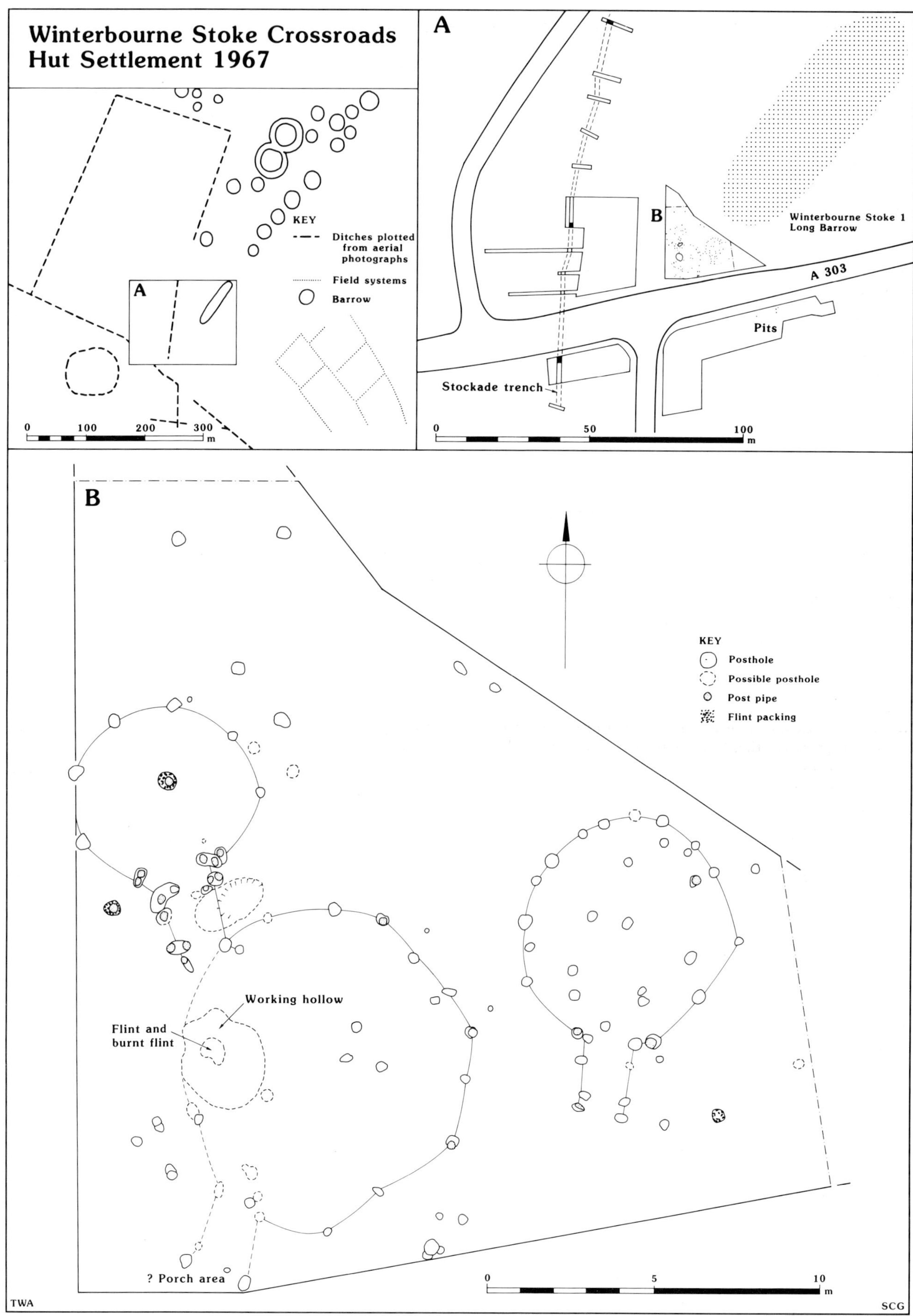

Fig 148 Winterbourne Stoke Crossroads 'hut' settlement: location and plans

Finds

The excavation produced very small quantities of worked flint (*c* 5 pieces) and animal bone, details of which are contained in archive. The pottery, the majority of which appears to have been recovered from the group of pits in the south-eastern quadrant, appears to be primarily of similar fabrics to those recovered from W34 (this vol, 4.14 c), and includes the Deverel-Rimbury rim sherd (P366).

On the basis of the limited evidence for economy and date, this settlement appears to be directly comparable with W34.

4.16 W17–22, W25–26: dry valley research

This project was the first research aspect of the Stonehenge Environs Project, and was initiated in 1981 with the intention of investigating the potential both for and within colluvial deposits in the study area.

Localised colluvial deposits had already been recorded within the study area, specifically within Durrington Walls (Wainwright and Longworth 1971) and could be inferred from the occurrence of 'Celtic' field lynchets (RCHME 1979). In addition, the sample excavation at Coneybury Henge (W2, this vol, 4.9) in 1980 had demonstrated localised colluvium within the slight hilltop saddle occupied by the monument.

Previous work by Martin Bell in Sussex (Bell 1981a) had shown the value of dry valleys as environmental catchment areas, their value highlighted where adjacent areas of intensive activity could be expected to generate datable horizons within associated deposits.

4.16 a Site description

The original methodology for the Stonehenge area, developed in discussion with Martin Bell, was to involve four elements after the selection of areas of potential.

1 Contour survey of a transect spanning the area of assumed colluvial deposits and including the adjacent slopes.
2 Surface collection (where the area was under arable cultivation) of the contoured transect, to be collected as a transect of 5m by 5m squares.
3 The excavation of test pits at the highest and lowest points of the transect indicated by the contour survey.
4 If substantial and datable deposits were located by 3, then a more extensive excavation would be carried out, employing the methodology devised by Bell (1981).

During the 1981 and 1982 seasons, a total of eight areas were investigated. These areas (W17–22, 25, and 26) are located on Figure 8, as are the position of eight auger observations (A 1–8, Table 113, MF2 G8) made by David Cope in the course of mapping the soils of the area (Colborne and Cope 1983). Four of the test pits excavated by the Stonehenge Environs Project were observed by either Martin Bell or David Cope and this report summarises their observations, details of which are contained within the project archive.

All of the areas investigated, with the exception of W26 (located in a side dry valley of the River Till to the west), were associated with the main Stonehenge Bottom/Spring Bottom dry valley system which dissects the study area. None, again with the exception of W26, produced more than 0.40m of deposits overlying natural chalk and, in consequence, no further excavation was carried out. As the first three areas to be investigated proved negative, the full methodology outlined above was discontinued and in subsequent areas test pits were excavated as an initial stage of investigation. In no case was this followed by contour survey and collection.

A summary of the sample areas is given below. Details of contour surveys and finds are contained within the project archive.

Transect 1 W17, Winterbourne Stoke Crossroads SU 104414

North–south 200m transect contoured, collected, and sampled through shallow depression south-west of Winterbourne Stoke Crossroads. Collection showed a correlation between a drop in artefact numbers and the edge of the apparent colluvium. Excavation proved that the fall-off in artefact numbers was real and did not represent 'masking' by colluvium.

Transect 2 W18, The Diamond (Wilsford Down) SU 108407

North-west–south-east 175m transect contoured, collected, and sampled across 'industrial' area. Exceptionally flinty but no colluvium recorded.

Transect 3 W19, Durrington Down SU 118438

East–west 240m transect contoured, collected, and sampled parallel to Fargo Road farm track. Collection produced 12 sherds of pottery, primarily of Middle and Late Bronze Age date, together with a barbed and tanged arrowhead.

The pits at the side of the valley produced shallow plough rendzina soils of the Icknield series, that to the west being flint-free, while that to the east was somewhat disturbed by a modern ditch. The profile in the centre of the valley was only 0.35m deep over a Pleistocene coombe deposit, and would probably be classified as an Icknield-Andover intergrade.

Transect 4 W20, Stonehenge Bottom SU 127420

Prior to sampling, Stonehenge Bottom was considered to show the highest potential for colluvial deposits within the study area. However, excavation in the centre of the eccentrically profiled dry valley produced negative results. The absence of colluvial deposits was suggested as possibly being the result of recent scouring by winterbourne streams.

Transect 5 W21, Stonehenge Bottom (side valley) SU 125414

This, a side coombe off the main Stonehenge Bottom dry valley, was investigated in order to determine whether or not such minor elements of the overall dry valley system contained the colluvial deposits absent from the main valley (eg W20). The results were again negative.

Transect 6 W22, Cursus Valley (Larkhill Sewage Farm) SU 128430

This consisted of a single sample trench excavated within an area of pasture immediately south of the point at which the Stonehenge Cursus crosses Stonehenge Bottom. Large quantities of worked flint were recovered unassociated with any colluvial soils.

Transect 7 W25, Stonehenge Bottom II (north of A303) SU 127421

This consisted of a single sample trench excavated within an area of pasture immediately north of where the A303 embankment crosses Stonehenge Bottom. This was excavated largely to prove once and for all that, despite initial preconceptions, there was no colluvium within the entire Stonehenge Bottom dry valley complex. The profile, classified as Icknield series, was 0.4m deep over a Pleistocene coombe deposit.

Transect 8 W26, Greenland Farm ('The Deep Hole') SU 098435

This consisted of a single trench excavated at the bottom of a narrow, steep-sided side valley of the River Till. This produced a profile, classified as Gore series (Cope 1976) over 1.3m deep. However, the upper colluvial levels (down to *c* 0.60m) were contaminated with recent debris and below this the deposits probably represent palaeosol predating the colluvium. This profile contained no worked flint at any level.

Discussion

The problem of explaining the paucity of colluvial deposits on dry valley floors within the study area is not a simple one. One possible explanation is that for reasons of land use little widespread erosion occurred over much of this gently sloping area. It can also be suggested that the position of the study area on the gently sloping dip slope may, together with the limited extent of superficial deposits on rounded slopes, account for thinner colluvial deposits than have been reported from escarpment valleys or those lower on the dip slope. A third possibility is that colluvial sediments may have been removed or thinned by the action of seasonal streams at times of higher water table. Water is recorded as having flowed in Stonehenge Bottom within living memory and further down towards Spring Bottom water still stands during wet periods. This idea is attractive in view of the very flinty nature of some of the valley floor deposits and evidence for periodic waterlogging from W26 (Greenland Farm). However, sediments appear equally thin near the heads of dry valleys where stream activity is unlikely (eg W19, Durrington Down), and the excellent state of preservation of the Stonehenge Cursus near to W22 also suggests that this hypothesis may be incorrect.

4.16 b Lithics

The methodology employed in the examination of dry valleys for colluvial potential involved the collection of surface finds from a 5m wide transect and the excavation of small soil pits. In no cases did these pits locate stratified deposits or significant colluvial soils and in consequence the material recovered has only been rapidly assessed for the production of a stage 1 catalogue. Details of the flint assemblages are contained within the archive.

The composition of the individual assemblages is shown in Table 115. In each case the amalgamated total of material from both collection and ploughsoil excavation is shown. Transects W17, W18, and W19 involved surface collection, and in consequence produced larger assemblages of worked flint. The character of these non-site-specific groups tends to reflect the overall lithic repertoire of the zones from which they were recovered, zones identified on the basis of surface collection results. This is particularly noticeable in the case of W19, located adjacent to the Durrington Down (65) collection area, an area in the centre of a zone of extensive Bronze Age activity. Although the scrapers from W19 failed to exhibit any coherent grouping, the eight other tools included Bronze Age type fossils in the form of four awls/borers and a barbed and tanged arrowhead.

Of the four remaining sample excavations which produced worked flint, W22, located immediately adjacent to the southern bank of the Cursus, produced an anomalously high number of worked flints from a very restricted area. The size of the sample area was too small for any wider observations to be made with confidence.

5 Lithic studies

5.1 Introduction

The fieldwork and excavation carried out during the Stonehenge Environs Project inevitably generated considerable quantities of lithic debris, primarily of worked (struck) flint. The approach developed for material from surface collection has been described above (this vol, 3.1). This involved the sorting of material by collection unit into a series of categories based on aspects of reduction and utilisation (Table 5). The end product of this sorting, itself a labour-intensive activity, was a number of basic catalogues which enabled assemblages to be rapidly quantified and an assessment made of their functional and chronological range. In addition to the programme of extensive surface collection, more detailed collection and the excavation of both surface scatters and specific monuments also generated large quantities of lithic debris. The volume of the assemblages has necessitated a realistic approach to analysis, and a distinction between those needs related to the production of this publication and those more orientated towards research. In consequence, very little of the material recovered has been exhaustively analysed, full analysis here being taken as a combination of metrical and technical assessment, and including full exploitation of refitting potential.

The final approach, the results of which are contained within this section and within the project archive, has three stages of investigation.

Stage 1 involves the production of a basic catalogue of recovered finds by context. This stage also involves the removal and individual record of any typologically or technologically diagnostic pieces. When applied to excavated material, even from unstratified contexts, this analysis has generally included a subjective assessment of the total assemblage, including the potential for, and advantages of, further stages of analysis.

This level of investigation aimed to provide a quantification of assemblage which, in relation to the stratigraphic and spatial record of the area/site, would suggest the location, intensity, and potential continuity, of areas of activity. This quantification should also provide an assessment of the suitability of the group for statistical tests.

Stage 2 involves the re-examination of a sample of the stage 1 catalogued material, spatially or stratigraphically defined, and may focus on a specific element of the assemblage, for example, tools/cores/complete flakes. This re-examination is intended to provide clarification or quantification of specific technological or morphological trends identified during initial (stage 1) examination.

Stage 3 involves a full examination of a specific group of material, including metrical analysis and refitting where possible and appropriate. The aims and methodology of this stage of analysis are introduced below (Harding, this vol, 5.2).

Application

All worked flint recovered during the project has been catalogued and tabulated by appropriate unit of collection (Stage 1, summarised in Table 114). Tabulated breakdowns are contained within text or fiche and more detailed information is contained within the project archive. All scrapers have been recorded as described below and a catalogue has been created for all petit tranchet derivative arrowheads (Riley, this vol, 5.3).

Beyond this basic assessment, the level of analysis has largely been dictated by the volume of material involved, and by a strict interpretation of the nature of closed groups for which stage 3 analysis would be appropriate. Material from the excavation of ploughsoil contexts is obviously unstratified and only in rare cases (Harding forthcoming a) has been treated as a

Table 114 Assessment of flint assemblages from project excavations

Site/type	*Context of lithic group*				*Report*	*Potential*
	topsoil	*accumulative subsoil*	*closed*	*refitting*	*stage*	
W2 henge	**	**			2	**
W2 (1981) pit	**		**		3	
W17, etc	**				1	
W31 scatter	**	*		**	2/3	
W32 scatter	**				2	
W34 scatter	**				2	
W51 ditch	**	*			1	
W52 ditch	**	**	*	*	2	**
W55 cursus		**			1	
W56 cursus	**	**			1	
W57 barrow	**		*		2	
W58 barrow	**	**	**	**	2/3	**
W59 scatter	**		**		3	
W83 scatter	**		**		3 (interim)	**

** major assemblage
* minor assemblage

Table 115 Composition of flint assemblages from project excavations

Site	*Cores*		*Flakes*				*Scrapers*	*Other*	*Total*
	complete	*fragments*	*complete*	*broken*	*burnt*	*retouched*		*tools*	
W2	108	132	7552	5760	724	185	195	104	14760
W2(1981)	2	13	550	648	251	N/R	54	9	1545
W17	54	16	176	195	19	11	16	4	491
W18	48	25	179	295	1	12	7	6	573
W19	62	45	305	433	22	7	14	8	896
W20	18	8	145	67	0	5	0	0	243
W21	17	5	143	52	0	3	0	0	220
W22	17	7	345	144	16	31	6	2	568
W25	0	2	32	19	1	3	0	0	57
W31	366	187	9762	9987	615	150	182	94	21343
W32	175	117	2377	833	129	160	57	26	3874
W34	289	159	5257	1607	271	150	69	41	7843
W51	4	1	42	18	1	1	1	1	69
W52	26	22	448	126	12	20	12	7	673
W55	39	6	582	68	14	16	16	9	750
W56	6	4	216	59	0	6	3	0	294
W57	86	101	2761	1696	82	121	34	15	4896
W58	75	19	2541	537	30	16	14	18	3250
W59	168	84	4327	2333	487	199	117	61	7776
Totals	1578	953	37740	24877	2675	1096	797	405	70121

group suitable for detailed analysis. However, the nature of the deposits encountered in the project excavations, the majority of them gradually accumulative rather than distinctly episodic, means that few groups of worked flint can be considered as potentially without residual elements or uncontaminated by intrusive material. Even where individual residual pieces are identifiable, for example specific retouched forms or pieces exhibiting differential patination or technological attributes, elimination of all residual elements is unlikely to be possible. Stage 2 analysis has, in consequence, been applied to assemblages from the sites shown in Table 115, while only a restricted, but carefully chosen, series of stratified groups has been examined in greater detail.

The aims of the programme of stage 3 analysis were to attempt the definition of technological change through time by the detailed examination of a series of closed groups. If possible such groups were to relate to single phases of flint reduction, or to short phases of deposition, preferably with datable associations. Employing such a strict definition, groups fulfilling these criteria were inevitably few in number, consisting of two deposits of conjoining knapping debris from W31 Wilsford Down and W58 Amesbury 42 long barrow, and three pits or groups of pits: W2 (1981) Coneybury 'Anomaly', W59 King Barrow Ridge, and W83 Robin Hood's Ball settlement site (this vol, 4.10 b, 4.7 b, 4.1 b, 4.8 b, and 4.2 b). The comparative analysis of these groups (Harding, this vol, 5.2) provides an independent study of great value. It also serves to highlight the as yet unexploited potential within many of the excavated project flint assemblages, potential which it is hoped will be realised in future as specific research projects. The potential value of the wider application of the results contained within this volume has also been enhanced by the recovery of additional lithic assemblages subsequent to 1984 (Richards in prep b).

The flint reports, with the exception of the detailed studies by Philip Harding and the report for W2, Coneybury Henge (this vol 5.9 b), which was prepared by Joshua Pollard, have been prepared by Julian Richards. The stage 1 cataloguing of material from W2, Coneybury Henge, and W57, Durrington Down round barrow, was carried out by Mark Edmunds. All other stage 1 catalogues were prepared by either Julian Richards or Philip Harding.

5.2 The comparative analysis of four stratified flint assemblages and a knapping cluster

by Philip Harding

This report presents a comparative analysis of groups of stratified material from W2 (1981) Coneybury 'Anomaly', W83 Robin Hood's Ball settlement site, W59 King Barrow Ridge flint scatter, and W31 Wilsford Down flint scatter. Reference is also made to the detailed report of an *in situ* knapping scatter from W58, Amesbury 42 long barrow. Individual flint reports appear separately within the site reports.

Within this comparative report, sites will be referred to by site code only, and consistently in their defined or assumed chronological sequence: W2 (1981), W83, W58, W59, and W31. The composition of the analysed samples is shown in Table 116. The analysed samples from W2 (1981), W83 and W59 were recovered from pits, of which only W2 (1981), a large feature, contained an adequate sample within its primary fills. Material from amalgamated pit fills was therefore included in

Table 116 Composition of the analysed flint assemblages

Site	Cores analysed	Not analysed	Core fragments	Measured flakes	Whole flakes (not measured)	Broken flakes	Burnt flakes	Chips no	Chips (wt)
W2 (1981)									
Basal	13	–	11	305	6	365	193	–	(–)
Others	–	7	2	–	239	283	58	–	(–)
W83									
Pit 102	11	–	1	142	–	101	9	140	(–)
Pit 104	1	–	–	59	–	69	3	74	(–)
Pit 106	1	–	–	48	–	44	4	36	(–)
Pit 108	10	–	–	170	–	141	17	230	(–)
Pit 114	3	–	–	72	–	66	6	63	(–)
W58	2	–	–	74	–	?	–	135*	(59)
W59									
Pit 418	8	–	1	69	1	43	7	257	(170)
Pit 430	5	–	1	74	–	59	12	230	(73)
Pit 432	10	–	4	68	–	74	35	259	(83)
Pit 438	3	–	2	33	–	29	7	311	(85)
Pit 440	5	–	3	45	1	40	9	175	(72)
W31									
Area L	37	13	10	446	228	784	72	311	(181)
Area R	2	5	4	71	95	207	34	184	(96)
Area T	19	2	2	281	53	391	131	67	(34)

* identifiable chips
() weight includes all chips

the samples from W83 and W59, although at neither site were intrusive artefacts thought to be a serious problem. The sample from W31 was taken from undisturbed contexts within natural truncated subsoil features.

Analysis of retouched material from each site was restricted to scrapers and chisel arrowhead groups from W31 and W59. The samples, with the exception of W2 (1981), included finds from excavated ploughsoil contexts. Totals are shown in Table 123.

Finds were recorded by context with, in the majority of cases, implements recorded in three dimensions. Bulk sieving through 4mm mesh for artefact retrieval was undertaken at W83, W31, and W59. Additional samples from W31 and W59 were also sieved through 1mm mesh. These differences in sample and mesh size are reflected in the quantities of chips recovered from each site.

Aims

The general aims of the analyses have been to examine the raw material source and type, the technology, and the products of each assemblage. The raw material source is particularly relevant if products from local industrial sites were being transported to domestic sites. The limited quantity of some assemblages has made it difficult to interpret details of the technology and products; however, broad comparisons have been made.

Limited refitting has been possible from all sites but its potential has not been fully exploited, particularly with regard to the material from W31. The refitting that has been carried out has identified *in situ* knapping at W58, provided evidence of both core tool production at W31 and scraper sharpening at W2 (1981), and has shed light on the processes of pit fill formation. The pits at W59, for example, contained very little flint in their primary fills, and refitting material may have silted in from the surface. In contrast, the basal fills of W2 (1981) were shown to include individual deposits of material within which refitting was possible. This demonstrated the way in which the feature was backfilled and that, despite vertical compression, no significant vertical mixing of contexts had occurred. Other pit fills were more homogeneous and again vertical movement may have occurred within them. Refits from adjacent subsoil hollows at W31 also indicated that material was contemporary and that the material from within them represented the remains of originally more extensive activity areas.

Technological evidence has also been recovered, particularly from W58.

Raw material

Flint occurs naturally and prolifically within the Stonehenge area: within chalk, in surface deposits of clay with flints, and in the river gravels. These sources provided a wide range of raw material of sufficient quality to produce a complete range of domestic tools. The flint, which occurs in a variety of shapes and sizes, was probably available in sufficient quantity as surface nodules weathered from the chalk or as fresh flint found during the digging of pits and ditches. Deliberate mining was both unnecessary and unprofitable as trial flint mines north of Durrington Walls show (Booth and Stone 1952). These shallow and apparently short-lived mines produced only poor quality tabular flint.

Nodules of flint from the area are irregular, rounded or subangular in shape, mostly weighing between *c* 200g and 400g. They occur either as isolated nodules or in consistent seams within the chalk. The flint is dark grey to black in colour, with irregular paler grey cherty inclusions. Cortex is usually chalky, and up to 12mm thick, but is often weathered and thinner on surface nodules and those from river gravels. Thermal fractures and inclusions are common, with obvious effects on knapping quality, although thermal fractures were often used as unmodified striking platforms. The occurrence of thermal fractures varies across the study area; the scar patterns on flakes (Fig 149) indicate that thermal flaws were more common at W31 than elsewhere, a possible reflection of the nature of the raw material at this site.

Thin vertical bands of poor quality tabular flint outcrop on the surface of the upper chalk of Coneybury Hill. This was sometimes worked bifacially but was also flaked down the edge for the production of blades/bladelets.

The southern half of the study area has a greater density of natural surface flint and also includes thick seams of tabular flint in the chalk. Flint of this type often has a coarser cherty interior although the exterior of the nodule is suitable for producing large flakes. Tabular flint, which may belong to the same seam, was seen outcropping at about 100m OD on the north side of Rox Hill, at W31 and to the north of Stonehenge. There is no evidence that it was exploited at W31; in fact, the general flake size shows no variation from sites with small raw material. The southern area does, however, show a greater level of industrial activity (this vol, 3.5), and some of the larger flakes and an assortment of surface tools from W59 may represent the products of this zone. It cannot be established, however, whether they were transported as finished tools, blanks, or cores. The size of the nodules in the north part of the area make it likely that ground axes and fragments from W59 and W83 were also manufactured elsewhere. This suggestion may be substantiated by flakes, classified as thinning flakes, from W2 (1981), which are lighter in colour than flint from the immediate area.

Gravel flint was used at W2 (1981), the closest site to a river, and one core was made on a gravel flint flake at W83. Occasional flakes and tools of Portland chert have also been found, which indicates some movement of this raw material into the study area. Some flint may have been obtained as a by-product of field clearance in the Bronze Age and evidence from W57, Durrington Down round barrow, suggests that the barrow cairn was being exploited as a source of raw material.

Flint from all primary and secondary ditch or pit fills was in mint condition, with most surfaces covered by a mottled white to light blue or grey patina. Some material from the deeper primary silts of W2 and W83 were covered by calcium carbonate concretion, which results from ground water precipitation. Flakes from tertiary deposits were more often patinated light blue to white. The term 'patina' is here used to describe post-depositional chemical discoloration of the surface of the flint; the term 'cortex' is reserved for the natural outer surface of the flint.

Hammer mode

Flakes were probably removed by direct percussion using flint hammerstones. There is no evidence of imported hammerstones or of organic hammers. Analysis (Fig 149) has produced consistent results for the four assemblages, with an average of 44% of flakes identifiably removed by hard hammer. Flint produces characteristics similar to those of a hard hammer: clear point and cone of percussion, pronounced conchoidal fracture marks on the bulb, unlipped butt and pronounced bulb (Ohnuma and Bergman 1982, 169). The effects of cortical surfaces, however, can produce results which are comparable to soft hammers: lipped butt and diffuse bulb, vague or no point/cone of percussion, and diffuse bulb (Ohnuma and Bergman 1982, 166). These characteristics have been used to interpret the hammer mode in sequence 3, W58 (Fig 69). However, there are also a consistently large number of indeterminate flakes (an average of 45%), the characteristics of which are likely to form a larger proportion of flakes in any assemblage where flint and cortical surfaces are used randomly. Retouch was probably also by direct percussion, although some implements were undoubtedly made by using pressure flaking.

Table 117 Flint core typology used in analysis and percentage of cores 50–99g in analysed groups

	Total cores	*Single platform A ii %*	*Two platforms B %*	*Multi platform C %*	*'Keeled' D %*	*Misc*	*%50–99g*
W2(1981)	13	38	23	–	–	38	38
W83	26	28	32	20	12	8	46
W59	31	19	6	39	19	16	42
W31	58	45*	17	9	11	17	45

* includes bladelet cores made on flakes

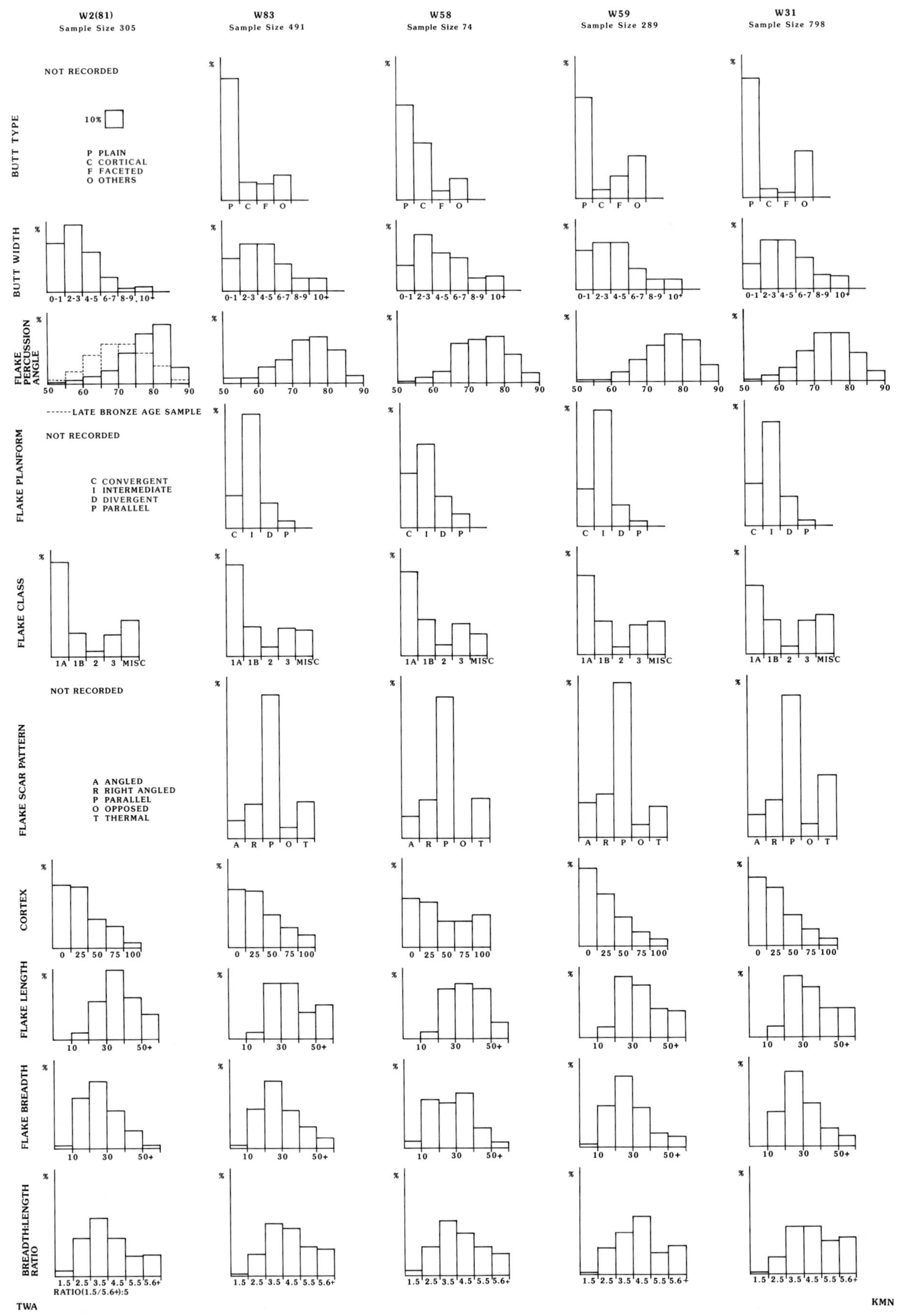

Fig 149 Comparative flint flake analysis

Table 118 Ratio of flint flakes and burnt flakes to cores in analysed groups

Analysed groups	*W2(1981)*	*W83*	*W58*	*W59*	*W31*
Average of all flakes: core	57	42	29	19	49
Average whole and burnt flakes: core	33	26	–	12	23

Table 119 Flint core striking platform types in analysed groups

Total cores		*Percentage*			
		prepared	*neg. faceted*	*unmodified*	*unknown*
W2 (1981)	13	25	12	61	12
W83	26	65	8	19	8
W59	31	48	34	18	–
W31	58	44	18	35	3

Cores

Table 117 shows the basic core typology as defined by J G D Clark (1960) and the percentage of cores weighing 50–99g. Core numbers at most sites are lower than might have been expected, particularly as some are failed pieces. Such under-representation of cores is also suggested at W31, where waste and rejuvenation flakes of a distinctive flint appear for which there are no apparent cores. Table 118 shows that W2 (1981) has the largest ratio of all flakes to cores and of whole and burnt flakes to cores, again consistent with an assemblage of selected pieces. In contrast, W58, where the complete sequence was recovered, shows the variations that can occur between successful and failed cores, 18 flakes from sequence 2 and 50 flakes from sequence 3.

The numbers of cores are, with the possible exception of those from W31, too small to provide reliable technological or typological results. All groups include both exhausted and failed cores, neither of which reflect the appearance of core in their productive stages. Productive cores are, however, less likely to be discarded. Many of the failed pieces, which are neither chronologically nor technologically diagnostic, are included in the miscellaneous category. With the exception of those from W58, no complete knapping sequences – which demonstrate how flakes were produced – have been reconstructed. The diversity of the cores confirms that there was no consistent method of flake production. The flake cores require less core control to maintain production if the form of the blank is not predetermined precisely. The refitting of W58 suggests that many began as single-platform cores, but developed into multi-platform cores by rotating the piece during rejuvenation. The single platform cores from W83 include those of Clark's flat-faced A2 type (J G D Clark 1960, 217, fig 10). Alternate flaking was also used both in flake production, as with 'keeled' or biconical cores, and in platform preparation. A similar technology was also used to produce discoidal/semi-discoidal cores, examples of which were found in pre-excavation surface collection at W59. Evidence of the Levallois technique (Manby 1974, Gardiner 1984) was restricted to one flake from a ploughsoil context at W59 and was probably an off-site product, from a more industrial area.

Table 119 shows the types of striking platform recorded on the analysed cores from W83, W31, and W59. Most platforms were prepared unless suitable thermal fractures were available. At W31, the nodules appear to have a higher frequency of thermal fractures and, consequently, of thermal platforms. Here, some of these thermal platforms have a similar patina to the flake surfaces, which may imply that they were freshly broken surfaces at the time of knapping. Also recovered from this site were two small cores which refit to a waste fragment and which could only have been worked after the nodule had been broken. It is uncertain whether or not these nodules were smashed deliberately. Cores from W58 demonstrate both the removal of single flakes and alternate flaking to create a striking platform. A specific technique of blade/bladelet manufacture at W31 involved the removal of 'burin spalls' from flakes or thin fragments (Fig 118). Eleven cores of this type were found with striking platforms prepared by a truncation if a suitable platform was not already available, the result being blades/bladelets with faceted butts. The production of similar blades/bladelets with trapezoidal or triangular cross sections has been described from the Linear Bandkeramik site of Omal, Belgium (Cahen 1987, 3, fig 1.3).

The general absence of specific end-products is accompanied by a lack of specialised core preparation techniques (*lame à crête*) or shaping of the base and back of the core.

Blank production can be divided into two main types, blades/bladelets and flakes. The direction of percussion was not always parallel to the longest axis of the nodule, although ridges were utilised to maintain overall length, particularly for the production of blades/bladelets.

Blanks for flake tools require few specific attributes and were produced from single- and multi-platformed cores as well as being produced by alternate flaking. Refitting sequences which demonstrate flake production are rare. The illustrated core from W31 (Fig 118) is produced by a similar technique to one from an Early Neolithic context at Rowden, Dorset, where the technology was reconstructed by refitting waste flakes (Harding forthcoming b, fig 43, pl 31 and 32). The core from this sequence was absent. The 'tea-cosy' core from W31 is similar in all aspects except that some flakes from Rowden had been prepared by faceting.

Platform abrasion, which strengthens the striking platform and allows a blow near the core edge, is present at most sites, although its use is not extensive. There is a strong correlation between abrasion and narrowness of butts, with both attributes associated with blades/bladelets rather than flakes. The use of platform abrasion is also evident on some of the cores, however, most particularly those from W31 and W83. These have irregular edges which show that the point of percussion was often set back from the edge of the striking platform. Faceting, used as a technique to modify or maintain the flaking angle, appears to have been used sparingly and is especially rare on prepared flakes. A refitted flake from W31 shows that faceted butts sometimes result from rotating the core during rejuvenation. A second faceted butt from the same site has a low flaking angle which suggests that the faceting is unconnected with the preparation of the flaking angle.

Platform rejuvenation flakes, which indicate a systematic attempt to prolong flake production from each core, are present but not common at all sites. Such flakes can also include flakes removed during alternate flaking. The proportion of cores with at least two striking platforms indicates that most rejuvenation involved rotating the core and the resumption of production from a new striking platform. Crested flakes, a by-product of this form of rejuvenation, are found at most of the examined sites. These forms of rejuvenation are both represented in the refitting sequences from W58 (sequence 2 and sequence 3c, Figs 68 and 69).

On all sites examined, measurement of the longest complete flake scars on each core indicates that the flakes produced would have been long enough for conversion into scrapers without the necessity of introducing blanks from 'industrial' sites.

Most cores were rejected when the flaking angle had increased to 90°. In some cases this occurred during initial preparation and usable flakes were therefore not produced. In other cases, cores were rotated and a new striking platform prepared. An increase in the flaking angle affects 34% (W83), 23% (W31), and 30% (W59) of all striking platforms. Recession of the striking platform edge, accompanied by edge crushing, step and hinge fractures, results from continued percussion when the flaking angle is already too steep. This is present on only 7% (W83), 3% (W31), and 6% (W59) of striking platforms, which suggests that there was an appreciation of the point at which the core became unworkable. Comparable observations from five industries on the Marlborough Downs, Wiltshire (Harding forthcoming a), show that edge recession had increased to on average 15% of all striking platforms by the later Bronze Age.

Additional reasons for core rejection are more difficult to assess. Core size associated with exhaustion, when no more flakes can be produced, and potential, when preparation would leave the core too small to produce blanks, are particularly variable. Refitted core fragments from both W2 (1981) and W31 show that core fragments were re-used to produce small blanks if the flint looked sound. Results of assessed core size, exhaustion, and potential, together with details of raw material flaws, are contained within the archive.

Flakes

The total number of flakes analysed from each assemblage is shown in Table 116. The sample from W31 represents 68% of all whole flakes from the areas examined. All complete flakes were analysed using the system later standardised for the South Dorset Ridgeway (Harding forthcoming b). The system records details of identifiable hammer mode, as defined by Ohnuma and Bergman (1982), the type and width of the butt, the presence of platform preparation, and the angle of percussion, expressed as the 'operative' angle (Warren 1951, 12). The dorsal surface of the flake shows details of the core from which it was removed. This information is contained in the flake scar pattern, the proportion of cortex remaining, and the presence or absence of a ridge which guides the length (or breadth) of the flake (Gingell and Harding 1979). Some of these observations can be confirmed in the planform (Isaac 1977, fig 57), according to whether the edges converge, are widest at the mid-point (intermediate), diverge, or are parallel. Hinged and plunged distal ends were recorded from all of the analysed assemblages, with the exception of W2 (1981). Measurements of flake length, at right angles to the butt, breadth, parallel to it, and maximum thickness were also taken. Breadth:length ratios were calculated according to Bohmers (1956). They are shown to reflect blades as breadth:length 2.5:5.

Refitting has also allowed flakes to be divided according to their position and supposed function on the core. This classification is currently at an early stage and will be modified as necessary. Results are presented from W83 and W31. Flakes have been placed into the following broad groups.

Preparation flakes

These are often the largest flakes removed during debitage. They have large areas of cortex or thermal fracture on the dorsal surfaces. They are produced during the construction and shaping of primary or secondary striking platforms and flaking surfaces. W58 sequence 3 suggests that preparation flakes struck parallel to the long axis of the nodule, possibly in the preparation of the flaking surface, are likely to be more elongated than flakes struck across the axis of the nodule in platform preparation. Preparation flakes show the greatest susceptibility to hinge fractures at both W83 (19%) and W31 (26%), figures in broad agreement with those from Rowden (29%).

Side trimming flakes

These have cortex or thermal fractures along the edge. They result from shaping or broadening flaking faces or striking platforms (Bordes 1979, pl 37.9, *Couteau à dos naturel*). Flakes of this type from W58 show that they can also have negative flake scars from a previous striking platform in cases where the core has been rotated. These flakes are mainly ridged, 71% (W83) and 62% (W31) (Classes 1A/1B), with an intermediate planform 67% (W83) and 57% (W31).

Distal trimming flakes

These flakes have cortex at the distal end. They overshoot the flaking surface accidentally or are produced to lengthen the flaking surface. They include the highest proportion of plunged flakes, 11% at W83. Flakes from the main flaking surface (Phase 3) of W58 sequence 3 were all distal trimming flakes, many of which terminated in a hinge fracture. Some of the blades from W2 (1981) also had cortical distal ends, indicating that blade length could be maintained, presumably by careful platform preparation. At W83 these flakes are predominantly ridged (56% 1A), but at W31 are of ridged or miscellaneous classes (43% 1A, 29% misc). Intermediate planforms (59% W83, 60% W31) predominate, but both sites have 20% with divergent edges.

Miscellaneous trimming flakes

These form the bulk of the core trimming and shaping flakes. They maintain the shape of the core following preparation and therefore have less cortex than side or dorsal trimming flakes (above). They are also smaller and figure less frequently as blanks for tools. They can be identified more easily where a deliberate blank form is produced. The refitted material from W58 shows that miscellaneous trimming varies according to the need to achieve control over the core and that failed cores may have produced almost entirely miscellaneous trimming flakes. W83 and W31 both contain miscellaneous trimming flakes of intermediate planform (62% and 55% respectively) but show a strong contrast in flake class. In class 1A the difference is between 62% (W83) and 39% (W31), and for miscellaneous 11% (W83) and 20% (W31). The reasons for this contrast are not immediately apparent.

Blanks

Blanks are either selected for use in an unmodified form, and are therefore difficult to distinguish from flakes of other groups, or are modified by retouch. The total number of unretouched flake tools in an assemblage relies on incontestable microwear traces. The assemblages from the Stonehenge Environs offer no more than occasional evidence, for example that from W2 (1981), of unspecialised blanks ('waste flakes') (E Moss pers comm). This indicates that even where blade production or selection was important, unretouched flakes were also of considerable value. Flake tools of this type were presumably used in greater numbers where blade production was less specialised.

Attributes sought from retouched tools included the selection of specific blanks. The flakes from W83 were compared with the mean length, breadth and thickness of the scrapers, here, as with all the examined groups, the largest retouched group. This showed that only 19% of the flakes lay within one standard deviation of the mean for two or more of these measured attributes, compared with 81% of scrapers with zero or one failed attribute. This indicates that suitable scraper blanks were rare among the flakes from the pits. Core preparation flakes (24%) and side trimming flakes (40%) were shown to include the least number of failed attributes and were therefore more suited for scrapers than miscellaneous trimming flakes (22%). A similar analysis of scrapers from the South Dorset Ridgeway (Harding forthcoming b) shows that 28% were made on side trimming flakes and 22% on preparation flakes, but that 31% were made on some form of miscellaeous trimming flake. These flakes contrast with the shorter, thinner, elongated miscellaneous trimming waste flakes which were found within the pits. Scraper blanks may therefore represent a part of the normal flake production not evident in the contents of the pit, or they may signify deliberate blank production elsewhere.

Specialist blanks are represented by blades, ridged pieces with parallel edges. Of the examined groups, these are best represented at W2 (1981) where the numbers present suggest their use as tools. Their technique of manufacture is unsophisticated, especially at W31 where their production on flakes relies on the removal of unprepared 'burin spalls'.

Rejuvenation flakes

Such flakes, in the form of core rejuvenation tablets, were recorded in limited numbers from all sites. It should be noted, however, that rejuvenation by rotation of the core reduces the need to remove tablets. Additional rejuvenation flakes are contained in groups 2, 3, and 4 above, and result from alternate flaking. Rejuvenation tablets are not shown in the results of the analysis.

Core tool thinning flakes

These are described by Newcomer (1971) as thin flakes with a dipping profile, feathered edges, multidirectional flake scars, and narrow butts. Flakes of this type were recorded at W2 (1981) and core tool manufacture was also evident at W31 where the refitting 'roughing-out flakes' are among the broadest analysed and have some of the lowest angles of percussion. The failure to recognise identifiable thinning flakes may result from the use of a hard hammer, which is unlikely to produce the broad invasive flakes characteristic of a soft hammer.

Flakes which resemble thinning flakes were also found at W59, but here cores suggest that flakes of this type may have been produced from biconical or discoidal cores. Chips of a similar form are also present which may result from faceting or retouch.

Most flakes are undoubtedly waste products although unretouched flake tools are probably present at most sites. Tools of this type are more likely to occur within domestic rather than industrial contexts.

Figure 149 shows the amalgamated results of analysis of preparation, side, distal, and miscellaneous trimming flakes from each site. Details of each group are contained within the archive. The results show considerable consistency throughout, which probably reflects similarities in technology and raw material.

Flake butts are predominantly plain and average 63% at W83, W59, and W31. Faceted butts range from a maximum of 13% (W59) down to only 3% (W31), which confirms that faceting was not a significant technique. Refitting from W59 has indicated that some faceted butts result from alternate flaking of cores with abraded striking platforms.

Percussion angles from the examined groups are shown compared with the mean of four later Bronze Age assemblages from the South Dorset Ridgeway (Harding forthcoming b). This clearly shows that whereas Late Bronze Age industries group between 65°–74°, the Neolithic assemblages lie mainly between 70°–90°, the highest being from W2 (1981), the earliest analysed group. Such higher percussion angles help to maintain flake length. The detailed analysis of groups from W58 and W31 show that preparation flakes are associated with lower angles of percussion than are miscellaneous trimming flakes and blades. Flaking at a high angle of percussion requires more core control and platform preparation helps to achieve this. Platform abrasion, which strengthens the striking platform by removing overhang and allowing a blow to be placed near the core edge, is present at most sites. Its occurrence is more common on miscellaneous trimming flakes and blades which suggests an association with blank production. Forty-one per cent of blades at W2 (1981) have abraded butts and 90% of the blades have butts less than 4mm wide. Butts are generally broader at W31 (32% are wider than 5mm) and platform abrasion accounts for only 4.5%, of which 66% are miscellaneous trimming flakes. The absence of platform abrasion from W58, however, demonstrates that its use was not universal.

W2 (1981) has more ridged pieces (Classes 1A and 1B) which typify blades, while W31 with the broadest flakes has more of classes 3 and miscellaneous.

Scar patterns on the dorsal surfaces of the flakes also show the incidence of thermal fractures and confirm that W31 contained a higher proportion of thermally fractured flint than the other examined sites. There is no proportional decrease in cortical cover on flakes from W31. The remaining figures show considerable similarity. Negative scars at the distal ends of flakes are sometimes lost because successive flake removals became shorter. However, the analysis appears to confirm the rarity of cores with opposed striking platforms and of discoidal cores, most flakes apparently having been struck from cores worked in a single direction. The material from W58 also shows that, apart from alternate flaking, which is unlikely to be recordable by observing waste flakes, cores were worked through no more than 90°, a figure confirmed by the scar patterns on the flakes.

The greatest variability in length and breadth exists at W2 (1981), where blades (24%) form a significant proportion. The breadth:length ratios do not show the marked differences demonstrated between the earlier Neolithic at Windmill Hill (I F Smith 1965, fig 38) and the Late Neolithic at the West Kennet Avenue (ibid) or Durrington Walls (Wainwright and Longworth 1971, fig 68). However, Farley (1979) has suggested that blades may account for no more than 10% of the material at Windmill Hill and broad flakes only 21% at Durrington Walls. He consequently concludes that the shift to broader flakes in the Late Neolithic is less marked than has been suggested, and that the proportion of blades may not be a reliable indicator of date. The Stonehenge Environs groups reflect this gradual increase in flake width, with an increase in breadth:length ratio from 3.5:5 to 4.5:5 between W2 (1981) and W59. The groups from W2 (1981), W83, and W58 are very similar, while those from W59 and W31 include a second accumulated peak beyond 5.6:5, although the proportion of blades remains fairly constant. The broadest range, 12% between the blades and 16% between the broad flakes of W2 (1981) and W31, may substantiate the trend for broader flakes in the later Neolithic but may also result from the comparison of two sites of differing function. The analysis has indicated that the samples, particularly those from W2 (1981), W83, and W58, are similar in all recorded categories. Detailed comparisons with other industries are more difficult to make, however, as results are published only as lengths and breadths, factors affected by raw material size, and breadth:length ratios. Comparable sites, dominated by narrow flakes, include Hembury, Whitehawk (Whittle 1977, 71), Bury Hill (Drewett 1981, fig 6), Carn Brea (Saville 1981, table 21), and the old land surface at Mount Pleasant (Wainwright 1979, fig 60). The trend towards broader flakes at W59 can be paralleled with later groups at Mount Pleasant (enclosure ditch, north entrance) (Wainwright 1979, fig 67) and Durrington Walls (Wainwright and Longworth 1971, fig 68), where, although blades averaged 10%, the histograms peak at 4:5.

It should be noted, however, that these comparisons indicate similarities in flake shape, but not necessarily in technology.

The percentage occurrence of flakes broken by 'Siret' (accidents) (Bordes 1979, fig 4.2) is shown in Table 120. Such breakages, often associated with the use of hard hammers, averaged 5% in both Neolithic and later Bronze Age industries at Rowden (Harding forthcoming b). Measured flakes with plunged or hinged distal ends are also shown. The results for hinge fractures are similar to those from the Early Neolithic industry at Rowden, where 18% were hinged, in contrast to 24% for the Middle/Late Bronze Age industries.

Chips

The total numbers of chips from each site are shown by both quantity and weight in Table 116, except those from W2 (1981) and W83. Direct comparison between sites is not possible owing to variation in sample size and sieving technique. The total for W58 shows only recognisable chips, although others which are little more than coarse grit are included in the weight. This small component is typical of knapping scatters that are found *in situ* and illustrates the size range and total weight of chips which might be expected from flake or blade production where platform abrasion and faceting are not part of the technology.

Most chips from the sites examined are undiagnostic and probably result from impact around the point of percussion. Diagnostic chips do exist in sufficient numbers to confirm identified technological features. Faceting chips, short, fan-shaped pieces with a hinge or step fracture at the distal end (Newcomer and Karlin 1987, 33), and, occasionally, a faceted butt, are generally scarce. Platform abrasion chips which have small butts, feathered edges, parallel or converging lateral edges, and straightish profiles (ibid) are more common. Some carry evidence of earlier abrasion on the butt (10% at W83). Bulbar scars, which are also diagnostic of debitage phases (ibid) were found at W83, W59, and W31.

Table 120 The occurrence of Siret fractures, plunged and hinged flint flakes in analysed groups from W83, W59, and W31

	% of broken flakes with Siret fractures (accidents)	*% of measured flakes plunged*	*hinged*
W83	11	2	13
W59	11	4	11
W31	12	1	12

Retouch chips, which are often short and cortex-free with curved profiles and feathered edges (Newcomer and Karlin 1987, 33), are more difficult to identify with certainty. Chips from the manufacture or resharpening of end scrapers at W2 (1981) included one which could be refitted to its tool (Fig 27). The presence of unfinished tools at W31 suggests that blanks were retouched at the site, but, with the exception of one Janus flake, no retouch chips were identified.

Chisel arrowheads

The small groups of petit tranchet derivative arrowheads of chisel form (J G D Clark 1934, types B, C, and D) from W59 and W31 were examined in detail and were found to be remarkably similar on technological as well as typological grounds.

Although there is no evidence that deliberate blanks were produced, some flakes were obviously more suitable than others. Those selected were flat, broad, and unridged, with an upright profile and proportionally more scars at right angles to the axis of percussion (50% at W31) than miscellaneous trimming flakes. Blanks of this type can be, but are not exclusively, removed from discoidal cores (Green 1974, 84) examples of which were recorded from W59. Levallois technology (Manby 1974, Gardiner 1984) was not, however, used to produce these blanks.

Flakes were converted into tools by retouching the ends, most commonly with straight or oblique truncations. The proximal end often required bifacial thinning, although some arrowheads suggest that the blank originally had a crushed, linear, or punctiform butt. Some of these may have resulted from accidents of debitage. The position and distribution of retouch, together with the results of metrical analysis, is shown in Table 121. Length and breadth are measured according to the axis of percussion of the blank. No explanation is offered for why, within the sample examined, a disproportionate number of truncations converge on the left edge of the arrowhead (when viewed with the blank dorsal surface up). There is no evidence that an anvil was used to support the blank during retouch.

Table 121 Flint arrowheads of chisel form from W59 and W31

	W59 (21 examples)	*W31 (17 examples)*
Retouch		
Proximal bifacial	15	11
Distal bifacial	9	6
Distal direct	6	6
Truncations		
% converge on left	57	76
% converge on right	24	12
Length 20–29mm	14	14
Breadth 20–29mm	11	6
Thickness		
30–39mm	6	9
5–7mm	17	9

Table 122 Composition of the analysed flint scraper assemblages

	W2 (1981)	*W83*	*W59*	*W31*
Scrapers	47	153	106	67
Burnt	3	1	5	2
Broken/not recorded	3	35	21	15
Analysed	19	116	80	50
Stratified (primary)	25	35	–	–
Secondary	22	11	4	10
Surface	–	106	102	57

Table 123 Flint tools from analysed assemblages

	W2 (1981)	*W83 (all contexts)*	*W59 (all contexts)*	*W31 (analysed squares R, T, K/L)*
Miscellaneous				
Scrapers	47	152	106	67
Retouch	21	12	51	59
Knives	5	3	14	11
Piercers	–	–	5	2
Arrowheads				
Leaf	1	2	1	1
Tranchet	5	1?	23	10
B and T	–	–	1	–
Microdenticulate	–	1?	9	6
Axes and axe fragments	1	4	4	–
Grand tranchet tools	1	–	2	–
Broken tools	–	1	11	12
Fabricators	–	1	1	2
Others	3	2	1	14

Table 124 Typology of the analysed flint scraper assemblages

	W2 (1981)	*W83*	*W59*	*W31*
End scrapers	37	108	86	50
Side scrapers	2	12	8	6
End (proximal) scrapers	–	6	–	1
End/side scrapers	–	16	4	5
Double end scrapers	–	4	1	–
Double side scrapers	–	2	–	–
Others	3	3	3	5

Scrapers

The number of scrapers from each site is listed in Table 115. These formed the basis of the analysed samples, except for W2 (1981), where only 25 scrapers from the primary fills were considered. The composition and typology of the analysed flint scraper assemblages are shown in Tables 122 and 124.

These implements are the most common retouched tool type and as such maintain the dominance of scrapers in Neolithic assemblages. The proportion of scrapers to flakes varies from 1:11 at pit 108 (W83) to 1:199 from the subsoil hollows at W31.

Most scrapers were made on flakes which have a slightly dipping profile. Flakes with plunged or hinged distal ends were normally avoided. The results of the analysis of the scrapers and their retouch is shown in Figs 150 and 151.

Blanks were generally of intermediate planform, with a proportional increase in the use of flakes with divergent edges. The selection of broader flakes is reflected in the decreasing number of ridged flakes. These can be produced by maintaining a flatter flaking surface to the core and by placing the point of percussion well on to the striking platform. Scraper butts are noticeably broader than those of waste flakes at all sites. Many scrapers have considerable cortical cover; for example, 27% at W2 (1981) have 75% cortex, suggesting that some suitable blanks were removed during core preparation stages.

Analysis of scraper size from the groups examined has provided no clear indication of chronological variability. Most implements measure over 400mm in both length and breadth. Scrapers of similar dimensions were found at Windmill Hill and the West Kennet Avenue (I F Smith 1965, 95) and Durrington Walls (Wainwright and Longworth 1971, 168). Healy (1985, 190, table 11) has shown that scrapers frequently exceed the size of unretouched flakes in both Neolithic and Bronze Age assemblages.

The scraper shapes as expressed by breadth:length ratios show considerable uniformity by the selection of squat flakes, but rarely of broad flakes. The scrapers from W59 and W31 are, however, more elongated than those from W2 (1981) and W83, both of which contain a higher proportion of blades.

Measurement has partly confirmed that scrapers of later Neolithic date tend to be thinner than those of the earlier Neolithic. This is in accord with results from Windmill Hill, the West Kennet Avenue (I F Smith 1965, 95) and Durrington Walls (Wainwright and Longworth 1971, 168), although Smith's suggestion that this results from elaborate core preparation and platform faceting cannot be confirmed. Six per cent of the scrapers from W83 had faceted butts, whereas those from W59 and W31 had 12% and 8% respectively. Scrapers from W59 often showed maximum thickness towards the distal end.

The general form of the blanks indicates that some were probably removed from deliberate flake cores rather than from blade cores. Although these cores and some of their technological attributes have been recognised, the blanks that they produced, particularly when broken, are difficult to recognise.

Blanks were usually modified by direct, abrupt or semi-abrupt, regular continuous retouch to form a convex scraping edge. Figure 151 shows that most retouch on end scrapers from W83, W59, and W31 is located at the distal end or is extended partially along the edges. This is most frequently on the right edge, a feature which may be indicative of its method of use, possibly by a predominantly right-handed population. Additional retouch is rare and is limited to simple modification of the butt.

Figure 151 also shows the relationship of scraper blade length to scraper blade angle. This shows only minimal variations in scraper blade length between W83, W59, and W31, although those from W2 (1981), despite the small sample, do appear to have more extensive retouch and are particularly well made. Angles of retouch are also similar but are marginally lower at both W2 (1981) and W83, which minimises the number of scrapers with undercut edges. Retouch of this type has been replicated by the author using low angle direct percussion with a flint hammerstone.

Scraper manufacture/resharpening is represented at W2 (1981). Three scrapers made on cortical flakes of a distinctive flint were found in close proximity. At least two were broken during or after manufacture while a third was made on a flake with a hinged distal end. It is possible that these represent failed examples of tools produced in bulk. A retouch chip was also found which refits to its scraper (Fig 27), although, in the absence of visible wear on the scraper edge it is not possible to establish whether this is a product of manufacture or resharpening. It does, however, indicate the expendability and possible life span of retouched flake tools, including well-made pieces which show no obvious reason for rejection. The retouch chips show similarities in hammer mode with the blanks.

Conclusions

The analysed groups of flint from the project represent material from several sources of production. Within the stratified contexts at W31, the proportion of waste material to retouched tools (199 flakes:1 scraper) probably represents industrial activity. This suggestion is reinforced by refitting material, much of which is associated with core preparation or correction/rejuvenation. The groups from W2 (1981), W83, and W59 all contain mixed debitage and tools (Table 123) which, in combination, probably represent small-scale knapping for domestic purposes. This is particularly marked at W2

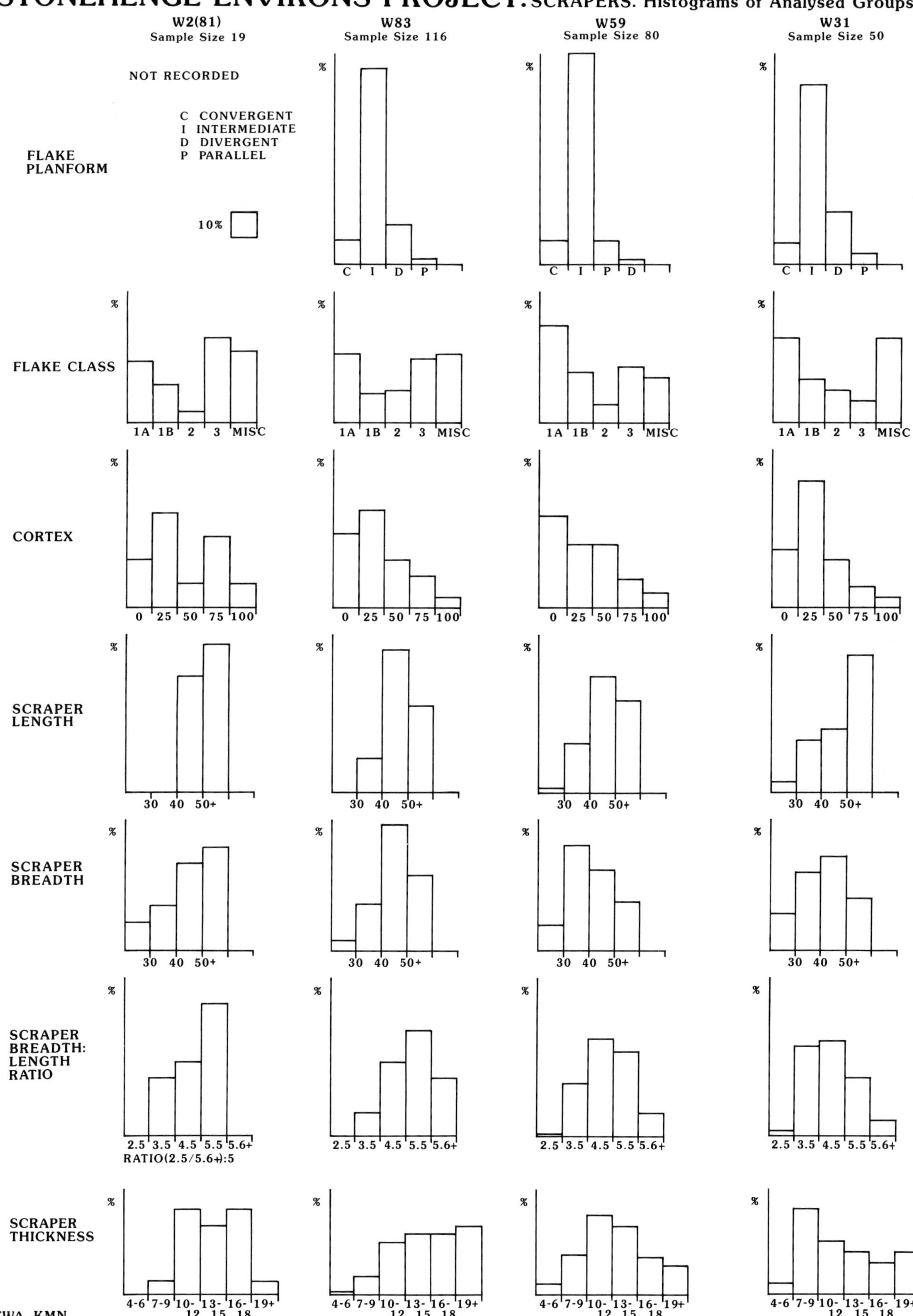

Fig 150 Comparative flint scraper analysis

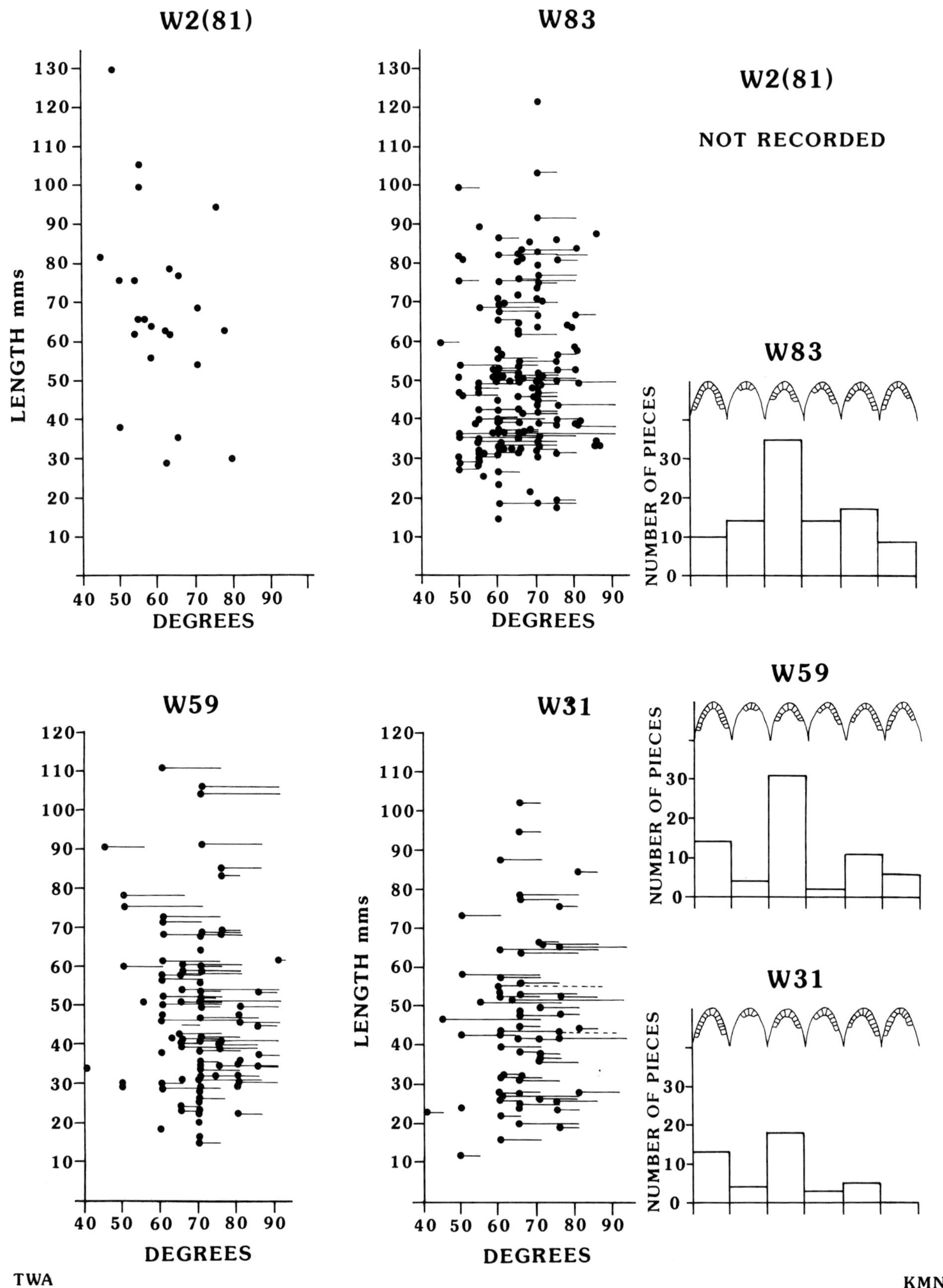

Fig 151 Flint scrapers: blade length, angle, and location of retouch

(1981), where blades, unretouched tools (identified by microwear traces), and retouched tools were found in association with other domestic refuse. The assemblages examined were all flake industries and no evidence of predetermined blank production was found. Blank selection could therefore only be determined from retouched material.

Blades and bladelets account for between 24% (W2 (1981)) and 10% (W31) of each industry, although the ratio of blades to flakes produced at each site cannot be accurately assessed. The evidence of blade waste and bladelet cores made on flakes from W31, the material from W2 (1981), and the refits from W58 indicate that some blades/bladelets were produced at most sites, possibly for use in composite tools. There were no specialised techniques for controlling the end-product.

Core tools were manufactured at W31, the evidence here provided by refitting material, while at W2 (1981) ten probable thinning flakes also indicate production or reworking. Similar flakes were also recovered from W59, although here their function is less certain. Core tools were presumably produced as they were required at locally available flint sources. This supports the evidence of analysis (Sieveking *et al* 1972) which suggests that axe factories account for only a small proportion of core tool production. Ground tool fragments occur at W2 (1981), W83, and W59.

Retouch phases or resharpening can be demonstrated by refitting at W2 (1981) and can be assumed at W31 where failed flake tools were recovered.

5.3 The scraper assemblages and petit tranchet derivative arrowheads

by Hazel Riley

Scrapers are the most common retouched tools in all of the flint assemblages recovered from the project. In particular, extensive surface collection produced a total of 2553 scrapers, *c* 78% of all flake tools. With a view to obtaining some form of broad chronological information from the scrapers recovered from surface collection, the classification scheme outlined below was devised, within which all of the scrapers recovered

Table 125 Flint scraper classification scheme

Class 1	on a flake of length: breadth ratio 2 : 1 or greater, with retouch on both the distal and proximal ends
Class 2	on a flake of length: breadth ratio 2 : 1 or greater, with retouch on the distal end
Class 3	on a flake of length: breadth ratio of *c* 1 : 1, the retouch may be on the sides and/or distal end
Class 4	on a flake of length: breadth ratio of between 1 : 1 and 2 : 1, with retouch on the distal end, the retouch may extend to one or both of the sides
Class 5	on a flake of length: breadth ratio of less than 1 : 1, the retouch may be on the sides and/or distal end
Class 6	on a flake of length: breadth ratio of between 1 : 1 and 2 : 1, with retouch on one of the sides
Class 7	on a flake of dimensions less than *c* 30mm long and *c* 30mm wide, with fine, shallow invasive retouch on the sides and/or distal end
Class 8	on a flake of length: breadth ratio of between 1 : 1 and 2 : 1, with very steep or undercutting retouch on the distal end
Class 9	on an irregular flake, often large and thick, with a proportionately small amount of coarse retouch, which may be denticulate
Class 10	scrapers which cannot be classified according to this scheme, including those made on thermal pieces, broken flakes or cores, those with retouch on the proximal end only, and broken scrapers

Table 126 Dated flint scraper assemblages

Site	*Date*	*Scraper assemblage*
W2 (1981) Coneybury 'Anomaly'	Early Neo: pottery, flint and C14 date	54 stratified
W83 Robin Hood's Ball	Early Neo: pottery, flint and C14 date	53 stratified 92 topsoil
W59 King Barrow Ridge	later Neo: pottery, flint and C14 date	12 stratified 121 topsoil
W31 Wilsford Down	later Neo: flint and pottery	12 stratified 168 topsoil
W84 Robin Hood's Ball	Beaker: pottery	4 stratified 45 topsoil
W34 Fargo Wood II	later Bronze Age: pottery	3 stratified 66 topsoil

Table 127 Flint scraper class by dated assemblage

Scraper	*W2 (1981)*		*W83*		*W59*		*W31*		*W84*		*W34*	
class	*No*	*%*	*No*	*%*	*No*	*%*	*No*	*%*	*No*	*%*	*No*	*%*
1	2	4	2	1	1	1	0	0	0	0	0	0
2	0	0	5	3	3	2	7	4	0	0	3	4
3	13	24	32	22	9	7	12	7	2	4	5	7
4	24	44	58	40	66	50	58	32	12	24	27	39
5	4	7	16	11	11	8	12	7	1	2	4	6
6	5	9	6	4	10	8	24	13	10	20	9	13
7	2	4	0	0	1	1	5	3	9	18	1	1
8	0	0	1	1	1	1	7	4	0	0	0	0
9	0	0	12	8	17	13	27	15	4	8	3	4
10	4	7	13	9	14	11	28	16	11	22	17	25
Total	54		145		133		180		49		69	

from the project were recorded. The records are available in the archive. The absence of mainframe computing facilities suggested that a scheme based on metrical analysis of all of the scrapers recovered from the project (a total of 4005) would be impracticable. It was therefore decided to use a morphological classification, based on dated associations from sites outside the study area where possible, and to test this classification for its utility as a broad chronological indicator against scraper assemblages of known date from excavated sites in the study area.

The classification scheme

Reference to published flint reports (discussed below) and a rapid assessment of the scraper assemblage from the project, based on the first level of flint analysis, suggested that the main attributes to be considered were the flake length:breadth ratio and the position and type of retouch. Six classes of scraper were defined on this basis, with an additional four classes to accommodate expedient, irregular, and broken scrapers, and obvious functional types which were noted during the level one flint analysis. The classes are described in Table 125 and illustrated in Figure 15.

A survey of the literature suggests that little work has been done on assessing the broad chronological implications of the range of scraper types found from both surface collection and excavation. The scraper classification scheme devised by Clark for the Hurst Fen assemblage (J G D Clark 1960) has also been used for a number of other assemblages, such as Windmill Hill and Durrington Walls (I F Smith 1965, Wainwright and Longworth 1971).

Class 1 and 2 scrapers, on long flakes, are suggested to be earlier Neolithic, given the metrical analysis of flakes from both earlier and later Neolithic assemblages. At Durrington Walls, the most common scrapers are short end scrapers, a type which encompasses all of Class 4 (Wainwright and Longworth 1971, 164). The ubiquity of this type of scraper is obviously to some extent a product of blank availability and selection, but its possible association with later Neolithic assemblages is considered in more detail below. The association of 'thumbnail' scrapers (Class 7) with Beaker assemblages has been recognised for many years (Gibson 1982). As working hypotheses, scrapers of Classes 6 and 8 were thought to be products of flake blank and scraper function, while the expedient and unclassifiable scrapers of Classes 9 and 10 were considered more likely to occur in larger numbers in assemblages of the second millennium BC.

The excavated scraper assemblages

The sites with reasonably well-dated flint assemblages used to assess the chronological integrity of the scraper classification are shown in Table 126. Six sites were chosen, two of earlier Neolithic date (W2 (1981) and W83), two of Middle/later Neolithic date (W59 and W31), one of Beaker date (a preliminary examination of W84, a Beaker pottery scatter, Richards in prep a) and one dating to the later Bronze Age (W34). Only one of the sites, W2 (1981), has the majority of scrapers from stratified contexts. For the rest of the sites, the small numbers of stratified scrapers has meant that those from topsoil excavation have been included in the analysis.

The first stage of the analysis was to look at the association of each defined scraper class with the assemblages of known date. The results are shown in Table 127, which suggests a number of associations. In very broad terms, the association of the Class 1 and 2 with the earlier Neolithic was shown, although very low numbers make any further inference difficult. More useful in this case is the association of Classes 3 and 5 with the two earlier Neolithic assemblages. All of the assemblages have high numbers of Class 4 scrapers, which was expected given its definition, and some form of refinement, discussed below, was sought. Interestingly, Class 6, originally thought to be a function of flake blank, shows an association with the Beaker site and, to a lesser extent, the later Bronze Age site. Only the Beaker site has high numbers of Class 7 scrapers, emphasising its usefulness as a type fossil. The very low numbers of Class 8 scrapers for all the assemblages negate inference, while the rise in the numbers of expedient and unclassifiable scrapers through time is particularly marked for Class 10 scrapers.

Figure 152 shows the scraper classes arranged in these broad chronological groups, with the percentages of each class in each assemblage shown. Classes 4 and 8 have been excluded from this plot. At a very general level, some of the scraper classes have been shown to have utility as chronological indicators for the earlier Neolithic (Classes 1, 2, 3, 5), the Beaker period (Classes 6, 7), and the later Bronze Age (Classes 9, 10). The problem of refining the Class 4 scrapers to look for a distinctive later Neolithic component remains.

Given the work from Durrington Walls and the observations on stratified scraper groups of later Neolithic date from the project, it was felt that a useful attribute to consider was the thickness of the scraper blank. It was observed in a comparison of scraper assemblages of earlier and later Neolithic date that later Neolithic scrapers tended to be thinner than those from earlier assemblages (Wainwright and Longworth 1971, 164; Harding, this vol, 5.2). A comparison of the mean thicknesses of the Class 4 scrapers from the six assemblages agreed with this observation (Table 128), with the qualification that while large numbers of thin Class 4 scrapers may indicate a later Neolithic component, the converse does not automatically follow.

Table 128 Mean thickness of class 4 flint scrapers

Site	*Mean thickness (to nearest mm)*
W2 (1981) Coneybury Anomaly	15
W83 Robin Hood's Ball	14
W59 King Barrow Ridge	8
W31 Wilsford Down	12
W84 Robin Hood's Ball	12
W34 Fargo Road II	13

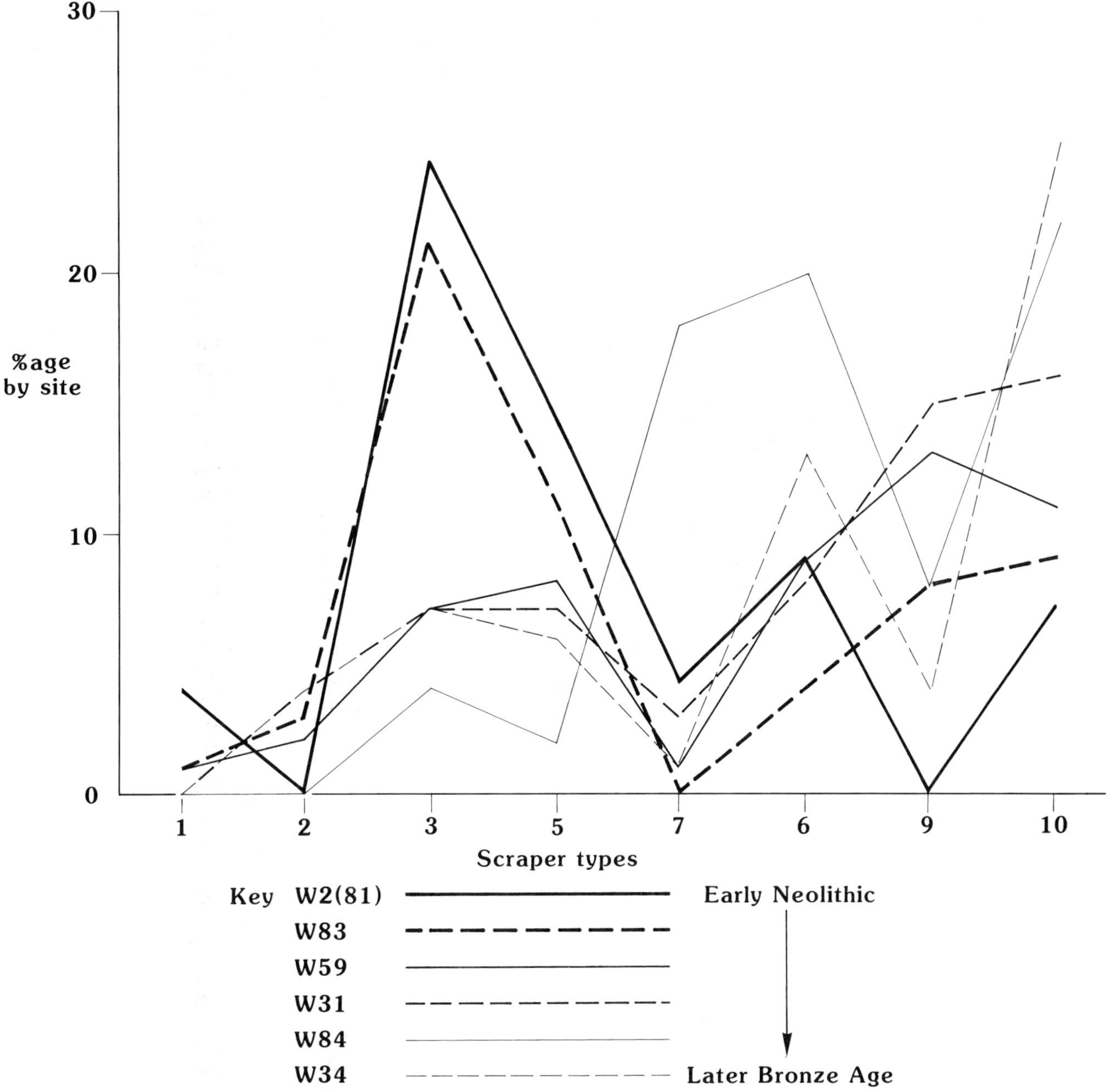

Fig 152 Analysis of flint scrapers for chronological attributes

Applications and limitations

The aim of this analysis was to produce a classification scheme for scrapers which would have some chronological value and which would be simple enough to allow large numbers of scrapers to be assessed. Within the constraints of working manually with the data thus obtained, it is felt that the broad chronological scheme outlined above has some validity within the study area. To this end, the classification has been used on the scraper assemblage from surface collection to indicate broad areas of activity within a particular chronological period on the composite maps (Figs 156–9). Given the relatively few chronologically diagnostic flint tools and the dearth of prehistoric pottery recovered from surface collection, this method of assessing general chronological trends within the scraper assemblage has proved to be of some value.

It must be said, however, that while the author feels that the classification has utility in suggesting, very broadly, the date of a large sample of scrapers in terms of proportions of different scraper classes, it would be meaningless to single out a particular scraper from an assemblage and assign it, for example, to the later Neolithic on the grounds of its thickness. Such factors as the availability of flake blanks and the intended function of the flint tool must influence scraper production.

The petit tranchet derivative arrowheads

A detailed comparative study of the petit tranchet derivative arrowheads of chisel form from W59 and W31 has been carried out (Harding, this vol, 5.2). Beyond this detailed technological analysis, it was felt that all

Table 129 Flint arrowheads of petit tranchet derivative form from extensive surface collection

Field no	*Petit tranchet*	*Chisel*	*Oblique*	*?*	*Total*
50		1			1
51		5	1	1	7
52		3	1		4
54	1	4	6		11
55			1		1
57		1	1	1	3
59		1			1
61		1			1
62		2			2
63		4	2		6
65		4	2		6
68		1			1
71		1	2	1	4
72		1	2		3
77			1		1
78		4	1		5
82		1	1		2
84		1			1
86				1	1
Total	1	35	21	4	61

Table 130 Flint arrowheads of petit tranchet derivative form from intensive surface collection and excavation

Site	*Petit tranchet*	*Chisel*	*Oblique*	*?*	*Total*
W2 Henge					
topsoil	4	8	2		14
stratified		1	1		2
W2 'Anomaly'					
upper fill		1	2		3
W17		1		1	
W31					
topsoil		13	5	2	20
stratified		5			5
W32					
topsoil		4			4
W34					
topsoil		5	1		6
stratified		1			1
W52					
stratified	1	1			2
W57					
topsoil		2			2
W59					
total collection		5	2	3	10
topsoil	1	15	3	1	20
stratified		1	1		2
Total	6	62	18	6	92

of the petit tranchet derivative arrowheads from surface collection, topsoil excavation, and stratified deposits should be examined and classified according to J G D Clark (1934). The results of this classification are available in the archive. A useful distinction is between chisel arrowheads (Clark types B to D) and oblique arrowheads (Clark types E to I). The results of the classification of the petit tranchet derivative arrowheads from the project according to this distinction are shown in Tables 129 and 130, and the oblique and chisel arrowheads from surface collection are shown on the period map for the later Neolithic, Figure 158.

Some work has already been carried out on the association of specific petit tranchet derivative arrowhead types with varying styles of Late Neolithic pottery, particularly Grooved Ware (Wainwright and Longworth 1971, fig 95). Within the study area, this work suggested two associations: first, between henge monuments, Grooved Ware, and oblique arrowheads (Durrington Walls: 51 oblique, 5 chisel; Woodhenge: 20 oblique, 3 chisel); and second, between pits, Grooved Ware, and Clark type D petit tranchet derivative arrowheads (Ratfyn pit: 2 type D; Woodlands pit: 6 type D, 1 petit tranchet). Wainwright and Longworth also suggested (1971, 259) that there was an association between sites where Grooved Ware was a minor component of the ceramic assemblage, and higher proportions of chisel arrowheads. This appears to be confirmed by the material from W2, Coneybury Henge, where small quantities of Grooved Ware (Ellison, this vol, 4.9 c) are associated with 9 chisel and 2 oblique arrowheads. The arrowheads from W59, King Barrow Ridge (21 chisel, 2 of these type D, and 6 oblique) also agree with this suggested association. These arrowheads are all from surface or ploughsoil contexts, but within a zone where Grooved Ware is consistently found (Cleal, this vol, 6.3).

5.4 Worked flint assemblages: an overview

The studies reported above, while concentrating individually on widely differing aspects of the overall project flint assemblage, all serve to highlight both the benefits and the limitations of study within a restricted landscape zone. It is clear that lithic artefacts, by virtue of their durability and general lack of secondary use potential, represent a powerful tool for the location and identification of Neolithic and Bronze Age activity.

Harding's study (this vol, 5.2) emphasises the consistent use of immediately available raw material, the only apparent exception being that used for the production of ground axes. With a common source of raw material, even allowing for slight variation in quality, other factors must be sought in explanation for observed changes in both technology and typology.

With the exception of identifiable, and generally isolated, episodes of core tool manufacture, production appears to be of blades/flakes, with Harding's study re-emphasising previously observed trends towards broader flakes throughout the Neolithic. Some variations can be observed, however, between broadly contemporaneous groups (W2 (1981) and W83), where Harding suggests that a greater proportion of blades indicates a higher standard of technology. The nature of the activity taking place at these two 'sites' may, however, have greater bearing on this observed technological variation, with blades representing more mobile aspects of the Neolithic subsistence/economy.

It is inevitable that the material record of the majority of the wide range of activities which can be suggested as forming part of everyday prehistoric life will not be incorporated within deposits capable of preserving archaeological integrity. It can be argued that the activities represented within ditch fills, and to a lesser extent those contained within deliberately filled pits, may be far from representative. Flint procured during the excavation of a ditch may be of a type of raw material not normally encountered, and may equally embody spiritual or ceremonial significance. As such the technological aspects of its reduction, which may not necessarily involve any concept of utilisation, should be interpreted with some caution, and may not necessarily typify those employed under more normal circumstances. A cautious approach should not, however, diminish awareness of the opportunities for detailed technological reconstruction offered by such episodes as that recovered from W58 (this vol, 4.7 b).

The lithic assemblage from this project has offered the opportunity to integrate both technological and typological approaches, the latter more appropriate to the rapid assessment and interpretation of surface tools, particularly of the more ubiquitous types. Within this context, Riley's study (this vol, 5.3) of the large scraper assemblage has provided a valuable and potentially more widely applicable model of fundamental importance in attempts to refine the chronology of surface lithic scatters.

In retrospect, the greatest problem encountered in carrying out the project lithic studies lay in the intensity and extent of the record created by a wide variety of activities. The palimpsest created by these activities was, by virtue of its extent and occasional intensity, only susceptible to broad study, with more restricted and detailed studies inevitably serving to indicate the potential still remaining.

5.5 Non-local stone

The majority of the material recorded as foreign (non-local) stone was recovered by surface collection or from the excavation of unstratified contexts. The recovery, during the first season of surface collection, of large quantities of material subsequently discarded as road metalling, forcefully introduced the problem of field identification, previously encountered by the excavators at Durrington Walls (Wainwright and Longworth 1971, 185). In subsequent seasons of fieldwork the desire to maximise the retrieval of useful data had, of necessity, to be tempered by the inadvisability of both collecting and identifying quantities of recently introduced rocks.

The surface collection programme at least in part confirmed the suggestion made by Bowen and Smith (1977) that sarsen was a local occurrence. The sarsen recorded, but not collected, during project fieldwork tended to be in the form of small rounded boulders of hard 'rooty' sarsen (Pitts 1982, 121). These, in general no larger than 0.3–0.4m in diameter, occurred most frequently within dry valley bottoms. In contrast to this distribution, the scatter of broken sarsen recorded during surface collection and subsequent excavation on the King Barrow Ridge (W59, this vol, 4.8) is both anomalous and difficult to explain.

With the exception of the hard sarsen, the material consequently defined as non-local stone fell into three categories: stone axe fragments, recognised as much for their morphological characteristics as their distinctive stone types; specific types of 'bluestone'; and fragments of querns, rubbers, and 'potential' quern material. These categories are discussed below.

5.5 a *Stone axe fragments*

Eight fragments of stone tools were recovered by excavation and surface collection. Following conventional assumptions concerning the developed stone axe trade (Bradley 1984, 53), they are suggested as having later Neolithic associations.

The fragments, none of which are illustrated, were examined by Mrs F Roe, who has provided the following identifications. Four axes were subsequently examined by Dr Olwen Williams-Thorpe as part of a programme of bluestone analysis and comments are appended.

Surface collection

North of the Cursus (52) SU 112431/A SF392

Flake from a polished stone axe
Laboratory no R198. Petrological no 1837/W1 416
Petrology – macroscopic: fine-grained, light coloured siliceous rock with white phenocrysts; microscopic: Group VII augite granophyre
(The matrix of this rock is basically siliceous, but it is now mainly altered and contains a good deal of chlorite. There are also grains of iron ore and leucoxene throughout, while scattered grains of colourless pyroxene can be seen and possible traces of feldspar crystals. A few grains of calcite also occur. This sample lacks the clusters of augite grains that are more typical of Group VII.)
Source: Penmaenmawr area, Gwynedd

King Barrow Ridge (57) SU 140431/E SF375

Axe fragment
Laboratory no R199. Petrological no 1838/W1 417
Petrology – macroscopic: an altered, medium-grained igneous rock, dark-coloured on the freshly broken surface – greenstone; microscopic: Group 1 greenstone
(There is still some residual pyroxene in this altered gabbro, but it is mainly altered to green uralite. The feldspar is either clouded, or filled with needles of green amphibole. Skeletal ilmenite is scattered throughout. Typical Group 1.)
Source: Cornwall, probably near Penzance

Stonehenge Triangle (54) SU 118421/E SF382

Reworked stone axe fragment
Laboratory no R200. Petrological no 1839/W1 418
Petrology – macroscopic: fine-grained, light-coloured siliceous rock; microscopic: devitrified rhyolite
(The rock contains a cryptocrystalline, siliceous, felsitic groundmass consisting of quartz, feldspar, and chlorite. There are phenocrysts up to 0.3mm in

diameter of quartz and two feldspars. Scattered grains of iron ore are to be found, while slight traces of perlitic structure can be seen. There are accessory grains of epidote and calcite.)
Source: possibly relates to other Pembrokeshire rhyolite.
(This axe is not chemically identical with the Stonehenge rhyolite bluestones, four of which were analysed.)

The Diamond (59) SU 105409/B SF251

Reworked stone axe fragment
Laboratory no R201. Petrological no 1840/W1 419
Petrology – macroscopic: fine-grained, light-coloured siliceous rock; microscopic: devitrified rhyolite
(The matrix is cryptocrystalline and felsitic, consisting of quartz, feldspar, and chlorite, and containing phenocrysts of quartz, plagioclase, and alkali feldspar, with the latter predominating. Carbonate is present as an alteration product, and there are scattered grains of iron ore. The carbonate sometimes forms rims around the iron ore. There are possible traces of perlitic structure and banding.)
Source: as R200, possibly relates to other Pembrokeshire rhyolite
(This axe is not chemically identical with the Stonehenge rhyolite bluestones, but does show some similarity with one Stonehenge rhyolite.)

The Diamond (59) SU 10104140 SF246

Butt of ground stone axe
Laboratory no R202. Petrological no 1841/W1 420.
Petrology – macroscopic: light-coloured, medium-grained weathered igneous rock. There are no true spots in this small specimen, though some lesser spots can be seen in the cut section; microscopic: ophitic dolerite
(The augite forms plates up to 3mm across, and these are mainly unaltered. The plagioclase though is too altered for certain identification, and a fair amount of chlorite can be seen in the thin section. The iron ore varies between discrete grains, skeletal ilmenite, and leucoxene. A little quartz is present.)
Source: unknown, but possibly in the Preselau Hills, Dyfed, Pembrokeshire.
(This axe is not chemically the same as any of the analysed Stonehenge dolerites. Although the analysis does not fall within the spotted dolerite Preseli area of Carn Meini, it does just fall within the range of other Preseli rocks.)

West Field (68) SU 104396/B SF763

Fragment of pebble-hammer
Laboratory no R203 (not sectioned). Petrological no 1842/W1 421
Petrology – macroscopic: reddish-coloured quartzite

Excavation

W34B Fargo Wood II SU 11184317 Context 221, SF66

Flake from a stone axe
Laboratory no R204. Petrological no 1843/W1 422
Petrology – macroscopic: light-coloured fine-grained siliceous rock with white phenocrysts; microscopic: Group VII augite granophyre
(Chlorite grains occur throughout in an altered matrix of siliceous material. Much of this now appears clouded, with a scatter of small grains of iron ore. Larger fragments in the matrix include possible feldspar and pyroxene, perhaps also glass.)
Source: Penmaenmawr area, Gwynedd

W58 Amesbury 42 SU 137432 SF3

Flake from a stone axe
Laboratory no R205. Petrological no 1844/W1 423
Petrology – macroscopic: light-coloured, fine-grained siliceous rock with phenocrysts; microscopic: ash or tuff
(The glassy matrix contains a large rock fragment, a shard of devitrified glass, and smaller crystals of chlorite, pyroxene, and possibly altered feldspar.)
Source: unknown

5.5 b 'Bluestones'

The most recent and most detailed consideration of the Stonehenge 'foreign' stones is that prepared by Hilary Howard (Pitts 1982, 104–26). Howard proposes a broad terminology consisting of three rock types: ophitic ('spotted') dolerite, rhyolitic rocks, and basic tuffs. The corpus of finds of such rocks from the Stonehenge area (Pitts 1982, 125–6) is heavily biased towards the first two groups, and the results from the present project reflect this bias towards the essentially more distinctive types. The identification of both dolerite and rhyolite, the occurrence of which is shown in Table 131, has been purely visual, and made by reference to a collection of positively identified specimens loaned from the Alexander Keiller Museum, Avebury.

Table 131 Bluestone from surface collection and excavation

Dolerite				
Excavation				
W31	context 87			33g
W52	context 18	SF7	flake	24g
	context 33	SF53	fragment	1g
	context 37	SF32	flake	22g
Surface collection				
Stonehenge Triangle (54)	116424/B	SF381	flake	84g
Rhyolitic rock				
Excavation				
W2	context 720	SF187	flake	3g
W59	context 8	SF3	flake	21g
	context 503	SF333	chip	1g
Surface collection				
North of the Cursus (52)	116433/E	SF388	slab	662g
	119436/A	SF390	hammerstone	215g
	111433/B	SF410	?tool	49g
South of Stonehenge (55)	124414/B	SF9	flake	1g
The Diamond (59)	104411/G	SF250	bifacial tool	175g
Fargo Road (63)	11404426	SF309	slab	72g
Horse Hospital (64)	114437/B	SF917	tool	111g
Spring Bottom (78)	125402?E	SF705	flake	50g
New King (87)	135422/G	SF1332	tool	137g
Wood End (90)	108437/C	SF511	flake	1g

The distribution of surface finds and those from excavation suggest that fragments of both rhyolite and dolerite have a wide distribution within the Stonehenge area. Finds from the western half of the Stonehenge Cursus may provide some confirmation of the 'bluestone scatter' recorded by Stone (1947, 17) the specific location of which, now within an area of reintroduced pasture, cannot be checked. The only pieces recovered from a stratified context were the three fragments of spotted dolerite from the old ground surface beneath the bank of the North Kite (W52, this vol, 4.12). The occurrence of three fragments, two of which appear to be flakes, within an area of less than $10m^2$ suggests that dolerite was being worked nearby. Perhaps in this context it is worth noting the recovery of a dolerite battle axe from the excavation of a round barrow less than 300m to the east (Greenfield 1959).

Some evidence was recovered from surface collection of the use of bluestone for the manufacture of tools. Four examples, all of rhyolite, are illustrated in Figure 153.

North of the Cursus (52) 119436/A SF390
Apparently laminated slab with bifacial retouch and showing signs of considerable battering at both ends. ?Possible hammerstone.

North of the Cursus (52) 111433/B SF410
Flake with abrupt bifacial retouch at distal end to produce roughly lozenge profile point. ?Piercer.

The Diamond (59) 104411/G SF250
Apparently laminated slab with bifacial retouch. ?Axe roughout.

New King (87) 135422/G SF250
Possible flake with bifacial retouch. ?'Y'-shaped tool.

If the identifications suggested above are correct, then, by analogy with flint tool types, SF1332 and SF410 are chronologically diagnostic tools and can be suggested as dating to the later Neolithic and Early Bronze Age periods respectively (this vol, 3.3 d, Table 6, and Fig 11b and e).

5.5 c *Chert*

It has been noted above that flint is a readily available resource, and thus with the exception of the truly 'exotic' rocks considered above, alternative sources of flaking material are unlikely to have been of great significance. This suggestion appears to be confirmed by the recovery of a mere 23 pieces of identifiable worked chert in the course of project fieldwork. It must be noted, however, that, when patinated, the distinction between flint (some decidedly 'cherty'), and true chert is far from clear. Only one chert tool was recovered, a petit tranchet derivative arrowhead from surface collection on Coneybury Hill (51) (Riley, this vol, 5.3). The majority of the identified chert is fine and grey, and may have originated either in Portland or from the Tisbury area, the latter only 15km to the south-west.

5.5 d *Querns and quern fragments*

Querns in a complete, or partly complete, state are not difficult to recognise in the field. Certainty as to their precise location should, however, be tempered by an

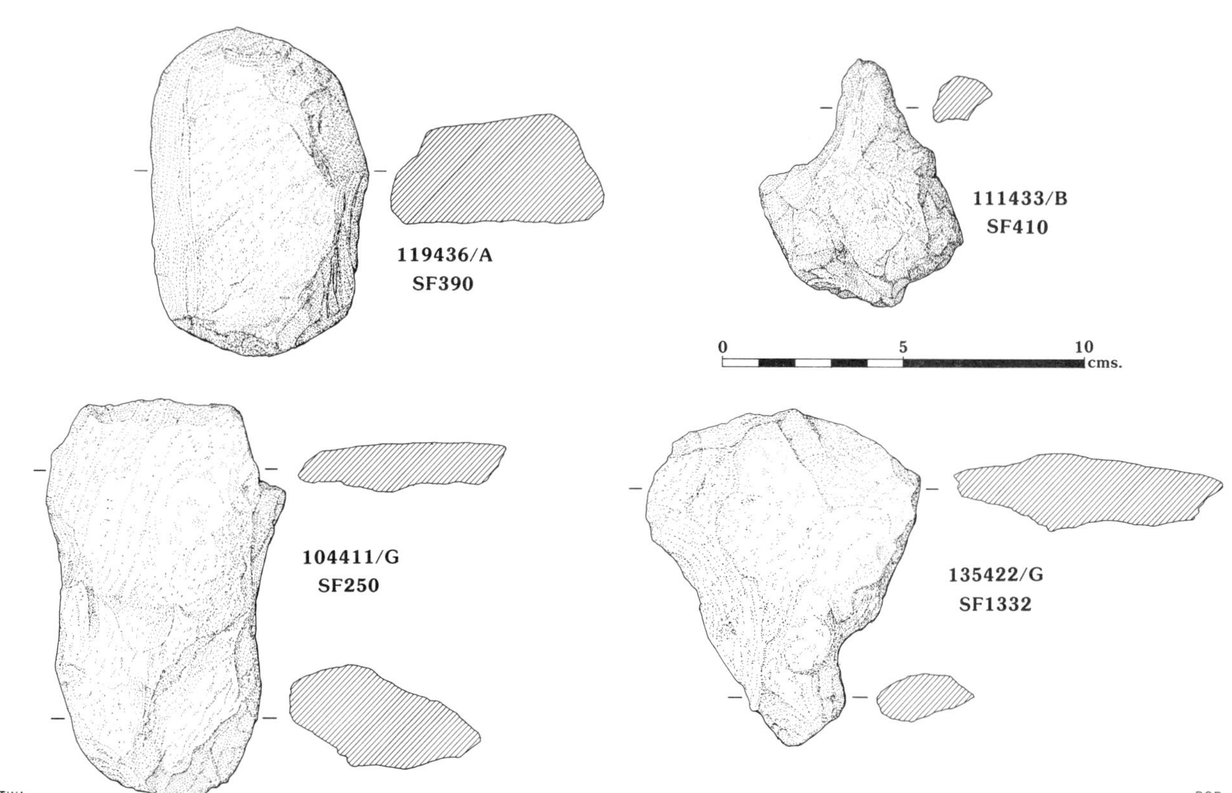

Fig 153 'Bluestone' tools from extensive surface collection

awareness of their portability and their nuisance value to the farmer, a combination which may explain the occurrence of some examples towards the edges and corners of fields. Quern fragments were identified on the basis of surviving prepared and/or smoothed surface, in some cases enabling very small fragments to be identified. The majority recovered during project fieldwork were of sugary or saccaroid sarsen (Pitts 1982, 120) and, where form could be determined, were of saddle type. This type of sarsen is most likely to have been introduced from the Marlborough Downs, where quern manufacture, associated with Bronze Age clearance, has been recorded recently at Dean Bottom and Rockley Down (Gingell forthcoming). As a non-local and heavy resource, querns appear to have been used until considerably worn down, their reduction in size possibly associated with changing function. Many of the fragments exhibiting a small area of quern surface appear to be flakes, possibly removed in the course of pecking (refacing) the quern too close to the edge.

Saddle querns need not necessarily be associated with the processing of extensively produced cereals, and alternative uses in the processing of wild plant resources can be suggested. Fragments of sarsen querns or rubbers occur within earlier Neolithic contexts at W83 (Richards in prep a), but here they do not appear to be associated with cereal remains. None the less, querns do show a strong association with areas of later Bronze Age activity, themselves integrated with areas of 'Celtic' fields, and often, in surface assemblage, showing considerable evidence for burning. The surface combination of later Bronze Age pottery, burnt flint, and quern fragments which identified the site of Fargo Wood II (W34, this vol, 4.14) was also repeated within a specific area of the Robin Hood's Ball intensive surface collection (Richards in prep a). Sample excavation at the former site produced over 60% of all quern fragments recovered from excavations, and surface collection within the surrounding fields to the north of the Cursus reinforce this emphasis.

Three fragments of rotary querns were recovered, all of old red sandstone, and it is likely that other unfeatured fragments of this rock were originally part of similar querns. The distribution of these querns and this type of rock corresponds well with that of Roman pottery (Figure 17) concentrated around Rox Hill (82), Winterbourne Stoke Crossroads (50), and Woodhenge (60).

6 The prehistoric pottery

by Rosamund Cleal with Frances Raymond

The principal concern in the following discussion is the pottery recovered during the Stonehenge Environs Project, through both surface collection and excavation, but comparable material from both within and outside the area studied is cited throughout. It was not possible, within the scope of the project, to provide an exhaustive study of all published and unpublished pottery found within the Stonehenge area. This must be borne in mind when distribution patterns are considered. Even with this proviso, it is clear that by using the material recovered by the Stonehenge Environs Project, combined with published material from the area, it is possible to discern overall patterns which are unlikely to be much altered by subsequent work.

In the following discussion the sections on location, fabric, and distribution refer principally to material recovered during the project, with the addition of the King Barrow Ridge Neolithic pit excavated by the Vatchers. The discussion throughout will concentrate on featured sherds, as it is only these which can be certainly classified to ceramic style and period, but the distribution of featureless sherds will also be noted. Sites within the general study area which have been investigated in the past, but did not form part of the project, may be mentioned in these sections, but a distinction will be made between them and the sites covered by the project. Comparative material from outside the immediate area is only discussed in the sections on relationships.

6.1 The Early–Middle Neolithic: South-Western style, Decorated style

Locations

Featured sherds: W2 Coneybury Henge; W2 (1981) Coneybury 'Anomaly'; W59 King Barrow Ridge pit 418 (possibly earlier Neolithic); King Barrow Ridge (Vatcher pit). Surface collection: South of Stonehenge (55)

Featureless sherds: Fargo Road (63); Luxenborough (84)

Fabric

Among the certainly identifiable Neolithic pottery only flint, sand, and chalk occur as inclusions, with flint and sand together occurring in most of the pottery. A small number of plain sherds containing sand and shell were recovered from the fill of the Coneybury 'Anomaly' and are therefore almost certainly earlier Neolithic in date, but no diagnostic sherds occurred in that fabric (SSh:Indet/1). However, the problematic flat piece (P263) from pit 418, at W59 King Barrow Ridge, is in a fabric similar to this, and must be of Early to Middle Neolithic date, as it is associated with the radiocarbon date of 3510–2910 BC (OxA 1397). There are parallels, although not close ones, for such a piece in assemblages of the Early to Middle Neolithic, and none within the Grooved Ware tradition, but the presence of sherds apparently of Woodlands style bowls of the Grooved Ware tradition in the same layer and in a similar fabric is difficult to explain. There are no dates for Woodlands style assemblages in this area, and it is likely that only future dating of such material could shed light on this problem, as the association between the sherds and the dated material in pit 418 seems secure, and it is difficult to envisage the two cordoned sherds as belonging to anything other than Woodlands style vessels (Dr I F Smith pers comm).

The sources of the clays and inclusion types are unknown, but all, with the exception of the shelly fabrics, could be local.

Distribution and context

The earlier Neolithic material recovered by the project is concentrated in a fairly small part of the study area to the east of Stonehenge, and all but one sherd was recovered from pits. This preponderance of pit finds is a common pattern with earlier Neolithic material and cannot be entirely due to post-depositional processes as much of the pottery is moderately well-fired and robust, and is likely to survive in topsoil at least as well as other earlier prehistoric pottery.

The emphasis on the area around King Barrow Ridge is also apparent in previously recovered material. Barrow Amesbury G132, east of King Barrow Ridge, and Amesbury G39, just west of it, have both produced earlier Neolithic pottery (Gingell 1988, Ashbee 1981). Elsewhere in the study area, earlier Neolithic activity is attested by the pottery excavated by Greenfield from Wilsford barrows 51, 52, and 54 (I F Smith in prep); by the assemblage from Robin Hood's Ball (N Thomas 1964) and the area immediately outside it (W53 and W83, Richards in prep a); by an isolated find of two earlier Neolithic rims at Winterbourne Stoke barrow 46 (Gingell 1988, fig 34: 1, 2); and by finds at both Durrington Walls (Wainwright and Longworth 1971) and Woodhenge (Cunnington 1929) henge monuments.

Relationships

As already noted, the largest earlier Neolithic assemblage from the area, that from the Coneybury 'Anomaly' W2 (1981), clearly belongs within the South-Western style of earlier Neolithic pottery. This style is characterised by unthickened rims, rarity of decoration, and common use of lugs; the trumpet form of the latter is especially characteristic. Both carinated and uncarinated bowl forms occur in the South-Western style, although not all sites have carinated forms, and even some large assemblages, such as that from Maiden Castle, have very few (Wheeler 1943; Cleal forthcoming a).

The nearest earlier Neolithic assemblage of any considerable size to the 'Anomaly' is that from Robin Hood's Ball, Shrewton, 5.5km to the north-west of Coneybury. There is some similarity between the fabric of one of the Robin Hood's Ball vessels (Thomas 1964, fig 4.1) and Fabric FS:Neo/1 from the 'Anomaly', but overall the differences between the two assemblages seem to outweigh the general similarity which serves only to identify them as both belonging to the same regional style. The Robin Hood's Ball assemblage shows a marked similarity to the pottery from Maiden Castle, Dorset, both in form and in the presence of gabbroic ware, the source of which is The Lizard, Cornwall. The pits outside the enclosure (W83), as well as the assemblage from the enclosure itself, contain gabbroic ware. At Maiden Castle certain forms from Robin Hood's Ball (Thomas 1964, figs 4:1, 4:2, 4:4, 4:7, 4:9, and 4:17) are fairly common, and elongated lugs with concave upper surfaces (Thomas 1964, fig 4:2) also occur. The pottery from the Coneybury 'Anomaly' is not, however, so readily paralleled at Maiden Castle, where carinated forms such as P1 are rare, except in gabbroic ware. A closer parallel is provided, at least for P1, by the assemblage from Rowden, Dorset, near Maiden Castle (Woodward forthcoming), where there are several such vessels in non-gabbroic fabrics.

The forms of P7 and P6 from the 'Anomaly' are also unusual: P6 is a neutral necked bowl, and P7 a closed bowl or, possibly, a jar (the terms used are as defined by Whittle 1977, 77). There is a close parallel for P6 among the South-Western style component of the Windmill Hill assemblage (I F Smith 1965, P79), and Smith points out the occurrence (ibid, 60) of two rims from necked jars at Maiden Castle (Wheeler 1943, fig 30:77 and one not illustrated). In the case of P7 it is more difficult to find a close parallel, but all the elements of the vessel (closed bowl form, rolled-over rim, and perforated lug) are represented in the South-Western style.

In the immediate area around Coneybury there is little earlier Neolithic pottery, but both the Decorated (ie Windmill Hill) and South-Western regional styles are represented. At Robin Hood's Ball the recent excavation of pits outside the causewayed enclosure (W83, Richards in prep a) has produced at least one thickened, decorated rim of Abingdon Ware, as well as gabbroic ware and light-rimmed pottery. Thickened rims, although in this case not decorated, occur on vessels from the ditch of a long barrow at Woodford, approximately 5km to the south (barrow G2, Gingell 1986), and from the pre-enclosure settlement at Durrington Walls, approximately 2.5km to the north-east. There, about 21 vessels are represented, of which about half have some thickening of the rim (Wainwright and Longworth 1971, 53–55, figs 30–31). Although some simple rims are present, the assemblage does not show any marked resemblance in form or fabric to the Coneybury 'Anomaly' pottery. At Woodhenge, however, the small assemblage of earlier Neolithic pottery includes vessels of the South-Western regional style (eg Cunnington 1929, pl 32: no 43, pl 32: no 58, and possibly nos 56 and 57), and a small number of thickened rims. This pottery much more closely resembles that from Coneybury 'Anomaly' than does that from Durrington Walls, and it includes sherds in fabric FS:Neo/1. There is also a finer element, not represented at W2 (1981), which in form and fabric appears almost to be an imitation of gabbroic ware (eg Cunnington 1929, pl 32 no 43); this reinforces the impression that the assemblage belongs firmly within the South-Western regional style.

Three Neolithic bowls belonging to the South-Western style, and one probably of that style, were found in a pit beneath barrow Amesbury G132 (Gingell 1988, fig 18), east of the Avenue, just under 1km from the 'Anomaly'. These are in a fabric with flint and sand inclusions which is not dissimilar to FS:Neo/1. The vessels themselves are not directly comparable to those from the 'Anomaly', but clearly belong to the South-Western style, and are comparable to vessels such as P52, P54, P62, and P64 at Windmill Hill (I F Smith 1965), which belong to the South-Western component of that assemblage. The pottery from the barrow mound of Amesbury barrow G39, a barrow only 500m to the north-west of W2 (1981), is not illustrated in the excavation report (Ashbee 1981), but includes both light- and heavy-rimmed vessels; a few sherds are in a fabric comparable to FS:Neo/1. On the King Barrow Ridge, less than 400m from the 'Anomaly', a pit excavated during road widening produced a small assemblage of pottery which shows a considerable degree of similarity to that from the 'Anomaly'. In this pit, a minimum of four earlier Neolithic vessels, two of which certainly have lugs (P53–P56), are represented by 34 sherds. The fabric of the majority of the sherds from the pit lies within the range of FS:Neo/1, and it would seem likely that similar sources of raw material were utilised, although this cannot be established with certainty as the inclusion types are common ones.

To the south-west of Coneybury, on Wilsford Down, an area which produced no earlier Neolithic pottery during excavation and surface collection by the project, a minor concentration of earlier Neolithic pottery occurs in the barrow group comprising Wilsford 51–54 (I F Smith in prep). Both simple and thickened rim forms are represented among this material, as are a vessel with an oval perforated lug, a vessel decorated with multiple round impressions, and rims with slight incision or slashing obliquely across the rim. The types of decoration present can be paralleled at Maiden Castle, both among the material excavated by Wheeler (round impressions: Wheeler 1943, fig 28: 34) and among the material excavated more recently (rims with slashes or incision, Cleal forthcoming a). The fabrics of this group have not been compared with those of the 'Anomaly', but on the grounds of form and decoration alone, and in spite of the presence of lugs at both Wilsford and Coneybury, it would seem likely that the strongest local parallels for the Wilsford material are with the Robin Hood's Ball assemblage, rather than with Coneybury.

6.2 Middle–Late Neolithic: Peterborough Ware

Locations

Featured sherds: W31 Wilsford Down (Mortlake, ?Ebbsfleet); W32 Fargo Wood I (indeterminate substyle); W34 Fargo Wood II (Fengate); W52 North Kite (Fengate, Mortlake); W59 King Barrow Ridge (Mortlake). Surface collection: Horse Hospital (64) (Ebbsfleet/Mortlake, Fengate); Fargo Road (63) (indeterminate substyle); Stonehenge Triangle (54) (indeterminate substyle); The Diamond (59) (Ebbsfleet/Mortlake); King Barrow Ridge (57) (indeterminate substyle)

Featureless sherds: North of the Cursus (52); West Field (68); Wood End (90)

Fabric

As with the fabrics of the earlier Neolithic, flint is the commonest inclusion type in the Peterborough Ware from the area and occurs in almost all fabrics. However, ferruginous and micaceous clays were used at several of the sites, in contrast to the earlier Neolithic fabrics, in which iron oxides occur only as very occasional inclusions, and from which mica is absent. Only 8 out of the 24 Peterborough Ware fabrics identified contained sand (Table 32, MF1 C1–14), in comparison to the occurrence of sand in almost every sherd of earlier Neolithic pottery recovered by the project from the area. The sand appears likely to be a natural inclusion in the clay because of its restricted size range and the evenness of its distribution throughout the fabrics, which is in sharp contrast to the unevenness of much of the flint temper. This may indicate a change in preference between the traditions and raises the possibility that different clay sources were being exploited. The differences in fabric types within the Peterborough Ware do not appear to be reflected in their distribution, nor are they related to the ceramic substyles within the tradition. The micaceous fabrics in the FfeM: and FM: series occur at W31 Wilsford Down, in the south of the area covered by the project; at W59 King Barrow Ridge, in the east; and at Horse Hospital (64) and W32 Fargo Wood I to the north. Ferruginous fabrics, which include some with mica, also occur at W31 Wilsford Down, W52 North Kite, at W59 King Barrow Ridge, and in Stonehenge Triangle (54). As the preceding section shows, these sites include all but one or two of the findspots of Peterborough Ware within the project area.

Vessels of different substyles occur on the same sites at W52 North Kite and at Horse Hospital (64). At the North Kite the substyles represented are Mortlake Ware and Fengate Ware, and both occur in fabric FS:Pet/1 (P199, P200, P208, P209); P200, P208, and P209 were recovered from beneath the bank of the enclosure, and P199 from an unstratified context. In the material from Horse Hospital (64), where the sherds are from surface collection, the Ebbsfleet or Mortlake Ware sherds (P270, P282), differ markedly from the Fengate-related bowl (P273) and the sherd of indeterminate Peterborough Ware, P272 (which could belong to a Fengate Ware vessel), P270 and P282 are both in fabric FM:Pet/1, while P273 and P272 are in GV:Pet/1, in which the voids represent calcareous inclusions, including shell, some of which survives. This suggests a source outside the immediate area for these sherds, unlike the Fengate Ware from the North Kite (P199, P200), which could have been made locally. The Peterborough Ware from Horse Hospital is also unusual in that it includes one sherd, P282, from the neck of either an Ebbsfleet Ware or a Mortlake Ware bowl, which is in a fabric type more usual among the Beaker pottery from the area (feGS:Bkr/2). All four illustrated sherds were found in a 500m band across the southern part of the collection area.

Distribution and context

The Peterborough Ware recovered by the project is concentrated in three main areas: 1, Wilsford Down (W31, W52, and from the surface in The Diamond(59)); 2, Fargo Wood and the area between it and the Packway (W32 and the surface in Horse Hospital (64) and Fargo Road (63)); and 3, the King Barrow Ridge area (W59 and surface on King Barrow Ridge (57)). A small concentration of sherds also occurs within Stonehenge Triangle (54). At the northern limit of the study area there is also Peterborough Ware among the material from W53 (Richards in prep a). At none of the sites was the pottery found within man-made features, and most occurred as scatters of material within ploughsoil.

Pottery recovered from within the study area by other excavators includes a single sherd of Mortlake Ware from a high level in the ditch of the Normanton Down Long Mortuary Enclosure (F de M Vatcher 1961, fig 6) and sherds of Peterborough Ware, including Ebbsfleet, Mortlake, and Fengate Ware, reported from Wilsford G51, G52, and G54 (RCHME 1979, 5–6, and information from Dr I F Smith), where they occur in derived positions (in mound make-up and ditch silts). Several vessels are represented, and decorative techniques include paired fingernail impression, whipped and twisted cord impression, grooving, and end-to-end linear fingernail impressions. Although the location of this material is within 400m of the section excavated across the North Kite, there are no particularly close stylistic parallels between the two groups of pottery. In the assemblage from the barrows there are no heavy rims of classic Mortlake type such as P212 from W52, nor at W52 the range and variety of decoration exhibited by the barrow group material. The occurrence of Fengate Ware at both is notable, however, and at both sites curvilinear motifs are present: in end-to-end fingernail at the barrows, and in twisted cord at W52 (P199). Peterborough Ware was also recovered from the excavation of seven barrows in the Lake barrow group (Grimes 1964), and includes at least one Ebbsfleet Ware rim with herringbone and lattice decoration (fig 7.1). This further emphasises the area of Wilsford Down, and indicates its importance in the late fourth to early third millennia BC. The importance of the King Barrow Ridge area is likewise highlighted by the finds from previously examined sites. A large quantity of Peterborough Ware was found in the loam core of the barrow Amesbury G39, which lies just at the western edge of the Ridge, and in ploughsoil at the same site (Ashbee 1981). This material includes body sherds from several Peterborough Ware bowls, probably of the Mortlake substyle, and at least one rim sherd certainly of that style; all are decorated with twisted cord impressions (not illustrated in Ashbee 1981). Peterborough Ware, including sherds of Ebbsfleet or Mortlake Ware bowls, has also recently been recovered from a modern tree-throw hole on barrow Amesbury G30, in the middle of the New King Barrows. The finds of Peterborough Ware, including two sherds of the Fengate substyle, recovered by the Project from the Fargo Wood area, are similarly augmented by the Fengate Ware rim from the mini-henge in Fargo Wood (Stone 1938).

Relationships

Peterborough Ware does not occur in large quantities within the study area, although it is quite widely spread. Beyond the study area there is a large assemblage from Downton, approximately 21km to the south-east, which includes Ebbsfleet and Fengate Ware (Rahtz 1962), and to the east, a site at Winterbourne Dauntsey, 8km to the south-east, produced sherds of six or seven Mortlake Ware vessels from shallow pits cut in the chalk, one of which was surrounded by stakeholes (Stone 1934).

6.3 Later Neolithic: Grooved Ware

Locations

W2 Coneybury Henge; W59 King Barrow Ridge, pits 418 and 440. Occasional find: King Barrow Ridge (rabbit hole in Amesbury G34)

Fabric

The only large assemblage to include Grooved Ware from the study area is that from W2 Coneybury Henge, where most of the Grooved Ware sherds contain shell, mixed in most cases with grog and sand; the probable Grooved Ware from pit 418 at W59 King Barrow Ridge also contains shell and sand. The sherd from Amesbury G34 differs from this in that it contains flint and sand. Both shell and flint occur as inclusions in the much larger assemblage of this tradition at Durrington Walls (Wainwright and Longworth 1971, 55), although grog with sand and/or shell is the commonest inclusion type there. The assemblage from Woodhenge appears to be dominated by shelly fabrics (Cunnington 1929, description of plates), which also figure in the Grooved Ware from pits near Durrington Walls (Larkhill Married Quarters; Longworth 1971). The only petrological examination of sherds from the area is that of samples from Durrington Walls (Finch 1971), but although the shell there is noted as probably fossil, no possible sources are suggested.

The use of shelly clays and/or the use of shell as a tempering material appears to have been a common practice among the makers of Grooved Ware generally, as the frequency of shelly fabrics is much higher in this tradition than in either the Peterborough or Beaker traditions. However, without some detailed analysis of the shell inclusions in the Stonehenge area Grooved Ware, and a survey of possible sources for them, which are outside the scope of the project, it is impossible to speculate further about sources for the pottery.

Distribution and context

Both the material from Coneybury Henge and that from King Barrow Ridge form part of a concentration of Grooved Ware finds to the east of Stonehenge and west of the Avon, which is made up in part by the assemblages from the henge monuments at Durrington Walls and Woodhenge, and also by finds from isolated pits and other contexts. This pattern is also reflected in the material excavated from barrows in the area. Grooved Ware was recovered from the mound make-up of Amesbury G39 (Ashbee 1981), just to the west of the King Barrow Ridge, and from the old ground surface beneath G133 (Gingell 1988), just to the east, and sherds have recently been recovered from a tree-throw hole in Amesbury G30, within the New King Barrows group itself. Sherds of several Grooved Ware vessels were also found in association with two decorated chalk plaques in a pit beside the A303, close to the New King Barrows (Harding 1988). The only exception to this pattern appears to be the few sherds from Stonehenge (Atkinson 1979, 88), and a minor concentration of finds on Wilsford Down. Grooved Ware occurred at both Wilsford G51, where sherds were found in the ditch (unpublished, but one vessel illustrated in Annable and Simpson 1964, no 10) and in the fill of the large grave at the neighbouring site, Wilsford G52 (RCHME 1979, 6).

Relationships

The Grooved Ware from the area, both that recovered by the project and that found at other times, is dominated by vessels of the Durrington Walls substyle. The assemblage from Coneybury Henge, both that from the ditch and from the pits in the interior, falls within that substyle, as do vessels from Amesbury G133 (Gingell 1988, fig 16:3), from the tree-throw hole in Amesbury G30, from Wilsford G51 (Annable and Simpson 1964, no 10), and from Amesbury G39 (Ashbee 1981). The material from Amesbury G39 also includes at least two vessels with collars (Ashbee 1981, fig 7: 2, 8; the latter is drawn in section as if it has a worn surface, but this is not the case). This is a rare attribute, occurring most notably in the assemblage from Woodhenge, and one which Longworth did not include in his list of diagnostic features because of its rarity and the fact that it occurs on vessels of both the Durrington Walls and Clacton substyles (Wainwright and Longworth 1971, 240).

The two other southern British substyles of Grooved Ware are represented within the study area. In the Chalk Plaque Pit (Harding 1988) only one vessel out of a possible six is of the Durrington Walls substyle, the remainder being of the Clacton substyle, and a Clacton style element also appears to be present at Amesbury G39 (Ashbee 1981, fig 7: 3, 4). These two sites are adjacent to one another and it seems likely that both formed part of one area of occupation. The Clacton substyle is also represented in the Wilsford Down area, as much of the Grooved Ware from Wilsford barrow 52 may be of this style, although it is difficult to reconstruct vessel form (information from Dr I F Smith).

The type site for the Woodlands substyle lies within the study area at Woodlands, Amesbury (Stone and Young 1948; Stone 1949), and at least one vessel from Durrington Walls is noted as having Woodlands style attributes (Wainwright and Longworth 1971, P384, 287). Apart from this there are only one certain, and one possible, occurrence of the style within the study area: at Wilsford barrow 51 a single rim sherd belongs to an unusually thick-walled Woodlands style vessel (information from Dr I F Smith), and at King Barrow Ridge (W59) two sherds of thin-walled vessels with cordons (P261, P262) seem likely to belong to this style.

Outside the study area there is very little Grooved Ware recorded from the region: the catalogue compiled by Wainwright and Longworth (1971, 268–306) notes sherds only from Snail Down, Everleigh, 13km to the north-east, and one sherd is now known from the barrow cemetery at Shrewton (Green and Rollo-Smith 1984, fig 27: P35).

6.4 Beakers

Although the majority of the material excavated and collected by the project is fragmentary and difficult to classify, it is possible to identify sherds of specific Clarke (1970) groups and Lanting and van der Waals (1972) Steps. However, there is much more material which it is possible to assign to broadly defined Styles (Case 1977), and it is that classification which is preferred here. In order to highlight any differences in distribution and use of the area at least between the Early Style and the Middle and Late Styles, these are considered separately. It should be stressed that although Case's Early, Middle, and Late Styles are chronologically successive, they are not necessarily the same as the Early, Middle, and Late Phases described by him. As Case notes (1977, 72) there is some evidence for the manufacture of Early and Middle Style vessels into the phases succeeding the ones of which they are characteristic: for instance, Early Style vessels may still occasionally have been made even in the Late Phase, if the evidence of the ditch silts at Mount Pleasant is correct (Longworth 1979, 90).

6.4 a Early Style Beakers

Locations

W31 Wilsford Down; W52 North Kite. Surface collection: The Diamond (59)

Fabric

Only three fabrics are represented among the Early Style Beakers from the area, and all belong to the feGS: fabric group (ie feGS:Bkr/1,4, and 8); all are moderately fine and compact, and contain a moderate amount of finely crushed grog.

Distribution and context

Only five sherds can be attributed to this Style, and all were found in the Wilsford Down area. Only the four sherds from W52 were in a stratified context, beneath the bank of the enclosure, in layers which also contained Peterborough Ware and Late Style Beaker sherds.

Very little Early Style Beaker has been found within the study area at other times. One sherd of AOC Beaker was recovered from Wilsford barrow 54 (information from Dr I F Smith), and Lanting and van der Waals comment on the occurrence of a true Maritime Beaker, of their Step 1, at this site (1972, 36; Clarke 1970, fig 60). Finds of AOC Beaker also occur at Wilsford 36(f), 37, 38, and 39 (Grimes 1964), and five small sherds, possibly representing three vessels, were recovered during the excavations of the North Kite by Ernest Greenfield (information from Dr I F Smith). This concentration of finds on Wilsford Down is all the more remarkable in view of the dearth of Early Style Beaker from the rest of the area, and the occurrence of a concentration of Peterborough Ware finds in the same area seems unlikely to be purely coincidental, although the dating of the Peterborough Ware is more uncertain than that of the Beakers. Although there is no direct dating evidence for the Early Style Beakers either within or immediately outside the study area, AOC Beakers generally are likely to appear no earlier than the second quarter of the third millennium BC.

Early Style Beakers have been found at Durrington Walls, Stonehenge, and Woodhenge, but the total number of sherds is small. Only two sherds (Wainwright and Longworth 1971, P568 and P569) of AOC Beaker were found at Durrington Walls, both from the surface of the Platform, and therefore not in a datable context. Two sherds were also recovered from Woodhenge, although neither is illustrated in the report (Cunnington 1929; listed in Clarke 1970, corpus no 1107). At least one sherd of AOC Beaker was also recovered from the excavations of Stonehenge by Professor Atkinson (material in the Salisbury and South Wiltshire Museum).

Relationships

Outside the study area Early Style Beakers are not particularly well-represented: a scatter of such finds occurs across Wessex, but the only major concentration is around the monuments of the Avebury area in north Wiltshire, although compared with the dearth of Early Style material from southern Britain as a whole, even the scatter in south Wiltshire appears significant (Clarke 1970, 529, 557, map 1), and the concentration within the study area itself is almost equal in quantity to that around Avebury. In the immediate region one reconstructable AOC Beaker was found at Bulford, 7km to the east, and another, possibly from a destroyed grave, was recovered during the excavation of a Saxon cemetery at Winterbourne Gunner, 9km to the east, in the Bourne Valley (Salisbury Museum index 1963). Two sherds and one fragment of AOC Beaker were also recovered, apparently in a settlement context, from Downton, Wiltshire (Rahtz 1962, 137, fig 13: 15, 16), although there does not appear to have been any separation between the findspots of these sherds and the Beaker sherds of other Styles at the site. AOC Beaker sherds are also recorded by Clarke from Winterbourne Stoke 12, and from Codford St Mary, 14km to the west (Clarke 1970, 529).

6.4 b Middle and Late Style Beakers

Locations

Featured sherds: Because of the fragmentary nature of both the excavated pottery and that from surface collection, it is impossible to assign the majority of it to either the Middle or Late Styles. However, a small number of sherds, all of which are illustrated, can be classified, and the presence of sherds of the two Styles within the study area can be summarised by site (Table 132)

Featureless sherds: West Field (68)

Table 132 Presence of Beaker Styles by site and surface collection area

(Where sites or surface collection areas have no sherds attributable to Style, presence is shown by decorative technique.)

Coneybury Hill					
W2 Coneybury Henge	–	Middle	Late	–	FN
W2(1981) Coneybury 'Anomaly'	–	–	–	Indet	–
Fargo Wood area					
W32 Fargo Wood I	–	–	–	Indet	Imp
W34 Fargo Wood II	–	Middle	–	–	Imp
Cursus West End (62)	–	–	–	Indet	–
W55 Lesser Cursus	–	Middle	Late	–	FN; Imp
North of the Cursus (52)	–	–	–	Indet	–
Horse hospital (64)	–	–	–	Indet	–
Fargo Road (63)	–	Middle	–	–	–
Wood End (90)	–	–	–	Indet	–
Durrington Down (65)	–	Middle	–	–	–
Wilsford Down area					
W52 Wilsford Down North Kite	Early	–	Late	–	–
W31 Wilsford Down	Early	–	–	Indet	Inc; Imp
The Diamond (59)	Early	–	Late	–	–
Stonehenge Triangle (54)	–	–	–	–	–
W58 Amesbury 42	–	–	–	Indet	Imp

FN Fingernail impression
Indet Indeterminate
Imp Impressions
Inc Incision

Fabric

Among the sherds certainly identifiable as Middle or Late Style Beaker there is little differentiation of fabric; it is not possible to identify fabric types which are exclusive to either Style. The inclusion types utilised are limited. Tempering materials include grog, which occurs in all but a few fabrics, possibly sand, and possibly flint (always a sparse inclusion); sand is almost certainly a natural inclusion in some fabrics, and may be natural in all. In addition, clays containing visible grains of iron oxides appear to have been favoured. Micaceous clays also occur in a minority of fabrics. These fabric groups do not appear to be exclusive to particular parts of the study area, as most occur in all the areas where Beaker sherds are found, although not necessarily on every site. Beaker sherds in micaceous fabrics, for instance, occur in the Wilsford Down area (at W31 and W52), and around the Fargo Wood/Cursus area (W32, W34, W55, Wood End (90), Horse Hospital (64), and Cursus West End (62)), while ferruginous fabrics occur in every area. Only the fabric with possible bluestone inclusions has a limited distribution, as it is found only at W31 Wilsford Down, in sherds of indeterminate Beaker (P105–P106).

There does not appear to be a positive relationship between specific fabrics or inclusion types and the two Styles, nor between them and Early Style Beakers in the same area. Two of the Early Style Beaker fabrics (feGS:Bkr/4 and 8) certainly also occur in the Middle and Late Styles: in indeterminate comb-decorated Beaker at W52 (P216, P220) and in certainly Late Style Beaker at The Diamond (59) (P323, P327). If only the certainly classifiable sherds are considered, ferruginous fabrics occur in both Styles (at W34 and Fargo Road in Middle Style Beakers, and at W52, W55, and The Diamond (59) in Late Style Beakers). Grog and sand also occur in most cases, in both Styles. This might be taken as an indication that certain clay sources (ie the ferruginous ones) remained in use throughout the Beaker period.

Distribution and context

The major concentration of Middle and Late Style sherds, and indeed of most of the Beaker pottery, within the study area is around Fargo Wood and between there and the Packway. A small but relatively well-preserved group of sherds also occurs at W2 Coneybury Henge, and another on Wilsford Down (W31 and W52). Other than the material recovered from these areas all the Beaker pottery recovered by the project is small and undiagnostic.

There is no stratigraphical separation between the Middle and Late Style Beakers at any of the sites, but in most cases this is due to the contexts in which the material is found, that is in general layers of ploughsoil and topsoil. Only at Coneybury Henge and the North Kite are the sherds in stratified contexts with no other later material present; at the former, sherds of both Middle and Late Styles occur together. There, the sherds are contained in the secondary fills of the enclosure ditch, in the upper part of which Early and Middle Bronze Age sherds were found. The Late Style sherds (P77–P79), which may represent only one vessel, were found at the top of the secondary silts (context 1444) in a thin layer of silty clay loam representing a period of stabilisation in the fill. Middle Style Beakers also occurred in the secondary silts, and two sherds of unclassifiable Beaker (one illustrated as P82) were recovered from the top of the primary silts.

At the North Kite the latest material preserved under the bank is Late Style Beaker, in fairly fresh condition, and therefore probably only just pre-dating the construction of the bank. Two sherds (P214, P221), possibly of the same vessel, are certainly of this style: they are identifiable as being of Clarke's Southern tradition, probably of the S2 group, and possibly belonging to a vessel such as Clarke 1970, fig 898, from Winterbourne Monkton, Wiltshire, which has both a filled bar chevron above the base and filled triangles. The North Kite buried soil also contained sherds of Early Style Beaker (P220, P223, P224), although these appear to be in a more abraded state than the certainly Late Style sherds; the sorted horizon below the buried soil contains no Late Style Beaker, and does contain AOC sherds (P225, P226).

It is impossible to be certain that the Middle and Late Styles represent successive phases of use at any of the sites at which they occur, nor is it certain that even the Early Style Beaker represents a separate phase. The fact that sherds of Early Style Beaker are restricted to the Wilsford Down area, in contrast to the more widespread occurrence of the other two Styles, the slightly more worn appearance of the Early Style sherds in the buried soil at the North Kite in contrast to the freshness of the Late Style sherds, and the occurrence of the only Early Style Beaker in the sorted horizon at the same site, might be taken as indications that there is some difference in date between the Early and Middle/Late Beaker. It is much less tempting to postulate a difference in date between the Middle and Late Style Beaker on the evidence available within the project.

Relationships

Within the study area a fairly large number of reconstructable or partially reconstructable Beakers have been recovered from funerary contexts during the many barrow excavations which have taken place during the past two to three hundred years. Because these vessels are less fragmentary than those represented by the project material it is possible to classify them according to the more refined typology of Lanting and Van der Waals (Lanting and van der Waals 1972) and to Clarke (1970) groups, rather than to simple Early, Middle, and Late Styles (Case 1977). The pattern which emerges, however, does not contradict that suggested on the basis of finds from the project.

The majority of reconstructable vessels from the area fall into Steps 3 and Steps 5–6 in the Lanting and van der Waals scheme, and into Clarke's W/MR group and Southern tradition. Almost all the Southern tradition Beakers belong to his Developed Southern Group, and to the Western style within that group (ie S2(W)). The only vessel within the area illustrated by Clarke which possibly belongs to Lanting and van der Waals' Step 7 is fig 1036, from Wilsford 62, but this is an odd vessel which, with its marked internal rim bevel, could be classed as a Beaker/Food Vessel hybrid. One other vessel is noted as possibly from Winterbourne Stoke (Clarke 1970, fig 1002), but its exact provenance is unknown. A small number of vessels, all from the Wilsford area (including Clarke 1970, figs 60 and 67), belong to Clarke's AOC and European Beaker groups and to Lanting and van der Waals' Steps 1 or 2. The presence of Beakers which are early in the Beaker sequence, and the near absence of very late Beakers, is notable, and contrasts with the Shrewton barrow group just to the north-west of the study area, where none of the Beakers is earlier than Step 4/5, and there are two Step 7 vessels (Green and Rollo-Smith 1984; P36 from Shrewton is illustrated by Lanting and van der Waals as a Step 4 Beaker, using the Clarke illustration, but the vessel as illustrated in the final report differs so markedly from the stylised Clarke drawing that it must be placed in the succeeding Step, ie Step 5). However, Step 7 is poorly represented almost everywhere in central southern Britain except the Oxford area (Lanting and van der Waals 1972, 42), so that its poor representation in the vicinity of Stonehenge may not be remarkable.

The apparent gap in the record between the Step 3 and the Step 5/6 Beakers in the Stonehenge environs may well not represent a real hiatus in the use of the area, as Step 4 is barely represented anywhere in the Wessex region, or in the south generally. Although Lanting and van der Waals' scheme is presented as a series of chronologically successive steps, they do allow that Beaker development differed in different parts of the country, and that all stages are not equally important everywhere; in their rough outline of the chronology in radiocarbon years they envisage the likelihood that Step 5 will immediately succeed Step 3 in some areas (ie Step 3 – *c* 1900–1800 bc, Step 5 – 1800–1650 bc: Lanting and van der Waals 1972, 44). In calendar years the period encompassing both Step 3 and Step 5–6 use is likely to be within the range 2400–1700 BC.

Overall, it is apparent that the Beaker presence in the Stonehenge area does differ somewhat from that existing elsewhere in the region at the same period. Although there are few AOC Beakers within the area, the concentration on Wilsford Down is obviously important, if viewed in the light of the general scarcity of such material from southern Wiltshire, and in view of the fact that Beakers within the area may have been mainly entering henge monuments at this date. It is tempting to link this concentration of finds with the presence of Grooved Ware on Wilsford Down, and of a concentration of Peterborough Ware in the same area. The plethora of Middle Style Beaker finds, especially of Step 3, and of 'early' Late Style Beakers of Steps 5 and 6, is consistent with Wessex generally, but the number of Beakers found outside a funerary context seems small. With the exception of the area outside Robin Hood's Ball, at the northern extremity of the study area, there are, for instance, no sites of the nature and scale of Downton, 21km south-east of the area (Rahtz 1962), or Easton Down (Stone 1933), 13km east. This lack of sites which might on the grounds of the amount and type of pottery be likely to represent settlements, although to some degree a feature of the Beaker period in this region, seems particularly marked within the immediate area of Stonehenge, and becomes more apparent within the Early Bronze Age.

6.5 Early Bronze Age: Collared Urns, Food Vessels, Biconical Urns

Locations

Featured sherds: W2 Coneybury Henge (Collared Urn, Food Vessel, Biconical Urn); W31 Wilsford Down (Collared Urn); W58 Amesbury 42 long barrow (indeterminate). Surface collection: Durrington Down (65) (Food Vessel, indeterminate); Fargo Road (63) (Collared Urn); The Diamond (59) (Collared Urn)

Featureless sherds: King Barrow Ridge (57); North of the Cursus (52); Winterbourne Stoke Crossroads (57)

Fabric

As few as eight vessels of Early Bronze Age date may be represented among the featured sherds excavated and collected by the project. Among these sherds five fabrics are identifiable, four of which contain grog. The four grog-tempered fabrics are typical of the Early Bronze Age, and the only exception, fabric fe:Bkr/1, which is a sandy fabric similar to those typical of coarser

Beakers, occurs in a rim sherd (P288) of unequivocally Early Bronze Age type.

Distribution and context

With the exception of the sherds from W2 Coneybury Henge, all the finds could be derived from disturbed burials. The Fargo Road, Durrington Down, and Wilsford Down finds are all from the vicinity of barrows which have been ploughed. The only hint that non-funerary material may be present among this material is the presence of 16 other, featureless, sherds in fabrics typical of the Early Bronze Age, at W31 Wilsford Down (Fig 120). At Coneybury Henge, however, sherds belonging to several vessels of Early Bronze Age type appear to have entered the ditch in antiquity, and long before ploughing of the nearby barrows is likely to have redistributed any pottery from them. The sherd of Collared Urn from Coneybury (P86), which is unlikely to belong to an early vessel (Burgess 1986) or to Longworth's Primary Series (Longworth 1984) was found in the uppermost levels of the ditch terminal, but sherds of Food Vessel (P85) and possible Biconical Urn (P84) occur much lower in the fill in the main section through the ditch (cut 934), and appear to have entered the ditch as early in the sequence as most of the Beaker pottery.

Relationships

In an area in which the ceramics of the Early Bronze Age are overwhelmingly funerary, and in which non-ceramic finds are so important to the understanding of the period, it is meaningless to attempt to draw any firm conclusions from the few sherds recovered during the project. Although poor survival of sherds in surface scatters might partly account for the paucity of material of this period, it might be expected that the coverage of large areas both close to and away from barrow cemeteries, and the excavation of sites in several locations within the study area, would have produced more than the few sherds it has, if there had been widespread activity not associated with the barrows. Unfortunately, although the pattern is admittedly clear in this area, the lack of non-funerary pottery of the Early Bronze Age is a general phenomenon in Wessex; this problem has not been resolved for the region as a whole and so the area around Stonehenge cannot be seen as particularly exceptional in this respect.

Within the study area, and in terms of the published pottery alone, some patterning within the Early Bronze Age is apparent. Of four certainly early Collared Urns (using the classification of Burgess 1986), two are from Winterbourne Stoke 38 (Gingell 1988, 47–50), a barrow close to the Lesser Cursus, and one is from Winterbourne Stoke 28, 1km to the south-east, just to the south of the Cursus (Longworth 1984, pl 5b). It is likely that the Food Vessels from the area were deposited at a similar time (Burgess 1986, 350), and within the same part of the study area. In the mini-henge in Fargo Wood a food vessel is apparently associated with a Step 6 Beaker (Stone 1938), and other examples were found in Winterbourne Stoke 24, and in Barrow 13 of the Winterbourne Stoke Crossroads cemetery. Apart from the three Collared Urns of Burgess's early group from the western part of the study area, only one other published urn, probably found in Wilsford 80 (Longworth 1984, pl 52f), can be classified as early, although it lacks the strong internal moulding which the other three possess and which is considered by Burgess a particularly characteristic early trait (Burgess 1986, 345). Subsequent to this, Burgess's Middle Style of Collared Urns is represented only by two vessels, both from the Wilsford Down area: a vessel associated with Bush Barrow type grave goods from Wilsford 7 (in the Normanton Down group; Longworth 1984, pl 10a) and one from Wilsford 65 (in the Wilsford group; Longworth 1984, pl 19a). It is particularly interesting, in view of the occurrence of the Early Collared Urn with the marked internal moulding and externally convex collar from Winterbourne Stoke 28, to note that the Fengate Ware rim recovered from the mini-henge in Fargo Wood, approximately 300m from Winterbourne Stoke 28, is of an unusual form, possessing a markedly convex collar and an internal moulding (Stone 1938; the Fengate rim is not illustrated, and is in Salisbury and South Wiltshire Museum). The Fengate Ware rim is decorated on the interior and external surfaces with herringbone executed in twisted cord impression; the fabric is quite unlike Collared Urn fabrics, as it contains dense shell inclusions and is extremely friable. The stylistic similarities are so marked, however, that in view of the fact that Collared Urns are still thought to derive at least some features from Peterborough Ware, and the Fengate substyle in particular (Burgess 1986, 342), it is very tempting to suggest that the activity in the area south of the Cursus associated with the deposition or discard of the Fengate Ware was not far removed in time from the deposition of the Collared Urn in Winterbourne Stoke 28. The remainder of the Collared Urns from within the study area are classifiable as belonging to Burgess's Late group.

6.6 Early–Middle Bronze Age: Deverel-Rimbury

Locations

Featured sherds: W2 Coneybury Henge; W2 (1981) Coneybury 'Anomaly'; W32, W34 Fargo Wood I and II; W57 Durrington Down barrow. Surface collection: Durrington Down (65); Fargo Road (63); Horse Hospital (64); Normanton Gorse (61); North of the Cursus (52); Rox Hill (82); Stonehenge Triangle (54); The Diamond (59)

Featureless sherds: W55 Lesser Cursus. Surface collection: Ammo Dump (80); Cursus West End (62); Whittles (73); Winterbourne Stoke Crossroads (50)

Fabric

Most of the fabrics occurring in the Deverel-Rimbury pottery are typical of that tradition, and contain dense flint temper, mainly crushed to 4mm or less in diameter. Shell also occurs, but is not a common inclusion, occurring only at W57 (Durrington Down), Stonehenge Triangle (54), Rox Hill (82), Ammo Dump (80), and The Diamond (59) (Table 32, MF1 C1–14). Micaceous clays are not common, but are used in fabrics from W32 (Fargo Wood), W55 (Lesser Cursus), W57 (Durrington Down barrow), Rox Hill (82), North of the Cursus (52), Cursus West End (62), Fargo Road (63), and Durrington Down (65). Several fabrics appear to be confined to the area of the field system which straddles Fargo Road (ie FfeS:DR/2, FfeMV:DR/1, SSh:DR/1, FS:DR/1, FSV:DR/1), but others show a more widespread distribution. Fabric Ffe:DR/1, for instance, occurs in the area of the Fargo Road field system and at Winterbourne Stoke Crossroads (50) and The Diamond (59). This is unusual, however, as other fabrics which occur in the surface collection areas of Group 2 (ie between the Cursus and the Packway) and Group 3 (ie Stonehenge Down) tend not to occur elsewhere: this is true of fabrics FS:DR/5 and FGS:DR/2 (only at The Diamond (59)), FfeMsh:DR/1 (only at Rox Hill (82)), and FfeS:DR/3 and Fsh:DR/1 (only at Stonehenge Triangle (54)).

Distribution and context

Although pottery of this tradition is widely scattered across the study area, the amount of pottery is small, with only a few sherds occurring at most sites. The major concentration of material is in the Fargo Wood area, at sites W32 and W34, and in collection area 52, North of the Cursus. This coincides with the location of a field system, centred on Fargo Wood, but extending westwards to the Lesser Cursus (RCHME 1979 map 1), and southwards, to overlie the Stonehenge Cursus. Other findspots of Deverel-Rimbury pottery may also be related to field systems in the Fargo Road/Durrington Down area, in The Diamond collection area (59), and in the Stonehenge Triangle (54). However, with the exception of the excavated sites W32 and W34, where the considerable amount of pottery and other finds clearly suggest the presence of a settlement of Middle to Late Bronze Age date, the amount of pottery recovered from field collection is too small to warrant this interpretation. Even at Fargo Wood the presence of a large amount of pottery which seems more likely to belong to Late Bronze Age plain jar traditions complicates the picture; this is also the case at W53, where the large amount of pottery recovered, both of Deverel-Rimbury and plain jar styles, does suggest the existence of a settlement.

The small number of finds from Coneybury, both from the henge (W2) and from the very uppermost fill of the 'Anomaly' (W2 (1981)), do not appear to be related to a nearby settlement, as there is no trace of a field system on Coneybury Hill, and the number of even plain body sherds likely to be of this date from the field collection is small. Although it is possible that there are completely destroyed field systems in this area, this is considered to be extremely unlikely (RCHME 1979, xiii), and the number of barrows in the immediate vicinity, from which funerary vessels might have been derived, is small. Although it would seem improbable that the henge itself would still be a focus for activity at this time, when the ditches were almost completely filled in, there is some evidence that recutting of the top of the ditch terminal took place during the Bronze Age.

Relationships

Within the study area there is certainly one vessel of True Barrel Urn type and therefore probably of later Early Bronze Age, rather than Middle Bronze Age, date. This vessel was found with a cremation at Amesbury 3 (Annable and Simpson 1964, fig 576). One other vessel may also be of this type, although its upper body did not survive; it was found in a small hole close to the Durrington Egg and contained only a few scraps of unburnt bone (Stone *et al* 1954). The majority of Deverel-Rimbury pottery from the area is likely to belong to the Middle Bronze Age, although the material is so fragmentary that the possibility of there being unrecognisable vessels of South Lodge type within the sherd material cannot be entirely dismissed. However, there are also some grounds for suspecting that much of the Deverel-Rimbury pottery from the area was in use late in the Middle Bronze Age, as the same locations appear also to be in use during the currency of Late Bronze Age forms. The apparently transitional nature of the assemblage from W57 (Durrington Down) also strongly suggests that that site at least must date to the late Middle/early Late Bronze Age.

The area immediately around Stonehenge is notable for a general lack of Middle Bronze Age cemeteries around barrows, such as occur outside the area, at, for instance, Heale Hill, Middle Woodford (Musty and Stone 1956), and Shrewton 5a, and possibly 5k (Green and Rollo-Smith 1984, 258–65, 278). It is possible that this is in part because so much of the pottery from the Stonehenge area is from early excavations centred solely on the barrow mound. However, if any large cemeteries did exist in the area it would seem likely that over the past few decades, with the more complete excavation of several barrows, some indication of their existence would have emerged.

6.7 Late Bronze Age

Locations

Featured sherds: W2 Coneybury Henge; W32, W34 Fargo Wood I and II; W55 Lesser Cursus; W57 Durrington Down barrow. Surface collection: The Diamond (59), Cursus West End (62); Fargo Road (63)

Featureless sherds: W31 Wilsford Down; W56 Stonehenge Cursus; W58 Amesbury 42 long barrow. Surface collection: Ammo Dump (80), Durrington Down (65), Horse Hospital (64), North of the Cursus ((52), Railway (71), Rox Hill (82), Stonehenge Triangle (54), West Field (68), Woodhenge (60)

Fabric

Flint is the commonest inclusion type in pottery of this period, although shell and, rarely, grog and chalk also occur. The fabrics are generally less heavily tempered than those of the Deverel-Rimbury pottery. There is considerable sharing of fabrics between W32, W34 (Fargo Wood), and W55 (Lesser Cursus), and some also between W34 and W57 (Durrington Down), and between W34 and material from surface collection in the

Fargo Road area (63). The common use of fabrics at least between sites W32, W34, and W55 seems likely to be related to the location of all three sites within a single block of 'Celtic' fields, with which, presumably, the settlement represented was associated.

Distribution and context

With the exception of a single vessel in the uppermost ditch fill at the Coneybury Henge (W2) and three small sherds from The Diamond (59) (two illustrated: P332, P333), all the featured sherds identifiable as Late Bronze Age were found in the Fargo Wood area or between there and the Packway. The pattern of distribution of all sherds is so similar to that shown by the Deverel-Rimbury ceramics that it is difficult to envisage the two as entirely unconnected. If not actually contemporary it would seem reasonable to assume that the pottery represents continuing use of the same settlement areas over a period spanning the Middle Bronze Age (perhaps only the later part of that period) and the earlier part of the Late Bronze Age.

As with the Deverel-Rimbury pottery, it seems likely that the few stray finds elsewhere in the study area are also connected with the field systems known from survey and aerial photographs, with the exception of the find from Coneybury Henge, which cannot be explained in this way.

Relationships

All the Late Bronze Age pottery is extremely fragmentary and it is impossible to reconstruct vessel forms in most cases. There are certainly a small number of round-shouldered bowls or jars, such as P134 (from W32, Fargo Wood), P163, or P166 (W34, Fargo Wood), jars with finger-smeared surfaces (P176, W34), and with slashes and finger-tipping around the rim (P133, W32; P181, W34). However, the majority of vessels are represented by small rim sherds, and do not have reconstructable profiles.

Elsewhere in the area very little Late Bronze Age pottery has been recovered, although the factors which may have militated against Deverel-Rimbury ceramics being discovered (ie the methods and the emphasis of past research and antiquarian activity in the region) may also have operated in this case. However, Late Bronze Age material was found during the excavation of Winterbourne Stoke 32, 33, 38, and 46 (Gingell 1988); the material from barrows 32 and 38, which lie 700m to the west of Fargo Wood, could belong to the same period within the Late Bronze Age as the pottery recovered by recent fieldwork, although the pottery from the two other barrows is probably slightly later in date. At Winterbourne Stoke 32 two Late Bronze Age sherds were found in the upper fill of the ditch, one of which belongs to a slack-shouldered jar with finger impression around the shoulder, while at Winterbourne Stoke 38 several Late Bronze Age sherds were recovered from the upper ditch fill, including sherds of a vessel showing some Deverel-Rimbury traits on an apparently non-Deverel-Rimbury form, and a jar in a sandy fabric with impression around the shoulder (Gingell 1988, fig 23:3, and fig 28: 5, 6). Both Winterbourne Stoke 33 and 46, however, produced sherds of vessels which are likely to be of slightly later date, and belong to the phase of the Late Bronze Age typified by the All Cannings Cross assemblage (Cunnington 1923). At Winterbourne Stoke 33, which is only 20m from barrow 32, the sherds were of a haematite-coated bowl, and at barrow 46 of a necked bowl in a sandy micaceous fabric (Gingell 1988, 47, fig 34:6). Although the evidence is slight, it is possible that this represents a continuing use of the area into the latest phase of the Bronze Age, perhaps on a much reduced scale, before its apparent abandonment in the early first millennium BC.

6.8 The ceramic sequence: summary and discussion

by Rosamund Cleal

The pottery recovered by surface collection and during excavation by the Stonehenge Environs Project comprises 5709 sherds, weighing 16104.4g (581, weighing 2332.2g, from surface collection; 5128, weighing 13772.2g, from excavation). Much of this is diagnostic material which can be assigned to the ceramic styles described in the preceding sections. However, the material does not lend itself so readily, by virtue of the contexts in which it occurs, to the construction of a firm ceramic sequence. Much of the pottery was recovered from spreads of material within ploughsoil, there were few stratified groups, and only a small number of the radiocarbon dates have firm ceramic associations (Fig 6). In spite of this, and, to some extent, by drawing on information from outside the study area, it is possible to identify a broad ceramic sequence which can be related to other types of evidence for activity within the region, albeit lacking in fine detail.

Three phases may be distinguished within the Neolithic: an Early Neolithic, in which only Neolithic Bowl pottery was in use; a Middle phase, in which Peterborough Ware appeared, probably alongside the continued use of Neolithic Bowls, and during which the earliest Grooved Ware may have appeared; and a Late phase, during which Grooved Ware was the dominant ceramic, Peterborough Ware continued for a period of unknown duration, and the first Beakers entered the area. This scheme is based largely on the radiocarbon dates with ceramic associations used to construct Figure 6, and on the likely dating of Peterborough Ware and Early Style Beakers, for which there are no radiocarbon determinations within the study area. However, because the dating of these phases is so unrefined, and the dates for the clearly discernible Middle Neolithic phase lack firm ceramic associations, the ceramic evidence has been conflated for the purposes of Figure 154 into two major phases: later and earlier Neolithic, the former comprising sites with Neolithic Bowl, and the latter those with Grooved Ware and Peterborough Wares.

The earliest Neolithic Bowl assemblage within the area is clearly that from the Coneybury 'Anomaly', which, on the evidence of the radiocarbon dates, may pre-date the Neolithic activity represented by the dates from the Lesser Cursus and the Robin Hood's Ball pits by two to three centuries. Uniquely among the Neolithic Bowl pottery from the study area, it is an assemb-

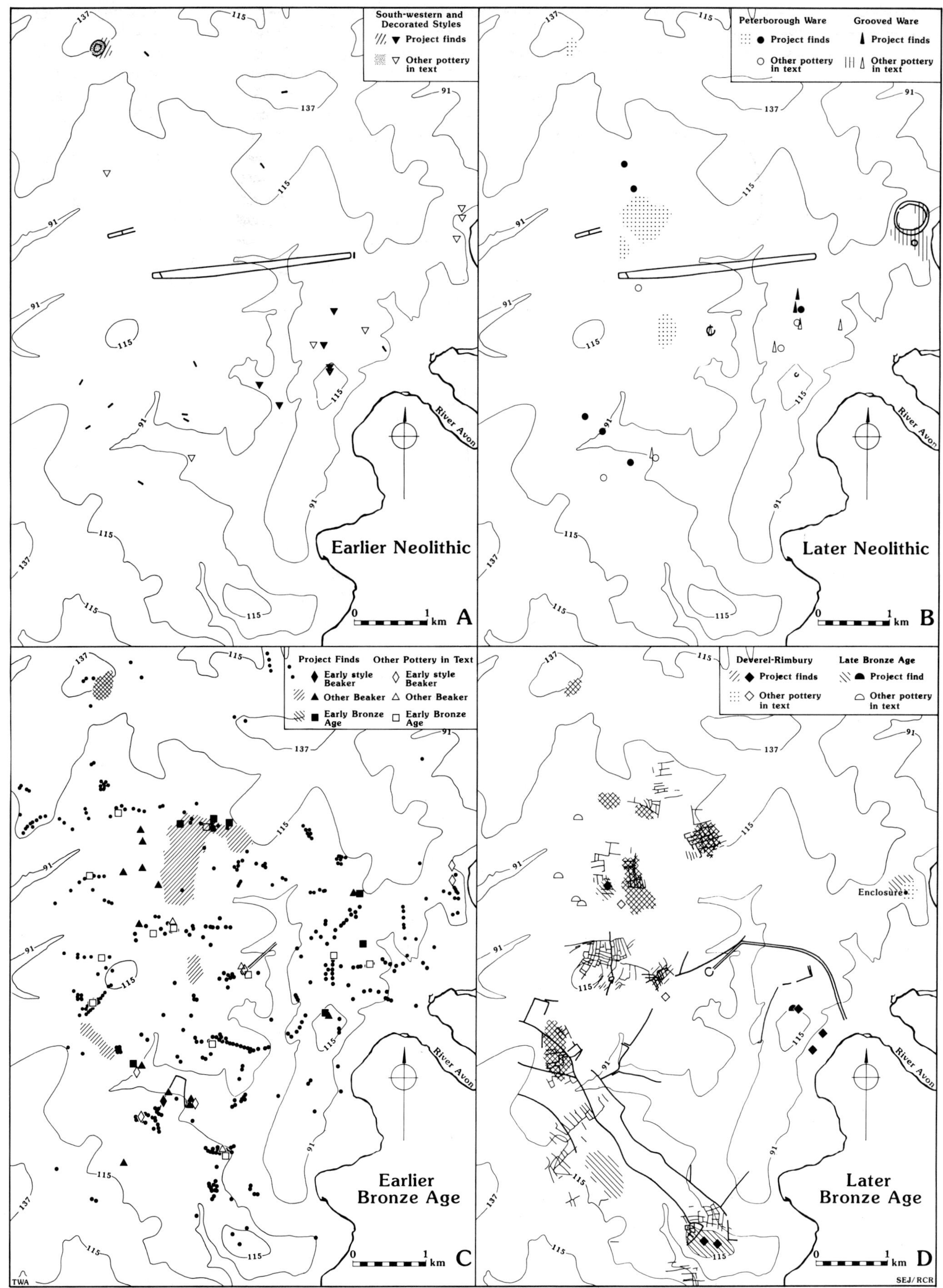

Fig 154 Prehistoric ceramic groups by period

lage with plain carinated forms; this difference may be owing to its early date, although the decorated vessels, both carinated and uncarinated, from Fussell's Lodge long barrow, Clarendon Park, 11km to the south-east (I F Smith 1966, 18–23) may be broadly contemporary (Ashbee 1966, 27). Carination is not a common feature on plain bowls in southern Wessex: it is rare at Maiden Castle (Cleal forthcoming a) and Hambledon Hill (information from Dr I F Smith), absent from Cranborne Chase (Cleal forthcoming b) and from the area between there and the south coast. Only at Rowden, Dorset, is there a small group dominated by plain carinated forms (Woodward forthcoming). The dates from Carn Brea for gabbroic ware, including plain carinated forms, cover almost half a millennium, from the early to mid-fourth millennium BC (Mercer 1981, 63), and so cannot be used to support an argument for carination necessarily being an early feature. The Coneybury 'Anomaly' assemblage, like that from Rowden, is unusual in that plain carinated open bowls occur in local fabrics in assemblages with no gabbroic ware. At Maiden Castle and Hambledon Hill carination is mainly a feature of gabbroic vessels; even those vessels in local fabrics could be explained as influenced by the gabbroic forms. The situation within the Stonehenge area must remain unclear while there are no dates for the causewayed enclosure at Robin Hood's Ball. The assemblage from the pits outside Robin Hood's Ball, which does include gabbroic ware, is certainly later than the Coneybury 'Anomaly' (Fig 156), but the relationship of this complex to the enclosure is unknown.

In the late fourth millennium or very early third millennium BC, vessels with heavy rims were in use at Durrington Walls, and at least one vessel of Abingdon Ware is represented among the material from the pits outside Robin Hood's Ball, which also date to the mid- to late fourth millennium BC. It is tempting to envisage the heavy rim forms from Woodhenge (Cunnington 1929) and Wilsford 51, 52, and 54 (I F Smith in prep), as belonging to the same broad period (the mid- to late fourth millennium BC), but this may be mistaken, as simple rim forms and occasional South-Western style features also occur at most of these sites.

Because of the uncertainty of the chronology, it is not clear how much of the Peterborough Ware was present in the area towards the end of the fourth millennium, but at least two of the areas in which Neolithic Bowl pottery occurs are also foci of activity in the Middle to Late Neolithic. On the King Barrow Ridge, use of the area is attested in the middle to late fourth millennium BC by two dates, and although the one date with ceramic associations is from a pit with only problematic pottery, the large amount of Peterborough Ware from the vicinity is likely to belong to the succeeding few centuries, if it is not actually contemporary. Other locations at which Peterborough Ware vessels may represent a use of the area either contemporary with, or, more likely, slightly later than, the Neolithic Bowls, are around Wilsford Down and outside Robin Hood's Ball causewayed enclosure. The zone of high ground directly to the west of the Avon, however, which seems to show a late use by makers of Neolithic Bowls (ie by the dated occupation at Durrington Walls), is completely devoid of Peterborough Ware; the single sherd at Durrington Walls (Wainwright and Longworth 1971, 24; see also this vol, P337) appears to be a perforated, decorated lug set immediately below the rim, and therefore more likely to be Grooved Ware than Mortlake Ware. Conversely, around Fargo Wood, Peterborough Ware finds are common in an area where there are no certain finds of Neolithic Bowl pottery.

It is difficult to discern any marked differences in the distribution of the different substyles of Peterborough Ware, although this may be in part due to the fragmentary nature of the material, which in most cases renders identification of substyle extremely difficult. All three substyles of the tradition are represented within the area. Sherds of several Fengate Ware vessels were recovered by Greenfield from his excavations at Wilsford barrows 51–54 (I F Smith in prep), and Fengate Ware also occurs around Fargo Wood, where, in addition to the material collected by the project, it was also found at the Fargo Wood mini-henge, in the upper ditch fill (Stone 1938). Only on King Barrow Ridge is Fengate Ware absent.

The first appearance of Grooved Ware in the area may be represented by the pottery from King Barrow Ridge (W59), but this, as noted elsewhere in this volume, is extremely problematic. The thin-walled sherds with cordons from pit 418 do not seem readily assignable to any ceramic style other than Woodlands style Grooved Ware, although the rather prominent cordons are not absolutely typical. One very small sherd from this context was considered to be in a Peterborough Ware fabric, but this association must remain doubtful. The flat piece, P263, is more readily paralleled by odd pieces from South-Western style assemblages such as Carn Brea, Cornwall (I F Smith 1981, P137) and Helman Tor, Cornwall (Dr I F Smith pers comm). In view of the fact that Woodlands style traits are not well represented in the large assemblages in the area, and that the Woodlands style groups in the area are not dated, it is possible that the separation between the two substyles is largely a temporal one, with the currency of the Woodlands style Grooved Ware preceding the large assemblages at Durrington Walls and Woodhenge perhaps by several centuries. This could be resolved by the dating of material from the pits at the Woodlands type-site (Stone and Young 1948; Stone 1949) and at Ratfyn (Stone 1935), Amesbury.

From the evidence of the radiocarbon dates it would seem that the Grooved Ware in the Coneybury Henge pits, and possibly also that from the ditch silts, may pre-date that from the main phase of use at the henge monument at Durrington Walls, so that the wealth of material at the latter must not be regarded as necessarily contemporary with the much smaller quantity of material from the Coneybury and Stonehenge henge monuments. The activity at Coneybury and at the first phase of Stonehenge, both associated with small quantities of Grooved Ware, can be suggested as taking place in an area in which Grooved Ware was not yet the dominant ceramic. The dating of the smaller assemblages in the area, however, is unknown.

The appearance of Beakers is likely to be marked by those of AOC type, and by the true Maritime Beaker from Wilsford barrow 54, but no direct dating evidence is available for this introduction. However, it is notable that in each case the AOC Beaker sherds occur at sites where either Peterborough Ware, or, more commonly,

Grooved Ware, or both, are already represented (ie Wilsford Down: Peterborough Ware and Grooved Ware; Woodhenge: Grooved Ware; Durrington Walls: Grooved Ware; Stonehenge: Grooved Ware), and that in three cases these sites are henges. Of the major Peterborough Ware concentrations only one, that around Wilsford Down, occurs in the same area as Early Style Beakers. If, as seems likely from evidence in central southern England generally, Peterborough Ware is a long-lived tradition, the absence of Early Style Beaker from two of the Peterborough Ware concentrations (ie King Barrow Ridge and the Fargo Wood/Cursus area) might be taken as an indication that activity there was earlier than that at Wilsford Down. There is some evidence, from Cranborne Chase, that both Mortlake Ware and Fengate Ware were in existence by the early third millennium BC, when features within a complex of pits at Down Farm, Woodcutts, were filled with Grooved Ware and some Mortlake and Fengate Ware – although, as at King Barrow Ridge, the dating association is not direct (Cleal forthcoming b). As the dating, and even the sequence of development, of Peterborough Ware remains uncertain, the relationship between the different areas of Peterborough Ware and Grooved Ware within the study area must remain unresolved. The extraordinary concentration of material on Wilsford Down and the occurrence not only in that general area of AOC Beakers, but their presence on almost every site within that zone with Peterborough Ware (and Grooved Ware in one case), strongly suggests that little time elapsed between the use of the Peterborough Ware and Grooved Ware and the appearance of Beakers. The fact that elsewhere in the region, and probably at a similar date, the earliest Beakers were being used at henges, raises the intriguing question of the nature of the activity on Wilsford Down, a question not resolvable from the ceramics alone.

The nature of the activity represented by the Middle and Late Style Beaker and Early Bronze Age ceramics is to some extent more readily identifiable, although its chronology is uncertain. Beakers, Food Vessels, and Collared Urns occur within the area primarily in funerary contexts, particularly in the case of the latter two styles; in addition, miniature vessels of Early Bronze Age type occur only with burials. The relationship between the three major ceramic styles of the Early Bronze Age is not generally well defined, and nor is it clear within the study area. Although Late Style Beakers, at least from Step 6 onwards, must be contemporary with at least some Food Vessels and Collared Urns, the extreme paucity of Step 7 Beakers within the Stonehenge area, and the fact that the dates for both the Step 6 Beaker from Amesbury 51 and the Stonehenge Beaker phase burial calibrate to the late third millennium BC, suggests the existence of something of a hiatus in the early second millennium BC. If the majority of the Beaker sherds from the area are no later than Step 6, as seems to be the case, there is then little evidence from the immediate environs of Stonehenge for occupation during the remainder of the Early Bronze Age, during which time the ceramic evidence is confined almost entirely to the extremely rich and varied funerary record. This is not the situation immediately outside the area, as Step 7 Beakers occur with burials at Shrewton (Green and Rollo-Smith 1984); outside Robin Hood's Ball, at the very edge of the area, there appears to be some Early Bronze Age pottery occurring in a general spread of occupation debris, unassociated with burials; and around Durrington Walls and Woodhenge the Bronze Age activity represented by the Durrington 'Egg', a ring ditch, and an isolated pit which produced a South Lodge type Barrel Urn may also belong to the latter part of the Early Bronze Age (Stone *et al* 1952, 164–6).

The position of the pottery of the Middle and Late Bronze Age in the ceramic sequence is difficult to establish with certainty. Since the case was argued some years ago for the development of Deverel-Rimbury ceramics having occurred in the Early Bronze Age (principally by Barrett 1976, 1980, and Barrett and Bradley 1980) the situation has not become markedly clearer. Undoubtedly some Deverel-Rimbury pottery must be contemporary with at least the latter part of the Wessex Culture, on the evidence of the radiocarbon dates presented by Barrett and others, and Ellison has dated at least South Lodge type Barrel Urns to the Early Bronze Age, but a clear Middle Bronze Age phase can still be recognised (eg by Ellison 1981), characterised by the three traditional Deverel-Rimbury forms and Taunton phase (ie Stage IX) metalwork. It is to this stage that the sites such as Boscombe Down East (Stone 1936) and Thorny Down (Stone 1941), 11km to the south-east of the Stonehenge area, seem to belong, but there are no comparable sites within the study area itself, unless perhaps the settlement at Winterbourne Stoke Crossroads belongs to this phase. Very little pottery now remains from the excavation of this site, but at least one sherd (P336) appears to be of a Deverel-Rimbury fabric. Classic Deverel-Rimbury pottery does occur within the region, as in the Wilsford Shaft, where it is dated to the fifteenth century BC (Fig 6), and in isolated finds, such as a recent find of a large sherd of Globular Urn from a fox's earth in Fargo Wood, apparently unassociated with a barrow (Salisbury and South Wiltshire Museum, acc no 54/1977; NGR SU 11004304). Deverel-Rimbury pottery was recovered by the project in the vicinity of Stonehenge, but its distribution overlaps with that of recognisably non-Deverel-Rimbury forms, which appear to belong to Barrett's Post-Deverel-Rimbury complex (Barrett 1980). This is true in particular of the concentration of material to the east of Fargo Wood (W32 and W34) and of the Durrington Down barrow (W57) assemblage. The relationship between these two types is unclear, as the lack of stratigraphy would disguise any temporal distinction that might exist. The Deverel-Rimbury element itself is not identical to the pottery from classic Deverel-Rimbury sites in the same region (ie Thorny Down, Boscombe Down East), and it is possible that what is represented is a late stage of that tradition, contemporary with the emergence of post-Deverel-Rimbury forms. If this is the case, and taking into account the radiocarbon dates for the Wilsford Shaft, which date the classic Deverel-Rimbury pottery from that site firmly to the fifteenth century BC, such assemblages might be expected to occur in the last few centuries of the second millennium BC. Similar assemblages appear to occur at some of the enclosures on the Marlborough Downs (eg Burderop Down and Rockley Down, Gingell forthcoming).

Acknowledgements Rosamund Cleal would like to express her particular thanks to Dr Isobel Smith for providing details of the pottery from Wilsford Down barrows 51–54 and from the North Kite (material from the Greenfield excavations); to Dr Paul Robinson (Wiltshire Archaeological and Natural History Society Museum, Devizes) for access to the material from Amesbury 39; and to Christopher Gingell for discussing the Bronze Age pottery.

7 The exploitation of animals in the Stonehenge Environs in the Neolithic and Bronze Age

by Mark Maltby

The animal bone assemblages from all the excavated sites have been studied and written up as separate reports. These are presented either as individual reports by excavated site, or, in the case of very small assemblages, are integrated within the site description. All the metrical, ageing, and butchery information has been computer-recorded, and is available in the archive. The samples were generally too small to contribute to observations on size and mortality patterns.

In addition to the major groups from W2 (1981), W59, W2, and W34, a sample of animal bones from W83, Robin Hood's Ball settlement site, has been included here for purposes of comparison with the Early Neolithic assemblage from W2 (1981) Coneybury 'Anomaly'; the complete bone report from this and other sites in the Robin Hood's Ball area will be presented elsewhere (Richards in prep a).

On the basis of these five bone assemblages, considered large enough for more detailed analysis to be carried out, an attempt has been made to compare possible changes and variations in the exploitation of animals in the Stonehenge area during the fourth to second millennia BC.

7.1 Earlier Neolithic

Of the sites that produced evidence for earlier Neolithic activity, the tiny faunal sample from W32, Fargo Wood I, was probably contaminated by later material. This leaves the small sample from the earlier Neolithic settlement at W83, Robin Hood's Ball, and the substantial and very early sample from W2 (1981), the Coneybury 'Anomaly', described above.

These samples were quite different. That from W83 contained only 73 fragments, and only domestic species (cattle, sheep/goat, and pig) were identified. These bones were scattered in small numbers in several pits. The only articulated group consisted of two tarsals and metatarsals of a pig. The primary deposits of the Coneybury 'Anomaly', on the other hand, produced 1715 fragments, mainly of cattle and roe deer, with red deer, beaver, pig, and brown trout also represented in small numbers. No sheep/goat bones were found. The deposit contained a dense accumulation of bones from the butchery of over 20 animals, which were processed over a short period of time. If the meat processed from these bones was destined for immediate consumption, it follows that the remains represent evidence for the preparation for a substantial feast.

The contrast between these two assemblages can be highlighted in two ways. The first is by simply comparing the relative species abundance and the second by considering the type of activities involved in the formation of these faunal assemblages.

Sheep bones have been identified in Early Neolithic contexts in southern England. They have been recovered, for example, on several sites in the Avebury area, including Windmill Hill, in both the causewayed enclosure and in pre-enclosure deposits (Jope 1965), and in the long barrows at Horslip and South Street (R W Smith 1984). There is, however, no evidence from the Coneybury 'Anomaly' for the exploitation of sheep in the early fourth millennium BC. If, as is argued, the assemblage was derived from one butchery event, it could simply be that sheep were not culled on that occasion. However, given the large-scale procurement of wild animals as well as domestic cattle, including calves, and the evidence for the intensive processing of the carcases to extract all the valuable meat and marrow content, it seems surprising that if sheep were available they were not culled, perhaps implying the operation of some form of ritual taboo. Alternatively, sheep may not have been kept in this area. It could also be suggested that domestic pigs were not available in any numbers either, since only one animal appears to have been butchered during this event. If this was the case, the only domestic species kept in any numbers in the area around Coneybury at the time was cattle. The abundance of wild species would also suggest that the area may still have been heavily wooded.

In addition, if we follow the argument that sheep remains were unusually common on the Early Neolithic sites in the Avebury area where *in situ* cereal growing could be proven (R W Smith 1984, 109), the lack of sheep bones in the Coneybury 'Anomaly' could suggest the lack of cereal production in that area at the time.

In contrast, sheep bones were found, albeit in small numbers, in the earlier Neolithic pits at W83. Here, at a later date than the assemblage from the Coneybury 'Anomaly', reliance seemed to be principally on domestic stock. It cannot be conclusively demonstrated, however, whether the apparent change in the exploitation of animals in the region is a function of chronology or of varying economy.

The presence of a mixture of domestic and wild species in the Early Neolithic deposit at Coneybury may be indicative of a transitory period in animal exploitation, during which there was a shift away from the hunting of wild animals to a strategy that relied principally on the resources of domesticated stock.

The evidence from the Coneybury 'Anomaly' would clearly suggest some sort of communal activity took place there. This may have involved co-operative hunting and communal sharing or redistribution of meat, amongst other activities. It has been suggested that communal activities and exchanges commonly took place in the earlier Neolithic at causewayed camps such as Windmill Hill and Hambledon Hill (Legge 1981a). The evidence from Coneybury suggests that such activities were not necessarily restricted to such sites. Indeed, Coneybury has produced better evidence for the actual butchery of animals in some numbers than any of the causewayed enclosures investigated to date. Legge has argued that the types of bone represented in the cattle assemblage from Hambledon Hill, with their low numbers of skull and mandible fragments, are indicative of an emphasis upon meat consumption as opposed to carcase processing (1981a, 174). The results from Coneybury further demonstrate how different bones can be deposited in quite separate locations.

Legge (1981a, 179; 1981b) has also suggested that the high proportion of calf bones in some Neolithic and Bronze Age collections, and the general dominance of adult females, indicates that there was a dairy basis to cattle husbandry during these periods. Perhaps in support of this, we should note that calves were well represented in the Coneybury 'Anomaly' and were also recorded at W83. The three fused distal metacarpi in the Coneybury 'Anomaly' all fell within the range suggested to belong to cows at Windmill Hill (Legge 1981a, 176). However, the presence of older but still immature cattle could equally suggest that meat production was an important component in the exploitation of cattle. Both strategies would result in the slaughter of a relatively high proportion of immature males.

7.2 Later Neolithic

A total of 510 animal bone fragments were recorded from Neolithic features found in association with the King Barrow Ridge flint scatter (W59). The two radiocarbon dates available from this site place it in a transitional period between that discussed above, and those sites more strictly of later Neolithic date. One pit contained the remains of at least four pigs, with an emphasis on the disposal of bones of low meat value of two of the animals. This is perhaps indicative of the primary butchery of their carcases. The tiny samples from the other pits contained more cattle bones than pig, including some articulated vertebrae. Again, few immature cattle were represented. Sheep bones were poorly represented and their bones were found no more commonly than those of red deer.

The most extensive sample for this period, and for the subsequent earlier Bronze Age, was obtained from W2, Coneybury Henge. The sample was dominated by cattle and there is evidence from the ditch terminal of the disposal principally of upper limb bones, some of which appear to have been roasted. Pigs appear to have been the only other species eaten in any numbers. Sheep bones were found only in small numbers and not in any of the interior features nor in any of the primary fills of the ditch sections. The cattle sample was dominated by bones of adult animals. Dog, red, and roe deer were represented in small numbers. Deer were now at most only a supplement to the meat diet.

Any consideration of the assemblage from Coneybury Henge should be seen in comparison with the large sample from Durrington Walls (Harcourt 1971; Richards and Thomas 1984). Pig bones were by far the most abundant, followed by cattle. As at Coneybury, sheep were poorly represented. Richards and Thomas (1984, 206) suggest that there was a correlation between the abundance of pigs used as a feasting animal and ritual sites with Grooved Ware pottery. Although the Coneybury Henge is within the zone of ritual activity defined by Richards (1984b, 182), it contained only small amounts of Grooved Ware pottery and comparatively fewer pig bones were represented. Evidence, however, for the deposition of different types of cattle bones in different locations was encountered at both sites. Both cattle samples contained a large proportion of the major upper limb bones in some deposits and correspondingly low numbers of skull and mandible fragments. Although Thomas shows that loose teeth were well represented at Durrington Walls, his explanation that the low representation of skull fragments was due to taphonomic factors (Richards and Thomas 1984, 206) cannot be used to explain the low numbers of mandibles, which survive well even in poorly preserved assemblages. Nevertheless, intra-site variability in the composition of the cattle assemblage resulting from differential disposal strategies does appear to have taken place (Richards and Thomas 1984, 210–11). The emphasis, however, appears to have been on meat consumption on both these sites.

By analogy, butchery deposits like those recorded in the earlier Coneybury 'Anomaly' are likely to have been created in association with these later Neolithic assemblages. Communal feasting around Coneybury, therefore, seems to have taken place in both the Early and later Neolithic periods. In the latter period, cattle still appear to have been the most important species, but pigs had replaced roe deer in secondary importance.

The low representation of sheep in the Stonehenge area appears to have continued throughout the Neolithic. The suggestion that, owing to wide ecological changes, pigs became more important while sheep declined during the Late Neolithic period (Grigson 1982c; R W Smith 1984) cannot be substantiated by the recently examined sites. These consistently provide little evidence that sheep were kept in the area in any great numbers throughout the Neolithic period. Even the upper colluvial fills of the Coneybury 'Anomaly' support this view. These fills must have accumulated over a substantial proportion of the Neolithic period, yet only two sheep/goat fragments were identified. They were outnumbered by aurochs bones in these fills, whereas pig and cattle in particular were better represented.

The ratio of pig and cattle bones has varied on different Neolithic sites in the Stonehenge area. It has been argued (Grigson 1982c) that pigs become relatively more important in the later Neolithic. Certainly pig bones dominated at Durrington Walls and ranked behind cattle on all the earlier sites considered in this report apart from the King Barrow Ridge (W59). There, it is perhaps significant that the pit which contained the large number of pig bones was the one which produced the later radiocarbon date and was spatially distinct from the other pits. Pig bones were particularly poorly represented in the earliest Neolithic assemblage studied, that from the Coneybury 'Anomaly'. However, we must note these observations with caution. Several of the samples are clearly biased by the deposition of particular skeletal elements. The fact that several of the sites may have been associated with feasting activities may have had a significant bearing on species representation.

7.3 Bronze Age

Earlier Bronze Age material was encountered mainly in secondary fills of features at the sites discussed above. At Coneybury Henge, for example, context 1501 in the ditch terminal produced Beaker pottery in association with a similar type of cattle assemblage to that encountered in the lower layers. This suggests that the site continued to function as a focus for meat consumption at this date. The same layer also produced the first evidence for the presence of sheep in that ditch section.

The fact that there is no evidence that pigs became more important in the later phase of this site also suggests that a chronological explanation for their high levels at Durrington Walls may be over-simplistic. However, the evidence from a single deposit such as that at Coneybury Henge must be treated with great caution.

The appearance of sheep in the ditch deposits at Coneybury in many ways sets the tone for the developments in animal husbandry that must have taken place during the Bronze Age. In the later Bronze Age at W34, Fargo Wood II, a poorly preserved faunal sample derived from ploughsoil contexts produced 1019 fragments. Of the identified sample, restricted almost entirely to loose teeth, cattle and sheep/goat were represented in roughly equal numbers whereas pig was poorly represented. Although it is unwise to place too much weight on the interpretation of such a sample to extrapolate general regional trends for changes in animal exploitation, the increased importance of sheep and the corresponding decline in pigs must have been developments that took place in the Bronze Age as a more settled mixed farming system developed on the chalklands. A corresponding decline in woodland can also be suggested. A similar emphasis on the exploitation of cattle and sheep has been observed in Beaker and later Bronze Age assemblages from the Marlborough Downs (Maltby forthcoming).

Unfortunately, the other sites of Bronze Age date produced little in the way of animal bones, so it is not possible to study the rate at which these changes took place, or how variable they were between different parts of the region. The upper fills of the terminal ditch of W55, the Lesser Cursus, produced 109 fragments of Middle to Late Bronze Age date, but only 20 of these were identifiable, and the secondary deposits at W57, the Durrington Down round barrow, produced even fewer identified bones. The upper fills of W58, the Amesbury 42 long barrow, produced more sheep/goat than pig bones but both were comfortably outnumbered by cattle in another unreliably small sample. Conversely, W52, the North Kite linear earthwork, only contained cattle and pig bones amongst its identifiable assemblage, although these totalled only 11 fragments.

7.4 Conclusions

The animal bones from the sites investigated by the Stonehenge Environs Project have demonstrated the value of such a detailed regional approach. Although several of the faunal samples were too small for individual detailed analysis, in combination with the more substantial assemblages they have provided new insights into the exploitation of animals in the fourth to second millennia BC, particularly within the Neolithic period. This study has created a broader basis for further investigation of the complex variations in animal exploitation and carcase disposal strategies which appear to have been prevalent throughout the Neolithic period in Wessex.

The study has highlighted some of the priorities for future work on Neolithic and Bronze Age assemblages in Wessex. The detailed examination and comparison of material from a restricted area of the chalklands are the means by which we can achieve a much better understanding of the development of animal domestication and husbandry in such a landscape. Such studies have to take into account localised variations in exploitation practices. Only by finding out the extent of this variability and by examining its possible causes will we be able to have greater confidence in our assertions about long-term trends.

Bearing this in mind, it is important to concentrate our research on well-dated assemblages. Too often it has been the practice to consider all bones from a site as an entity, especially when sample sizes are small. This overlooks the possibility that some of the bones may have been deposited at a substantially later date than others. In the study of animal bones from the Stonehenge Environs Project, close attention was paid to contextual information. Through this approach it has been possible to demonstrate, for example, the rarity of sheep bones in the earlier deposits at Coneybury Henge and in some of the primary fills of features from other Neolithic sites.

The question of contextual variability in faunal assemblages is an important one. The most remarkable aspect of the material studied in this project is the number of instances where it could be demonstrated that particular types of animal bones were dumped in discrete locations. Most of these assemblages reflect the processing of carcases of a number of animals at one time, and on such occasions it is more likely that such material will be buried and survive. Waste from smaller processing and consumption events has less chance of survival since, as it represents less of a disposal problem, it is more likely to have been abandoned on the ground surface rather than being buried. The question of whether material from such a large-scale processing represents a typical pattern of exploitation of the animals involved needs to be considered carefully.

The results of the analyses have also indicated that certain sites may have been on occasion the focus for such processing events over a very long period of time. Within and around the site of Coneybury Henge we have evidence for such activity that stretches over a period of approximately 2000 years. Food exchanges and redistributions were probably important components in the maintenance and development of the social and economic interactions of the people involved. It would not be surprising that a particular location was repeatedly chosen for such interchanges.

Acknowledgements Thanks are due to Jennie Coy for the identification of the bird and fish bones.

8 Plant and molluscan remains

8.1 Carbonised plant remains

by Wendy Carruthers

Samples for the recovery of plant remains were taken from suitable deposits encountered during project excavations. Unfortunately, due partly to the nature of the shallow chalk soils in the region, very few carbonised remains were recovered. In many cases these were poorly preserved.

The samples were processed by flotation, with the flot recovered in a 250 micron meshed sieve. In addition, the residues were sieved through a 1mm sieve and later sorted for plant remains and artefacts. Where cohesive soils were encountered, the samples were broken down in a solution of hydrogen peroxide prior to processing. A summary of the carbonised plant remains recovered from six sites is given in Table 133.

Since only a small number of carbonised remains were recovered in total, it has not been possible to establish the nature of the local economy throughout the Neolithic and Bronze Age periods. It is also impossible to know how representative the assemblages are of the area as a whole, since few deposits proved to be suitable for sampling. However, some of the remains are worthy of further comment, if only because of the paucity of evidence for crop husbandry from the early prehistoric period in Britain.

Cereal remains

Samples from the primary deposits of the Early Neolithic pit, W2(81), the Coneybury 'Anomaly', produced some poorly preserved cereals whose vesicular nature indicated that they had been subjected to intense heat. The identifiable caryopses were all glume wheats (*Triticum dicoccum/spelta*). As there is only a single, dubious record of spelt wheat from British sites of this period, at Hembury (Helbaek 1953), the grains are most likely to be emmer wheat. The presence of emmer (*Triticum dicoccum* Schubl.) was confirmed by the recovery of a single emmer glume base.

A sample from earlier Bronze Age deposits in the ditch of the Coneybury Henge (W2) contained a deposit of naked and hulled barley in the ratio of 3:2. The presence of twisted grains amongst both varieties indicated that six-row barley was present (*Hordeum vulgare* var *nudum* and *H vulgare* L emend). As no chaff fragments or arable weed seeds were recovered with the grain, this appears to have been a fully processed crop or crops. However, the possibility of differential preservation resulting in the destruction of the chaff fragments cannot be ruled out. The deposition of this clean sample of grain within the henge ditch may be of ritual significance, similar to the placed artefacts found in the causewayed enclosure ditch at Etton (Pryor *et al* 1986), or it may represent the deposition of waste from a domestic accident.

Most of the naked barley previously recovered from archaeological deposits has occurred mixed with hulled barley and other cereals. However, the Middle Bronze Age site at Rowden, Dorset (Carruthers forthcoming), produced a pure deposit of processed naked barley. Mixed samples of straight and twisted grains were used in a comparison of the size of 300 caryopses from Rowden and 90 from Coneybury. The results showed that they were of very similar dimensions (Table 134, MF2 G9).

At present, only a small amount of evidence is available for cereals grown in the early prehistoric period. Data amassed by Helbaek (1953) for southern England, primarily from seed impressions, suggested that emmer was the predominant cereal during the Neolithic. During the first half of the Bronze Age, naked barley had taken over in this capacity, but by the end of the Bronze Age hulled barley was the most frequently occurring cereal. More recent evidence (summarised by Moffett *et al* 1989) in the form of carbonised remains from a number of Neolithic sites supports the suggestion that these cereals were the principal crops in southern England and also demonstrates that a free-threshing bread-type wheat (*Triticum aestivum* s l) was grown on several sites. The recovery of large quantities of hazelnut shell fragments and fruit remains from these sites indicates that wild food sources continued to play a major role in the early prehistoric diet.

As no crop processing debris was recovered, it is not possible to be certain that the cereals recovered had been grown in the immediate vicinity of the sites examined around Stonehenge. However, molluscan evidence from this area consistently indicates that a primarily open landscape with some scrub growth existed from the Neolithic period onwards. Waterlogged and carbonised plant remains from the nearby site at Wilsford Shaft (Robinson, in Ashbee *et al* 1989) provided evidence for pasture and arable cultivation in the Middle Bronze Age, the cereals grown being emmer and six-row hulled barley.

Of the wheats, emmer is the most suitable for growing on the light calcareous soils of Salisbury Plain, although barley also grows well on such soils. In addition, at Coneybury the alluvial soils near the River Avon would have been available for cultivation, perhaps hinted at during the Neolithic by the pre-enclosure environmental sequence at Durrington Walls (Wainwright and Longworth 1971, 329–37).

Hazelnuts

Both earlier and later Neolithic contexts at W83 Robin Hood's Ball, W59 King Barrow Ridge, and W31 Wilsford Down, produced almost exclusively carbonised fragments of hazelnut shell (*Corylus avellena* L). These remains are common in Neolithic pit fills and indicate the use of scrub and hedgerow resources.

Molluscan analyses at Coneybury Henge (Bell and Jones, this vol, 4.9 f) indicate that the local habitat was probably shaded to some extent in the earlier Neolithic pre-henge environment, and soon after the construction of the henge. Dense shading can inhibit the flowering of hazel and so limit the production of nuts. Since fragments of hazelnut shell and charcoal were recovered from sites of Early Neolithic to Late Bronze Age date (Gale, this vol, 8.2), it seems likely that this species was growing in scrub, hedgerow, or woodland clearing habitats in the area for much of the period examined.

Table 133 Carbonised plant remains

Period	*Site*	*Type of context*	*Taxa*	*No*	*Total quantity sieved (litres)*
Earlier Neolithic	W2 (1981) Coneybury 'Anomaly'	pit	*Triticum dicoccum Schubl* (emmer glume base)	1	61
			Triticum dicoccum/spelta (emmer/spelt caryopses)	10	
			Indeterminate cereals	40	
	W31 Wilsford Down	pit	*Corylus avellana* L (hazelnut shell frag)	2	10
	W83 Robin Hood's Ball	pits	Indeterminate cereals	1	102
			Corylus avellana L (hazelnut shell frag)	26	
			tubers	2	
Middle Neolithic	W55 Lesser Cursus	ditch	tubers	5	hand picked
	W59 King Barrow Ridge	pits	*Triticum dicoccum/spelta* (emmer/spelt)	1	125
			Corylus avellana L (hazelnut shell frag)	160	
			Prunus spinosa L (sloe stone frag)	1	
			Bilderdykia convolvulus L Dumort (black bindweed)	1	
Later Neolithic	W2 (1981) Coneybury 'Anomaly'	pit upper fills	Indeterminate Gramineae (grass)	2	25
	W2 Coneybury Henge	ditch	*Hordeum vulgare* var *nudum* (naked six-row barley)	159	26
			H vulgare L emend (hulled six-row barley)	102	
			Hordeum sp (barley)	43	
			Arrhenatherum elatius var *bulbosum* (onion couch)	1	
			Stellaria media L (chickweed)	3	
			Urtica dioca L (stinging nettle)	1	
			Viola sp (violet)	1	
			cf *Crataegus monogyna* L (hawthorn)	1	
Earlier Bronze Age	W2 Beaker pit	pit	*Corylus avellana* L (hazelnut shell frag)	1	10
Later Bronze Age	W34 Fargo Wood II	post-holes	*Triticum dicoccum/spelta* (emmer/spelt)	1	6
			Indeterminate cereals	2	
			Corylus avellana L (hazelnut shell frag)	1	

Other possible food remains

A carbonised fragment of a sloe stone (*Prunus spinosa* L) was recovered from a later Neolithic pit at W59, King Barrow Ridge. *Prunus* sp charcoal was recovered from all of the sites sampled (Gale, this vol, 8.2), and it is likely that this refers to sloe rather than wild cherry in most cases, as blackthorn/sloe is a common shrub of hedgerows and open woodlands.

A possible fragment of hawthorn stone (cf *Crataegus monogyna*) was present in the Coneybury Henge ditch. Pomoideae sp (which includes hawthorn) was common in samples from most of the sites. Hawthorn would have occupied similar habitats to hazel and sloe.

Two carbonised tuberous stem-bases of onion couch (*Arrhenatherum elatius* var *bulbosum*) were recovered from a later Neolithic pit at W59, King Barrow Ridge, and another was found in a sample from the ditch of W2, Coneybury Henge. This grass is commonly associated with abandoned arable land. Such carbonised tubers are often recovered from Bronze Age cremation deposits and have also been recovered from the Neolithic long cairn at Hazleton (Straker 1985). It is uncertain to what extent these remains represent an interruption in the cultivation of cereals, or merely human disturbance.

A number of other carbonised tubers were recovered from two earlier Neolithic pits at W83, Robin Hood's Ball, and from the ditch of W55, the Lesser Cursus. These appeared to the author to be of a single species on the basis of their gross morphology, but anatomical examination (by Jon Hather at the Institute of Archaeology) was unable to confirm this due to the poor state of preservation of some of the tubers.

The best-preserved tuber examined by Hather was said to be similar to root tubers of bitter vetch (*Lathyrus montanus* Bernh.) or stem base tubers of pignut (*Conopodium majus* (Gouan) Loret). Both these kinds of tuber are edible, and documentation of their use both raw and cooked exists, dating from at least the Middle Ages. Mabey (1972) notes that bitter vetch tubers have been used as a subsistence crop in the Scottish Islands, and also for flavouring whisky. Both species are common in meadows and woodlands throughout most of the British Isles. It is not possible to determine whether the tubers were gathered for consumption, although pignut tubers at least are not easily recovered by pulling the plant up by its stem, but must be carefully dug out from some depth. According to Hather, the poor state of preservation of the tubers indicates that the tissues were charred when in a fresh state.

Weeds of arable and cultivated land

Very few weed seeds were recovered from the samples. The taxa represented were common weeds of cultivated or disturbed land, such as chickweed (*Stellaria media*) and black bindweed (*Bilderdykia convolvulus* L Dumort).

Summary

Evidence for the cultivation of emmer wheat in the Early Neolithic and naked and hulled barley in the later Neolithic was recovered from sites around Stonehenge. No chaff fragments and few weed seeds were found to indicate whether or not the cultivation occurred locally.

In addition, large numbers of carbonised fragments of hazelnut shell were present, indicating the continued use of scrub and woodland resources throughout the Neolithic period.

Tubers of onion couch grass and other tubers resembling those of bitter vetch or pignut were present in several Neolithic samples.

With the exception of the deposit of barley from Bronze Age contexts at Coneybury Henge (W2), the few Bronze Age remains recovered consisted of hazelnut shell fragments and cereal caryopses.

Acknowledgements I am grateful to Jon Hather for identifying the carbonised tubers and to Mark Robinson for providing details of unpublished work.

8.2 Charcoals

by Rowena Gale

Methodology

Charcoal from both manually excavated contexts and wet-sieved samples was identified by comparative anatomical methods. The condition of the samples was generally good, with little infiltration of extraneous matter or fungal hyphae. A few samples had undergone vitrification, making identification impossible. Some fragments were too small for positive identification; in some of these instances tentative identifications have been suggested.

Material was prepared by pressure fracturing in three directions to expose clean, flat surfaces in the transverse, tangential longitudinal, and radial longitudinal planes. These were mounted on microscope slides and examined using an epi-illuminating microscope at magnifications up to × 400. A list of the main taxa identified is given in Table 135 (MF2 G10), and Table 136 shows the genera present at the sites in chronological order. A more detailed breakdown of the species present by context is contained within the archive.

The species identified are all characteristic of calcareous soils and suggest that a mixed woody vegetation was present throughout the Neolithic and Bronze Age periods.

Oak, blackthorn/cherry, and hawthorn/rowan/whitebeam were present at most of the sites, together with hazel, yew, and field maple.

The elm decline was probably not so marked on the chalklands (Pennington 1974), although the single occurrence of elm in the earlier Neolithic at W83, Robin Hood's Ball, is interesting. The presence of ash at both earlier Neolithic (W83) and earlier Bronze Age (W57) sites is also of interest, since the two main periods of expansion of ash seem to be at these times, following the elm decline and during regeneration of the secondary forest following initial clearance.

The Neolithic period saw the development of woodland management in many areas (Godwin 1975, 267–8) although this phenomenon cannot be supported by the charcoal recovered by the Stonehenge Environs Pro-

Table 136 Charcoals: genera present by site

Period	*Site*	*Quercus*	*Prunus*	*Pomoideae*	*Corylus*	*Acer*	*Fraxinus*	*Taxus*	*Carpinus*	*Rhamnus Cathartica*	*Cornus*	*Ulmus* sp.
Earlier Neolithic	W2 (1981) Coneybury 'Anomaly'	*	*	*	*			*				
	W83 Robin Hood's Ball		*	*		*	*					*
	W55 Lesser Cursus		*									
	Total genera	*	*	*	*	*	*	*				*
Later Neolithic	W59 King Barrow Ridge	*	*	*	*	*			*	*		
	W2 Coneybury Henge	*	*	*	*						*	
	W2 (1981) Coneybury 'Anomaly'							*		*		
	Total genera	*	*	*	*	*		*	*	*	*	
Earlier Bronze Age	W2 Coneybury Henge	*	*	*	*							
	W52 North Kite	*	*									
	W57 Durrington Down round barrow	*	*		*							
	Total genera	*	*	*	*							
Later Bronze Age	W34 Fargo Wood II	*	*	*		*	*	*			*	

ject. Much is in a fragmentary state and in consequence the original dimensions of each piece and therefore the part of the tree or shrub from which it came are difficult to establish. Certainly, considerable quantities of stemwood are present, but the inclusion of shrubs such as buckthorn, which was unlikely to have been coppiced, suggests that some of the material was gathered from the wild.

Very little material relates to the Middle Neolithic and much of this was vitrified. Wood charred at temperatures higher than 800°C becomes vitrified, resulting in the loss of cell structure and morphology, and thus is unidentifiable (Prior and Alvin 1983).

Relatively few genera were present at the earlier Bronze Age sites; oak was used for the cremations at W57, Durrington Down round barrow; hazel, blackthorn and hawthorn/rowan/whitebeam were also identified. A much wider variety of species were identified from the later Bronze Age site at W34, Fargo Wood II.

8.3 Molluscan studies

by M J Allen, Roy Entwistle, and Julian Richards

This study integrates the available data from molluscan analyses, discussed below, together with those from the study of plant remains and charcoals. Its aim is an understanding of the evolution of and human impact upon the Stonehenge landscape throughout later prehistory.

8.3 a Site description

The study area, with one remarkable and localised exception (the Wilsford Shaft; Ashbee *et al* 1989), is exclusively one of dry chalkland. Consequently, the data for the study of environmental change have been derived principally from the analysis of terrestrial mollusca.

A number of individual studies were undertaken as part of the Stonehenge Environs Project, and have been presented within the appropriate site reports. These can be summarised as follows:

W2 (1981) Coneybury 'Anomaly' (Bell and Jones, this vol, report in 4.9 f): pit fill

W55 Lesser Cursus (Entwistle, this vol, 4.5 e): three ditch sequences

W56 Stonehenge Cursus: two ditch sequences

W58 Amesbury 42 long barrow (Entwistle, this vol, 4.7 e): ditch sequence and buried soil

W2 Coneybury Henge (Bell and Jones, this vol, 4.9 f): ditch sequence and subsoil hollow

W52 Wilsford Down North Kite (Allen, this vol, 4.12 e): buried soil

Additional data are available from previous studies and from work carried out subsequent to the completion of project fieldwork. The major contributions can be summarised as follows:

Durrington Walls (Evans 1971): buried soil beneath henge bank

Woodhenge (Evans and Jones 1979): buried soil beneath henge bank and ditch sequence

Stonehenge (Evans 1984): ditch sequence

Wilsford Shaft (Ashbee *et al* 1989): wide range of environmental data from fill of well

Durrington 3 (Allen *et al* forthcoming): ditch sequence from round barrow

These analyses represent a surprising lack of emphasis on environmental studies, particularly in an area where monuments are both densely concentrated and in certain cases much investigated. The lack of previous environmental analysis is due partly to the relative youthfulness of certain aspects of this area of study, but also reflects the material and structural approach of some previous archaeological investigators. In some cases within the Stonehenge Environs, round barrows appear to have been comprehensively sampled during excavation, but this has not been followed by appropriate, or indeed any, analysis. This appears to be the case, for example, with the majority of the 12 round barrows excavated by the Vatchers between 1959 and 1961 (Gingell 1988, 23).

Thus, although there is 'some sort of regional background available' (Evans 1984, 7), as Figure 155 demonstrates, this is still far from comprehensive. Further, all the suites of molluscan samples taken within the Stonehenge area are derived from identified monuments, assumed to be centres of human activity, and may, therefore, by their very nature, be biased towards felled and open country areas within the landscape. Any overall interpretation of the molluscan evidence may therefore over-estimate or over-emphasise the open nature of the area. This bias can be partially overcome by the use of other sources of environmental information, and by the examination of mollusca from buried soils. Unfortunately there is a paucity of such evidence, despite the potential which clearly exists in those old land surfaces buried beneath the many extant barrows within the study area. Attempts to provide suites of off-site and non-site-specific data was attempted via the dry valley research project (W17–W25, this vol, 4.15). This demonstrated the absence of the typical chalkland colluvial deposits described by Bell (1981, 1983) and Allen (1988, 1989), and consequently forces reliance upon the site-specific data.

The technique of molluscan analysis for palaeoenvironmental study is well tested and has been applied to archaeological sites for over 25 years (Evans 1972, 1984). Although individual molluscan interpretations will tend to be site-specific, the availability of a number of sequences enables the reconstruction of spatial and chronological patterning on a more regional scale. The resolution of such interpretation depends upon the nature and context, both spatial and temporal, of the data. Although, as described above, the Stonehenge area provides a basis, the spatial and temporal resolution of the interpretation falls far short of the potential for this landscape.

Analysis of specific sites provides some indication of the nature of their general setting and the statistical analyses applied by Entwistle were used to enhance the potential level of interpretation and reconstruction. These methods are reviewed below.

8.3 b Statistical appraisal

by Roy Entwistle

In order to separate fluctuations in the size and composition of the sub-fossil assemblages caused by varying rates of sedimentation from those reflecting environmental change, two diversity indices have been calculated. The results are given in Tables 42, 43, and 53 (MF1 D10, D11, E7). The indices used are those proposed by Hurlbert (1971) and applied to the analysis of sub-fossil molluscan assemblages by Gordon and Ellis (1985). The two measures used are D2, the probability of non-lethal interspecific encounters, and D4, the ratio of interspecific to intraspecific competition. It is argued that these are more applicable to biological populations than other indices and therefore are more sensitive indicators of environmental change (Gordon and Ellis 1985, 153–6).

However, although potentially useful in molluscan palaeoecology, ecological inference can be complicated and misleading (Thomas and Foin 1982). One of the main problems is that the range of species and individuals in a sub-fossil snail assemblage are assumed to represent a single living population. Unfortunately there is no way of knowing exactly what proportion of the sub-fossil assemblage were living at the same time, and therefore competing with each other in the same range of habitats. There is also an element of ambiguity in the results produced by the calculations. For example, in autochthonous assemblages low diversity indices could be interpreted in quite different ways: they could represent habitats of relatively low stability unfavourable to molluscan life, or habitats of high stability which favour a few competitively superior species (K D Thomas 1985, 144), but this may be a largely hypothetical consideration. In practice low-stability habitats would also produce assemblages with few individuals and probably higher numbers of juveniles, while high-stability habitats are more likely to be characterised by fewer species but larger numbers of individuals. Perhaps the most valuable contribution of diversity indices is in helping to separate autochthonous and allochthonous elements in an assemblage. This is particularly useful when dealing with accumulated ditch deposits, because it is essential to be able to separate faunal changes representing a response to transient conditions in the ditch from those reflecting a wider area and more long-term trends.

8.3 c Landscape development and modification

Although more a process of gradual development and alteration, the changing nature of the Stonehenge landscape will be reviewed within a similar broad chronological framework employed for comparative artefact studies. Chronological sections subsequent to the later post-glacial make reference to Fig 6.

The later post-glacial

It is assumed, on the basis of extensive evidence from the chalkland of southern England (Evans 1975), that the entire Stonehenge area was once heavily forested. There is, however, little direct evidence for primary post-glacial woodland, or for Mesolithic intervention in the form of woodland modification or small-scale clearance of the type recorded at Gatcombe withy beds (Scaife 1982, 1987). A subsoil hollow beneath the bank at Woodhenge provides clear evidence for ancient woodland, suggested, on the basis of a single artefact, to date to the Mesolithic period (Evans and Jones 1979). This evidence, together with abundant charcoal, appears to indicate some form of disturbance and activity. Close by, at Durrington Walls, both buried soil profiles again show clear evidence for ancient woodland (Evans 1971). Palynological analysis of one of the soil profiles (DWII) (Dimbleby 1971), indicates a hazel- (*Corylus*-) dominated woodland, including birch (*Betula*), pine (*Pinus*), oak (*Quercus*), lime (*Tilia*), and elm (*Ulmus*).

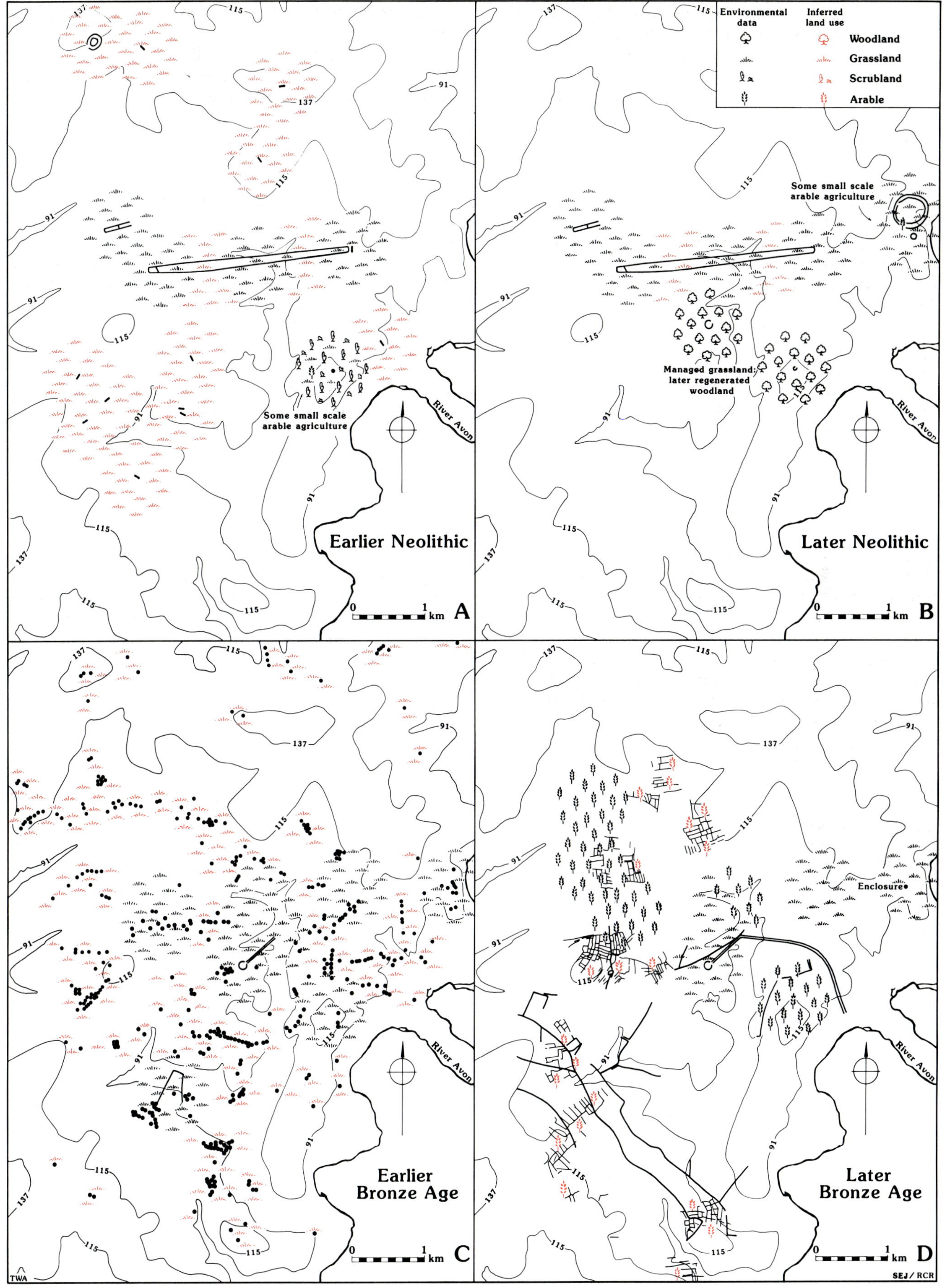

Fig 155 The changing prehistoric environment

Ferns (*Dryopteris*-type), bracken (*Pteridium*), and grasses (*Gramineae*) were also recorded. Although the pollen spectra was sparse, it is suggestive of the type of woodland resulting from regeneration of Mesolithic clearance (cf Smith 1970). The extent of such clearance has often been underestimated (Radley and Mellors 1964). In addition, the predominance within this woodland of hazel, typical of the Boreal *Corylus* maxima, can be attributed directly to human activity (cf Scaife 1982). This may therefore strengthen the evidence for Mesolithic activity on the margins of the Avon Valley, similar to the emphasis on river margin and valley locations noted in the Avebury area (R W Smith 1984).

Earlier Neolithic (Fig 155a)

By the beginning of the Neolithic, it can be assumed that the area was still extensively wooded, although, as discussed above, it appears likely that some limited and possibly ephemeral clearance had already been carried out. It can also be suggested that soils within the study area were appreciably thicker and possibly belonged to a different pedogenic regime (cf Allen 1988).

The human impact on the lowland zone throughout the Neolithic has been conceptualised in terms of progressive deforestation in response to agricultural exploitation of an increasingly intensive and extensive nature (Limbrey 1978). This basic concept requires radical re-examination.

As suggested above, localised clearance can certainly be detected, but may be undertaken for reasons other than intensification or extensification of tillage and farming practices (R W Smith 1984, 114). Although appropriate clearance is presumably required prior to the construction of monuments, neither crop production nor animal husbandry require large-scale open areas (Rowley-Conwy 1982). It is perhaps therefore more relevant to attempt to examine the specific nature and function of clearance than to record clearance activity *per se*. The environmental data for the earlier Neolithic is sparse, but adequate for interpretation at a local and sub-regional level.

The earliest dated environmental evidence is that available from W2 (1981), the Coneybury 'Anomaly', which, although difficult to interpret fully, appears to indicate localised clearance and the presence of grassland and scrub in the early fourth millennium BC (Bell and Jones, this vol, 4.9 f). The evidence here appears to suggest an example of early small-scale clearance, of the type discussed by Rowley-Conwy (1982), and carbonised cereal grains (Carruthers, this vol, 8.1) may indicate an arable component. The frequency and extent of such clearance elements within the Stonehenge Environs is as yet unquantified.

Additional evidence for the earlier Neolithic is provided by the environmental sequences recovered from specific monuments, the earliest datable example of which is W55, the Lesser Cursus (Entwistle, this vol, 4.5 e). This monument was constructed within a broadly open environment, although the paucity of shells in the primary fills of all the examined ditch sections does not allow the nature of the open environment to be more precisely determined. Nevertheless, the evidence from the lower secondary fills, likely to date only shortly after the construction and apparent partial backfilling of the ditches, shows that the surrounding environment was one of open, probably grazed, grassland. The extent of this grassland regime is suggested by data from W56, the Stonehenge Cursus, and from W58, Amesbury 42 long barrow (Entwistle, this vol, 4.7 e). The buried rendzina beneath the latter monument was distinctly lacking in shade-loving species, indicating that the barrow was constructed in a pre-existing and well-established grassland. Nevertheless, the lack of any woodland species, with the exception of fragments, indicates either long-term established and grazed grassland, or the existence of a non-calcareous soil (ie a brown earth) which supported a woodland flora but which was not conducive to the preservation of a molluscan fauna.

The limited range of sites discussed above provide positive data for the earlier Neolithic. In these sites the consistent appearance of grassland molluscs indicates that, within a landscape still extensively wooded, considerable areas of grassland had been established and were capable of providing colonising faunas. Beyond this positive data, communal monuments such as long barrows and the causewayed enclosure at Robin Hood's Ball are assumed to have been constructed in areas already cleared of woodland, if not cleared specifically for construction. This suggests that certain areas, for example Wilsford/Normanton Down, where long barrows are in close proximity, may have been more extensively cleared. The true extent of earlier Neolithic clearance can only be guessed at, however, and Figure 155a offers no more than informed speculation. This figure also reflects the inevitable bias caused by the assumption that monuments, at this period almost exclusively hilltop sited, represent the full extent of clearance. Valley bottoms, where evidence is totally lacking, may also have been as extensively cleared.

Later Neolithic (Fig 155b)

Although a more limited number of monuments were constructed during the later Neolithic, their construction, spanning the later fourth and third millennia BC, indicates a wider variety of pre-existing land use, albeit within a more restricted topographic zone, biased towards the eastern part of the study area.

The first phase of Stonehenge was constructed within an area of grassland, possibly hinting at the extent of the grassland zone suggested by the Cursus to the north and the long barrow 'cluster' to the south and south-west. In contrast, Coneybury Henge appears to have been constructed within a recent, and probably localised woodland clearing, suggesting some regeneration during the earlier fourth millennium BC. This may be a reflection of the ephemeral nature of such early clearance episodes hinted at above.

Despite the dissimilarity of the environment within which they were constructed, the contemporaneous environmental records from both Stonehenge and Coneybury show a distinct and unequivocal phase of woodland regeneration. This suggests the proximity of such habitats to both sites, and that Stonehenge was not constructed within a totally open landscape. It is tempting to view this regeneration as part of a regional phenomenon, especially in the light of previous models for site abandonment during the later Neolithic (P J Whittle 1978). This does not appear to be the case in the Stonehenge area, however, as the regeneration seems quite short-lived and is not paralleled in any other monument in the area. The data from Woodhenge suggest continuous open grazed grassland subsequent to construction, whilst, although some shadier elements can be seen at both the Lesser Cursus and at Amesbury 42 long barrow, these are very localised, and probably represent the colonisation of the ditches by natural vegetation (cf Evans 1972, 323–6), rather than a wider landscape phenomenon. Further, in these two instances, the dating of ditch colonisation is poor, but probably significantly later than the episodes of regeneration seen at both Coneybury and Stonehenge.

Close to the River Avon, and at a slightly later date in the Neolithic, both Durrington Walls and Woodhenge appear to have been constructed in grassland. At Durrington the establishment of grassland is preceded by a limited phase of agriculture, this evidence providing the single exception to the indications of grazed grass and shrubland which now appear to predominate in the exploited portions of the landscape.

Earlier Bronze Age (Fig 155c)

Positive data relating to the earlier Bronze Age are sparse, and, with the exception of the buried soil from the Wilsford Down North Kite, are derived from secondary ditch fills. Not surprisingly, the one buried soil and the ditch deposits from Stonehenge, Coneybury, and Woodhenge all indicate dry, probably grazed grassland. Some indication of the extent of this managed grassland can be extrapolated from the numerous monuments, specifically round barrows, which were constructed during this period. Although peripheral to the main study area, the evidence from Boscombe Down (Newell 1931), Earl's Farm Down (Christie 1964), and Greenland Farm (Christie 1970), all indicate open downland.

Once again, the position of many of the cemeteries of round barrows on hilltops provides a topographic bias to any overall understanding of the environment, but still serves to indicate the apparent extent of managed grassland. It can be suggested that this now extensively cleared landscape provides the ideal vehicle for the introduction of more extensive and formalised arable cultivation. However, the evidence for such economic change does not appear in the environmental record of the earlier Bronze Age.

Later Bronze Age (Fig 155d)

From the mid-second millennium BC onwards, the majority of the environmental data are again derived from ditch deposits, the one major exception being the remarkable suite of data from the primary fills of the Wilsford Shaft. As well as more local indicators such as molluscs, the Wilsford Shaft includes seeds and insects, perhaps derived from a more extensive area, and pollen, providing a more regional picture. The consistent picture from virtually all sources of information is one of a basically open landscape with very few trees. A major component of this landscape is short, grazed grassland, although seeds suggest a significant proportion of arable land, some recently abandoned. The Wilsford Shaft therefore seems to be sited close to a fluctuating boundary between areas of pastoral and arable land, both regimes indicating an open landscape.

In the absence of comparable data, it is impossible to suggest how widely this picture might be applicable within the Stonehenge area. At a general level, it may be acceptable to extend the broad indications of a primarily open landscape. Within this simple framework, the nature of subsistence will inevitably be constrained by more local factors, some purely economic but including those related to ideology and the by now highly structured landscape.

The development of definable settlement foci during the later Bronze Age shows some spatial association with areas of 'Celtic' fields, and it is assumed here that these represent areas of formalised arable activity. In the case of the Wilsford Shaft area, the fields to the north and west may represent such a stabilisation, here of the fluctuating arable/pastoral boundary embodied within the environmental data. Arable evidence from the Stonehenge area is reinforced by the presence of what have been interpreted as wind-blown silts from the Y-holes at Stonehenge (Cornwall 1953), possibly from the Stonehenge ditch (Evans 1984), and more recently from a long barrow close to Robin Hood's Ball (Richards in prep a) and from the western terminal of the Stonehenge Cursus (Richards in prep b). Similar possible deposits have been identified in the Stonehenge ditch (Evans 1984) where, although the mollusc fauna is one of grazed grassland, the wind-blown deposits indicate the proximity of areas of arable fields, possibly those some 500m to the west.

In general, these deposits are almost certainly the product of soil deflation from ploughed land. As such, it is interesting to note that their distribution, biased heavily towards the eastern half of the study area, shows a broad correspondence with that of 'Celtic' fields.

Summary

The fourth millennium BC effectively introduces the modification of the Stonehenge landscape on an extensive scale. The environmental data show clearly that certain specific locations, and by inference some broader zones, were cleared of woodland and that grassland was both established and maintained, the latter presumably by grazing. The faunal remains suggest that this was by cattle rather than by the extensive use of sheep. It also seems likely, based on the small amount of evidence from cereal remains, that some arable cultivation was being carried out. The location, nature, and extent of this activity are uncertain, and are likely to remain so.

A mosaic of land use is thus created, the emphasis within this period being on woodland and on newly created areas of grassland. A simple model, based on the maintenance of existing clearances, a gradual reduction in the amount of woodland, and an increasing emphasis on arable cultivation, would quite happily accommodate the pattern discernible in the later Bronze Age. This model is over-simple, however, and does not take into account episodes of regeneration, evidence for which appears in the later Neolithic.

As noted above, however, the regeneration which does appear within the environmental record appears to be short lived and localised, the overall pattern moving towards the largely open landscape of the earlier Bronze Age. The open environment of the second millennium BC can be suggested as one in which the conflicting demands of pastoralism and cultivation, initially reflected in shifting patterns of land use, are eventually reconciled within a formalised and zoned landscape. The constraints imposed by the ideological landscape, itself moulded by topographic considerations, appear to result in the patterns demonstrated by fields and their associated settlements.

The subsequent land use history of the study area appears to be one again largely of open grassland, with the exception of an undated arable episode at Coneybury and similar activity inferred from the existence of deep colluvial soils within Durrington Walls. This grassland regime appears to have been maintained until arable cultivation encroaches in the post-medieval period, this time from the east, reflecting the early extent of the open fields of the villages within the Avon Valley.

9 Dating evidence

The many excavations which have been carried out within the Stonehenge Environs over the last three decades have produced a large number of radiocarbon determinations. In addition, 14 radiocarbon accelerator dates are now available for sites examined as part of the Stonehenge Environs Project (OxA 1396–1409) and a sequence is available for the Wilsford Shaft (Ashbee *et al* 1989).

Table 137 provides contextual information for all available project area dates and Figure 156 shows all dates, calibrated according to the method recommended by Pearson *et al* (1986) and plotted at one and two sigma ranges.

Of the dates available from past excavations, one (NPL 239) lies beyond the range of the calibration programme, and a cautioning emphasis has been placed on those clearly stated as being either from bulked samples, or where there is a suggestion of contamination. The latter helps to explain the extremely late dates for Grooved Ware obtained from the Durrington Married Quarters pits (BM 702, 703).

With the exception of the antler sample from Stone's 1947 excavation of the Stonehenge Cursus, which produced the only anomalous date from the recent accelerator series, the samples were all recovered during project excavations. All samples were selected for their stratigraphic integrity and to provide a date for a specific event. All samples were taken from larger pieces of bone or antler, the residue of each of which is within the project archive. When selecting bone or antler to subsample, care was taken, and faunal remains records were employed, to select pieces which appeared to be fresh rather than those showing signs of gnawing and surface erosion which might have suggested bone from a secondary rubbish context. This careful approach has meant that the dates produced can be employed with confidence.

Within the text of the report all dates quoted are calibrated, and in most cases are used generally, for example 'early third millennium BC'. Where a specific date is being referred to, then the one-sigma calibrated range and the laboratory identification are appended, enabling reference to be made to Table 137 and Figure 156.

Table 137 The context of all radiocarbon dates from the Project area

Calibration carried out using the University of Washington Quaternary Isotope Lab Radiocarbon Calibration Program 1987

OxA 1402	Coneybury 'Anomaly' Bone sample from primary deposit	5050 ± 100 BP; 3980–3708 (1 sigma), 4040–3640 (2 sigma) cal BC
OxA 1407	Netheravon Bake Antler from base of Phase 1 ditch	4760 ± 90 BP; 3646–3378 (1 sigma), 3776–3350 (2 sigma) cal BC
OxA 1400	Robin Hood's Ball Bone sample from pit	4740 ± 100 BP; 3640–3370 (1 sigma), 3776–3194 (2 sigma) cal BC
OxA 1396	King Barrow Ridge Bone sample from pit	4700 ± 150 BP; 3650–3340 (1 sigma), 3790–2948 (2 sigma) cal BC
OxA 1405	Lesser Cursus Antler from base of ditch (Phase 2)	4640 ± 100 BP; 3606–3200 (1 sigma), 3640–3044 (2 sigma) cal BC
GRO 901	Durrington Walls Earlier Neolithic settlement	4584 ± 80 BP; 3494–3135 (1 sigma), 3611–3040 (2 sigma) cal BC
GRO 901a	Durrington Walls Earlier Neolithic settlement	4575 ± 50 BP; 3371–3144 (1 sigma), 3499–3100 (2 sigma) cal BC
OxA 1404	Lesser Cursus Antler from base of ditch (Phase 1)	4550 ± 120 BP; 3496–3042 (1 sigma), 3627–2920 (2 sigma) cal BC
OxA 1401	Robin Hood's Ball Bone sample from pit	4510 ± 90 BP; 3361–3039 (1 sigma), 3502–2920 (2 sigma) cal BC
BM 505	Normanton LME	4510 ± 103 BP; 3370–3040 (1 sigma), 3510–2920 (2 sigma) cal BC
OxA 1397	King Barrow Ridge Bone sample from pit	4500 ± 120 BP; 3370–2930 (1 sigma), 3607–2900 (2 sigma) cal BC
BM 1583	Stonehenge 1 30cm above base of ditch	4410 ± 60 BP; 3291–2924 (1 sigma), 3340–2910 (2 sigma) cal BC
NPL 191	Durrington Walls Earlier Neolithic settlement	4400 ± 150 BP; 3340–2900 (1 sigma), 3500–2618 (2 sigma) cal BC
BM 1617	Stonehenge 1 Antler from base of ditch	4390 ± 60 BP; 3097–2920 (1 sigma), 3326–2910 (2 sigma) cal BC

Table 137 continued

OxA 1409	Coneybury Henge Bone from interior pit	4370 ± 90 BP; 3254–2911 (1 sigma), 3340–2707 (2 sigma) cal BC
NPL 192	Durrington Walls Midden	4270 ± 95 BP; 3021–2705 (1 sigma), 3255–2611 (2 sigma) cal BC
OxA 1408	Coneybury Henge Bone from primary ditch fill	4200 ± 110 BP; 2917–2615 (1 sigma), 3075–2491 (2 sigma) cal BC
I 2328	Stonehenge 1 Ditch	4130 ± 105 BP; 2890–2508 (1 sigma), 2920–2460 (2 sigma) cal BC
OxA 1403	Stonehenge Cursus Antler from Stone's excavations (Stone 1947)	4100 ± 90 BP; 2878–2502 (1 sigma), 2910–2460 (2 sigma) cal BC
BM 400	Durrington Walls Enclosure ditch	4000 ± 90 BP; 2853–2459 (1 sigma), 2875–2290 (2 sigma) cal BC
OxA 1406	Lesser Cursus Destruction phase Antler from ditch fill	4000 ± 120 BP; 2860–2398 (1 sigma), 2890–2147 (2 sigma) cal BC
BM 399	Durrington Walls Enclosure ditch	3965 ± 90 BP; 2586–2365 (1 sigma), 2866–2200 (2 sigma) cal BC
MPL 77	Amesbury 71 Barrow ? Beaker phase charcoal	3960 ± 110 BP; 2600–2330 (1 sigma), 2875–2142 (2 sigma) cal BC
BM 396	Durrington Walls Southern Circle Phase 2	3950 ± 90 BP; 2580–2343 (1 sigma), 2863–2149 (2 sigma) cal BC
BM 398	Durrington Walls Enclosure ditch	3927 ± 90 BP; 2572–2308 (1 sigma), 2857–2144 (2 sigma) cal BC
NPL 240	Durrington Walls Northern Circle	3905 ± 110 BP; 2571–2207 (1 sigma), 2861–2043 (2 sigma) cal BC
BM 395	Durrington Walls Southern Circle Phase 2	3900 ± 90 BP; 2559–2283 (1 sigma), 2851–2140 (2 sigma) cal BC
BM 397	Durrington Walls Southern Circle Phase 2	3850 ± 90 BP; 2466–2147 (1 sigma), 2577–2039 (2 sigma) cal BC
BM 677	Woodhenge Antler, ditch floor	3817 ± 74 BP; 2456–2143 (1 sigma), 2480–2039 (2 sigma) cal BC
C 602	Aubrey Hole Cremation	3798 *cannot be calibrated*
NPL 239	Durrington Walls Southern Circle Phase 1 *bulked sample*	3760 ± 148 BP; 2460–1974 (1 sigma), 2590–1766 (2 sigma) cal BC
BM 678	Woodhenge Animal bone in primary rubble on ditch floor	3755 ± 54 BP; 2283–2047 (1 sigma), 2350–2030 (2 sigma) cal BC
BM 287	Amesbury 51 Barrow Wood with burial	3738 ± 55 BP; 2275–2042 (1 sigma), 2330–1984 (2 sigma) cal BC
HAR 2013	Stonehenge 2 SE avenue ditch; antler	3720 ± 100 BP; 2290–1979 (1 sigma), 2460–1880 (2 sigma) cal BC
BM 1582	Beaker burial (ST) in ditch, human bone	3715 ± 70 BP; 2271–2033 (1 sigma), 2340–1930 (2 sigma) cal BC
OxA 1398	Durrington Barrow 7; adult inhumation, unassociated with grave goods. Human bone	3700 ± 100 BP; 2275–1958 (1 sigma), 2470–1782 (2 sigma) cal BC
BM 1164	Stonehenge 2 NW Avenue ditch, antler	3678 ± 68 BP; 2190–1972 (1 sigma), 2290–1890 (2 sigma) cal BC
BM 46	Stonehenge 3a Antler below erection ramp	3670 ± 150 BP; 2290–1880 (1 sigma), 2480–1680 (2 sigma) cal BC

Table 137 continued

BM 286	Durrington Walls Hearth in secondary fill of ditch	3630 ± 110 BP; 2183–1880 (1 sigma), 2340–1705 (2 sigma) cal BC
HAR 1237	Amesbury 39 Barrow Charcoal from pyre	3620 ± 90 BP; 2135–1885 (1 sigma), 2279–1750 (2 sigma) cal BC
BM 702	Durrington MQ Pit 27, antler	3597 ± 76 BP; 2117–1883 (1 sigma), 2192–1750 (2 sigma) cal BC
MPL 75	Amesbury 71 Barrow Food Vessel phase (fire in the mound)	3590 ± 90 BP; 2123–1787 (1 sigma), 2199–1705 (2 sigma) cal BC
I 2384	Stonehenge 2 Antler	3570 ± 110 BP; 2123–1760 (1 sigma), 2274–1670 (2 sigma) cal BC
BM 285	Durrington Walls Hearth in secondary fill of ditch	3560 ± 120 BP; 2123–1750 (1 sigma), 2279–1620 (2 sigma) cal BC
BM 703	Durrington MQ Pit 27, animal bone	3473 ± 72 BP; 1890–1697 (1 sigma), 2018–1630 (2 sigma) cal BC
HAR 4879	Stonehenge Stone floor Charcoal	3400 ± 150 BP; 1900–1520 (1 sigma), 2133–1410 (2 sigma) cal BC
NPL 74	Wilsford Shaft Wood from bottom of shaft	3330 ± 90 BP; 1740–1518 (1 sigma), 1880–1430 (2 sigma) cal BC
I 2445	Stonehenge 3b Y hole, antler	3190 ± 105 BP; 1603–1400 (1 sigma); 1734–1225 (2 sigma) cal BC
WS 1	Wilsford Shaft 5 accelerator dates from the lower fills, which group as:	3151 ± 29 BP; 1446–1415 (1 sigma), 1513–1399 (2 sigma) cal BC
OxA 1399	Durrington burial Human bone from crouched burial adjacent to River Avon	3070 ± 90 BP; 1436–1135 (1 sigma), 1520–1052 (2 sigma) cal BC
BM 1079	Avenue 4 North ditch, West Amesbury	3020 ± 180 BP; 1506–1000 (1 sigma), 1690–820 (2 sigma) cal BC
I 3216	Avenue 4 By-pass, *bulked sample*	2750 ± 100 BP; 1010–810 (1 sigma), 1212–790 (2 sigma) cal BC
WS 2	Wilsford Shaft 4 accelerator dates from the upper fill which group as:	2413 ± 32 BP; 751–405 (1 sigma), 760–399 (2 sigma) cal BC

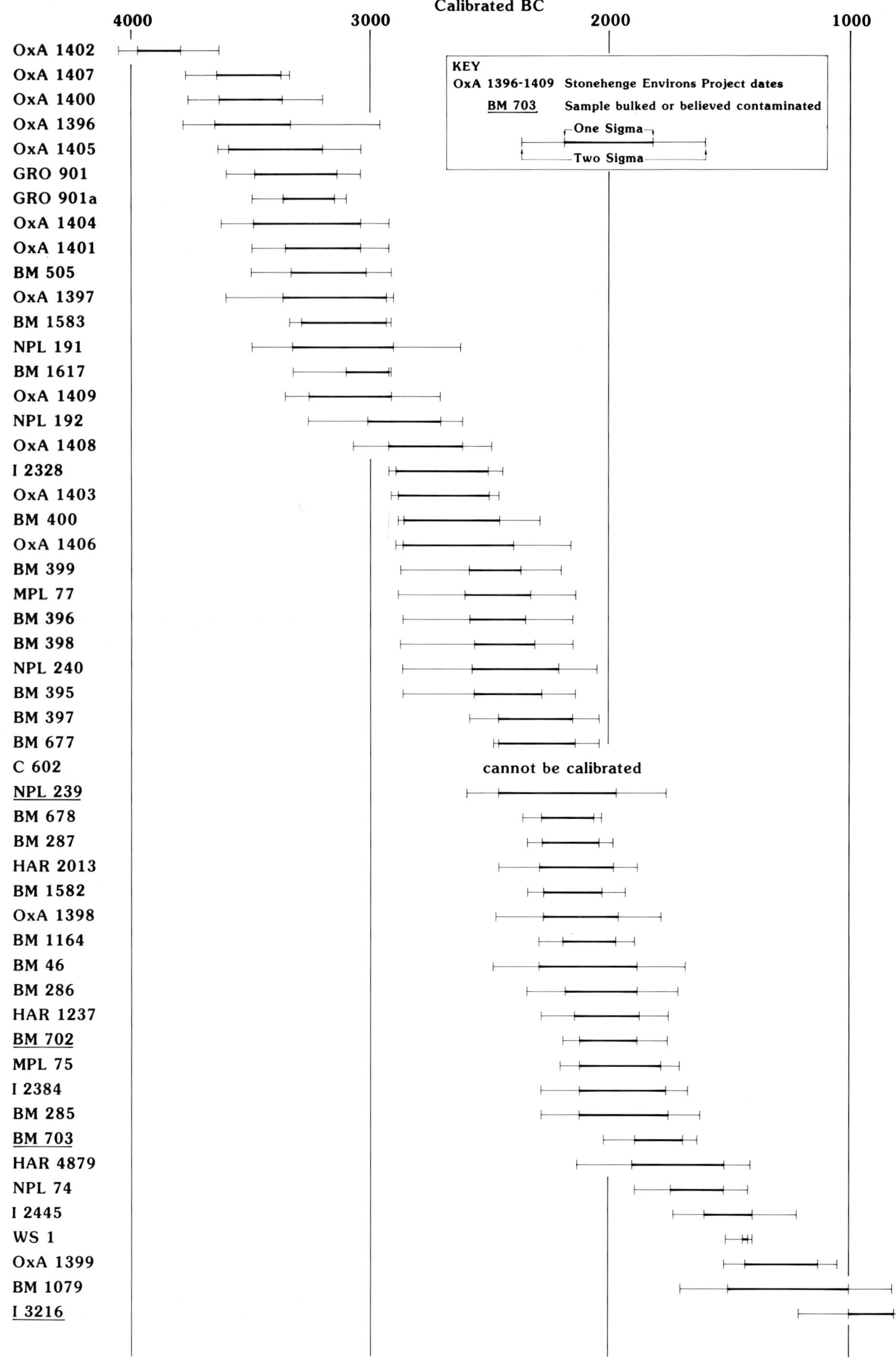

Fig 156 Calibrated radiocarbon dates for the Stonehenge Environs Project area

10 Landscape development and prehistoric societies in the Stonehenge Environs

Data recovered by the project fieldwork vary considerably in their interpretative capacity. Those from extensive surface collections, despite acknowledged limitations, can still provide indications of broad zones of activity, whether at a regional (Wessex) or micro-regional scale. On the latter scale, the analytical framework outlined in chapter 3 has been employed in the construction of a series of phased landscape plans for the Stonehenge Environs (Figs 157, 158, 159, and 160). Subsequent fieldwork and excavation (chapter 4) provide data of increasing refinement but of decreasing extent, with consequently greater analytical requirements.

The stages of development within which the various levels of data are considered and presented are based initially on conventional chronological divisions. The division of the Neolithic has long been a subject for debate, with belief or disbelief in the existence of the 'Middle' Neolithic largely a matter of personal choice. The chronological framework employed below involves a split into 'earlier' and 'later' Neolithic for the consideration of broad trends in landscape development, with the terms Early and Late Neolithic reserved for more specifically dated or associated events or material.

A similar approach is adopted for the Bronze Age, where divisions of the majority of the second millennium BC owe much to established ceramic traditions. Figure 6 shows the range of monuments and ceramic styles represented within the study area, together with their suggested currency and specific dating evidence. This figure suggests the basis for the period divisions employed within the following chapters.

10.1 The earlier Neolithic (Fig 157)

With the exception of the three pits/postholes in the Stonehenge car park (Vatcher and Vatcher 1973), dated earlier than the eighth millennium BC, previously recorded finds provide little evidence for Mesolithic activity on the chalk areas adjacent to the River Avon. This pattern is confirmed by the relative paucity of finds from the recent extensive surface collection programme which produced only very occasional individually diagnostic flint pieces (details in archive), in all cases unassociated with apparently contemporary debitage. The sporadic distribution of such pieces, the majority suggested as elements of composite tools, and including one microlith from Fargo Road (63), can provide little firm evidence for mobile exploitation of this particular chalk zone. There is no evidence for the type of small-scale, mosaic clearance suggested by R W Smith (1984, 113) for the pre-Neolithic landscape around Avebury. In contrast, an indication that late hunter-gatherer activity was concentrated on the Avon Valley has recently been provided by the sample excavation of a colluvial bench on the western side of the river below Durrington Walls. Here an apparently *in situ* flint industry of blade form was associated with microliths (Roy Entwistle, pers comm).

There seems therefore to be little background against which to place the activity and associated monuments of the Early Neolithic, if this period is introduced by the construction of communal monuments, even if of a restricted range. Both causewayed enclosures and, more specifically, early forms of long barrows have been suggested as representing a response to the stresses of a 'pioneering' phase of the Early Neolithic. In contrast, it can be suggested that their construction represents a period of stabilisation and consolidation and may therefore not represent the earliest phase of the Neolithic.

Although the latter hypothesis cannot be confirmed on the basis of a single event, the nature of the assemblages of both flint and animal bone from the Coneybury 'Anomaly' (W2 (1981), this vol, 4.1) does lend support. Here, the pit contents of the early fourth millennium BC appear to demonstrate the coexistence of elements of both mobile and more sedentary economies. A strong emphasis on the river valley is provided by bones of beaver and brown trout, and by the use of small quantities of river gravel flint. Cleal notes (this vol, 4.1 c), that the pottery indicates a group potentially outside the exchange networks within which gabbroic pottery circulates, a network in which enclosures play a significant role. It is equally possible that the activity represented in the 'Anomaly' pre-dates any element of more formal monument construction within the area.

The framework within which a range of subsistence activity can be placed is provided for the Stonehenge area by the causewayed enclosure of Robin Hood's Ball, lying in the north-western corner of the study area, by ten long barrows of varying size and form, and by one long mortuary enclosure. The few available radiocarbon determinations suggest that this framework is unlikely to date from very much earlier than the middle of the fourth millennium BC (Fig 156).

Excavations at Robin Hood's Ball (Thomas 1964) showed that construction was associated with plain pottery of South-Western style, but provided no absolute dating evidence. Although not directly associated with the enclosure, the area of extra-mural activity recently excavated (W83, Richards in prep a) can be dated to the second half of the fourth millennium BC. By analogy with other dated examples, an earlier date for the causewayed enclosure could be expected, but the features and pottery recorded under the bank Thomas 1964, 8–10) may suggest that the enclosure, or at least the outer ditch and bank, represents the formal incorporation of an already defined activity area. The description of the pre-enclosure soil profile at this site suggests a well-formed grassland profile (ibid, fig 3). A preliminary assessment of the excavated data from W83, the extra-mural site, assemblages of animal bone, flint, and pottery, suggests a strong contrast with those from the 'Anomaly'. The pottery, in particular, including gabbroic and Abingdon wares, suggests access to wider networks of exchange, potentially developed through time. The range of more sedentary activities which can be suggested at W83 may reflect a degree of stability associated with the formal construction,

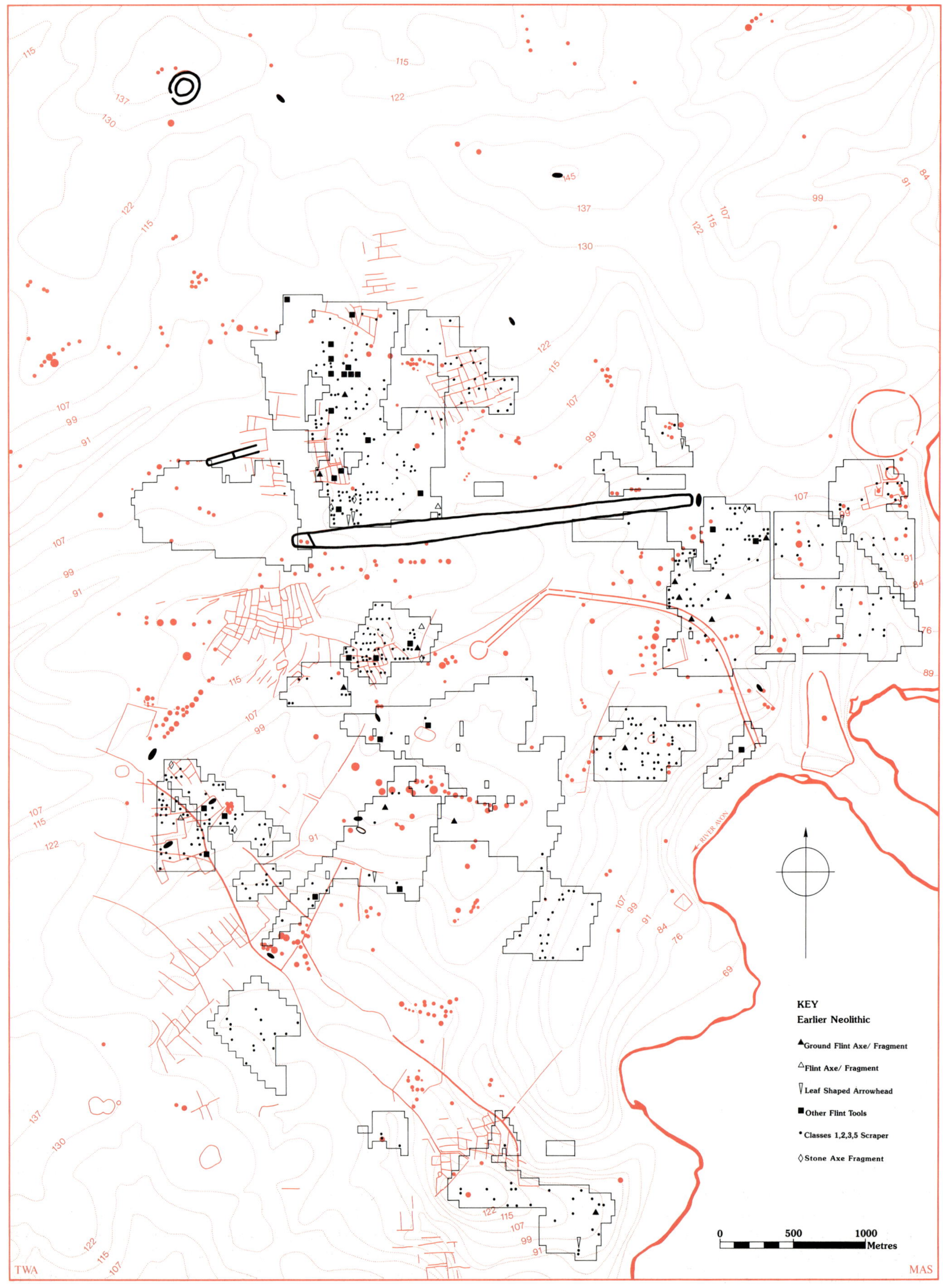

Fig 157 The prehistoric landscape: earlier Neolithic

possible extension, and maintenance of an enclosure complex.

Until recently, only one of the long barrows and associated sites, the Normanton Down long mortuary enclosure, had been investigated. This site produced a radiocarbon date in the late fourth millennium BC, placing the enclosure in the centre of the date range for conventional long barrows. A similar date could perhaps have been suggested for the Netheravon Bake long barrow, sampled as part of the research project in the Robin Hood's Ball area (Richards in prep a). Although it is essentially of 'short' form, at least two Neolithic phases can be identified prior to its modification to a round barrow. The first phase has, however, been dated to the mid-fourth millennium BC. The morphological variety exhibited by the remaining examples in the study area, ranging from massive examples such as Winterbourne Stoke 1 (the 'Crossroads' long barrow), down to Wilsford 13, barely 20m long and potentially U-ditched, suggests a wide range of both chronology and association. Later, developed types, perhaps exemplified by the spatially discrete cluster to the south-west of Stonehenge on Normanton, Wilsford, and Stonehenge Downs may be more firmly associated with subsequent phases of earlier Neolithic monument construction, specifically that during which the Lesser Cursus, if not the Stonehenge Cursus, was constructed.

Prior to recent survey work, earlier Neolithic activity of a non-monumental nature had been recorded in the form of both isolated artefacts and of archaeological deposits. The former, primarily casual finds of specific and easily recognised tools, such as ground flint axes and leaf-shaped arrowheads, inevitably correlate with areas of more recent cultivation and also demonstrate the effects of concentrated fieldwork on one specific area, in this case that carried out by Laidler and Young on the King Barrow Ridge (Laidler and Young 1938). Stratified deposits, both pits and spreads of occupation material of earlier Neolithic date, have consistently been recorded during the excavation of sites of later date, primarily round barrows on the King Barrow Ridge, but also at Durrington Walls.

The extensive excavations at Durrington Walls in 1966 and 1967 produced evidence for pre-enclosure activity (Wainwright and Longworth 1971, 192–3). Plain pottery, a ground axe, and leaf-shaped arrowheads, unassociated with any subsoil features, were recovered from under the bank in both areas examined, but primarily in the northern cutting. The radiocarbon dates from both areas suggest an area of extensive and potentially mobile settlement, spanning a period in the second half of the fourth millennium BC, lying within the area of the later enclosure.

In addition to this suggestion of intensive activity, with its apparent focus on the river valley, pits containing a similar range of artefacts have been recorded in several post-war excavations and watching briefs, most consistently in the area of the King Barrow Ridge. Amesbury barrow 132 produced sherds of plain pottery from a small pit (Gingell 1988) and similar pottery was recovered from Amesbury 39 (Ashbee 1981). Further emphasis on pit finds is provided by the 'Vespasian's Ridge pit' and a similar feature recorded to the west of the King Barrow Wood, both located during construction of the A303 (this vol, 4.3).

The artefacts contained within these pits, and in an isolated example located during the excavation of W31, Wilsford Down (this vol, 4.10), appear to be of a domestic nature. Bones are primarily those of domestic stock, although there is evidence of the exploitation of wild animals. The small quantities of pottery can all be suggested as local products. Unfortunately, the flints demonstrate a degree of selectivity on the part of the excavators.

Isolated from their immediate context, the initial function of the scattered pits noted above is difficult to determine. The broad context of the examples in the King Barrow Ridge area can be suggested by the distribution of elements of the worked flint assemblages recovered by surface collection (Fig 14). As the programme of extensive surface collection produced only a single sherd of earlier Neolithic pottery (P305) from south of Stonehenge (55), the isolation of earlier Neolithic elements inevitably rests heavily on individually diagnostic and, it is hoped, unambiguous tools, primarily leaf-shaped arrowheads and ground flint axes. Greater numbers of scrapers of potentially early type (Riley, this vol, 5.3) are available, but here are interpreted with caution.

In attempting to interpret the data from surface collection, specifically in order to isolate chronologically and functionally discrete areas, an awareness of the range of potential subsistence activities is essential. The available data, discussed below, suggest a wide range of exploitation, including both sedentary and mobile activities.

The King Barrow Ridge provides the most positive evidence of extensive earlier Neolithic activity, here in the form of ground flint axes, those from recent work augmented by further examples recovered by Laidler and Young (1938). This concentration of axes appears to be relatively restricted, and the overall ridgetop distribution of earlier Neolithic material continues south on to Coneybury Hill (51), primarily in the form of scrapers. To the east, close to the River Avon and to the area of occupation at Durrington Walls, surface evidence suggests little activity, a pattern repeated at the edge of the valley in Whittles (73).

Within the eastern half of the study area, for which Stonehenge Bottom appears to form a westerly boundary, the combined evidence suggests a range of activities, potentially representing the exploitation of differing resource zones. The varied resources of the river valley, including flint, water, and wild animals, both fish and other game, may offer sufficient potential for the development of more stable areas of settled activity. The pre-enclosure settlement at Durrington Walls can be suggested as being associated with a phase of woodland clearance and possibly of cultivation (Wainwright and Longworth 1971, 329–37), although the latter appears rather nebulous. Some investment in extensive clearance can be demonstrated, however, perhaps representing the creation and maintenance of a base area from which more mobile and sporadic exploitation of the chalk to the east was carried out. Entwistle suggests (this vol, 4.7 e) an expansion of grassland within the zone from Durrington to the King Barrow Ridge. Here, suggestions that

Amesbury 42 long barrow lies at the junction of differing ecological zones, together with the distribution of axe fragments, may suggest the exploitation of a wooded margin of an extensive area of grassland.

To the east of the King Barrow Ridge, the distribution of earlier Neolithic flint tools surprisingly shows very little emphasis on the area adjacent to the River Avon, discussed above in the context of the evidence from Durrington Walls. To the west, beyond the area of the King Barrow Ridge, the combined data suggest that earlier Neolithic activity, although perhaps sporadic, may have been concentrated within three specific areas:

1 Around Winterbourne Stoke Crossroads (50) and The Diamond (59), some activity can be identified within an area containing the most coherent cluster of long barrows within the study area, six examples within an area of less than $2km^2$. A single pit, potentially of earlier Neolithic date, was also recorded during the excavation of W31, Wilsford Down flint scatter (this vol, 4.10). The interpretation of the surface material, in contrast to the King Barrow Ridge, relies very heavily on scraper type, with an absence of ground axes.

2 The area of Stonehenge Triangle (54) is similar to the above area, characterisation again resting primarily on scraper types. Within this particular area, the occurrence of surface Peterborough Ware (see this vol, 10.2, the later Neolithic) may suggest that the scrapers cannot positively be associated with the phase of earlier Neolithic activity.

3 In contrast, data from surface collection in the area North of the Cursus (52) led to the suggestion that discrete, nucleated flint scatters were identifiable within more extensive patterns of earlier Neolithic activity. The suggestion was largely prompted by the location, early in the programme of surface collection, of the Fargo Wood I flint scatter (W32, this vol, 4.4). This hypothesis was appealing in what now appears to be its over-simplified social implications; a pattern of small-scale, mobile activity becoming increasingly sedentary and, in consequence, more extensive and potentially recoverable during the later part of the Neolithic. Although subsequent analysis has failed to confirm such scatters as recurrent elements within the surface collection data, their recognition may be more a function of the intensity of later activity. Within what is effectively a palimpsest landscape subsequent scatters may dilute the diagnostic blade element of early scatters to a level at which crude sampling may fail to identify it.

The developing Neolithic

The activity and monuments discussed above belong primarily within the first half of the fourth millennium BC, and are conventionally associated with forms of both pottery and flint tools, the longevity of which are still debated. Later in this millennium, the development of a distinctive suite of artefacts, including initially the range of Peterborough styles and followed by Grooved Ware, can be associated with novel monument types. The first appearance of such monuments leaves a chronological void, the 'Middle Neolithic', often devoid of firm associations with distinctive ceramic or lithic styles. This period has been suggested as one of hiatus, representing profound and far-reaching social change caused by factors including competition and over-population (Bradley 1978, 1982; Thomas and Whittle 1986; Whittle 1978, 1981).

It is within this period that the final development of linear monuments appears to take place, manifest in the two extremes of the 'short' long barrow and of Cursus monuments. Newly available radiocarbon dates place the Lesser Cursus in the second half of the fourth millennium BC, where, despite the somewhat ambiguous date recently obtained (Table 137, Figure 156), it is suggested the Stonehenge Cursus should also be placed. In their primary phases neither of these two sites demonstrate any association either with pottery or with specific forms of flint artefact. In the absence of positively identifiable elements of the surface collection data, the two cursus monuments appear potentially isolated. However, project excavations have demonstrated the contemporaneity of more extensive activity (W59, this vol, 4.8), and environmental sequences spanning this apparently transitional period (W58, this vol, 4.7) show little or no sign of a phase of dereliction and regrowth. The evidence from the Stonehenge area suggests that the latter part of the earlier Neolithic is a phase of modification, one which sees the development, extension, and final form of a range of soon-to-be archaic linear monuments. These may be associated with what must now be regarded as 'traditional' forms of pottery; the Dorset Cursus, for example, has plain Early Neolithic pottery in its primary fill (Bowden *et al* 1983). However, despite the total lack of pottery from primary contexts in the ditches of the two Cursus excavated in the Stonehenge area, there are suggestions, based solely on the distribution of surface material, that an association with early forms of Peterborough-style pottery is possible. A positive association has been demonstrated at the Springfield Cursus, Essex (Hedges and Buckley 1981, 5 and fig 3), although here the description of a 'primary' silt position for the predominantly Mortlake-style pottery does not seem to be confirmed by the drawn section. Pottery of the Ebbsfleet and Mortlake substyles has recently been recovered from the primary fill of the Drayton Cursus, Oxfordshire (Ros Cleal, pers comm).

Current understanding of the environmental background and economy of the earlier Neolithic is based on limited data. Molluscan analysis applied to specific monuments may reflect little more than an extremely localised sequence. In addition the nature of the recent fieldwork has failed to produce stratified deposits containing a suitable range of data. However, when the individual suites of data which, considered in isolation, are of limited interpretative value, are considered together, then some indication of economic and environmental trends can be determined.

The precise nature and extent of clearance during the earlier Neolithic cannot be determined. However, even clearance related to individual monuments, in conjunction with the positive data from the early settlement at Durrington Walls, suggests an extensive clearance mosaic. With the exception of the possible short-lived episode of cultivation at Durrington Walls (Wainwright and Longworth 1971, 329–338), there is little direct evidence of cereal cultivation within the Stonehenge area. Small quantities of heavily burnt emmer wheat came from the Coneybury 'Anomaly' (W2 (1981)) although in contrast only one indeterminate cereal fragment was recovered from the sieving of 102 litres of soil from pits at W83, Robin Hood's Ball (Carruthers, this vol, 8.1). This does not suggest a strong association between cereal cultivation and the stability represented by the construction of enclosures. The occurrence within earlier Neolithic contexts of fragments of what appear to be querns or rubbers may indicate the processing of wild grains or alternatively such activities as axe grinding.

The evidence from the earlier Neolithic in the Stonehenge area suggests little progress towards a formalised cereal-based economy that has occasionally been suggested as developing during this phase of prehistory. If extensive clearance is suggested, and the evidence for cereal cultivation is so conspicuously absent, then the widespread establishment of grassland can be envisaged. R W Smith (1984, 109) notes the association of early sheep with evidence for cereal cultivation elsewhere in southern Britain, and comments on the similar requirements for extensive openings on well-drained land. The establishment, within an area which can be suggested as grassland, of the enclosure at Robin Hood's Ball would appear to suggest the potential for more formalised agricultural practices. The nearby pits, despite containing a faunal assemblage of entirely domestic animals, showed no evidence of cereals.

The ecological requirements of both cattle and pigs are little different from those of their wild counterparts, and the occurrence within the Stonehenge area of both domestic cattle, to a lesser degree pig, and wild species suggests a continuing emphasis on the exploitation of areas of largely unmodified environment. The ubiquity of hazelnuts within pits of this phase also points to the continuing use of scrub and woodland resources during this period and re-emphasises Hillman's conclusion that most early agricultural communities were heavily dependent on wild food resources (Hillman 1981, 189).

10.2 The later Neolithic (Fig 158)

The concept of a later Neolithic, characterised by a range of novel enclosure forms and by the development of associated styles of decorated pottery, should not be taken to suggest any discontinuity from the period discussed above as the 'earlier Neolithic'. In pottery styles, in particular, the overlapping 'Middle Neolithic' demonstrates an association of early examples of the Peterborough style with monuments, the origins of which lie firmly in an Early Neolithic tradition.

Within the later Neolithic the sequence of major monument construction demonstrates a change in emphasis from the construction, extension, and abandonment of linear monuments, to a return to the construction of enclosures. Many recent authors (for example, Wainwright and Longworth 1971, 201–3), have suggested an evolutionary scheme linking causewayed enclosures and those of the later Neolithic. This argument suggests that the development of two independent traditions, each involving the construction of non-utilitarian enclosures, is unlikely. Within the Stonehenge area some direct continuity may be suggested if, as discussed above, Robin Hood's Ball is as late as the extra-mural dates suggest. This dating, when compared to that available for the first phase of Stonehenge, discussed below, suggests the possibility of a direct line of development.

Although this sequence of monument development is essentially local, both this and the parallel development of both Peterborough and Grooved Ware ceramics may potentially reflect more regional, or even national trends.

Before considering the constituent monuments of the later Neolithic landscape, it is appropriate to introduce the distribution of Peterborough Ware within the study area. Here, the chronology of this pottery is no better defined than elsewhere, in part resulting from the nature of the contexts from which this particular type of pottery is consistently recovered. Within the study area Peterborough Ware has not been recovered from pits, only occurring as surface finds, in buried soils, and within amorphous subsoil hollows. Spatially, three main areas can be identified: on Wilsford Down, between Fargo Wood and the Packway (north of the Stonehenge Cursus), and on the King Barrow Ridge. A less concentrated and stylistically indistinguishable group occurs on the Stonehenge Triangle to the west of Stonehenge. Of the three main areas, only that on the King Barrow Ridge fails to demonstrate an association with monuments of the later stages of the earlier Neolithic and, although no chronological variation can be assumed, is the only group not to include pottery of the Fengate substyle. The less defined area on the Stonehenge Triangle will be discussed below in association with other data from surface collection.

Within the study area five enclosures of later Neolithic date can be identified. Grouped broadly as 'henges', and exhibiting a wide range of size, morphology, and date typical of this ill-matched class of monument, these five examples span three of Harding's classes (Harding 1987, 26–31):

1 Stonehenge (Atkinson 1979), Coneybury (this vol, 4.9), and Woodhenge (Cunnington 1929), are 'classic henges';
2 Durrington Walls (Wainwright and Longworth 1971) is a henge-enclosure;
3 The Fargo Plantation 'hengiform' (Stone 1938) is a mini-henge.

The most anomalous, complex, and, in terms of its initial construction, the earliest of these monuments is Stonehenge. Although it is perhaps premature to reconsider aspects of the detailed sequence at Stonehenge in advance of the definitive publication, an examination of the currently available data (summarised in RCHME 1979, 8–13) enables some general phasing to be integrated into the current discussion.

It has long been recognised that the earthwork enclosure at Stonehenge represented the earliest definable phase of the monument, suggested on the basis of the single radiocarbon determination to date to the early third millennium BC (RCHME 1979, 8). Stratigraphi-

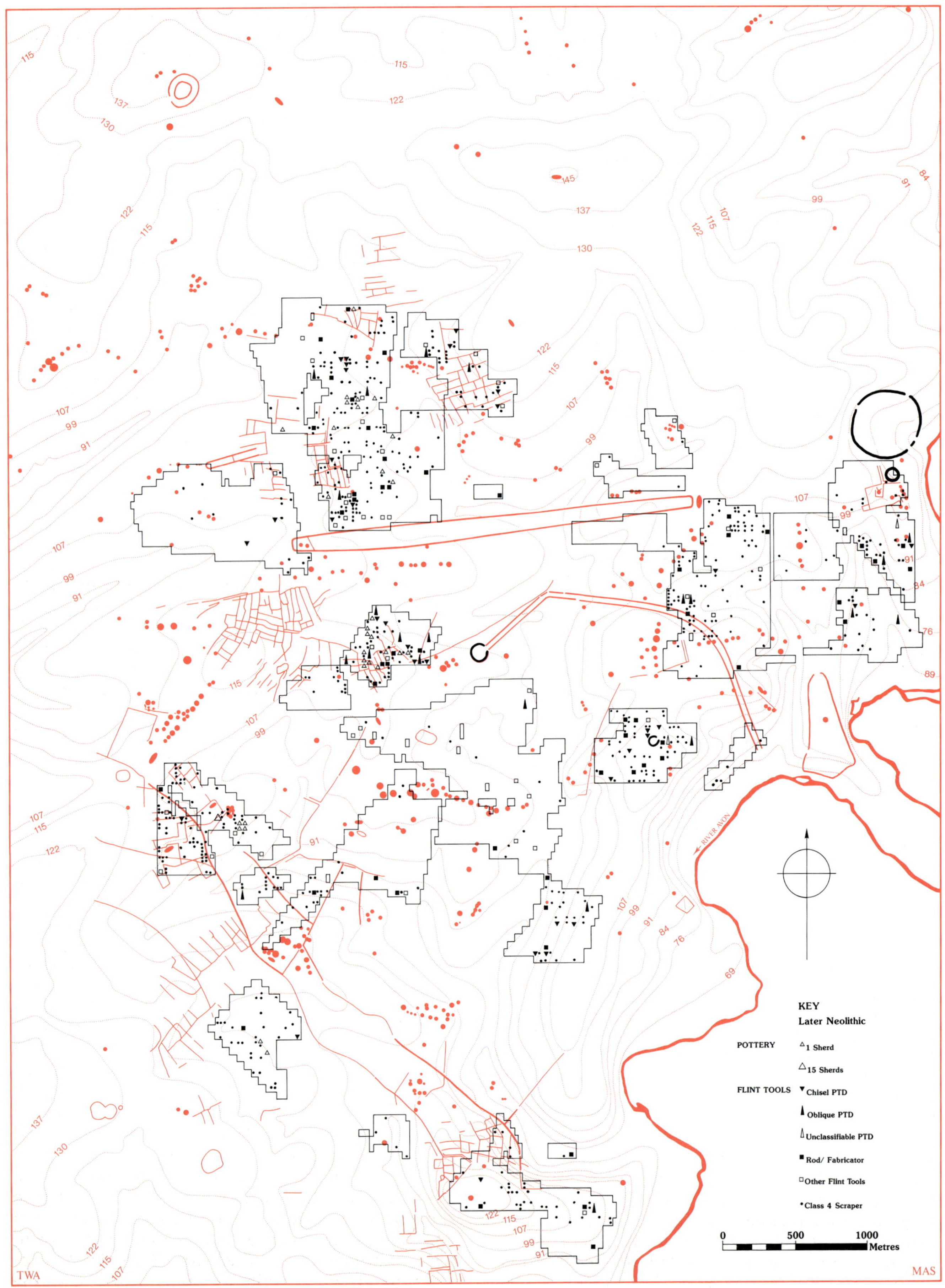

Fig 158 The prehistoric landscape: later Neolithic

cally, however, this date is not from a primary position in the ditch, and more recently available determinations (Evans 1984) indicate that the ditch was constructed in the late fourth millennium BC. This places Stonehenge I within the same date bracket as Balfarg Riding School, Fife (Harding 1987, 353), Llandegai, Gwynedd (ibid, 331–4), and Stenness, Orkney (Ritchie 1976), rather than within the later Wessex Group, perhaps typified in this area by Woodhenge and Durrington Walls.

Additional elements suggested as belonging to this first phase include the excavation and rapid backfilling of the Aubrey Holes, the Heel Stone and its paired stone (Pitts 1982), and a 'possible indeed probable' timber structure (Atkinson 1979). Currently available data allow only speculation about the internal structure of the enclosure, although the insertion of cremations into Aubrey Holes and into the ditch and bank suggests the possibility of an enclosed cremation cemetery. The accompaniment of some cremations with Late Neolithic objects provides some indication of date for this aspect of the monument, although the only available radiocarbon date (for an Aubrey Hole) unfortunately lies beyond the range of currently recommended calibration (Pearson *et al* 1986). Of whatever form and significance, the enclosure itself appears to have had a relatively short period of maintenance prior to abandonment. Environmental data from the ditch (Evans 1984) indicates an uninterrupted sequence which demonstrates the rapid recolonisation of the monument by rank grass and scrub.

There is, however, a considerable period of time within which such dereliction could have taken place. Figure 156 shows that (disregarding the single radiocarbon date relating to the Aubrey Hole) the phase of abandonment can be suggested as having lasted between 400 and 600 years. The evidence for subsequent reconstruction at Stonehenge, conventionally described as periods II and III, cannot be demonstrated as occurring until well into the second half of the third millennium BC.

In its earliest phase Stonehenge has little in common in both form and chronology with other classic henges, although the recent excavations at Coneybury (this vol, 4.9) have demonstrated some similarities between Stonehenge and this example. Both have early dates for their initial phases, demonstrate an association with Grooved Ware only in very small quantities, and, from environmental data, appear to be rapidly abandoned and overgrown. The similarity in ceramic association is particularly striking, as extensive excavations at both sites have produced groups of Grooved Ware minute in comparison to the assemblages from both Woodhenge and, more specifically and strikingly, from Durrington Walls. Although the association at Coneybury appears to be with a primary phase of the monument, it is possible that the position of the pottery is essentially secondary, and relates to a re-use of part of the ditch and to subsequent filling of internal features. Likewise, at Stonehenge Grooved Ware is noted as coming from pits cut into the silted-up ditch and from recuts in the top of Aubrey Holes (Atkinson 1979). Such a range of contextual data for this pottery is, however, difficult to reconcile with the quantities involved, recorded as a maximum of six sherds.

A final area of comparison between these two sites lies in their later re-use, broadly contemporaneous, although in the case of Stonehenge involving a more formal reconstruction, whereas at Coneybury only the ditch appears to have represented a focus for activity.

The riverside complex of Woodhenge and Durrington Walls, together with associated nearby pit groups, represents the most conspicuous single focus of later Neolithic activity within the study area. Woodhenge itself appears to represent the development of an increasingly complex ideology, identifiable not only in the nature of its contained artefacts, but in the circumstances and structured nature of their deposition (Richards and Thomas 1984). The complexity of Woodhenge, combined with its relatively small size, may suggest the final and declining display of the ritual authority which had developed and maintained such sites as Durrington Walls. This site, representing a massive investment in labour and a considerable monument to social cohesion, was originally interpreted by the excavators as having been constructed for communal or ceremonial purposes (Wainwright and Longworth 1971, 203). The massive internal structures were regarded as being unlikely to be purely domestic, and the considerable quantities of debris associated with both these structures and with formal areas of deposition was seen as resulting from ceremonial practices (ibid). Although the large-scale and extremely well-defined, if not understood, activity at Durrington Walls was seen as being a starting point in the search for later Neolithic settlement, it was not thought to represent a manifestation of everyday life. An alternative interpretation, in which the size of Durrington-type enclosures, together with the elements originally interpreted as ceremonial, are allowed a more secular function, appears in the Mount Pleasant report (Wainwright 1979, 237). Both seem perfectly reasonable interpretations, although there are arguments against each. The ceremonial interpretation denies the possibility of a cohesive social order which could produce and maintain a complex nucleated settlement. Alternately, the entirely domestic interpretation fails to explain the absence of Woodhenge/Durrington-type timber structures beyond the confines of such enclosures, and the quantities and status of contemporary artefacts from what appear to be non-ceremonial areas of activity. Durrington Walls may best be interpreted in a way which accommodates both concepts, as an area of rigidly defined settlement activity, constructed and used in a manner embodying equally rigid ideological codes. The contrast provided by this structured and highly recognisable activity, and the extensive but ephemeral activity represented beyond the confines of the enclosure, suggests more than simple status divisions operating within later Neolithic society.

Whatever the interpretation of Durrington Walls, the later Neolithic ceremonial focus within the Stonehenge area appears to concentrate in the zone stretching from the King Barrow Ridge eastwards to the River Avon. This 'Durrington Zone' (Richards 1984b, fig 11.2) appears to represent a shift of emphasis away from the areas within which lie the identifiable foci of the earlier Neolithic and the abandoned first phase of Stonehenge.

Prior to recent survey work the Durrington Zone had also produced the sole evidence for later Neolithic activity beyond the group of ceremonial monuments introduced above. Traces of occupation extending for about 150 metres south of Woodhenge were located during the excavation of a series of ring ditches (Cunnington 1929, 41–8). Also within the same area, but slightly further south, the Woodlands pits (Stone and Young 1948; Stone 1949) should perhaps be regarded as additional evidence for processes of formal, ideologically motivated deposition, rather than being domestic in nature. These pits contained, in addition to Grooved Ware, an exceptional range of animal bones, bone points, marine shells, a Group VII axe fragment, and transverse flint arrowheads. The capping of flint nodules placed over two pits provides further emphasis on the formality of such deposits.

Effectively within the same zone, the contents of the 'Chalk Plaque pit' (F de M Vatcher 1969; Harding 1988) appear undistinguished, with the exception of the plaques themselves and of sherds of Grooved Ware. Although few details of the pit itself are available, there seems little to suggest that the circumstances under which the finds were deposited showed any of the elements of formality represented in the Woodlands examples.

The evidence from the Durrington Zone can be taken to suggest not an exclusively ritualised landscape, but one within which ceremonial monuments and activities played a significant role within a wider domestic context. Evidence for this context is provided by lithic data from the programme of extensive surface collection augmented, within this particular area, by pottery recovered in the course of the excavation of later monuments, particularly round barrows.

Constraints within the extensive sampling strategy, particularly those of field availability, have inevitably placed some restrictions on the patterns related to local topography. It can be suggested, however, that Stonehenge Bottom, the major north–south dry valley, may have acted as a conceptual if not physical barrier to separate zones of varying activity, emphasis, and association.

With two exceptions, a minor concentration on Wilsford Down and the small quantity of material from Stonehenge itself, the distribution of Grooved Ware is exclusively within the eastern part of the study area. Concentrations of diagnostic flint tools are again concentrated on the King Barrow Ridge, with greater emphasis to the south on Coneybury Hill (51) where 'PTDs' (petit tranchet derivative arrowheads) and fabricators are perhaps associated with the construction and use of Coneybury Henge. Although the pattern on the central part of the King Barrow Ridge is less coherent than for the preceding period, the excavation at W59 demonstrated a consistent later Neolithic element within the ploughsoil assemblage, specifically in the quantities of PTDs recovered.

Towards what must be regarded as a major focus, the area of Durrington Walls and Woodhenge, within an area where surface pottery cannot be expected to survive, the distribution of later Neolithic flint becomes extremely sparse. Scattered PTDs and fabricators show no indication of extensive activity or of more nucleated foci, and immediately adjacent to Woodhenge, the fields were characterised by an almost total absence of worked flint. It can be suggested that many of the later Neolithic activities in this particular area are of an enclosed nature. In this area the material tightly contained within the flint-capped Woodlands pits appears to have no extensive associated scatters of artefacts, providing a contrast with patterns observed in the western half of the study area.

To the west of Stonehenge Bottom the data from extensive surface collection suggest that a number of areas of activity can be identified. Within some of these, where post-medieval land use has been less intensive, surface pottery of later Neolithic date survives. The distribution of this exclusively Peterborough-style pottery has been introduced earlier in this chapter, but in the light of its insecure chronology, this distribution must be reviewed within a more specifically Late Neolithic context.

The most identifiable and discrete concentration of flint tools occurs within the northern side of the Stonehenge Triangle (54). Here, immediately to the west of Stonehenge, a concentration of PTDs, of both oblique and chisel form, are associated with fabricators, other less specific tools, occasional stone axe fragments (Roe, this vol, 5.5 a), and surface pottery including indeterminate Peterborough Ware. Given the suggested chronological range of Peterborough styles of pottery, this strong association with transverse arrowheads may reflect an area of activity related to the earliest phase of Stonehenge. The classic Wessex Peterborough-associated material, suggested by Richards and Thomas (1984, 77) as including stone axes and chisel-ended PTD arrowheads, is demonstrated here. The extent of this area, within which a slightly undulating topography suggests the potential for variable preservation, appears to correspond with the low ridge of Stonehenge Down to the south, and to the north approximately with the line of the modern road.

The area to the north of the Stonehenge Cursus as far north as Durrington Down suggests extensive activity, extending over an area of at least 50 hectares. Within this broadly defined scatter, individual foci can be identified, represented by a variety of artefact combinations, potentially indicating a range of individual functions. Pottery of Ebbsfleet, Mortlake, and Fengate substyles occurs in combination with PTDs, fabricators, and scrapers suggested as being of later Neolithic date. One specific area which lies immediately north of the Cursus adjacent to Fargo Wood may have a corresponding scatter of worked flint just to the south. Young's diary for December 1934 (Stone 1947, 17) records 'flinting' in the field to the north-west of Stonehenge, where nothing was found until he approached the Cursus near Fargo Wood. Here 'implements, flakes and cores became plentiful'.

A cluster of PTDs, all of chisel form and largely unassociated with any other flint tools, lies on the northern periphery of the area under consideration. Such clusters are popularly regarded as representing game hunting, specifically within woodland, an interpretation rejected by Clark (1963) who points out the unsuitability of such arrowheads for this purpose, and more recently by Edmunds and Thomas (1984, 193). To the north and north-east the pattern of diagnostic finds breaks up, but still includes scattered PTDs. Fargo

Wood appears to mark the westerly extent of the scatter as the eastern side of Cursus West End (62) contains only occasional PTDs, possibly reflecting a similar, peripheral pattern to that observed to the north and north-east.

To the south-west, pottery within the Wilsford Down area suggests widespread activity, although the consistent circumstances of its recovery provide no associated economic or environmental data, and no opportunity for radiocarbon dating.

Under these circumstances, the interim interpretation of the data from surface collection (Richards 1984b), which proposed a simple scheme in which the Wilsford Down area, a Peterborough 'zone', performed a purely industrial function, need not be radically revised. The scheme, within which the contrast was provided by the ritual/domestic Durrington Zone with its emphasis on Grooved Ware, is inevitably an over-simplification. The industrial function for the Wilsford Down area must be seen as less exclusive, and the area supported a wider range of functions, some, identified from the excavation of an 'industrial' site (W31, this vol, 4.10), clearly of a more domestic nature.

The identification of the dry valley running up towards Wilsford Down as a topographical focus for major flint exploitation does not need revision, however. Although, as discussed in chapter 3, flint working on an industrial scale may contain little chronologically indicative material, this area does contain occasional later Neolithic flint tools associated with quantities of knapping debris. An indication of the extent of this activity can be gained by the recognition of a dense and tightly nucleated scatter of large flint knapping debris at Well House (83), further east down the dry valley system, closer to the point at which it joins with the valley of the River Avon.

In summary, the data from surface collection suggest extensive later Neolithic activity, perhaps characterised by broad surface scatters, some of which, even on initial examination, appear to exhibit some internal structure. The nature of the activity which could have generated such patterns is, however, open to speculation, although some insight into the subsistence base has recently been gained.

Environmental and economic data for the later Neolithic within the Stonehenge area are almost exclusively derived from the excavation of a range of sites, concentrated in the eastern half of the area, and of essentially non-domestic function.

Within this eastern area, the pre-enclosure soil at Durrington Walls indicates a grassland environment, suggested above as part of an extensive cleared and maintained zone. In contrast, and perhaps indicative of the southerly extent of this zone, the ditch sequence from Coneybury indicates that if the henge was constructed in a cleared area, then the area was likely to have been of small size and seems to have become overgrown in a generation. Although not precisely dated, and potentially only representative of a localised sequence, the evidence of scrub regeneration at Stonehenge provides a further indication that the later Neolithic is not represented solely by increased clearance.

Recent work in the project area has provided no indication of later Neolithic woodland management, including coppicing, although the continuing use of woodland food resources is evident throughout this phase. Wild animals, particularly deer, can be regarded as no more than a supplement to diet, with cattle and pig dominant, the pig particularly so at Durrington Walls, where it is seen as a source of meat for feasting (Wainwright and Longworth 1971, 189–90). Apart from the evidence from Durrington Walls, there is no confirmation of the suggestion made by Grigson (1982c) and re-emphasised by R W Smith (1984), that pig became more important than sheep. Evidence from the Stonehenge area suggests that sheep were very poorly represented throughout the Neolithic (Maltby, this vol, chapter 7).

There are unfortunately no economic or environmental data available for the later Neolithic in the western half of the study area.

The dynamics of the Late Neolithic have been the subject of much recent discussion, with attention focused on the wider implications of the relationship between varying ceramic styles (Richards and Thomas 1984). The interim project assessment, published not long after the completion of fieldwork (Richards 1984b), suggested a major reorganisation of the landscape associated with the introduction of Beaker pottery and its associated artefacts, monuments, and social implications. The nature and effects of this reorganisation will be discussed in the following section.

10.3 The earlier Bronze Age (Fig 159)

The final stage of the traditional Neolithic, as discussed in the preceding section, is a period which incorporated a wider range of developments than those represented in the Stonehenge study area. Elsewhere in southern Britain it seems clear that this period saw the introduction of metalwork, Beakers, and also of round barrows in perhaps greater numbers than the current record suggests (Kinnes 1979). Of these elements, only the earliest styles of Beakers (discussed by Cleal, this vol, 6.4, following Case 1977) can consistently be identified within the project area. Sherds, primarily of AOC Beakers, occur in small quantities, their distribution, with the exception of a single example at Stonehenge, entirely in the area of Wilsford Down.

An earlier interpretation of the developing landscape (Richards 1984b) identified the major shift in emphasis which marked the transition from the later Neolithic to the earlier Bronze Age. The potential motivation, whether economic or ideological, will be reconsidered below.

This section, called for convenience and by tradition the 'earlier Bronze Age', is less clearly defined than previous episodes in the evolution of the social and environmental landscapes, and even the evidence from Stonehenge itself is more ambiguous than might be expected. The employment of any of the more refined chronological schemes recently offered (for example, Burgess 1980) is largely inappropriate.

The available evidence on which to base this stage of the discussion lies largely within the developing complex of monuments represented by Stonehenge itself, and the funerary landscape which surrounds it. Within this complex, elements of which show evidence of continuity into the subsequent later Bronze Age, a

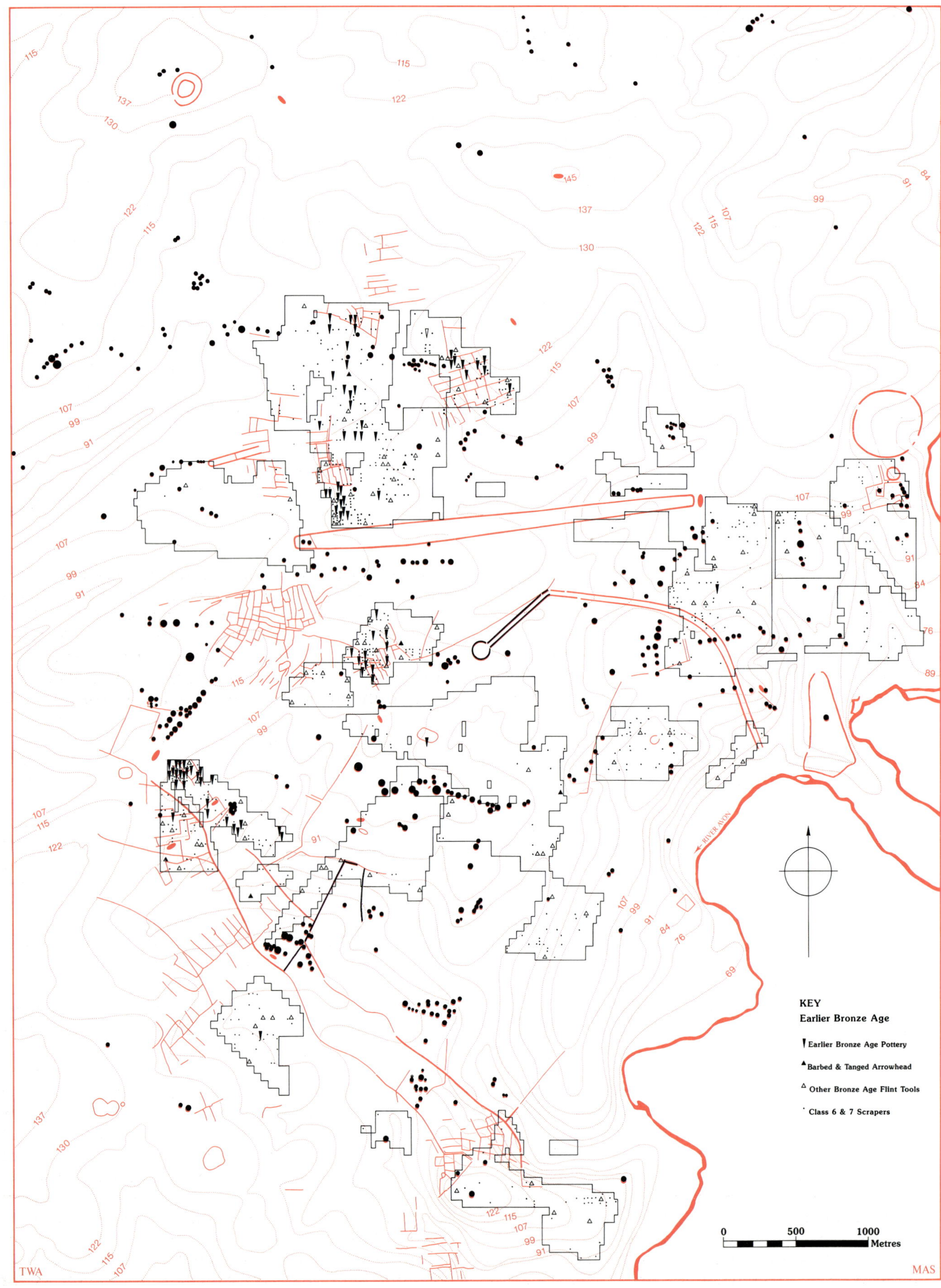

Fig 159 The prehistoric landscape: earlier Bronze Age

small number of radiocarbon determinations together with a range of positive and more closely datable ceramic associations provide a chronological sequence.

The earlier Bronze Age phase at Stonehenge itself is represented by a series of major events involving the remodelling and augmentation of the original, long-abandoned enclosure. These events, the precise sequence and form of which it is inappropriate to discuss in this volume, are conventionally described as belonging to periods II to IIIa (RCHME 1979, 8–11) and can be summarised as follows (events which are not positively dated are italicised):

Period II

- Modification of the original enclosure entrance
- Construction of the first straight stage of the Avenue
- *Erection of the station stones*
- Resetting of the two entrance stones
- Partial construction and dismantling of double bluestone circle

Period IIIa

- Erection of outer sarsen ring
- Erection of horseshoe of five sarsen trilithons
- *Erection of close-set pair of sarsens in enclosure entrance*
- Replacement of station stone 93

Also belonging to this general phase is the Beaker period burial from the enclosure ditch (Evans 1984).

Figure 156 shows available radiocarbon dates for this phase, dates which suggest that this intensive activity spans a period at the end of the third and beginning of the second millennia BC, and shows a strong correlation with available dates for primary burials in round barrows in the immediate area.

In chronological terms, it appears that the construction of this extensive ceremonial and funerary landscape overlaps with the final phases of identifiable activity at Durrington Walls, Woodhenge, and at Coneybury, all of which produced Beaker pottery from secondary contexts in both their interiors and ditches. Both Durrington Walls and Woodhenge produced sherds of AOC Beaker, in neither case from a datable context. Durrington Walls, Woodhenge, and Coneybury, particularly the former two, have been suggested as forming focal elements of a zone (the 'Durrington Zone', Richards 1984b, 182), within which ideology can be identified in both the structure and contents of specific monuments. Perhaps one of the most dramatic aspects of the shift which now takes place is the abandonment of this zone, demonstrated not only by the disuse of the monuments themselves, but in their environmental sequences and within the data from extensive surface collection.

Durrington Walls shows evidence of the abandonment of the long-established pasture (Wainwright and Longworth 1971, 337), and the environmental sequence from Coneybury shows little evidence of the maintenance of the clearing within which the henge is assumed to have been constructed (Bell and Jones, this vol, 4.9 f). The surface evidence east of the King Barrow Ridge shows a scattered pattern, predominantly of less specifically earlier Bronze Age flint tools. The secondary activity at Coneybury henge, represented by earlier Bronze Age deposits in the ditch terminal (this vol, 4.9), cannot be matched with more extensive activity recovered from surface collection within the same area.

For evidence of more positive developments, it is necessary to turn to the eastern half of the study area. Here, the available data must be reviewed within the context of a rapidly developing ceremonial and funerary landscape, of which Stonehenge and the Avenue, discussed above, represent the focal elements.

The area defined as the Stonehenge Environs could quite justifiably be regarded as a single extensive round barrow cemetery, being one of the greatest concentrations of such monuments anywhere in Britain (Fleming 1973; RCHME 1979, map 2). The development of this, on currently available evidence, took place predominantly during the second millennium BC. There has long been an awareness, however, developed initially during the period of antiquarian study (Hoare 1810), of a number of discrete clusters of barrows, consequently identified as individual cemeteries. The major examples within the Stonehenge area are the linear ridgetop cemeteries of the King Barrows (including both the Old and New King Barrows), the Normanton Down group, the Winterbourne Stoke Crossroads group, and the Cursus group (Fig 2). More clustered groups lie further south on Wilsford and Lake Downs and to the north on Durrington Down.

A detailed analysis of individual barrows, many of which were excavated in the early nineteenth century, or the establishment of an accurate sequence of cemetery development, would be a major study in itself and is beyond the remit of this survey. Some elements such as the rich burials of the so-called 'Wessex Culture' are well known, but they are few in number even within the Stonehenge area, and it is clear that the majority of the excavated examples were originally constructed in the earlier Bronze Age.

As noted by many previous observers, perhaps most recently in the interim project report (Richards 1984a, 185–6), the King Barrows, the Normanton Down group, and the Cursus Barrows are carefully positioned on the crests of low ridges to the east, south, and north-west of Stonehenge respectively, positions in which the mounds of the more substantial barrows are silhouetted against the skyline. This positioning emphasises the primary position, within the development of each cemetery, of barrows of bell and bowl form, and potentially of the larger examples of these forms. In many cases, the Lake group being a classic example, barrows of disc, saucer, and pond form appear peripheral to what can be suggested as the originally conceived linear layout of bowl or bell barrows.

Of the groups introduced above, the King Barrows and, to a lesser degree, the Cursus Barrows appear anomalous in their failure to develop into true Wessex cemeteries, which should be exemplified by the full range of fancy barrow forms. This failure on the part of the King Barrows may be seen as reflecting their somewhat peripheral position at the easterly edge of the ceremonial/funerary zone centred on Stonehenge. Certain features of these barrows, the only effectively undisturbed group within the study area, and potentially of early date, also suggest a differing perception of their group function, part cemetery, part boundary, perhaps acting to close off the area formerly of such ideological significance. Recent observations have shown that many of the mounds, including some of the extremely large examples (Amesbury 30, 34), are entirely turf-built, implying the stripping and potentially the consequent 'sterilisation', whether in a practical or symbolic manner, of a considerable area. This method of construction does not seem to be consistently represented within any of the other barrow cemeteries in the Stonehenge area.

The topographic relationship between Stonehenge and its peripheral barrow cemeteries is easily demonstrated; less easy to characterise positively is the concept, previously introduced (Richards 1984b, fig 11.3), of a complementary focal area on Wilsford Down, to which the cemeteries of Lake, Normanton Down, and Winterbourne Stoke Crossroads appear to be related. Focal to this suggested zone is the Wilsford Down North Kite (this vol, 4.12), a unique incomplete enclosure of unknown function, the construction of which is associated with Late Style Beaker.

The barrow cemeteries within this area, to the south and south-west of Stonehenge, demonstrate considerable morphological variety. Two cemeteries, Winterbourne Stoke Crossroads and Lake, contain a focal long barrow, the large example at the former providing the axis for the alignment of the linear group of presumably primary bowl and bell barrows. A consistent feature of these groups, however, is the evidence for accretion and development throughout the earlier Bronze Age with the addition of a variety of barrow forms.

It seems likely that the type of monuments described above would, either individually or collectively, impose local or more widespread constraints on human activities such as settlement or cultivation. The potential for linear cemeteries functioning as boundaries has already been introduced in relation to the King Barrows, implying a possible duality in land use. In order to assess the validity of this idea it is necessary to examine the data from surface collection, and the meagre environmental evidence available for this period.

With the exception of the data from the eastern half of the study area discussed above, the only direct evidence for the earlier Bronze Age environment relates to the re-use of Stonehenge (Evans 1984). Here, perhaps not surprisingly, evidence indicates the localised creation and maintenance of open grassland, a pattern which it is tempting to extend as far as the assumedly visible barrow cemeteries, the King Barrows, Normanton Down, and the Cursus Barrows, to suggest a zone of grassland surrounding Stonehenge (Richards 1984b, fig 11.3). The extent of this zone is, however, unproven, as is any firm indication of extensive and formalised arable cultivation during the earlier Bronze Age. The evidence, whether inferred from the many descriptions of soil profiles beneath round barrows (eg Ashbee 1978, 1981) or from molluscan analysis, consistently indicates an extensive grassland regime within the western half of the study area. Recently obtained data from the primary silts of round barrow Durrington 3 (Allen *et al* forthcoming) confirm this impression. Even the faunal remains from this phase at Coneybury Henge (this vol, 4.9 e), on the margins of this environmental zone, indicate the first significant appearance of sheep/goats as indicators of extensive areas of maintained grassland.

Previous statements (Richards 1984b, 185), have suggested the appearance of arable cultivation in the earlier Bronze Age, based largely on the evidence from the eastern end of the Lesser Cursus (this vol, 4.5). The molluscan evidence now available (Entwistle, this vol, 4.5 e) suggests only a minimal impact caused by cultivation at this early date, and the independent evidence provided by the incorporation of this part of the Lesser Cursus into a field system (Fig 43) should, owing to its more direct relationship with the Fargo Wood later Bronze Age settlement, more appropriately be discussed in that section. Within the western half of the study area the data from extensive surface collection must therefore be examined against a background of extensive and maintained grassland. Within this zone a wide range of ideological constraints may have operated and, in addition, despite the absence of positive dating evidence, physical boundaries, potentially representing the formalisation of agricultural units, may have started to develop.

The evidence from surface collection differs considerably from that employed in the discussion of the Neolithic period. Arrowheads of barbed and tanged form are extremely rare surface finds, in contrast to the considerable quantities from casual past collections in other southern chalkland areas, for example the Berkshire Downs (Bradley and Ellison 1975, fig 5.1), the Avebury area (Alexander Keiller Museum collection index), and Sussex (Gardiner 1984, 37). The pattern is, however, similar to that from Cranbourne Chase, where transverse arrowheads outnumber later forms by a ratio of about five to one (Gardiner 1984, 37). Assessment of an earlier Bronze Age lithic element within the surface collection material therefore relies on a small number of additional tool types, for example borers and 'tool kits' (borer/scrapers), which may be associated with later Bronze Age activity, and specific scraper types. Of these (types 6 and 7, Fig 15; Riley, this vol, 5.3), the more numerous type 7 'thumbnail' scrapers (Gibson 1982) can be regarded as providing the most reliable indicator of date, if not of specific function. Additional surface evidence is provided by pottery, the increasingly extensive survival of which provides both the potential for independent spatial assessment and a more refined chronology for the activities suggested by less datable lithic artefacts.

Although the combined surface data for the earlier Bronze Age (Fig 158) show a similar broad emphasis on those areas which demonstrated extensive later Neolithic activity, a greater degree of nucleation is now apparent. Foci can be identified in three locations:

1 Immediately south and south-east of Winterbourne Stoke Crossroads, primarily within The Diamond (59). Here a nucleated scatter of pottery and of type 7 scrapers, also including one of the few plano-convex knives recovered from surface collection, lies close to the area of later occupation, the 'hut settlement', recorded in 1967 during road construction (Vatcher and Vatcher 1968; this vol, 4.14). Although close, the absence of any earlier Bronze Age pottery from within the admittedly small assemblage from this site suggests settlement shift within an established focal area. Further indication that the patterns of fields and boundary earthworks, thought in

their initial phases to be associated with the later Bronze Age settlement, may originate earlier, may be inferred from the more sporadic surface data recorded to the south and south-east. Here earlier Bronze Age pottery was recorded on the north-east side of a main 'spinal' linear, its distribution reflecting that of the earthwork. The lack of similar pottery on the south-west side of the linear may be the result of differential survival or recovery, but could equally well be used to suggest the existence of a boundary, if not at this early stage a physical one, along this alignment.

2 Within a restricted area on the Stonehenge Triangle (54). Again the primary association is between pottery and type 7 scrapers, occurring within an area which here can be suggested as tightly defined and not associated with areas of apparently contemporary, but more extensive and less defined activity. The sole barbed and tanged arrowhead from within this scatter was an unfinished example, suggesting either manufacture or loss/discard within a settlement context, rather than as part of an essentially off-site activity.

3 Immediately north of the Stonehenge Cursus, adjacent to Fargo Wood. The area, identified primarily by a surface scatter of pottery, again with associated flint tools, lacks definition to the south, where it could possibly extend over the Stonehenge Cursus, and to the west into Fargo Wood. There is a marked similarity here with 1 (above), the establishment of a broadly preferred settlement location showing evidence of both continuity and slight settlement shift. To the north extensive scatters of pottery and flint tools can also be identified, the interpretation of which depends largely on a perception not only of the scatter described above, but also of its potential subsistence base. Cleal (this vol, 6.5) suggests that certain small elements of the pottery assemblage from this area may represent ploughed-out burials, as they rarely occur outside a funerary context. The absence even of a potential context for the remainder of the material, largely unfeatured sherds and therefore not considered within Cleal's discussion, makes functional assessment more of a problem.

The extensive zone of grassland within which both the scatters lay would have provided a suitable cleared and potentially territorially defined area for the establishment of a more formal regime of arable cultivation. The date for the establishment of the 'Celtic' field systems which lie within this area and more extensively in a broad band to the west and south of Stonehenge is uncertain, although identifiable relationships with settlement elements of the later Bronze Age suggests a more direct association. However, these fields, established initially through processes of definition and clearance, later enhanced by localised colluviation, may reflect the formalisation of established arable cultivation patterns rather than their introduction.

Within such a landscape, primarily of grassland, but with an uncertain but increasing arable component, the more scattered surface patterns of pottery and flint represent a range of activities, within which manuring of outfields, well-documented in later periods (Figs 18 and 19), can be suggested.

Whatever the activities represented by the scatters extending north across Horse Hospital (64) and Fargo Road (53), it seems likely that they are not all associated with the potential settlement area as much as 1.5km to the south. Additional foci may lie north of the Packway Road, within the area unavailable for surface collection, and the potential for a further focus in the area of the Larkhill Army Camp is perhaps suggested by the data from Durrington Down (65). Surface material here, the south-westerly extent of which appears to be defined by a shallow dry valley, is also associated with field systems, some elements of which are more strongly developed than others within the study area.

The physical and ideological constraints imposed by the construction of round barrows, either in groups or individually, can be demonstrated within the area to the north of the Stonehenge Cursus. Here too, a pragmatic integration of the needs of both agriculture and ideology can be demonstrated.

The sample excavation of the remains of round barrow Durrington 7, the primary burial from which can be dated to the late third millennium BC, demonstrated that the barrow was unditched and originally consisted of a cairn constructed of flint nodules. This form of construction is unusual within the study area and may suggest a duality of function: the construction of a funerary cairn combined with field clearance. This barrow appears to form the focus for a field boundary which, running down a shallow slope, cannot be considered to be purely accumulative and may therefore have incorporated elements of deliberate construction, possibly associated with linear clearance. Approximately 700m to the east of Durrington 7, a number of dense and nucleated scatters of flint nodules were recorded during surface collection. Although potentially solely the result of field clearance, they may also incorporate the dual function suggested for the barrow described above.

The evidence from this area, although slight, does point to the origins of arable cultivation within the Stonehenge area in the earlier Bronze Age. In common with much of Britain, the form of settlements and structures of the earlier Bronze Age has proved elusive. This period appears, however, to mark a changing emphasis within the broad subsistence base, and a stabilisation of patterns of settlement and land use which see their final development within the subsequent later Bronze Age.

10.4 The later Bronze Age (Fig 160)

Any discussion of the later Bronze Age landscape around Stonehenge involves an assumption of continuity and evolution in the more complete development of the patterns of fields and boundaries, the origins of which have been suggested as lying within the earlier Bronze Age. In some cases settlement shows evidence, if not of strict continuity, then of the maintenance of preferred locations, and the first enclosed settlements can also be identified. Stonehenge continues to be maintained and modified into the later Bronze Age, providing both a local and more widespread ideologi-

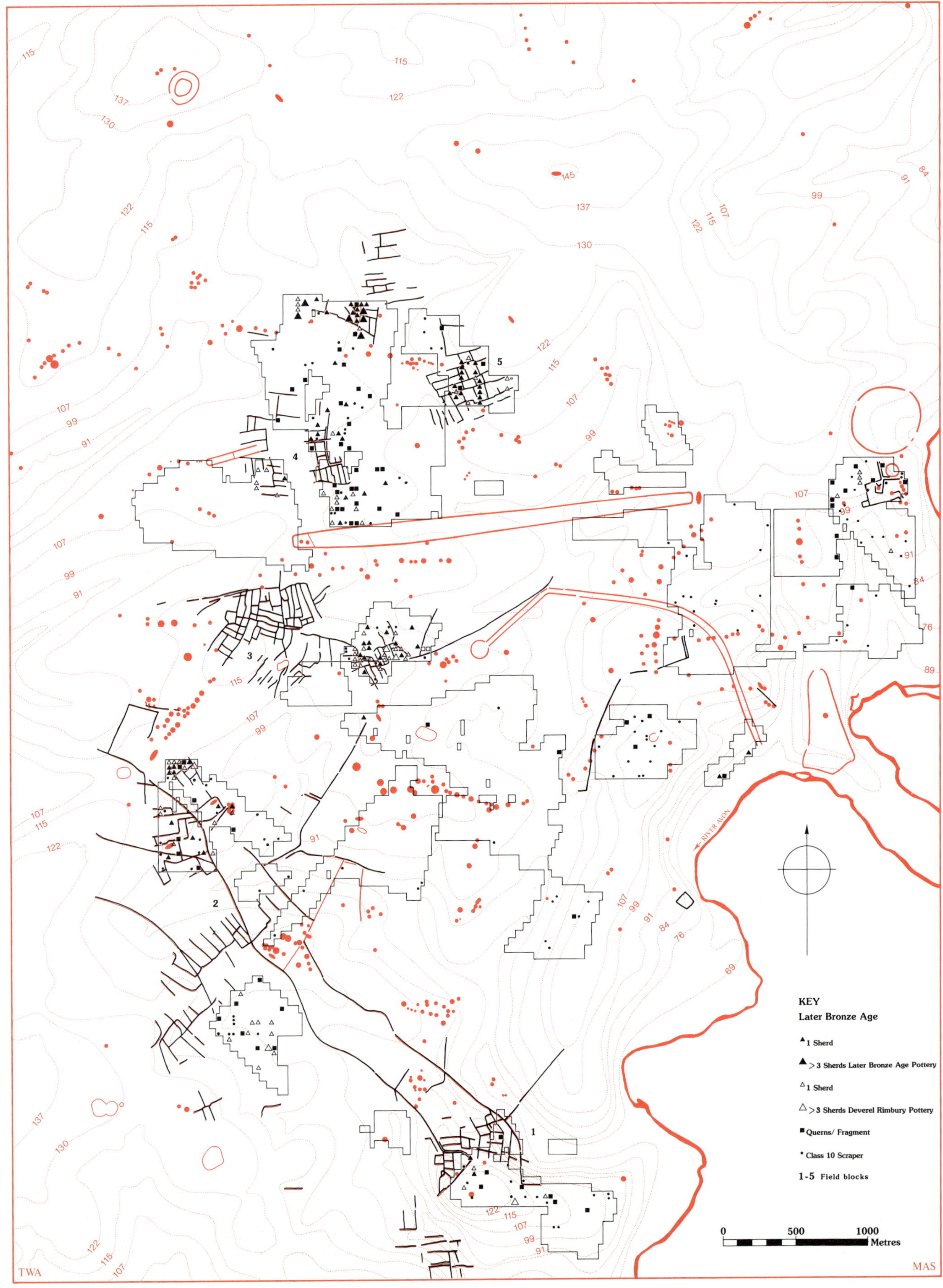

Fig 160 The prehistoric landscape: later Bronze Age

cal focus long after its resurrection in the Early Bronze Age.

The precise nature and date of the later sequence of construction and modification at Stonehenge is again uncertain. A clustering of the available radiocarbon dates for periods II–IIIa suggested their inclusion, as a phase of reconstruction, within the earlier Bronze Age. The events relating to periods IIIb, IIIc, and IV (RCHME 1979, 8–11), appear to lie as a chronologically discrete phase within the second half of the second millennium BC and can be summarised as follows (events which are not positively dated are italicised):

Period IIIb
Erection of oval bluestone structure
Digging of Y-holes
Digging of Z-holes

Period IIIc
Rearrangement of bluestones in circle and horseshoe

Period IV
Extension of the Avenue to the River Avon at West Amesbury

Of the events relating to Stonehenge itself, only the digging of the Y-holes in period IIIb can be dated on the basis of a single radiocarbon determination (I 2445, Fig 156, Table 137) to the mid-second millennium BC. Two radiocarbon determinations are available for the Avenue from the end of the straight section in Stonehenge Bottom to the point close to the River Avon. Of these dates, only the earlier (BM 1079) can be employed, despite a large standard deviation, as the other date is clearly stated as deriving from a bulked sample of bone and antler recovered from both ditches of the monument (RCHME 1979, 11). It can be suggested that the extension of the Avenue, which may have been carried out in a piecemeal manner, is likely to be associated with the final dated phase of construction at Stonehenge itself. As noted by the RCHME (1979, 11), the course of the Avenue east of the King Barrow Ridge suggests that it postdates specific round barrows, most probably of earlier Bronze Age date. A critical appraisal of the available radiocarbon dating does, however, suggest that the latest phases of the Avenue are unlikely to lie as late in the Bronze Age as has previously been suggested.

It is difficult, within a later Bronze Age ideology of continuing funerary emphasis, to integrate the maintenance of an archaic monumental tradition, apparently represented at Stonehenge. Of whatever form and precise date, the final phases represent a unique longevity.

There is less positive evidence available for a parallel development of the funerary landscape, and the addition of barrows of Wessex form to many of the Early Bronze Age cemeteries represents the final easily identifiable phase of extension. However, small bowl barrows, many of which appear to have at most a very slight ditch, can be seen in peripheral positions at some barrow cemeteries, and may be, as suggested by Annable and Simpson (1964, 30), of Deverel-Rimbury date. The excavation of ploughed barrows peripheral to the Lake group (Grimes 1964) clearly demonstrated the scale of some late barrows. Wilsford-cum-Lake 36g, a ditched bowl barrow containing a cremation associated with a fragmentary Barrel Urn, was only 6m in diameter.

The occurrence of Deverel-Rimbury material within the Winterbourne Stoke Crossroads cemetery has previously been noted (Barrett and Bradley 1980, 195), and small barrows within the cluster Winterbourne Stoke 17–21b, to the north-west of the main linear group with its Wessex additions, may be suggested as being of this date. A self-contained cluster of small barrows, apparently of bowl form but now ploughed out, lies only 600m to the south-east of the Winterbourne Stoke Crossroads long barrow. Nearly all these barrows (Wilsford 35–36e) are recorded by Colt Hoare as containing simple unaccompanied cremations (Hoare 1810).

Less obvious to assess, both from surface evidence and from the records of past excavation, in which the emphasis lay in the burial record of the barrow mound, is the potential for peripherally placed secondary burials. The area around Stonehenge is notable for a lack of Middle Bronze Age cemeteries, although the ditch of Shrewton 5a, approximately 4km to the north-west of Stonehenge, produced at least 18 cremations associated with Bucket and Globular Urns (Green and Rollo-Smith 1984, 258–65). Also to the north of Stonehenge, sample excavation of round barrow Durrington 7 and its immediate context (W57, this vol, 4.11) produced considerable evidence for a wide variety of secondary funerary activities, here broadly associated with Deverel-Rimbury pottery.

In the absence of more consistent sample excavation of both the immediate context of individual barrows and of barrow cemeteries, the possibility cannot be dismissed that they were later used as foci for later Bronze Age inhumation or cremation cemeteries. It is consequently extremely difficult to suggest the nature of the relationship of Stonehenge to its surrounding funerary landscape.

The relationship of Stonehenge to the developing agricultural landscape is easier to assess, as 'Celtic' fields, boundary earthworks, and enclosures, many of which can now only be recorded by aerial photography (RCHME 1979, map 1), provide an extensive if strictly undated framework. For the purposes of this discussion, unless specifically proven to the contrary, it will be assumed that this evidence relates to the later Bronze Age phase of the Stonehenge landscape.

The components of this framework, settlements and enclosures, boundary earthworks and ditches, and 'Celtic' fields, are discussed individually and in detail by the RCHME (1979, 20–31). The current discussion will review the combined patterns and suggestions of sequence and association, in conjunction with the data from surface collection. The latter inevitably relies on a more restricted range of artefacts, within which no firmly diagnostic flint tools can be included. As Riley notes (this vol, 5.3), expedient flint scrapers may equally well reflect a range of less specific functions rather than a consistently inept technology. Surface material regarded as diagnostic includes Deverel-Rimbury and Late Bronze Age pottery, which appears to survive well, even occurring in areas where no other surface pottery of prehistoric date was recovered, together with querns (excluding rotary types) and rubbers. This latter class of artefact has been included on the basis of its strong association with the only excavated site of this phase (W34, this vol, 4.14). However, as individual items within this class are undatable, the distribution may only strictly be used as an adjunct to more firmly dated evidence.

The overall distribution of fields is concentrated in the western half of the study area, although the RCHME (1979, map 1) do note 'traces of "Celtic" fields' on the ridgetop and west-facing slopes centred on SU 130405. The overall bias in distribution seems unlikely to have been produced by the total destruction of fields within the eastern half of the study area. This area was more intensively cultivated during the historic period, but it can be assumed that fields, had they existed, would have survived sufficiently to have been recorded by aerial photography. Molluscan evidence from this area does suggest some cultivation at Coneybury Henge associated with the slighting of the enclosure bank and dating to the later Bronze Age (Bell and Jones, this vol, 4.9 f). In contrast, the evidence from Amesbury 42 long barrow (Entwistle, this vol, 4.7 e) suggests that cultivation cannot be positively identified until the Roman period. This suggested pattern of land use may be reinforced by the total lack of colluvial deposits from Stonehenge Bottom where sampled in three places (this vol, 4.16). It seems unlikely that extensive cultivation could have taken place on Coneybury Hill and the King Barrow Ridge without producing some evidence in the form of hillwash in adjacent catchment zones.

The discussion of fields and their association with the range of identifiable landscape and settlement elements noted above must therefore concentrate on a broad zone within which five relatively discrete blocks of fields can be identified. These are, from the south (located as blocks 1–5 on Fig 160): 1 Rox Hill; 2 Winterbourne Stoke Crossroads (south); 3 Stonehenge Down; 4 Fargo Wood; 5 Durrington Down.

1 Rox Hill. The majority of the fields lying on the slopes of Rox Hill are contained by, and integrated with, a pair of parallel boundary earthworks. Hoare (1810, 213) found evidence of settlement, assumed to be of prehistoric date, possibly associated with a small enclosure which appears to postdate some of the fields. Surface collection produced evidence of a small Roman settlement on the summit of Rox Hill (Fig 17, details in archive), as well as small quantities of later Bronze Age pottery.

2 Winterbourne Stoke Crossroads (south). Over 120 hectares of fragmentary fields have been recorded to the south of Winterbourne Stoke Crossroads, but they should strictly be considered as two blocks, (a) and (b), separated by a shallow east–west dry valley to the north-west of the Lake Barrows.

The most southerly block, (a), appears to be cut by both the main linear ditch running from Rox Hill to Winterbourne Stoke Crossroads and by a parallel but more westerly example. Suggestions of Late Bronze Age settlement activity were recorded from the ditch of round barrow Wilsford-cum-Lake 38 (Grimes 1964) which contained pottery and animal bones.

The complex of fields and boundary earthworks immediately south of Winterbourne Stoke Crossroads, (b), can be suggested as directly associated with the 'hut' settlement recorded in 1967 (Vatcher and Vatcher 1968; this vol, 4.15). The settlement, within which three post-built round houses and associated features were identified, is of Thorney Down type (Stone 1941), a parallel reinforced by the admittedly tiny assemblage of associated pottery. This suggests a Deverel-Rimbury date, and surface collection produced a restricted scatter of pottery of similar date immediately to the south. However, it has already been suggested that this settlement focus may originally have developed during the earlier Bronze Age, and surface collection, which produced not only Late Bronze Age pottery but also a small nucleated scatter of Roman material within the nearby field system (Fig 17, details in archive), suggests that it remained a preferred location. The complex of fields, settlements, and boundaries can be suggested as having considerable potential for development and modification over a long period of time, perhaps suggested by the inconsistent relationships exhibited by specific elements. Linear earthworks appear both to respect and to cut fields, their boundary function perhaps emphasised by the variation in field alignment to either side. Surface collection produced little later Bronze Age material from the area of the field systems. It is unfortunate that the examination of the 'stockade trench' associated with the Crossroads settlement, here potentially part of the linear earthwork complex (Fig 148), produced only ambiguous dating evidence, mainly from the upper ditch fills.

Further south, on Wilsford Down, the excavation of two small sections through linear earthworks (W31, area M, and W51, this vol, 4.13) produced no dating evidence at all. It does appear, however, that the North Kite enclosure (this vol, 4.12) is an independent Early Bronze Age structure, later integrated into a more extensive system of boundary earthworks. The date of the North Kite cannot be employed to suggest a similarly early date for the entire system. Within the area of Wilsford and Normanton Downs the layout of some boundary earthworks, here unassociated with 'Celtic' fields, and incorporating 'funnelled' entrance gaps, strongly suggests elements of stock control. Potentially associated with this pastoral zone is the Wilsford Shaft, which, although possibly embodying some ideological significance, may, on the basis of the currently available information (Ashbee 1963; RCHME 1979, 19 and fig 12; Ashbee *et al* 1989), equally plausibly be regarded as a well. Recently available radiocarbon dates from the primary fill confirm a date in the mid-second millennium BC.

3 No information concerning potential date is available for the majority of the complex group of fields on Stonehenge Down, which includes a linked enclosure and boundary earthwork, the latter marking the most northerly extent of this type of feature within the study area. The well-defined northern boundary of the field block incorporates a round barrow (Winterbourne Stoke 81), and the south-western corner of the fields exhibits a similar relationship with Winterbourne Stoke 23a which, on excavation, produced a primary unaccompanied cremation (Hoare 1810). A linked but less structured

block of fields to the east, elements of which lie less than 600m from Stonehenge, is, however, strongly associated with surface pottery of both Deverel-Rimbury and Late Bronze Age date. Further evidence of a later Bronze Age date for these particular fields may be provided by their apparent relationship with the south-western end of the Stonehenge 'underpass' boundary earthwork (Vatcher and Vatcher 1968, 108). Pottery from this ditch, which also included a palisade and an intrusive crouched burial in a terminal, appears to be of Deverel-Rimbury date.

4 The Fargo Wood field systems are in reality more extensive and coherent than Figure 160 suggests. Traces of fields can be identified within Fargo Wood, linking the easterly and westerly blocks, and also to the south where it can be suggested (W56a, this vol, 4.6) that the earthworks of the Stonehenge Cursus were utilised as field boundaries during the later Bronze Age. The integration of the eastern end of the Lesser Cursus into this field system has already been noted, this area producing direct evidence for a phase of Bronze Age cultivation (Entwistle, this vol, 4.5 e). The settlement evidence associated with this field block was not located during the programme of extensive surface collection and consequently does not appear on Figure 160. Subsequent sample excavation (W34, this vol, 4.14) failed to produce structural evidence or strictly stratified deposits, but did confirm an association with both Deverel-Rimbury and Late Bronze Age pottery and with considerable numbers of quern fragments, the latter suggesting a greater emphasis on cereal cultivation. The limited evidence from faunal remains (Maltby, this vol, 4.14 e) shows an almost equal balance of cattle and sheep/goat, an indication of a classic mixed farming assemblage. Beyond the immediate area of the settlement focus, there is little evidence from surface collection for the extent of associated activity. The sole evidence for use of the surrounding fields has come from the sample excavation of a flint scatter approximately 200m to the north of W34 (W32, this vol, 4.4). Here, a field boundary appeared to relate to a localised soil change, and associated pottery suggested the use of the field during the later Bronze Age. The alignment of the field block to the east of Fargo Wood on an isolated round barrow (Amesbury 113) 250m east of the settlement area is strongly reminiscent of the consistent spatial relationship between barrows and settlements of this date suggested by Barrett and Bradley (1980, 195).

5 To the north, the area of Durrington Down includes two blocks of fields separated by a nucleated cemetery of round barrows (Durrington 10–23), some of which contained inurned cremations (Hoare 1810). The most westerly block, (a), has already been discussed in relation to round barrow Durrington 7 (W57, this vol, 4.11) on which one element of the field system appears to be aligned. Other round barrows, Durrington 6, 8, and 9, also appear to be firmly integrated with this particular block. Related surface evidence consists predominantly of Deverel-Rimbury pottery, which occurs in several discrete clusters, including an easterly example which lies beyond the area of the field system. One cluster, directly associated with a round barrow and consequently assumed to relate to funerary practices, was sampled by excavation (W57A, this vol, 4.11). Although not appearing to be of domestic character, this scatter could not be interpreted as the remains of an urnfield and may more realistically be suggested as representing an area of structured pottery deposition, potentially related to funerary practices. The remaining clusters of pottery, if unassociated with existing funerary foci, may equally well represent domestic areas within the field system. The more coherent field block to the east, (b), is also associated with pottery predominantly of Deverel-Rimbury date, but here more scattered and failing to exhibit the degree of clustering noted from the previous field block.

The general impression gained from the field systems discussed above is that they exhibit a certain coherence in their initial form, primarily in the integration of round barrows and, in the hints from surface material, of an earlier Bronze Age origin. Once initiated, unless effected by a radical change either in the subsistence base or in territorial divisions, there is no reason for the development of fields to be anything but a process of piecemeal accretion. The uneasy relationship of some fields and boundary earthworks may hint at such radical changes, perhaps more a developing territoriality than the classic increased emphasis on pastoralism.

The remaining element of the settlement evidence for the later Bronze Age, and one for which a more pastoral emphasis has been suggested, lies in the far north-east of the study area. The Durrington 'Egg' (Cunnington 1929) is a small enclosure of Middle Bronze Age date, subsequently demonstrated to be part of a more extensive area of similarly dated activity (Stone *et al* 1954, 165–6; RCHME 1979, 23–4). The paucity of finds from the enclosure led to the original suggestion that it was for stock rather than for human habitation. The postholes recorded within the interior do, however, suggest the presence of a building, and consequently the original interpretation may not be totally appropriate. Economic evidence from the enclosure included charred grains of barley, indicating some involvement in cereal cultivation although the surrounding area appears to be devoid of identifiable 'Celtic' fields. The evidence from surface collection in the immediate area of this complex is slight, consisting of a very few sherds of later Bronze Age pottery and of fragments of querns. The latter, of uncertain form, may be associated with the nearby Roman settlement (Wainwright *et al* 1971), extensive traces of which were recorded by surface collection (Fig 17, details in archive).

The later Bronze Age landscape in the Stonehenge area appears to demonstrate a considerable degree of stability, the evidence for which can be seen in the established areas of cultivation, and in the continuity of settlement location from the earlier Bronze Age onwards. The area cannot be considered as marginal in any way, although the thin soils would have had a limited productive capacity without periods of fallow and the application of manure to enhance fertility. It is difficult therefore to suggest the cause, if environmental, for the consistent lack of evidence from the Iron Age for the core Stonehenge area.

10.5 The Stonehenge Environs in the final prehistoric and historic periods

The preceding sections have brought together the range of data available for the Stonehenge Environs on which to base discussion of the development of the prehistoric landscape throughout the Neolithic and Bronze Age periods.

This development has been demonstrated as one in which environmental and economic trends perhaps indicative of those occurring elsewhere in southern Britain are here played out against a background of increasing ideological, political, and social complexity. This would appear to reach a peak in the earlier Bronze Age with the extensive formality of the ceremonial and funerary landscape centred on a revitalised Stonehenge. Subsequent developments, admittedly involving the maintenance of an archaic monument, suggest a degree of conservatism, perhaps linked to the decline of the economic supremacy formerly enjoyed by the Wessex chalklands.

A stability is evident within the later Bronze Age landscape in the Stonehenge Environs, based apparently on mixed farming and with a number of identifiable settlement foci. It is perhaps therefore surprising that there is very little evidence of continuity of this apparently established pattern.

Evidence of Iron Age activity within the study area ranges considerably in scale, with the most coherent settlement evidence occurring in the eastern half of the study area close to the River Avon. Vespasian's Camp, a univallate hillfort possibly of earlier Iron Age date, lies on a prominent spur immediately above a meander of the river. To the north, traces of both enclosed and unenclosed settlement of later Iron Age date have been recorded within and around Durrington Walls (Stone *et al* 1954, 158, 164, 174–5; Wainwright and Longworth 1971, 307–28).

Despite this background, encompassing a wide range of settlement evidence, albeit from a restricted topographic zone, project fieldwork produced virtually no evidence of Iron Age activity. No pottery of this date was recovered by surface collection, and, beyond the areas of settlement noted above, only sporadic activity has previously been recorded, from Stonehenge (Atkinson 1979) and from the upper levels of the Wilsford Shaft (Ashbee 1963; Raymond in Ashbee *et al* 1989).

In the absence of dating evidence the environmental background for this period is difficult to determine, although available data suggest that the extensive grassland regime suggested for the later Bronze Age was largely maintained, not only in the Iron Age, but throughout the historic period.

Some indication of the sporadic nature and scale of Roman activity recovered by surface collection has been shown in Figure 17. Beyond this indication of a very scattered pattern of settlement, perhaps again based on pastoral activity, the only specific information previously recorded comes from the margin of the River Avon. Here, to the west of Woodhenge, the true extent of an area of recorded settlement (Wainwright *et al* 1971) was suggested by pottery and other finds recovered by surface collection. Some indication of cultivation at this period comes from the ditch of Amesbury 42 long barrow (W58, this vol, 4.7 e), and the occurrence of scattered Roman pottery within areas of 'Celtic' fields may indicate their continued use.

The pattern of settlement during the Saxon and medieval periods is focused firmly on the valleys of the Rivers Till and Avon, and it can be assumed that the pattern of valley edge cultivation and downland grazing, evidenced from post-medieval documentation (RCHME 1979, map 3), was long established.

This generally benevolent pattern of land use can thus be seen to have existed for several millennia, dating back to the Bronze Age if not before. It was not until the present century that the palimpsest began to be damaged through dramatic and widespread changes in the farming regime.

11 Summary, assessment, and continuing threats

11.1 Summary of the project results and assessment in the light of the original objectives of the project

The original aim of the Stonehenge Environs Project was to identify the prehistoric settlements within the study area, and to present a report on their state of preservation, in order that a management strategy could be developed by the relevant authorities.

These objectives were quite explicit, and relate both academically and more practically to the identification of prehistoric settlement. Academically the settlements were seen as fundamental to the investigation of major themes of subsistence, population, and social organisation, whereas the requirements of cultural resource management related more to definition and evaluation.

The report here presented has been devoted almost entirely to the theme of landscape and social evolution through time; the more specific recommendations for preservation and management were presented to the Historic Buildings and Monuments Commission for England in 1984 (Richards 1984a).

The basis of the investigation involved a number of stages:

1 Location, by means of extensive surface collection;
2 Definition, by means of intensive 'total' surface collection;
3 Geophysical survey, location of subsoil features;
4 Geophysical/geochemical survey, further characterisation of the ploughsoil;
5 Sample excavation –
   a ploughsoil for artefact recovery and refinement of spatial patterning
   b subsoil features for recovery of closed groups of robust artefacts (flint/stone), fragile artefacts (pottery), and associated environmental and economic data (animal bones, seeds, charcoals, and snails)

In combination, the component elements all serve in the construction of an overall assessment of the extent, nature, chronology, and economy of each 'site'. Once identified and assessed, a wider context could be sought within the results from extensive field survey.

In terms of the general objectives restated above, a number of settlements, or at least settlement activities, of the Neolithic and Bronze Age were located by the fieldwork carried out by the project. Each of these has its own individual characteristics and they serve to highlight the variability of prehistoric settlements. It is clear that our perception of the structure and character of settlement of the fourth to second millennia BC is influenced heavily by external evidence from the first millennium BC. Within southern England excavated sites such as Blackpatch (Drewett 1982) show stable settlements set within organised agricultural landscapes, a pattern repeated in a broadly contemporary but less investigated form within the Stonehenge area. However, this pattern is the product of a long period of landscape modification, and reflects a wide range of changing social, economic, and ideological factors. It simply cannot be projected back into the fourth millennium BC.

With the exception of areas of activity such as Robin Hood's Ball and Durrington Walls, where enclosure may simply serve to define already identified areas of activity, the shifting patterns of subsistence and settlement suggested by the work of the project for the Neolithic and earlier Bronze Age periods do not lend themselves to conventional methods of location and definition. In this alone, the project results may be seen to have a wider significance.

The identification of broadly preferred areas of activity and an assessment of their chronology and functional range is certainly within the capacity of the extensive surface collection data, and has been demonstrated above. What is less certain, however, is the capacity of this level of data, and of that generated by more intensive surface collection, to define more precisely specific foci and to isolate areas of activity within them. The problems lie not only in the nature of the ploughsoil artefacts, the majority of which are not chronologically or functionally specific enough, but in the palimpsest effect of intensive activity in many areas over several millennia. Many of the problems of interpretation can be alleviated, if not overcome, where associated closed groups of material can be recovered in association with the surface material that provided the initial location and subsequent definition.

Therefore, given the nature of the settlement evidence for the Neolithic and Bronze Age, the methodology developed by the project was entirely appropriate. The results are positive and the data generated available for the pursuit of ancillary research themes. This does not mean that a modified approach would not be adopted if the project, or any other project with similar objectives, was to be carried out again.

An awareness, if not a complete understanding, of the economic and environmental background for any settlement under investigation is fundamental. The value of ploughsoil data for environmental and economic studies is slight and, within a chalkland area, restricted essentially to more robust animal bones datable solely on the grounds of spatial association. In contrast, stratified deposits, particularly those which represent single or short-term episodes, have the potential to provide a suite of data, individual elements of which may not be of great value but which in association make possible more confident interpretation.

11.2 Threats to the Stonehenge archaeological landscape

In company with considerable areas of the chalkland of southern England, the Stonehenge landscape has suffered the effects of changing patterns of land use during the medieval and post-medieval periods. The erosion of traditional extensive grassland by arable cultivation has had its most marked effect in the eastern half of the study area. This has meant that the effects of more recent arable extension can be seen more dramatically in areas where grassland survived up until the 1940s. This final phase of grassland conversion saw the deliberate destruction of many monuments, and the reduction of others to a barely recognisable state. In recent decades a state of relative equilibrium has been reached, with many of the surviving monuments scheduled as of national importance. While not guaranteeing immunity from marginal plough erosion, infestation by burrowing animals, or *ad hoc* tree planting, such legislative protection has ensured the survival of a large number of monuments, but only of a relatively restricted range of types.

The current threats from cultivation need to be examined in relationship to two aspects of the archaeological landscape, previously defined as 'monuments' and 'sites' (Richards 1986). The former are the built elements of the archaeological landscape, ditches, banks, mounds and quarries of varying forms, but having a recognisable morphology in their original form. The effect on monuments of destructive processes is therefore quantifiable: the height of a barrow decreases, the profile of a ditch blurs, and the effects even of a single destructive event can be assessed. In contrast, 'sites', areas of activity almost exclusively defined by surface collection, can only be located when some aspect of their archaeological record has been dislocated by cultivation. Even when this happens, it is difficult to define the extent of the 'site', and therefore quantification of the loss is not easy. The other element of such 'sites' lies in their potential for associated sealed deposits, again largely unquantified. Such deposits must be regarded as a hidden resource, of considerable interpretative potential.

Appendix 1 An introduction to the project archive

The archive, which is housed in the Salisbury and South Wiltshire Museum along with the finds, can be broadly divided into three main parts, relating respectively to surface collection, excavation, and post-collection/excavation analysis.

Surface collection

The records relating to this aspect of project fieldwork, which form the basic collection and catalogue record, consist of:

1 Hectare record forms recording details of collector, known archaeology, weather, light and soil conditions, and topographic observations. These are grouped by collection area, and are filed in the order indicated in Table 4, together with annotated field maps.
2 Fieldwalking finds records, grouped as above, which record the breakdown of finds from each collection unit (subdivision of each hectare). Employing the categories shown in Table 5, these form the basic lithic catalogue, and are linked to:
3 Fieldwalking special finds records, which record individual finds (flint tools, non-local stone, pottery).
4 Archival plots of all surface collection artefact classes (pottery by period or style, flint tools by type, flint scrapers by class, etc).

Excavation

The excavation records, which are grouped by individual site (see Table 9), are filed in 'W' number order and consist of:

a Context forms
b Abbreviated context forms
c Graphic registers
d Photographic registers
e Sample registers
f Sieving registers
g Burial records
h Context finds records
j Special finds registers

The graphic record consists of field drawings, indexed by drawing and sheet number to (c) above, and levels books.

The photographic record consists of colour transparencies and monochrome negatives/contact prints and selected prints, indexed to (d) above.

A context index for all sites, indexed in 'W' number order, is contained within a separate file.

Post-collection/excavation

Archival data relating to individual artefact classes are organised as follows.

1 Lithic studies

a Sort forms by site in context order, employing the categories shown in Table 5, and linked to the site special finds register
b Details of analysed flint groups (P A Harding)
c Scraper and transverse arrowhead analysis (H Riley)

2 Ceramic studies

a Individual sherd records indexed by collection area and by site
b Featured sherd records
c Fabric description records

3 Faunal remains

Computer files of individual bone records.

4 Other studies

Archival data relating to other individual studies are filed under two categories:

a Artefacts
b Environmental

The archive also contains the Wiltshire Sites and Monuments data for the study area at the time of survey. This consists of a series of annotated 1:2500 maps, together with related printout.

Appendix 2 Pottery concordance

Excavation

Pot no	*Fig*	*Site/context*	*Pottery type*
P1	28	W2 (1981) Coneybury 'Anomaly'/pit	Early Neo
P2	28	W2 (1981) Coneybury 'Anomaly'/pit	Early Neo
P3	28	W2 (1981) Coneybury 'Anomaly'/pit	Early Neo
P4	28	W2 (1981) Coneybury 'Anomaly'/pit	Early Neo
P5	29	W2 (1981) Coneybury 'Anomaly'/pit	Early Neo
P6	29	W2 (1981) Coneybury 'Anomaly'/pit	Early Neo
P7	29	W2 (1981) Coneybury 'Anomaly'/pit	Early Neo
P8	29	W2 (1981) Coneybury 'Anomaly'/pit	Early Neo
P9	29	W2 (1981) Coneybury 'Anomaly'/pit	Early Neo
P10	29	W2 (1981) Coneybury 'Anomaly'/pit	Early Neo
P11	30	W2 (1981) Coneybury 'Anomaly'/pit	Early Neo
P12	30	W2 (1981) Coneybury 'Anomaly'/pit	Early Neo
P13	30	W2 (1981) Coneybury 'Anomaly'/pit	Early Neo
P14	30	W2 (1981) Coneybury 'Anomaly'/pit	Early Neo
P15	30	W2 (1981) Coneybury 'Anomaly'/pit	Early Neo
P16	30	W2 (1981) Coneybury 'Anomaly'/pit	Early Neo
P17	30	W2 (1981) Coneybury 'Anomaly'/pit	Early Neo
P18	30	W2 (1981) Coneybury 'Anomaly'/pit	Early Neo
P19	30	W2 (1981) Coneybury 'Anomaly'/pit	Early Neo
P20	30	W2 (1981) Coneybury 'Anomaly'/pit	Early Neo
P21	30	W2 (1981) Coneybury 'Anomaly'/pit	Early Neo
P22	30	W2 (1981) Coneybury 'Anomaly'/pit	Early Neo
P23	30	W2 (1981) Coneybury 'Anomaly'/pit	Early Neo
P24	31	W2 (1981) Coneybury 'Anomaly'/pit	Early Neo
P25	31	W2 (1981) Coneybury 'Anomaly'/pit	Early Neo
P26	31	W2 (1981) Coneybury 'Anomaly'/pit	Early Neo
P27	31	W2 (1981) Coneybury 'Anomaly'/pit	Early Neo
P28	31	W2 (1981) Coneybury 'Anomaly'/pit	Early Neo
P29	31	W2 (1981) Coneybury 'Anomaly'/pit	Early Neo
P30	31	W2 (1981) Coneybury 'Anomaly'/pit	Early Neo
P31	31	W2 (1981) Coneybury 'Anomaly'/pit	Early Neo
P32	31	W2 (1981) Coneybury 'Anomaly'/pit	Early Neo
P33	31	W2 (1981) Coneybury 'Anomaly'/pit	Early Neo
P34	31	W2 (1981) Coneybury 'Anomaly'/pit	Early Neo
P35	31	W2 (1981) Coneybury 'Anomaly'/pit	Early Neo
P36	31	W2 (1981) Coneybury 'Anomaly'/pit	Early Neo
P37	31	W2 (1981) Coneybury 'Anomaly'/pit	Early Neo
P38	31	W2 (1981) Coneybury 'Anomaly'/pit	Early Neo
P39	31	W2 (1981) Coneybury 'Anomaly'/pit	Early Neo
P40	31	W2 (1981) Coneybury 'Anomaly'/pit	Early Neo
P41	31	W2 (1981) Coneybury 'Anomaly'/pit	Early Neo
P42	31	W2 (1981) Coneybury 'Anomaly'/pit	Early Neo
P43	31	W2 (1981) Coneybury 'Anomaly'/pit	Early Neo
P44	31	W2 (1981) Coneybury 'Anomaly'/pit	Early Neo
P45	31	W2 (1981) Coneybury 'Anomaly'/pit	Early Neo
P46	31	W2 (1981) Coneybury 'Anomaly'/pit	Early Neo
P47	31	W2 (1981) Coneybury 'Anomaly'/pit	Beaker
P48	31	W2 (1981) Coneybury 'Anomaly'/pit	Dev-Rim
P49	31	W2 (1981) Coneybury 'Anomaly'/pit	Early Neo
P50	31	W2 (1981) Coneybury 'Anomaly'/pit	Early Neo
P51	31	W2 (1981) Coneybury 'Anomaly'/pit	Early Neo
P52	31	W2 (1981) Coneybury 'Anomaly'/pit	Early Neo
P53	35	King Barrow Ridge/pit	Early Neo
P54	35	King Barrow Ridge/pit	Early Neo
P55	35	King Barrow Ridge/pit	Early Neo
P56	35	King Barrow Ridge/pit	Early Neo
P57	108	W2 Coneybury Henge/ditch terminal	Early Neo
P58	108	W2 Coneybury Henge/pit	Grooved Ware
P59	108	W2 Coneybury Henge/pit	Grooved Ware
P60	108	W2 Coneybury Henge/pit	Grooved Ware
P61	108	W2 Coneybury Henge/pit	Grooved Ware
P62	108	W2 Coneybury Henge/pit	Grooved Ware
P63	108	W2 Coneybury Henge/pit	Grooved Ware
P64	108	W2 Coneybury Henge/ditch terminal	Grooved Ware
P65	108	W2 Coneybury Henge/pit	Grooved Ware
P66	108	W2 Coneybury Henge/pit	Grooved Ware
P67	108	W2 Coneybury Henge/pit	Grooved Ware
P68	108	W2 Coneybury Henge/ditch	Beaker
P69	108	W2 Coneybury Henge/ditch	Beaker
P70	108	W2 Coneybury Henge/ditch	Beaker
P71	*108*	*W2 Coneybury Henge/ditch terminal*	*Beaker*
P72	108	W2 Coneybury Henge/ditch terminal	Beaker

Pot no	*Fig*	*Site/context*	*Pottery type*
P73	108	W2 Coneybury Henge/ditch	Beaker
P74	108	W2 Coneybury Henge/pit	Beaker
P75	108	W2 Coneybury Henge/ditch	Beaker
P76	108	W2 Coneybury Henge/ditch	Beaker
P77	108	W2 Coneybury Henge/ditch	Beaker
P78	108	W2 Coneybury Henge/ditch	Beaker
P79	108	W2 Coneybury Henge/ditch	Beaker
P80	108	W2 Coneybury Henge/ditch	Beaker
P81	108	W2 Coneybury Henge/ditch	Beaker
P82	108	W2 Coneybury Henge/ditch	Beaker
P83	108	W2 Coneybury Henge/pit	Beaker
P84	108	W2 Coneybury Henge/ditch	?Biconical Urn
P85	108	W2 Coneybury Henge/ditch	Food Vessel
P86	108	W2 Coneybury Henge/ditch terminal	Collared Urn
P87	108	W2 Coneybury Henge/ditch terminal	Globular Urn
P88	108	W2 Coneybury Henge/ploughsoil	Late Bronze Age
P89	108	W2 Coneybury Henge/ditch terminal	Bucket Urn
P90	119	W31 Wilsford Down/U/S	Peterborough
P91	119	W31 Wilsford Down/ditch	Peterborough
P92	119	W31 Wilsford Down/ditch	Peterborough
P93	119	W31 Wilsford Down/?posthole	Peterborough
P94	119	W31 Wilsford Down/ploughsoil	Peterborough
P95	119	W31 Wilsford Down/ploughsoil	Peterborough
P96	119	W31 Wilsford Down/ploughsoil	Peterborough
P97	119	W31 Wilsford Down/ditch	Peterborough
P98	119	W31 Wilsford Down/ploughsoil	Peterborough
P99	119	W31 Wilsford Down/ploughsoil	Peterborough
P100	119	W31 Wilsford Down/feature	Peterborough
P101	119	W31 Wilsford Down/feature	Peterborough
P102	119	W31 Wilsford Down/ploughsoil	Peterborough
P103	119	W31 Wilsford Down/ploughsoil	Peterborough
P104	119	W31 Wilsford Down/ploughsoil	LN/EBA
P105	119	W31 Wilsford Down/feature	Beaker
P106	119	W31 Wilsford Down/feature	Beaker
P107	119	W31 Wilsford Down/ploughsoil	LN/EBA
P108	119	W31 Wilsford Down/feature	LN/EBA
P109	119	W31 Wilsford Down/feature	LN/EBA
P110	119	W31 Wilsford Down/ploughsoil	Beaker
P111	119	W31 Wilsford Down/ploughsoil	Beaker
P112	119	W31 Wilsford Down/ploughsoil	Beaker
P113	119	W31 Wilsford Down/ploughsoil	Beaker
P114	119	W31 Wilsford Down/ploughsoil	Beaker
P115	119	W31 Wilsford Down/feature	LN/EBA
P116	119	W31 Wilsford Down/ploughsoil	Collared Urn
P117	119	W31 Wilsford Down/feature	LN/EBA
P118	40	W32 Fargo Wood I/sorted horizon ploughsoil	Peterborough
P119	40	W32 Fargo Wood I/sorted horizon below ploughsoil	Peterborough
P120	40	W32 Fargo Wood I/ploughsoil	Beaker
P121	40	W32 Fargo Wood I/sorted horizon below ploughsoil	Beaker
P122	40	W32 Fargo Wood I/sorted horizon below ploughsoil	Beaker
P123	40	W32 Fargo Wood I/sorted horizon below ploughsoil	Beaker
P124	40	W32 Fargo Wood I/sorted horizon below ploughsoil	Beaker
P125	40	W32 Fargo Wood I/sorted horizon below ploughsoil	Beaker
P126	40	W32 Fargo Wood I/sorted horizon below ploughsoil	Beaker
P127	40	W32 Fargo Wood I/sorted horizon below ploughsoil	Beaker
P128	40	W32 Fargo Wood I/sorted horizon below ploughsoil	Dev-Rim
P129	40	W32 Fargo Wood I/sorted horizon below ploughsoil	Dev-Rim
P130	40	W32 Fargo Wood I/ploughsoil	Dev-Rim
P131	40	W32 Fargo Wood I/ploughsoil	Dev-Rim
P132	40	W32 Fargo Wood I/sorted horizon below ploughsoil	Dev-Rim
P133	40	W32 Fargo Wood I/sorted horizon below ploughsoil	Late Bronze Age
P134	40	W32 Fargo Wood I/sorted horizon below ploughsoil	Late Bronze Age
P135	40	W32 Fargo Wood I/sorted horizon below ploughsoil	Indeterminate
P136	40	W32 Fargo Wood I/sorted horizon below ploughsoil	Late Bronze Age
P137	40	W32 Fargo Wood I/surface collection	Beaker
P138	40	W32 Fargo Wood I/surface collection	Beaker
P139	144	W34 Fargo Wood II/ploughsoil	Peterborough
P140	144	W34 Fargo Wood II/sorted horizon	Peterborough
P141	144	W34 Fargo Wood II/ploughsoil	Beaker
P142	144	W34 Fargo Wood II/ploughsoil	Beaker
P143	144	W34 Fargo Wood II/ploughsoil	Beaker
P144	144	W34 Fargo Wood II/ploughsoil	Beaker
P145	144	W34 Fargo Wood II/ploughsoil	Beaker
P146	144	W34 Fargo Wood II/ploughsoil	Beaker
P147	144	W34 Fargo Wood II/sorted horizon	Beaker
P148	144	W34 Fargo Wood II/sorted horizon	Beaker
P149	*144*	*W34 Fargo Wood II/ploughsoil*	*Beaker*
P150	144	W34 Fargo Wood II/ploughsoil	Beaker

Pot no	*Fig*	*Site/context*	*Pottery type*
P151	144	W34 Fargo Wood II/feature	Beaker
P152	144	W34 Fargo wood II/ploughsoil	Late Bronze Age
P153	144	W34 Fargo Wood II/ploughsoil	Late Bronze Age
P154	144	W34 Fargo Wood II/ploughsoil	Late Bronze Age
P155	144	W34 Fargo Wood II/ploughsoil	Late Bronze Age
P156	144	W34 Fargo Wood II/feature	Late Bronze Age
P157	144	W34 Fargo Wood II/feature	Late Bronze Age
P158	144	W34 Fargo Wood II/ploughsoil	Late Bronze Age
P159	144	W34 Fargo Wood II/ploughsoil	Late Bronze Age
P160	144	W34 Fargo Wood II/ploughsoil	Late Bronze Age
P161	144	W34 Fargo Wood II/ploughsoil	Late Bronze Age
P162	144	W34 Fargo Wood II/ploughsoil	Late Bronze Age
P163	144	W34 Fargo Wood II/ploughsoil	Late Bronze Age
P164	144	W34 Fargo Wood II/ploughsoil	Late Bronze Age
P165	144	W34 Fargo Wood II/ploughsoil	Late Bronze Age
P166	144	W34 Fargo Wood II/ploughsoil	Late Bronze Age
P167	144	W34 Fargo Wood II/ploughsoil	Late Bronze Age
P168	144	W34 Fargo Wood II/ploughsoil	Dev-Rim
P169	144	W34 Fargo Wood II/ploughsoil	Late Bronze Age
P170	144	W34 Fargo Wood II/ploughsoil	Late Bronze Age
P171	144	W34 Fargo Wood II/ploughsoil	Late Bronze Age
P172	144	W34 Fargo Wood II/ploughsoil	Dev-Rim
P173	144	W34 Fargo Wood II/ploughsoil	Late Bronze Age
P174	144	W34 Fargo Wood II/ploughsoil	Late Bronze Age
P175	144	W34 Fargo Wood II/ploughsoil	Late Bronze Age
P176	144	W34 Fargo Wood II/ploughsoil	Late Bronze Age
P177	144	W34 Fargo Wood II/ploughsoil	Late Bronze Age
P178	145	W34 Fargo Wood II/ploughsoil	Late Bronze Age
P179	145	W34 Fargo Wood II/sorted horizon	Late Bronze Age
P180	145	W34 Fargo Wood II/sorted horizon	Late Bronze Age
P181	145	W34 Fargo Wood II/sorted horizon	Late Bronze Age
P182	145	W34 Fargo Wood II/sorted horizon	Late Bronze Age
P183	145	W34 Fargo Wood II/sorted horizon	Late Bronze Age
P184	145	W34 Fargo Wood II/sorted horizon	Late Bronze Age
P185	145	W34 Fargo Wood II/sorted horizon	Late Bronze Age
P186	145	W34 Fargo Wood II/sorted horizon	Late Bronze Age
P187	145	W34 Fargo Wood II/sorted horizon	Late Bronze Age
P188	145	W34 Fargo Wood II/sorted horizon	Late Bronze Age
P189	145	W34 Fargo Wood II/layer beneath sorted horizon	Late Bronze Age
P190	145	W34 Fargo Wood II/ploughsoil	Late Bronze Age
P191	145	W34 Fargo Wood II/ploughsoil	Late Bronze Age
P192	145	W34 Fargo Wood II/ploughsoil	Late Bronze Age
P193	145	W34 Fargo Wood II/ploughsoil	Late Bronze Age
P194	145	W34 Fargo Wood II/ploughsoil	Late Bronze Age
P195	145	W34 Fargo Wood II/U/S	Late Bronze Age
P196	145	W34 Fargo Wood II/ploughsoil	Late Bronze Age
P197	145	W34 Fargo Wood II/ploughsoil	Late Bronze Age
P198	145	W34 Fargo Wood II/U/S	Late Bronze Age
P199	136	W52 Wilsford Down North Kite/layer	Peterborough
P200	136	W52 Wilsford Down North Kite/buried soil beneath bank	Peterborough
P201	136	W52 Wilsford Down North Kite/primary ditch silt	Beaker
P202	136	W52 Wilsford Down North Kite/buried soil beneath bank	Peterborough
P203	136	W52 Wilsford Down North Kite/buried soil beneath bank	Peterborough
P204	136	W52 Wilsford Down North Kite/buried soil beneath bank	Peterborough
P205	136	W52 Wilsford Down North Kite/sorted horizon beneath buried soil	Peterborough
P206	136	W52 Wilsford Down North Kite/sorted horizon beneath buried soil	Peterborough
P207	136	W52 Wilsford Down North Kite/sorted horizon beneath buried soil	Peterborough
P208	136	W52 Wilsford Down North Kite/buried soil beneath bank	Peterborough
P209	136	W52 Wilsford Down North Kite/sorted horizon beneath buried soil	Peterborough
P210	136	W52 Wilsford Down North Kite/shallow depression	Peterborough
P211	136	W52 Wilsford Down North Kite/sorted horizon beneath buried soil	Peterborough
P212	136	W52 Wilsford Down North Kite/sorted horizon beneath North Kite	Peterborough
P213	136	W52 Wilsford Down North Kite/sorted horizon beneath buried soil	Peterborough
P214	136	W52 Wilsford Down North Kite/buried soil beneath bank	Beaker
P215	136	W52 Wilsford Down North Kite/mound (?turf dump)	Beaker
P216	136	W52 Wilsford Down North Kite/buried soil beneath bank	Beaker
P217	136	W52 Wilsford Down North Kite/buried soil beneath bank	Beaker
P218	136	W52 Wilsford Down North Kite/buried soil beneath bank or sorted horizon beneath buried soil	Beaker
P219	136	W52 Wilsford Down North Kite/buried soil beneath bank	Beaker
P220	136	W52 Wilsford Down North Kite/buried soil beneath bank	Beaker
P221	136	W52 Wilsford Down North Kite/buried soil beneath bank	Beaker
P222	136	W52 Wilsford Down North Kite/sorted horizon beneath buried soil	Beaker
P223	136	W52 Wilsford Down North Kite/buried soil beneath bank	Beaker
P224	136	W52 Wilsford Down North Kite/buried soil beneath bank	Beaker
P225	136	W52 Wilsford Down North Kite/sorted horizon beneath buried soil	Beaker
P226	*136*	*W52 Wilsford Down North Kite/sorted horizon beneath buried soil*	*Beaker*
P227	53	W55 The Lesser Cursus/ditch	Beaker

Pot no	*Fig*	*Site/context*	*Pottery type*
P228	53	W55 The Lesser Cursus/feature	Beaker
P229	53	W55 The Lesser Cursus/feature	Beaker
P230	53	W55 The Lesser Cursus/feature	Beaker
P231	53	W55 The Lesser Cursus/feature	Beaker
P232	53	W55 The Lesser Cursus/feature	Beaker
P233	53	W55 The Lesser Cursus/feature	LN/EBA
P234	53	W55 The Lesser Cursus/feature	Beaker
P235	53	W55 The Lesser Cursus/feature	Beaker
P236	53	W55 The Lesser Cursus/ploughsoil	Late Bronze Age
P237	53	W55 The Lesser Cursus/feature	Late Bronze Age
P238	53	W55 The Lesser Cursus/feature	Late Bronze Age
P239	53	W55 The Lesser Cursus/feature	Late Bronze Age
P240	130	W57 Durrington Down Barrow/ploughsoil	LN/EBA
P241	130	W57 Durrington Down Barrow/ploughsoil	Dev-Rim
P242	130	W57 Durrington Down Barrow/ploughsoil	Dev-Rim
P243	130	W57 Durrington Down Barrow/ploughsoil	Dev-Rim
P244	130	W57 Durrington Down Barrow/ploughsoil	Dev-Rim
P245	130	W57 Durrington Down Barrow/ploughsoil	Dev-Rim
P246	130	W57 Durrington Down Barrow/ploughsoil	Dev-Rim
P247	130	W57 Durrington Down Barrow/ploughsoil	Dev-Rim
P248	130	W57 Durrington Down Barrow/ploughsoil	Dev-Rim
P249	130	W57 Durrington Down Barrow/ploughsoil	Dev-Rim
P250	130	W57 Durrington Down Barrow/ploughsoil	Dev-Rim
P251	130	W57 Durrington Down Barrow/ploughsoil	Dev-Rim
P252	130	W57 Durrington Down Barrow/ploughsoil	Dev-Rim
P253	130	W57 Durrington Down Barrow/ploughsoil	Dev-Rim
P254	130	W57 Durrington Down Barrow/ploughsoil	Dev-Rim
P255	130	W57 Durrington Down Barrow/ploughsoil	Dev-Rim
P256	130	W57 Durrington Down Barrow/ploughsoil	Saxon
P257	85	W59 King Barrow Ridge/feature	Peterborough
P258	85	W59 King Barrow Ridge/ploughsoil	Peterborough
P259	85	W59 King Barrow Ridge/feature	Peterborough
P260	85	W59 King Barrow Ridge/feature	Peterborough
P261	85	W59 King Barrow Ridge/feature	?Grooved Ware
P262	85	W59 King Barrow Ridge/feature	?Grooved Ware
P263	85	W59 King Barrow Ridge/feature	?Early Neo
P264	85	W59 King Barrow Ridge/feature	Grooved Ware
P265	85	W59 King Barrow Ridge/feature	Grooved Ware
P266	85	Occasional find No 1/Amesbury barrow 34 (rabbit scrape)	Grooved Ware
P267	85	King Barrow Ridge surface collection	Peterborough
P268	85	W58 Amesbury 42 long barrow/ditch	Beaker

Surface collection

Pot no	*Fig*	*Collection area no/name*	*Pottery type*
P269	21	(63) Fargo Road	Peterborough
P270	21	(64) Horse Hospital	Peterborough
P271	21	(63) Fargo Road	Peterborough
P272	21	(64) Horse Hospital	Peterborough
P273	21	(64) Horse Hospital	Peterborough
P274	21	(90) Wood End	Beaker
P275	21	(62) Cursus West End	Beaker
P276	21	(90) Wood End	Beaker
P277	21	(63) Fargo Road	Beaker
P278	21	(63) Fargo Road	Beaker
P279	21	(52) North of the Cursus	Indeterminate
P280	21	(63) Fargo Road	Beaker
P281	21	(52) North of the Cursus	Beaker
P282	21	(64) Horse Hospital	Peterborough
P283	21	(64) Horse Hospital	Beaker
P284	21	(64) Horse Hospital	Beaker
P285	21	(63) Fargo Road	Collared Urn
P286	21	(65) Durrington Down	Early Bronze Age
P287	21	(65) Durrington Down	Beaker
P288	21	(65) Durrington Down	Food Vessel
P289	21	(65) Durrington Down	LN/EBA
P290	21	(64) Horse Hospital	Dev-Rim
P291	21	(52) North of the Cursus	Dev-Rim
P292	21	(63) Fargo Road	Dev-Rim
P293	21	(63) Fargo Road	Dev-Rim
P294	21	(63) Fargo Road	Dev-Rim
P295	21	(63) Fargo Road	Dev-Rim
P296	21	(63) Fargo Road	Dev-Rim
P297	21	(63) Fargo Road	Dev-Rim
P298	21	(52) North of the Cursus	Dev-Rim
P299	*21*	*(65) Durrington Down*	*Dev-Rim*
P300	21	(65) Durrington Down	Dev-Rim

Pot no	*Fig*	*Site/context*	*Pottery type*
P301	21	(65) Durrington Down	Dev-Rim
P302	21	(62) Cursus West End	Late Bronze Age
P303	21	(63) Fargo Road	Late Bronze Age
P304	21	(64) Horse Hospital	Indeterminate
P305	22	(55) South of Stonehenge	Early Neo
P306	22	(54) Stonehenge Triangle	Peterborough
P307	22	(54) Stonehenge Triangle	Peterborough
P308	22	(54) Stonehenge Triangle	Peterborough
P309	22	(54) Stonehenge Triangle	Beaker
P310	22	(54) Stonehenge Triangle	Beaker
P311	22	(54) Stonehenge Triangle	LN/EBA
P312	22	(61) Normanton Gorse	Dev-Rim
P313	22	(54) Stonehenge Triangle	Dev-Rim
P314	22	(54) Stonehenge Triangle	Dev-Rim
P315	22	(54) Stonehenge Triangle	Dev-Rim
P316	22	(54) Stonehenge Triangle	Dev-Rim
P317	23	(59) The Diamond	Peterborough
P318	23	(59) The Diamond	LN/EBA
P319	23	(59) The Diamond	LN/EBA
P320	23	(59) The Diamond	LN/EBA
P321	23	(59) The Diamond	LN/EBA
P322	23	(59) The Diamond	Collared Urn
P323	23	(59) The Diamond	Beaker
P324	23	(59) The Diamond	Beaker
P325	23	(59) The Diamond	Beaker
P326	23	(59) The Diamond	Beaker
P327	23	(59) The Diamond	Beaker
P328	23	(59) The Diamond	Beaker
P329	23	(59) The Diamond	Dev-Rim
P330	23	(59) The Diamond	Dev-Rim
P331	23	(82) Rox Hill	Dev-Rim
P332	23	(59) The Diamond	Late Bronze Age
P333	23	(59) The Diamond	Late Bronze Age
P334	23	(59) The Diamond	Indeterminate
P335	23	(82) Rox Hill	Indeterminate

Additional sherds

P336	23	Winterbourne Stoke Crossroads settlement	Dev-Rim
P337	23	Durrington Walls henge monument, previously published as P24 in Wainwright and Longworth 1971	Grooved Ware

Appendix 3 Prehistoric pottery fabric description

The pottery from the Stonehenge Environs Project is described throughout using a single descriptive system, although the material from W2 (1981), the Coneybury 'Anomaly' and the King Barrow Ridge pit were examined by Cleal (this vol, 4.1 c and 4.3 c), and all other sites were examined by Raymond. Coneybury Henge (W2) is the single exception to this, as the pottery assemblage was examined and described by Ellison (this vol, 4.9 c) before the system was established by Cleal and Raymond.

The fabrics identified by Cleal and Raymond are referred to throughout by an alpha-numeric code, plus an abbreviation of ceramic style. The codes are made up as follows:

Initial letters of inclusion type(s):ceramic style abbreviation/fabric number

The inclusion types are listed in alphabetical order. In fabrics described by Cleal only those inclusions visible at × 10 magnification are used (excluding rare inclusions). In fabrics described by Raymond all inclusions visible at × 30 are used, with the exception of rare types. Fabrics are generally assigned to ceramic style groups on the basis of diagnostic sherds occurring in that fabric. In the case of fabrics described by Cleal, diagnostic sherds (ie featured sherds) were present in all fabrics assigned to ceramic style. In the case of fabrics described by Raymond, some fabrics without diagnostic material were assigned to ceramic styles on the basis of their similarity to fabrics which did have diagnostic material. Fabric numbers, which are to distinguish one fabric from another with the same inclusion type and are listed in the descriptive tables in microfiche, run in a series within each style group, eg FS:Neo/1 is a different fabric from FS:Bkr/1.

Small sherds and fragments which it is impossible to assign to particular fabrics are referred to by inclusion type alone, eg FS:- is material which can be seen to contain flint and sand inclusions.

Examples of the use of the system are as follows:

FS:Neo/1 is the first (or only) earlier Neolithic fabric identified with flint and sand inclusions.

S:Bkr/1 is the first (or only) Beaker fabric identified with sand inclusions.

It should also be noted that the term 'inclusion' is used throughout to refer to non-plastic material in the fabric, which may be a natural inclusion or an addition by the potter. Where it is likely or certain that the material was added by the potter this will be made clear in the text.

Abbreviations

Inclusion types

C	Chalk
F	Flint
fe	Iron oxides
G	Grog
M	Mica
S	Sand
Sh	Shell
V	Voids

Ceramic styles

Neo	earlier Neolithic
Pet	Peterborough Ware
GW	Grooved Ware
LN/EBA	Late Neolithic/Early Bronze Age (indeterminate style)
Bkr	Beaker
DR	Deverel-Rimbury
LBA	later Bronze Age
Indet	indeterminate

Summary

This report summarises the results of the Stonehenge Environs Project, a programme of archaeological investigation carried out by the Trust for Wessex Archaeology between 1980 and 1984 in the immediate vicinity of Stonehenge.

The main objective of the project, which was substantially funded by English Heritage, was to identify the location of prehistoric settlements in the Stonehenge region. Such sites, once identified, were to be evaluated with a view to developing appropriate strategies for their preservation and management. Similar strategies were to be developed for previously identified monuments, where their condition was uncertain, and in specific cases these too were evaluated.

Additional research objectives, primarily the expansion of environmental themes, but also including the investigation of linear ditches within the study area, were identified and pursued from 1981 onwards. Research into the Neolithic landscape around Robin Hood's Ball causewayed enclosure commenced as part of the main project but is continuing and will be reported on in a separate publication.

The location of areas of prehistoric activity within a primarily modern agricultural landscape was by means of surface collection, initially extensive. The subsequent intensive surface collection of more restricted sample areas was almost exclusively carried out as a prelude to excavation and formed part of a suite of investigative techniques including geophysical and geochemical survey.

Sample excavation formed the ultimate stage of investigation of both surface scatters and defined monuments and, with only one exception, involved the gridded manual excavation of all deposits overlying natural chalk. This approach resulted in the recovery of data which, although unstratified, retain some spatial integrity and enable aspects of site function and chronology to be more fully explored.

The project fieldwork has demonstrated an intensity of Neolithic and Bronze Age activity beyond the framework of funerary and ceremonial monuments which characterise the Stonehenge area. The concept of a ritual landscape, reserved solely for the ceremonial, is now no longer tenable, as the analysis of surface collections, primarily of worked flint, has provided evidence for extensive activity, both domestic and industrial in nature.

The excavation of monuments and other stratified deposits has provided a range of comparative data, economic, environmental, technological, and ideological, linked to a series of radiocarbon dates. The data have been employed in a number of comparative studies, emphasising the benefits of a consistent and thematic approach.

Résumé

Ce compte-rendu résume les résultats d'un programme de recherches archéologiques entreprises par la Société Archéologique du Comté de Wessex, entre les années 1980 et 1984, à proximité immédiate de Stonehenge, programme intitulé 'Projet des Environs de Stonehenge'.

L'objectif principal de cette étude, qui a reçu de substantiels crédits d'English Heritage, était de localiser les sites d'occupation préhistorique dans la région de Stonehenge. Après les avoir identifiés, on devait évaluer ces sites, afin de mettre en place des méthodes appropriés pour leur préservation et leur gestion. On prévoyait de développer des méthodes similaires pour les monuments déjà identifiés, mais dont l'état de conservation n'était pas satisfaisant, et, dans certains cas particuliers, ceux-ci devaient également être évalués.

A partir de 1981, les recherches se sont fixé et ont poursuivi des objectifs supplémentaires, à savoir, d'une part, l'élargissement des thèmes liés à l'environnement et, d'autre part, l'étude des fossés rectilignes à l'intérieur de la zone concernée. Au départ, les recherches portant sur le paysage néolithique autour de l'enceinte avec digue de Robin Hood's Ball faisaient partie du projet principal, mais elles se poursuivent et feront l'objet d'un rapport distinct dans une publication ultérieure.

C'est d'abord grâce à un ramassage extensif sur une surface étendue que nous avons pu localiser les aires d'activité préhistorique dans un paysage à présent essentiellement consacré à l'agriculture. Le ramassage de surface intensif sur des aires échantillon plus restreintes n'a pratiquement été effectué que comme un prélude aux fouilles, et faisait partie d'une série de techniques d'investigation qui comprenait aussi des relevés géophysique et géochimique.

La dernière étape des recherches, aussi bien en ce qui concernait les trouvailles de surface que les monuments déterminés, a consisté en une excavation localisée et, à une seule exception près, on a chaque fois dégagé manuellement après quadrillage tous les dépôts qui se trouvaient au-dessus de la couche de craie naturelle. Cette méthode a eu comme résultat la récupération de données qui, bien que non stratifiées, avaient gardé une certaine intégrité spatiale et permettaient d'approfondir l'étude de certains aspects de la fonction et de la chronologie du site.

Le travail de terrain lié à ce projet a montré qu'il existait, au Néolithique et à l'Age du Bronze, une activité intense dépassant le cadre des monuments associés aux rites funéraires et aux cérémonies et caractéristiques de la région de Stonehenge. Le concept de lieu rituel, réservé seulement aux cérémonies, n'est plus tenable car l'analyse des collections trouvées en surface, en particulier des silex travaillés, a fourni la preuve de l'existence d'activités variées, de nature à la fois domestique et artisanale.

La mise au jour de monuments et d'autres dépôts stratifiés a fourni un champ de données comparatives, concernant l'économie, l'environnement, la technologie et l'idéologie, dont on a pu établir la datation au radiocarbone. Ces données ont été utilisées dans un certain nombre d'études comparatives qui insistent sur les avantages d'une approche thématique et logique.

Zusammenfassung

Der vorliegende Bericht faßt die Ergebnisse des Forschungsprojektes 'Stonehenge Environs' zusammen. Eine Reihe gezielter archäologischer Untersuchungen wurde zwischen 1980 und 1984 von dem 'Trust for Wessex Archaeology' in der unmittelbaren Umgebung von Stonehenge durchgeführt.

Das Hauptanliegen diese Untersuchungsprojektes, das von English Heritage großzügig unterstüzt wurde, war es, die Lageorte vorgeschichtlicher Siedlungsplätze im Gebiet von Stonehenge festzustellen. Diese Siedlungsplätze, erst einmal bekannt, sollten dann bewertet werden mit Hinblick darauf, geeignete Maßnahmen für ihre Erhaltung und Verwaltung zu entwickeln. Ähnliche Maßnahmen sollten für schon bekannte Bodendenkmäler, wo der Erhaltungszustand ungewiß war, ausgearbeiten werden und in besonderen Fällen wurden diese dann ebenfalls bewertet.

Weitere Forschungsziele, hauptsächlich eine Auswertung umweltbestimmter Themen, die aber auch die Untersuchung gradliniger Gräben innerhalb des Forschungsareals entschließen, wurden festgelegt und von 1981 an verfolgt. Untersuchungen in die neolithische 'Landschaft', die 'causewayed' (mit Durchlässen versehene) Einfriedung Robin Hood's Ball umgab, begannen als Teil des zentralen Forschungsprojektes, wurden jedoch fortgeführt und werden später als sebstständiger Bericht veröffentlicht werden.

Die Lagebestimmung von Arealen mit vorgeschichtlichem Befund innerhalb einer in erster Linie modernen Agrarlandschaft wurde mit Hilfe von Feldbegehungen und Streufunden anfänglich extensiver Art vorangetrieben. Das nachfolgende intensive Sammeln von Streufunden auf beschränkten Arealen wurde dann fast ausschließlich als Vorbereitung für Grabungen durchgeführt und war Teil einer Reihe von Forschungstechniken, die auch geophysikalische und geochemische Untersuchungen einschlossen.

Ausgrabungen im kleinen Rahmen bildeten dann die letzte Phase der Untersuchungen von Streufunden wie auch festgelegten Bodendenkmälern. Diese Grabungen wurden, mit einer Ausnahme, ohne Maschinen in einem Rastersystem durchgeführt, wobei alle Ablagerungen oberhalb der gewachsenen Kreide entfernt wurden. Diese Verfahrensweise brachte die Sicherstellung von Daten, die, obwohl unstratifiziert, eine gewisse räumliche Einheit beibehielten und es so erlaubten, alle Aspekte der Nutzung der Fundstelle sowie ihre Chronologie genauer untersuchen zu können.

Die Feldbegehungen während des Forschungsprojektes haben eine Intensität jungsteinzeitlicher und bronzezeitlicher Aktivität aufgezeigt, die über den Rahmen der funeralen und zeremoniellen Denkmäler, die das Gebiet um Stonehenge kennzeichnen, hinausreicht. Die Vorstellung einer kultischen Landschaft, die ausschließlich dem Zeremoniell vorbehalten ist, kann nicht länger aufrechterhalten werden, da die Analyse der Streufunde, hauptsächlich Feuersteinartifakte, Beweise für eine extensive Nutzung ergeben hat, die sowohl häuslicher wie industrieller Art war.

Die Ausgrabungen von Bodendenkmälern und anderen stratifizierten Ablagerungen haben eine Reihe von vergleichbaren Daten, wirtschaftlicher umweltlicher, technologischer und ideologischer Art erbracht, die mit eine Reihenfolge von Radiokarbondaten verknüpft sind. Diese Daten sind in einer Anzahl von vergleichenden Untersuchungen benutzt worden und weisen so mit Nachdruck auf die Vorteile hin, die eine folgerichtige und thematische Verfahrensweise bringen kann.

Bibliography

Allen, M J, 1986 Magnetic susceptibility as a potential palaeo-environmental determinant, *Circaea*, **4**, 18–20

——, 1988 Archaeological and environmental aspects of colluviation in south-east England, in *Man-made soils* (eds W Groenmann-van Waateringe and M Robinson), BAR, **S410**, 69–94, Oxford

Allen, M J, Heaton, M, and Richards J C, forthcoming Durrington Barrow 3, *Wiltshire Archaeol Natur Hist Mag*

Anon, 1920 Interment at Durrington, *Wiltshire Archaeol Natur Hist Mag*, **41**, 184

Annable, F K, and Simpson, D D A, 1964 *Guide catalogue of the Neolithic and Bronze Age collections in Devizes Museum*, Wiltshire Archaeol and Nat Hist Soc, Devizes

Ashbee, P, 1963 The Wilsford shaft, *Antiquity*, **37**, 116–20

——, 1966 The Fussell's Lodge Long Barrow, *Archaeologia* **100**, 1–80

——, 1978 Amesbury barrow 51: excavation 1960, *Wiltshire Archaeol Natur Hist Mag*, **70**, 1–60

——, 1981 Amesbury barrow 39: excavations 1960, *Wiltshire Archaeol Natur Hist Mag*, **74–5**, 1–34

Ashbee, P, Bell, M, and Proudfoot, E, 1989 *Wilsford Shaft: excavations 1960–62*, HBMC Archaeological Report No 11, London

Atkinson, R J C, 1965 Waylands Smithy, *Antiquity*, **39**, 126–33

——, 1979 *Stonehenge*, London

——, 1984 Barrows excavated by William Stukeley near Stonehenge, *Wiltshire Archaeol Natur Hist Mag*, **79**, 244–6

Atkinson, R J C, and Evans, J G, 1978 Recent excavations at Stonehenge, *Antiquity*, **52**, 235–6

Atkinson, R J C, Piggott, S, and Stone, J F S, 1952 The excavation of two additional holes at Stonehenge, and new evidence for the date of the monument, *Antiq J*, **32**, 14–20

Bamford, H M, 1982 Beaker domestic sites in the Fen Edge and East Anglia, *East Anglian Archaeology Report* **16**, Norfolk Archaeology Unit, Dereham, Norfolk

Barrett, J C, 1976 Deverel-Rimbury: problems of chronology and interpretation, in *Settlement and Economy in the third and second millennia BC* (eds C Burgess and R Miket), BAR, **33**, 289–307, Oxford

——, 1980 The pottery of the later Bronze Age in lowland England, *Proc Prehist Soc*, **46**, 297–320

Barrett, J C, and Bradley, R, 1980 Later Bronze Age settlement in south Wessex and Cranborne Chase, in *Settlement and society in the British later Bronze Age* (eds J Barrett and R Bradley), BAR, **83**, 181–208, Oxford

——, forthcoming *Cranborne Chase*, Cambridge University Press, Cambridge

Barton, R N E, and Bergman, C, 1982 Hunters at Hengistbury: some evidence from experimental archaeology, *World Archaeol*, **14**, 237–48

Bedwin, O, 1981 Excavations at the Neolithic enclosure on Bury Hill, Houghton, West Sussex, 1979, *Proc Prehist Soc*, **47**, 69–86

Bell, M G, 1977 Excavations at Bishopstone, *Sussex Archaeol Collect*, **115**

——, 1981a Valley sediments as evidence of prehistoric land use: a study based on dry valleys in south-east England, unpubl PhD thesis, Univ London

——, 1981b Valley sediments and environmental change, in *The environment of man: the Iron Age to Anglo-Saxon period* (eds M Jones and G W Dimbleby), BAR, **87**, 75–91, Oxford

——, 1983 The land mollusca and other palaeoenvironmental evidence, in *Excavations at Condicote Henge Monument, Gloucestershire, 1977*, (A Saville), *Trans Bristol Gloucestershire Archaeol Soc*, **101**, 39–45

——, forthcoming Sedimentation rates on the English chalk: ditches and Wilsford Shaft, in *Experimentation and Reconstruction in Environmental Archaeology* (ed D Robinson), BAR, Oxford

Binford, L R, 1981 *Bones: ancient men and modern myths*, New York

Bohmers, A, 1956 Statistics and graphs in the study of flint assemblages. Part 1. Introduction, *Palaeohistoria*, **5**, 1–5

Bond, D, 1983 An excavation at Stonehenge, 1981, *Wiltshire Archaeol Natur Hist Mag*, **77**, 39–44

Booth, A St J, 1951 Excavation notes, unpubl MS, Salisbury Museum

Booth, A St J, and Stone, J F S, 1952 A trial flint mine at Durrington, Wiltshire, *Wiltshire Archaeol Natur Hist Mag*, **54**, 381–8

Bordes, F, 1979 *Typologie du Paléolithique. Ancien et Moyen*, Centre Nationale de la Recherche Scientifique, Paris

Bowden, M, Bradley, R, Gaffney, V, and Mepham, L, 1983 The date of the Dorset Cursus, *Proc Prehist Soc*, **49**, 376–80

Bowen, H C, and Smith, I F, 1977 Sarsen stones in Wessex: the Society's first investigation in the evolution of the landscape project, *Ant J*, **57**, 185–96

Bradley, R, 1976 Maumbury Rings, Dorchester: the excavations of 1903–1913, *Archaeologia*, **105**, 1–98

——, 1978 *The Prehistoric Settlement of Britain*, London

——, 1982 Position and possession: assemblage variation in the British Neolithic, *Oxford Journ Archaeol*, **1.1**, 27–38

——, 1984 *The social foundations of prehistoric Britain*, London

Bradley, R and Ellison, A, 1975 *Rams Hill*, BAR, **19**, Oxford

Braun, D P, 1982 Radiographic analysis of temper in ceramic vessels: goals and initial methods, *Journ Field Archaeol*, **9**, 183–92

——, 1983 Pots as tools, in *Archaeological hammers and theories* (eds J A Moore and A S Keene), 107–34, New York

Britton, D, 1967 Heathery Burn Cave, Co Durham (England), *Inventaria Archaeologica*, **GB.55**, British Museum

Bronitsky, G, and Hamer, R, 1986 Experiments in ceramic technology. The effects of various tempering material on impact and thermal-shock resistance, *American Antiquity*, **51**, 89–101

Bull, G, and Payne, S, 1982 Tooth eruption and epiphyseal fusion in pigs and wild boar, in *Ageing and sexing animal bones from archaeological sites* (eds B Wilson, C Grigson, and S Payne), BAR, **109**, 55–72, Oxford

Burgess, C, 1980 *The Age of Stonehenge*, London

——, 1986 'Urnes of no small variety': Collared Urns reviewed, *Proc Prehist Soc*, **52**, 339–52

Cahen, D, 1987 Refitting stone artefacts: why bother?, in *The human uses of flint and chert: papers from the fourth international flint symposium* (eds G de Sieveking and M H Newcomer), 1–9, Cambridge

Calkin, J B, 1962 The Bournemouth area in the Middle and Late Bronze Age, with the 'Deverel-Rimbury' problem reconsidered, *Archaeol Journ*, **119**, 1–65

Cameron, R A D, and Morgan-Huws, D T, 1975 Snail faunas in the early stages of a chalk grassland succession, *Biol J Linnaean Soc*, **7**, 215–29

Carruthers, W J, forthcoming The carbonised plant remains, in Woodward forthcoming

Case, H J, 1977 The Beaker culture in Britain and Ireland, in *Beakers in Britain and Europe* (ed R Mercer), BAR, **S26**, 71–84, Oxford

Catt, J A, 1978 The contribution of loess to the soils in lowland Britain, in *The effect of man on the landscape: the lowland zone* (eds S Limbrey and J G Evans), CBA Res Rep, **21**, 12–20, London

Chippindale, C, 1983 *Stonehenge Complete*, London

Christie, P M, 1963 The Stonehenge Cursus, *Wiltshire Archaeol Natur Hist Mag*, **58**, 370–82

——, 1964 A Bronze Age round barrow on Earl's Farm Down, Amesbury, *Wiltshire Archaeol Natur Hist Mag*, **59**, 30–45

——, 1970 A round barrow on Greenland Farm, Winterbourne Stoke, *Wiltshire Archaeol Natur Hist Mag*, **65**, 64–73

Clark, A J, 1983 The testimony of the topsoil, in *The impact of aerial reconnaissance on archaeology* (ed G S Maxwell), CBA Res Rep, **49**, 128–35

——, 1986 Archaeological geophysics, *Geophysics*, **51**, 1404–13

Clark, J G D, 1934 Derivative forms of the petit tranchet in Britain, *Archaeol J*, **91**, 32–58

——, 1960 Excavations at the Neolithic site at Hurst Fen, Mildenhall, Suffolk, 1954, 1957, and 1958, *Proc Prehist Soc*, **19**, 202–45

——, 1963 Neolithic bows from Somerset, England, and the prehistory of archery in North-Western Europe, *Proc Prehist Soc*, **29**, 50–98

Clarke, D L, 1970 *Beaker pottery of Great Britain and Ireland*, Cambridge

Clay, R C C, 1927 Stonehenge Avenue, *Antiquity*, **1**, 342–4

Cleal, R M J, forthcoming a The earlier prehistoric pottery, in Sharples forthcoming

——, forthcoming b The earlier prehistoric pottery, in Barrett and Bradley forthcoming

Colborne, G J N, and Cope, D W, 1983 *Soils of south western England*, Soil Survey 1:250,000, Sheet 5, Harpenden

Cope, D W, 1976 Soils in Wiltshire 1: Sheet SU 03 (Wilton), (Harpenden) Soil Survey Record no 32

Cornwall, I W, 1953 Soil science and archaeology with illustrations from some British Bronze Age monuments, *Proc Prehist Soc*, **19** 129–47

Cox, P, and Hawkes, J, forthcoming *The Isle of Purbeck Survey*

Crabtree, K, 1971 Overton Down experimental earthwork, Wiltshire 1968, *Proc Univ Bristol Spelaeol Soc*, **11**, 237–44

Craddock, P T, 1980 The soil phosphate survey at the Newark Road subsite, in Pryor 1980, 213–17

Crawford, O G S, 1928 *Air survey and archaeology*, 2 edn, Southampton

Crawford, O G S, and Keiller, A, 1928 *Wessex from the air*, Oxford

Crummy, N, 1983 *The Roman small finds from excavations in Colchester 1971–9*, Colchester Archaeol Rep, **2**, Colchester Archaeological Trust and DoE

Cunliffe, B, 1987 *Hengistbury Head, Dorset*: **1**, *The prehistoric and Roman settlement, 3500 B C–A D 500*, Oxford University Committee for Archaeology, Monograph **13**, Oxford

Cunliffe, B, and Phillipson, D W, 1968 Excavations at Eldon's Seat, Encombe, Dorset, England, *Proc Prehist Soc*, **34**, 191–237

Cunnington, M E, 1923 *The Early Iron Age inhabited site at All Cannings Cross Farm, Wiltshire*, Devizes

——, 1929 *Woodhenge*, Devizes

——, 1935 Note on a burial at Amesbury, *Wiltshire Archaeol Natur Hist Mag*, **47**, 267

Dimbleby, G W, 1967 Pollen analysis, in Tratman 1967, 121–2

——, 1971 Pollen analysis, in Wainwright and Longworth 1971, 332–4

Duffey, E, 1975 The effects of human trampling on the fauna of grassland litter, *Biol Conserv*, **7**, 255–74

Drewett, P L, 1981 The flint industry, in Bedwin 1981, 77–9

Edmunds, M, and Thomas, J, 1984 The Archers: an everyday story of country folk, in *Lithic analysis and Later British Prehistory* (eds A G Brown and M Edmunds), BAR, **162**, 187–99, Oxford

Ellison, A B, 1975 Pottery and settlements of the later Bronze Age in southern England, unpubl PhD thesis, Univ Cambridge

——, 1980 *A policy for archaeological investigation in Wessex*, unpubl report, The Trust for Wessex Archaeology

——, 1981 The Middle Bronze Age Pottery, in A Bronze Age Urn Cemetery at Kimpton, Hampshire, *Proc Prehist Soc*, **47**, 173–96

Entwistle, R, 1984 Soil phosphate analysis and lithic scatters, unpubl undergraduate dissertation, Univ Reading

Entwistle, R, and Richards, J C, 1987 The geophysical and geochemical properties of lithic scatters, in *Lithic analysis and later British prehistory* (eds A G Brown and M R Edmonds), BAR, **162**, 19–38, Oxford

Evans, W E D, 1963 *The Chemistry of Death*, Springfield

Evans, J G, 1971 The pre-henge environment, in Wainwright and Longworth 1971, 329–37

——, 1972 *Land snails in archaeology*, London

——, 1984 Stonehenge: the environment in the late Neolithic and early Bronze Age and a Beaker age burial, *Wiltshire Archaeol Natur Hist Mag*, **78**, 7–30

Evans, J G, and Jones, H, 1979 The land mollusca, in Wainwright 1979, 190–213

Farley, M, 1979 Flint flake dimensions in the British Neolithic, *Proc Prehist Soc*, **45**, 322–3

Farrer, P, 1917 Excavations in the Cursus July 1917, unpubl MS, Devizes Museum

——, 1918, Durrington Walls or Long Walls, *Wiltshire Archaeol Natur Hist Mag*, **40**, 95–103

Fasham, P, and Ross, J M, 1978 A Bronze Age flint industry from a barrow site in Micheldelver Wood, Hampshire, *Proc Prehist Soc*, **44**, 47–67

Field, E V, 1961 Excavation and fieldwork in Wiltshire, 1960, Wilsford, *Wiltshire Archaeol Natur Hist Mag*, **58**, 30–1

Field, N H, Matthews, C L, and Smith, I F 1964 New Neolithic sites in Dorset and Bedfordshire with a note on the distribution of Neolithic storage pits in Britain, *Proc Prehist Soc*, **30**, 352–81

Finch, L A, 1971 Report on the petrological examination of sherds from Durrington Walls, in Wainwright and Longworth 1971, 409–10

Fischer, A, Hansen, P V, and Rasmussen, P, 1984 Macro and micro wear traces on lithic projectile points. Experimental results and prehistoric examples, *Journ Danish Archaeol*, **3**, 19–46

Fleming, A, 1973 Tombs for the living, *Man*, **8**, 177–93

Foley, R, 1981 Off-site archaeology and human adaptation in Eastern Africa: an analysis of regional artefact density in the Amboseli, Southern Kenya, BAR, **S97**, Oxford

Ford, S, Bradley, R, Hawkes, J, and Fisher, P, 1984 Flint working in the Metal Age, *Oxford J Archaeol*,**3**, 157–73

Gardiner, J, 1984 Lithic distributions and Neolithic settlement patterns in central southern England, in *Neolithic studies: a review of some current research* (eds R Bradley and J Gardiner), BAR, **133**, 15–40, Oxford

——, 1985 Intrasite patterning in the flint assemblage from the Dorset Cursus, 1984, *Proc Dorset Natur Hist and Archaeol Soc*, **107**, 87–93

——, 1987a Tales of the unexpected: approaches to the assessment and interpretation of museum flint collections, in *Lithic analysis and later British prehistory*, BAR, **162**, 49–65, Oxford

——, 1987b The occupation 3500–1000bc, in Cunliffe 1987, 22–60

Gibson, A M, 1982 *Beaker domestic sites. A study of the domestic pottery of the late third and early second millennia BC in the British Isles*, BAR, **107**, Oxford

Gingell, C J, 1980 The Marlborough Downs in the Bronze Age: the first results of current research, in *The British later Bronze Age* (eds J Barrett and R Bradley), BAR, **83**, 209–22, Oxford

——, 1986 A long barrow, Woodford G2, south of Druid's Lodge, in Harding and Gingell 1986, 15–21

——, 1988 Twelve Wiltshire round barrows. Excavations in 1959 and 1961 by F de M and H L Vatcher, *Wiltshire Archaeol Natur Hist Mag*, **82**, 19–76

——, forthcoming *The Marlborough Downs*, Wiltshire Archaeol Natur Hist Soc monograph

Gingell, C J, and Harding, P A, 1979 A method of analysing the technology of flaking in Neolithic and Bronze Age flint assemblages, *Staringia*, **6**, Nederlandse Geologische Vereniging, Maastricht, 73–6

Godwin, H, 1975 *The history of the British flora*, 2 edn, Cambridge

Gordon, D, and Ellis, C, 1985 Species composition parameters and life tables: their application to detect environmental change in fossil land molluscan assemblages, in *Palaeoenvironmental investigations* (eds N R J Fieller, D D Gilbertson, and N G A Ralph), BAR, **258**, 157–74, Oxford

Gowland, W, 1902 Recent excavations at Stonehenge, *Archaeologia*, **58**, 37–105

Grant, A, 1982 The use of toothwear as a guide to the age of domestic ungulates, in *Ageing and sexing animal bones from archaeological sites* (eds B Wilson, C Grigson, and S Payne), BAR, **109**, 91–108, Oxford

Gray, H St G, 1935 The Avebury excavations, 1908–1922, *Archaeologia*, **84**, 99–162

Green, C, and Rollo-Smith, S, 1984 The excavation of eighteen round barrows near Shrewton, Wiltshire, *Proc Prehist Soc*, **50**, 255–318

Green, H S, 1974 Early Bronze Age burial, territory and population in Milton Keynes, Buckinghamshire, and the Great Ouse Valley, *Archaeol J*, **131**, 75–139

——, 1980 *The flint arrowheads of the British Isles*, BAR, **75**, Oxford

Greenfield, E, 1959 Excavation and fieldwork in Wiltshire, 1958, Wilsford Down and Normanton Down, Amesbury, *Wiltshire Archaeol Natur Hist Mag*, **57**, 228–9

Grigson, C, 1965 Measurements of bones, horncores, antlers and teeth, in *Windmill Hill and Avebury: excavations by Alexander Keiller 1925–1939* (ed I F Smith), 145–67, Oxford

——, 1982a Sex and determination of some bones and teeth of domestic cattle: a review of the literature, in *Ageing and sexing animal bones from archaeological sites* (eds B Wilson, C Grigson, and S Payne), BAR, **109**, 7–24, Oxford

——, 1982b Sexing Neolithic domestic cattle skulls and horn cores, in *Ageing and sexing animal bones from archaeological sites* (eds B Wilson, C Grigson, and S Payne), BAR, **109**, 25–36, Oxford

——, 1982c Porridge and pannage: pig husbandry in Neolithic England, in *Archaeological aspects of woodland ecology* (eds M Bell and S Limbrey), BAR, **146**, 297–314, Oxford

Grimes, W F, 1964 Excavations in the Lake Group of barrows, Wilsford, Wiltshire, in 1959, *Bull Inst Archaeol Univ London*, **4**, 89–121

Harcourt, R A, 1971 Animal bones from Durrington Walls, in Wainwright and Longworth 1971, 338–50

Harding, A F, 1987 *Henge Monuments and Related Sites of Great Britain: Air Photographic Evidence and Catalogue*, BAR, **175**, Oxford

Harding, P A, 1986 The worked flint, in Woodward forthcoming

——, 1988 The Chalk Plaque Pit, Amesbury, *Proc Prehist Soc*, **54**, 320–7

——, forthcoming a The flint, in Gingell forthcoming

——, forthcoming b The flint, in Woodward forthcoming

Harding, P A, and Gingell, C J, 1986 The excavation of two long barrows by F de M and H F W L Vatcher, *Wiltshire Archaeol Natur Hist Mag*, **80**, 7–22

Haslam, J P, 1960 Notes on excavations, 1959, Wilsford, Westfield Farm, *Proc Prehist Soc*, **15**, 344

Hawley, W, 1921 The excavations at Stonehenge, *Antiq J*, **1**, 19–39

——, 1922 Second report on the excavations at Stonehenge, *Antiq J*, **2**, 36–51

——, 1923 Third report on the excavations at Stonehenge,*Antiq J*, **3**, 13–20

——, 1924 Fourth report on the excavations at Stonehenge, *Antiq J*,**4**, 30–9

——, 1925 Report on the excavations at Stonehenge during the season of 1923, *Antiq J*, **5**, 21–50

——, 1926 Report on the excavations at Stonehenge during the season of 1924, *Antiq J*, **6**, 1–25

——, 1928 Report on the excavations at Stonehenge during 1925 and 1926, *Antiq J*, **8**, 149–76

Hazelgrove, C, Millett, M, and Smith, I, 1985 *Archaeology from the ploughsoil*, Sheffield

Healey, E, and Robertson-Mackay, R, 1987 The flint industry, in Robertson-Mackay 1987

Healy, F, 1985 The struck flint, in Shennan *et al* 1985, 177–207

Healy, F, 1987 Prediction or prejudice? The relationship between field survey and excavation, in *Lithic analysis and later British prehistory* (eds A G Brown and M R Edmonds), BAR, **162**, 9–17, Oxford

Hedges , J, and Buckley, D, 1981 *Springfield Cursus and the cursus problem*, Essex County Council Occasional Paper, **1**, Essex County Council

Helbaek, H, 1953 Early crops in southern England, *Proc Prehist Soc*, **18**, 194–233

Higham, C F W, 1967 Stock rearing as a cultural factor in prehistoric Europe, *Proc Prehist Soc*, **33**, 84–106

Hillman, G, 1981 Crop husbandry: evidence from the macroscopic remains, in *The environment in British prehistory* (eds I G Simmons and M J Tooley), 183–91, London

Hoare, R Colt, 1810 *The history of ancient Wiltshire: Part 1*, London

Hodder, I, and Orton, C, 1976 *Spatial analysis in archaeology*, London

Hodgson, J M, 1976 *Soil survey field handbook*, Soil Survey Technical Monograph, **5**, Harpenden

Howard, H, 1981 In the wake of distribution: towards an integrated approach to ceramic studies in prehistoric Britain, in *Production and distribution: a ceramic viewpoint* (eds H Howard and E Morris), BAR, **S120**, 1–30, Oxford

Hurlbert, S H, 1971 The nonconcept of species diversity: a critique and alternative parameters, *Ecology*, **52**, 577–86

Isaac, C L I, 1977 *Olorgesailie. Archaeological studies of a middle Pleistocene lake basin in Kenya*, Chicago

Jewell, P A, 1963 Cattle from British archaeological sites, in *Man and cattle* (eds A E Mourant and F E Zeuner), Royal Anthropological Institute Occasional Paper, **18**, 80–91, London

Jewell, P A, and Dimbleby, G W, 1966 The experimental earthwork on Overton Down, Wiltshire, England: the first four years, *Proc Prehist Soc*, **32**, 313–24

Jope, M, 1965 Faunal remains: frequencies and ages of species, in *Windmill Hill and Avebury: excavations by Alexander Keiller 1925–1939* (ed I F Smith), 142–5, Oxford

Kerney, M P, 1966 Snails and man in Britain, *J Conchology*, 26, 3–14

Kerney, M P, and Cameron, R A D, 1979 *A field guide to the land snails of Britain and north-west Europe*, London

King, A N, 1970 Crop-mark near West Amesbury, *Wiltshire Archaeol Natur Hist Mag*, **65**, 190–1

Kinnes, I, 1979 *Round Barrows and Ring-ditches in the British Neolithic*, British Museum Occasional Paper, **7**, London

Krebs, C J, 1972 *Ecology*, New York

Krogman, W M, 1962 *The Human Skeleton in Forensic Medicine*, Springfield

Laidler, B, and Young, W E V, 1938 A surface flint industry from a site near Stonehenge, *Wiltshire Archaeol Natur Hist Mag*, **48**, 151–60

Lanting, J N, and van der Waals, J D, 1972 British Beakers as seen from the continent, *Helinium*, **12**, 20–46

Legge, A J, 1981a Aspects of cattle husbandry, in *Farming practice in British prehistory* (ed R Mercer), Edinburgh, 169–81

——, 1981b The agricultural economy, in *Grimes Graves, Norfolk: excavations 1971–72*, **1** (ed R Mercer), DoE Archaeol Rep, **11**, 79–103

Liddell, D M, 1930 Report on the excavations at Hembury fort, Devon, 1930, *Proc Devon Archaeol Explor Soc*, **1**, 39–63

——, 1931 Report on the excavations at Hembury fort, Devon. Second Season, 1931, *Proc Devon Archaeol Explor Soc*, **1**, 90–119

——, 1932 Report on the excavations at Hembury fort. Third Season, 1932, *Proc Devon Archaeol Explor Soc*, **1**, 162–90

——, 1935 Report on the excavations at Hembury fort. Fourth and Fifth Seasons, 1934 and 1935, *Proc Devon Archaeol Explor Soc*, **2**, 135–75

Limbrey, S, 1975 *Soil science and archaeology*, London

——, 1978 Changes in quality and distribution of the soils of lowland Britain, in *The effect of man on the landscape: the Lowland Zone* (eds S Limbrey and J G Evans), CBA Res Rept, **21**, 21–7

Lobb, S, and Rose, P, in prep *The Kennet Valley Survey*, Berkshire Arch Trust monograph

Longworth, I H 1979 The Neolithic and Bronze Age pottery, in Wainwright 1979, 75–124

——, 1984 *Collared Urns of the Bronze Age in Great Britain and Ireland*, Cambridge

Mabey, R, 1972 *Food for Free*, Glasgow

Maltby, J M, nd Animal bones from four late Bronze Age sites on the Marlborough Downs, Wiltshire, unpubl report, Ancient Monuments Laboratory

——, forthcoming The animal bones, in Gingell forthcoming

Manby, T G 1974 *Grooved Ware sites in Yorkshire and the north of England*, BAR, **9**, Oxford

Mercer, R J 1980 *Hambledon Hill*, Edinburgh

——, 1981 Excavations at Carn Brea, Illogan, Cornwall, 1970-73, *Cornish Archaeol*, **20**

Moffett, L, Robinson, M A, and Straker, V, 1989 Cereals, fruit and nuts: charred plant remains from neolithic sites in England and Wales and the neolithic economy, in *The Beginnings of Agriculture* (eds Annie Milles, Diane Williams, and Neville Gardner), BAR Int Series, **496**, 243–61, Oxford

Moore, C N, 1966 A possible Beaker burial from Larkhill, Durrington, *Wiltshire Archaeol Natur Hist Mag*, **61**, 92

Mortimer, J R, 1905 *Forty years researches into British and Saxon burial mounds of East Yorkshire*, London

Musty, J W G, and Stone, J F S, 1956 An Early Bronze Age Barrow and Late Bronze Age Urnfield on Heale Hill, Middle Woodford, *Wiltshire Archaeol Natur Hist Man*, **56**, 253–61

Musty, J, and Stratton, J E D 1964 A Saxon cemetery at Winterbourne Gunner, near Salisbury, *Wiltshire Archaeol Natur Hist Mag*, **59**, 86–109

Newcomer, M H, 1971 Some quantitative experiments in hand axe manufacture, *World Archaeol*, **3**, 85–94

Newcomer, M H, and Karlin, C, 1987 Flint chips from Pincevent, in *The human uses of flint and chert: papers from the fourth international flint symposium* (eds G de Sieveking and M H Newcomer), 33–6, Cambridge

Newcomer, M H, and Sieveking, G de G, 1980 Experimental flake scatter patterns: a new interpretative technique, *J Field Archaeol*, **73**, 345–52

Newell, R S, 1931 Barrow 85, Amesbury (Goddard's List), *Wiltshire Archaeol Natur Hist Soc Mag*, **45**, 253–61

Ohnuma, K, and Bergman, C, 1982 Experimental studies in the determination of flaking mode, *Bull Inst Archaeol Univ London*, **19**, 161–70

Osborne, P J, 1969 An insect fauna of late Bronze Age date from Wilsford, Wiltshire, *J Animal Ecol*, **38**, 555–66

Passmore, A D, 1940 A disc barrow containing curious flints near Stonehenge, *Wiltshire Archaeol Natur Hist Mag*, **49**, 238

Pearson, G W, Pilcher, J R, Baille, M G, Corbett, D M, and Qua, F (1986) High Precision ^{14}C Measurement of Irish Oaks to show the Natural ^{14}C Variations from AD 1840–5210 BC, *Radiocarbon*, **28**, 911–934

Pennington, W, 1974 *The history of British vegetation*, London

Pitts, M W, 1978 Towards an understanding of flint industries in post-glacial England, *Bull Inst Archaeol Univ London*, **15**, 179–97

——, 1979–80 On two barrows near Stonehenge, *Wiltshire Archaeol Natur Hist Mag*, **74–5**, 181–4

——, 1982 On the road to Stonehenge: report on the investigations beside the A344 in 1968, 1979 and 1980, *Proc Prehist Soc*, **48**, 75–132

Prior, J, and Alvin, K L, 1983 Structural changes on charring

woods of Dichrostachys and Salix from Southern Africa, *IAWA Bulletin*, n s, **4**, 197–206
Pryor, F, 1980 *Excavation at Fengate, Peterborough, England. The third report*, Northamptonshire Archaeol Soc Monograph, **1**
——, 1987 Etton 1986 Neolithic metamorphoses, *Antiquity*, **61**, 78–9
Pryor, F, French, C, and Taylor, M, 1986 An interim report on the excavations at Etton, Maxey, Cambridgeshire, 1982–4, *Antiq J*, **65**, 275–311
Radley, J, and Mellors, P, 1964 A Mesolithic structure at Deepcarr, Yorkshire, England, and the affinities of its associated flint industries, *Proc Prehist Soc*, **30**, 1–24
Rahtz, P A, 1962 Neolithic and Beaker sites at Downton, near Salisbury, Wiltshire, *Wiltshire Archaeol Natur Hist Mag*, **58**, 116–42
Richards, C, and Thomas, J, 1984 Ritual activity and structured deposition in later Neolithic Wessex, in *Neolithic studies* (eds R Bradley and J Gardiner), BAR, **133**, 189–218, Oxford
Richards, J C, 1982 The Stonehenge Environs project: the story so far, *Scot Archaeol Rev*, **1**, 98–104
——, 1984a Stonehenge Environs: a preservation and management policy, unpubl report, The Trust for Wessex Archaeology
——, 1984b The development of the Neolithic landscape in the environs of Stonehenge, in *Neolithic studies* (eds R Bradley and J Gardiner), BAR, **133**, 177–88, Oxford
——, 1985a Scouring the surface: approaches to the ploughzone in the Stonehenge Environs, *Archaeol Rev Cambridge*, **4**, 27–42
——, 1985b *Beyond Stonehenge*, Salisbury
——, 1986 Sites and monuments in the Stonehenge Environs, in *The management and presentation of field monuments* (eds M Hughes and T Rowley), Oxford
——, in prep a Past and present landscapes around Robin Hood's Ball causewayed enclosure
——, in prep b New light on the Stonehenge Cursus
Ritchie, J N G, 1976 The Stones of Stennes, Orkney, *Proc Soc Antiq Scotland*, **107**, 1–60
Robertson-Mackay, R, 1987 The Neolithic causewayed enclosure at Staines, Surrey: excavations 1962-63, *Proc Prehist Soc*, **53**, 23–128
Robinson, M, 1989 Seeds and other plant macrofossils, in Ashbee *et al* 1989, 78–90
Roe, F E S, 1966 The Battle-Axe Series in Britain, *Proc Prehist Soc*, **32**, 199–245
RCHME 1970 *An inventory of the historical monuments in the county of Dorset*, **II**, *South-east*, part 3, Royal Commission on the Historical Monuments of England, London
——, 1979 *Stonehenge and its environs*, Edinburgh
Rowley-Conwy, P, 1982 Forest grazing and clearance in temperate Europe with special reference to Denmark: an archaeological view, in *Archaeological Aspects of Woodland Ecology* (eds M Bell and S Limbrey), BAR Int Series, **146**, 199–216, Oxford
Ruddle, C S, 1901 Notes on Durrington, *Wiltshire Archaeol Natur Hist Mag*, **31**, 331–42
Saville, A, 1980 Five flint assemblages from excavated sites in Wiltshire, *Wiltshire Archaeol Natur Hist Mag*, **72/73**, 1–28
——, 1981a Grimes Graves, Norfolk. Excavations 1971–72, **II**, *The flint assemblage*, London
——, 1981b The flint and chert artefacts, in Mercer 1981, 101–52
Scaife, R G, 1982 Late-Devensian and early Flandrian vegetational changes in Southern England, in *Archaeological Aspects of Woodland Ecology* (eds M G Bell and S Limbrey), BAR Int Series, **246**, 57–74, Oxford
——, 1987 A review of later quaternary plan microfossil and macrofossil research in southern England: with special reference to environmental archaeological evidence, in *Environmental Archaeology: a regional review*, **II** (ed H C M Keeley), HBMC Occasional Paper no 1, 125–203, London
Semenov, S A, 1964 *Prehistoric technology*, Bath
Sharples, N, forthcoming *Maiden Castle*, HBMC Archaeological Reports series
Shennan, S J, Healy, F, and Smith, I F, 1985 The excavation of a ring ditch at Tye Field, Lawford, Essex, *Archaeol J*, **142**, 150–215
Shepard, A O, 1956 *Ceramics for the archaeologist*, Carnegie Institute of Washington, publication 609
Shortt, H de S, 1946 Bronze Age Beakers from Larkhill and Bulford, *Wiltshire Archaeol Natur Hist Mag*, **41**, 381–3
Sieveking, G de G, Bush, P, Ferguson, J, Craddock, P T, Hughes, M J, and Cowell, M R, 1972 Prehistoric flint mines and their identification as sources of raw material, *Archaeometry*, **14**, 151–76
Sieveking, G de G, Longworth, I H, Hughes, M J, Clark, A J, and Millett, A, 1973 A new survey of Grimes Graves: first report, *Proc Prehist Soc*, **39**, 192–218
Silver, I A, 1969 The ageing of domestic animals, in *Science in archaeology* (eds D Brothwell and E Higgs), 2 edn, 282–302, London
Smith, A G, 1970 The influence of Mesolithic and Neolithic man on the British vegetation: a discussion, in *Studies in the vegetational history of the British Isles* (eds D Walker and R G West), Cambridge, 81–96
Smith, G, 1973 Excavation of the Stonehenge Avenue at West Amesbury, Wiltshire, *Wiltshire Archaeol Natur Hist Mag*, **68**, 42–56
——, 1979–80 Excavations in Stonehenge car park, *Wiltshire Archaeol Natur Hist Mag*, **74-5**, 181
Smith, I F, 1965 *Windmill Hill and Avebury: excavations by A Keiller 1925–39*, Oxford
——, 1966 The pottery, in Ashbee 1966
——, 1981 The Neolithic pottery, in Mercer 1981, 161–85
——, in prep Wilsford barrows 51–54, excavations by Ernest Greenfield
Smith, R W, 1984 The ecology of Neolithic farming systems as exemplified by the Avebury region of Wiltshire, *Proc Prehist Soc*, **50**, 99–120
Stevens, F, 1919 Skeleton found at Fargo, *Wiltshire Archaeol Natur Hist Mag*, **40**, 359
Stone, J F S, 1933 A Middle Bronze Age urnfield on Easton Down, Winterslow, *Wiltshire Archaeol Natur Hist Mag*, **46**, 218–24
Stone, J F S, 1934 Excavations at Easton Down, Winterslow, 1931–32, *Wiltshire Archaeol Natur Hist Mag*, **46**, 225–42
——, 1935 Some discoveries at Ratfyn, Amesbury and their bearing on the date of Woodhenge, *Wiltshire Archaeol Natur Hist Mag*, **47**, 55–67
——, 1936 An enclosure on Boscombe Down East, *Wiltshire Archaeol Natur Hist Mag*, **47**, 466–89
——, 1938 An early Bronze Age grave in Fargo Plantation near Stonehenge, *Wiltshire Archaeol Natur Hist Mag*, **48**, 357–70
——, 1941 The Deverel-Rimbury settlement on Thorney Down, Winterbourne Gunner, S Wilts, *Proc Prehist Soc*, **7**, 114–33
——, 1947 The Stonehenge Cursus and its affinities, *Archaeol J*, **104**, 7–19
——, 1949 Some Grooved Ware pottery from the Woodhenge area, *Proc Prehist Soc*, **15**, 122–7
Stone, J F S, and Young, W E V, 1948 Two pits of Grooved Ware date near Woodhenge, *Wiltshire Archaeol Natur Hist Mag*, **52**, 287–306
Stone, J F S, Piggott, S, and Booth, A St J, 1954 Durrington Walls, Wiltshire: recent excavations at a ceremonial site of the early second millennium BC, *Antiq J*, **34**, 155–77
Straker, V, 1985 Carbonised cereals and charcoal from Hazleton chambered long cairn, Gloucestershire, unpubl report, Ancient Monuments Laboratory
Stukeley, W, 1740 *Stonehenge: a temple restor'd to the British Druids*, London
Thomas, K D, 1977 A preliminary report on the mollusca from the lynchet section, in Bell 1977, 258–64
——, 1982 Neolithic enclosures and woodland habitats on the South Downs in Sussex, England, in *Archaeological aspects of woodland ecology* (eds M G Bell and S Limbrey), BAR, **146**, 147–70, Oxford
——, 1985 Land snail analysis in archaeology: theory and practice, in *Palaeoenvironmental investigations* (eds N R J Fieller, D D Gilbertson, and N G A Ralph), BAR, **258**, 131–48, Oxford
Thomas, N, 1964 The Neolithic causewayed camp at Robin Hood's Ball, Shrewton, *Wiltshire Archaeol Natur Hist Mag*, **59**, 1–27
Thomas, W R, and Foin, T C, 1982 Neutral hypotheses and patterns of species diversity: fact or artefact?, *Palaeobiology*, **8**, 44–55
Thomas, J, and Whittle, A, 1986 Anatomy of a tomb – West Kennet revisited, *Oxford J Archaeol* **5(2)**, 129–56
Thurnam, J, 1868 On ancient British barrows, especially those of Wiltshire and adjoining counties. Part 1, Long barrows, *Archaeologia*, **42**, 405–21
Toms, H S, 1926 Valley entrenchments east of the Ditchling road, *Brighton and Hove Archaeologist*, **3**, 42–61
Tratman, E K, 1967 The Priddy Circles, Mendip, Somerset. Henge monuments, *Proc Univ Bristol Spelaeol Soc*, **11**

Vatcher, F de M, 1960 Excavation and fieldwork in Wiltshire, 1959, barrows east of Stonehenge Avenue, *Wiltshire Archaeol Natur Hist Mag*, **57**, 394

——, 1961 The excavation of the long mortuary enclosure on Normanton Down, Wiltshire, *Proc Prehist Soc*, **27**, 160–73

——, 1962 Excavation and fieldwork in Wiltshire, 1961, Winterbourne Stoke, Greenlands Farm, *Wiltshire Archaeol Natur Hist Mag*, **58**, 241

——, 1969 Two incised chalk plaques near Stonehenge Bottom, *Antiquity*, **43**, 310-1-1

Vatcher, F de M, and Vatcher, H L, 1968 Excavation and fieldwork in Wiltshire, 1967, Winterbourne Stoke/Wilsford, *Wiltshire Archaeol Natur Hist Mag*, **63**, 108–9

—— and ——, 1969 Excavation and fieldwork in Wiltshire, 1968, Amesbury, King Barrow Wood to Stonehenge, *Wiltshire Archaeol Natur Hist Mag*, **64**, 123

—— and ——, 1973 Excavation of three postholes in Stonehenge car park, *Wiltshire Archaeol Natur Hist Mag*, **68**, 57–63

Vatcher, H L, 1962 Excavation and fieldwork in Wiltshire, 1961, Winterbourne Stoke, *Wiltshire Archaeol Natur Hist Mag*, **58**, 242

von den Driesch, A, 1976 *A guide to the measurement of animal bones from archaeological sites*, Peabody Mus Bull, **1**, Cambridge, Massachusetts

Wainwright, G J, 1971 The excavation of a late Neolithic enclosure at Marden, Wiltshire, *Antiq J*, **51**, 177–239

——, 1979 *Mount Pleasant, Dorset: excavations 1970–71*, Rep Res Comm Soc Antiq London, **37**

Wainwright G J, and Longworth, I H, 1971 *Durrington Walls: excavations 1966–1968*, Rep Res Comm Soc Antiq London, **29**

Wainwright, G J, Donaldson, P, Longworth, I H, and Swan, V, 1971 The excavation of prehistoric and Romano-British settlements near Durrington Walls, Wiltshire, 1970, *Wiltshire Archaeol Natur Hist Mag*, **66**, 76–128

Walden, H W, 1976 A nomenclatural list of the land mollusca of the British Isles, *J Conchology*, **29**, 21–5

Warne, C, 1866 *The Celtic Tumuli of Dorset*, London

Warren, S H, 1951 The Clacton flint industry: a new interpretation, *Proc Geol Assoc*, **62**, 107–33

Waton, P V, 1982 Land snail evidence of post-glacial environmental change on the Hertfordshire chalklands, *Trans Hertfordshire Natur Hist Soc*, **28**, 63–75

Wheeler, R E M, 1943 Maiden Castle, Dorset, Rep Res Comm Soc Antiq London, **12**

Whittle, A, 1977 *The earlier Neolithic of southern England and its continental background*, BAR, **S35**, Oxford

——, 1981 Later Neolithic Society in Britain: a realignment, in *Astronomy and society during the period 4000–1500 BC*, BAR, **88**, 297–342, Oxford

Whittle, P J, 1978 Resources and population in the British Neolithic, *Antiquity*, **52**, 34–42

Woodward, P J, forthcoming *The south Dorset Ridgeway survey and excavations 1977–1983: The pre-Iron Age landscapes*, Dorset Natur Hist Archaeol Soc Monograph Series

Index

compiled by Lesley Adkins and Roy Adkins